*Dudley Randall, Broadside Press, and the
Black Arts Movement in Detroit, 1960–1995*

Dudley Randall, Broadside Press, and the Black Arts Movement in Detroit, 1960–1995

by
JULIUS E. THOMPSON

McFarland & Company, Inc., Publishers
Jefferson, North Carolina, and London

To the writers and artists of Broadside Press

Frontispiece: Dudley Randall in the early 1990s (courtesy Dudley Randall)

The poems that appear in this volume are reproduced by permission of Broadside Press, with the following exceptions: Nikki Giovanni, "Nikki-Rosa," "Knoxville Tennessee" and "The Funeral of Martin Luther King, Jr." from *The Selected Poems of Nikki Giovanni* (compilation ©1996 by Nikki Giovanni), by permission of William Morrow & Co., Inc.; Sonia Sanchez, "right on: wite america" by permission of Sonia Sanchez; Haki R. Madhubuti (Don L. Lee), "Message to a Black Soldier" and "But He Was Cool or: he even stopped for green lights" by permission of Third World Press; Dudley Randall, "The Rite" and "A Poet Is Not a Jukebox" by permission of Dudley Randall and Lotus Press, Inc.; and Dudley Randall, "The Profile on the Pillow," "Nationalist," "On a Name for Black Americans" and "Detroit Renaissance" by permission of Dudley Randall. An excerpt from *Devil's Night: And Other Tales of Detroit* by Ze'ev Chafets, ©1990 by Ze'ev Chafets, is reprinted by permission of Random House, Inc. Photographs are reproduced by permission of Broadside Press.

LIBRARY OF CONGRESS CATALOGUING-IN-PUBLICATION DATA

Thompson, Julius E.
    Dudley Randall, Broadside Press, and the Black arts movement in
Detroit, 1960–1995 / by Julius E. Thompson.
        p.   cm.
    Includes bibliographical references and index.

    ISBN 0-7864-2264-5 (softcover : 50# alkaline paper) ∞

    1. Randall, Dudley, 1914–   — Knowledge — Publishers and publishing.
2. American literature — Afro-American authors — Publishing — Michigan —
Detroit.   3. Literature publishing — Michigan — Detroit — History — 20th
century.   4. Afro-American arts — Michigan — Detroit.   5. Broadside Press.
I. Title.
PS3568.A49Z85   2005   811'.54 — dc21 [B]   98-9306

British Library cataloguing data are available

On the cover: Collage by Broadside Press artists and photographers *(courtesy Broadside Press)*

Manufactured in the United States of America

McFarland & Company, Inc., Publishers
Box 611, Jefferson, North Carolina 28640
    www.mcfarlandpub.com

Table of Contents

Also by Julius E. Thompson

Hopes Tied Up in Promises (1970)
Blues Said: Walk On (1977)
Hiram R. Revels, 1827–1901: A Biography (1982)
The Black Press in Mississippi, 1865–1985: A Directory (1988)
The Anthology of Black Mississippi Poets (1989)
The Black Press in Mississippi, 1865–1985 (1993)
Percy Greene and the Jackson Advocate: The Life and Times of a Radical Conservative Black Newspaperman, 1897–1977
(McFarland, 1994)

List of Tables and Figures

Tables

Figures

Preface

The name of Dudley F. Randall holds a unique place among American poets, editors, and publishers who have profoundly influenced American life and culture since World War II. Randall's key contribution was made during the Civil Rights Movement and the Black Arts Movement of the sixties and seventies, with his establishment in 1965 in Detroit of Broadside Press, a company devoted to publishing, distributing, and promoting the works of black poets and other writers. In the mid–1960s under his leadership Broadside Press first produced a series of broadsides (poetry on a single sheet of paper), reasonably priced at 50 cents each, and soon followed with books of poetry in pamphlet form, generally priced at $1 to $2 each. The African-American community and other readers responded enthusiastically to these literary efforts, and Broadside became a major institution in the struggle of the black community to achieve justice, equality, and self-determination in the United States.

Dudley Randall displayed a genius in being able to organize Broadside with very few funds, and he brought a wealth of skills and talents to bear on his work as an editor and publisher. These included his training as a librarian, decades of work in studying and writing poetry, and a deep love for literature and the fine arts. His total commitment to the advancement of black poetry and freedom encouraged other black poets, both famous and unknown, to seek out Broadside Press as an outlet for the publication of their poems, books and tapes of black literature. The list of Broadside poets between 1965 and 1995 reads like a who's who among African-American poets of the twentieth century: Gwendolyn Brooks, Haki R. Madhubuti (formerly Don L. Lee), Margaret Walker, Etheridge Knight, Sonia Sanchez, James A. Emanuel, Audre Lorde, Clarence Major, Nikki Giovanni, Marvin X (aka Marvin Ellis Jackmon, Marvin Portman, Nazzam al Fitnah of Nazzam A Sudan), Johari Amini, Sterling D. Plumpp, Mae Jackson, Alvin Aubert, Melba J. Boyd, Lance Jeffers, and some four hundred other voices.

American culture is much richer today because of the work of Dudley Randall and Broadside Press. Like earlier black pioneers in the black freedom struggle from the seventeenth to the twentieth centuries, Randall waged a battle against the odds to promote black identity and independence and a reform of American society. His efforts across sixty years have helped to promote literacy, understanding, love and appreciation for black literature in the United States and around the world. Randall's contributions to American culture serve as a link between the generation which grew up in the days of the Great Depression of the thirties, the activists of the Civil Rights era of the fifties through the seventies, and the contemporary generation of the eighties and nineties. His life's work serves as a model of the human possibilities still available in our own troubled times. In a period of great hardship, he sacrificed much in terms of his own personal comfort to help hundreds of writers to lift their voices so that the world might hear their songs of freedom, joy, peace, love, hope, trust, and faith through struggle for the future. The present book seeks especially to bring Dudley Randall's work and contributions through Broadside Press to the attention of contemporary readers and students, and the academic community. Americans owe Dudley Randall a great debt for his foresight in helping to promote many new voices, and in reinvigorating some older ones, in black literature of the modern era.

The book is divided into six chapters and covers the time period of 1900 to 1995. Chapter 1, "Dudley Randall, Black Life and Culture in Detroit, 1900–1959," explores the early life and work of Dudley Randall within the context of the growth and development of the black community in Detroit from the opening decades of the twentieth century through the fifties. Chapter 2, "The Early Development of Broadside Press, 1960–1969," follows Randall's career as a librarian, poet and creator of Broadside Press, and denotes the significance of his work against the background of the Black Arts Movement and the Freedom struggle of African-Americans during the sixties. Chapter 3, "The Growth of Broadside Press, 1970–1975," delineates the golden years in the company's development and the stimulation of Randall's acceptance as a major poet of the Black Arts Movement. Chapter 4, "Crisis and Decline of Broadside Press, 1976–1979," discusses the turbulence of the seventies and the varied reasons for the decline of Broadside during this period. Chapter 5, "Revival and Rebirth, 1980–1995," notes the historical, social and cultural changes of the contemporary period, and the impact of those changing conditions on Broadside in its struggle to survive and carry forward the work of Dudley Randall to a new generation of readers and thinkers. Chapter 6, "The Achievement of Broadside Press, 1965–1995," highlights the contributions to American literature and black life of thirty years of publishing activities at Broadside Press, and notes the immense historical and literary significance of Dudley Randall to the Black Arts Movement in America.

The author owes a debt of great gratitude to many writers, editors, and publishers for their assistance with this study. Dudley and Vivian Randall have extended many courtesies to me during the preparation of this book, and I wish to express my most heartfelt appreciation for their kindness. Many writers and editors in Detroit were helpful with leads, interviews, letters, and questionnaires, including Naomi Long Madgett, Alvin Aubert, Melba Joyce Boyd, Stella Louise Crews, Ronald Snelling, Hilda and Donald Vest, and Willie Williams. Other writers who were extremely helpful for this study include Samuel Allen, Gwendolyn Brooks, Margaret Burroughs, James A. Emanuel, Paul Breman, Nikki Giovanni, Lance Jeffers, Ntozake Shange, Doughtry Long, Audre Lorde, Clarence Major, Raymond Patterson, Sterling D. Plumpp, and James A. Randall, Jr.

A number of other scholars, poets, and creative artists have also provided the author with data and encouragement. I wish to acknowledge their assistance here. Jerry W. Ward, Jr., Lawrence Durgin Professor of Literature, Tougaloo College, Mississippi, has been a valuable colleague and wise counsel for my historical and literary efforts since 1973; he has played a similar role with this book, and has been tireless in his encouragement of my scholarly work. Several of my former students have aided my efforts, and I am thankful for their support across the years, including James N. Conyers, Gena Cox, Curtis Franks, Sr., Dorothy V. Smith, Martin Torain, and Colia L. LaFayette Clark. Last, but not least, a word of appreciation goes to my colleagues Wendell P. Holbrook of Rutgers University, David A. Gerber of SUNY–Buffalo, Henry Lewis Suggs of Clemson University, and James M. McPherson of Princeton University, for their pacesetting examples of scholarship and encouragement. For editorial assistance, I am thankful for the aid of Deborah LeSure-Wilbourn of Coldwater, Mississippi, and for the encouragement received from Camille A. Jones of Carbondale, Illinois.

More than fifty American libraries were used in the preparation of this book. I thank librarians everywhere for their kindness to scholars. This book especially benefited from work in the collections of the following libraries: Wayne State University, Detroit Public Library, University of Detroit; New York Public Library, SUNY–Albany, University of Rochester; Southern Illinois University at Carbondale; Carbondale (Ill.) Public Library; Washington University (Mo.); Clark Atlanta University; Howard University; Jackson State University; Tougaloo College; Alcorn State University; Millsaps College; Jackson (Miss.) Public Library; Natchez (Miss.) Public Library; Department of Archives and History, Jackson, Miss.; Cleveland State University; Indianapolis (Ind.) Public Library; and the Ward M. Canaday Center, University of Toledo.

Finally, two research grants were influential in helping me to complete the research for this study. A National Endowment for the Humanities Summer Seminar for College Teachers grant allowed me to work with historian David M. Katzman at the Joyce and Elizabeth Hall Center for the Humanities, University of Kansas, Lawrence, during the summer of 1992, and an NEH Fellowship for University Teachers allowed me to work full-time on this book during the period June–December, 1994.

Julius E. Thompson
Columbia, Mo.
Fall 1998

Chapter 1
Dudley Randall,
Black Life and Culture
in Detroit, 1900–1959

The life of Dudley Felker Randall began on January 14, 1914. Born in Washington, D.C., Dudley was the third of five children of Ada Viola Bradley Randall and Arthur George Clyde Randall. His siblings were James (born in 1910), Arthur (1912), Esther (1916), and Philip (1920).[1]

Dudley's father was born in 1878 in Macon, Georgia, and educated at Talladega College, Alabama. He was a teacher, school principal and Congregational minister. His mother was born in 1883 in Boston, Massachusetts. She attended an African-American Normal School in Buffalo, New York, and was a kindergarten teacher and housewife.[2] The Randalls resided in a city where African-Americans faced discrimination and segregation in housing, education, employment, police protection, and the use of such public facilities as hotels, restaurants, and amusement centers. Yet, between 1910 and 1920, 95,000 to 110,000 blacks lived in Washington, a city with a total population of 437,571 in 1920.[3]

Dudley's first four years were spent in this thriving metropolis, where his mother often took the children to concerts. It was there that he recalls a visit to Towson, Maryland, a suburb of Washington, D.C., where he was inspired to compose words to the song "Maryland, My Maryland."[4] Dudley said, "This is the earliest instance I can remember of my composing a poem."[5]

Arthur Randall moved the family to East St. Louis, Illinois, in either 1919 or 1920, to secure employment with the YMCA.[6] The Randalls were thus among the hundreds of thousands of African-Americans who migrated from one region to another during and after World War I. In fact, between 1916 and 1930, over one million blacks migrated from the South in order to escape the great violence, poverty, segregation, and economic deprivation of the region.[7] However, the Randall family's migration from Washington, D.C. to East St. Louis was like that of many other migrants, in that they moved not from the South, but from one urban center to another. Scholar Carole Marks notes that "a majority of the migrants of the Great Migration were urban, non-agricultural laborers, not the rural peasant usually assumed."[8] In July 1917, before the Randalls' arrival, East St. Louis experienced a bitter race riot. The casualties included eighty African-Americans beaten and thirty-nine killed, along with nine whites. Scholar Allan H. Spear assesses the event as "the deadliest urban race riot of the twentieth century. Historians attribute the riot to exaggerated fears of black competition [for] jobs, and to the political corruption and mismanagement that had bred disrespect for law."[9]

After a year in East St. Louis, where Dudley began his early schooling, the Randall family moved again in 1921 to Detroit, Michigan.[10] Arthur Randall's main goal with this new move was to secure greater economic opportunity in the Motor City, with hopes of a full-time job in the personnel department of Ford Motor Company. However, when Arthur Randall eventually secured a position with Ford, sometime during his mid-forties, it was as a common laborer. He was one of the approximately 5,000 to 6,000 black males who worked for Ford between 1923 and 1925, and made a salary of $3.50 to $10 daily.[11]

During the Randall's move in the twenties, Detroit was a major American industrial center and held a leading position in producing automobiles. Prior to World War I, the black population in the city of Detroit and in the state of Michigan had been small. In 1910, there were only 17,115 blacks in Michigan (0.6 percent of the state's total population), but this number increased to 169,453 in 1930 (3.5 percent of the state's residents).[12] While in Detroit there were 5,741 blacks in 1910, and 40,838 in 1920, an increase of 611.3 percent in ten years.[13] Thus, many blacks were drawn to the area because of the growth of jobs in the auto industry.

Dudley attended five elementary schools in Detroit during the twenties: Columbian and Deerfield (1921), Jackson (1922), Barstow (1923), and Capron (1926).[14] Conditions were difficult after the war for many blacks, and one scholar observes that in Detroit "almost all were engaged in unskilled labor and earned two to five dollars less a week than whites doing the same work."[15] Perhaps economic hardships and locating reasonable housing forced the Randall family to move often during this period. Both issues were common problems for urban blacks.

In 1926, Dudley entered Eastern High School in Detroit. His apprenticeship as a poet began in 1927, when he reached the age of thirteen. In that same year one of his early sonnets was selected as a first prize winner for publication on the "Young Poets' Page" of the *Detroit Free Press*. He also received a cash award of $1.[16] Scholar D. H. Melhem notes that Dudley's early talents and consciousness were shaped by the influences of, "Music, religion, politics and poetry," on the development of his personality. Dudley took writing seriously and studied prosody.[17]

During the decade known as the Harlem Renaissance in African-American letters, Dudley was especially influenced by two of the giant poets of that era: Countee Cullen, for "the skill" of his ability in writing "the sonnet and his use of language"—first recognized by Dudley at age thirteen, when his father gave the children a copy of Cullen's *Copper Sun* (1927); and Jean Toomer, because of the power and imagery of his work, as represented in his most famous book, *Cane* (1923), which Dudley first read at age sixteen. He later believed that Toomer was "our best poet" produced from the period. He was also influenced by the work of Paul Laurence Dunbar.[18] Dudley's political consciousness was also influenced by his father, who encouraged his son's intellectual curiosity and political awareness by taking an early interest in bringing his children to hear outstanding black intellectuals, such as W. E. B. Du Bois, James Weldon Johnson, and Walter White, among others, when they lectured in Detroit churches and other institutions.[19] Yet, Dudley was also inspired during these early years by the activities of local blacks in Detroit. "A roomer in my home was the janitor at Marcus Garvey's UNIA [Universal Negro Improvement Association] Hall down Russell Street, and he had me help him clean the hall after the meetings, and I heard the men talk and saw the parades."[20]

Arthur Randall was also active in local Detroit politics, which had an impact on Dudley's social, political, and poetic sensibilities. In an interview with critic Charles H. Rowell, he notes:

> It's hard to say unequivocally my background made me political. Of course, I unlike the child who was brought up in a home where there is no politics, was aware of politics. But my mother used to fuss at my father about being out in the streets all the time — about his going out to meetings instead of staying at home taking care of family business. So that may have turned me off a little toward being a public person as opposed to a private or family person. A child is influenced by his mother as well as his father. When the child is small, he has more contact with his mother than his father. I think that as I grew older, as I said in the interview, I looked back on those circumstances and remembered that I, as a boy, preferred playing baseball to hearing Du Bois or Johnson. But as I grew older I appreciated the opportunity I had to hear these people. You are right: I was made conscious of politics and social change. I suppose it shows in my poetry.[21]

The young poet was cognizant, however, of the ambivalent attitude of many in the community toward the creative process of poets and writers. "I was thirteen when I started writing seriously and studying other poets. In my neighborhood, prizefighters, not poets, were respected. I wrote my poetry secretly and hid it under a loose plank in the attic."[22] During the late twenties Dudley was a very active member in Eastern High School's ROTC program.[23] Perhaps, with such physical activity, he was able to find solace (and protection) from community eyes. Dudley may also have been influenced in his military outlook by the experiences of his father and one of his uncles.

> My father was a theological student at Talledega [*sic*]. He led a student strike before the Spanish-American War and was kicked out of college. He took his class and his brother who was also a student there and they enlisted in the army for the Spanish-American War in 1898. After coming back and getting a job and doing well on his job, he was invited to go back to Talledega and he went back and got his degree.[24]

Dudley's life during the twenties was also impacted by the tremendous range of political, social, and economic developments which were taking place in Detroit and elsewhere. In general, life in Detroit was tough for most blacks. These conditions during 1925 are representative of the black situation in cities throughout the United States during this period. The Sweet case was the most famous court case of the year for the black community in Detroit. The case grew out of the efforts of Dr. Ossian W. Sweet, a local African-American dentist, to buy a home on Garland Avenue in Detroit in May 1925. After his family moved into the home on September 8, 1925, a local white mob surrounded the house for two days. However, on September 9, one white man was killed and another wounded. The police department arrested all ten occupants of the house on murder charges. The NAACP secured the services of Clarence Darrow to defend the Sweets and their supporters in court. Darrow won the case.[25] Dudley Randall was eleven years old during this time of the black community's continued struggle for justice and fair housing.

Young Dudley's outlook was also influenced by the discrimination and racism as exhibited by the Detroit Police Department and the Ku Klux Klan. During 1925, fourteen local blacks were killed by the Detroit Police Department. The department, as a matter of course, had fourteen black policemen out of its 3,000 officers.[26] The migration of large numbers of southern whites to northern states such as Michigan during World War I, mixed with northern whites' fears of black migrants, also helped to foster a revival and growth of the Ku Klux Klan in the state, and throughout the nation. One author suggests that Michigan may have had as many as 875,130 Ku Klux Klan members in 1925 — the highest estimated membership for any state.[27] Other scholars believe that this figure is too high, and suggest a more conservative figure of 80,000 by mid-decade.[28] Whatever figures are accurate, they indicate another level of violence, opposition and oppression with which black citizens in Detroit (where half of the state's 32,000 official Ku Klux Klan members lived) and the state of Michigan, had to contend during the twenties. Although Michigan was not known in the United States as a major lynching state, four whites and four blacks were officially listed as lynch victims there between 1882 and 1930.[29] Such gloomy statistics were active news stories during the roaring twenties.

Nevertheless, the black community had a number of meaningful institutions to help address the political, cultural, social, and economic conditions of the period. These included the black church, press, social clubs, businesses, and voluntary and community organizations. Historian Richard W. Thomas identifies the ten largest black churches in Detroit as having a total membership of 19,200 in 1926. The two largest and oldest in the city were the Second Baptist Church (established in 1836, with 4,000 members), and Bethel AME (founded in 1841, with 3,500 members).[30] The weekly black press of Detroit reached out from Paradise Valley, a part of Detroit's oldest black district, and other sections of the city, to carry black opinions on the news of the day to black Detroiters. The best known black organs in the city during the twenties were the *Detroit Owl* (1926–30), and the *Detroit Independent* (1921–32).[31] There were eight other organs also active in the city during this period, including the *Detroit Tribune* (established in 1922), and the *Northwest News* (1922–38).[32] Many blacks, including young Dudley, also read the two major historically white daily newspapers of the city, the *Detroit News* and the *Detroit Free Press*.

Dudley's world view during the twenties was also influenced by the many activities of black organizations in Detroit. The major black community organizations of the city were the NAACP's Detroit branch, established in the city in 1911, and active in pressing for black legal rights and fighting cases of racial discrimination against blacks; the Detroit Urban League, first organized in the city during 1916, and very active under the leadership of its executive secretary John C. Dancy in promoting better economic and social improvements for blacks in Michigan; and more radical groups, such as the Detroit branch of the National Negro Congress and the UNIA (which had 5,000 active members in Detroit alone).[33] Additionally, black Detroiters had hundreds of smaller organizations to meet their needs and interests. These included social clubs, Greek letter fraternities and sororities, women's clubs, and voluntary organizations, such as the YMCA and YWCA, and cultural outreach groups like the Detroit branch of Carter G. Woodson's Association for the Study of Negro Life and History, organized in Detroit in 1926.[34]

Black Detroit was a vibrant part of a city on the move in the twenties. There were major problems and challenges for its black citizens to overcome, but the future looked bright to many young people, like Dudley Randall, who graduated from Miller Junior High School in 1927 and from Eastern High School in 1930 at age sixteen. But it would take the poet many years of hard work before he could achieve his desire to become a professionally trained librarian.[35]

Two years out of high school, Dudley Randall finally landed a full-time job in 1932 at the Ford Motor Company foundry in Dearborn, Michigan.[36] These were extremely difficult years for Americans, but especially so for blacks, who were generally "the last hired and first fired" at many jobs. The additional burdens created by the Great Depression, which extended throughout the thirties, did not make matters any easier. Yet, the Great Migration continued from the south to the north, and the black population of Detroit increased to 120,066 in 1930, 7.7 percent of the city's total. Detroit now held the seventh largest concentration of blacks among American cities.[37]

Dudley was very lucky to have a job, for between 1929 and 1931, 225,000 workers lost their positions in the Detroit area auto plants. Blacks were in the worst position. Their unemployment rates reached 80 percent in Detroit during the decade.[38] However, their daily lives were made even more miserable by discriminatory practices in meeting their needs, even among relief agencies.[39] One scholar notes the severe nature of the period: "...one Detroit hotel dismissed their Negro employees and hired whites to take their place."[40]

Yet, Dudley's success at gaining a position with Ford highlights the paradoxical history of this period in the black experience. On the one hand, scholar Joyce Shaw Peterson reveals the almost hopeful aspect of the situation:

> The auto industry's domination of the economic life of Detroit created a situation which meant that the black population of the city was more highly industrialized than in any other large Northern city. By 1920 over 79% of Detroit's male, black workers were employed in manufacturing and mechanical jobs. In Detroit ... by 1930 14% of all auto workers were black.[41]

However, these same workers faced a work environment where they were

> concentrated in the most unskilled and unpleasant jobs in the auto industry. They were hired into those jobs that had the lowest pay scales, required the greatest physical exertion, had the highest accident rates, and the largest number of health hazards. A great many black auto workers were employed in foundry departments. Others were hired in paint departments as sprayers and sanders or in maintenance departments as janitors. Auto workers considered the foundry to be the most undesirable place in the whole factory in which to work because of its noise, heat and filth. Many plant managers expressed a belief in the superior ability of black workers to withstand extreme heat and to display superior stamina on particularly exhausting and difficult jobs. Black workers understood, however, that their main qualification for foundry work was the color of their skin, and finding themselves in the foundry was often their first disillusioning experience with Northern equality.[42]

Dudley worked at the Ford River Rouge plant for five years. Ford was the largest employer of blacks in the auto industry, but by 1937 had concentrated 99 percent of them at the River Rouge plant.[43] In all, 40 percent of the auto industry's black employees worked at Ford's Dearborn operations, where over 50 percent of them were assigned to the most difficult plant jobs.[44] Most workers in the auto industry also received lower wages during the depression. Scholars have estimated that in 1929 the average yearly wages in the auto industry was $1,638, but in 1931 this fell to $1,228, and in 1933 to $1,035. Others suggest that these figures are too high, and that a more realistic average is $900 in 1934. One study notes, "Where hourly wages at the Ford River Rouge plant had averaged 92¢ in 1929, in 1933 the norm was 59¢ per hour."[45] Nonetheless, people in Michigan were proud of the fact that as late as 1939–40, the state manufactured 60 percent of all the cars produced in the world.[46]

While employed with Ford, Dudley married Ruby Hands on May 27, 1935. Ruby was born in 1917 at Valdosta, Georgia. She grew up in Detroit, was graduated from Miller High School, and became an x-ray technician and social worker aide in the city. Her career interests have included music, and she has been active in church choirs. They were soon the parents of a daughter, Phyllis Ada Randall. However, her marriage to Dudley ended in divorce.[47] On the economic front, Dudley was laid off from Ford in 1937.[48] The next year, in 1938–39, he secured new employment at the U.S. Post Office in Detroit as a carrier, and later as a clerk.[49] After the auto industry and the Detroit Department of Public Works, the U.S. Post Office was the third largest employer of blacks in the Detroit area. As early as 1926, 454 black men and 31 black women worked for the local post office.[50] Such positions were highly valued for the economic stability and job security which they brought during an era of financial crisis.

Meanwhile, life in the urban center continued at a brisk pace for Dudley and other blacks. Two developments which took place in the community are suggestive of the impact of the experiences of black Detroiters on the national culture during this period. First, Detroit blacks witnessed the 1930 establishment of the Lost-Found Nation of Islam in the Wilderness of North America (also known as the Nation of Islam and the Black Muslims), under the teaching of W. D. Fard, both led in 1934 by Elijah Muhammad (Elijah Poole).[51] This new organization called for the complete separation of blacks from "the white slave-masters" of America, and for the development of black controlled institutions, outlook, and identity. Scholars suggest that the group had a membership of 10,000 before World War II. However, its growth and influence would be far reaching in the fifties and sixties.[52] Second, the boxing career of Joe Louis, known affectionately as the "Brown Bomber," had a wide following in the black community. Louis, who grew up in Detroit, became internationally famous in 1937, when he won his first heavyweight championship, which he successfully defended until 1949.[53] He became a cultural icon in the black world both at home and abroad. These domestic events, and world conditions, such as the role of black Americans in the Spanish Civil War, and the crisis facing Ethiopia with Italy's invasion in 1935, were shaping ideas in the minds of many African-Americans during the thirties.[54]

At home in Detroit, Dudley Randall continued his efforts to develop as a poet by reading extensively and writing. However, it was an effort that he was in no hurry to reveal to the world. His studies continued to be influenced by the works of Countee Cullen and Jean Toomer; Dudley remembers that he

> also read [Countee] Cullen's anthology *Caroling Dusk* [1927] and [Robert T.] Kerling's anthology [1935]. Of course I read other poets too, the ones we studied in school assignments. I heard Countee Cullen read at old Detroit City College, and heard Langston Hughes read. Bob Hayden was bold enough to invite him to lunch and to show him his poetry, but I was too much in awe of the great man even to shake his hand.[55]

Robert Hayden, who was born in Detroit in 1913, became a friend of Dudley's in the thirties. He is perhaps the best known African-American poet who was born or lived in Detroit during the twentieth century. During this period, Dudley remembers that he and Hayden, "used to write poems and show them to each other and talk about poetry. That was the only communication I had [with other poets]."[56] Dudley first met Hayden when a mutual friend introduced them at the Detroit YMCA, because they "both were interested in poetry and should [therefore] get together." Randall feels that "Hayden was made aware of more advanced poets by people he met in Ann Arbor [at the University of Michigan]— Kiman Friar, John Malcolm Brinnin, and his teacher W. H. Auden. He suggested we do a book together, but we never got around to it." Randall and Hayden occasionally communicated with each other by letter across the years.[57]

Dudley was basically a "shy and self-centered" person during his developing early years. However, by 1939 he was twenty-five years of age, and still unpublished as an active poet. His work remained largely hidden in his notebooks. Nevertheless, his poetic voice would grow stronger in the forties, when he would compose a number of new poems, which would slowly begin to reach the public-at-large through their publication in small magazines. In the thirties, Dudley was comfortable being in a position where he "was learning to write."[58] Fame could come later.

In the early forties, Dudley continued his work as an employee of the U.S. Post Office, still considered to be an excellent position for a black American. On December 20, 1942, he married his second wife, Mildred Pinckney, a clerk-typist. Mildred was born in Silver Springs, Colorado, in 1919, and was a high school graduate. This marriage also ended in divorce. Dudley's daughter Phyllis Ada was educated in Detroit, and later received a B.A. degree from Dillard University in New Orleans, Louisiana; and two M.A.'s, one in education, and a second in nursing from the University of Michigan at Ann Arbor, and had a successful career as a registered nurse and teacher in Detroit.[59]

The forties were a decade filled with changes, yet a host of older problems still confronted blacks in Detroit. Although many of these issues were economic in origin, they also covered social and political concerns of the African-American community. But none of these problems were able to prevent the continued migration of blacks to the city from the South. During the decade, the black population of Detroit rose from 149,119 in 1940 (9.2 percent) to 300,506 in 1950, or 16.2 percent of the city's total.[60] The Randall family and other blacks in Detroit lived in a very modern city where they generally had more rights than did their cousins in the South, but where discrimination and the customs of segregation still prevented many of them from enjoying the full range of benefits of American citizenship. At the center of the black world stood the church, the press, and the business community. In 1942, the black Detroit community contained:

> five Negro artists, 25 barber shops, 71 beauty shops, two bondsmen, seven building contractors, two corsetiers, four chiropodists, 25 dress makers and shops, ten electricians, four employment agencies, two dairy distributors, 12 coal dealers, 13 confectioners, 36 dentists, 30 drug stores, 15 fish and poultry markets, five flower shops, three furriers, 14 garages, 12 hat shops, ten hospitals, 20 hotels, nine insurance companies, three jewelers, 16 laundries, 14 manufacturers and distributors, 24 moving and express companies, 18 music teachers, 112 clubs and societies, 33 real estate brokers, 57 restaurants, 11 shoe repair operators, 49 tailors, cleaners and dyers, three upholsterers and furniture makers, six variety and art shops, 47 fraternities and clubs, five beauty schools, 18 engineers, eight veteran posts, three newspapers, 85 lawyers, 151 physicians, 140 social workers, two business schools, and three night clubs.[61]

Such services were vital in helping to fulfill psychological and economic needs, as well as the interests of many blacks. Clearly, however, civil rights organizations, such as the NAACP and the National Urban League, had their work cut out for them. In Detroit, police brutality, housing discrimination, and other ills impacted on the well-being of the black community. Then came World War II. In the new decade of the forties, it would be World War II which would be the shaping experience in Randall's life.

Dudley Randall was inducted into the U.S. Army in July 1943, and received his basic training in North Carolina and Missouri. In February 1944, he was sent overseas to the South Pacific theater, and saw duty on a number of islands, including New Caledonia, the Spice Islands, Admiralty Island, the Bismarck Archipelago, and the Philippines. Randall was a supply sergeant in the headquarters branch of the Signal Corps, and did not see active combat, although the war was often close at hand. He later described the work of the Signal Corps as "put[ting] up telephone line between airports, and I was in the headquarters detachment. The headquarters detachment didn't even do that. They kept the records and sent out reports in quintuplicate."[62]

Black soldiers faced many restrictions and segregation during World War II, but by 1945, 2,438,831 of them had registered for the draft, over one million were drafted, and 1,154,720 served in the war, with a half million going overseas.[63] A major goal of the black community during the war was to end discrimination against blacks in the military, while battling segregation at home.[64] The black press came under tremendous pressure to support the war aims, and to remain quiet on the grievances of blacks in and out of the Armed Forces.[65] Black activists were caught in a complex situation, for they could see clearly what had happened to one group of American citizens, who happened to have been of Japanese descent: the forced "relocation" of 120,000 West Coast Japanese-Americans to detention and interment centers in twelve states.[66] Could it happen to black Americans as well? Nobody knew for sure.

At home in Detroit the news was also not good. Two major events in the early forties depict the black and white mood in Detroit. In an effort to relieve a serious housing shortage in Detroit for black workers and their families, the federal government approved $1 million for the Detroit Housing Commission to build a housing project, named in honor of Sojourner Truth, the nineteenth century anti-slavery crusader. However, it was decided that the 200-unit housing project, located in a white area of the city, would be totally segregated, with only black residents allowed to live in it. Local whites objected to having blacks in their neighborhood, and were successful in having the housing given to whites only. Blacks fought back with a campaign to regain the project for black workers and were able to force housing officials to reopen the project again for blacks. In February 1942, a series of mob actions by whites against black tenants preparing to move into the Sojourner project resulted in a riot. Many blacks believed that the police department's handling of the affair was one-sided, because more blacks were arrested than whites. But due to black coalition building and fortitude, by the end of April 1942, black workers were finally able to move into the project.[67]

Although the extreme conditions produced by the Great Depression of the thirties had eased somewhat in Detroit with an increase in jobs due to war production in the early forties, racial tensions and the continued migration of both blacks and whites to Detroit, created an ebb and flow situation. Segregation and racism created problems for blacks, and some whites viewed blacks as a major source of competition for jobs and public services. Some white extremists, such as the Ku Klux Klan in Michigan, were opposed to any perceived black progress in the state. Blacks pushed ahead anyway — by 1945, they had increased their membership in the United Automobile Workers Union to 5,000. The local Detroit branch of the NAACP increased its presence in the city by increasing its membership from 2,860 in 1938 to 20,500 in 1944.[68] Perhaps historian Rayford W. Logan of Howard University best summarized what blacks desired in America, when he wrote in 1944 that "first-class citizenship" was their goal in a land where African-Americans would have:

1. equality of opportunity;
2. equal pay for equal work;
3. equal protection of the laws;
4. equality of suffrage;
5. equal recognition of the dignity of the human being; [and]
6. abolition of public segregation.[69]

In spite of these hopes, however, a major war-time riot erupted in Detroit on June 20–21, 1943, in which thirty-four people were killed, twenty-five of them black; and of this latter number, seventeen died as a result of police actions.[70] Among the Detroiters arrested during the riot, 85 percent were blacks.[71] Editor Louis Martin of Detroit's *Michigan Chronicle*, wrote of the black reaction to the riot:

> The race riot and all that has gone before have made my people more nationalistic and more chauvinistic and anti-white than ever before. Even those of us who were half liberal and were willing to believe in the possibilities of improving race relations have begun to have doubts — and worse, they have given up hope.[72]

Events such as these on the home front were another burden which black soldiers had to carry with them throughout the war. When peace finally came in 1945, with the defeat of the Axis powers by the Allied powers, thousands of black Americans had given their lives to help win the struggle.

In 1946, Dudley Randall returned to the United States from the Pacific front, and resumed his duties in the post office at Detroit.[73] Now at thirty-one years old, Dudley decided to continue his education, and he selected Wayne State University in Detroit for its strong undergraduate program in English. He continued to hold his position at the post office, where he now served as a clerk, which allowed him to attend day classes as a full-time student. The G.I. Bill of Rights aided the educational needs of thousands of ex-service persons after World War II, and Dudley received such assistance while a student at Wayne.[74]

Although Dudley was older than the average student among the 26,542 individuals who attended Wayne State University in the late forties, he nonetheless maintained a busy college life outside of the classroom. He became a member Kappa Alpha Psi Fraternity, the black social organization for men. This fraternity was established in 1911 by ten black male students who attended Indiana University (Bloomington, IN).[75] Dudley also devoted a great deal of his creative time to service as a staff writer for the *Daily Collegian* at Wayne; he was also the poetry editor of *Panorama Magazine*; and one writer observes that "he was, in 1949, the first chairman of the Miles Poetry Club, a group of Wayne students who met to read and exchange manuscripts."[76] Dudley successfully completed his undergraduate studies at age thirty-five in 1949, and received an B.A. in English from Wayne.[77]

Dudley's two brothers, James and Arthur, and their sister Esther, were also highly educated, with both brothers holding an B.A. from the University of Michigan, Ann Arbor, and Esther earning her B.A. from Talladega College in Alabama. James also received an M.A. in sociology from the University of Michigan, while Esther held an M.A. in social work from the same institution.[78]

As in the thirties, Dudley's writing career did not fully blossom in the forties. However, he did expand his contacts with literary circles, as is evident by his student days and writing activities at Wayne State University. By the late forties, Randall had also increased his productivity of poems, and in fact, composed some of his finest work, which would later become world famous. Such poems included "Roses and Revolutions" and "The Southern Road," both written in 1948. In 1949, "Roses and Revolutions" became one of his first published poems, when it appeared in *Milestone I*, a Wayne State University publication.[79]

ROSES AND REVOLUTIONS

Musing on roses and revolutions,
I saw night close down on the earth like a great dark wing,
and the lighted cities were like tapers in the night,
and I heard the lamentations of a million hearts
regretting life and crying for the grave,
and I saw the Negro lying in the swamp with his face blown off,
and in northern cities with his manhood maligned and felt the writhing
of his viscera like that of the hare hunted down or the bear at bay,
and I saw men working and taking no joy in their work
and embracing the hard-eyed whore with joyless excitement
and lying with wives and virgins in impotence.

And as I groped in darkness
and felt the pain of millions,
gradually, like day driving night across the continent,
I saw dawn upon them like the sun vision
of a time when all men walk proudly throughout the earth
and the bombs and missiles lie at the bottom of the ocean
like the bones of dinosaurs buried under the shale of eras,
and men strive with each other not for power or the accumulation of paper
but in joy create for others the house, the poem, the game of athletic beauty.

Then washed in the brightness of this vision,
I saw how in its radiance would grow and be nourished and suddenly
burst into terrible and splendid bloom
the blood-red flower of revolution.

According to critic R. Baxter Miller, this free verse poem "addresses both the Civil Rights Movement [of an earlier era] and personal conscience."[80]

THE SOUTHERN ROAD

There the black river, boundary to hell,
And here the iron bridge, the ancient car,
And grim conductor, who will surly yell
Forbids white soldiers where the black ones are.
And I re-live the enforced avatar
Of shuddering journey to a dark abode
made by my sires before another war;
And I set forth upon the southern road
To a land where shadowed songs like flowers swell
And where the earth is scarlet as a scar
Friezed by the bleeding lash that fell (O fell)
Upon my fathers' flesh. O far, far far
And deep my blood has drenched it. None can bar
My birthright to the loveliness bestowed

Upon this country haughtily as a star.
And I set forth upon the southern road.
This darkness and these mountains loom a spell
Of peak-roofed town where yearning steeples soar
And the holy holy chanting of a bell
Shakes human incense on the throbbing air
Where bonfires blaze and quivering bodies char.
Whose hair crisped black like cotton, and fiercely glowed?
I know it; and my entrails melt like tar
And I set forth upon the southern road.

O fertile hillsides where my fathers are,
From which my griefs like troubled streams have flowed.
I have to love you, though they sweep me far.
And I set forth upon the southern road.

Randall recalled in an interview that he "conceived 'The Southern Road' while traveling to a basic training center in the South in 1943, but I didn't write the poem until after the war, in 1948." Critic D. H. Melhem describes "The Southern Road" as "a brilliant poem," which explores the "emblems of his people's suffering," yet expresses their historic love for the fertile land of the South.[81]

Like black writers in the country who lived outside the leading artistic centers of New York and Chicago, Dudley found that a communication gap existed in the forties in Detroit for black poets. Besides Robert Hayden and the student poets at Wayne State University, he did not know of other black writers in Detroit; and Hayden departed Detroit in 1946 to accept a teaching post in the English Department at Fisk University, in Nashville, Tennessee.[82] There were important black writers in Chicago who communicated with each other and held writers' workshops and conferences. The Chicago group included Richard Wright, Gwendolyn Brooks, Margaret Danner, Margaret Walker, Frank Marshall Davis, Margaret Burroughs and others.[83] However, it was almost impossible for a struggling worker, student, and writer like Dudley to travel back and forth to Chicago (a distance of 275 miles from Detroit) to meet the group. In addition, economic conditions were a major factor, as well as the psychological barriers of making contacts with writers who were better known and more widely published than Randall.

A more realistic option for Dudley was to submit his work to black journals for possible publication. But, the economics of publishing black poetry were not easy in the 40s. In one interview, Dudley stated,

> There were no markets. *Opportunity* folded [in 1949, in spite of a circulation of 10,000] and *Crisis* ceased publishing poetry. However, I wasn't much concerned with publishing. I wrote because I enjoyed writing, and was learning how to write. When I would show Robert Hayden a new poem and he would ask where I was going to publish it, I'd be amazed. Why was he so eager to be published? As a result of our varying attitudes, his first book was published in 1940. [Randall's would come 26 years later.] But Bob doesn't allow his early poems to be reprinted now.[84]

The fifties were an eventful decade in the life and work of Dudley Randall and in the continuation of his growth and development as an American poet. Life in the black community of Detroit and throughout the nation also continued to move at a breathless pace, as blacks promoted major activities to address their political, social and economic needs.

These activities involved efforts to break the back of Jim Crow and *de jure* segregation in the South and of *de facto* segregation in the North, through the Civil Rights Movement.

In 1950, Dudley Randall's hometown of Detroit had a population of 1,800,000 of which 300,506 (16.4 percent) were blacks. However, over the next ten years, 542,000 whites would move out, and only 82,000 non-whites would move into the city.[85] Such population shifts would bring profound changes in the history of the city. Scholar Jacqueline Jones characterizes the regional impact of the migration patterns from this period:

> ...in the 1950's, the decade of greatest out-migration from the South, 15 percent of the white population of Kentucky and West Virginia left, while 25 percent of all blacks from the Deep South states of Mississippi and Alabama headed North. Nevertheless, the dynamics of black and white migration were similar in the sense that kin relations served as the vital link sustaining self-generating patterns of movement.[86]

A significant number of such migrants continued to travel to Michigan in search of jobs and a better life — free from the poverty and hardships of conditions back home.

Yet, Detroit was not the promised land, as some local blacks could well testify (nor for that matter was it the hellhole that Mississippi, Arkansas, or Alabama were either). Life for many blacks in 1950s Detroit fell somewhere in the middle of these extremes. Police brutality remained a serious issue for black Detroiters during the decade,[87] as did continued housing and economic discrimination. One study notes that by 1959, "the cycle of deprivation was also accompanied by a cycle of dependence.... In Detroit, blacks constituted 30 percent of the population but 80 percent of the welfare recipients."[88] In 1956, the average black family in Detroit and the rest of the nation had a yearly median income of $4,085, while their white neighbors had $7,698 to use for family support.[89] Nevertheless, in spite of such issues, in 1954 black Detroiters were able to use their political strength to elect Charles Diggs, Jr., to represent the city in the U.S. House of Representatives.[90] It was the first of many political breakthroughs which blacks in Detroit would make in the years ahead.

After graduating from Wayne State University in 1949, Randall decided to continue his studies for a Master of Arts degree in library science at the University of Michigan, Ann Arbor, located twenty-four miles west of Detroit. He enrolled at Michigan during the fall of 1950, while still working as a post office clerk in Detroit.[91] During the fifties, a small number of black undergraduate and graduate students attended the University of Michigan, which had over 20,000 yearly students during the decade, and a faculty of 2,500 in 1959.[92] Since Detroit was so close to the university, Dudley could commute to Ann Arbor, which, by 1960, was a small university town of 67,000 inhabitants. Only 1,085 blacks lived in Ann Arbor in 1950, and they suffered housing and economic discrimination as did blacks in Detroit.[93] Some blacks did well in the town, since the university setting created the illusion of a liberal community open to all groups. However, most black lives in Ann Arbor were "bound within understood limits: they worked in largely unskilled, blue-collar jobs, lived almost exclusively in a half-dozen areas on the northside and along the river, and knew they would be ignored or insulted if they entered certain restaurants."[94] Such conditions, however, did not prevent Randall from completing his program, and he graduated from the University of Michigan in 1951 with his M.A. in library science.[95]

On receiving his professional degree, Randall resigned his post office position in Detroit, and in 1951 accepted an appointment to the library staff at Lincoln University

(Jefferson City, Missouri), where he served as a reference librarian, cataloger, and instructor in the library science program.[96] Lincoln University was established in 1866 as an African-American public land-grant institution; later it offered fields of study at the undergraduate level in agriculture and applied technology, education, business, and the arts and sciences.[97] In 1951, the school, which had a small student body and faculty, offered five degrees, including the B.A., B.S., LL.B, M.A., and B.J.[98]

Randall's father died in 1952, just as he settled into Lincoln with his library service routines. Dudley traveled to his father's hometown in Macon, Georgia, for the funeral.[99] Dudley's service at Lincoln continued for three years, but in 1954, he resigned and assumed a new post at Morgan State College (now University), in Baltimore, Maryland, as the associate librarian for technical services, 1954–55, and in 1955–56, as associate librarian for public services.[100]

Morgan State was established in 1867 by the Methodist Church, but later became a public institution in Maryland. In the early fifties Morgan was a coeducational, liberal arts college which offered B.A. and B.S. degrees in ten majors, including the sciences, social sciences, humanities, home economics, and physical education.[101] The school had an enrollment of 3,000 students, and an excellent academic reputation. Historian August Meier, who taught at Morgan State between 1957 and 1963, observes that in the fifties the institution "probably had more Ph.D.'s on its faculty than any other black school except for Howard University, a situation that was the result of three factors: the growing number of blacks earning doctorates; the threat of desegregation which led many southern states to raise salaries at black colleges, including Morgan; and Morgan's location in a border state, where blacks voted and the racial lines were not drawn as rigidly as farther South."[102] Obviously, Dudley had been attracted to Morgan because of its many positive advantages for his career, and the larger urban setting which Baltimore provided (its population in 1960 was just under a million people, one-third of them African-Americans).[103] He remained at Morgan for two years, until 1956.[104]

A new position in 1956 with the Wayne County (Michigan) Public Library, later renamed as the Wayne County Federated Library System, brought Dudley back to Detroit.[105] During the late fifties he served as assistant, and later as head librarian at the Eloise Hospital Library. His services at Eloise had an impact on his literary interests: "Some of my poems came out of my library experience. I was hospital librarian to the patients at Eloise, the Wayne County General Hospital."[106] On April 4, 1957, Dudley married Vivian Barnett Spencer, his third wife. Vivian was a psychiatric social worker in Detroit who had received a B.A. and M.A. in social work from Wayne State University. Vivian was born in 1923, in Lexington, Kentucky.[107] The Randalls enjoyed a black middle-class lifestyle in Detroit during the late fifties. The incomes of two black professional people made this possible. Dudley's work in a public library also offered him an opportunity to further refine his interests in books, art, music, and literature. It also allowed him to expand his work as a poet, and he began to see his work published in little magazines.[108]

Dudley Randall's cultural, intellectual, and aesthetic interests were influenced by the ongoing Civil Rights Movement of the fifties. Major events such as the 1954 Supreme Court decision in *Brown v. Board of Education* in Topeka, Kansas, and the work of Rosa Parks, Edgar D. Nixon, and Martin Luther King, Jr., in the Montgomery Bus Boycott, 1955–56, and, other momentous events, greatly influenced his rising consciousness as an African-American poet.[109] During his years of preparation to become a fully recognized poet, Dudley sometimes became discouraged. However, he had enough faith in his work to enter "books in the Yale University Younger Poets Competition, for poets under forty, and everytime I said if I didn't win that prize, then I wasn't a poet and couldn't write ... but I never gave up, so I suppose I'll just keep on writing poetry all my life."[110] Yet the fifties were a relatively quiet period for African-American poets. Gwendolyn Brooks' *Annie Allen* (1949), which won the Pulitzer Prize for Poetry in 1950, had a strong impact. But it was the major novelists of the period, especially James Baldwin (1924–87), author of *Go Tell It on the Mountain* (1953), and Ralph Ellison (1914–94), author of *Invisible Man* (1952), which won the National Book Award in 1953, who set the pace for the decade — followed in 1959 by Lorraine Hansberry's (1930–65) play *A Raisin in the Sun*.[111]

For Dudley, it was a matter of getting some of his work into print. This was a critical matter, since most of the major black poets among his contemporaries were widely published by the fifties. This group consisted of such poets as Melvin B. Tolson, Robert Hayden, Margaret Walker, Owen Dodson, and Gwendolyn Brooks. Two of Randall's translations of poems by the Russian poet K. M. Simonov, "Wait for Me, and I'll Return" and "My Native Land," were published in the winter 1951-52 issue of *Midwest Journal*. His best known poem, "Booker T. and W. E. B." (Booker T. Washington, 1856–1915, and W. E. B. Du Bois, 1868–1963), had its first appearance in the winter 1952-53 issue of *Midwest Journal*.[112] These were published while Dudley was on the staff at Lincoln University, Jefferson City, Missouri, the home base of the organ. The journal was created at Lincoln in 1947 as a faculty research organ in the social sciences, arts, and sciences, with the black historian Lorenzo J. Greene (1899–1988) as its editor until 1956. During the fifties the *Midwest Journal* broadened its fields of interests, and published a wide range of writers from both inside and outside of Lincoln. These included Oliver Cox, Armstead Pride, Rayford Logan, Herbert Aptheker, Carol Holman, and Melvin B. Tolson. The journal, which appeared quarterly, had a circulation of 1,500.[113]

Since the fifties, scholars, students, and the general public have responded enthusiastically to Randall's most anthologized poem, "Booker T. and W. E. B."

BOOKER T. AND W. E. B.

(Booker T. Washington and W. E. B. Du Bois)

"It seems to me," said Booker T.,
"It shows a mighty lot of cheek
To study chemistry and Greek
When Mister Charlie needs a hand
To hoe the cotton on his land,
And when Miss Ann looks for a cook,
Why stick your nose inside a book?"

"I don't agree," said W. E. B.
"If I should have the drive to seek
Knowledge of chemistry or Greek,
I'll do it. Charles and Miss can look
another place for hand or cook.
Some men rejoice in skill of hand,
And some in cultivating land,
But there are others who maintain
The right to cultivate the brain."

"It seems to me," said Booker T.,
"That all you folks have missed the boat
Who shout about the right to vote,
And spend vain days and sleepless nights
In uproar over civil rights.
Just keep your mouths shut, do not grouse,
But work, and save, and buy a house."

"I don't agree," said W. E. B.,
"For what can poverty avail
If dignity and justice fail?
Unless you help to make the laws,
They'll steal your house with trumped-up clause.
A rope's as tight, a fire as hot,
No matter how much cash you've got.
Speak soft, and try your little plan,
But as for me, I'll be a man."

"It seems to me," said Booker T.—
"I don't agree"
Said W. E. B.[114]

Critic R. Baxter Miller observes that this poem:

> presents one voice's call and another's response. In alternating stanzas in the poem the
> two Black leaders ... express opposite views. While Booker T. Washington favors agri-
> culture and domestic service, Du Bois emphasizes the human quest to learn liberally.
> Despite Washington's focus upon property, Du Bois proposes dignity and justice. Ran-
> dall, who tries to present each man realistically, favors Du Bois, to whom the narrator
> gives the last line intentionally.[115]

Such an historical consciousness would become a trademark of Randall's poetry in the years
ahead. Dudley also published another historical poem, "Legacy: My South" during the
fifties. It appeared in *Free Lance*, in 1954.[116]

In 1959, Dudley Randall reached the age of forty-five. At this stage of his life, he had
seriously studied and written poetry for thirty-two years, since the age of thirteen. However, he had published very little of his growing body of work, which filled many notebooks in his Detroit home. As a creative person, foremost, Dudley's concentration had been
on writing, not publishing widely in the small magazines, or having a book of poetry published. Perhaps he took solace in his family life and work experiences as a professional librarian. However, in the sixties, he would emerge as "the father of the black poetry movement"
of that era.[117] All of his prior hard work in developing as a writer, and training in library
science, would be harnessed to give birth to the most important publishing company ever
created by an African-American to promote the publication, distribution and enjoyment
of black poetry—Broadside Press. It was a challenge which Dudley Randall was uniquely
qualified to fulfill.

Chapter 2

The Early Development of Broadside Press, 1960–1969

When Dudley Randall reached the age of forty-six in 1960, a shaping decade in American history was about to unfold. He continued his work as the head branch librarian of the Eloise Hospital Library (1960–63); and he was promoted to Librarian IV, on July 1, 1963.[1] With his promotion also came a new position as the head reference-interloan department librarian of the Wayne County Federated Library System at Wayne, Michigan.[2] Randall's supervisor, Clarence Cady, reviewed Dudley's work on October 31, 1963: "his professionalism and personal characteristics have won him the whole hearted respect of his staff."[3] Randall's commitment to the field of librarianship was also expressed by his active membership in such guild organizations as the American Library Association, and the Michigan Library Association. These two significant organizations have been historically devoted to promoting the development of libraries, expanding reading, and aiding efforts to increase literacy in the United States.[4] These interests would remain a major concern of Randall throughout the sixties, as would Dudley's continuous efforts to improve himself intellectually.[5] In 1962, he entered the Master of Arts program in the Humanities at Wayne State University.[6] He completed all of the course requirements, but dropped out of the program before writing a thesis required for the degree. During this period Dudley considered writing a "translation of Chopin['s] preludes and waltzes into 'songs without words'—lyrics so totally expressive of the music that they would merge with it," for his M.A. thesis, but this work was never finished.[7] Yet in 1962, in recognition of his writing talents, the Department of English at Wayne State University presented Dudley with its Tompkins Award for Poetry and Fiction.[8]

In 1964, Dudley and Vivian Randall moved into their new home at 12651 Old Mill Place, Detroit. They were active participants in local Detroit organizations, such as the NAACP, the Michigan Poetry Society, and the Detroit Society for the Advancement of Culture and Education. Dudley also remained active in Kappa Alpha Psi Fraternity during these years; politically he was an Independent, and his religious affiliation was with the Congregational Church.[9]

In the early sixties the Randalls lived in a city which continued to attract black migrants from other regions of the country, and to lose whites to the suburbs. In fact, by 1960, Detroit had a black population of 482,233 (28.8 percent) of the city's total population of 1,670,144. Detroit ranked fourth among U.S. cities in terms of its black population.[10] Statewide in 1960, there were 717,581 blacks (9.2 percent) of Michigan's total population of 7,823,194. Blacks concentrated in the urban areas of the state numbered 686,591.[11]

Black Detroiters were a politically active group in the period between 1960 and 1964. As one study notes "a coalition of [democratic] black, labor, and liberal organizations worked to elect blacks to state and city political and judicial positions."[12] However, during the sixties, "the number of black elected and appointed officials [was] not commensurate with their percentage of the population."[13] Yet, several significant black Detroit figures were elected to office during this period. The list included William Patrick, who was the first black elected to the Detroit City Council in 1957, and served to 1964; George H. Edwards, a black state representative throughout the sixties; Coleman Young, a state senator from 1964 to 1973; and two blacks in Congress, Charles Diggs, first elected in 1954, and John Conyers, elected in 1964. A special moral force in the city was provided by Rosa Parks (1913–) of the Montgomery, Alabama, bus boycott fame, who migrated to Detroit in 1957.[14] Such figures were important influences on the political scene of black Detroit during the sixties.

Although Dudley and Vivian Randall were able to lead a comfortable middle-class lifestyle in Detroit because of their professional careers, conditions were mixed for a large percentage of other blacks in Detroit. Nevertheless, according to scholar Robert H. Brisbane, by the early sixties Detroit held a reputation as a "model" city "in the matter of living conditions for blacks. Enjoying high employment in the automobile industry, Detroit blacks were considered to be among the most affluent in the nation. More than half of them owned automobiles and almost half of them owned their own homes." Yet, Brisbane also gives the testimony that "there were also lesser blacks in the city" who suffered from tremendous housing overcrowding, population density, unemployment, crime, and narcotic addiction.[15] Economic discrimination was indeed a matter of life and death for many blacks. They faced racism in the economic arena at union halls, industrial sites, and in the amount of the black median family income in comparison to whites. For example, in 1960, the white median family income in the United States stood at $8,152, while blacks averaged only $4,562.[16] Furthermore, one recent study estimates that "in 1960, employed black men averaged 49 percent of what employed white men made."[17] Such harsh economic factors made life difficult for many of those in Detroit's black community.

The social realities were also stern for black Detroiters. Segregation in housing was a fact of life for many. For example, in 1960, the indexes of black-white residential segregation stood at 85 percent in Detroit; ten years later it reached 82 percent. Many white Detroiters sought to keep "black representation" to a "minimum" in white neighborhoods. Furthermore, Dearborn, Michigan, stood as an extreme "anti-black" example among the suburban areas, which wished to remain "white only" during this period.[18] Educational matters were of utmost importance to blacks in Detroit, for in 1960 only 34.4 percent of the city's residents were high school graduates, (and 41.8 percent in 1970). Dudley and Vivian Randall stand out from the crowd in Detroit because they were college graduates. In 1960, only 5.3 percent of their fellow citizens also held college degrees, and a decade later the figure was still only 6.2 percent.[19] The state of race relations was also a major concern of blacks in the city in the early sixties. The *Crisis* noted in 1961 that "a chronic, major problem" existed in the "general mistreatment" of Detroit blacks by the police department.[20]

Two of the most powerful black institutions in Detroit during this period were the black church and press. According to historian Richard W. Thomas, a number of key black leaders emerged in Detroit from major black churches. Among the most powerful churches in the black community were the Second Baptist Church, St. Matthew, Bethel A.M.E., St. Paul A.M.E.Z., Ebenezer A.M.E., Scott M.E., St. John's C.M.E., Shiloh Baptist, Hartford

Avenue Baptist, New Bethel Baptist, and Plymouth Congregational. One of the most important contemporary movements among black churches in the city was the Black Christian Nationalist Church (later known as the Shrine of the Black Madonna). This church was created by the Rev. Albert Cleage, Jr. (later known as Jaramogi Abebe Agyeman). Other well-known national black church leaders of this era in Detroit include the Rev. C. L. Franklin, the Rev. James Bristah, the Rev. Ralph J. Boyd, and Prophet Jones.[21]

During the sixties blacks in Michigan were served by eighteen major black newspapers with fifteen of these being concentrated in Detroit.[22] The most dominate of these was the *Michigan Chronicle*, which had a weekly circulation of 48,000 in 1966.[23] The paper was edited by Longworth Quinn, who served as general manager, Louis E. Martin, publisher, and John H. Sengstacke, president.[24] The editorial policy of the *Chronicle* was very progressive and liberal during the sixties, and placed a special emphasis on news items of the Civil Rights Movement, in both the South and the North. Thus, in spite of an environment which contained many economic, political, and social problems, black Detroiters could still depend on institutions like the black church and press, which "served a purpose that was often much larger in scope than that of parallel white institutions." Indeed, both institutions "in the twentieth century [have] been invaluable as a force for racial advancement and as the focal point of every controversy and every concern of black people."[25]

Nonetheless, a rising tide of black anger, disappointment, and resolve to bring about greater reforms in society were also taking place during this period. The Black Freedom Movement in America had two major branches during the sixties. On the one hand stood the traditional civil rights organizations (NAACP, CORE, National Urban League, SCLC, and SNCC) which hoped to bring about an end to segregation and a more integrated society; and on the other the black nationalistic groups (Nation of Islam, Republic of New Africa, the Pan African Congress, Freedom Now Party — Detroit, League of Revolutionary Black Workers, Black Christian Nationalists, and the Organization of Afro-American Unity) which were generally in agreement about ending forced segregation of blacks, but also demanded a more independent, or self-determinative stance for American blacks.[26]

Yet, the average black working-class person in Detroit was less concerned with ideology and more interested in exactly when a real change would take place in their daily lives. Scholar Rhoda Lois Blumberg's suggested list shows the "most pressing demands" which many blacks sought a solution to in the Freedom Movement:

1. Freedom from enslavement and destruction of family.
2. The right to earn a living.
3. Freedom from harassment, terror, and violence.
4. Equal justice.
5. The right to vote.
6. The right to quality education.
7. The movement toward integration, or alternatively, escape from oppression.
8. Recognition of the African cultural heritage.
9. The right to self-pride and an end to stereotyping.[27]

Nevertheless, ideological divisions among blacks would remain a source of concern for many within the black community of the sixties and beyond.

Dudley Randall's life and work were of course, greatly impacted by all of the factors discussed above. It is also significant that during the years 1960–64, Randall's influence as an emerging African-American poet from Detroit began to grow in the consciousness of the black literary community in America. This was a period which witnessed the rapid publication of Dudley's poetry and short stories in journals and anthologies. Table 2.1 shows the full range of Randall's publications for 1960–64. In 1960 and 1961, none of his work appeared in a national publication. However, he was very active in 1962, when eight poems and one short story were published; followed in 1963 with sixteen published poems; and in 1964 with six published poems and one short story.[28]

A breakthrough came for Randall when his work was selected for publication in the three important anthologies of the early sixties: Rosey E. Pool's *Beyond the Blues* (1962), Arna Bontemps' *American Negro Poetry* (1963), and Langston Hughes' *New Negro Poets: USA* (1964).[29] With his work published in these important anthologies, Randall was guaranteed a national and international mass audience, where his poetic voice would be viewed by many for the first time. Similarly, the fact that six of his poems were published in *Negro Digest* and another three in the *Negro History Bulletin* during this time also brought his work to the attention of both the general public and critics of black literature. *Negro Digest* was the largest mass-distributed social and cultural magazine produced by blacks in the early sixties.[30] Created in 1942 by publisher John H. Johnson and edited by Detroit native Hoyt W. Fuller, *Negro Digest* had a general circulation of over 35,000 in 1968.[31] Fuller was very receptive to publishing Randall's work in the sixties, and he was a major influence in helping to advance Dudley's career as a serious writer in the United States. Likewise, Dudley's publications in *Negro History Bulletin* (established in 1937), brought his work to the attention of teachers, scholars and students, and to the membership of Carter G. Woodson's organization, the Association for the Study of Negro Life and History (later renamed in the seventies as the Association for the Study of Afro-American Life and History). This organ had a circulation of 8,070 in 1969.[32] The publication of his work in *Umbra* in 1963 also signaled that Dudley was an accepted (although older) member of the newer generation of black writers who came of age in the early sixties.

Curiously, as Table 2.2 indicates, Randall had an early interest in seeing his very best poems repeatedly republished in the journals and anthologies of the time. In 1960–64, eight of his poems, "I Loved You," "Hymn," "Memorial Wreath," "The Southern Road," "Booker T. and W. E. B.," "The Trouble with Intellectuals," "Souvenirs," and "The Rite," were published twice. These were first in a magazine and then usually in an anthology, or vice versa.[33] As a very serious and committed poet, Dudley still believed that poets should not overpublish their new work.

Randall's broad interests in the humanities continued during the sixties with his translation of poetry from the Russian, Latin, and French languages into English: "He has translated some of Catullus into the hendecasyllabics and Sapphic Strophes of the original. In translating, whether from Aleksandr Pushkin or Konstantin M. Simonov or Paul Verlaine, Randall tries to render the form as well as the content."[34]

Such concerns, however, did not distract Dudley from his main task of capturing and interpreting the African-American experience in poetic form. His body of poetic work, according to scholars James A. Emanuel and Theodore Gross, "is usually meditative, rhythmical, formally designed. His racial material tends to be somber, historical, and morally urgent, although tempered with sympathy and occasional humor."[35]

In 1964, when Dudley Randall reached the age of fifty, the Black Arts Movement had

Table 2.1
Dudley Randall's Publications, 1960–1964

Journals and Anthologies	Number of Published Poems	Number of Published Short Stories
American Negro Poetry (A) (1963)	3	
Beyond the Blues: New Poems by American Negroes (A) (1962)	3	
Correspondence (J) (1963)	3	
Negro Digest (J) (1962)	2	
(1963)	1	
(1964)	3	1
Negro History Bulletin (J) (1962)	3	1
New Negro Poets: USA (A) (1964)	3	
Ten: An Anthology of Detroit Poets (A) (1963)	8	
Umbra (J) (1963)	1	

Table 2.2
Republication of Dudley Randall's Poems, 1960–1964

Poem	Published in
"I Loved You"	*Negro Digest* (Sept. 1962); and corrected copy (Dec. 1962)
"Hymn"	*Negro History Bulletin* (Oct. 1962); and *Ten: An Anthology of Detroit Poets* (1963)
"Memorial Wreath"	*Negro History Bulletin* (Oct. 1962); and *New Negro Poets: USA* (1964)
"The Southern Road"	*Negro History Bulletin* (Oct. 1962); and *New Negro Poets: USA* (1964)
"Booker T. and W. E. B."	*Beyond the Blues* (1962); and *Ten: An Anthology of Detroit Poets* (1963)
"The Trouble with Intellectuals"	*Correspondence* (March 1963); and *Ten: An Anthology of Detroit Poets* (1963)
"Souvenirs"	*Ten: An Anthology of Detroit Poets* (1963); and *Negro Digest* (March 1964)
"The Rite"	*Ten: An Anthology of Detroit Poets* (1963); and *Negro Digest* (Sept. 1964)

been in progress for five years in the United Sates. Often compared to the Harlem Renaissance Movement of the twenties — and a flowering of African-American cultural production in this country — the Black Arts Movement of the sixties was larger, in that it took place in many parts of the nation, whereas the Harlem Renaissance was concentrated in the major cities along the Atlantic seaboard. Geographic considerations aside both movements have continued to have an immense impact on black life and culture.

In essence, the Black Arts Movement was perhaps best defined by Larry Neal, one of its major theoreticians as "a Movement concerned with artistic responsibility to a Black community, employing an aesthetic derived from Black experience."[36] Central writers and editors of the movement during the sixties, in addition to Neal, were Hoyt W. Fuller, Addison Gayle, Jr., Don L. Lee (later named Haki R. Madhubuti), and Amiri Baraka (LeRoi Jones). Black women writers who made major contributions to the movement were Carolyn Rodgers, Sonia Sanchez, Sarah Webster Fabio, and Carolyn Fowler [Carolyn F. Gerald].[37] Thousands of students, artists, workers, and writers were influenced by the efforts of the movement to promote black consciousness, and to create a black aesthetic in order to achieve "a Distinctive code for the creation and evaluation of black art."[38] Abroad, the campaign for an independent Africa also greatly shaped the Blacks Arts Movement, as did the writings of the black psychiatrist and revolutionist, Frantz Fanon. His books *The Wretched of the Earth* (1966), *Black Skins, White Masks* (1967), and *Toward the African Revolution* (1969) were a major international influence on the Black Arts Movement, because of their analysis of the need for black people everywhere to use struggle, resistance, and violence to overcome colonialism, discrimination, and racism.[39]

Randall was familiar with the Black Arts Movement and its advocates in the United States.[40] Detroit also had its own component of the movement. Chief influences in the city's movement were the playwrights and directors Woodie King, Jr., David Rambeau, and Ron Milner, active at Concept East Theatre; poet Margaret Danner; the black staff members at *On the Town* (a radical black-owned publication active in 1963–64); and jazz and other musicians in the Detroit Artists' Workshop, among others.[41]

Four formative events between 1962 and 1964 contributed to the ongoing development of Dudley Randall as a poet, critic, and cultural seer in Detroit. First, in 1962, he became a regular member of Margaret Danner's Boone House, a black cultural center active in Detroit between 1962 and 1964.[42] Dudley described Boone House in an interview:

> There were a number of activities at Boone House from jazz sessions to creative writing classes for children. Since the federal government had not begun to fund community projects at this time, Margaret had to rely on membership fees and donations. Boone House was an old abandoned parish house lent to Margaret by Dr. Theodore S. Boone, pastor of New Bethel Baptist Church in the inner city of Detroit. In the winter, the place would be insufficiently heated, and we would come early to the meetings in order to break up pieces of wood to make a fire in the fireplace.[43]

On Friday or Sunday night sessions at Boone House, Dudley was able to read his own work and to meet a considerable number of the black writers currently living in or formerly from Detroit. These writers included Oliver LaGrone, Ed Simplins, Harold Lawrence, James Thompson, Betty Ford, and Woodie King.[44]

Secondly, in 1962 Randall and other Detroit area writers were invited to submit work for a special October 1962 issue of the *Negro History Bulletin*, featuring black Detroit writers. Dudley remembers that until this time he had not "met many black writers. I then discovered that there were other black writers in Detroit. It was a revelation to me."[45] In this year Dudley's work also appeared in Rosey E. Pool's anthology, *Beyond the Blues*. This collection also contained work by other black Detroit poets: Margaret Danner, James Edward McCall, Robert Hayden, Oliver LaGrone, Naomi Long, and James W. Thompson.[46] Randall believes that this book "was the first comprehensive anthology of black poetry published since Langston Hughes' and Arna Bontemps' *The Poetry of the Negro, 1746–1949*."[47]

Thirdly, Randall was greatly moved by the Civil Rights Movement in the South during 1963, and like many Americans he was shocked when the news was announced on September 15, 1963, that the Sixteenth Street Baptist Church in Birmingham, Alabama, had been bombed injuring twenty-one persons. Four young black girls (Carol Robertson, Cynthia Wesley, Addie Mae Collins [all fourteen years old], and Denise McNair [age eleven]) were killed in this attack by the Ku Klux Klan.[48] This tragic event was captured by Randall in one of his most famous poems, the "Ballad of Birmingham."

BALLAD OF BIRMINGHAM
(On the bombing of a church in Birmingham, Alabama, 1963)

"Mother dear, may I go downtown
Instead of out to play,
And march the streets of Birmingham
In a Freedom March today?"

"No, baby, no, you may not go,
For the dogs are fierce and wild,
And clubs and hoses, guns and jails
Aren't good for a little child."

"But, mother, I won't be alone.
Other children will go with me,
And march the streets of Birmingham
To make our country free."

"No, baby, no, you may not go,
For I fear those guns will fire.
But you may go to church instead
And sing in the children's choir."

She has combed and brushed her night-dark hair,
And bathed rose petal sweet,
And dawn white gloves on her small brown hands,
And white shoes on her feet.

The mother smiled to know her child
Was in the sacred place,
But that smile was the last smile
To come upon her face.

For when she heard the explosion,
Her eyes grew wet and wild.
She raced through the streets of Birmingham
Calling for her child.

She clawed through bits of glass and brick,
Then lifted out a shoe.
"O, here's the shoe my baby wore,
But, baby, where are you?"[49]

Randall was also inspired to write "Dressed All in Pink" after the assassination of President John F. Kennedy on November 22, 1963.

DRESSED ALL IN PINK

It was a wet and cloudy day
when the prince took his last ride.
The prince rode with the governor,
and his princess rode beside.

"And would you like to ride inside
for shelter from the rain?"
"No, I'll ride outside, where I can wave
and speak to my friends again."

They ride among cheering crowds,
the young prince and his mate.

The governor says "See how they smile
and cheer you where they wait."

The prince rides with the governor,
his princess rides beside,
dressed all in pink as delicate
as roses of a bride.

Pink as a rose the princess rides,
but bullets from a gun
turn that pink to as deep a red
as red, red blood can run,

for she bends to where the prince lies still
and cradles his shattered head,
and there that pink so delicate
is stained a deep, deep red.

The prince rides with the governor,
the princess rides beside,
and her dress of pink so delicate
a deep, deep red is dyed.[50]

Later Jerry Moore, a folksinger, secured Dudley's permission to set the "Ballad of Birmingham" and "Dressed All in Pink" to music for publication.[51] The fourth event between 1962 and 1964 which had an impact on Randall's career was a collaboration with Margaret Danner on a joint collection of poetry, whereby each poet would pair an individual poem to the other's work, to create a full poetry volume. However, as the poets circulated the book to various publishers in 1962–64, "all of them rejected the manuscript."[52] Thus, the above factors had an influence on the idea that perhaps Dudley could become a new publisher of not only his own work, but that of other black poets as well. The crystallization of his thoughts on these matters would lead to the creation of Broadside Press a year later, in 1965.[53]

The initial spark for the creation of Broadside Press came in 1965, when Randall decided to publish the "Ballad of Birmingham" as a broadside, that is, a single poem on one sheet of paper. This poem was followed by his second broadside (#2), "Dressed All in Pink," which reflected his concerns growing out of the assassination of President John F. Kennedy in 1963. The early broadsides sold for between thirty-five and fifty cents.[54] As Randall soon began to publish other broadsides, thus was born the name of the new company. At first the focus was on his own poetry, but later he turned his attention to the more established blacks poets of the period, such as Langston Hughes, Margaret Walker, Gwendolyn Brooks, Melvin B. Tolson, Amiri Baraka (LeRoi Jones), and Robert Hayden, also adding original new works by younger poets.[55] Certainly his work was aided by the fact that many of the older generation of black poets allowed him to reprint their work. This enabled the publisher to begin the process of developing the new company.

Randall began Broadside Press without "a blueprint," or savings, nor any investments from other writers or investors. In fact, he paid for the first broadside with "twelve dollars" that he "took out of his paycheck" as a librarian in Detroit.[56] Such were the humble beginnings of "the major black press in America" during the period 1965–75.[57]

The new company had many objectives, but central to its goals was Randall's desire "to bring poetry to the people," because "poetry is the most effective form of writing."[58]

RACE RESULTS, U.S.A., 1966:

**White Right—A Favorite—Wins;
Lurline—A Long Shot—Places;
Black Power—A Long Shot—Shows.**

For Stokely Carmichael

BY SARAH WEBSTER FABIO

Blistering,
the lone black jockey's
ear deafens beneath
the roar of torments
hurled from Birmingham
bleachers by the helmeted
keepers of the leashed
law as their white hot
screams dare him dare
run the race; those
killers of his dreams
invade the bugle's blare,
spooking his steed; yet,
he's off!

Galloping,
furiously, the horses round
the curves and come into
the homestretch: in the
lead, it's White Right;
Lurline, in line for second;
and, wait, the black jockey,
eyeing the hateful hurdles
blocking him, grips tight
his reins for a quickening
thrust:

noses forward,
testily, heads out from
the dusty herd, and jeers
back at those who mourn
the lost purses of their
thoroughbreds. He spurs
on the dark horse to
the finish, toward his
fully reckoned, time-honed
hour of triumph.

AT BAY

MY SIRENS
AIN'T NEVER STOPPED SCREAMIN'
MY SEARCHLIGHTS
AIN'T GOT TO NO SKY
MY PISTOL
AIN'T HUNG UP FOR DREAMIN'
MY TEAR GAS
AIN'T MADE NOBODY CRY.

COME ON, COPS.
AIN'T BUT ONE WAY
TO LIVE AND TO DIE.

JAMES A. EMANUEL

Two examples of early broadsides: *(left)* Sarah Webster Fabio's "Race Results, U.S.A., 1966" and *(right)* James A. Emanuel's "At Bay" (courtesy Broadside Press).

He also wanted "to give people joy, because poetry gives joy." Broadside Press also existed to help in creating African-American literature, "and pride in black literature, therefore, pride in" black people. Furthermore, the company sought to aid the black struggle "to create black consciousness, and values for black people to live by." Such aid was meant to reach the widest possible audience in the black community — not just "college professors and other poets."[59]

Randall viewed Broadside Press' role as that of an active participant both in the Black Arts Movement and in the ongoing struggles of the Civil Rights Movement. Randall and the writers and artists who published under the Broadside label became major shapers of the cultural and intellectual developments fostered by the Black Arts Movement. In fact, in the area of black published poetry produced during the sixties and seventies, no other American city can match the record created in Detroit by Dudley Randall and the Broadside Press.

Besides the factors previously emphasized, Broadside Press' creation and early successes were also influenced by the strong cultural base in Detroit's black community. Most noteworthy during this period was the production of music created by Barry Gordy's Motown Records, and by the work of the city's other outstanding soul (especially Aretha Franklin), blues, jazz, and religious musicians.[60] Along with strong chapters of the traditional black Civil Rights Movement organizations in Michigan (the National Association for the Advancement of Colored People, the Congress of Racial Equality, the National Urban League, the Southern Christian Leadership Conference, and the Student Non-violent Coordinating Committee), Detroit also contained a wide variety of other black organizations — from conservative black fraternities and sororities, to activist nationalist groups.

Table 2.3 is a selected list which indicates the range of organizations operated by blacks in Detroit during the sixties and seventies. Such organizations, be they radical, moderate, or conservative, served the community as educationally minded institutions, which generally supported reading and literacy activities among their members. They also served as another possible outlet for Dudley Randall and other black publishers to expand their marketing strategies for selling books and other publishing materials in the community, especially since highly motivated individuals may also have had some funds with which to purchase poetry and other reading materials. (For the national situation see Table 2.4.[61])

Yet, in spite of the availability of such a wide diversity of black institutions, Randall and other black artists and cultural workers were always faced with the fact that Detroit was not one of the four national centers of African-American culture. New York City, Chicago, Los Angeles, and Washington, D.C., were the thriving centers of wealth, and business, and institutions controlled by blacks. These cities were also the nerve centers for black college and university graduates and professionals, and even writers (with older black writers' workshops, black newspapers, magazines, and publishers. Such factors served to remind black Detroiters that they had to carefully nurture and cherish the black arts in Detroit — for other black artistic centers including Newark, New Orleans, Philadelphia, and Cleveland, among others, stood ready to claim the honor of being a "national" center of black artistic endeavors.[62]

Dudley Randall's early years as editor and publisher at Broadside Press were thus affected by local, state, regional, national, and even international issues. A black publisher could never take anything for granted.[63] Perhaps Randall's publishing endeavors during the mid-sixties were made easier by the goodwill which the new company received from a number of individuals. In fact, Randall credits the help of individuals as having been more important to the survival of Broadside Press between 1965 and 1969 than was the support received from institutions.[64] Two national figures played a dramatic role in promoting Broadside Press in the sixties. They were Hoyt W. Fuller (1923–81), the editor of *Negro Digest/ Black World* (1961–76); and writer Gwendolyn Brooks, who left her publisher, Harper and Row, in 1969 to join the ranks of black poets who published with Dudley Randall.[65] The strong commitment of these individuals was extremely valuable in validating the work of the new company, in attracting new talent to Broadside Press, and in fostering a long-term degree of public acceptance.

When Dudley Randall began his publishing activities as editor of Broadside Press in 1965–66, he worked "from a single room in his home" in Detroit.[66] However, over the next few years he developed a staff of young associates and professionals, who also played a major role in the early success of the company. For Randall, "people, not institutions, made a difference in the day to day operations of the company." Three associates were essential to the early organization of Broadside: "They were Malaika Wangara, librarian, who devised standard forms, such as a reply to queries on publication; her sister Mrs. Ruth Foundren who wrote out procedures for different tasks; and her brother Bill Whitsitt who made out pay rolls and tax forms."[67] During the first ten years of Broadside, ten workers were employed

Table 2.3
Selected Black Organizations in
Detroit During the 1960s and 1970s

Traditional "Big Five"	Conservative to Moderate	Radical
NAACP (1909–)	Alpha Kappa Alpha Sorority (1908–)	Black Panther Party (1966–)
National Urban League (1910–)	Alpha Phi Alpha Fraternity (1906–)	Citizens Action Committee (Summer 1966–)
CORE (1942–)	Association for the Study of Afro-American Life & History (1915–)	Concept East Theater (1960s–)
SCLC (1957–)	Delta Sigma Theta Sorority (1913–)	Detroit Artist's Workshop (1960s–)
SNCC (1960–73)	Improved Benevolent Protective Order of Elks of the World (1898–)	Detroit Metropolitan Welfare Rights Organization (1967–)
	International Conference of Grand Chapters Order of Eastern Star (1907–)	Federation of Self-Determination (1960s)
	Kappa Alpha Psi Fraternity (1911–)	League of Revolutionary Black Workers (mid–1960s)
	Michigan Chronicle (1936–)	The Malcolm X Society (mid–1960s)
	National Bar Association (1925–)	Nation of Islam (1930–)
	National Business League (1900–)	Organization of Afro-American Unity (1964–)
	National Council of Negro Women (1935–)	Radical Education Program (1970–)
	National Dental Association (1913–)	The Republic of New Africa (1969–)
	National Insurance Association (1921–)	SNCC (After 1965–73)
	National Medical Association (1895–)	Universal Negro Improvement Association (1916–)
	National Newspaper Association (1940–)	Vaughn's Bookstore (1960s–80s)
	Omega Psi Phi Fraternity (1911–)	
	Operation Push (1972–)	
	Phi Beta Sigma Fraternity (1914–)	
	Shaw College of Detroit (1936–83)	
	Zeta Phi Beta Sorority (1920–)	

at different stages in the development of the company. Perhaps the next most important person to aid the company's work was Melba Boyd, an assistant editor between 1972 and 1976.[68]

The major publication focus of Broadside Press between 1965 and 1969 was on producing inexpensive, but high quality broadsides, pamphlets (chapbooks), cloth books, and

Table 2.4
Major Black Publishers in Select Cities and States During the 1960s and 1970s

Chicago	Detroit	Washington, D.C.	Los Angeles	New York
Afro-Am Pub. Co. (1963–)	Agascha Prods. (1970–1978)	Afro-American (1933–)	Black Liberation Pubs. (1960s)	African World Distributors (1978–)
Black Books Bulletin (1971–)	Black Arts Magazine (1971–)	Associated Pubs. (1930s–)	Black Panther (1970–)	Afro-Arts (1971–)
Chicago Defender (1905–)	Black Arts Pubs. (1969–)	Drum & Spear Press (1969–1974)	Black Scholar (1967–)	Black Creation (1970s–)
College Peoples Press (1970s–)	Black Graphics International (1968–)	Howard Univ. Mag.	Black Scholar Press (1970s–)	Black Dialogue Press (1965–)
DuSable Museum Press (1971–)	Black Star Pubs. (1970?–1978)	Howard Univ. Press (1972–)	Journal of Black Poetry (1967–)	Black Theatre (1968–72)
Free Black Press (1971–)	Broadside Press (1965–)	Journal of Black Psychology (1974–)	Journal of Black Poetry Press (1967–75)	Blyden Press (1967–)
Johnson Pub. Co. (1961–)	Ink & Spot Pubs. (1976–)	Journal of Negro Education (1931–)	Journal of Black Studies (1970–)	The Crisis (1910–)
Negro Digest/Black World (1942–51, 1961–76)	Lotus Press (1972–)	Negro History Bulletin (1937–)	Julian Richardson Associates (1960s–)	Emerson Hall Publishers (1969–)
Nommo (1969–)	Michigan Chronicle (1936–)	Three Continents Press (1973–)	L.A. Sentinel (1934–)	Freedomways (1961–)
Third World Press (1967–)	Tribune (1922–66)		Yardbird Press (1972–)	Liberator (1961–)
				N.Y. Amsterdam News (1909–)
				Third Press (1970–)

cassette tapes of poetry.[69] In total, the company produced thirty-three broadsides by twenty-eight poets; nineteen paperbacks and three hardback or cloth editions of books; and twelve tapes of poetry during this period.

During the first five years of Broadside Press, the Broadside Series played an important part in the production of works of poetry published by Randall. Table 2.5 illustrates the range of single poems which were selected for publication by Broadside.[70] The editor was especially pleased with the first six poems printed, which he entitled "Poems of the Negro Revolt," because this group of broadsides contains "outstanding poems by some of our finest poets." Poets in this group included Dudley Randall, Robert Hayden, Margaret Walker, Melvin B. Tolson and Gwendolyn Brooks. According to playwright Woodie King, Jr., these are the "Forerunners" among contemporary black American poets, from the period of the late thirties and forties — and were among the leaders of the generation to succeed the poets produced by the Harlem Renaissance of the twenties and the early thirties.[71]

The first set of thirty-three broadsides includes work by most of the leading black poets in the United States since World War

Gwendolyn Brooks was born on June 7, 1917, in Topeka, Kansas, but has lived most of her life in Chicago, Illinois. In 1950, she became the first African-American recipient of a Pulitzer Prize, for her second book of poetry, *Annie Allen.* In 1968, she was appointed the poet laureate of Illinois. Today she remains one of the most highly respected black poets in the United States (photo by Roy Lewis; courtesy Broadside Press).

II. However, Randall clearly likes the poetry of Gwendolyn Brooks and Don L. Lee (Haki R. Madhubuti). Thus, the poets with the largest number of broadsides published in the sixties include Randall, with three, numbers 1, 2, and 8; Brooks with two, numbers 6 and 19; and Lee with three, numbers 16, 25, and 33.

The twenty-eight Broadside Series poets published during this decade include twenty men and eight women; or 72 percent for the former, and 28 percent for the latter. Eight poets who published broadsides with the company in the sixties also had work selected later by the press for full-length poetry books. The poets in this group were Dudley Randall, Margaret Walker, Gwendolyn Brooks, Don L. Lee, Etheridge Knight, Margaret Danner, James A. Emanuel, and Doughtry Long. Among this group five, or 62.5 percent were men and three, or 37.5 percent were women.

The social backgrounds of the Broadside Series poets offers an interesting portrait of a select group of black poets at the end of the sixties. Four groups of distinct black poets emerge from the data. Group one consists of ten major black poets, including Gwendolyn Brooks, Robert Hayden, Langston Hughes, LeRoi Jones (Amiri Baraka), Naomi Long Madgett, Raymond Patterson, Dudley Randall, Melvin B. Tolson, Jean Toomer and Margaret

Table 2.5

Broadside Series Poets 1965–69

Author	Title	Year	Price	Gender
1. Dudley Randall	"Ballad of Birmingham"	1965	$0.35	M
2. Dudley Randall	"Dressed All in Pink"	1965	.50	M
3. Robert Hayden	"Gabriel"	1966	.50	M
4. Margaret Walker	"Ballad of the Free"	1966	.50	F
5. Melvin B. Tolson	"The Sea Turtle and the Shark"	1966	.50	M
6. Gwendolyn Brooks	"We Real Cool"	1966	.50	F
7. LeRoi Jones (Amiri Baraka)	"A Poem for Black Hearts"	1966	.50	M
8. Dudley Randall	"Booker T. and W. E. B."	1966	.50	M
9. Bobb James Hamilton	"A Child's Nightmare"	1966	.50	M
10. Naomi Long Madgett	"Sunny"	1966	.50	F
11. Julia Fields	"I Heard a Young Man Saying"	1967	.50	F
12. Carolyn Reese	"Letter from a Wife"	1967	.50	F
13. Langston Hughes	"Backlash Blues"	1967	.50	M
14. Sarah E. Webster Fabio	"Race Results, U.S.A., 1966"	1967	.50	F
15. Jean Toomer	"Song of the Sun"	1967	.50	M
16. Le Graham (Ahmed A. Alhamisi)	"The Black Narrator"	1967	.50	M
17. Harold Lawrence (Harun Kofi Wangara)	"Black Madonna"	1967	.50	M
18. Gwendolyn Brooks	"The Wall"	1967	.50	F
19. Don L. Lee (Haki R. Madhubuti)	"Back Again, Home"	1968	.50	M
20. Raymond Patterson	"At That Moment"	1968	.50	M
21. Etheridge Knight	"2 Poems for Black Relocation Centers"	1968	.50	M
22. Margaret Danner	"Not Light, Nor Bright, Nor Feathery"	1968	.50	F
23. James A. Emanuel	"At Bay"	1968	.50	M
24. Rolland Snellings (Askia Muhammad Toure)	"Earth"	1968	.50	M
25. Don L. Lee	"Assassination"	1968	.50	M
26. Bahala T. Nkrumah	"Black Unity"	1968	.50	M
27. B. Felton (Elmer Buford)	"Ghetto Waif"	1968	.50	M
28. Tony Rutherford (Umar Hassan)	"Black and White"	1968	.50	M
29. Carl Killibrew	"The Squared Circle"	1969	.50	M
30. Alicia L. Johnson	"Our Days Are Numbered"	1969	.50	F
31. Walter Bradford	"T.C. (Terry Callier, True Christian)"	1969	.50	M
32. Doughtry Long	"Ginger Bread Mama"	1969	.50	M
33. Don L. Lee	"One Sided Shoot-out"	1969	.50	M

Walker. Group two is composed of four established writers: Margaret Danner, James A. Emanuel, Sarah E. Webster Fabio, and Julia Fields. Group three has five members, who because of their poetic talents, very quickly assumed positions during this period as established (new) writers: Etheridge Knight, Harold Lawrence (Harun Kofi Wangara), Don L. Lee (Haki R. Madhubuti), Doughtry Long, and Askia Muhammad Toure (Rolland Snellings). A list of nine new writers makes up the fourth group portrait, or status position of the poets in the sixties. These included: Le Graham (Ahmed Alhamisi), Walter Bradford, B. Felton (Elmer Buford), Bobb James Hamilton, Alicia L. Johnson, Carl Killibrew, Bahala

T. Nkrumah, Carolyn Reese, and Tony Rutherford (Umar Hassan). All of the twenty-eight poets are African-Americans.

A large number of the poets, eleven of twenty-eight, or 39 percent, were born in the Midwest; eight, or 29 percent, in the South; and seven, or 25 percent, in the East. Data are not available on two of the poets, or 7 percent of the sample. Certainly since Broadside Press is located in a central city in the Midwest, the company greatly promoted the work of poets from that region. Yet, Dudley Randall was fair in publishing broadsides of poets from all parts of the country: eleven poets, or 39 percent, lived in such Midwestern locations as Detroit (six), Chicago (three), Indianapolis, Indiana (one), and East St. Louis, Illinois (one); eight, or 29 percent lived in Eastern cities, such as New York City and its suburbs (five), Newark and Trenton, New Jersey (one each), and Cleveland, Ohio (one); three, or 17 percent, lived in southern cities, such as Jackson, Mississippi, Scotland Neck, North Carolina, and Nashville, Tennessee; and one poet resided in Berkeley, California. Two others, or 7 percent, were deceased by the end of the decade, and the whereabouts of three are unknown for this period.

The Broadside Series poets during the sixties were a highly educated group: sixteen of them, or 57 percent attended historically white colleges and universities, while ten, or 35 percent, were students at historically black institutions. By 1969, sixteen of the poets, or 57 percent had attended a historically white graduate school. Two poets, Emanuel and Walker, held the Ph.D. degree, and only one poet, Knight, did not attend college prior to the end of this period.[72]

Although the Broadside Series poets explore many themes in their personal lives, and in the experiences of black people, the following topics are central to understanding their poetic voices in this format: the African heritage of black Americans; criticism of American racism; black life in Chicago; black art; the complexity of the black experience; the struggle for racial pride; the Civil Rights Movement; the prison experience; the triumphs and setbacks of black women; war and peace; fostering black consciousness and culture; the nature of the urban experience; the South; and among others, the role of the Islamic faith in black life.

Margaret Walker's "The Ballad of the Free" (Broadside No. 4) brings forth many of these themes:

> Bold Nat Turner by the blood of God
> Rose up preaching on Virginia's sod;
> Smote the land with his passionate plea
> Time's done come to set my people free.
>
> > The serpent is loosed and the hour is come
> > The last shall be first and the first shall be none
> > The serpent is loosed and the hour is come
>
> Gabriel Prosser looked at the sun,
> Said, "Sun, stand still till the work is done.
> The world is wide and the time is long
> And man must meet the avenging wrong."
>
> > The serpent is loosed and the hour is come
> > The last shall be first and the first shall be none
> > The serpent is loosed and the hour is come

Denmark Vesey led his band
Across the hot Carolina land.
The plot was foiled, the brave men killed,
But Freedom's cry was never stilled.

   The serpent is loosed and the hour is come
   The last shall be first and the first shall be none
   The serpent is loosed and the hour is come

Toussaint L'Ouverture won
All his battles in the tropic sun,
Hero of the black man's pride
Among those hundred who fought and died.

   The serpent is loosed and the hour is come
   The last shall be first and the first shall be none
   The serpent is loosed and the hour is come

Brave John Brown was killed but he
Became a martyr of the free,
For he declared that blood would run
Before the slaves their freedom won.

   The serpent is loosed and the hour is come
   The last shall be first and the first shall be none
   The serpent is loosed and the hour is come

Wars and Rumors of Wars have gone,
But Freedom's army marches on.
The heroes' list of dead is long,
And Freedom still is for the strong.

Randall's innovation with the Broadside Series introduced a new element of excitement and enjoyment among black poetry lovers everywhere. Yet, it was Broadside's work in publishing a string of new poetry books during the sixties which really set the company apart from other like-minded ventures. Table 2.6 denotes the volumes of poetry published by the press in the sixties.[73] The first Broadside book planned for publication was *For Malcolm X,* an anthology of poems collected in honor of the fallen leader. *For Malcolm X* germinated out of Randall's attendance in 1966 at the Fisk University First Black Writer's Conference, in Nashville, Tennessee.[74] However, because of a printer's delay, the actual first book to appear was a joint work of Margaret Danner and Dudley Randall, *Poem Counterpoem,* in December 1966. Critic R. Baxter Miller observes that this book was "Perhaps the first of its kind" with "ten poems each by Danner and Randall. The poems are alternated to form a kind of double commentary on the subjects they address in common. Replete with allusion to social and intellectual history, the verses stress nurture and growth."[75]

When the anthology *For Malcolm X,* edited by Dudley Randall and Margaret G. Burroughs, was widely distributed in 1967–68, it too aided the growth of Broadside Press.[76] Many American poets had something to say about the life, work, and death of one of the ten top black American leaders of the twentieth century. (The others were Booker T. Washington, 1856–1915; W. E. B. DuBois, 1868–1963; Ida B. Wells-Barnett, 1862–1931; Marcus Garvey, 1887–1940; Mary McLeod Bethune, 1875–1955; Elijah Muhammad, 1897–1975; Fannie Lou Hamer, 1917–77; Martin Luther, King, Jr., 1929–68; and Ella Baker, 1903–86.) Author John Oliver Killens (1916-87) sums up the impact of this book when he wrote that:

Table 2.6

Broadside Press Books, 1965–1969

Authors	Publication	Genre	Price of Book	Price of Tape	Pages	Gender of Author
1966						
Margaret Danner & Dudley Randall	Poem Counterpoem	Poetry	$1.00	$5.00	26	F, M
1967						
Margaret G. Burroughs & Dudley Randall, eds.	For Malcolm X, Poems on the Life and Death of Malcolm X	Poetry Anthology	$2.95 (Cloth, $4.95)		136	F, M
1968						
Margaret Danner	Impressions of African Art Forms	Poetry	$1.00		24	F
James A. Emanuel	The Treehouse and Other Poems	Poetry	$1.00	$5.00	26	M
Nikki Giovanni	Black Judgement (Distributor of in the U.S.A.)	Poetry	$1.50		40	F
Etheridge Knight	Poems from Prison	Poetry	$1.00	$5.00	34	M
Don L. Lee	Black Pride	Poetry	$1.00		36	M
Dudley Randall	Cities Burning	Poetry	$1.00	$5.00	18	M
1969						
Gwendolyn Brooks	Riot	Poetry	$1.00	$5.00	26	F
Jon Eckels	Home Is Where the Soul Is	Poetry	$1.00	$5.00	28	M
Mae Jackson	Can I Poet with You	Poetry	$1.00		22	F
Keorapetse Kgositsile	Spirits Unchained	Poetry	$1.00	$5.00	26	M
Don L. Lee	Think Black! (Second Edition)	Poetry	$1.00		26	M
	Don't Cry, Scream!	Poetry	$1.50 (Cloth, $4.50)	$5.00	66	M
Marvin X	Black Man Listen	Poetry	$1.00	$5.00	30	M
Beatrice M. Murphy & Nancy L. Arnez	The Rocks Cry Out	Poetry	$1.00	$5.00	26	F, F
Dudley Randall, ed.	Black Poetry, a Supplement to Anthologies Which Exlcude Black Poets	Poetry Anthology	$0.95 (Cloth, $4.00)		50	M
Sonia Sanchez	Home Coming	Poetry	$1.00	$5.00	34	F
Stephany Fuller	Moving Deep	Poetry	$1.00	$5.00	34	F

> From the preface by Ossie Davis to the very last poem, this book is a great tribute to a
> great man, a man who so loved the black and disinherited of this world that he gave his
> life that they might live their own lives more abundantly. And yet these poems are tes-
> taments to his life, not to his death.... "Malcolm lives!"[77]

The number of copies sold also spoke of the book's power and inspiration. In 1967, 8,000
copies were purchased from Broadside.[78]

For Malcolm X contained the work of thirty-one men and fourteen women. Poetry
appeared in the anthology from such major writers as Gwendolyn Brooks, Margaret Burroughs, Margaret Danner, Mari Evans, Julia Fields, Sonia Sanchez, and Margaret Walker.
Seven major African-American men were represented in the volume. Ossie Davis contributed a "Preface" and "Eulogy" to Malcolm X; Randall, the "Introduction"; and Joe
Goncalves, Robert Hayden, Ted Joans, LeRoi Jones, and Raymond Patterson, poems. Seven
newer women poets were selected for the book, as were thirty-three younger males.[79]

In 1968, Broadside Press published eight books; these were followed by another eleven
new works in 1969. (See Table 2.6.) The authors or editors were divided equally in number
between men and women. Three writers of this group produced two or more Broadside books
during the sixties. Dudley Randall was the coauthor of *Poem Counterpoem*, the coeditor of *For
Malcolm X*, the editor of *Black Poetry*, and the author of *Cities Burning*. Broadside published
three of Don L. Lee's books during this era—*Black Pride*, the second edition of *Think Black*,
and *Don't Cry, Scream!*. Margaret Danner was the coauthor with Randall of *Poem Counterpoem*
and the author of *Impressions of African Art Forms*. Of the above group of sixteen authors who
wrote Broadside books, twelve also made cassette tapes of their work for the company.[80]

The titles selected by Broadside authors and editors during the sixties reveal a clear
linkage between the Africa past, present, and future; and an emphasis on "Black" issues of
identity, historical consciousness, struggle, and uplift. The social backgrounds and career
choices of the sixteen authors are also revealing and interesting in the details which they
provide about the lives of the poets. (See Table 2.7.)[81]

During the late sixties many of the younger writers waged a vigorous campaign to
force the public to discontinue the use of the term "Negro" when referring to African-
Americans, and replace it with "black" for everyday usage. Gradually, in the late sixties and
early seventies the use of the term "black" became the common term to use in reference to
African-Americans. Critics of the terms Negro and "colored" argued that "black" symbolized a more positive self-image for African-Americans in a racist society.[82]

As Dudley proceeded to develop Broadside Press in the late sixties, economic, political, and social conditions continued to gain momentum in Detroit. Black Detroiters were
in all economic classes, but the very poor and the working poor faced daily hardships in
their struggles to survive. Although *Look* magazine viewed Detroit in 1966 as the "all–American city," another source saw that "the limitations of black capitalism were especially visible" in the Motor City where:

> 65 percent of the inner-city population was black, but only 38 percent of the businesses
> were owned by blacks. Of these—mostly small retail and service operations—
> 60 percent had an annual net income of less than $8,000. Urban renewal programs have
> hurt black business. Fifty-seven percent of the Negro-owned businesses failed to sur-
> vive urban renewal compared with only 35 percent of white businesses. Thus federal or
> private programs to foster black capitalism are offset by the impact of urban renewal
> developments.[83]

Still another study notes that "Calculations made for Detroit in the late 1960s suggested that perhaps as much as six percent of the city's budget — amounting to $80 per resident household — was spent providing services for suburban residents."[84]

The general plight of blacks in America, in spite of the achievements of the Civil Rights Movement, brought a demand in 1966–69 for "Black Power," by Stokely Carmichael and other blacks in the United States.[85] This new black movement demanded that blacks shift their focus from an earlier effort to integrate and assimilate with white Americans, to a more black nationalist and separatist (and in some cases, socialist) program of action for radical change in black America and in American life and institutions.[86] In Detroit, such groups and works as the Detroit Metropolitan Welfare Rights Organization (1967), *The Inner City Voice* edited by John Wetson, Uhuru, SNCC (Detroit branch), the League of Revolutionary Black Workers (1968–73), the Republic of New Africa (1968), the Freedom Now Party, the Black Panther Party (Detroit branch), CORE (Detroit branch), the black studies movement and Wayne State University, and the Radical Black Student Union, among others, expanded the impact of the Black Power concept throughout black Michigan society.[87]

However, the black citizens of Detroit took matters into their own hands on July 23, 1967, in what became known as the most extensive urban rebellion in twentieth century American history. The toll was sweeping:

> 44 deaths [39 of them black], over 2,000 known injuries, over 7,331 arrests [5,000 were left homeless], and property damage estimated at $500 million. In both numbers and range, the law enforcement personnel called in also reached new peaks: 4,300 local police officers, 370 state troops, 1,100 National Guardsmen, and 4,700 army paratroopers were placed on alert.[88]

But, in general, the deterioration of the city continued — and its educational crisis, poor police relations with the community, substandard housing, and other ills remained in place.[89] Some black Detroiters were hopeful that the growing black political power base in Detroit would somehow help to make a difference in the long run.[90] However, blacks in the city were not able to elect a black mayor in the sixties.[91]

Against this backdrop and besides his work at Broadside Press, Dudley Randall led a very active life as a poet, lecturer, and librarian during the late sixties. He was often invited to read and talk about poetry at various high schools and libraries in the Detroit area.[92] Such contacts with the public, and especially with young people, widened as his fame and work became greater known in the late sixties. One of his most ambitious years was 1966, when he traveled widely throughout the United States and Europe. Randall was a poetry panelist on three occasions during the year. He spoke at the Black Arts Convention in Detroit during April, the Oakland University (Mich.) Writer's Conference in October, and at the Alabama A&M College Writer's Conference (Montgomery) in December 1966. As has been noted, he was a participant at the May 1966 First Negro Writer's Conference at Fisk University in Nashville, Tennessee.[93]

Dudley's trip to Russia was made in the summer of 1966, when Margaret Burroughs was able to intercede on his behalf with the Institute for Soviet-American Relations to secure a place for him with an artistic tour group, after sculptor and poet Oliver LaGrone of Detroit was unable to go.[94] The party of nine departed the United States in early August, and made a one-week visit to Paris, before traveling on to Moscow. Their tour of the Soviet Union included stops in Leningrad, Baku in the Republic of Azerbaijan, and Alma-Ata in the Republic of Kazakhstan. The highlights of the tour included visits to cultural centers

Table 2.7

Social Backgrounds of Authors at Broadside Press, 1965–1969

Name	Place of Birth	Date of Birth	Education	Occupation(s)	Resident	Status of a Writer
Nancy L. Arnez	Baltimore, MD	July 6, 1928–	B.A., M.A., Ed.D.	Teacher, writer	Chicago, IL	Established writer
Gwendolyn Brooks	Topeka, KA	June 7, 1917–	A.A.; many hon. doctorates	Writer, teacher	Chicago, IL	Major Est. writer
Margaret G. Burroughs	St. Rose, LA	Nov. 1, 1917–	B.A.E., M.A.E.; hon. doctorate	Artist, writer, teacher	Chicago, IL	Established writer
Margaret Danner	Pryorsburg, KY	Jan. 12, 1915–88	B.A. studies	Writer, teacher	Detroit, MI	Established writer
Jon Eckels	Indianapolis, IN	circa 1940	B.A., M.A., Ph.D.	Writer, teacher	Palo Alto, CA	New writer
James E. Emanuel	Alliance, NB	June 14, 1921–	B.A., M.A., Ph.D.	Writer, teacher	White Plains, NY	Established writer
Stephany Fuller	Chicago, IL	Oct. 23, 1947–	B.A., M.A.	Writer, teacher, business	Chicago, IL	Established new writer
Nikki Giovanni	Knoxville, TN	June 7, 1943–	B.A., M.A.; hon. doctorate	Writer, teacher	New York City, NY	Established new writer
Mae Jackson	Earl, AR	Jan. 3, 1946–	B.A. studies	Writer, teacher	New York City, NY	Established new writer
Keorapetse W. Kgositsile	Johannesburg, South Africa	Sept. 19, 1938–	B.A., M.A.	Writer, teacher	New York City, NY	Established writer
Etheridge Knight	Corinth, MS	April 19, 1931–91	grade school, self-taught; B.A.	Prisoner, writer, teacher	Indiana State Prison; Indianapolis, IN	Established new writer
Don L. Lee	Little Rock, AR	Feb. 23, 1942–	B.A., M.F.A.	Writer, teacher, publisher	Chicago, IL	Established new writer
Marvin X	Fowler, CA	May 29, 1944–	B.A., M.A. studies	Writer, theater director, teacher	San Francisco, CA	Established new writer
Beatrice M. Murphy	Monessen, PA	June 25, 1908–	High School diploma	Writer, editor	Washington, DC	Established writer
Dudley Randall	Washington, DC	Jan. 14, 1914–	B.A., M.A.L.S.	Teacher, writer, librarian, publisher	Detroit, MI	Established writer
Sonia Sanchez	Birmingham, AL	Sept. 9, 1934–	B.A., M.A. studies; hon. doctorate	Writer, teacher	Pittsburgh, PA	Established new writer

(i.e., museums, galleries, and schools), the studios of local artists and artistic events and a visit to the circus in Leningrad.[95] Dudley was enchanted by the respect and honor extended to creative artists on his European tour. Certainly this was not the case back home in the United States. When he later reflected on the visit, Dudley noted that:

> I think I got a little more self-respect from being a poet, and just from this visit to Russia. I would think that that was one of the great influences that this visit had on me.[96]

After the tour of Russia, the group also made a visit to Prague before returning to Paris, and then back to the United States on August 26.[97]

During the late sixties Dudley's hobbies were reading and tennis. The birth of his two grandchildren also took place during this period, with Venita Sherron King born in 1966, and William Sherron, III, in 1968, both in Detroit.[98] Randall was also active in Detroit in a number of social and cultural organizations, such as Kappa Alpha Psi Fraternity, the Michigan Poetry Society, and New Detroit Inc., Committee for the Arts (formed after the 1967 rebellion to help rebuild Detroit).[99]

However, the march of events during the last half of the sixties was unrelenting in its furor and impact. In February 1965, Malcolm X was assassinated in New York; on May 27, 1967, Langston Hughes died in New York; Dudley's sister, Easter B. Randall LaMarr, died in 1968; Martin Luther King, Jr., was assassinated on April 4, 1968, in Memphis, Tennessee, and Robert Kennedy in June 1968, in Los Angeles, California.[100] Such national and personal events certainly impacted the lives of many people, as well as Randall himself during this crucial decade.

For Randall, working conditions and the stress of doing two major jobs—head reference-interloan department librarian with the Wayne County Federated Library System and his so-called "part-time" duties at Broadside, which actually demanded most of his time—became too much for him in 1969. Accepting an appointment in the spring of 1969 as a visiting professor in the English Department at the University of Michigan, Ann Arbor, Randall found the much needed flexibility to completely free his creative influence. Then the University of Detroit (a historically private Catholic institution) invited Dudley to join the university as a part-time reference librarian and poet-in-residence during the fall of 1969.[101] He accepted the offer, with appreciation. The new position allowed him to work three days a week as a reference librarian, and to have Mondays and Fridays off to "write poetry."[102] This arrangement allowed the poet to more effectively use his time at Broadside, and to concentrate on his writing. He also enjoyed working with young writers, and offered cash prizes to the very best of them at the University of Detroit. Randall took his duties in this regard very seriously:

> I feel that it's my duty to help promote poetry on the campus. So, I teach a course in poetry. (They [the University of Detroit] told me that I didn't have to teach when I went there but that if I felt like teaching, I could just volunteer. However, I was asked to teach, so I've been teaching one course a year) ... I have a contest every year for poetry and I think that helps to channel the interest of the students in poetry. I read manuscripts that student-poets give to me to read; I have had poets read there; and generally in my class I have one or two poets come and talk to the class every year.[103]

Yet, Randall also viewed his position at the University of Detroit as an outgrowth of the Civil Rights Movement and the demands of black students. In an interview, he told the news bureau director of the University of Detroit that:

Dudley Randall, seen here ca. 1971, took a hands-on-approach to his operation of Broadside Press (courtesy of Broadside Press).

> I understand quite clearly that if there were not the increasing number of black students at the University of Detroit, I would not be here. I think that it is very important that I realize that, that the black students realize that there is a black poet there, that he understands their hopes and purposes in going to college.[104]

Nonetheless, Dudley was able to make a new academic home for himself at an institution that was physically close to his residence on Old Mill Place (near Livernois and Davison avenues) in Detroit.

At the same time, his efforts were tireless in the continuous struggle to promote the growth of Broadside Press. To increase the community's awareness of the company's work, he established *Broadside News* in 1969 as a monthly newsletter.[105] To aid the efforts of other writers and publishers, Randall also assumed new responsibilities as the U.S. distributor for such publishing endeavors as the Heritage Poetry Series of Paul Breman Limited, London, England; select works of Black Arts Publications, Detroit; select books of Third World Press, Chicago; select works of 5X Publishing Company, New York; and the first two books of

Gabriel

(HANGED FOR LEADING A SLAVE REVOLT)

Black Gabriel, riding
To the gallows tree,
In this last hour
What do you see?

I see a thousand
Thousand slaves
Rising up
From forgotten graves,
And their wounds drip flame
On slavery's ground,
And their chains shake Dixie
With a thunder sound.

Gabriel, Gabriel,
The end is nigh,
What is your wish
Before you die?

That rebellion suckle
The slave-mother's breast
And black men
Never, never rest
Till slavery's pillars
Lie splintered in dust
And slavery's chains
Lie eaten with rust.

Gabriel, Gabriel,
This is the end,
Your barbarous soul,
May God befriend.

The blow I struck
Was not in vain,
The blow I struck
Shall be struck again.

Gabriel hangs
Black-gold in the sun,
Flame-head of
Rebellion.

The black folk weep,
The white folk stare:
Gabriel is
A sword in the air.

His spirit goes flying
Over the land
With a song in his mouth
And a sword in his hand.

A sample of Robert E. Hayden's poetry, here reprinted as Broadside No. 3 (courtesy of Broadside Press).

poet Nikki Giovanni, *Black Feeling, Black Talk* (1968), and *Black Judgement* (1968).[106] The largest producer of literary materials among the above mentioned publishers was Paul Breman Limited. A European, Breman was born in 1931 in Amsterdam, Holland and educated at Amsterdam University. He is a noted specialist in the antiquarian book trade, as well as an editor and publisher. He has lived in London, England, since 1959, and has operated his own company there since 1968. Breman's interest in black music and poetry extends from 1946, and he has edited several important anthologies in the field. He established the Heritage Poetry Series in 1962 to focus public attention on and to promote the work of significant black writers, especially from the United States, who were often ignored by white American editors and publishers.[107]

The first seven volumes in the Heritage Poetry Series published during the sixties are listed in Table 2.8. Breman was especially attracted to the work of Robert Hayden, and Hayden's volume, *A Ballad of Remembrance*, inaugurated the series in 1962. This was the first commercial book published by Hayden since his forties collection, *Hearthshape in the*

Table 2.8

The Heritage Poetry Series, London, England, 1962–1969

(Distributed in the United States by Broadside Press)

(arranged by year of publication)

Author	Publication	Year of Publication	Price of Book	Pages	Gender of Author
Robert Hayden (1913–80)	*A Ballad of Remembrance*	1962	$2.50	72	male
Paul Breman, ed. (1931–)	*Sixes and Sevens: An Anthology*	1962	$2.50	96	male
Frank Horne (1899–74)	*Haverstraw*	1963	$2.50	40	male
Arna Bontemps (1902–73)	*Personals*	1963	$2.50	40	male
Conrad Kent Rivers (1933–68)	*The Still Voice of Harlem*	1968	$2.50	24	male
Mari Evans (1923–)	*Where Is All the Music?*	1968	$2.50	24	female
Russell Atkins (1927–)	*Heretofore*	1968	$2.50	32	male

Dust (although his second and third books had been privately printed in 1948 and 1955). Breman ranks Robert Hayden's poetic achievements among the best yet produced by an African-American writer. In fact, he feels that Hayden "is the only black American poet to range with [Léon Gontran] Damas," the French Guianese poet (1912–84) associated with the Negritude movement.[108] *A Ballad of Remembrance* was awarded the grand prize for poetry in English at the First World Festival of Negro Arts in Dakar, Senegal, in 1966, but only after a campaign, according to Breman, of "tireless promotion by Rosey Pool and Langston Hughes" on Robert Hayden's behalf.[109] In 1967, Hayden dedicated his anthology, *Kaleidoscope,* to Paul Breman.[110] Broadside Press played a key role in expanding the public's ability to buy the Heritage Poetry Series books in the United States. Thus, Dudley Randall's work touched the lives of at least six major black poets and a white editor, none of whom ever published a major book under the Broadside imprint.

Dudley Randall's own creative writing career rapidly increased in its productivity in several areas during the years 1965–69, when the poet published at least fifteen poems in seven journals, three short stories, twelve articles, thirty-two poems in anthologies, two book reviews, three broadsides; two introductions [in Don L. Lee's *Black Pride* in 1968, and Stephany Fuller's *Moving Deep* in 1969], and four books, one published each year during 1966–69.[111] "Booker T. and W. E. B." continued to be his most popular poem, at least in terms of its appearance in seven anthologies during the late sixties.[112] His two best-selling books during the decade were the first two anthologies published by Broadside Press — *For Malcolm X: Poems on the Life and Death of Malcolm X,* edited with Margaret Burroughs in 1967, and *Black Poetry: A Supplement to Anthologies Which Exclude Black Poets,* edited by Randall in 1969.[113] *Black Poetry*'s history began when Randall and Robert Hayden were teachers at the University of Michigan in 1969. According to Randall, they were both "asked by the chairman of the Department of English to compile a small collection of black poetry, students had pointed out that the anthologies used in the introduction-to-poetry courses contained no black poets. Because of pressures of time in moving to different teaching posts, Mr. Hayden had to withdraw from the project, but I completed it, and the new anthology can be used by students and by the general reader."[114]

Twenty-five poets appeared in the anthology, and at the time of publication four of them were deceased: Countee Cullen, Langston Hughes, Claude McKay, and Melvin B. Tolson. Only six black women poets appear among the twenty-five poets: Gwendolyn Brooks, Margaret Danner, Nikki Giovanni, Naomi Long Madgett, Sonia Sanchez, and Margaret Walker. It can be taken for granted that all of them are great poets in black history, but it is also interesting to note that they were all Broadside Press poets. In addition, ten of the nineteen black male poets were also major Broadside Press authors, including James A. Emanuel, Etheridge Knight, Don L. Lee, Doughtry Long, Clarence Major, Dudley Randall, Ahmed Alhamisi, Robert Hayden, LeRoi Jones, and Melvin B. Tolson. The latter four poets either had a broadside poem published by Broadside, or were the authors of books distributed by the company. Thus, of the twenty-five poets selected for the anthology, sixteen, or 64 percent had been previously published by Broadside. Randall believes that an editor has a responsibility to "publish poems only because they're good, not because they're historical."[115] Yet, the anthology met a favorable public reception, was moderate in price ($0.95), and helped to fill a void in the black poetry anthology field.

A random sample of seven anthologies also published in the sixties offers an interesting contrast with Randall's *Black Poetry*. The anthologies include Paul Breman, ed., *Sixes and Sevens: An Anthology* (1962); Rosey E. Pool, ed., *Beyond the Blues* (1962); Arna Bontemps, ed., *American Negro Poetry* (1963); Langston Hughes, ed., *New Negro Poets: USA* (1964); Robert Hayden, ed., *Kaleidoscope: Poems by American Negro Poets* (1967); Arnold Adoff, ed., *I Am the Darker Brother* (1968); and Clarence Major, ed., *The New Black Poetry* (1969). Table 2.9 lists the names of the most anthologized poets in the eight collections of poetry reviewed here.[116]

By far the most popular poets among the eight editors during the sixties were LeRoi Jones, Dudley Randall, Conrad Kent Rivers, Calvin Herton, Ray Durem, Paul Vesey, Arna Bontemps, Gwendolyn Brooks, Countee Cullen, Margaret Danner, James A. Emanuel, Mari Evans, Julia Fields, Robert E. Hayden, Langston Hughes, and Margaret Walker. Greatly respected poets of the period include Sterling A. Brown, Ted Joans, Audre Lorde, Naomi Long Madgett, Raymond Patterson, Oliver Pitcher, and Melvin B. Tolson. Like Dudley Randall, editors Langston Hughes (1964) and Clarence Major (1969), were more favorable toward including younger poets of the era, such as Nikki Giovanni, Don L. Lee, David Henderson, Etheridge Knight, and Sonia Sanchez.

Black male poets dominate the pages of the eight anthologies. The following figures of the percentages of male to female poets within each anthology are strikingly one-sided. Black male poets represent from 70 percent of the contributors in Langston Hughes' volume to 92 percent in Paul Breman's collection. Breman also has the lowest percentage of black female poets in his book (one of thirteen, or 8 percent). Langston Hughes, on the other hand, has the highest percentage of black women poets in his anthology, at 30 percent (eleven of thirty-seven poets). The most published black female poets among the editors are Gwendolyn Brooks, Margaret Danner, Mari Evans, Julia Fields, Margaret Walker, Audre Lorde, Naomi Long Madgett, and Gloria Oden. Only two of the above poets (Lorde and Fields) were among the younger group of black female writers of the sixties who were born during the Great Depression years or after (all of the other poets noted above were born prior to 1929). In general, publishing opportunities were fewer for black female poets than for their male counterparts during this period.

Table 2.9
Eight Anthologies of Black Poetry Published in the 1960s

Poets Selected	BREMAN	POOL	BONTEMPS	HUGHES	HAYDEN	ADOFF	MAJOR	RANDALL	TOTALS
LeRoi Jones (Amiri Baraka)		x	x	x	x	x	x	x	7
Dudley Randall		x	x	x	x	x	x	x	7
Conrad Kent Rivers	x	x	x	x	x	x	x		7
Ray Durem	x	x		x		x	x	x	6
Calvin C. Hernton	x	x		x	x	x	x		6
Paul Vesey (Samuel Allen)		x	x	x	x	x		x	6
Arna Bontemps		x	x		x	x		x	5
Gwendolyn Brooks		x	x		x	x		x	5
Countee Cullen		x	x		x	x		x	5
Margaret Danner		x	x	x	x			x	5
James A. Emanuel	x		x	x	x			x	5
Mari Evans		x	x	x	x	x			5
Julia Fields		x	x	x	x		x		5
Robert E. Hayden		x	x		x	x		x	5
Langston Hughes		x	x		x	x		x	5
Margaret Walker		x	x		x	x		x	5
Sterling A. Brown		x	x		x	x			4
Ted Joans		x	x	x	x				4
Audre Lorde	x	x		x			x		4
Naomi L. Madgett		x		x	x			x	4
Raymond Patterson	x			x		x	x		4
Oliver Pitcher		x	x	x	x				4
Melvin B. Tolson			x	x	x			x	4
Russell Atkins	x		x					x	3
Julian Bond		x	x	x					3
Frank M. Davis			x		x	x			3
Owen Dodson		x			x	x			3
Paul L. Dunbar			x		x	x			3
Frank Horne		x	x		x				3
Fenton Johnson			x		x	x			3
James W. Johnson			x		x	x			3
Claude McKay	x		x		x				3
Gloria Oden			x	x	x				3
Myron O'Higgins			x	x			x		3
A. B. Spellman		x		x			x		3
James Vaughn			x	x	x				3
Charles Anderson	x	x							2
Waring Cuney		x	x						2
Nikki Giovanni							x	x	2
David Henderson				x			x		2
Lance Jeffers		x				x			2
Percy Johnston	x	x							2
Bob Kaufman				x			x		2
Etheridge Knight							x	x	2
Oliver LaGrone		x		x					2
Don L. Lee (Haki R. Madhubuti)							x	x	2
Clarence Major							x	x	2
Allen Polite	x			x					2
Sonia Sanchez							x	x	2
James W. Thompson	x	x							2
Jean Toomer				x				x	2
Richard Wright			x			x			2

Dudley Randall's work at Broadside Press placed him in the forefront of sixties black writers, editors, and publishers of the Black Arts and Black Aesthetic Movements. He was in a unique position, given his generation and age (fifty-five) in 1969, in light of the general attitudes about "anyone over thirty" of the many young activists during the time. Dudley was able to break down such barriers, and to foster communication between the generation of poets who came of age after the Harlem Renaissance in the mid-thirties and the forties. Randall seemed to symbolize for many the strong voice of an older poet, who could understand the need for, and work to help achieve, a change in modern society. Thus, he served as one of a number of important sages to the black cultural movements of the era, along with other such important personalities as Gwendolyn Brooks, Hoyt Fuller, Arna Bontemps, Langston Hughes, Margaret Walker, John Oliver Killens, and John Henrik Clarke. Although independent thinkers, writers, and intellectuals, such figures were definitely a part of the Black Arts Movement. Addison Gayle, Jr., understood this well when he sought to give a definition for the Black Aesthetic:

> The Black Aesthetic is a corrective — a means of helping black people out of the polluted main-stream of Americanism, and offering logical, reasoned arguments as to why he [and she] should not desire to join the ranks of a Norman Mailer or a William Styron. To be an American writer is to be an American, and, for black people, there should no longer be honor attached to either position ... the black artist due to his [and her] historical position in America at the present time, is engaged in a war with this nation that will determine the future of black art ... [and African-American's] unique experiences produce unique cultural artifacts, and that art is a product of such cultural experiences ... [which] mandates unique critical tools for evaluation.[117]

But even a sage has to be in a position to offer advice, and Randall was willing to suggest to younger black writers and artists that

> precision and accuracy are necessary for both white and black writers.... "A black aesthetic" should not be an excuse for sloppy writing. [He believes that for writers who adhere to the "black aesthetic" there is a future], as long as their rejection of "white standards" rejects only what is false.... How else can a black writer write than out of black experience? Yet, what we tend to overlook is that our common humanity makes it possible to write a love poem, for instance, without a word of race, or to write a nationalistic poem that will be valid for all humanity.

Ron Welburn further acknowledges that Randall has brought to [his poetry] a good heart, ear and eye for sensitive observation, all [of] which enhance his lyricism. Young black poets who read him should be influenced by him to some degree, for his voice alone is infectious, more so, he is contributing something to black literature that has a long lasting value.[118]

By 1969, Broadside Press held a major position among national Black Arts Movement publishers. Table 2.10 lists a selection of these and their founders, and related major cultural workshops in ten central cities. Randall's publishing activities at Broadside were considered by many activists, students, intellectuals, and professionals as among the best of black companies in the United States, especially in the area of black poetry.[119] Broadside published a broader variety and a larger number of broadsides, anthologies, books, and tapes of poetry than did any other black publisher in the United States during the sixties. Such a huge achievement at Broadside brought increased prestige to Dudley Randall in the Black Arts Movement: *(cont. on page 50)*

Table 2.10

Major Black Arts Movement Publishers, 1960–1969

Location	Major Publisher	Founder(s)	Year	Major Cultural Workshop(s)	Founder(s)	Year
Atlanta, GA	Institute of the Black World	Vincent Harding	1965	Black Image Center for Black Art (*The Journal of Rhythm*), 1970	A. B. Spellman	1960s 1960s
Chicago, IL	Third World Press	Don L. Lee, Carolyn Rogers, Johari M. Amini	1967	The Organization of Black American Culture Writer's Workshop (*Nommo*, 1969)	Hoyt Fuller, Carolyn Rogers, Johari M. Amini, Don L. Lee, Alicia Johnson, David Llorens, Gerald McWorter, Conrad Kent Rivers, Ronald Fair, Keorapetse Kgositsile	1967
	Free Black Press		1960s			
Cleveland, OH	Free Lance Press	Russell Atkins	1950	Free Lance Poets and Prose Workshops, Inc. (*Free Lance*, 1950s)	Casper Leroy Jordan & Russell Atkins, with the aid of Helen J. Collins, Beatrice Augustus, & Helen Dobbins	1953
	Vibration Press	Norman Jordan	1960s	Karamu Theatre	Norman Jordan	1960s
Detroit, MI	Broadside Press	Dudley Randall	1965	Boone House	Margaret Danner	1962
	Black Arts Publications	Ahmed Alhamisi & Harun K. Wangara	1969	Concept East Theater	Woody King, Ron Miller & David Rambeau	1962
Los Angeles, CA	House of Respect		1960s	Watts Writer's Workshop	Budd Schulberg, Harry Dolan & Herbert Simmons; later, Quincy Troupe, Stanley Crouch, & Jayne Cortez	1965

Location	Major Publisher	Founder(s)	Year	Major Cultural Workshop(s)	Founder(s)	Year
Newark, NJ	Jihad Press	Amiri Baraka	1967	Spirit House	Amiri Baraka	mid–1960s
New Orleans, LA	Black Arts South Press	Kalamu Ya Salaam, Tom Dent, Isaac Black, Nayo (Barbara Malcolm), & Raymond Washington	1969	Free Southern Theater (*Nkombo*, 1969)	John O'Neal, Jr. Tom Dent	mid–1960s
New York City, NY	The Third Press	Joseph O. Okpaku	1969	Society of Umbra–The Umbra Workshop (*Umbra magazine*,1963)	Tom Dent, Calvin Hernton, and David Henderson; with William E. Day, Rolland Snelling, Pritchard and Nora Hicks	1963
				Harlem Writer's Club (Guild)	John Henrik Clarke, John Oliver Killens, William Patterson, Johnny Moore	1950s
San Francisco, CA	Journal of Black Poetry Press Free Black Press of California	Joe Goncalves	1966	Black Arts West	Ed Bullins and Marvin X	1964
			1960s	The Negro Student Assoc., San Francisco State College (*Black Dialogue*)	Arthur A. Sheridan, Edward Spriggs	1967
Washington, DC	Drum and Spear	Carolyn Carter	1969	Dasein Poets, Howard Univ. (Dasein Literary Society)	Percy Johnston, Walter Delegall, with Al Fraser, Oswald Govan, Lance Jeffers, LeRoy O. Stone & Joseph White	1950s–1960s

But no account of the black arts movement of the 1960s would be creditable without an acknowledgment of the indispensable role played by black publisher Dudley Randall and his Detroit-based Broadside Press. Himself an older poet of note, Mr. Randall originated his outfit for the printing of single poem broadsides. But history made him into a "man of destiny," the right man with the right idea in the right place at the right time: he was flexible and imaginative enough to move rapidly from single-poem broadsides to small pamphlets of powerful, expressive poetry inexpensively produced and relatively easy to market. The general ferment in black communities across the nation provided him with an almost inexhaustible supply of good material and a new awakened public hungry for good black literature. A distribution system within the black community — bookshops, community cultural centers, and the poets themselves peddling their books at lectures and readings and street corners, all independent of the established distribution networks controlled by the large white publishing houses — demonstrated something of the possibilities of black-controlled publishing of black literature. Virtually all of the young black poets who gained national reputations and national followings between 1967 and 1972 were first and sometimes exclusively published by Broadside Press. This black control of black publishing, minimal as it has been in the case of Broadside Press [and its offshoot, Don Lee's Third World Press], has been of incalculable importance in insulating the movement from the pressure-demands of the "larger audience," thus making possible a degree of autonomous development unprecedented in the history of Afro-American literature.[120]

The editors of *Negro Digest* were also prophetic in an analysis of the impact of the Black Arts Movement on the sixties, and of the role of such individuals as those who published their works under the imprint of Dudley Randall's Broadside Press. In 1968, the editors noted that:

nowhere is the new Black Renaissance more evident than in the number of talented poets who are emerging upon the scene. Most of them are confronting their experiences and giving vent to their imaginations without apology, thanks — in large measure — to the growing number of literary outlets for their works.... It goes without saying that only a few of the poets now being given exposure will develop into artists of the first rank; that is always the case; but what is important is that, for the first time in America, black people themselves are being provided the opportunity of deciding who their "best" poets are and when those poets are speaking to and for them.[121]

This statement still stands as a testament to the courage and vision which Dudley Randall displayed — as he led the good fight from Detroit to help bring more momentum to the African-American struggle to decrease illiteracy in the community and to increase social and cultural awareness in the years ahead.

By the end of 1969, Dudley Randall had published nineteen books, and Broadside Press was the U.S. distributor for another ten books. All of Randall's work with Broadside was achieved at home, "quartered in a converted bedroom of his tri-level" dwelling with the aid of "two employees and no printing plant of its own." Broadside Press was organized to serve the community, and for Randall this meant that "the business isn't organized on the profit motive and keeping it small-staffed makes it easier to make decisions. If I like an idea I can say 'Let's do it,' without arguing with some board of directors."[122] Yet, once Broadside's books were produced, it became necessary to promote and sell them, to inform the public of their existence, and to secure where possible favorable critical commentary on the works in the media. This task was a major challenge for Randall and the company.

In the late sixties most of the historically white media, especially the literary periodicals of the United States, were uninterested in small black publishers such as Broadside

Haki R. Madhubuti was born (as Don L. Lee) on February 12, 1942, in Little Rock, Arkansas, but grew up in Detroit, Michigan, and has lived most of his adult life in Chicago, Illinois. Madhubuti continues to enjoy a wide success as one of the most influential black writers of his generation. Since 1967, he has written and edited nineteen books. He currently serves as publisher of Third World Press, established in 1968 in Chicago, and is professor of English and director of the Gwendolyn Brooks Center at Chicago State University. Here he is pictured ca. 1991 (courtesy Third World Press).

Press. Randall also had trouble during this period in securing reviews at such traditional black publications as the academic-oriented *College Language Association Journal*, or even the more liberal and historically focused *Negro History Bulletin*.[123] He basically had to rely instead on the little black magazines of the Black Arts Movement, and on an occasional review in the white radical underground press, for book reviews of most Broadside Press publications. News about Broadside books also reached black people through their "underground" communication system: by word of mouth on the urban streets of America.[124] Broadside authors also worked hard to promote their own books, for Broadside did not have a large advertising budget. Bookstores in black communities also promoted Broadside publications, and requests for Broadside titles at public and private libraries also increased an awareness of the company's products. In fact, during 1969, Broadside sold over 1,200 volumes to libraries and stores in the United States. Table 2.11 describes the range of Broadside volumes sold by 1969. The three best-sellers at the company were the first three books of Don L. Lee, *Think Black!*, *Black Pride*, and *Don't Cry, Scream!*; followed by the anthologies *For Malcolm X*, and *Black Poetry*. Most of the best-sellers at Broadside were in the range

Table 2.11

Copies in Print of Select Broadside Press Books, 1965–1969

Author(s)	Book	Copies in Print by 1969
Margaret G. Burroughs and Dudley Randall, eds.	*For Malcolm X* (1967)	8,000
Margaret Danner and Dudley Randall	*Poem Counterpoem* (1966)	1,500
Nikki Giovanni	*Black Feeling, Black Talk* (1968); *Black Judgement* (1968)	Over 3,000
Etheridge Knight	*Poems from Prison* (1968)	1,500
Don L. Lee	*Black Pride* (1968) *Think Black!* (Second Edition, 1968); *Don't Cry, Scream!* (1969)	55,000 to 80,000
Dudley Randall, ed.	*Black Poetry* (1969)	5,000
Sonia Sanchez	*Home Coming* (1969)	1,500

of 1,500 to 8,000 copies sold; however, Don L. Lee's work sold between 55,000 and 80,000 titles in the late sixties.[125]

The greatest outlet in the sixties for book reviews of Broadside publications were six Black Arts Movement periodicals. They were *Negro Digest* (Chicago), *Soulbook* (Berkeley), *Journal of Black Poetry* and *Black Dialogue* (San Francisco), and *Liberator* and *Freedomways* (New York City). These journals were edited by some of the most influential Black Arts Movement personalities of the sixties, and included Hoyt W. Fuller, Carole A. Parks, Donald Freeman, Bobb Hamilton, Julia Fields, Joe Goncalves, Edward S. Spriggs, Abdul Karim, Aska Toure, Nikki Giovanni, Daniel H. Watts, Clayton Riley, Larry Neal, Clarence Major, LeRoi Jones, Ed Bullins, Don L. Lee, Shirley Graham, Esther Jackson, Ernest Kaiser, John Henrik Clarke, and Jack O'Dell. However, another significant group of twenty-five black magazines were also active in publishing book reviews during this period. Poet and critic Eugene Redmond believes that a key problem which faced most black nationalist journals of the sixties was their "on-again-off-again publication schedule [which] attested to the problems they faced as the first black literary magazines in history to try sustaining themselves purely on black resources."[126] Their commitment to the black aesthetic called for most of them to support a policy of being "exclusively for black writers and readers."[127] This meant, for the most part, cutting them off from a consideration of white advertisement dollars. The leader among the journals both in circulation size (68,000 in 1969) and influence was *Negro Digest*, which was "the only national black literary magazine with a paid staff and a reliable publishing history" during the sixties.[128]

Reviews of Broadside Press books in such organs as *Negro Digest* and the *Journal of Black Poetry*, helped to fortify the development of Broadside. The company was also aided by the fact that its publishing list of black poetry was the strongest in the United States. By 1969, not only did Broadside have such established poets as Gwendolyn Brooks, Margaret Danner, James A. Emanuel, and Dudley Randall on its list, but it also contained at least eight of the most exciting and promising younger poets of the new black poetry movement in America. These included Don L. Lee, Nikki Giovanni, Sonia Sanchez, Marvin X, Etheridge Knight, Mae Jackson, Stephany Fuller, and Keorapetse Kgositsile. As Eugene

Redmond notes, during the sixties Dudley Randall emerged to figure "prominently in the development of an audience for the new black poetry."[129] However, it was up to the critics to assess, analyze, and place this body of work within the traditions of African-American poetry in America.

A sample of seven critics (James Cunningham, David Llorens, Ron Welburn, Jewel Latimore [Johari Amini], Houston A. Baker, Jr., Nikki Giovanni, and Sonia Sanchez) reviewed five Broadside books in 1968, in such publications as *Negro Digest* and *Liberator*. Later, in 1969, six critics (Houston A. Baker, Jr., Carolyn Gerald [Carolyn Fowler], Johari Amini [Jewel C. Latimore], David Llorens, Ron Welburn, and Nikki Giovanni) wrote eight reviews of Broadside publications in *Liberator*, *Negro Digest*, *Black World* (a title change for *Negro Digest*), and *Ebony*. (See Table 2.6 for a list of Broadside books produced in the sixties, and Table 2.12 for critical commentary on the books by a random sample of critics.[130]) In general, the critics were highly favorable and positive toward Broadside books and authors. Only one book, Beatrice M. Murphy and Nancy L. Arnez's *The Rocks Cry Out* (1969), received an unflattering review by Nikki Giovanni, herself a Broadside author. The work of older poets was sometimes criticized for being too conservative by some younger black critics during the Black Arts Movement. However, the overall tone of the reviews was explicitly in Broadside's corner, and helped the company to build a market and public following in the United States and other countries.

The social backgrounds of the eight critics are striking for the details which they supply about the younger generation of African-American black aesthetic critics who came of age during the sixties. (See Table 2.13.) This group is composed of four men and four women.

Their philosophic backgrounds range from Gerald's black aesthetic/Marxist critical perspectives to Sonia Sanchez's black nationalist/separatist ideology (with the added influence of Elijah Muhammad's Nation of Islam program), to Houston A. Baker's more academically inclined approach to advanced theories about the nature and interpretation of black literature. Their professional careers in the sixties included contributions as practicing poets, editors, teachers, and as critics. They were among the best and brightest of the several hundred active publishing black poets and book reviewers during this period.

In 1969, the average age of this group of critics was thirty, and five of them were born in the thirties and the other three in the forties.[131] A majority of this group was born in the South — five of eight critics (Baker, Cunningham, Gerald, Giovanni, and Sanchez), or 62.5 percent — and three in the North (Latimore, Llorens, and Welburn), with 37.5 percent of the total. Yet, the continuing impact of the Great Migration can also be observed by the 1969 regional residences of the critics. Although a majority of this sample once lived in the South, they had to leave in order to advance their careers. Like their fellow artists and writers of the earlier black cultural movements, most notably of the Harlem Renaissance, they migrated to northern cities, where they could also secure employment, especially at the university level. All eight of the critics taught at the university level in the late sixties; none lived in the South.[132] Six of the eight critics published creative works at Broadside Press.[133] This is another indication of the unrivalled position of Broadside as a publishing outlet for U.S. black poets during the heyday of the black poetry movement.

Dudley Randall's first five years (1965–69) as publisher and editor of Broadside Press were impressive for the range of accomplishments which he achieved with so few financial resources. He was able to create a new company in spite of his lack of business acumen in *(cont. on page 60)*

Table 2.12

Critical Commentary on Broadside Press Books and Authors During the 1960s

Critic	Author and Title of Broadside Book	Viewpoint of the Critic
Johari Amini (Jewel C. Latimore) in *Negro Digest* 18, no. 11 (September 1969)	Mae Jackson, *Can I Poet with You* (1969)	"Sistr Mae Jackson is a serious poet.... *Can I Poet with You* ... is a book of poetry with serious intent, which is neither missed nor misdirected, whether she is creating a 'Black Genesis' or letting her sarcasm rap about our growth processes as in 'There Was a Time.' ... Also, being a blk woman writing of positives hard —...."
Johari Amini, in *Negro Digest* 19, no. 1 (November 1969): 87–89	Dudley Randall, ed., *Black Poetry: A Supplement to Anthologies Which Exclude Black Poets* (1969)	Amini notes Randall's anthology "supplements the more-than-few anthologies which are black. Which is so because approximately two-thirds of the volume is composed of poetry which is new: from 1966 to 1969, as well as several selections which are taken from manuscript. Which really makes this volume welcome and necessary.... Yea, the poetry is on time. And Brother Dudley Randall is too, with this anthology. (And so is Broadside Press.)"
Houston A. Baker, Jr., in *Liberator* 10, no. 9 (September 1970): 22	Gwendolyn Brooks, *Riot* (1969)	"*Riot* is concerned primarily with a single event, which becomes an event through the poetry of Gwendolyn Brooks. In dealing with 'the disturbances in Chicago after the assassination of Martin Luther King in 1968,' the poet has shown her word magic and technical virtuosity once again." Baker suggests that Gwendolyn Brooks does not need to be placed in a "classification," because the "range, mastery of language, and maturity" of her work "defy categorization."
Houston A. Baker, Jr., in *Liberator* 10, no. 9 (September 1970): 22	Dudley Randall, *Cities Burning* (1968)	"Dudley Randall's *Cities Burning* [has] a deceptive title. With one or two exceptions, Randall's volume has little to do with cities burnings. Randall does have a good deal to say about the role of the poet, and he has some ironic and bitter comments to make about the pretensions of poets.... There is also a reprinting of the 'Ballad of Birmingham' and one or two reflective pieces that show fine polish." Baker classifies Randall under the label "the reflective literary lion."
Houston A. Baker, Jr., in *Liberator* 10, no. 9 (September 1970): 22	Sonia Sanchez, *Home Coming* (1969)	"Sonia Sanchez is almost flawless in 'home coming,' 'poem at thirty,' 'summary,' 'malcolm,' and one or two others in her volume, but she resorts to tricks of style ... on the whole, *Home Coming* could have been profitably shortened." Baker classifies Sanchez under the label "the dynamic sister."

Critic	Author and Title of Broadside Book	Viewpoint of the Critic
James Cunningham (Olumo), in *Negro Digest* 18, no. 3 (January 1969): 70–76	James A. Emanuel, *The Treehouse and Other Poems* (1968)	Cunningham suggests that Emanuel's poems "reveal the perceptions and sensibilities of a poet who conducts his thought and expression very much in the manner of an apparently unassuming gadfly — which is to say that in Emanuel we are to encounter yet another kind of Ellison who's individuality of viewpoint and smoothness of expression is bound to offend the more tribal-minded among the black conscious. Indeed, a poet is revealed whose singular toughness and keenness of mind and fancy is almost hidden by an apparent absence of any interest in the current fondness for, and preoccupation with, stunning spatial innovations, that stress uniqueness in form and word arrangement. Indeed, in Emanuel, we encounter a poet who leans in the very unfashionable direction of not so very-long-ago traditional devices such as rhymed quatrains and regularity of line and stanza length. Yet, for all of this, we are faced with a formidable, deadly serious and technically assured, and even mischievous talent. There is here a verbal dexterity and tightness not unworthy of a Brooks, and an emotional steadiness and resiliency underneath the light, humorous, gentle unassuming surface that will grip your fondest notions and make them SCREAM OUT as they are carried unceremoniously under."
Carolyn Gerald (Carolyn Fowler), in *Black World* 19, no. 10 (August 1970): 51–52	Gwendolyn Brooks, *Riot* (1969)	"*Riot*, by Gwendolyn Brooks, is a poem in three parts whose title refers to the Chicago rebellion after the death of Martin Luther King in 1968.... The poem speaks for itself as poetry. It is poetry, and poetry in the ultimate sense of the word, since it connects instantly with our feelings, since it activates a whole potential world of new perceptions, since it stirs in us all kinds of mysterious associations with our past experiences of the world."
Nikki Giovanni, in *Negro Digest* 18, no. 10 (August 1969): 97–98	Beatrice M. Murphy and Nancy L. Arnex, *The Rocks Cry Out* (1969)	With this book, critic Nikki Giovanni suggests that Broadside Press "had ... run out of steam. Even the little engine who thought he could couldn't forever, neither the little red hen — even she had to have one seed that didn't come up right. And *The Rocks Cry Out* is the seed that doesn't flower. Authors Beatrice M. Murphy and Nancy L. Arnex seem to just miss the whole point of being Black in the beginning of Blackness.... And I suppose I resent the despair and helplessness in this poetry more than anything else. I believe 'we're a winner.' And as we move we will move as a group to build our nation. I'd like to think this pleases Black people, not frightens or depresses them. The Rocks Cry Out, and so do I, against their level of despair."
Nikki Giovanni, in *Negro Digest* 18, no. 11 (September 1969): 96	Dudley Randall, *Cities Burning* (1968)	"Seems like every age has its new Black poetry 'cause no one cares for us to know that we are just one more car, neither engine nor caboose, in the struggle for freedom. Well, we are turning a curve and we can see how many cars have gone before us. And we know that missing any car will cause a terrible accident 'cause we'll be thrown off the track. Dudley Randall ... is an important link in the total hook-up that we are needing.... He knows us a lot better than we know him, which is why, really, we should become aware of him.... That's a great part of Randall's poetic reality ... he can compliment and teach ... he doesn't have to compete.... *Cities Burning* is a total poem. Both the man and the book."

Critical Commentary on Broadside Press Books and Authors During the 1960s (continued)

Critic	Author and Title of Broadside Book	Viewpoint of the Critic
Jewel C. Latimore (Johari Amini) in *Negro Digest* 17, no. 9 (July 1968): 82–84	Etheridge Knight, *Poems from Prison* (1968)	Jewell Latimore observes that "Etheridge Knight brings the strength and hardness of black existence through his poetry to his people." The black writer's methods, Latimore notes, "are not of necessity confine in traditional 'mainstream' garb — but are the forms and constructs created by him, or adapted, as a set form like the Japanese Haiku." The critic concludes: "Etheridge Knight's poetry is just that — poetry. And as such, it is art, and a living experience for the reader."
Jewel C. Latimore (Johari Amini), in *Black World* 19, no. 7 (May 1970): 52, 98	Stephany Fuller, *Moving Deep* (1969)	"*Moving Deep* ... is a book of love poems ... Stephany is less than 21, /in 1970/ and a good deal of her work reflects her youthfulness. *Moving Deep* is illustrated with six sensitive drawings of the poet's, which complement the poetry; in most instances, they are more penetrating than the poetry.... Her rhythms are structured with care, but feel in places like structured rather than flowing.... Yet, there is a missing perspective — a needed one; in spite of the depth of awareness to feeling, there is no awareness here of the unlovely which is an intense part of our reality, our existence where we are...."
Jewel C. Latimore (Johari Amini), in *Black World* 19, no. 10 (August 1970): 92–93 94	Sonia Sanchez, *Home Coming* (1969)	Amini views *Home Coming* as a major contribution which aids African-Americans in moving "away from and out of unreality fantasized by the master fakers toward and into a real (solid in terms of placement) concretized consciousness of what we got to be about to survive just being here."
David Llorens in *Ebony* 24 no. 5 (March 1969): 72–80	(Overview of Don L. Lee's work to 1969)	David Llorens called Don L. Lee (Haki R. Madhubuti) "a lion of a poet who splits syllables, invents phrases, makes letters work as words, and gives rhythmic quality to verse that is never savage but often vicious and always reflecting a revolutionary black consciousness.... With monkeylike single-mindedness and extraordinary passion Don L. Lee casts an unsparing eye on the events of our times.... Don Lee has no energy for crying in appeal to the conscience of the white world. He is a screaming, urgent, appeal to the reason of dark victims everywhere."
David Llorens, in *Negro Digest* 18, no. 6 (April 1969): 82–84	Nikki Giovanni, *Black Judgement* (1968)	"When I met Nikki Giovanni some three years ago she was still giving Fisk University hell. She was something then. Running around challenging God, anybody's God. She's something else now; poet, short story writer, book reviewer bad enough to keep some niggers from writing a sellout novel. And if I say 'ain't this child a bitch' and your imagery don't do better than dogs, you better check yourself all the way out. Or better, get next to *Black Judgement* ... a book of poems by the sister from Cincinnati that's one more fast number."

Critic	Author and Title of Broadside Book	Viewpoint of the Critic
Sonia Sanchez, in *Negro Digest* 19, no. 6 (April 1970): 51–52, 88–89	Marvin X, *Black Man Listen* (1969)	"So brothers and sisters, if u'd like to have 28/survival/lessons on hand, be readen on the pages of *Black Man Listen* by Marvin X (Broadside Press, $1.00) and be taught as i have been taught by a Great/Poet/Teacher."
Ron Welburn, in *Liberator* 9, no. 8 (August 1969): 20	Nikki Giovanni, *Black Judgement* (1968)	"About half of these poems were written between March and June 1968, and most of the remaining during the last three months of that year of transition for Black America. Like all Black poets, Nikki had a number of things to say about what was happening in the wasteland during those earlier months. What we have, then, are two distinct moods in this book: poems of war and poems of love. *Black Judgement* is an appropriate title for what the two moods generate, and in some cases the line of demarcation between them fades … this Black sister is at her poetic best when she relates the observations that only a Black woman can take the time to understand and intuitively appreciate … there is a sensitive brilliance that stands out when her creations are feelings which initially gave impetus to her total span of judgements."
Ron Welburn in *Negro Digest* 19, no. 2 (December 1969): 91–94	Don L. Lee, *Don't Cry, Scream!* (1969)	"Don L. Lee is a technician, poet-linguist continuing the development of a new language for black poetics, the language of familiar experience, the same language black readers have grown up speaking."
Ron Welburn, in *Negro Digest* 19, no. 2 (December 1969): 94–95.	Dudley Randall, *Cities Burning* (1968)	"Randall possesses a firm sense of the lyric, and *Cities Burning* is more appropriately a book of songs or psalms than a rugged razor-edged batch of poetry that might correspond to the title of the collection itself. The lyrical tone dominates throughout; it is so strong that the poem 'Ballad of Birmingham' is one example of the kind of Randall piece that has been set to music. Randall is a contemporary of Gwendolyn Brooks, and so not in the new school of black poets; but all schools aside, his is a keen functional awareness of what black poetry has been and remains, and there is no hint of an alienation from the ethos being developed by the new stylists. In theme and passion, black poetry has always had its own thing going in sound, sense, imagery, metaphor, and content, and there are many different styles or ways of 'doing the thing.' … Randall's verse is closer to the feeling of the rhetoric or the Scriptural prophets than the spontaneous rap.… Randall has brought to [his poetry] a good heart, ear and eye for sensitive observation, all [of] which enhance his lyricism.…"

Table 2.13

Social Backgrounds of the Critics Surveyed on Broadside Press Publications, 1965–1969

Name	Birth Place	Birth Date	Education	Book Reviews in	Publications in	Resident/Occupation
Houston A. Baker, Jr.	Louisville, KY	March 22, 1943–	Howard Univ., B.A.; UCLA, M.A., Ph.D.; grad. studies, Purdue Univ.	Negro Digest; Black World; Yale Review; Liberator; Journal of Popular Culture	UCLA Graduate Journal (1968); Victorian Poetry (1968, 1970); Liberator (1969–70); Phylon (1971) Black World (1971–73)	New Haven, CT; teacher, writer
James Cunningham (Olumo)	Webster Grove, MO	January 4, 1936–	Butler Univ., B.A.	Negro Digest	Nommo; Black Voices; To Gwen with Love; Jump Bad; Broadside Series #63; The Blue Narrator (1973)	Chicago, IL; teacher, writer, Univ. of Wis. and Cornell Univ.
Carolyn Gerald (Carolyn Fowler)	Lafayette, LA	January 27, 1937–	UC-Berkeley, B.A., M.A.; Univ. of Pa., Ph.D.	CLA Journal; Black World; Negro Digest; Freedomways	Negro Digest; Black World Phylon; Journal Black Poetry (1968–70s)	Philadelphia, PA; Atlanta, GA; teacher, writer, Atlanta Univ.
Nikki Giovanni	Knoxville, TN	June 7, 1943–	Fisk Univ., B.A.; Univ. of Pa.	Freedomways; Black Dialogue; Encore; Negro Digest; Black World	Black Dialogue; Journal of Black Poetry; Black Arts; Soulscript; Black Feeling, Black Talk (1968)	New York City; teacher, writer, Rutgers Univ.
Jewel Latimore (Johari Amini) [Kungjufu]	Philadelphia, PA	February 13, 1935–	A.A., Chicago City College; Chicago St. College, B.A.; M.A., Univ. of Chicago	Negro Digest; Black World; Black Expression; Pan African Journal	Black Expression; Black World; Journal of Black Poetry; Nommo; Black Arts; Jump Bad; Black Essence (1960s)	Chicago, IL; teacher, writer, Kennedy-King College; co-founder of Third World Press

Name	Birth Place	Birth Date	Education	Book Reviews in	Publications in	Resident/Occupation
David Llorens	Chicago, IL	October 12, 1939– November 27, 1973	G.E.D.H.S.; college level certificates	Negro Digest; Ebony	American Ed.; Black Books Bulletin; Ebony; Nommo; Black Fire; For Malcolm X (1960s)	Chicago, IL; editor, writer, teacher
Sonia Sanchez	Birmingham AL	September 9, 1934–	Hunter College, B.A.; grad. studies, N.Y.U.	Negro Digest; Black World	Black World; Journal of Black Poetry; Muhammad Speaks; Black Fire; Home Coming (1969)	San Francisco, CA; Pittsburgh, PA; teacher, writer, Univ. of Pittsburgh
Ron Welburn	Bryn Mawr, PA	April 30, 1944–	Lincoln Univ. (PA), B.A.; Univ. of Arizona, M.A.; N.Y.U., Ph.D.	Negro Digest; Black World; Liberator; Black Review; Nickel Review; Syracuse New Times	Guerrilla; The New Black Poetry	Tucson, AZ; Oxford, PA; Syracuse, NY; teacher, writer

Dudley Randall's genius at Broadside Press was expressed in his emphasis on producing inexpensive, pamphlet-size books, generally priced between $1 and $3, such as those pictured above.

the field of publishing. In fact, Randall had to overcome twelve major barriers, which have historically prevented most blacks from entering and surviving in the field of publishing and in other businesses for more than a year, or two, under the best of circumstances.[134] In general, when Randall created Broadside Press in the middle of the sixties, he faced a challenge in dealing with the high costs of entering the field — including printing, advertising, and lack of funds. Other obstacles included competition from other publishers (both black and white), the limited market for poetry books, price barriers (low income levels of many blacks); lack of a good national distribution system, and lack of office technology (especially computers). Additional challenges included discrimination (barriers to breaking into the information market, especially in securing fair advertisement rates in white owned publications and book reviews of Broadside publications), a small office staff (and labor costs), lack of ownership of a printing press and accounting and dealing with the tax system. An equally problematic challenge was gaining readers and a market for Broadside's products while being aware of black literacy rates, reading behavior, and issues of ideology growing out of the Civil Rights Movement, Black Power, and Black Arts movements of the period. The surveillance of black press institutions by American security agencies, such as the FBI, and local and state police departments further complicated the situation.[135] Thus, Randall faced a variety of pitfalls, as he struggled to create a viable black publishing company in Detroit.

But Randall was a visionary, a highly educated person, a professional librarian, and a poet. He was also a student of African-American history, and like many black men and women before him, who had met the challenges of their times — such as Frederick Douglas with his *North Star* newspaper (1847), and Ida B. Wells-Barnett with her lynching publications (1890s) — Dudley was willing to assume the risks involved in creating something new which might help to improve the lives of black writers, while promoting the cultural needs of black people everywhere.

Randall began Broadside Press with petty cash from his librarian's paycheck, while his prosperous white counterparts were making huge profits in the publishing business. One scholar notes that "From 1963 to 1969 publishing industry sales increased by 59 percent, from $1.7 billion to $2.7 billion. Many factors worked together to benefit the various segments of the industry. Research projects supported by government and foundation grants encouraged acquisition of professional books; generous federal and state budgets, bringing unaccustomed affluence to colleges, universities, and their faculties, augmented sales of scholarly materials. There was, in addition, the factor of growing export and foreign sales."[136] However, during this period, such a market was not available to black publishers in the United States. Indeed, U.S. blacks had fewer than a dozen major publishing companies within this nation in 1969. The majority of such firms were located in just six cities, including New York (Joseph Okpaku's The Third Press); Newark (Amiri Baraka's Jihad Productions); Chicago (Don L. Lee's Third World Press, and John H. Johnson's Johnson Publication Company); Washington, D.C. (Drum and Spear Press); San Francisco (Joe Goncalves' Journal of Black Poetry Press); and Detroit (Randall's Broadside Press).[137] Black Americans did find publication outlets in black journals and weekly newspapers, but few black publications were able to survive for long under U.S. market conditions:

> Carolyn Gerald, a Philadelphia poet and free-lance writer, reported in 1969 that she could list as many as thirty "revolutionary" journals which appeared (almost none survived) between 1966 and 1969.[138]

This fact highlights again the noble achievement of Randall's work at Broadside: he was a survivor in the cutthroat world of U.S. publishing.

Broadside was able to survive because of its success in effectively building a mail order for its products around the world.[139] The cashflow was always small, but sufficient to keep old products moving, and new ones in production, since profits at Broadside went back into the operation of the company.[140] Randall also displayed a genius for promoting diversity of talent among Broadside authors, and this was a factor in creating good book sales for the company. Randall seems to have understood American historian Benjamin Quarles' idea on black individuality: "Aside from their common cause against an adversary and a shared sense of having been wronged ... American blacks have been marked historically by diversity. Within themselves, they fall into a congeries of groups reflective of a typically American individualism."[141]

Randall had a special eye for selecting new poetic talent, while maintaining a flexibility and appreciation for the work and service of the older generation of poets. He published and promoted the work of both groups.

Broadside was also able to secure for its publications the services (often at minimum charges) of black artists and illustrators. Table 2.14 lists the contributions of black artists to Broadside in the 1960s.[142] Such services by Detroit artists helped to improve *(cont. on page 64)*

Table 2.14

Broadside Press Artists, 1965–1969

Name	Publication	Year	Artistic Contribution
Kenneth Benson	*Black Pride* by Don L. Lee	1968	Photograph (back cover)
Bill Day	*Black Judgement* by Nikki Giovanni	1968	Cover
Jeff Donaldson	*Riot* by Gwendolyn Brooks	1969	Frontispiece
Emory	*Home Coming* by Sonia Sanchez	1969	Cover
Eugene Feldman	*Think Black!* by Don L. Lee	1968	Cover
LeRoy Foster	"Black Madonna" by Harold Lawrence	1967	Design for Broadside #18
Stephany Fuller	*Moving Deep* by Stephany Fuller	1969	Cover and Illustrations
Doug Harris	*Spirits Unchained* by Keorapetse Kgositsile	1969	Photograph (back cover)
Bruce Heath	*Spirits Unchained*	1969	Cover
Henri [Umbaji] King	*Impressions of African Art Forms* by Margaret Danner	1968	Cover and Illustrations
Talita Long	"Ballad of the Free" by Margaret Walker	1966	Design for Broadside #4
Art McFallan	*Don't Cry, Scream!* by Don L. Lee	1969	Cover
John Porter	*Black Pride* by Don L. Lee	1968	Cover
Gerald L. Simmons, Jr.	*Cities Burning* by Dudley Randall	1968	Photograph, and back cover
Johnny Smith	*Black Judgement* by Nikki Giovanni	1968	Photograph
Shirley Stark	"At Bay" by James A. Emanuel	1968	Design for Broadside #23
Frederick Gerald Stepp	*Poems from Prison* by Etheridge Knight	1968	Cover
Cledie Taylor	"Gabriel" by Robert Hayden	1966	Design for Broadside #3
	"The Sea Turtle and the Shark" by Melvin B. Tolson	1966	Design for Broadside #5
	"We Real Cool" by Gwendolyn Brooks	1966	Design for Broadside #6
	Riot	1969	Cover
James D. Wilson	*For Malcolm X; Poems on the Life and Death of Malcolm X*, eds., Dudley Randall and Margaret Burroughs	1967	Photograph of Malcolm X
Shirley Woodson	"Ballad of Birmingham" by Dudley Randall	1965	Design for Broadside #1
	"Dressed All in Pink" by Dudley Randall	1965	Design for Broadside #2

Broadside Press artists and photographers were a key element in the success of the company. This collage shows a sample of their work (courtesy Broadside Press).

the overall artistic and physical appearance, and thus the sales of Broadside's
books, broadsides, posters, and tapes produced during this period. Painter Shirley
Woodson offers an enlightened perspective on her work with Broadside Press:

For H. W. Fuller
by Carolyn M. Rodgers

> In December, 1965 I received a
> phone call from Dudley Randall
> asking me whether I could letter
> in Old English. After several
> practice sheets with a speed ball
> pen I tackled the job. I hand let-
> tered the poem, "Dressed All in
> Pink," and my collaboration with
> Broadside Press began. Since that
> time I have had the privilege to
> design eight book covers, six
> Broadsides and one poster.
> Working with a publisher was a
> challenging and rewarding expe-
> rience. Artists are trained essen-
> tially to express personal view-
> points and when called upon to
> express ideas around the work of
> another artist, in this case the
> poet, the process of creativity
> becomes broadened. Traditional
> art schools don't necessarily pre-
> pare you for the "public" art of

Shirley Woodson's cover art for Broadside No.
50 (courtesy of Broadside Press).

> the book cover. I wanted my art for Broadside to be more than illustration — I wanted
> it to transmit the power of the poetry visually.[143]

Thus, Dudley Randall and Broadside Press were major forces in the Black Arts Movement, where in the making of books, the company successfully demonstrated that "small
can be beautiful."[144] Indeed, as writer Michael Loudon observes:

> Randall's idea succeeded in bringing poetry to the ordinary citizens of the community:
> the venture was more educational than commercial. [This idea has since been imitated by
> small presses all over the country.] Within a few years, Broadside was publishing antholo-
> gies, volumes of new poets, criticism, and recordings. By example, other black writers also
> began to establish independent presses that specialized in reaching the black community
> with inexpensive editions of poetry, most notable Haki R. Madhubuti's Third World Press.
> One can fairly credit Randall, then, as one of the most influential black publishers of his
> time: his refusal to place commercial interests ahead of literary education has helped to
> inform a whole generation of the richness and diversity of black poetic traditions. In doing
> so, he has introduced new Afro-American writers, and he has fostered an awareness of the
> reciprocity between black writers in the United States and Africa.[145]

Broadside Press produced nineteen books between 1965 and 1969; seventeen collections of poetry by fifteen authors; and two anthologies. (See Table 2.6.) These works can
be classified into three major groups: traditional black poetry, radical new black poetry, and
liberationist black poetry.

The traditional school of black poetry is represented by seven Broadside books produced in the sixties. They are Margaret Danner and Randall, *Poem Counterpoem* (1966); Danner, *Impressions of African Art Forms* (1968); James A. Emanuel, *The Treehouse and Other Poems* (1968); Randall, *Cities Burning* (1968); Gwendolyn Brooks, *Riot* (1969); Beatrice M. Murphy and Nancy L. Arnez, *The Rocks Cry Out* (1969); and Stephany Fuller, *Moving Deep* (1969). This body of work extends the range of the black experience and connects the historical consciousness of African-Americans to the poetry created by earlier generations of black poets. Two central role models and influences on the poets in this group are Martin Luther King, Jr., and Langston Hughes, described by poet and critic Eugene Redmond as "the literary father of all modern black writers."[146] Curiously, only two men are this group, Randall and Emanuel, while five women are centered here — Brooks, Danner, Murphy, Arnex, and Fuller. Did this group of black women poets bring to their work a special sensitivity toward the historical triumph of black survival in America? Margaret Danner expresses the motif of this group and perhaps answers this question in her poem, "This Is an African Worm."[147]

THIS IS AN AFRICAN WORM

This is an African worm
but then a worm in any land
is still a worm.

It will not stride, run, stand
before the butterflies, who
have passed their worm-like state.

It must keep low, not lift its head.
I've had the dread experience, I know.
A worm can do nothing but crawl.

Crawl, and wait.

Further enhancement of this central theme of struggle and overcoming oppression is reflected in James A. Emanuel's poem, "The Negro."[148]

THE NEGRO

Never saw him.
Never can.
Hypothetical,
Haunting man:

Eyes a-saucer,
Yessir bossir,
Dice a-clicking,
Razor flicking.

The-ness froze him
In a dance.
A-ness never
Had a chance.

The radical new black poetry school of Broadside books produced during the sixties, includes four authors: Don L. Lee, with three books, *Think Black* (1968), *Black Pride* (1968), and *Don't Cry, Scream!* (1969); Nikki Giovanni, *Black Judgement* (1968); Mae Jackson, *Can I Poet with You* (1969); and Sonia Sanchez, *Home Coming* (1969); and other younger poets represented in Randall's anthology *Black Poetry* (1969).[149] Critic Trudier Harris offers an excellent recent assessment of the new black poetry school:

> The New Black Aesthetic movement of the 1960s brought a poetic revolution in its wake. It introduced a group of poets who are still publishing today. Nikki Giovanni, Haki Madhubuti (formerly Don L. Lee), Amiri Baraka (formerly LeRoi Jones), Sonia Sanchez, and others fashioned the poets' response to social change during this period. Advocating a nationalistic approach to literature, they called upon black people to take an active role in freeing themselves from a racist, undemocratic society. They also provided a path by which blacks were to arrive at being a nation of African-Americans. They were to change their hair and clothing styles, their patterns of behavior, and even their names; it became the age of dashikis and afros. The nationalist bent was reflected in the language of the poetry itself; it attempted to imitate speech patterns and colloquialisms of the common black folk, and it consciously sought to dissociate itself with the conventions of western poetry.[150]

Radical black poets were especially challenged by the ideas and philosophies growing out of the black power movements of the mid-sixties, and were also influenced by the work of LeRoi Jones (Amiri Baraka). This group of writers, represented at Broadside by one male, Don L. Lee (Haki R. Madhubuti), and three women — Giovanni, Jackson, and Sanchez — were all very young. In 1968, Lee was twenty-six, Giovanni twenty-five, Jackson twenty-two, and Sanchez thirty-four. Ten radical new black poets (out of twenty-five writers) are represented in Randall's *Black Poetry*. They were also younger writers, and included Etheridge Knight (age thirty-seven in 1968); LeRoi Jones (thirty-four); Edward S. Spriggs (thirty-four); Sanchez; Clarence Major (thirty-two); Ahmed Alhamisi (twenty-eight); Lee; Ebon (Ebon Dooley) (twenty-six); Doughtry Long (twenty-six); and Giovanni. In 1968, the average age of this group of eleven writers was twenty-nine years old. Writer John Oliver Killens welcomed this younger generation of black writers onto the sixties scene.

> I am most impressed with their anger. They are questioning the status quo. Years ago, writers wrote because they wanted to be "in." This generation ... is working to change the world.... They are moving away from whiteness and affirming their black identity. I think this is a healthy trend.[151]

Critic Eugene Redmond suggests that there are six major ways to example and critique the new black poetry. This work can be approached by its major themes, types of poetry produced (structure and saturation), the important names of the movement, the goals and objectives of the black aesthetic approach, "the magic of black poetry," and music.[152] A central focus nonetheless dominates the radical new black poetry: black self-assertiveness. Two of Broadside's brightest lights in this regard were Don L. Lee (later Haki R. Madhubuti) and Nikki Giovanni. Two of their best known poems from this period are reflective of this group's efforts to promote black consciousness and direction for black people in the United States. First, Lee's poem:

BUT HE WAS COOL OR: HE EVEN
STOPPED FOR GREEN LIGHTS

super-cool
ultrablack
a tan/purple
had a beautiful shade

he had a double-natural
that wd put the sisters to shame.
his dashikis were tailor made
& his beads were imported sea shells
   (from some blk/country i never heard of)
he was triple-hip.
his tikis were hand carved
out of ivory
& came express from the motherland.
he would greet u in swahili
& say good-by in yoruba.

wooooooooooooo-jim he bes so cool & ill tel li gent
cool-cool is so cool he was un-cooled by
other niggers' cool
cool-cool ultracool was bop-cool/ice box
cool so cool cold cool
his wine didn't have to be cooled, him
was air conditioned cool
cool-cool/real cool made me cool — now
ain't that cool
cool-cool so cool him nick-named refrigerator.

cool-cool so cool
he didn't know,
after detroit, newark, chicago,
we had to hip
cool-cool/super-cool/real cool
that
to be black
is
to be
very-hot.[153]

And Giovanni's masterpiece:

NIKKI-ROSA

childhood remembrances are always a drag
if you're Black
you always remember things like living in Woodlawn
with no inside toilet
and if you become famous or something
they never talk about how happy you were to have your mother
all to yourself and
how good the water felt when you got your bath from one of those
big tubs that folk in chicago barbecue in
and somehow when you talk about home

it never gets across how much you
understood their feelings
as the whole family attended meetings bout Hollydale
and even though you remember
your biographers never understand
your father's pain as he sells his stock
and another dream goes
and though you're poor it isn't poverty that
concerns you
and though they fought a lot
it isn't your father's drinking that makes any difference
but only that everybody is together and you
and your sister have happy birthdays and very good christmasses
and I really hope no white person ever has cause to write about me
because they never understand Black love is Black wealth
and they'll probably talk about my hard childhood and never understand that
all the while I was quite happy[154]

     The last major group of Broadside books published in the sixties falls between the radical new black poetry school and the liberationist black poetry school, due to its emphasis on the issue of freedom for the black community — and the special role and responsibility of African-American men in securing a new life for black people on the planet Earth. The books of four men appear under the liberation school: Jon Eckels, *Home Is Where the Soul Is* (1969); Keorapetse Kgositsile, *Spirits Unchained* (1969); Etheridge Knight, *Poems from Prison* (1968); and Marvin X, *Black Man Listen* (1969). In addition to these books, most of the collective works represented in Randall and Burroughs' anthology, *For Malcolm X*, falls under the liberationist school of poetry. The four major authors in the liberationist school were all young men in 1968: Echels (under thirty), Kgositsile (thirty), Knight (thirty-seven), and Marvin X (twenty-four). Three key leaders are paramount as role models and influences on the poets of this group: Elijah Muhammad, Nelson Mandela, and Malcolm X. According to critic Stephen E. Henderson such writers from the sixties believed that:

> to write black poetry is an act of survival, of regeneration, of love. Black writers do not write for white people and refuse to be judged by them. They write for black people and they write about their blackness, and out of their blackness, rejecting anyone and anything that stands in the way of self-knowledge and self-cele-bration.[155]

The liberationist black poets at Broadside were also a part of the new intellectual movement of the sixties, which historian Vincent Harding describes as a part of the total black liberation struggle in this country — growing out of the civil rights movement on the one hand (mass struggle), and the search for new knowledge and direction (intellectual struggle) on the other — in the schools, in black community institutions, such as the church, cultural centers, and think tanks, and on the streets.[156]

     Black liberationist poets believed strongly in black self-help and communal cooperation. They were generally critical of the exploitive characteristics of American capitalism, and of blacks working for the system. This theme is treated in such poems as Jon Eckels' "White Collar Job."[157]

WHITE COLLAR JOB

Willie works
in an office
the
First and
Only
course
he's
Different
the
Best Neegrow
ever-
third there
in line
to a paper
clip

Few poets of the era were as effective as
Etheridge Knight in capturing the exploita-
tion theme as represented in the thousands
of black lives in American prisons during
the sixties, as in his "Haiku."[158]

HAIKU

1

Eastern guard tower
glints in sunset; convicts rest
like lizards on rocks.

The anti–Vietnam War mood and the
spread of American imperialism is also
documented in Marvin X's untitled
poem.[159]

Keorapetse W. Kgositsile was born on September 19, 1938, in Johannesburg, South Africa. Since
1961, he has lived in many parts of the world, including the United States, Tanzania, and Bostswana.
Kgositsile is widely known for his work as an activist
in the cause of freedom for South Africa, and he is
one of the best-known poets of his generation from
his native country. In 1969, his poetry won the Conrad Kent Rivers Memorial Award (photo by Doug
Harris; courtesy of Broadside Press).

The white man's enemy is the Black man's friend. Have the people of Vietnam ever called
us a nigger? Did the people of Vietnam lynch our fathers and rape our mothers? Did
the people of Vietnam kidnap us from Africa and rob us of our righteous names, our
God (Allah), and our religion, Islam? Why should we go 10,000 miles to risk our lives
defending the freedom of someone else when we have never enjoyed freedom, justice,
and equality ourselves.

No, whitey is not our friend. He is not our brother. He is our open enemy, our
natural enemy. How can the slave be friends with his master? How can the slave be his
master's brother?

South African poet Keorapetse Kgositsile sums up the work of this school of poets in his
classic poem, "For LeRoi Jones, April, 1965," which incorporates the transatlantic liberation theme — from America to Africa.[160]

FOR LEROI JONES, APRIL, 1965

Because finally things have come to this
White world gray grim cold turning me into a killer

Because I live love
Puerto Ricans and Black captive people piss
In the hallways and project elevators
This is the white face they vomit on
Not knowing but feeling the truth
Watchout,
There comes the Blackman!

In your airconditioned grotesque monstrosities
I cannot breathe
Your cold bricks are made of the pulp of my bones
The water my sweat and blood

All the machinegun happy verwoerds and johnsons
All the housewives at pta coldwar meetings
All the butcher criminals who sat in judgement
Over Lumumba, Mandela, Sobukwe, Brother Malcolm
All the infernal priests teaching Blackmen
Never to know the truth
All the apologists for obscene hatred
And domination by white faggots
All these ghosts are dying
I discovered the truth one more time

Watchout,
Here comes the Blackman!
Can you do the dog?
Did you ever drink skokian?
Is Harlem a vice-infested nigger ghetto
Or a house of truth?
Is that Christ I saw in your bedroom?
Are you looking forward to
THE DESTRUCTION OF AMERICA,
A concrete act by LeRoi Jones?

Watchout,
Here comes the Blackman!
He has seen the truth
He beats his drums without embarrassment
Swinging to the rhythm of his birth pangs.

As a group, the liberationist poets were influenced by socialism, Islam, and militant black nationalism:

> Theirs is not a poetry for comfort-loving academicians or gentle intellectuals with bourgeois graces.... For these young poets, no traditional institution Western civilization needs to be preserved or venerated or protected or enshrined or respected. Western history for them is a curse and the American here-and-now an abomination. Like other revolutionaries, they are grouping for some coherent and disciplined approach to an understanding of the particular aspects of their human condition... Their "thing" is protest — strident, articulate, arrogant, bitter, caustic protest.[161]

American readers, especially black youth, responded very well to the poetry creations of Broadside poets. This was most certainly the case with many of the poets within the radical new black poetry group. One key that aids an understanding of their impact during the sixties lies in the fact that like the work of Langston Hughes, their "poetry was popular because it could be read easily by people of all ages and backgrounds."[162] Among the over 150 poets published in Broadside publications during the sixties, scholars Richard Barksdale and Kenneth Kinnamon note in *Black Writers of America* (1972) that four were introduced "with remarkably provocative results." They were Don L. Lee, Sonia Sanchez, Nikki Giovanni, and Etheridge Knight. "Rarely has a group of Black poets had such a constructively emotional impact on the collective racial ego of Black America."[163] Lee, Giovanni, Knight, and Sanchez were able to produce a new sound and tone in their urban poetry that was timely, and which spoke to the needs of young Americans. Their positive influence was also affected by the public's perception that they were:

> committed in their poetry to the cause of political, social, and moral revolution. And all believe that poetry and other forms of artistic expression should serve the ends of revolution. All express a deep pride in Blackness, and all believe that poetry should be written from a racial perspective and should probe the full range of racial confrontation. This they do using ghetto folk speech, without literary embellishments. Theirs is a language of confrontation in which are to be found irony, understatement, and satiric portraiture.[164]

Thus, Dudley Randall and Broadside Press played a significant role, during a key decade of American history, in helping to promote and expand the humanizing function and impact of poetry on American readers. It is a legacy that lives in the texts created by the poets of the sixties published by Broadside Press. As such, each succeeding generation brings a different set of responses to the texts as readers. This can be further noted in "the complex relation between a present reader and past work, especially the pastness of the past." Each generation of readers must therefore attempt "to understand the questions a past work asks and the answers it gives ... [and] the reader reconstructs."[165]

The production of Broadside's publications during the sixties were immensely dominated by black writers who lived in northern urban centers. Few southern-based black poets were published by the company. Therefore, a particular northern-based urban experience is concentrated in the poetry produced at Broadside. Several factors help to account for this situation. First, most black poets and other creative writers and artists lived in northern (and Californian) cities during the sixties. Secondly, even most black poets born in the South had to leave the region in order to be able to write about it. In the South, black writers faced a host of special problems, including a lack of publishing opportunities, few writer's workshops, an insufficient number of black oriented bookstores, few networks of other black writers, and few employment opportunities for writers (except at some black colleges, universities, and public schools). There was also a lack of major cultural centers for black writers, except for Houston, Texas; New Orleans, Louisiana; and Atlanta, Georgia (which were three of the largest southern cities with historically significant black arts and cultural bases).

A geographical review of Broadside's major authors (those who published, or edited books for the company) in the sixties, reveals the following data: six authors lived in Chicago (Arnez, Brooks, Burroughs, Kgositsile, Lee and Fuller); four lived in New York City (Emanuel, Giovanni, Jackson, and Sanchez); two lived in Detroit (Danner and Randall); two were from California (Eckels from Palo Alto, and Marvin X from San Francisco); and one each

Sonia Sanchez and sons, ca. 1974. Sanchez was born on September 9, 1934, in Birmingham, Alabama, but grew up in New York City. She has been a major voice in African-American poetry since the mid-sixties, and is the author of fourteen books. Sanchez has read her poetry and delivered lectures at more than 600 universities, colleges and other institutions in the United States and abroad. She currently holds the Laura Carnell Chair in English at Temple University, Philadelphia, Pennsylvania (photo by Ed Sherman; courtesy Broadside Press).

from Indianapolis (Knight), and Washington, D.C. (Murphy). Therefore, during the six-ties Broadside did not publish a poet who lived in the South. However, it did publish eight poets who were born in the South, but had moved elsewhere by the time of the publica-tion of their books with the company.

Black women writers were well represented in the diversity of Broadside Press publica-tions of the sixties. (See Table 2.6.) Nine black women writers had nine books produced at Broadside during this period; followed by seven black men writers, who had twelve works pub-lished by the company. These figures include the joint editorship of *For Malcolm X* by Ran-dall and Burroughs, and the joint authorship of *Poem Counterpoem* by Randall and Danner.

Black writers at Broadside Press received royalties on their publications with the com-pany. The amounts were generally small, and an author of a book of poems could gener-ally expect to receive a royalty payment of 10 to 15 percent on the number of volumes sold, while poets with poems in anthologies or single published poems received at least $10 for their work.[166] The average price of a Broadside book during the sixties was $1.00. If an author's book sold 500 copies, he or she would receive $50 at a royalty rate of 10 percent, or $75 at 15 percent. Writers thus had to have other sources for their livelihood — gener-ally everyday jobs. The vast majority of the Broadside writers listed on Table 2.6 were eco-nomically dependent on teaching positions from the university to the high school and lower levels in the sixties. In fact, all of the major Broadside poets have been teachers during some stage of their careers.[167]

In 1969, Dudley Randall could look back on five years of outstanding achievements at Broadside Press. For one thing, the company had surmounted the economics of pub-lishing during the sixties. In spite of a lack of capital, by the end of 1969, Broadside had produced two anthologies, *For Malcolm X* and *Black Poetry*; published seventeen volumes of poetry; printed thirty-three broadsides of poetry; produced twelve tapes of poetry; cir-culated *Broadside News*, a monthly newsletter; and distributed thirteen books of other pub-lishers and authors.[168] Truly, Randall could be proud of the fact, that "just about every major black poet to emerge out of the sixties sprouted with Broadside Press."[169]

As a publisher and editor, Randall was especially helpful in promoting the careers of four giant Black Arts Movement poets: Don L. Lee, Etheridge Knight, Nikki Giovanni, and Sonia Sanchez; and in advancing the careers of major writers such as Gwendolyn Brooks, James Emanuel, Audre Lorde, and Margaret Danner. He was also influential in giving direc-tion to at least a dozen other poets during the sixties, including Jon Eckels, Mae Jackson, Keorapetse Kgositsile, Stephany Fuller, and Marvin X, among others. Yet, Randall, in the final analysis, must be given an extraordinary amount of credit for recognizing the early tal-ents of Don L. Lee and Etheridge Knight. The case of Knight was especially meritorious, given the fact that his career as a poet began in the Indiana State prison, where he had been serving a twenty-year sentence since 1960 for a robbery in Indianapolis, Indiana. Randall corresponded with, and later visited Knight at the prison. "In a small room reserved for con-sultations with death row inmates, with riot doors slamming and prisoners shouting in the background, Randall convinced a hesitant Knight of his talent."[170] Randall also worked very hard to foster the career of Don L. Lee (Haki R. Madhubuti) who according to critic Stephen Henderson is "more widely imitated than any other Black poet with the exception of Amiri Baraka (LeRoi Jones). His unique delivery has given him a popular appeal which is tanta-mount to stardom. His influence is enormous and is still growing."[171] In the beginning of these two significant careers, Randall was there to give a helping hand.

A number of Broadside authors and books won prestigious awards and nominations for prizes in the sixties. Top honors in 1969 went to Keorapetse Kgositsile and Mae Jackson, winners respectively of the Second and Third Conrad Kent Rivers Memorial Award, administered by the editors of *Negro Digest*, and "presented once or twice a year to young writers who are notably striving to achieve the highest literary goals despite economic disadvantages or against unusual odds." The winners were awarded $500.[172]

Dudley Randall was the recipient of many dedications during the sixties. In 1967, Gwendolyn Brooks dedicated her poem "Malcolm X" to him, and followed in 1969 with a second notation in her Broadside book *Riot*.[173] Don L. Lee included Randall among the persons honored in his 1969 collection of poems, *Don't Cry, Scream!*[174]

At the end of the sixties, Randall was recognized nationally and internationally as a major African-American poet in his own right, and as an important publisher of black literature. In 1969, Nikki Giovanni wrote of Randall and Broadside that "only a true poet could assemble poets to create an organ for poetry. Broadside is one of our more vital organs and the man who created it one of our more vital men."[175]

Life had been good to Dudley Randall. At age fifty-five, as the sixties ended, he could look back on over a half-century of struggle to educate himself, to prepare and work in a career as a professional librarian, and to develop into a significant black poet and publisher of leading books by black American writers. It was no small feat, for Randall lived in a country known for its historical discrimination against and mistreatment of African-Americans. Yet, like so many before him, Dudley had succeeded against the odds, to create a valuable community institution — Broadside Press — which was needed to promote black literacy and the writings of black thinkers in America. The challenge in the near future for Randall and his small staff at Broadside was to keep the dream and vision of black literature alive, as economic hardships gathered added force in the seventies. But Randall had demonstrated in the sixties that a small black press devoted to black literature could survive with hard work and dedication. Randall was a true pioneer in a time of rapid social change and cultural outlook. He gave leadership and direction in the field of black publishing, and produced a body of work which offered his own people, his fellow Americans, and people everywhere an opportunity to explore the literature and thus the lives of the African-American community. This is his lasting legacy from the sixties to the present.

Chapter 3

The Growth of
Broadside Press, 1970-1975

The period from 1970 to 1975 represented the golden years of Broadside Press, when the company produced its greatest volume of literary materials, and extended its influence as the major publisher of black poetry in the United States. Dudley Randall continued at the helm of Broadside, while also serving as a reference librarian and poet-in-residence at the University of Detroit until 1974.[1] His duties at the University of Detroit as librarian and teacher were performed between Tuesday and Thursday of each week during the academic term. While teaching a course on black poetry, Randall's dedication to both poetry and his students was exemplified as he awarded poetry prizes (cash from his own pocket) to deserving student writers.[2]

Dudley and his wife, Vivian Barnett Spencer-Randall, remained active in Detroit community affairs during the early seventies. With a background in the arts, Dudley was a participant between 1971 and 1976 in the work of the New Detroit Inc. Committee, established after the Detroit rebellion of 1968 to promote economic and social improvements in the city. He also served as an advisory panel member for the Michigan Council for the Arts, 1970–76.[3] Vivian's own career as a psychiatric social worker kept her very busy, but she and the family were supportive and very proud of Dudley's accomplishments as a writer and publisher.[4]

Dudley's daughter (from a previous marriage), Mrs. Phyllis Ada (Randall) Sherron, II, continued to live in Detroit with her family, husband William Sherron, II, and their two children, Venita Sherron (King) and William Sherron, III. Phyllis' careers have included service as a registered nurse in Detroit, and as a teacher at the Highland Park, Michigan High School.[5]

The early seventies were very intensive travel years for Randall. His third major foreign trip took place in August 1970, when he traveled to West Africa on a group tour with the American Forum to Ghana. Over 100 Americans made the trip, and they were based at the University of Ghana near Accra.[6] Dudley later described the group's daily activities:

> In the morning, we attended lectures; in the afternoons we were free; sometimes in the evenings there would be cultural events like the National Ballet of Ghana would come to dance for us or dance groups form the villages would come to dance for us; or, we would see plays; we would also go on other side trips, by bus usually; we spent a few days, about a week, at the University of Kumasi, in the City of Kumasi, in the Ashanti country; a group of about nine of us went on a trip to Togo, and Dahomey; and we stayed several days on that trip; another separate group went down to Abidjan in the

Ivory Coast. The whole group was scheduled to go to Nigeria and stay for about a week, but we were not able to get visas, I think because of the feeling in Nigeria about the United States, after their [Nigeria's] civil war.[7]

This trip allowed Dudley to study African arts, to explore three African societies up close, and to expand his intellectual and cultural exchanges with African writers.[8]

Domestically, Randall was an extremely active traveler in the early seventies. He maintained a heavy schedule of poetry readings, and attendance at conferences and seminars.[9] He was a poetry festival participant at such institutions as Howard University, Washington, D.C., in May 1972; Southern University, Baton Rouge, Louisiana, in 1974, and with a group of Broadside poets at the Studio Museum in Harlem, New York, on October 27.[10]

On the homefront Dudley faced a health crisis in October 1972. Poet and Broadside assistant editor Melba Boyd summarized the events leading up to his mild coronary insufficiency:

> Randall was rushing between the University of Detroit, the printer and Broadside Press, preparing for the Paul Laurence Dunbar Festival at the University of Dayton. After changing a flat tire, loading and unloading heavy boxes of books, a sharp pain pierced his heart.[11]

Besides being overworked, Dudley enjoyed smoking cigarettes, but obviously his health now demanded that he slow down a bit and try to give up smoking. While working on these areas, Dudley also took the family dog, Butch, for walks and began to make the two mile trip to work at the University of Detroit by bike.[12] Such efforts enabled Randall to make a rapid recovery.[13]

Dudley Randall's status as a major American poet and outstanding publisher was exemplified in the early seventies by the comments of two critics. Donald Gibson wrote in 1973 that Randall "is a well-known and frequently anthologized poet who founded and operates the most significant outlet for the writing of black authors, the Broadside Press in Detroit."[14] Howard University professor Stephen Henderson notes that Randall's work with Broadside Press created a base "where many of the poets of the present generation first broke into print. Among these are Don L. Lee, Sonia Sanchez, Nikki Giovanni, and Etheridge Knight. The importance of this venture is easily grasped when one tries to imagine what the state of Black publication would be without the Broadside poets, and without works like the collection *For Malcolm [X]: Poems on the Life and Death of Malcolm X*, which he edited with Margaret Burroughs."[15] Indeed, during the years 1970–75, there was an explosion in the quantity and range of places where Randall's poetry and other writings were published. He was thus able to consolidate his position as both a poet and publisher.

During the six years between 1970 and 1975, Randall published six books: *Love You* (poems), 1970; *More to Remember* (poems), 1971; editor, *The Black Poets* (a poetry anthology), 1971; *After the Killing* (poems), 1973; *Broadside Memories: Poets I Have Known* (autobiography), 1975; and with Gwendolyn Brooks, Keorapetse Kgositsile, and Haki R. Madhubuti, *A Capsule Course in Black Poetry Writing* (criticism), 1975.[16] This body of work was well received by the public and critics. For example, Jim Walker, writing in *Black Creation*, called Randall's *The Black Poets* "an excellent compilation of the entire range of Black American poetry from slave songs to the present, it is especially welcome and sorely needed in the Afro-American poetic archives."[17] Poet Frank Marshall Davis spoke eloquently of Randall's work too:

In his brief but potent new book, *After the Killing*, Dudley Randall again offers visual proof of why he should be ranked in the front echelon of Black poets. His words are the distinctive reaction of a sensitive Afro-American to the world he has come to know, both at home and abroad. He has an African Suite composed of impressions received in Ghana and the Ivory Coast, and in such poems as "Words, Words, Words" and "Tell It Like It Is," he comes down hard on some of the sham current in today's world of American Blacks. And there is plenty.... Mr. Randall knows how to intelligently use Black lingo without it becoming annotated graffiti. He also has a gift for irony. The poems in this brief collection are militant and memorable.[18]

Randall was also one of the most anthologized poets of his generation during this period. In fact, he published over ninety-three poems in at least thirty-three or more anthologies between 1970 and 1975.[19] As in previous years, editors were especially attracted to his signature poem, "Booker T. and W. E. B.," which appeared in eleven anthologies in the early seventies. They were also favorably disposed to the following poems as well: "The Profile on the Pillow" (selected by seven editors for publication) "Primitives" (in six anthologies) and "Legacy: My South," "The Melting Pot," "Ballad of Birmingham," and "The Southern Road" (in four anthologies each). "The Profile on the Pillow" is an example of Randall's work which displays "the application of his fine lyricism to free verse."[20]

THE PROFILE ON THE PILLOW

After our fierce loving
in the brief time we found to be together,
you lay in the half light exhausted, rich,
with your face turned sideways on the pillow,
and I traced the exquisite
line of your profile, dark against the white,
delicate and lovely as a child's

Perhaps you may cease to love me,
or we may be consumed in the holocaust,
but I keep, against the ice and the fire,
the memory of your profile on the pillow.[21]

Two of Dudley's poems which appeared in *More to Remember* (1971), seem to capture his place in and central feelings during the Black Arts Movement — these are "An Answer to Lerone Bennett's Questionnaire on a Name for Black Americans" and "Nationalist."[22]

AN ANSWER TO
LERONE BENNETT'S QUESTIONNAIRE
ON A NAME FOR BLACK AMERICANS

Discarding the Spanish word for black
and taking the Anglo-saxon word for Negro,
discarding the names of English slavemasters
and taking the names of Arabian slave-traders
won't put a single
bean in your belly
or an inch of steel
in your spine.

Call a skunk a rose,
and he'll still stink,
and make the name stink too.
Call a rose a skunk,
and it'll still smell sweet,
and even sweeten the name.

The spirit informs the name,
not the name the spirit.

If the white man took the name Negro,
and you took the name Caucasian,
he'd still kick your ass,
as long as you let him.

If you're so insecure
that a word makes you quake,
another word
won't cure you.

Change your mind,
not your name.

Change your life,
not your clothes.

NATIONALIST

"Black
is beautiful,"
he said,
as he stroked
her white
breasts.

Some of his poetry from this period ranged outside the subject of race relations, however:

GREEN APPLES

What can you do with a woman under thirty?
It's true she has a certain freshness, like a green apple,
but how raw, unformed, without the mellowness of maturity.

What can you talk about with a young woman?
That is, if she gives you a chance to talk,
and she talks and talks and talks about herself.
Her self is the most important object in the universe.
She lacks the experience of intimate, sensitive silences.

Why don't young women learn how to make love?
They attack with the subtlety of a bull,
and moan and sigh with the ardor of a puppy.
Panting, they pursue their own pleasure,
forgetting to please their partner, like an older woman.

It's only just that young women get what they deserve.
A young man.

Dudley's poetry continued to appear widely in periodicals. He published over twenty poems during the early seventies, in such journals as *Black World, Michigan in Books, Journal of Black Poetry, Hoo Doo,* and *Okike: An African Journal of New Writing.*[23] He also published seven major essays, one short story, two broadsides, a poetry tape, five significant interviews, six introductions to new books, and over a dozen book reviews, in such organs as *Black World,* and *Okike,* during the first half of the decade.[24] Such an immense literary production increased both the literary world's and the general public's appreciation both for Randall's artistic work as a poet and critic, and for his publishing activities at Broadside Press.

While Randall's achievements brought him many personal rewards during the early seventies, blacks in Detroit also experienced a series of triumphs over the course of the decade, in the midst of continued poverty, discrimination, and social misery for many, In 1970, the black population in Detroit increased to 660,481, or 43.7 percent of the city's total population of 1,514,063. During this same year, there were 838,877 whites and 12,177 other racial groups in the city. On the state level, blacks represented 991,066 (11.2 percent) of Michigan's total population of 7,833,474.[25]

Politically, there were some bright moments during the decade. In 1972, blacks in Detroit sent thirteen black representatives and three senators to the Michigan legislature in Lansing. (The Michigan house of representatives contained 113 members, and the Senate, 38.) *Black Enterprise* wrote in 1972 that "Detroit was the first city in modern times to send two black men — Charles C. Diggs, Jr. and John Conyers, Jr. — to the U.S. Congress."[26] Then in November 1973, after a brilliant campaign by Coleman Young, aided with the skills of the "political wizard" Robert L. Millender, blacks captured the office of the mayor of Detroit for the first time.[27] This victory brought great psychological relief to the city's black community, burdened by such enduring practices as white police brutality, which received official toleration "from a police agency called STRESS" (Stop the Robberies and Enjoy Safe Streets).[28] Mayor Young disbanded STRESS in 1973, and initiated an active program to increase the presence of black police officers in the Detroit Police Department, and to improve public safety in the city.[29] Perhaps journalist Remer Tyson best sums up the mood of the era with his observations that

> Coleman A. Young's first year as the first black Mayor of Detroit was one of notable achievement: the city remains intact, mostly, and survived his worst fear: that some hate-eyed white sharpshooter from within his own Police Department might try to assassinate him. The city payroll was met each week, with the help of a few hundred layoffs. The garbage got picked up. The teachers didn't strike. The police didn't revolt. Blacks increased their share of high-paying City Hall jobs about 50 percent without losing the 90 percent they already held on the garbage trucks.[30]

Social conditions were nonetheless painful for large numbers of Detroit's citizens. Educationally, desegregation remained a key problem from the past, highlighted in the early seventies, when the Supreme Court ruled on July 25, 1974, "in the 'Detroit Case' that integration could not be achieved by linking city schools with those of surrounding suburbs."[31] With increasing white flight to the suburbs and a weakened financial base, by 1973, black students composed 70 percent of the city's school population. They were taught by a teaching staff which was 56 percent white and 43.2 percent black. Yet, in 1970, only 41.8 percent of students graduated from Detroit's high schools.[32]

Other social ills expressed themselves in the city's high crime rates (693 homicides in 1972), in its serious drug culture (over 40,000 addicts), and, as in many other cities, its "deplorable housing, hunger and inadequate medical care" for many of the low-income residents of Detroit.[33] Many blacks in the city remained gloomy about the state of the criminal justice system. The greatest mistrust was held for the Detroit Police Department, which in 1972 totaled "5,300 men, 560 [of them] black, about 13 percent, far below proportional representation. However, this was far above the 146 blacks on the 4,400-man force of 1966. In 1959 there were only 95 black policemen on a then 2,500-man force."[34]

Detroit's black economic situation was a complex one in the early seventies. At least 20 percent of blacks in the city had incomes below the poverty level.[35] Unemployment was high and was measured for blacks in Detroit at 10.3 percent in 1970. But according to a mid-seventies report, "unemployment among Detroit's black youth over age sixteen is extremely high, variously estimated at from 50 to 75 percent. Precise figures are unknown because officials simply have lost track of thousands of these youngsters."[36] Detroit had a strong black middle class, since it was a blue collar industrial town; however, "only 0.1 percent of the black American population had a household income of $50,000" in 1970.[37] Nonetheless, a significant element of black Detroiters were interested in operating businesses. But, sadly, as one report observes, "of the 59,000 business enterprises in the metropolitan Detroit area, some 6,000 (slightly more than ten percent) are black owned."[38] Many of these very were small business operations.

In the mid-seventies, one black-owned bank was active in Detroit, the First Independence National Bank of Detroit, established in 1970, which had assets of $35,378,000, and outstanding loans of $14,658,000. Blacks also owned the Home Federal Savings and Loan Association, created in 1947, and which had assets of $21,663,000, and loans of $18,699,000.[39] In 1974, *Black Enterprise* listed six black-owned Detroit business firms on its list of the "Top 100" black businesses in the United States. They were G.E. Wash Construction, Conyers Ford, Porterfield Wilson Pontiac, Clipper International Corp. Component Manufacturing, Renmuth (metal fabrication), and Bowers Realty and Investment Company. Jointly, these six companies employed 385 people, and had total 1973 sales of $30,900,000.[40] Yet, as Carlton B. Goodlett, publisher of the *San Francisco Sun-Reporter* reported, "in 1972 Black America earned $51.8 billion and spent $46 billion."[41] However, this sum was minuscule in comparison to white Americans, and most of it went to meet the daily needs of black people.

Detroit in the early seventies was becoming a black city surrounded by a white fortress — the suburbs. The challenge became one of living with the suburbs in the distance, as race relations deteriorated, and conditions became more destitute in Detroit.[42] The economic power of the region lay in the suburbs, yet Detroit remained a great city, with outstanding cultural, educational, and business interests. Within this orbit, one small black publisher, Dudley Randall, and company, Broadside Press, continued during the early seventies to carry the message of black literature out to the world.

This was the scene and state of affairs from which Randall worked to promote black literature in America. His goals for the seventies were a carry-over from the sixties: to help foster, create, and publish black literature.

> It [Broadside Press] has always been a sustenance, a teacher, an inspiration, and a joy.... it helps in the search for black identity, reinforces black pride and black unity, and is helping to create the soul, the consciousness and the conscience of black folk.[43]

Four of the major voices among African-American poets of the Black Arts Movement appear together, ca. 1975. From left to right, Haki R. Madhubuti, Dudley F. Randall, Sterling A. Brown (1901–1989), and Etheridge Knight (1931–1991) (courtesy Broadside Press).

In this "period of self-assertive Blackness of the early 1970's" stood Dudley Randall. He was a person of the hour who served his community "as a bridge connecting an older generation of poets with a younger generation."[44]

Although Randall had begun Broadside Press "to open a channel of publication for individual poems by young [and established] black poets for classroom circulation and personal collections," he had now advanced greatly from those original humble goals.[45] For in reality he was now a full-time publisher of black literature in many artistic forms. In truth, he became a living witness and example of the new "black aesthetic" of the Black Arts Movement, which fostered helping men and women "in becoming better than they are."[46]

A central ingredient in the work of Broadside remained the Broadside Series, the monthly sheets of poetry first produced by Randall in 1965 to establish the company:

> A broadside is something printed on one sheet of paper, on a single leaflet. The significance of them is that they can be very timely. They can be produced very rapidly since they're only one page and they can be sold very inexpensively because they're only one page. That was what I started publishing in Broadside Press, because I had only twelve dollars and broadsides were all I could afford to publish…. At that time my intention was to publish famous familiar poems in an attractive format so that people could buy their favorite poems in a form worth treasuring. A reviewer in *Small Press Review*, however, suggested that I could serve contemporary poetry better by publishing previously unpublished poems. Beginning with Broadside twenty-five, that is what I have attempted to do. I try to make the format of the Broadside harmonize with the poem in paper, color, and typography, and often employ artists to design or illustrate the

> Broadsides.... The purpose has changed.... This year we've started publishing more than
> one poet in a Broadside. We'll change as we go along. But it's a convenient format in
> which to present a classic, a timely poem, a new poem, a new poet, or a group of poems
> or poets.[47]

Broadside Press published 59 broadsides (numbers 34 to 92) by 81 poets between 1970 and
1975. They were distributed yearly with nine poems appearing on nine broadsides in 1970;
twenty-seven poems on twelve broadsides in 1971; eighteen poems on twelve broadsides in
1972; sixteen poems on twelve broadsides in 1973; twelve poems on twelve broadsides in
1974; and two poems on two broadsides in 1975. The low prices of the Broadside Series,
generally 50 cents each, or $6 to $12 for the yearly series, continued to make them a favorite
with many poetry lovers. The average number of a broadside's circulation was 500 copies;
however, nine poets — Paula Denise Alexander, Ronda M. Davis, Nikki Giovanni, Etheridge
Knight, Kuweka Amiri Mwandishe, Arthur Pfister, Helen Pulliam, Carolyn Rodgers, and
Jill Witherspoon — were the authors of broadsides with printed editions of 1,000 each. The
physical size of the broadsides varied greatly, from 8½ × 11 to large poster broadsides; and
the page numbers also varied from one to four pages. Poets were paid $10 a poem for their
broadsides, but some authors may have also received copies of their work as form of payment by the company.[48]

Table 3.1 enumerates the Broadside Series poets of this period.[49] While the great
majority of the poets had only one broadside (as did most poets in the sixties) four poets
during the early seventies had more — with three publications by Carolyn Rodgers (numbers 37, 44, and 50); and two each by Melba Joyce Boyd (numbers 66 and 68), Chaka
Shango (Horace Coleman) (numbers 56 and 74), and Etheridge Knight (numbers 36 and
64). By 1975, three distinct groups of poets could be observed among the Broadside Series
writers. The standards of measurement of each poet are based on the following three cri-
terias for a position as either a major, established, or new black poet, during the period
1970–75: (1) Range of publications in books, anthologies, periodicals, and other formats;
(2) The public service records of the poets; (3) the response of critics and the public to the
body of work created by a poet.

Group one consisted of ten major African-American poets (four men and six women):
Sonia Sanchez, Etheridge Knight, Carolyn Rodgers, Nikki Giovanni, Sterling D. Plumpp,
Dudley Randall, Gwendolyn Brooks, June Jordan, Lucille Clifton, and Michael S. Harper.
The fifteen established poets in group two (six women and nine men) were Arthur Pfister,
Stephany Fuller, Bobb Hamilton, Johari M. Amini (Jewel Latimore), Alice Walker, Jim
Cunningham (Olumo), Judy D. Simmons, John Randall, C. Gene Drafts, Chaka Aku
Shango (Horace Coleman), Herbert Woodward Martin, Pinkie Gordon Lane, Eugenia Col-
lier, Charles H. Rowell, and George Barlow. Fifty-six new black poets — (thirty-five men
and twenty-one women) — were published in a third group with broadsides during this
time period. The best known poets of group three in the early seventies were Jill Witherspoon, Ronda Davis, Walter Bradford, Alice Walker, Jose-Angel Figuerosa, and Melba
Boyd. Randall was true to his word: he devoted a considerable amount of space for the
voices of new poets to be heard through the Broadside Series. The fifty-six new poets represented 69 percent of the broadsides produced in the Broadside Series in 1970–75. Overall, forty-eight men (75 percent) and thirty-three women (25 percent) were the authors of
"broadsides" during the seventies. Although the data sources are insufficient on the social
backgrounds of twenty-four of the eight-one Broadside Series poets, a clear picture emerges,

nonetheless, of the continued influence and impact of the earlier black migration waves from the South to the North. (See Table 3.1.)

Broadside also produced five posters during the early seventies. Larger and more expensive than the Broadside Series, the posters included literary work by the following poets: Etheridge Knight, "For Black Poets Who Think of Suicide," (illustrated by Talita Long), $1; Dudley Randall, "On Getting a Natural," (illustrated by Leonard Baskin), $1 for the regular poster, $10 for one of fifty copies signed by Randall and the artist; Pat Whitsitt, "Black Silhouette," $1; Talita Long, "Angela," $1; and Reginald Payne and Pearl Eckles, "Protect the Sister," $2.[50] Poets in the Broadside Series and poster series explored a multiplex of themes on the black experience in America and abroad. Collectively, their work represented the wide array of black social, political, economic, and cultural realities in America — from the struggles of blacks to overcome racism and discrimination in this country, to the everyday lives of those in poverty and the working classes, to the hopes and dreams of the middle class. All are represented, yet, as in the sixties, the central theme which runs through much of this work is a focus on the quest for black freedom and renewal, in a better world for the great grandchildren of the 4,000,000 African-American bondspersons of 1860.

Randall also made a serious effort in the seventies to promote the work of black poets with a series of new anthologies. In all, five were published between 1971 and 1974. Many of the anthologized poets were intent as Keorapetse W. Kgositsile expressed it, to forge ahead in the Black Arts Movement with "an urgency to make their art as potent a weapon as any in the assertion, not birth of their humanism." For many of them there was a close connection between black art and everyday black life — "in practical terms," a merging of black culture and black social institutions.[51]

In 1971, lending her skill to this effort, Gwendolyn Brooks edited two anthologies for Broadside Press. The volume, *A Broadside Treasury,* includes work by many of the most outstanding contemporary black poets (male and female) in the United States since World War II. This anthology contained the works of thirteen women poets, and twenty-nine men.[52] *Jump Bad* introduces readers to the younger generation of black Chicago poets, such as Johari Amini, Walter Bradford, James Cunningham (Olumo), Don L. Lee, and Carolyn Rodgers, among others. This anthology represented seven women poets and six male poets.[53]

Another effort on the company's part to reach even younger and newer poets came in 1972 and 1973, when Jill Witherspoon Boyer edited two new anthologies, *The Broadside Annual. The Broadside Annual, 1972* contained the poetry of thirteen poets; eight men and five women.[54] Boyer's 1973 volume consisted of the work of six women and six male poets.[55]

Embracing the whole of the Black Experience, Randall also printed works from black inmates. Twenty-one black American males who were incarcerated in New York's Attica Prison were published in a 1974 anthology entitled *Betcha Ain't*, edited by Celes Tisdale. Broadside Press placed a special value on the work of black prisoners and was consistent in publishing their work. Such an opening was certainly needed in the seventies — even in the state of Michigan, black males were incarcerated at the rate of 1734.7 per 100,000 in 1978.[56] While Michigan had a total male prison population of 14,323 in 1978, 8,101 or 56.6 percent of this total were black. New York State on the other hand, with a larger black population, imprisoned a total of 19,635 individuals, of whom, 10,485, or 54.4 percent, were blacks.[57] Such individuals were among the most dispossessed black people in America, and Broadside offered some of them a communication outlet to the world.[58] *(cont. on page 93)*

Table 3.1

Broadside Series Poets, 1970–1975

Name & Gender	Broadside & Number	Writer's Group	Birth Place	Birth Date	Residence during 1970–75	Education	Broadside Press Books
Jim Witherspoon (Boyer) (F)	"County Jail" No. 39 (1970)	New	Detroit, MI	April 18, 1947–	Detroit, MI	Michigan St. Univ., B.A., 1969; Wayne State Univ.	(ed.), *The Brookside Annual*, (1972), (1973)
Ronda M. Davis (F)	"Rip-Off" No. 40 (1970)	New	Chicago, IL	Oct. 31, 1941–	Chicago, IL	Roosevelt Univ.	none
Nikki Giovanni (F)	"All I Gotta Do" No. 41 (1970)	Major	Knoxville, TN	June 7, 1943–	New York City, NY	Fisk Univ., B.A., 1967; Univ. of Pa.	*Re: Creation* (1970) (*Black Feeling, Black Talk*, 1968; and *Black Judgement* 1968, were first distributed by Broadside Press)
Paula Denise Alexander (F)	"Goodnight" No. 42 (1970)	New	Las Vegas, NV	Jan. 6, 1951–	Washington, DC	Stephens Col., 1969–71; Howard Univ., 1972	none
Sterling D. Plumpp (M)	"Muslim Men" No. 43 (1971)	Major	Clinton, MS	Jan. 30, 1940–	Chicago, IL	Roosevelt Univ., B.A., 1968, and grad. studies	*Clinton* (1976)
Carolyn Rodgers (F)	"A Love Rap/Commonly Known as a Poetic Essay" No. 44 (1971)	Major	Chicago, IL	Dec. 14, 1942–	Chicago, IL	Roosevelt Univ.; Chicago State Univ., B.A., 1981, M.A., 1984	none
Kuweka Amiri Mwandishe (Sterling X) (M)	"The Nigger Cycle" No. 45 (1971)	New	Chester, PA	Feb. 4, 1953–	Chester, PA	Univ. of Pa.	none
Omari Kenyatta Tarajia (Richard C. James III) (M)	"Simple Poem to Mae" No. 46 (1971)	New	N/A	N/A	N/A	N/A	none

Name & Gender	Broadside & Number	Writer's Group	Birth Place	Birth Date	Residence during 1970–75	Education	Broadside Press Books
Rockie D. Taylor (Tejumola Ologboni) (M)	"Black Henry" No. 47 (1971)	New	Salina, KS	May 2, 1945–	Milwaukee, WI	Univ. of Wis., 1963–68, B.S., 1968; Ind. Univ., 1968–69; Univ. of Wis., 1973	none
Robert Kesby (M)	"Black Rebel" No. 48 (1971)	New	N/A	N/A	N/A	N/A	none
Stephanie Fuller (F)	Poem No. 48 (1971)	Established	Chicago, IL	Oct. 23, 1947–	Chicago, IL	Univ. of Ill., Chicago Circle; M.A., Atlanta U.	*Moving Deep* (1969)
Wilbert F. Rutledge, Jr. (M)	"Non-Violent Revolution" No. 49 (1971)	New	Kansas City MO	March 7, 1940–	Kansas City, MO	Lincoln Univ. (Mo.), B.S., 1965	none
James Amaker (M)	"I Reach Inside Myself" No. 49 (1971)	New	N/A	N/A	State Correctional Institution, Huntington, PA	High School diploma (G.E.D.)	none
Lori Lunford (F)	"Sister/Brother Good" No. 49 (1971)	New	N/A	N/A	N/A	N/A	none
Porter Kirkwood (M)	"The Search" No. 49 (1971)	New	N/A	N/A	N/A	N/A	none
Glenda Gracia (F)	Poem No. 49 (1971)	New	Philadelphia, PA	Dec. 31, 1948–	Philadelphia, PA	Cheyney St. Col., B.A., Univ. of Pa.; Temple Univ. Law School	none
Carolyn Rodgers (F)	"For Hoyt W. Fuller" No. 50 (1971)	Major	Chicago, IL	Dec. 14, 1942–	Chicago, IL	Roosevelt Univ.; Chicago State Univ.	none
Bobb Hamilton (M)	"A Father Tells" His Son About the Statue of Liberty" No. 51 (1971)	Established	Cleveland, OH	Dec. 16, 1928–	New York City, NY	Ohio State Univ., B.S., 1950; New School of Social Research	none

Broadside Series Poets, 1970–1975 (continued)

Name & Gender	Broadside & Number	Writer's Group	Birth Place	Birth Date	Residence during 1970–75	Education	Broadside Press Books
George Edward Buggs (M)	"Crossing the International Date Line" No. 51 (1971)	New	Brooklyn, NY	Jan. 27, 1947–	Suny-Oswego, NY	Hampton Univ., B.A., 1971; Suny-Oswego	none
Yusuf Burni (Joseph Pannell) (M)	"To My Immortality" No. 52 (1971)	New	Washington, DC	N/A	Chicago, IL	N/A	none
Jeanne Newkirk Smith (F)	"Attempted Genocide," "Sometimes When It Doesn't Work," and "Good Times" No. 52 (1971)	New	New York City, NY	Nov. 25, 1936–	Bronx, NY	Hunter College, B.A., 1959	none
Robert T. Bowen (M)	"Childhood" No. 52 (1971)	New	New Haven, CT	June 14, 1936–	Los Angeles, CA	Lincoln Univ. (Pa.), 1954–55; Univ. of Conn., B.A., 1958	none
Carol Gregory Clemmons (F)	Poem No. 52 (1971)	New	Youngstown, OH	March 18, 1945–	Brooklyn, NY	Youngstown Univ., B.A., 1968	none
Benjamin Howard Rogers (M)	"The Black Man's Life" No. 53 (1971)	New	Sioux City, IA	May 13, 1949–	Minneapolis, MN	Univ. of Minn. 1968–73	none
LaDonna Jean Tolbert (F)	"Unite" No. 53 (1971)	New	Detroit, MI	July 21, 1956–	Detroit, MI	Cass High School Detroit, 1974	none
Alvin Kingcade (M)	"Superblack" No. 53 (1971)	New	Philadelphia, PA	June 26, 1950–	Philadelphia, PA	Temple Univ., 1967–68; Univ. of Pa., B.S., 1972	none
Hodari Kinamo (M)	"Hoes Are for Raking Leaves" No. 53 (1971)	New	Jonesville, LA	Dec. 21, 1940–	Las Vegas, NV	Calif. St. Col., Los Angeles, B.A., 1967	none

Name & Gender	Broadside & Number	Writer's Group	Birth Place	Birth Date	Residence during 1970–75	Education	Broadside Press Books
Lawrence C. Riley (M)	"Ebony Woman" No. 54 (1971)	New	Detroit, MI	Oct. 26, 1947–	Detroit, MI	Ferris State Col. or Univ.	none
Thomas Washington, Jr. (M)	"Growing Pains" No. 54 (1971)	New	N/A	N/A	N/A	N/A	none
Robert L. Robinson (M)	"Convict Warrior No. 122088" No. 54 (1971)	New	Detroit, MI	Dec. 5, 1946–	Detroit, MI	Public schools of Detroit, MI	none
Mabarut Khalil Malik (M)	"Sisters Love to Rap" No. 54 (1971)	New	N/A	N/A	N/A	N/A	none
Julianne D. Perry (F)	"Black Song" No. 55 (1972)	New	Durham, NC	July 12, 1952–	Durham, NC	Barnard Col., Columbia Univ., 1972–	none
Chaka Aku Shango (Horace Coleman)	"Black Gifts for a Black Child" No. 56 (1972)	New	Dayton, OH	May 4, 1943–	Athens, OH	Bowling Green State Univ., 1961–65, B.A. & M.F.A. 1972	none
Evelyn Clarke (F)	"Gonna Free Him" No. 57 (1972)	New	Tarboro, NC	March 6, 1935–	North Plainfield, NJ	Newark St. Teachers Col.; Shaw Univ., Raleigh, NC	none
Karl W. Carter (M)	"Song," "The Old Woman," & "In Apology for All Black Women" No. 58 (1972)	New	N/A	N/A	N/A	N/A	none
Johari M. Amini (Jewel Latimore) (now Johari M. Amini Kunjufu) (F)	"A Hip Tale in the Death Style" No. 59 (1972)	Established	Philadelphia, PA	Feb. 13, 1935–	Chicago, IL	Chicago City, Col., A.A., 1968; Univ. of Chicago, 1968–69; Chicago St. Univ., 1970; Univ. of Chicago, M.A., 1972	none

Broadside Series Poets, 1970–1975 (continued)

Name & Gender	Broadside & Number	Writer's Group	Birth Place	Birth Date	Residence during 1970–75	Education	Broadside Press Books
Alice Walker (F)	"Revolutionary Petunias," "J, My Good Friend," "The Girl Who Died No. 1," "Lost My Voice?" & "He Said Come" No. 60 (1972)	Established	Eatonton, GA	Feb. 9, 1944–	Jackson, MS	Spelman Col., 1961–63; Sarah Lawrence Col., B.A., 1965	none
James Randall (M)	"The Ropy Plea for Status —Quo Anxiety Frustration" No. 61 (1972)	New	Bolton, NC	July 31, 1943–	Cedar Rapids, IA	N.C. A&T Col., B.S., 1965; Carnegie Mellon Univ., M.A., 1967; Ind. Univ.	none
Ray B. Oxford (M)	"Sandwedge," & "The Arms Race" No. 61 (1972)	New	Chicago, IL	March 29, 1935–	Cochelle, IL	High School diploma	none
Jerry Frosh (M)	"We'll Dance, We'll Sing, Our Own Way" No. 61 (1972)	New	Canton, GA	March 1, 1949–	Atlanta, GA	Tuskegee Univ.	none
Dudley Randall (M)	"Green Apples" No. 62	Major	Washington, DC	Jan. 14, 1914–	Detroit, MI	Wayne St. Univ., B.A.; Univ. of Michigan, M.S.L.S.	*Poem Counterpoem;* (1966) *For Malcolm X* (1967); *Cities Burning* (1968); ed., *Black Poetry* (1969); others
Jim Olumo Cunningham (M)	"Pearl Bailey Sings" No. 63 (1972)	Established	Webster Grove, MO	Jan. 4, 1936–	Ithaca, NY; Chicago, IL	Butler Univ.	none
Judy Dothard Simmons (F)	"Schizophrenia" No. 64 (1972)	Established	Westerly, RI	Aug. 29, 1944–	New York City, NY	Sacramento State Col., B.A., 1967	*Judith's Blues* (1973)
Lyn Knight (Lyn A. Levy) (F)	"The Final Indignity" No. 64 (1972)	New	Boston, MA	July 8, 1946–	Dorchester, MA	Northeastern Univ. 1968–72	none
Etheridge Knight (M)	"A Poem for Brother/Man" No. 64 (1972)	Major	Corinth, MA	April 19, 1931–1991	Pittsburgh, PA; Hartford, CT; Jefferson City, MO; Indianapolis, IN	Grade school; self-educated	*Poems from Prison* (1968); *Belly Song and Other Poems* (1973)

Name & Gender	Broadside & Number	Writer's Group	Birth Place	Birth Date	Residence during 1970–75	Education	Broadside Press Books
Habte Wolde (Alonzo Jennings) (M)	"For the Children…" No. 64 (1972)	New	Patterson, NJ	1945–	Princeton, NJ; Addis Ababa, Ethiopia	Montclair St. Col., B.A.; Princeton Univ., M.A., 1972	Enough to Die For (1972)
Gwendolyn Brooks (F)	"Aurora" No. 65 (1972)	Major	Topeka, KS	June 7, 1917–	Chicago, IL	Wilson Junior Col., Chicago, 1936	Riot (1970); Aloneness (1971); ed., A Broadside Treasury (1971); ed., Jump Bad (1971); Report from Part One (1972); others
Melba Joyce Boyd (F)	"1965, Dedicated to all my brothers & sisters of Southwest Detroit, who did not Survive." No. 66 (1972)	Established	Detroit, MI	April 2, 1950–	Detroit, MI	Western Mich. Univ., B.A., 1971, M.A., 1972; Univ. of Michigan, D.A.	none
Jose-Angel Figuerosa (M)	"X Pressing Feelin'" No. 66 (1972)	Established	Mayaguez, PR	Nov. 28, 1946–	Bronx, NY	New York Univ., 1970; SUNY-Buffalo	East 110th Street (1973)
George Barlow (M)	"Flowers at the Jackson Funeral Home" No. 66 (1972)	Established	Berkeley, CA	Jan. 23, 1948–	Oakland, CA	Calif. St. Col., B.A., 1970; Univ. of Iowa, M.F.A., 1972	Gabriel (1974)
Ruth Steed (F)	"Ain't No Mo Ain't" No. 67 (1973)	New	Marianna, FL	July 9, 1947–	Pontiac, MI	Oakland Comm. Col.; Fla. International Univ.; Wayne State Univ.	none
Chinosole (M)	"Impressions of Zambia" No. 67 (1973)	New	N/A	N/A	N/A	N/A	none

Broadside Series Poets, 1970–1975 (continued)

Name & Gender	Broadside & Number	Writer's Group	Birth Place	Birth Date	Residence during 1970–75	Education	Broadside Press Books
Tom Sellers (Thomas Peyton Sellers) (M)	"The Little Black Girl on the Subway" No. 67 (1973)	New	Summit, NJ	Dec. 8, 1949–	Boston, MA	Amherst Col., 1967–71	none
Melba Joyce Boyd (F)	"To Darnell and Johnny" No. 68 (1973)	Established	Detroit, MI	April 2, 1950–	Detroit, MI	Western Mich. Univ., B.A., 1971, M.A., 1972; Univ. of Michigan, D.A.	none
Walter Cox (M)	"Rosedale Street," "Love Poem for Patricia (Who I Dig)," "As of Late," & "Carmel" No. 69 (1973)	New	N/A	N/A	N/A	N/A	none
John Randall (M)	"Indigoes" No. 70 (1973)	New	Detroit, MI	March 26, 1942–	Evansville, IN	Univ. of Mich.; Wayne State Univ., B.S., 1969	Black Heart Blues (1974)
El Gilbert (M)	"Democracy" No. 71 (1973)	New	N/A	N/A	N/A	N/A	none
JoAnn Anderson (F)	"Summer Time Haiku, Not on Nature, But on Being Natural" No. 72 (1973)	New	Detroit, MI	Jan 1, 1953–	Detroit, MI	Marygrove Col., 1971–72; Univ. of Detroit, 1973–	none
C. Gene Drafts (Charles Gene Drafts) (M)	"But Not for Me" No. 73 (1973)	New	Boston, MA	Sept. 27, 1946–	Mattapan, MA	Mass. Bay Comm. College	none
Chaka Aku Shango (Horace Coleman) (M)	"The Sunflower Queen" No. 74 (1973)	New	Dayton, OH	May 4, 1943–	Athens, OH	Bowling Green State Univ., 1961–65, B.A. & M.F.A., 1972	none
Denise Alexander Burnett (F)	"Four Women," "Lorraine Hansberry," "Billy Holiday,"	New	N/A	N/A	N/A	N/A	none

Name & Gender	Broadside & Number	Writer's Group	Birth Place	Birth Date	Residence during 1970–75	Education	Broadside Press Books
Albert Wendt (M)	"Traders" No. 76 (1973)	New	N/A	N/A	N/A	N/A	none
Susan Cotrell (F)	"To My Man in Jail" No. 77 (1973)	New	N/A	N/A	N/A	N/A	none
Richard Alonso (M)	"Afro Blue" No. 77 (1973)	New	N/A	N/A	N/A	N/A	none
Jacelyn Lewis (F)	"Hold Me" No. 77 (1973)	New	N/A	N/A	N/A	N/A	none
June Jordan (F)	"Poem: On Moral Leadership as a Political Dilemma, Watergate 1973" No. 78 (1973)	Major	Harlem, NY	July 9, 1936–	New York City, NY	Barnard Col. 1953–55, 1956–57; Univ. of Chicago, 1955–65	none
Herbert Woodward Martin (M)	"At the Five and Dime" No. 79 (1974)	Established	Birmingham, AL	1933–	Dayton, OH	Univ. of Toledo; SUNY Buffalo	none
Pinkie Gordon Lane (F)	"A Quiet Poem" No. 80 (1974)	Established	Philadelphia, PA	Jan. 13, 1923–	Baton Rouge, LA	Spelman Col., B.A., 1949; Atlanta Univ., M.A., 1956; La. St. Univ., Ph.D., 1967	none
Lucille Clifton (F)	"All of Us Are All of Us" No. 81 (1974)	Major	Depew, NY	June 27, 1936–	Baltimore, MD	Howard Univ., 1953–55; Fredonia St. Teachers Col., 1955; hon. doctorates, Univ. of Md., Towson St. Col.	none
Deonne B. Wright	"Watermelon Poems" No. 82 (1974)	New	N/A	N/A	N/A	N/A	none
Eileen Tann (F)	"Counterpoem for Dudley Randall" No. 83 (1974)	New	N/A	N/A	N/A	N/A	none

Broadside Series Poets, 1970–1975 (continued)

Name & Gender	Broadside & Number	Writer's Group	Birth Place	Birth Date	Residence during 1970–75	Education	Broadside Press Books
Eugenia Collier (F)	"Hurl" No. 84 (1974)	Established	Baltimore, MD	April 6, 1928–	Baltimore, MD	Howard Univ., B.A., 1948; M.A., Columbia Univ., 1950; Univ. of Md., Ph.D.	none
Charles H. Rowell (M)	"Silent Words at My Mother's Grave" No. 85 (1974)	Established	Auburn, AL	1940–	Baton Rouge, LA	Alabama A&M Univ., B.A., 1961; Univ. of Missouri, Columbia, M.A., 1962; Ohio State Univ., Ph.D., 1972	none
Melvin Dixon (M)	"Climbing Montmartre" No. 86 (1974)	New	Stamford, CT	May 29, 1950– Oct. 29, 1992	Providence, RI	Wesleyan Univ., B.A., 1971; Boston Univ., M.A., 1973, Ph.D, 1975	none
Hurley X (Smith) (M)	"Poem for Patrice Lumumba" No. 87 (1974)	New	N/A	N/A	N/A	N/A	none
Donald Mosely (M)	"Strolling" No. 88 (1974)	New	N/A	N/A	N/A	N/A	none
Mozehin Tejani (M)	"African Mama" No. 89	New	N/A	N/A	N/A	N/A	none
Rhonda Mills (F)	"Love Deep" No. 90 (1974)	New	N/A	N/A	N/A	N/A	none
Michael S. Harper (M)	"To an Old Man Twiddling Thumbs" No. 91 (1975)	Major	Brooklyn, NY	March 18, 1938–	Providence, RI	Calif. St. Col., Los Angeles, B.A., 1961, M.A., 1963; Univ. of Iowa Writers Workshop, 1962	none
Betty H. Neals (F)	"The Great Gettin' Down" No. 92 (1975)	New	N/A	N/A	N/A	N/A	none
Dudley Randall (M)	"For Vivian" No. 93 (1982)	Major	Washington, DC	Jan. 14, 1914–	Detroit, MI	Wayne St. Univ., B.A.; Univ. of Michigan, M.S.L.S.	*Poem Counter-poem* (1966); *For Malcolm X* (1967); *Cities Burning* (1968); ed., *Black Poetry* (1969); others

The main body of Broadside's work between 1970 and 1975 consisted of sixty-three collections of the individual poetry and other books of black writers.[59] Table 3.2 complies a record of all Broadside paper and cloth editions of books published by the company during the seventies. The press placed a heavy concentration on publishing new single-authored books of black poetry, thirty-six in all. Of these, twenty-six (70 percent) were by black men, and ten (30 percent) by black women.

The list of thirty-six volumes of Broadside poetry includes some of the most important poetry published by black writers during the last stage of the Black Arts Movement. As with the Broadside Series poets, three groups of poets emerge from this period. (See Table 3.9.) Among the major poets (nine men and five women) who published Broadside books were Sterling A. Brown, James A. Emanuel, Nicholas Guillen (of Cuba), Keorapetse Kgositsile (of South Africa), Etheridge Knight, Don L. Lee (Haki R. Madhubuti), Lance Jeffers, Clarence Major, Dudley Randall, Gwendolyn Brooks, Nikki Giovanni, Audre Lorde, Sonia Sanchez, and Margaret Walker. Key figures among the established poets (two women and seven men) in this group include Frenchy Hodges, Judy Simmons, Alvin Aubert, Ahmed Alhamisi, George Barlow, Jon Eckels, Jose-Angel Figuerosa, Doughtry Long, and Arthur Pfister. The dozen new poets (ten men and two women) on Broadside's publication schedule were Henry Blakely (Gwendolyn Brooks' husband), Arthur Boze, C. E. Cannon, C. Gene Drafts, Everett Hoagland, James Randall, Jr., and Jon C. Randall (nephews of Dudley Randall), John Raven, William A. Thigpen, Jr., and Habte Wolde (Alonzo Jennings).

Of the thirty-six authors, twelve men and four women were born in the South (44 percent), seven men and two women in the Midwest, two men and two women in the mid-Atlantic states, two women and one male in New England, one male in the West, and one male each in Puerto Rico, Cuba, and South Africa. As in the sixties the majority of poets born in the South migrated from the region to seek jobs and build their writing careers in other parts of the country. Likewise, northern blacks found their greatest opportunities as writers in the central cities of that region. Between 1970 and 1975, most of the black poets of this survey lived in New York City (five poets), Detroit and Chicago (three each), San Francisco Bay area (three), and other northern cities. Even in the South, black poets were concentrated in the cultural centers and such key cities of the region as Houston, New Orleans, Jackson (Mississippi), Washington, D.C.; Chattanooga (Tennessee), and Greensboro (North Carolina). Such southern cities were also significant because they usually contained black colleges, which employed some black poets, such as Margaret Walker at Jackson State, Charles Rowell and Alvin Aubert at Southern University in Baton Rouge, Louisiana, and Arthur Pfister at Texas Southern University in Houston.

A large number of the thirty-six poets were born in the forties (nineteen, or 53 percent). Thus, continued the sixties tradition at Broadside of offering new opportunities for book publication to younger poets. The vast majority of the poets attended college and many held undergraduate degrees — twenty-four men and ten women. Twenty-four of the poets completed advanced studies beyond the B.A. degree — fourteen men and six women at the master's level; and three men and one woman at the Ph.D. level. Three men and five women were awarded honorary doctorates during the period. As in the previous generation, teaching and writing remained the dominant occupations of black poets during the seventies. Broadside writers were also employed as journalists, librarians, social workers, and arts administrators, and in such varied fields as business, publishing, manufacturing, and photography.

Left: Arthur Pfister was born on September 20, 1949, in New Orleans, Louisiana. His career has included periods of teaching and service as a writer-in-residence at such institutions as Southern University, Baton Rouge, Louisiana, and Texas Southern University, Houston, Texas. In 1969, he received a writing award from the National Endowment of the Arts (photo by T. W. Anderson; courtesy Broadside Press). *Right:* Alvin Aubert was born on March 12, 1930, in Luchter, Louisiana. He has been an active poet, essayist and playwright since the early sixties. He founded *Obsidian: Black Literature in Review* in 1975 and served for over ten years as its chief editor. In the fall of 1989, *The Black American Literature Forum* honored Aubert with a special issue devoted to his work. He is professor emeritus in the Department of English at Wayne State University, Detroit (courtesy Broadside Press).

In addition to the five anthologies previously discussed, the company published seventeen other books, in seven genre areas, during this era. (See Table 3.2.) Regina O'Neal's *And Then the Harvest: Three Television Plays* (1974) was the only drama publication to appear during the history of the company. Five books were published in the *Broadside Critics Series,* of which James A. Emanuel served as general editor. They included *Dynamite Voices, Black Poets of the 1960's* (1971), by Don L. Lee; *Claude McKay: The Black Poet at War* (1972), by Addison Gayle, Jr.; *A Many Colored Coat of Dreams: The Poetry of Countee Cullen* (1974), by Houston A. Baker, Jr.; *The Folk Roots of Contemporary Afro-American Poetry* (1974), by Bernard W. Bell; and *Phillis Wheatley in the Black American Beginnings* (1975), by William H. Robinson. There were three autobiographies, perhaps the most famous of which was Gwendolyn Brook's *Report from Part One* (1972); but an important contribution to black life and letters was also made with the publication in 1975 of Dudley's Randall's *Broadside Memories* and Chauncey E. Spencer's *Who Is Chauncey Spencer?* (Spencer served during World War II with the famed Tuskegee [Alabama] Airmen.)[60] *(cont. on page 99)*

Table 3.2

Broadside Press Books, 1970–1975

Author(s)	Publication	Genre	Price of Book	Price of Tape	Pages	Gender of Author
1970						
Gwendolyn Brooks	Family Pictures	Poetry	$3.00 (Cloth, $5.00)	$5.00	24	F
James Emanuel	Panther Man	Poetry	$1.00	$5.00	34	M
Nikki Giovanni	Black Feeling, Black Talk	Poetry	$1.00		26	F
	Re: Creation	Poetry	$1.50 (Cloth, $4.50)		50	F
Everett Hoagland	Black Velvet	Poetry	$1.00		34	M
Lance Jeffers	My Blackness Is the Beauty of This Land	Poetry	$1.00		26	M
Don L. Lee	We Walk the Way of the New World	Poetry	$1.50 (Cloth, $4.50)	$5.00	72	M
James Randall, Jr.	Don' Ask Me Who I Am	Poetry	$1.00		18	M
Sonia Sanchez	We a BaddDDD People	Poetry	$1.50	$5.00	74	F
Carolyn Thompson	Frank	Coloring Book	$1.00		42	F
Margaret Walker	Prophets for a New Day	Poetry	$1.00		34	F
1971						
Gwendolyn Brooks	Aloneness	Children's	$1.00 (Cloth, $3.00)		20	F
	Report from Part One	Autobio-graphy	$5.95 (Cloth)		220	F
Gwendolyn Brooks, ed.	The Black Position	Essays	$1.00		40	F
	A Broadside Treasury, 1965–1970	Poetry Anthology	$4.00 (Cloth, $6.00)		194	F
	Jump Bad, a New Chicago Anthology	Poetry Anthology	$4.00		194	F
Jon Eckels	Our Business in the Streets	Poetry	$1.00	$5.00	34	M

Broadside Press Books, 1970–1975 (continued)

Author(s)	Publication	Genre	Price of Book	Price of Tape	Pages	Gender of Author
Frenchy Jolene Hodges	Black Wisdom	Poetry	$1.00	$5.00	34	M
Don L. Lee	Directionscore: Selected and New Poems	Poetry	$3.75 (Cloth, $6.00; Deluxe Cloth, $15.00)		210	M
	Dynamite Voices, Black Poets of the 1960's	Literary Criticism (Broadside Critics Series I)	$2.75		98	M
Doughtry Long	Black Love Black Hope	Poetry	$1.50		42	M
	Song for Nia	Poetry	$1.50		42	M
Marion Nicholes	Life Styles	Poetry	$1.00		26	F
John Raven	Blues for Momma and Other Low Down Stuff	Poetry	$0.50		32	M
Sonia Sanchez	It's a New Day, Poems for Young Brothas and Sistuhs	Poetry	$1.25 (Cloth, $4.00)		34	F

1972

Author(s)	Publication	Genre	Price of Book	Price of Tape	Pages	Gender of Author
Ahmed Alhamisi	Holy Ghosts	Poetry	$1.95 (Cloth, $4.50)		66	M
Alvin Aubert	Against the Blues	Poetry	$1.50		34	M
Arthur Boze	Black Words	Poetry	$1.00		26	M
Gwendolyn Brooks, ed.	The Black Position	Essays	$1.50		50	F
C. E. Cannon	St. Nigger	Poetry	$1.00		26	M
Addison Gayle, Jr.	Claude McKay: The Black Poet at War	Literary Criticism (Broadside Critics Series 2)	$1.50		48	M
Lyn (Lyn Levy)	Singing Sadness Happy	Poetry	$1.50		34	F
Pearl Lomas	We Don't Need No Music	Poetry	$1.00		18	F
Clarence Major	The Cotton Club	Poetry	$1.25	$5.00	26	M
Bill Odarty	A Safari of African Cooking	Cookbook	$3.95 (Cloth, $5.95)		65	M

Author(s)	Publication	Genre	Price of Book	Price of Tape	Pages	Gender of Author
Arthur Pfister	*Beer Cans Bullets Things & Pieces*	Poetry	$1.25		32	M
William A. Thigpen, Jr.	*Down Nigger Paved Streets*	Poetry	$1.25		34	M
Jill Witherspoon, ed.	*The Broadside Annual*	Poetry Anthology	$1.00		26	M
Habte Wolde	*Enough to Die For*	Poetry	$1.50		50	M

1973

Gwendolyn Brooks, ed.	*The Black Position*	Essays	$3.00		65	F
Jose-Angel Figueroa	*East 110th Street*	Poetry	$1.75		50	M
Etheridge Knight	*Belly Song and Other Poems*	Poetry	$1.75 (Cloth, $4.95)		66	M
Audre Lorde	*From a Land Where Other People Live*	Poetry	$1.50		50	F
Haki R. Madhubuti (formerly Don L. Lee)	*Book of Life*	Poetry	$1.95		82	M
	From Plan to Planet	Essays	$1.95		162	M
James Randall	*Cities and Other Disasters*	Poetry	$1.50		34	M
Judy Simmons	*Judith's Blues*	Poetry	$1.25	$5.00	26	F
Margaret Walker	*October Journey*	Poetry	$1.50		40	F
Jill Witherspoon, ed.	*The Broadside Annual*	Poetry Anthology	$1.50		26	F

1974

Leaonead Pack Bailey, compiler & editor	*Broadside Authors and Artists, an Illustrated Bio-graphical Directory*	Reference Work	$9.95 (Cloth)		132	F
Houston A. Baker, Jr.	*A Many Colored Coat of Dreams: The Poetry of Countee Cullen*	Literary Criticism (Broadside Critics Series 4)	$2.75		66	M
George Barlow	*Gabriel*	Poetry	$2.00		66	M
Bernard W. Bell	*The Folk Roots of Contemporary Afro-American Poetry*	Literary Criticism (Broadside Critics Series 3)	$2.00 (Cloth, $5.00)		80	M

Broadside Press Books, 1970–1975 (continued)

Author(s)	Publication	Genre	Price of Book	Price of Tape	Pages	Gender of Author
Henry Blakely	*Windy Place*	Poetry	$2.50 (Cloth, $6.00)		16	M
Linda Bragg	*A Love Song to Black Men*	Poetry	$2.00		34	M
Sterling Brown	*The Last Ride of Wild Bill*	Poetry	$3.00 (Cloth $6.00)		58	M
Gene Drafts	*Bloodwhispers/ Black Songs*	Poetry	$1.50	$5.00	16	M
Nicolas Guillen (Translated by Richard J. Carr)	*Tango*	Poetry	$4.25 (Cloth $7.25)		148	M
Lance Jeffers	*When I Know the Power of My Black Hand*	Poetry	$1.95 (Cloth $5.00)		66	M
Andre Lorde	*The New York Head Shop and Museum*	Poetry	$3.50		60	M
Regina O'Neal	*And Then the Harvest, Three Television Plays*	Drama	$6.00		146	F
Sonia Sanchez	*A Blues Book for Blue Black Magical Women*	Poetry	$1.95 (Cloth, $5.00)		66	F
Celes Tisdale, ed.	*Betcha Ain't, Poems from Attica*	Poetry Anthology	$2.50 (Cloth, $5.00)		66	F

1975

Author(s)	Publication	Genre	Price of Book	Price of Tape	Pages	Gender of Author
Gwendolyn Brooks, with Keorapetse Kgositsile, Haki R. Madhubuti, and Dudley Randall	*A Capsule Course in Black Poetry Writing*	Literary Reference Work	$6.00		68	F, M, M, M
Gwendolyn Brooks	*Beckonings*	Poetry	$2.00		18	F
Dudley Randall	*Broadside Memories: Poets I Have Known*	Literary History & Auto-biography	$6.00		68	M
John C. Randall	*Indigoes*	Poetry	$2.00		18	M
William H. Robinson	*Phillis Wheatley in the Black American Beginnings*	Literary Criticism (Broadside Critics Series 5)	$3.50		98	M
Chauncey E. Spencer	*Who Is Chauncey Spencer?*	Auto-biography	$7.95		152	M
Jill Witherspoon	*Dream Farmer*	Poetry	$2.00		26	F

A specialty book, Bill Odarty's *A Safari of African Cooking*, was added to the Broadside list in 1972. Works devoted to children did not go unnoticed at Broadside; and Carolyn Thompson's *Frank* (1970), a coloring book, plus Gwendolyn Brooks' *Aloneness* (1971) helped to supply materials to reach this segment of the market. Two significant reference books helped to increase the amount of black biographical data available for students who wished to become black poets. Leaonead Pack Bailey edited the eminent *Broadside Authors and Artists, an Illustrated Biographical Directory* in 1974; and Gwendolyn Brooks, Keorapetse Kgositsile, Haki R. Madhubuti, and Dudley Randall wrote *A Capsule Course in Black Poetry Writing* in 1975. Broadside also published three collections of essays at the beginning of the decade. In 1971 and 1972, Gwendolyn Brooks edited *The Black Position*, a collection of essays on contemporary issues; and Don L. Lee's first book of essays, *From Plan to Planet, Life Studies: The Need for Afrikan Minds and Institutions*, appeared in 1973. The social backgrounds of the above authors are listed in Table 3.3.

Randall's interest in recording on tape the voices of Broadside poets reading from their books, continued in the seventies. (See Table 3.4.) Between 1968 and 1975, twenty-five Broadside books were recorded on tape. Dudley explained the history behind the tapes to Frenchy Hodges:

> I thought it would be very good if you could hear the voice of the living poet reading his tape. I got the idea from the Black Sparrow Press of John Martin in Los Angeles, who has a series of tapes. I wrote to him about it. He sent me a couple of his tapes and he advised me to sell them for $10.00 a piece. However, I put my price at $5.00 a piece, because our audience does not have as much money as the Black Sparrow audience has. We do not publish many of these because we haven't found a large audience of people that have tape recorders and buy tapes. Our original plan was to publish fifty tapes which would be autographed, and that would be that. But some of the tapes ran over fifty in sales and since we had orders, we continued to make the tapes. Usually, we make the tapes in small amounts — ten at a time. That's the way we did it, at first, until we'd used up the original fifty. Then it was necessary to go over the fifty. Now, because of changes in ownership in the tape company that we used, we have to use a company where we make a minimum of 100 tapes. One hundred tapes is plenty for the demand we get for tapes. We are now dividing these between tapes and cassettes. I think cassettes will be more the medium of the future because they're easier to use. You don't have to go through that trouble of unwinding the tape and trying to thread the tape, which is very hard for me. And then, the cassette-reorders are much smaller and much more handy to carry around than are reel-to-reel reorders.[61]

The twenty-five tapes of Broadside voices represented a good sample of the company's older and younger poetic talents; with recordings made by ten men and ten women poets. Frenchy Hodges observes that the tapes were

> informally recorded at Mr. Randall's home, when possible, or when visiting the city where a poet may be located. Many times, if this procedure is impossible to follow, the poet is instructed to make the recording and send it to Mr. Randall for further processing.[62]

The first tape in the series was made by James A. Emanuel of his book, *The Tree House and Other Poems* (1968). Two of the most popular tapes in the series were "Don L. Lee Reads *Don't Cry, Scream!*" and "Don L. Lee Reads *We Walk the Way of the New World.*"[63] *(cont. on page 104)*

Table 3.3

Social Backgrounds of Single Authors at Broadside Press, 1970–1975

Name	Place of Birth	Date of Birth	Education	Occupation(s)	Residence in the 1970s	Status as a Writer
Male Poets						
Ahmed Alhamisi	Savannah, GA	Feb. 18, 1940–	B.S., M.S.	Writer, teacher, artist, editor	Detroit, MI	Established
Alvin Aubert	Luchter, LA	March 12, 1930–	B.A., M.A., Ph.D. studies	Writer, teacher, editor	Fredonia, NY	Established
Houston Baker, Jr.	Louisville, KY	March 22, 1943–	B.A., M.A., Ph.D.	Writer, teacher, editor	Charlottesville, VA	Established
George Barlow	Berkeley, CA	Jan. 23, 1948–	B.A., M.F.A.	Writer, teacher	Oakland, CA	Established
Bernard W. Bell	Washington, DC	Feb. 7, 1936–	B.A., M.A., Ph.D.	Writer, teacher	Amherst, MA	Established
Henry Blakely	Chicago, IL	1916–1997	Public schools	Worker, writer	Chicago, IL	New
Arthur Boze	Washington, DC	July 23, 1945–	B.A.	Writer, social worker	Los Angeles, CA	New
Sterling A. Brown	Washington, DC	May 1, 1901–89	B.A., M.A.	Writer, teacher	Washington, DC	Major
C. E. Cannon	Durham, NC	Oct. 28, 1946–	B.A.	Writer, automotive worker	Chattanooga, TN	New
C. Gene Drafts	Boston, MA	Sept. 27, 1946–	B.A.	Writer	Mattapan, MA	New
Jon Eckels	Indianapolis, IN	1940s–	B.A., M.A., Ph.D.	Writer, teacher	Palo Alto, CA	Established
James A. Emanuel	Alliance, NE	June 14, 1921–	B.A., M.A., Ph.D.	Writer, teacher, editor	White Plains, NY	Major

Name	Place of Birth	Date of Birth	Education	Occupation(s)	Residence in the 1970s	Status as a Writer
Jose-Angel Figueroa	Mayaguaz, PR	Nov. 28, 1946–	B.S., M.A.	Writer, teacher	Bronx, NY	Established
Addison Gayle, Jr.	Newport News, VA	June 2, 1932–91	B.A., M.A.	Writer, teacher	New York City, NY	Major
Nicholas Guillen	Camaguey, Cuba	July 10, 1902– July 16, 1989	B.A.	Writer, editor, journalist	Havana, Cuba	Major
Everett Hoagland	Philadelphia, PA	Dec. 18, 1942–	B.A., M.A.	Writer, teacher	Pomona, CA	New
Lance Jeffers	Fremont, NE	Nov. 28, 1919–85	B.A., M.A.	Writer, teacher	Bowie, MD	Major
Keorapetse Kgositsile	Johannesburg, South Africa	Sept. 19, 1938–	B.A., M.A.	Writer, teacher	Chicago, IL	Major
Etheridge Knight	Corinth, MS	April 19, 1931–91	Public schools; B.A.	Writer, teacher	Indianapolis, IN	Major
Don L. Lee	Little Rock, AR	Feb. 23, 1942–	B.A., M.F.A.	Writer, teacher, publisher, editor	Chicago, IL	Major
Doughtry Long	Atlanta, GA	March 14, 1942–	B.S., M.A.	Writer, teacher	New York City, NY	Established
Clarence Major	Atlanta, GA	Dec. 31, 1936–	B.A., hon. doctorate	Writer, teacher, editor	New York City, NY	Major
Bill Odarty	Ghana, West Africa	1938–	B.A., M.A.	Writer, business	New York City, NY	New
Arthur Pfister	New Orleans, LA	Sept. 20, 1949–	B.A., M.A.	Writer, teacher	Houston, TX	Established
Don C. Randall	Detroit, MI	March 26, 1942–	B.S.	Writer, business	Evansville, IN	New
Dudley Randall	Washington, DC	Jan 14, 1914–	B.A., M.A.L.S.	Writer, teacher, editor, publisher, librarian	Detroit, MI	Major

Social Backgrounds of Single Authors at Broadside Press, 1970–1975 (continued)

Name	Place of Birth	Date of Birth	Education	Occupation(s)	Residence in the 1970s	Status as a Writer
James Randall, Jr.	Detroit, MI	Dec. 3, 1938–	B.A.	Writer, journalist, photographer	Brooklyn, NY	New
John Raven	Washington, DC	June 22, 1936–		Writer, computer operator	Bronx, NY	New
William H. Robinson	Newport, RI	Oct. 29, 1922–	B.A., M.A., Ph.D.	Writer, teacher	Providence, RI	Established
Chauncer E. Spencer	Lynchburg, VA	N/A	B.A.	Freelance artist	Detroit, MI	New
William A. Thigpen, Jr.	Detroit, MI	July 25, 1948–April 13, 1971	Wayne State Univ.	Writer, student	Detroit, MI	New
Habte Wolde	Patterson, NJ	May 29, 1944–	B.A., M.A.	Writer, museum director, teacher	Princeton, NJ & Addis Ababa, Ethiopia	New
Female Poets						
Leaonead Pack Bailey	Hinton, WV	Jan. 28, 1906–	B.A., B.S.L.S.	Librarian, writer	Detroit, MI	New
Linda Bragg	Akron, OH	March 14, 1939–	B.A., M.A.	Writer, teacher	Greensboro, NC	New
Gwendolyn Brooks	Topeka, KS	June 7, 1917–	A.A., hon. doctorate	Writer, teacher, editor	Chicago, IL	Major
Nikki Giovanni	Knoxville, TN	June 7, 1943–	B.A., M.A., hon. doctorate	Writer, teacher, journalist, editor	New York City, NY	Major
Frenchy Hodges	Dublin, GA	Oct. 18, 1940–	B.S., M.A.	Writer, teacher	Detroit, MI	Established
Lyn Levy	Boston, MA	July 8, 1946–	B.A.	Writer, social worker	Dorchester, MA	New
Audre Lorde	New York, NY	Feb. 18, 1934–92	B.A., M.A.	Writer, librarian, teacher	New York City, NY	Major

Name	Place of Birth	Date of Birth	Education	Occupation(s)	Residence in the 1970s	Status as a Writer
Marion Alexander Nicholes	New York, NY	July 19, 1944–	B.A.	Writer, social worker	Chicago, IL	New
Regina O'Neal	Detroit, MI	N/A	B.A., M.A.	Writer, journalist, teacher, director, broadcasting	Detroit, MI	New
Sonia Sanchez	Birmingham, AL	Sept. 9, 1934–	B.A., M.A., hon. doctorate	Writer, teacher, editor	Pittsburgh, PA	Major
Judy Simmons	Westerly, RI	Aug. 29, 1944–	B.A.	Writer, business, teacher	New York City, NY	Established
Carolyn Thompson	Detroit, MI	N/A	B.A.	Freelance artist	Detroit, MI	New
Margaret Walker	Birmingham, AL	July 7, 1915–	B.A., MA., Ph.D.	Writer, teacher	Jackson, MS	Major

Broadside also produced two additional recorded products during this period. First, Don L. Lee produced the company's only album of recorded poetry, "Rappin' and Readin'." In an interview, Randall recalled:

> That was recorded live at Wayne State University during a reading by Don [L.] Lee. I don't know exactly how the idea came. Lee is a very popular poet, so I thought that it would be a good idea to try another medium, a record. I'd had no experience with records and didn't know how they would sell. But so far, we have a first pressing of 500 and we're now in the second pressing of 500.... We may make other albums, too, since I think phonograph records are more popular with the public than cassettes or reel recorders.... That's the only album so far. It was experimental; I recorded it to see how it would sell. It entailed a whole new method of shipping. We had to get special containers for it.[64]

Second, in 1970, a cassette was made of seven Broadside poets (Dudley Randall, Jerry Whittington, Frenchy Hodges, Sonia Sanchez, Gwendolyn Brooks, Don L. Lee, and Margaret Walker) reading their poetry together at the Arts Extended Gallery in Detroit.[65] It was titled "Broadside on Broadway: Seven Poets Read." This tape became the only recording made by Broadside in which a group of poets read their poetry.[66] All Broadside tapes, albums, and cassettes were priced at $5.00.

Broadside also continued its sixties policy of serving as a United States distributor for selected poetry book titles from other publishers. (Table 3.5 gives a detailed description of authors and their backgrounds.[67]) Between 1968 and 1975, forty-three books were distributed by the company, including titles published by Paul Breman, Ltd., London, England; Third World Press, Chicago; Black Arts Publications, Detroit; and privately printed volumes by Nikki Giovanni, Barbara Mahone, Sonia Sanchez, McLane Birch, and Mae Jackson. Such efforts by Randall helped to promote the movement to publish black poetry, while increasing public awareness of new and older black poets from throughout the world, but especially those from the United States and the West Indies.

Out of the thirty-five authors of Broadside-distributed books, all of the poets worked in large cities, either in the United States, Europe, or Africa. Blacks born in the South migrated to northern cities; blacks from the West Indies and Africa migrated to Europe, especially to London and Paris, or to study and work in the United States (especially in New York and Chicago) during this period. In 1970, twenty-three poets (or 60 percent) were under the age of forty-one, thus, indicating that this group of poets, overall was a young one. Also, the continuing significance of the Great Migration can be observed in these poets in the fact that a large number were born in the North, and that a major portion of others born in the South during the thirties and forties, migrated from that region to such states as Illinois and New York. This was a highly educated group of writers—another theme which connects them to other groups of Broadside poets. Most earned their B.A.'s and master's degrees, and some achieved Ph.D.'s and honorary doctorates.[68]

Due to the tremendous problems which black writers, and especially poets, faced in finding publishers for their books, Broadside Press was inundated with manuscripts. However, Randall could only publish so many, in spite of the quality of materials which were submitted across the years. Among the several key aspects of this issue facing black publishers, according to Randall, was the fact that:

Table 3.4

Broadside Voices: Recorded Poetry 1968–1975

Men with Tapes	Women with Tapes
Gene Drafts	Nancy L. Arnex (with Beatrice Murphy)
John Eckels (2 tapes)	Gwendolyn Brooks (2 tapes)
James A. Emanuel (2 tapes)	Margaret Danner
Lance Jeffers	Nikki Giovanni
Keorapetse Kgositsile	Frenchy Jolene Hodges
Etheridge Knight	Sonia Sanchez (2 tapes)
Don L. Lee (2 tapes)	Judy Simmons
Clarence Major	Stephany (Jean Dawson-Fuller)
Marvin X	Margaret Walker
Dudley Randall	

> There have to be limits measured by literary quality, the publishers' interests, and their financial and editorial capabilities. I have set a limit of four books a year, in order to give satisfactory editorial attention and promotion. But last year [1974] I published 12.[69]

Thus, Randall was limited by such restrictions, but committed to advancing as many projects as he could handle at Broadside. In practical terms it came down to making a decision on a poetry manuscript because "…you can tell what is good to you by the gut feeling of enjoyment and discovery you get from reading it."[70] The publisher also recommended to poets that on the average they should submit about "16 pages of poetry because of his main interest in poetry, published in small booklets."[71] The publisher was also known for his advice that authors should seek "precision and accuracy" in preparing their manuscripts for publication.[72]

Furthermore, since Broadside Press could only publish a small number of black authors, Randall was appreciative of

> every good book the other [black] publishers
> put out. Every publishing company has its own
> personality, and attracts writers congenial
> to it. Drum and Spear favors children's books,
> Jihad is concerned with nation-building. Third
> World is interested in education, Broadside
> specializes in poetry…. We're the most literary
> of the publishers, and writers interested in
> creating good literature will gravitate to us.
> But I feel there's room for us all. After all,
> I receive at least 200 manuscripts a year, and
> can publish only ten or twenty. That leaves
> 180 or 190 for the other publishers.[73]

Nonetheless, Randall, like all black publishers, was faced with the everyday tasks of actually operating a publishing company in the most advanced capitalistic system on Earth! Meanwhile, he also held another job as a reference librarian and poet-in-residence at the University of Detroit. He was, indeed, a busy man. In order to effectively operate Broadside Press as a business, he needed funds to pay for both rental space and the daily expenses of running an office.[74] Such matters really demanded the services of a full-time publisher and editor, with a strong support staff to keep the company afloat. (cont. on page 110)

Table 3.5
Books Distributed by Broadside Press, 1965–1975

Author & Gender	Title of Book	Year	Publisher	Price	Pages	Birth Place of Author	Date of Birth	Education
Lloyd Addison (M)	*The Aura and the Umbra*	1970	Paul Breman	$2.50	25	Boston, MA	March 10, 1931–	B.A. studies
Ahmed Alhamisi	*Black Spiritual Gods*	1968	Black Arts	$1.00	N/A	Savannah, GA	Feb. 18, 1940–	B.S., M.A., Ph.D. studies
———	*Guerrilla Warfare*	1970	Black Arts	$1.00	N/A			
———	*Zizwe: A Little African Boy Born in a Foreign Land*	1974	Detroit: Wakweli Publications	$1.50	N/A			
———, with Kofi Wangara (M) eds.	*Black Arts: An Anthology of Black Creations*	1969	Black Arts	$3.50	160	Wangara: Detroit, MI	Dec. 14, 1928–	B.A., M.ed., Ph.D. studies
Samuel Allen (M)	*Paul Vesey's Ledger*	1975	Paul Breman	$2.50	24	Columbus, OH	1917–	B.A., LL.B.
Sonebeyatta Amungo (Robert Hagan) (M)	*Youth Makes the Revolution*	1971	Black Arts	$1.00	N/A	Detroit, MI	Sept. 30, 1956–	Detroit public schools
Russell Atkins (M)	*Heretofore*	1968	Paul Breman	$2.50	34	Cleveland, OH	Feb. 25, 1927–	B.A. studies
McLane Birch, III (M)	*The Kandi Man*	1970	Detroit: Black Star Printing	$1.00	30	Little Rock, AR	Jan. 31, 1942–	B.A., M.A., Ph.D.
Arna Bontemps (M)	*Personals*	1963	Paul Breman	$2.50	44	Alexandria, LA	Oct. 13, 1902–73	B.A., M.A.

Author & Gender	Title of Book	Year	Publisher	Price	Pages	Birth Place of Author	Date of Birth	Education
Paul Breman, ed. (M)	Sixes and Sevens: An Anthology of New Poetry	1962	Paul Breman, Ltd. (London)	$2.50	96	Bussum, Holland	July 19, 1931–	B.A. studies
Harold Carrington (M)	Drive Suite	1970	Paul Breman	$2.50	N/A	Atlantic City, NJ	1938–July 30, 1964	Reform schools/prison
Sebastian Clark (M)	Sun Song	1973	Paul Breman	$2.50	26	Trinidad	Dec. 1948–	
William Waring Cuney (M)	Storefront Church	1973	Paul Breman	$2.50	24	Washington, DC	May 6, 1906–76	B.A., grad. studies
Owen Dodson (M)	The Confession Stone: Song Cyles	1971	Paul Breman	$2.50	30	Brooklyn, NY	Nov. 28, 1914–	B.A., M.F.A., hon. doct.
Ray Durem (M)	Take No Prisoners	1971	Paul Breman	$2.50	21	Seattle, WA	Jan. 30, 1915–	B.A. studies
Eseoghene (C. Lindsay Barrett) (M)	The Conflicting Eye	1973	Paul Breman	$2.50	N/A	Lucea, Jamaica	Aug. 15, 1941–	Local schools
Marie Evans (F)	Where Is All the Music?	1968	Paul Breman	$2.50	24	Toledo, OH	1923–	B.A. studies
Ronald Fair (M)	Excerpts	1975	Paul Breman	$2.50	24	Chicago, IL	Oct. 27, 1937–	Public schools
Nikki Giovanni (F)	Black Feeling, Black Talk	1967	Privately printed	$1.00	40	Knoxville, TN	July 6, 1943–	B.A., M.A. studies, hon. doct.
————	Black Judgement	1968	Privately printed	$1.00	40			

Books Distributed by Broadside Press, 1965–1975 (continued)

Author & Gender	Title of Book	Year	Publisher	Price	Pages	Birth Place of Author	Date of Birth	Education
Robert Hayden (M)	A Ballad of Remembrance	1962	Paul Breman, Ltd. (London)	$2.50	72	Detroit, MI	Aug. 4, 1913–80	B.A., M.A., hon. doct.
———	The Night-blooming Cereus	1972	Paul Breman	$2.50	18			
Frank Horne (M)	Haverstraw	1963	Paul Breman	$2.50	40	New York City, NY	1899–	B.A.
Femi Funmi Ifetayo (Regina Micou) (F)	We the Black Woman	1970	Black Arts	$1.00	N/A	Detroit, MI	May 21, 1954–	Detroit public schools
Mae Jackson (F)	Can I Poet with You	1969	New York: Black Dialogue Press	$1.00	22	Earl, AR	Jan. 3, 1946–	Public schools
Frank John (M)	Light a Fire	1973	Paul Breman	$2.50	N/A	Trinidad	Nov. 14, 1941–	Local schools
Dolores Kendrick (F)	Through the Ceiling	1975	Paul Breman	$2.50	24	Washington, DC	Sept. 7, 1927–	B.S., M.A.T.
Le Graham (Ahmed Alhamisi) (M)	The Black Narrator	1966	Black Arts Publications (Detroit)	$1.00	N/A	Savannah, GA	Feb. 18, 1940–	B.S., M.A., Ph.D. studies
Audre Lorde (F)	Cables to Rage	1970	Paul Breman	$2.50	30	New York City, NY	Feb. 18, 1934–92	B.A., M.A., hon. doct.
Barbara Mahone (Barbara Diane [Mahone] McBain) (F)	Sugarfields	1970	Privately printed	$1.25	34	Chicago, IL	Feb. 27, 1944–	B.A., grad. studies
Clarence Major (M)	Private Line	1971	Paul Breman	$2.50	18	Atlanta, GA	Dec. 31, 1936–	B.A., hon. doct.
Mukhtarr Mustapha (M)	Thorns and Thistles	1972	Paul Breman	$2.50	18	Freetown, Sierra Leone, West Africa	Dec. 25, 1943–	Local schools

Author & Gender	Title of Book	Year	Publisher	Price	Pages	Birth Place of Author	Date of Birth	Education
Sterling D. Plumpp (M)	Black Rituals	1972	Chicago: Third World Press	$1.95	108	Clinton, MS	Jan. 30, 1940–	B.A., M.A.
Dudley Randall (M)	After the Killing	1973	Chicago: Third World Press	$1.25	18	Washington, DC	Jan. 14, 1914–	B.A., M.A.L.S., hon. doct.
_____	Love You	1970	Paul Breman	$2.50	18			
_____	More to Remember: Poems of Four Decades	1971	Chicago: Third World Press	$1.95	77			
Ishmael Reed (M)	Catechism of d Neoamerican Hoodoo Church	1970	Paul Breman	$2.50	30	Chattanooga, TN	Feb. 22, 1938–	B.A. studies, hon. doct.
Conrad Kent Rivers (M)	The Still Voice of Harlem	1968	Paul Breman	$2.50	25	Atlantic City, NJ	Oct. 15, 1933–67	B.A., M.A. studies
_____	The Wright Poems	1972	Paul Breman	$2.50	22	Atlantic City, NJ		
Sonia Sanchez, ed. (F)	Three Hundred and Sixty Degrees of Blackness Coming at You	1971	New York: 5X Publishing Co.	$3.60	92	Birmingham, AL	Sept. 9, 1934–	B.A., M.A., hon. doct.
Ellease Southerland (F)	The Magic Sun Spins	1975	Paul Breman	$2.50	24	Brooklyn, NY	June 18, 1943–	B.A., M.A.
James W. Thompson (M)	First Fire: Poems, 1957–1960	1970	Paul Breman	$2.50	21	Detroit, MI	Dec. 21, 1935–	B.A. studies

Randall also needed to be able to more effectively reach the book market potential of the 24 million African-Americans in the United States during the seventies. For indeed, although many members of this group faced economic hardships, they still contributed $30 billion to the U.S. economy in 1968, and $70 billion by 1978. Yet, as one student of the black economy points out, "the total income of black Americans [in the late 1970s was] 7.1 percent of total U.S. income, although blacks account[ed] for 12 percent of the total population."[75]

What Randall and other black businesses were up against was a harsh economic system which had historically excluded many blacks from positively gaining their share of the economic rewards of the system. In fact, prior to the successes of the Civil Rights Movement of the fifties through seventies:

> Racism in the United States had rendered Blacks nearly invisible to consumer econo-
> mists, to market research analysts, and to others concerned with consumer behavior.
> Blacks lacked access to and control of capital; job training and meaningful employment
> opportunities were denied them. The result was, for most Blacks, a level of income inad-
> equate for the purchase of even the bare necessities of life. Even Blacks with adequate
> incomes were not always welcomed by businesses as customers. Department stores in
> many cities prohibited the trying on of dresses and hats by black customers; hotels,
> restaurants, public and private social and recreational facilities refused to accept Blacks
> as patrons. Housing discrimination was universal, effectively limiting the black con-
> sumer's access to quality housing at reasonable prices.[76]

Such economic burdens, of course, did not end overnight. Frenchy Hodges describes the immediate problem facing Broadside Press in the early seventies as one of office space.

> Broadside Press was housed in an upper-floor room of Dudley Randall's home at 12651
> Old Mill Place from its beginning in 1965 to January, 1970 when it moved to the smaller
> quarters of an exterminating business owned by Ole Oja, located at 12652 Livernois. It
> soon outgrew the smaller quarters there, and in January, 1971 it moved to 15205 Liver-
> nois which offered slightly more floor space, fifty feet by twenty feet. By January 1973,
> Mr. Ole Ova had retired, closing his business; Broadside Press had again outgrown its
> housing. It then returned to 12652 Livernois, taking occupancy in the vacated and larger
> quarters, which are conveniently located just behind the Randall home. Still, every inch
> of usable space is quickly filling, which presupposes the need of additional space within
> the next two years. The floor space of the present location is sixty feet by thirty feet.[77]

Thus, the company had grown larger across the late sixties in spite of its lack of capital and personnel.[78] An improvement in its daily operations between 1970 and 1973 increased the company's effectiveness in meeting its business goals of producing excellent black poetry publications at an affordable price. However, financial matters were always a prime concern at Broadside. In 1970, Broadside received one of its largest development grants, when the Coordinating Council of Literary Magazines awarded the company $2,500 to aid its publication work.[79] Randall also submitted a proposal in 1970 to the New Detroit, Incorporated agency for a $9,000 grant "to enable Broadside Press to pay the salary of one full-time employee." However, Broadside only received $1,000 from New Detroit.[80] Such economic restrictions meant that Dudley Randall often did

> all the work, from sweeping floors, washing windows, licking stamps and envelopes, and
> packing books, to reading manuscripts, writing ads, and planning and designing books....[81]

However, in the early seventies, Randall was able to mobilize an excellent staff at Broadside, and to create two administrative units, or departments at the company: managerial and editorial. Obviously, Randall's outstanding contributions with Broadside Press during the sixties attracted a number of young and talented black Detroiters. In William T. Whitsitt, a local worker, he found a competent office manager to handle the managerial affairs of the office.[82] Whitsitt's service allowed Dudley to concentrate his time on editorial matters. On the advice of a representative of the Service Corps of Retired Employers, Randall hired Malaika Wangara as a full-time employee in charge of the daily clerical and office work at Broadside.[83] A number of other individuals aided the work of the company during its first ten years of operations. Hodges notes that Randall

Frenchy Jolene Hodges (here shown ca. 1971) was born on October 18, 1940, in Dublin, Georgia. She is a teacher as well as a poet. Scholars and students of African-American literature owe a special debut of gratitude to Hodges for her 1974 M.A. thesis on Broadside Press, written while at Atlanta University, which contains many important Broadside documents that are not available for study elsewhere. She currently teaches at the George Washington Carver High School in Atlanta, Georgia (courtesy Broadside Press).

had experienced the need for additional help long before the first move and had been using part-time personnel: Janice Robertson, a high school student; Ayuma McClure, a former creative writing student of Mr. Randall's; Ayuma's sister, Cynthia; a young neighbor, Mrs. Vernita Norris; and an older woman on pension, Mrs. Lottie Butler. Broadside Press has survived and has grown to its present expansion proportions [in 1973] with five full-time employees and three part-time employees: the publisher and editor, Mr. Randall, his full-time assistants Melba Boyd and Deidre Honore, the full-time general office manager, William T. Whitsitt, the full-time company secretary, Deborah McAfee, the part-time secretary, a high school work-study student, Janice Kayle, a part-time packer, John Clure, and part-time packer and general office-boy, James "Ricky" Robertson. The official office hours are from 9:00 A.M. to 5:00 P.M. However, in keeping with the lifestyle of which it is a part, the office has been observed to open earlier or later, more often later. Of course, it closes later many times, too.[84]

The editorial department at Broadside received hundreds of manuscripts between 1970 and 1975. A few were accepted for the book list, selected poems became part of the Broadside Series, and still other poems, especially by younger writers, were published in the *Broadside Annual* series, a yearly anthology edited by poet Jill Witherspoon Boyer in

```
                         BROADSIDE PRESS
            12651 Old Mill Place, Detroit, Michigan 48238


            Dear

            Thank you for letting us see your work.  We
            regret that we cannot use it.  This does not
            imply any lack of merit in your work, as
            there may be other reasons to prevent its use.


                                            Sincerely,


                                            The Editors
```

Figure 3.1. Form Letter of the Rejection Notice

1972 and 1973. Most manuscripts were not accepted for publication, and the author received a form letter, with regrets from the company. (See Figure 3.1.[85]) Broadside also produced a letter of response for writers inquires about the work of the company (See Figure 3.2.[86])

Once a book won approval for publication at Broadside, Randall worked to see that:

> The book is listed in bibliographical publications like *Books in Print*, for instance. That's one of the reasons why we have to plan so far in advance, because to get in *Books in Print* for 1974...we have to have our books listed, we have to send in the list, in May 1973, so that means that we have to know in advance up to November 1974 what our books are going to be. But then, since the next *Books in Print* will not be out until November 1975, we also try to plan what books will be out between November 1974 and November 1975.[87]

After further discussions with an author and suggested editorial work (by the staff, or the author), Randall generally wrote to offer a contract to a writer. (See Figure 3.3.[88]) Hodges delineates the next stages in a Broadside book's production:

> The book is immediately begun and is placed on the bulletin board under the proper year that it is to be published [see Fig. 3.4]. As each preliminary step is completed, the proper information is recorded on the posted form. By the time it goes to the printer, the book will have been assigned a Library of Congress Number (LCN), an International Standard Book Number (ISBN), the final title, a table of contents, and a selling price which will appear on the cover of the book, if it's a paperback.[89]

Randall's printer in Detroit was the Harlo Printing Company, affiliated with Harlo Press. This company was created in 1946, and specializes in printing poetry, prose, and how-to books.[90] Most Broadside books were priced after the company received Harlo's estimate of the printing costs. Randall notes that he

> started out pricing books at $1.00. Then I found out that the cost of the book should be at least one-fourth, ideally it should be one-fifth, of the selling price, in order for you to get your money back to make any kind of profit on the book. In addition to that, prices have gone up, printing prices. A quotation on a certain number of books in 1967 would be much less than a quotation on the same number of books in 1972. So,

BROADSIDE PRESS
12651 Old Mill Place, Detroit, Michigan 48238

Dear

In answer to your letter inquiring about the publication of your material by Broadside Press, I am sending you
the following information:

Broadside Press publishes broadsides of single poems;
posters; and books which can best be described as small
pamphlets. A typical Broadside Press book by a beginning
poet would consist of sixteen pages. Selections would be
made from a manuscript of about twenty of your best poems
submitted to us for consideration.

We are not printers and we are not a vanity press, so
the poet pays nothing. Royalties are ten percent of the
list price of books sold. We publish poetry by Black people
which is of the highest literary merit. Reading our publications (catalog and newsletter are enclosed) will give you a
better idea of the type and quality of work that we are
seeking.

May I further suggest, that as a beginning writer, you
attempt to have single poems published in sources at hand,
e.g., local newspapers and periodicals. Publication of
single poems in various sources enhances the possibilities
of publishing a complete book. Periodicals which offer
good possibilities of publication for beginning Black poets
are: Tan, Black Dialogues, Crisis, Freedomways, Journal of
Black Poetry, Liberator, Negro Digest, Negro History Bulletin,
Phylon, Soulbook, and any others which you may know of.

I hope that this will be of some help in enabling you
to make a decision about publishing with us, and, further,
that we can be of help to each other.

Thank you for considering us and power to you in the
future.

Cordially yours,

Dudley Randall, Editor

DR:cm
Enclosure

Figure 3.2. Broadside Press Inquiry Letter

therefore, you figure your unit cost of the book, and then your retail cost should be five
times that, and it'll come out to, according to the number you want printed, it'll come
out to $1.50 or $1.25.[91]

Finally, according to Hodges, a Broadside "manuscript then makes its first trip to the
printer."[92] Randall observes that the editorial department's role then becomes one of preparing the volume for Harlo:

That means, that besides the poems themselves we put in the preliminary matter.... And,
the poems, together with all the preliminary matter, the cover, the back cover, the poems

BROADSIDE PRESS
12651 OLD MILL PLACE
DETROIT, MICHIGAN   48238
(313) 431-0606

      Agreement between Broadside Press, hereafter known as
"the Publisher" and _____, hereafter
known as "the Author" for the publication of _____
_____ hereafter known as the book.

      The conditions of the agreement are as follows:

      1. The Author shall deliver the Book to the Publisher
before, or no later than _____.

      2. The Publisher shall cause to be printed and shall
publish _____ copies of the book within twelve (12) months
from the date in paragraph 1. The Publisher shall issue
additional printings of the book if sales so warrant.

      3. The Author shall receive in royalties from the
Publisher ten percent (10%) of the list price of all books
sold. These royalties shall be computed in January and July,
and statements sent and paid in April and October.

      4. Fees received for reprints and other copy rights
shall be divided equally between Publisher and Author (50% to
each). The Author shall refer to the Publisher all requests
for permission to reprint or to use any part of the book.
The Publisher shall act as the agent of the Author.

      5. The Author shall receive ten (10) free copies of
the book from the publisher.

      6. The Author shall have the right to purchase the
book from the Publisher at a forty percent (40%) discount
rate.

      7. The Publisher shall copyright the book in the
name of the Author and has the right to renew the copyright
in the Author's name before the expiration of the copyright.

      8. If the Publisher has not renewed the copyright
30 days before its expiration date, the Author may notify
the Publisher in writing and renew the copyright himself.

      9. The Publisher shall have sole control of the
physical format (cover design, illustration, layout, etc.)
of the book.

      10. The Publisher shall receive five (5) free
copies of the book.

      11. The Publisher may distribute or use free copies
of the book for review and publicity purposes.

Publisher's signature_____

                    Date_____

Author's signature _____

                    Date_____

Figure 3.3. The Broadside Publisher-Author Contract

BOOK RECORD FORM

AUTHOR:

TITLE:

MS Received_____Accepted_____

Contract sent_____Received_____

SBN_____LCN sent_____Received_____

PRINTERS ESTIMATE: Date_____

Copies_____Price_____Unit Cost_____Retail_____

MS to Printer: First Printing_____

Galley proofs received_____Returned_____

Page proofs received_____Returned_____

Copies_____Price_____Unit cost_____Retail_____

Reels: copies_____Price_____Unit cost_____

Cassettes: copies_____Price_____Unit cost_____

Flyers: copies_____Price_____

Advance Publicity: Publisher's Weekly
                    Wilson
                    Broadside News
                    Black World
                    Other

                    _____
                    _____
                    _____

Copyright: Applied_____Received_____

Ads: Bookstore Readings
                    Radio
                    Television
                    Book Review. PW____CBI____WLB____LJ____
                                  BIP____other:_____

Figure 3.4. Broadside Press Book Record Form

are sent to the printer. Then we get galley sheets which are corrected and also sent to the poet for correction. We get a second set of galley sheets which are cut up into pages and we paste them in the book, according to the number of pages, 16, 24, 32 pages. Then we get the page proofs from the printer in the form of separate pages. We revise these and send them to the poet for correction. Then, those are sent back to the printer and we wait for the finished book to come.[93]

The financing of new Broadside books and other materials came from the profits, made on previous sales of books, broadsides, posters and tapes at the company; plus royalties paid to reprint Broadside publications in other mediums. Generally, a first edition (printing) of a book at Broadside consisted of 2,000 printed copies, and totaled on the average between sixteen and twenty-four pages.[94] Most were paperbacks, however, beginning with Don L. Lee's *Don't Cry, Scream!* (1969), Broadside began a policy of also producing a cloth edition of its major books, to increase its sales with libraries and collectors of African-American literature. A majority of Broadside books sold for $1.00 to $1.50.[95] Such sums were in reality too small for the services and products which Broadside provided to the public. Yet, Broadside operated on the principle of the company as a labor of love for black literature and black people. Randall and his small staff, like most small black businesses, ran a race with the clock, to stay ahead of the mounting paper work and other countless chores, which occupied so much of their working time at Broadside.

Once a Broadside book was received from the printer, the staff now had to meet a new challenge of promoting the new work, by securing favorable book reviews and hopefully community support, often by word of mouth. The staff was thus responsible for selling the book. In the world of black book publishing nothing could be taken for granted, and this meant more work for Broadside's employees, and just about everything at the company was done by hand. Fifty review books were usually mailed by Broadside to various media outlets in the United States.[96] However, Broadside, like most black publishing companies, continued to experience a great difficulty in securing book review notices in most of the historically white-controlled media in the United States.[97] The end result, according to political scientist Marcus D. Pohlmann, was that whites enjoyed a "white press monopolization" in this country.[98] As in the sixties, Broadside depended greatly on "the Big Nine" (*Black World, Journal of Black Poetry, Liberator, The Black Panther, Muhammad Speaks, Freedomways, Black Creations*, the *Black Scholar*, and *Ebony*) among black-owned media, for book reviews and notices of publication. Randall could also depend on some coverage of Broadside in black newspapers, such as the *Detroit News, Michigan Chronicle*, the *Chicago Defender*, the *Pittsburgh Courier*, and others, and from Black Studies journals and newsletters, as well as black student publications from the high school to the college levels. Liberal elements among the white underground and alternative media also covered activities at Broadside.[99]

Frenchy Hodges' observations on Broadside's promotional activities are highly informative:

> Press releases are sent out on the book. These are in the form of flyers and are mimeographed. These releases or flyers are sent to people who have asked for ads or notification of new publications. Another method of promotion is the publication of a newsletter in which all new books are announced. The book is also listed in bibliographical publications. Copies of the book are sent to *Publisher's Weekly* and are listed in its Weekly Record. This listing has proved to be the source of a reputable number of sales. Books are sent to *Cumulative Book Index*, as well as *Books in Print*. As the book is copyrighted after it has been published, copies of it are sent to the Library of Congress so catalog cards can be made for the book.
>
> The next level of treatment that the newly published book receives is the filling of standing orders to bookstores and individuals who have asked to have this service. These are the first sales that the book will have.
>
> The filling of consignment orders is of importance here because it demonstrates Mr. Randall's cultural appreciation of the small black business: We send books on consignment to all the Black bookstores, because we figure they would be interested in the books and a lot of them don't have the time to read the trade publications and to order

the new books. So we just take it upon ourselves to send the new books to them. They're on consignment so they either send us the money or they send the books back at the end of thirty days.

Before Mr. Randall adopted this method of voluntary consignment, he had tried to establish agreements with the Black bookstores, but received very few replies from them. It is evident here that Mr. Randall's main concern is that the bookstore[s] shall have the book when it is requested. This area is a major concern of Mr. Randall's and he has voiced his opinions concerning the black book markets both in his interviews as well as in his article on the Press:

> Black publishers should try to build a stable base in their own communities. It is the black bookstores which are most genuinely interested in their books. In my own home town, Detroit, neither of the large department stores (in a black neighborhood, incidentally), and almost none of the white bookstores stock Broadside books, but Vaughn's Book Store (black) carries all of them. There is an interdependence between black booksellers and black publishers. One Chicago bookseller, who had just opened a store, told me, "Only Broadside and Free Black Press would give me credit. The white companies wouldn't do it."[100]

Jill Witherspoon Boyer, seen in a photograph taken around 1975, served as editor of the *Broadside Annual* series. Boyer was born in Detroit, Michigan, on April 18, 1947. She has worked as a social worker in Michigan and California, and continues to maintain an interest in writing and the fine arts (courtesy Broadside Press).

A shortage of funds at Broadside also prevented Randall from adequately advertising in the media. Five advertisements for Broadside books were purchased in 1970–75 from the *Black Academy Review*, *Black Theatre*, the *Black Scholar*, *Black Books Bulletin*, and *Black Creation*; and two book notices were printed by the *Black Academy Review* and the *College Language Association Journal*. (See Table 3.6.[101]) Five Broadside women writers appeared in the advertisements and notices, including Gwendolyn Brooks, Nikki Giovanni, Audre Lorde, Sonia Sanchez, and Margaret Walker — for a grand total of sixteen notices. These writers were among the most popular with Broadside. However, among the women writers, Nikki Giovanni was the best book seller at Broadside. The books of twelve Broadside male authors were advertised by the company, or received a book notice by a black journal. Don L. Lee was the leading writer at Broadside Press in terms of sales (and with advertisements at fourteen entries). Yet, clearly, such figures as James Emanuel, Etheridge Knight, Dudley Randall, and Lance Jeffers, among others, were all major voices among

Table 3.6

Advertisements and Notices of Broadside Press
Publications in Black Periodicals, 1970–1975

Organ	*Location*	*Date of Issue*	*Broadside Work Advertised or Noted*
Black Academy Review	Buffalo, NY	Spring, 1970 V. I, no.1, p. 39	"Advertisement": Gwendolyn Brooks, *Riot*; Don L. Lee, *Don't Cry, Scream!*; Nikki Giovanni, *Black Judgement*; Dudley Randall, ed., *Black Poetry*; Sonia Sanchez, *Homecoming*.
		V. 1, no. 3, Fall 1970, p. 63	"Books Received": Nikki Giovanni, *Black Judgement*; Don L. Lee, *Don't Cry, Scream!*; Dudley Randall and Margaret Burroughs, eds., *For Malcolm X: Poems on the Life and the Death of Malcolm X.*
Black Theatre	New York City, NY	No. 5, 1971, p. 54	"Advertisement": Margaret Walker, *Prophets for a New Day*; Don L. Lee, *We Walk the Way of the New World*; Gwendolyn Brooks, *Riot*; Nikki Giovanni, *Re: Creation*; Sonia Sanchez, *We a BaddDDD People*; Everett Hoagland, *Black Magic*; Dudley Randall, ed., *Black Poetry*.
College Language Association Journal	Baltimore, MD	V. 14, no. 3, March 1971, p. 362	*Broadside Work Advertised or Noted* "Notice: Books from Broadside Press": Gwendolyn Brooks, *Family Pictures*; James Emanuel, *The Treehouse and Other Poems*, and *Panther Man*; Nikki Giovanni, *Re: Creation*; Everett Hoagland, *Black Velvet*; Lance Jeffers, *My Blackness Is the Beauty of This Land*; Don L. Lee, *Directionscore: Selected and New Poems*; Doughtry Long, *Black Love Black Hope*; John Raven, *Blues for Momma and Other Low Downs.*
The Black Scholar	Sausalito, CA	V. 3, no. 6, Feb. 1972, p. 9	"Advertisement": Gwendolyn Brooks, *Aloneness*; Etheridge Knight, *Poems from Prison*; Margaret Walker, *Prophets for a New Day*; Sonia Sanchez, *We a BaddDDD People*; Don L. Lee, *Don't Cry, Scream!*; Gwendolyn Brooks, ed., *A Broadside Treasury*; Sonia Sanchez, *It's a New Day*; Nikki Giovanni, *Re: Creation.*

Organ	Location	Date of Issue	Broadside Work Advertised or Noted
Black Books Bulletin	Chicago, IL	V. 1, no. 4, 1973, p. 41	"Advertisement": Seven books by Don L. Lee: *From Plan to Planet*; *Think Black!*; *Black Pride*; *Don't Cry, Scream!*; *We Walk the Way of the New World*; *Directionscore: Selected and New Poems*; *Dynamite Voices: Black Poets of the 1960s*; and one album, "Rappin' & Readin'."
Black Creation: A Review of Black Arts and Letters	New York City, NY	V. 6, 1974–75, p. 97	"Advertisement": Etheridge Knight, *Belly Song*; Celes Tisdale, ed., *Betcha Ain't: Poems from Attica*; C. Gene Drafts, *Bloodwhispers/Blacksongs*; Haki R. Madhubuti (Don L. Lee), *Book of Life*; Jose-Angel Figueroa, *East 110th Street*; Audre Lorde *From a Land Where Other People Live*; Don L. Lee, *From Plan to Planet*; George Barlow, *Gabriel*; Gwendolyn Brooks, *Report from Part One*.

African-American poets. They deserved, as did black women poets at the company, wider exposure in the print media, in order to increase both the public awareness of their work and book sales. However, Broadside did not have the cash-flow to promote their work, or that of younger poets with any degree of sustained activity, with an effective advertisement campaign. Nevertheless, the company tried to promote the work of its poets, as demonstrated above, but these efforts were too small to reach the diverse markets among African-American (or general American) readers. Thus, Broadside largely depended on the poets themselves to promote their books and broadsides, and on the ancient underground communication networks among black people, to spread the word about the assets which the company and its artists offered the black community and the world.[102]

Profits and losses were a major issue at Broadside Press during the sixties and seventies, but the company always managed to keep going. One central problem lay in the under capitalization of the company. When Broadside was established by Randall in 1965–66, the company fit the pattern of many small businesses in Detroit. In fact, a 1966 study of 4,100 black businesspersons in Detroit found that 41 percent of them had starting investments of under $2,000 for their businesses. Fourteen percent managed to save, or raise between $2,000 to $5,000; and only 7 percent had over $5,000 in capital.[103] Randall, of course, began Broadside with $12 out of his paycheck. Dudley also began the company during his middle years, at age fifty-one in 1965; and he had little business experience. (The average age of businesspersons in the Detroit study, on the establishment of their companies was forty-six years.)[104] Randall was thus older than the average new black businessowner in the city. Dudley's special strengths lay, however, in his superior education, excellent training as a librarian, ability to work well with writers and other artists, willingness to take risks, knowledge of black networking techniques, and his cosmopolitan outlook. Such factors as these, and a committed office staff, plus several best-selling authors, enabled Broadside Press to weather the financial storms of the period.

A second significant concern at Broadside was collecting debts owed to the company, especially by black bookstore owners.[105] William Whitsitt, who served as the general office manager at Broadside in the early seventies, helped to eliminate part of this problem by organizing a strong filing and billing system at the company.[106] However, unpaid bills and unreturned books remained a central problem at Broadside throughout the seventies. As a last measure, Broadside hired the firm Dunn and Bradstreet, a commercial collection agency, to recover some of its losses.[107]

An examination of Broadside's ten top and bottom selling books during 1972 is revealing. (See Table 3.7.[108]) Without the selling power of five major Broadside writers, Nikki Giovanni, Don L. Lee, Gwendolyn Brooks, Dudley Randall, and Sonia Sanchez, the company might not have survived as a strong black publisher beyond its first five to seven years in operation.

If the top ten best-sellers are measured per unit at their paperback rates (only four books had cloth editions, Lee's *Don't Cry, Scream!* and *We Walk the Way of the New World* [$4.50 each], Brook's *A Broadside Treasury* [$6.00], and Randall's *Black Poetry* [$4.00]) the grand total of sales is $38,311, compared to only $1,952.50 for the lowest ten sellers at Broadside for the year.[109] Such sales figures were too drastically low to foster the development of a strong and vibrant black publishing company at Detroit. Indeed, Randall's pricing system was just too low. Nikki Giovanni's paperback best-sellers sold for $1.50 each. Don L. Lee's poetry was the same price, and his *Dynamite Voices* sold for only $2.75. Gwendolyn Brooks' anthology, *A Broadside Treasury*, was priced somewhat better at $4.00 per copy (but this too was almost a give away for a book just under 200 pages). Her children's book, *Aloneness*, sold at $1.00 — a gift. Randall's anthology, *Black Poetry*, was actually priced at $.95. Sonia Sanchez's *We a BaddDDD People* sold for $1.50. Nine of the lowest selling books were priced at $1.00 each, and Raven's *Blues for Mamma*, sold for $1.50.[110] Among the lowest selling books at Broadside in 1972, volumes by Emanuel, *The Treehouse and Other Poems*; Randall, *Cities Burning*; Danner, *Impressions of African Art Forms*; and Kgositsile, *Spirits Unchained*, are artistically speaking, ranked by this author with the best books published in the company's history. Although their works are, of high poetic quality, the bottom selling authors, especially the four noted above, suffered the transitory nature of the marketplace, due to no fault of their own; and of the cash flow problems at Broadside, which prevented the publisher from adequately advertising and fully marketing their books in the American marketplace.

Broadside and its authors continued to be challenged during the seventies by the Black Arts Movement, and by the stimulation provided by the Black Studies Movement from 1969 into the new decade.[111] Black cultural affairs were a central concern in the lives of most Broadside authors, and manifested itself most vividly in the kinds of literary materials which were produced by the writers — in their everyday dress, speech, political outlook, social interests. Some changed their American names to African or more black oriented names. The name change aided some individuals in their personal struggles to meet a special need to redefine themselves, and to move from "a slave mentality" to a black or African free state of mind.[112] Many were influenced by the teachings of Elijah Muhammad and Malcolm X, the Nation of Islam (the Black Muslims), and the Organization of Afro-American Unity (OAAU); others by such charismatic personalities as Maulana Ron Karenga and his organization called US in California; LeRoi Jones (Amiri Baraka) and Spirit House of Newark, New Jersey; radical SNCC leaders, such as H. Rap Brown (Jamil Abdullah Al-Amin), and

Stokely Carmichael (Kwame Toure); and among others, the Black Panthers and its leaders, Huey Newton, Bobby Seale, and Eldridge Cleaver.[113]

The economic position of many black writers and artists was impacted in the seventies by the Black Studies Movement. Scholar Robert H. Brisbane notes that many

> Black Studies budgets often [ran] into thousands of dollars [and] patronage [positions were now available in the form of] directorships, and administrative and faculty appointments.[114]

Some Broadside authors won such appointments, and were able to secure employment, or lecture dates, and thus were able to survive financially while developing their writing careers. Others, of course, taught in the more traditional departments (i.e., English, History, and Philosophy), and some served as poets-in-residence on many campuses.

Broadside's major authors, such as Nikki Giovanni, Don L. Lee (Haki R. Madhubiti), Sonia Sanchez, Dudley Randall, Marvin X, Gwendolyn Brooks, Carolyn Rodgers, Etheridge Knight, Audre Lorde, and Margaret Walker, among others, were a major feature on the college and university lecture circuit during the sixties and seventies. They were especially in great demand for poetry readings, and to serve as panelists at conferences, festivals, and other programs.[115] Such activities were a major contribution of Broadside authors to the Black Arts Movement and the Black Studies Movement.

Broadside's writers also played a significant part in promoting the development of Black Studies curriculums, and in the use and adoption of black texts (books and articles) as instructional materials for students in American schools. Many of the works written by Broadside authors became required reading on the syllabuses of many courses taught on black life and culture, black literature, and women studies.[116]

Many Broadside authors also served in key leadership positions in black organizations, and as publishers, editors, journalists, and board members to black periodicals.

Black writers at Broadside Press were also associated with and promoters of the new Black History Movement of the sixties and seventies; especially in the efforts of reformers among such black historians as Vincent Harding, Lerone Bennett, Jr., and Mary Frances Berry, among many others, to transform the Negro History Movement (nineteenth century to early sixties), into the changing emphasis on the Black History Movement and the Black Studies Movement of the late sixties and seventies. The new black history, according to Vincent Harding, was a call to black people to seek the truth of their historical memories and lives in America. Harding believed they had to face

> the chasm, the hard and unromantic reading of the experiences of black people in America. It is the groans, the tears, the chains, the songs, the prayers, the institutions. It is a recording of the hopes, even if we no longer participate in them. It is seeing clearly not only what we have done, but what has been done to us. It is the grasping of our history out of the hands of others and taking the responsibility of men [and women] for the shaping of our own past. For we insist on the future.[117]

Many of the Broadside writers were serious students of black history, from the African experience to the New World; and historical topics, issues, events, and concerns were a significant theme in the literary works created by the writers.[118] Black history and black literature were also the dominant academic subjects taught in many of the new Black Studies programs and departments of the era. As has been demonstrated, many Broadside

Table 3.7

Highest and Lowest Selling Broadside Books in 1972

TOP SELLING BOOKS			BOTTOM SELLING BOOKS		
No.	Title	Copies Sold	No.	Title	Copies Sold
1.	Re: Creation (Giovanni)	3,432	1.	The Treehouse and Other Poems (Emanuel)	134
2.	Don't Cry, Scream! (Lee)	3,078	2.	Song for Nia (Long)	173
3.	Black Feeling, Black Talk (Giovanni)	2,872	3.	The Rocks Cry Out (Murphy and Arnez)	189
4.	Black Judgement (Giovanni)	2,656	4.	Don't Ask Me Who I Am (Randall)	190
5.	Black Poetry: A Supplement... (Randall)	2,553	5.	Black Velvet (Hoagland)	191
6.	Dynamite Voices (Lee)	2,201	6.	Panther Man (Emanuel)	204
7.	We a BaddDDD People (Sanchez)	1,944	7.	Cities Burning (Randall)	207
8.	A Broadside Treasury (Brooks)	1,924	8.	Blues for Momma (Raven)	210
9.	Aloneness (Brooks)	1,674	9.	Impressions of African Art Forms (Danner)	230
10.	We Walk the Way of the New World (Lee)	1,409	10.	Spirits Unchained (Kgositsile)	243

writers were teachers, and some of them, such as Don L. Lee, Sonia Sanchez, Nikki Giovanni, and Jon Eckels, among others, worked to promote the new black consciousness in American schools, through teaching and writing about the new black history and literature of the Black Arts and Black Studies movements.[119]

Further evidence of the influences of the Black History and Black Studies movements are expressed in the pages of Broadside's annual periodical, *The Black Position*, edited by Gwendolyn Brooks between 1971 and 1976.[120] This publication was priced at $1.50 in 1971, $2.00 in 1972, and $3.00 in 1973; an average issue contained between 45 and 65 pages.[121] Its essays focused on the political, economic, cultural, and historical condition of black people. Its stated aim was to "feature important black thinking on this time. The substance of the drama — 'on this I stand. Now. This is my position.'"[122] Nine of the fifteen essays are rooted in the new historical and cultural consciousness of the intellectual and social struggles of the sixties and seventies.[123]

During the early seventies, a majority of the contributors lived in three cities: New York (Addison Gayle, Larry Neal, Saundra Towns, and Larry Darby); Detroit (Dudley Randall); and Chicago (Gwendolyn Brooks, Francis Ward, Val Gray Ward, Don L. Lee, George Kent, Sweiyi Fiddo [from Nigeria], W. Keorapetse Kgositsile [from South Africa], and Lerone Bennett, Jr.).[124] Eight of the authors were major figures in the Black Arts Movement of the period, including Gayle, Neal, Randall, Brooks, Lee, Kent, Kgositsile, and Bennett. Their intellectual and cultural influences have had a tremendous impact on the generations between the Civil Rights Movement of the fifties through the seventies.[125] The body of their contributions to black life and letters lives on in the many books, articles, and lectures which they gave to raise the consciousness of so many people, across so many decades.

As Broadside Press grew from 1968 to 1975, in the background stood the Vietnam War, which was of supreme importance to many of Broadside's writers and artists among the foreign policy decisions of the American government. The Vietnam War was unpopular among most of them. Many viewed the American effort there as an expansion of U.S. imperialism in a third world country, while at home some white Americans practiced discrimination and racism against blacks, Native Americans, Chinese-Americans, Puerto Ricans, Chicanos, and other groups.[126] Yet, they noted, whites expected these same groups to fight abroad even though the civil and human rights struggles to reform America were still unresolved.

Table 3.8 describes the range of military experience among a sample of Broadside authors. What is most striking about the list is that there is no clear indication that a large number of Broadside authors served in Vietnam, between 1965 and 1975. However, many Broadside writers did serve in previous U.S. conflicts, especially in World War II.[127]

Certainly, Broadside's authors were disturbed about the war — and this fact is documented in many of their books, articles, and speeches from the period. A random sample of poems by twelve of them reveals the importance of the anti-war theme in their work. (See Table 3.9.[128]) Three poems from this list express the international dimensions of the war, and the impact of the era on third world peoples. First, Audre Lorde's "Viet-Nam Addenda":

VIET-NAM ADDENDA

for/Clifford

Genocide doesn't only mean bombs
at high noon and the cameras
panning in on the ruptured stomach
of somebody else's pubescent daughter.
A small difference in time and space
names that war
while we live
117th street at high noon
powerlessly familiar.
We are raped of our children
in silence
giving birth to spots quickly
rubbed out at dawn
on the streets of Jamaica
or left
all the time in the world
for the nightmare of idleness
to turn their hands
against us.[129]

William Waring Cuney's "Say Amen" and Don L. Lee's "Message to a Black Soldier" are equally intriguing in their denouncement of the war.

Table 3.8

Military Service of Broadside Press Writers

Name	Branch of Service	Rank	Years of Service
Ahmed Akinwole Alhamisi	U.S. Army (Administrative Assistant, Army Education Center, Ansback, Germany, 1965)		1963–65
Samuel W. Allen (Paul Vesey)	U.S. Army	Lieutenant	World War II
Robert T. Bowen	Military Service		1958–62
Charles E. Cannon	U.S. Marine Corps (saw service on Okinawa and in Vietnam)		1966–68
Ray Durem	U.S. Navy (Note: Durem was a member of the International Brigade in Spain, 1937)		World War II
James A. Emanuel	U.S. Army (93rd Infantry Division; saw duty in the South Pacific; confidential secretary to General Benjamin O. Davis, Sr., the assistant inspector general of the U.S. Army)	Staff Sergeant	1942–46, 1951–53
Addison Gayle, Jr.	U.S. Air Force		
Lance Jeffers	U.S. Army (Company commander, 740th Medical Sanitary Company, saw duty in England)	First Lieutenant	1944–46
LeRoi Jones (Amiri Baraka)	U.S. Air Force (Weatherman and gunner on B-36 in Puerto Rico)		1954–56
Etheridge Knight	U.S. Army (Medical Technician, saw duty in Korea, Guam, and Hawaii)		1947–51
Don L. Lee (Haki R. Madhubuti)	U.S. Army		1960–63
Clarence Major	U.S. Air Force		1955–57
George E. Norman	U.S. Navy (Musician)		World War II
Dudley Randall	U.S. Army (Signal Corps, saw duty in the South Pacific, the Philippines, and other islands)	Sergeant	1943–46
James A. Randall	U.S. Navy (Journalist and photographer with the Public Information Office of the U.S. Navy; editor, U.S. Navy Aviation Journal)		1961–65
Jon C. Randall	U.S. Navy (Hospital Corpsman in California)		1961–65
William H. Robinson	U.S. Army (?)		World War II
Chauncey E. Spencer	U.S. Army (Air Corps; Trained at Tuskegee, Alabama)		World War II

SAY AMEN

Hear me talking
say Amen
hear me preaching
say Amen
there will be a day
of reckoning
say Amen
there will be a
Day of Reckoning
say Amen
hear me preaching
say Amen
hear me talking
say Amen[130]

MESSAGE TO A BLACK SOLDIER

The black brothers at home refuse
to go to war. They say:
"the Viet Cong never
called us a nigger."
As the black soldier shot the Cong,
the Viet cried:
"we are both niggers — WHY?"[131]

The most controversial Broadside author associated with the movement against the Vietnam War was Marvin X (Marvin Ellis Jackmon). Poet Lorenzo Thomas notes in a biographical sketch of Marvin X that the writer's commitment to the Black Arts Movement have emerged from his

> embrace of the Muslim religion taught by Elijah Muhammad's Nation of Islam and a personal confrontation in 1967 with issues of racial politics, pacifism, and the Vietnam War.[132]

Marvin X's opposition to the Vietnam War was expressed through his conscientious objection to the war — and by his refusal to be inducted into the Armed Forces of the United States. Thomas explains the consequences of this decision:

> Refusing induction, Marvin X was tried and convicted, and while awaiting sentence in 1967, he fled to Canada. "I departed from the United States," he wrote later, "to preserve my life and liberty, and to pursue happiness." He traveled from Canada to Honduras, where he was arrested and returned to the United States. For his court appearance (at which he was sentenced to five months at Terminal Island Federal prison) he prepared an angry and eloquent statement, which was later published in *Black Scholar* (April–May 1971). "There comes a time," Marvin X wrote, "when a man's conscience will no longer allow him to participate in the absurd!" He recalled with disgust the Supreme Court's 1857 Dred Scott decision, which pronounced that "a black man has no rights which a white man is bound to respect," and in ringing tones he challenged the court's authority to contravene his religious and philosophical principles. "But there you sit," he charged, "with the blood of my ancestors dripping from your hands! And you seek to judge me for failing to appear in a court for sentencing on a charge of refusing induction, of refusing to go 10,000 miles to kill my brothers in order to insure the perpetuation of White Power in Southeast Asia and throughout the world."[133]

Audre Lorde (Feb. 18, 1934–Nov. 20, 1992) was a giant among the poets of her generation and gave much of her time and energy to aid the struggles of other writers and of students. On her death, *The New York Times* wrote, "From the publication of her first book in 1968, Ms. Lorde's 17 volumes of poetry, essays and autobiography reflected her hatred of racial and sexual prejudice." She received many honors during her lifetime, and served as the New York State Poet from 1991 until her death (ca. 1973 photo courtesy Broadside Press).

The legacy of the Vietnam War was deeply felt in America throughout the sixties and seventies and beyond. As a group, Broadside's writers condemned the war, in which 274,937 African-Americans, between 1965 and 1974, had served in the Armed Forces of the United States; none could forget that 5,681 blacks were killed in combat, and could never return to this country to live out their lives with their loved ones. Many blacks could never forget the high death and service rates, (12.3 percent of U.S. totals) which blacks had experienced in Vietnam.[134]

As a group with shared interests and concerns, black women were a voice to be reckoned with at Broadside Press in the sixties and seventies. First, they held the largest number of staff positions in the early days of the company (Janice Robertson, Ayuma and Cynthia McClure, Vernita Norris, and Lottie Butler).[135] Later, in the early seventies, when the company had five full-time and three part-time positions, women occupied two full-time jobs as assistant editors at Broadside (Melba Boyd and Deidre Honore). Deborah McAfee served as secretary of Broadside; and Janice Kyle, then in high school, worked in the shipping department. Thus, women held three of the five full-time positions, and one of the three part-

time posts at Broadside in 1973.[136] Only two men were major figures at Broadside during these years: Dudley Randall, as publisher and editor, and Bill Whitsitt, as office manager. Black women were 50 percent of the staff at Broadside in the mid-seventies. They were among the key decision makers who determined what was published by the company; and their efforts helped to sell the literary products of the writers to the rest of the world.

Dudley Randall was also very positive in promoting the work of black women poets and editors at Broadside, as has been demonstrated in previous discussions in this book. While more men than women were published at Broadside Press between 1965 and 1975, the company published more black women poets than did any other publishing company in the United States. In fact, Broadside published at least 270 men and 140 women writers during its first decade.[137] Men were clearly the dominant group published, and authored 66 percent of all Broadside publications produced in the mid-sixties to the mid-seventies, compared to only 34 percent for women.

Table 3.9

Antiwar Poems by a Sample of
Broadside Press Authors, 1965–1975

Author	Poem	Year
Arna Bontemps	"The Day-breakers"	1963
C.E. Cannon	"Thank u lbj"	1972
William Waring Cuney	"Say Amen"	1973
Jon Eckels	"What Pueblo Means to Me"	1969
James A. Emanuel	"I Touched the Hand of a Soldier Dead"	1968
Nikki Giovanni	"The Great Pax Whitie"	1968
Lance Jeffers	"When I Know the Power of My Black Hand"	1974
Etheridge Knight	"A Poem to be Recited"	1973
Don L. Lee	"Message to a Black Soldier"	1968
Audre Lorde	"Viet-Nam Addenda"	1974
Marvin X	"Untitled Proverb"	1969
Dudley Randall	"Beasts"	1973
Habte Wolde	"Enough to Die for"	1972

Some black feminists believed that black men writers held an advantage over black women, since during the Black Arts Movement, more men than women were published in the black journals, and by American publishing companies, both black and white. Few could seriously argue that Dudley Randall and Broadside Press were not fair about this issue, since such a wide range of black women poets were published and distributed by the company. Thus, Randall and Broadside were somewhat sheltered from the harshest criticism of black feminist writers on this point. Also, all of America, and the rest of the world for that matter, could observe that half a dozen or more of the most famous and significant black women poets of the era were published by Broadside. By 1975, this list included Gwendolyn Brooks, Margaret Walker, Nikki Giovanni, Sonia Sanchez, Audre Lorde, Mae Jackson, Margaret Danner, and Carolyn Rogers, among many others.

Yet, the concerns of black feminist writers and thinkers were obviously not just centered on the number of black women who were published, or not, by American publishers. As scholar Patricia Hill Collins points out in *Black Feminist Thought* (1990), black women were committed to overcoming the centuries of their oppression based on their race, gender, class, and sexual orientation.[138] Central in the arguments and thinking of a diverse universe of black women, such as Gwendolyn Brooks, Alice Walker, Sonia Sanchez, Nikki Giovanni, June Jordan, Audre Lorde, and so many others, was a need for black women to foster greater racial solidarity among black women, to promote uplifting of black children and the community; to seek self-definition, self-reliance and self-valuation, while also fostering the black woman's perspective on life (through daily living, literature, the arts, work, and play). It was also important to promote the empowerment of black women, on the economic, political, social, and cultural arenas of public and private life; while challenging the levels of male domination in society.[139]

But the economic position of blacks was a major hurdle for many to overcome in the seventies. Educator Barbara Sizemore noted in 1975, that:

> Black women holding the same jobs black men, white men and women hold make less money. There are Bureau of Labor statistics that show this inequity. We're at

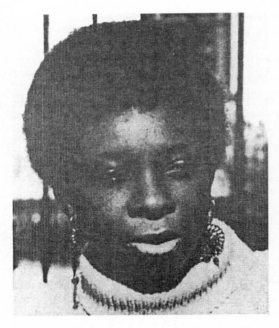

Mae Jackson was born on January 3, 1946, in Earl, Arkansas, but lives in New York City, where she is a teacher, essayist, and poet. Her major poetry collection, *Can I Poet with You* (1969), was awarded the Third Conrad Kent Rivers Memorial Award in 1970 by *Black World* magazine (courtesy Broadside Press).

the bottom of the barrel in the job market.... And on the three levels of American superiority — white, male and wealth — we're number four.[140]

Indeed, the median income in 1975 was only $7,297 for black women, contrasted with $7,614 for white women, $9,875 for African-American men, and $13,216 for white men (which was double that of black women).[141]

Such economic factors made life difficult for many black women. But most active and neophyte black writers — both male and female — were still hard pressed to make a living as writers in the seventies. Critic Bell Hooks observes that the task of "surviving economically while writing" has been greater for black women writers most of all.[142] The reality, she points out, is that

the difficulty of this process for black women has changed little through the years. For every one black woman writer that manages to [be] published, hundreds if not thousands cease writing because they cannot

withstand the pressures, cannot sustain the effort without affirmation, or because they fear that to risk everything in pursuit of one's creative work seems foolish because so few will make it in the end.[143]

Still, some black women have committed their lives to writing and promoting black literacy. As Patricia Hill Collins observes: "Mary Helen Washington points out that one distinguishing feature of black women's literature is that it is about African-American women."[144] Another significant task for such black women, which grows out of the black feminist movement, has been to develop an audience for that literature. Social critic Calvin C. Hernton takes a severe position on the mistreatment of black women authors by men and society. In *The Sexual Mountain and Black Women Writers* he writes,

> Except for Gwendolyn Brooks, and perhaps Margaret Walker, the name of not one black woman writer and not one female protagonist was accorded a worthy status in the black literary world prior to the 1970s, not even [Lorraine] Hansberry, first black woman to have a play on Broadway. Gwendolyn Brooks was the exception. Her age, her numerous prizes and awards and honors from the white literary world, the prestige she already had, plus her unquestionable genius, made her, per force, the acceptable exception.
>
> Although the 1960s witnessed a plethora of black female writers, especially poets, the legacy of male chauvinism in the black literary world continued to predominate. In fact, during the Black Power/Black Arts Movement of the 1960s, the unequal recognition and

treatment of women writers was enunciated more bigotedly than perhaps ever before. "The only position in the revolution for women is the prone position!" "The women's place is seven feet behind the men!" Pronouncements like these were reflected again and again in the writings, and deeds of the males of the period. In Stokely Carmichael and Charles Hamilton's *Black Power, The Politics of Liberation in America*, not one black woman is mentioned significantly, not even Angela Davis. In Harold Cruse's encyclopedia masterpiece, *The Crisis of the Negro Intellectual*, about thirty women are mentioned, largely in passing, most of whom are entertainers such as Josephine Baker and Lena Horne. There also occurred, if one remembers, the proliferation of macho pimp films and books, *Superfly, Sweetback, Shaft, Nigger Charlie*; Nathan Heard's *Howard Street* and Iceberg Slim's autobiographical works enjoyed lively sales. During the heyday, moreover, of the Black Power Black Revolution Black Arts Movement, one could go through the Black Studies Curriculum and learn all about the Black Experience, and encounter less than a handful of black females. The first issue of the *Black Scholar* magazine came out in 1969. The issue was entitled, "The Culture of Revolution." Nine articles were listed in the table of contents. All of them were authored by men. On the inside cover the editorial states:

"...A black scholar...is a man of both thought and action, a whole man who thinks for his people and acts with them, a man who honors the whole community of black experience, a man who sees the Ph.D., the janitor, the businessman, the maid, the clerk, the militant, as all sharing the same experience of blackness, with all its complexities and its rewards. THE BLACK SCHOLAR is the journal for such a man."*

*Changes in the editorial personnel of the *Black Scholar* since the first issue, plus the raising of consciousness, brought about a more egalitarian policy toward women that has become evident in subsequent issues.[145]

Scholar Skip Gates credits black women with not only being major shapers of increasing black literacy in America, but also observes that it was "the black women's movement [which] expanded the potential readership and 'market' for black studies, saving it from demise."[146] Still, the final reality for black women in publishing is that each generation must struggle constantly to keep the gains won in the past, while opening new opportunities for younger writers. According to scholar Erlene Stetson in this setting, black women

> are powerless to control the most basic aspects of our lives in a white male-run economy, we have little participation in and impact on the institution that enable writers to get their thoughts, visions, and creativity into print. If the routes to publication were not filled with obstacles, our way would still be blocked, for the publishing industry, academic as well as commercial, is run by white men with essentially two aims — making profits and preserving the status quo.[147]

In the final analysis, then, black women and men writers were in the same boat! Dudley Randall understood this point; and his work at Broadside Press sought to advance the literature of the African-American people, poem by poem, and book by book, in a very closed society. In essence, a key to understanding Dudley Randall's attitude toward black women writers is that he did not "talk about" doing something for them. In fact, he did do something: he published the works of over 140 black women writers between 1965 and 1975 at Broadside Press. Such accomplishments have not been achieved by anyone else in modern America.

The work of black gay writers, however, was not a priority issue at Broadside Press during the period of the sixties and seventies. In fact, the black gay liberation movement and the interests of black lesbians were often not even discussed publicly in black literary and publishing circles of the Black Arts Movement era. Two major problems were evident during these years. First, the problem of homophobia was pronounced in American life, and extended to some elements in the black community, especially among certain black intellectuals and activists in movement organizations. Scholar Manning Marable describes the situation:

> Like the vast majority of white Americans, most Blacks refused to acknowledge the presence of lesbians and gay males within their communities.... Black nationalist and radical writers condemned homosexuality in unambiguous terms. LeRoi Jones (Amiri Baraka) asserted that "most American men are trained to be fags...so white women become men-things, a weird combination..."; Eldridge Cleaver argued that homosexuality is "a sickness, just as baby-rape or wanting to become the head of General Motors.... Many Negro homosexuals are outraged and frustrated because they are unable to have a baby by a white man."[148]

Secondly, it was often physically dangerous for black gay persons to admit publicly that they were homosexual. Critic Patricia Hill Collins also notes that many black writers of both sexes were fearful of being stigmatized as lesbians or gays, because of the toll of the oppression which individuals could face when thus "charged" with this sexual preference in the black community.[149]

At Broadside, Dudley Randall's focus was on the publication of works by heterosexual black writers. However, the editorial policies of the company do not appear to have prevented authors from adding a diverse selection of their poetry — even on such controversial or perceived radical themes as homosexuality — in their individual or collected poetic works. But, the overwhelming conclusions which emerges from the published works of Broadside authors between 1965 and 1975 is that black gay liberation is not reflected as a major, or even a minor, concern among Broadside authors, except for the work of poet Audre Lorde, who was one of the major Broadside writers of the era. Yet, according to scholar Ann Allen Shockley:

> Audre Lorde, an established and notable poet, paved the way early through her excellent writing and Black woman['s] courage. Her poetry does not deal with exclusively Lesbian themes, encompassing others of love, women, race, family, children and places. The book, *From a Land Where Other People Live* (Detroit: Broadside Press, 1973), was nominated for the 1974 National Book Award.[150]

Perhaps the excellent quality of Lorde's writings, promoted the acceptance of her work at Broadside.

> Audre Lorde believed that: Dudley and Broadside began the flood of Black poetry publishing. He introduced voices that were important and would not otherwise have been heard, my own among them. Dudley and I did not always agree in philosophy, but I have the utmost respect for him and gratitude for the role Broadside Press played in bringing my work to a Black public.[151]

Nevertheless, Lorde was also of the opinion that Broadside Press did not foster equal treatment for the poetic works of both black men and women poets: "I feel this was one area in which the Press was derelict — women writers were not well represented or understood *at all*."[152] Lorde's perspective also included the observation that:

Dudley...never accepted or approved of my being a Lesbian, but he did publish the work and support it — altho it was only on the insistence and with the financial support of Gwendolyn Brooks that he accepted the manuscript of *From a Land Where Other People Live* for publication.[153]

During the sixties and seventies, silence on black gay issues remained the watchword at Broadside Press and most other black publishers in America. Although black gay people were active contributors to all aspects of African-American life, they were often invisible to the public at large; and their books and other artistic achievements, if they reflected a non-heterosexual preference or perspective, often remained unpublished. If published at all, they were not reviewed in the major black literary organs of the period. The black gay liberation movement was a taboo subject in most areas of the public life of black America, or held up to revulsion by many spokespersons in the black community, during the heyday of the Civil Rights and Black Power movements. But, in general, silence on black gay lifestyles was the norm of the era, and Randall and Broadside Press remained conservative on the issue.

During the Black Arts Movement, Dudley Randall and Broadside Press were targets of government surveillance because of the cultural, social, and political implications of the literary work published by the company.[154] Indeed, many of the poets, such as LeRoi Jones (Amiri Baraka), Marvin X, and Sonia Sanchez, among others, were considered as "well-known extremists" by such government agencies as the Federal Bureau of Investigation, and some local and state police agencies in Michigan.[155] The central problem for the black community lay in the observation of scholar Manning Marable that there was "a pattern of illegal surveillance acts which victimized" many blacks and their organizations, such as SCLS, CORE, SNCC, the Black Panthers, the Republic of New Africa, and others, during the decades of the sixties and seventies. Furthermore, the intensity of the repression reached new levels under President Richard M. Nixon's and J. Edgar Hoover's FBI Cointelpro Program and the IRS' Probe List, which "set about the task of systematically destroying the still powerful radical wing of the Black Power Movement."[156] Yet, black publishers, such as Broadside, had to carry on with their activities in spite of such outside pressure and tactics by governments agencies.

Black Detroit and Broadside Press authors and friends celebrated the tenth anniversary of the founding of the company with a series of programs in the city on September 26–28, 1975. Some of the most famous Broadside authors to attend the festivities were Gwendolyn Brooks, Haki R. Madhubuti (Don L. Lee), Audre Lorde, Etheridge Knight, and Sonia Sanchez.[157] Among the activities held during the anniversary celebrations were several writer's workshops, an awards banquet, and a poetry benefit reading. Other figures who honored Randall by participating in the programs included Mayor Coleman Young of Detroit; Hoyt W. Fuller, editor of *Black World*; and other writers, such as Melba Boyd, Frenchy Hodges, Chauncey E. Spencer, James Thompson, Naomi Long Madgett, C. Gene Drafts, Jill Witherspoon Boyer, John Randall, Arthur Pfister, James Randall, Stella Crews, Henry Blakely, Alvin Aubert, Sarah Webster Fabio, Pinkie Gordon Lane, Celes Tisdale, and Charles Rowell.[158]

Several special honors were bestowed upon Dudley Randall during this period. A testimonial resolution from the City of Detroit was read by City Councilperson Erma Henderson, which proclaimed September 27–28, 1975, as "Broadside Press Days." Rep. Barbara-Rose Collins read a special tribute from the Michigan Legislature in honor of

Margaret Walker (shown ca. 1970) was born on July 7, 1915, in Birmingham, Alabama, but has also lived in many other parts of the United States, including New Orleans, Chicago, and, since 1949, Jackson, Mississippi. Along with Gwendolyn Brooks, Walker is a "dean" among living black women poets born before 1920. In 1942, she won the Yale University Award for Younger Poets. She has produced ten books in a career spanning over fifty years.

Randall. Chicago's Kuumba Workshop awarded Randall a check for $150.00, and Governor William G. Milliken of Michigan published an Executive Declaration, which read, "In Observance of the contributions Dudley Randall has made to the literary world as a respected contemporary poet and publisher in Michigan."[159]

Carole A. Parks, an editor at *Black World*, summed up a decade of hard work at Broadside Press when she reflected on the fact that Dudley Randall had started out in 1965 to build a new company

with no outside funding, little mass advertising and frankly inadequate distribution. [But ten years later he had] managed to release nearly 70 volumes of poetry and criticism and 90 traditional broadsides, sold about 200,000 books, mostly to the black audience they are intended for; and published at least 230 writers, some (like Gwendolyn Brooks, Margaret Walker and Margaret Danner) with reputations established before they came to him, but the majority unknown until Mr. Randall "discovered" them.[160]

The period between 1965 and 1975, produced a profusion of excellent literary works from Broadside Press. The most prosperous Broadside author, in terms of the total number of books sold, was Don L. Lee (Haki R. Madhubuti), who by 1973, had over 100,000 books in print.[161] Dudley Randall's comment on this phenomenon was that it had "occurred without book reviews in the mass media," but only in "small black and underground magazines"; and, of course, by word of mouth in black schools, churches, entertainment centers—and on the streets.[162]

A key factor for Broadside Press' success was the trust and sincerity which Randall radiated to many black authors. They were attracted to and stayed with Broadside because many of them believed that Randall had displayed a "consistent dedication to Black American poetry." This brought or "won" for him the "personal and communal loyalty" of such writers as Madhubuti, Brooks, Margaret Walker, Sanchez, and Giovanni.[163] Such writers allowed Randall and Broadside Press to create an oasis for black poetry publishing in Detroit, which also helped to sustain the Black Arts Movement during its final days of artistic creation, and contributions to African-American life. Now at the age of sixty-one, Randall could look back from the vantage point of 1975 on over a half-century of reading and writing poetry, and on a decade of promoting the poetic talents of over 300 poets who had published poems and other works with Broadside Press. It was a magnificent record, but one which had been achieved at great personal costs to Randall, to which the final years of the seventies would bear witness.

Chapter 4

Crisis and Decline of
Broadside Press, 1976–1979

W hile the echoes of the 1975 tenth anniversary of Broadside Press were a positive indication of Dudley Randall's work in Detroit, such an acknowledgment did not reveal
or predict the difficulties which would soon face the company. Randall was overtaken in
early 1976 with a series of economic and personal setbacks. His assistant editor at Broadside, poet Melba Joyce Boyd, best summed up the situation with a penetrating analysis:

> the press fell into financial havoc as printing costs skyrocketed with inflation and small
> bookstores and businesses closed, leaving their balances due to Broadside unpaid. Black
> Studies programs across the country were severely cut or completely eliminated. Unem-
> ployment hit the Afro-American community with an economic eruption that echoed
> like the Great Depression crashing on top of Harlem and its cultural renaissance.
>   The $1.50 and $2.00 priced publications that had become almost as commonplace as
> *Ebony* magazines were no longer possible. Eighty titles and more that 500,000 books by
> Broadside had been distributed throughout the U.S. and the world, a cultural extension
> unprecedented in Afro-American literary history. But Randall was no business-man and
> the press did not operate on "profit principles." He overextended credit to bookstores
> and poets alike, and the tension of internal and external financial factors compounded
> by the national economy and decline in black cultural enthusiasm forced him to sell the
> press to prevent bankruptcy and total institutional collapse.
>   Being the self reliant and overly responsible editor that he was, he internalized this
> loss as a severe personal defeat. In 1977 Randall sold the press and slowly slipped into
> an emotional and creative depression that would approach suicide and loom for four
> years.
>   Broadside Press was sold to the Alexander Crummell Center, the cultural extension
> of a socially and politically active Episcopalian Church, which was named after the 19th
> century abolitionist. The center engaged Gloria House [Aneb Kgositsile] as the editor.
> But essentially the center assumed the responsibility of distribution and there were no
> new titles published under the auspices of the center.[1]

Indeed, Dudley Randall had simply made too many commercial commitments without
enough cash-flow, cash-reserves, or a large enough staff to reach the growth potential
which once had seemed so promising at Broadside. For Dudley, like so many other artists,
much of his effort at Broadside had been attempted through trial and error; and there was
always the huge problem of overcoming a "lack of capital in a capitalistic society where a
large proportion of small businesses fail every year."[2] When he set out in 1965–66 to create Broadside, Randall suggests, he was not thinking of "profits." Instead, his "strongest

motivations [were] to get good black poets published, to produce beautiful books, help create and define the soul of black folk, and to know the joy of discovering new poets."[3]

But, in 1976–77 the financial crisis of publishing sent a thunderbolt through Broadside. Also in 1976, Randall and many other black intellectuals had been horrified by the removal of *Black World* from the stable of Johnson Publishing Company organs in Chicago — and the end of Hoyt W. Fuller's association with that preeminent journal.[4] Now, a year later, for all practical purposes it seemed to many that Broadside Press would also become a victim of war in the historical struggles of the times.

> The *Detroit Free Press*'s synopsis of the situation revealed that: Randall's idealism was his undoing. He couldn't refuse to publish deserving poets, he insisted on keeping the price of books below $3 and he kept sending books to small bookstores that were behind in their accounts. By the mid–1970's, sales were dropping off, creditors were going broke and bills mounted.[5]

Randall's firm policy since the sixties of keeping Broadside's books as inexpensive as possible is highlighted in Table 4.1.[6] An average paperback edition of a Broadside book was priced at less than $2 between 1966 and 1976. In all, sixty-two paperback books were produced in this price range, while only twenty-three were priced at or above $2. During this period Broadside also issued sixteen cloth or hardback books that were sold at less than $6.00 each and eight priced at or above $6. Such market decisions helped to lead to the collapse of Broadside Press. Thus, the economic history of Broadside was not as positive as its literary portrait. In reflecting on these issues, Randall observed:

> When I started I was ignorant of business tenets. If I had known, perhaps I would not have started Broadside Press. Most small businesses fail within the first three years. One should expect to make no profit or, if lucky, to break even for the first few years. One should start with sufficient capital: $10,000, $50,000, $100,000. I started with only $12. Very unwise.
>   Besides rent, telephone, you have wages, supplies, postage, printers, deductions, and royalties to pay. Some small presses do not pay royalties or wages. I paid both. To make up the difference, I worked free, when I should have paid myself maybe $20,000 or $30,000 a year. Sometimes grants from Arts Councils help, but they cannot be depended on. Suppose you apply for a grant and don't get it?[7]

Philosophically, the issue of profits and directions was a major ideological issue in the struggles between black writers, activists, and publishers during the sixties and seventies. A leading black Detroit poet and editor, Ahmed Akinwole Alhamisi, demanded in the early seventies that black artists and publishers must focus on "creative Spiritualism" and the development of a "Revolutionary Spirit" in all of their activities. Alhamisi asked black writers two questions: "What do we write? Where do we write?" The responsibility of black writers and publishers, he argued, lay with abandoning all white publications and publishers — and supporting black ones, in the struggle for the "total liberation" of black people.[8] Juxtaposed against this argument was Dempsey J. Travis' observation that the major obstacles facing black businesses centered on the fact that:

> production and profits remain small and insignificant on the scale of total American businesses because racism and racist practices keep whites from patronizing black businesses. On the other hand, black consumers support black businesses to an extraordinary degree.

Table 4.1

Prices of Broadside Press Books, 1966–1976

Paperback Books		Cloth Editions	
Price of Book	*Number Sold at this Price*	*Price of Book*	*Number Sold at this Price*
$0.50	1	$ 3.00	1
$0.95	1	$ 4.00	2
$1.00	31	$ 4.50	4
$1.25	5	$ 4.95	2
$1.50	17	$ 5.00	5
$1.75	2	$ 5.95	2
$1.95	5	$ 6.00	4
$2.00	7	$ 6.95	1
$2.50	2	$ 7.25	1
$2.95	1	$ 9.95	1
$3.00	2	$15.00	1
$3.50	2		
$3.75	1		
$3.95	1		
$4.00	2		
$4.25	1		
$6.00	3		
$7.95	1		

...black families spend from 10% to 20% of their income with black businesses. [And yet these same concerns] provide only 2% of the goods and services needed by Americans.[9]

Dudley Randall took a middle course position, when he suggested in a 1972 interview that among the major problems facing black publishers are "(1) financing, (2) collecting what is owed them. These are interrelated." These publishers have always had to be cognizant of this central question: when might their clientele "promptly" pay them for their services? Yet, always lurking in the background have been such additional problems as "banks [which] are averse to lend, and anyway independent publishers don't worry to borrow or to beg for grants." In Randall's world view the greatest satisfaction comes "not so much in money as in achievements. Books contain ideas, and ideas move the world."[10] This was the state of affairs in the seventies, when a *Black Enterprise* article was headlined "Black Book Publishing: Protest, Pride and Little Profit."[11] Black book publishers were just too small and many, like Broadside Press, were operated with more regard for the substance of their publications than for a healthy bottom line. Even major black publishers were tiny in both size and wealth, in comparison to the major white American publishers. For example, in 1972, Harper and Row of New York published 1,426 titles, while Johnson Publishing Company of Chicago could only manage 5.[12] Still, in spite of everything, Randall expressed the dominant view shared by many in the black press on his concerns about an independent and black-focused press remaining in black hands.

> I've declined partnerships, mergers and incorporations. I want freedom and flexibility of action; want to devote the press to poetry; and I am afraid that stockholders in a

corporation would demand profits and would lower quality or go into prose in order to obtain profits. Income from the press goes into publishing new books in an attractive and inexpensive format. I pay royalties to other poets, but royalties on my own books go back into the press. I'm not against royalties for myself or profits for the company, if they ever come, but I'm most interested in publishing good poetry, including all viewpoints and styles. I deplore incestuous little cliques, where poets of a narrow school of ideology band together, cry themselves up and deride all others.[13]

But the lack of profits across the previous decade had now exhausted Randall and his small staff of workers, who numbered three in 1975. Even Randall had to admit later that "it was a mistake not paying myself a salary." Perhaps if he had done so early in the creation of the company the danger signals would have been more self-evident before Broadside was riddled with debt.

If I were paying myself, and I wasn't able to do so, then I would have said something is wrong. We've got to raise prices or sell more books or fire some of the staff. But I didn't pay myself and that never happened.[14]

However, Randall was not alone in navigating the dangerous economic, social and political currents of the seventies. At home, his city was now referred to in the national media as "The Deadliest City," and "Detroit: That Sinking Feeling."[15] Black scholars, such as economist Lloyd Hogan, and sociologist Alphonso Pinkney, traced the origins of the crisis deep within the American past. In economic terms, Broadside represented on the local level the national condition of black businesses in America. Hogan points out that "The first official national census of black owned businesses in 1969 identified some 200,000 such firms. Only 32,000 employed paid workers. Among the latter, a mere handful of less than 3,000 reported more than ten employees." Most of these were employed only "on a part-time or sporadic basis." But in reality, only "20,000 full time equivalents really had jobs." At the end of the sixties black business firms made $250,000,000.[16] Yet, very little of this total sum went to black publishers of poetry.

The economic situation in most black families left little room for buying poetry for enjoyment. In 1977, 21 percent of U.S. black families were measured to have had annual incomes between $15,000 and $24,999; and only 9 percent of black American families earned more than $25,000.[17] Hogan suggests that as late as 1981, only some 15,000 blacks could be accurately identified as being members of "the sum total of the black middle class — the alleged black bourgeoisie."[18] In any event, regardless of the true nature of the numbers, one circumstance stands out clearly: the numbers were small. And added to the impact of economic matters on the everyday struggle of black publishers to stay afloat in America were the concerns of the 1,500,000 "unemployed" blacks in 1976, and the daily pains of the 7,545,000 who lived "below the official poverty level" of the United States government.[19]

These local, state, regional, and national problems, in which blacks found themselves everywhere, did little to smooth over the aggrievement that many black artists must have felt with the turn of events at Broadside Press. After all, many black writers and artists had sacrificed a great deal to support the efforts for an independent black poetry company in Detroit. One had only to reminisce on the special contributions made by many of the Broadside authors themselves to witness what such devotion had meant to the life of the company. Gwendolyn Brooks' biographer, George E. Kent, notes that the poet laureate of

Illinois "gave her poem 'For Malcolm X' to Broadside, without fee, for inclusion in the anthology devoted to Malcolm X. Later she would recommend other poets for publication in the Broadside Press series and pay the printing costs for some of them. Through her would come several books, and Broadside would finally become her publisher. This collaboration brought her further out into the [main] stream of new Black literary movements."[20] Certainly Gwendolyn Brooks was one of Randall's major sources of inspiration during the sixties and seventies, but there were others as well. Key among them was Haki R. Madhubuti (Don L. Lee), who also received Brooks' support at his Chicago-based Third World Press.

Together, Brooks and Lee were a force of great service to Broadside's work. Kent relates that Brooks "and Don usually paid the expenses incurred by Broadside in publishing their work and helped at times to defray publication costs for other writers."[21] Interestingly, in 1972, Randall notes that "For Don's thirtieth birthday Gwen [Brooks] commissioned Broadside to publish Don's [Lee] selected poems, *Direction-score*, in paper, cloth, and deluxe editions."[22] Randall extends his warmest note of gratitude to support "from the grassroots, from poets who donated their poems to the anthology *For Malcolm X*, in honor of Malcolm X; from the poets in the first group of the Broadside Series, who steadfastly refused payment for their poems; from the many persons who subscribed in advance for the Broadside Series and the anthologies, so that they could be printed; and from others who donated sums above their subscriptions. It is the poets and the people who have supported Broadside Press."[23]

Indeed, Randall could look back on many book, tape, record, poster, and broadside poems purchase orders received "primarily by mail from buyers around the world."[24] For certainly, Broadside's publications, sold well "in Africa, Europe, the Caribbean, Latin America, Canada, Mexico, Australia and New Zealand."[25] One of the rich rewards of the Civil Rights Movement and the Black Nationalist Movement of the sixties and seventies was that the black struggle had helped to revitalize a market for black-oriented books in all segments of the black population. Randall's work and that of Broadside Press were a part of this struggle to reach all levels of black society with a message of hope and endurance for the work ahead. Randall was most contended when Broadside could cement such relationships with the black community.

> I often get orders for poetry books which are scrawled and misspelled on paper torn from notebooks, and once received an order scrawled on part of a brown paper bag. I am more pleased to receive such individual orders than a large order from a bookstore or a jobber, for they show that black people are reading poetry and are finding it meaningful, not an esoteric art.[26]

But the genuine hopes of Randall and other progressive-thinking Americans were dashed by the conservative mood of most of their fellow citizens in the seventies. An indecisiveness magnified itself even among many of the writers and artists of the period. At this point Randall could remark that "the poets of the 1970's are less angry. They seem to be taking stock of themselves. They're more concerned about building institutions and organizations that will endure. For example, LeRoi Jones [Amiri Baraka] helped elect the mayor of Newark, New Jersey, [Kenneth Gibson in 1970]. Now he's trying to get a housing project for the people there."[27] Others were just worn out — smashed by the tremendous physical and psychological costs which black Americans had paid to achieve a few openings in their civil and human rights struggle in America.

On a personal level, Randall became an observer of events, rather than a shaper of them, in the years between 1976 and 1979. He could only stand by and give encouragement to others at the Alexander Crummell Memorial Center of Highland Park, Michigan, as the church "paid Broadside's debts by selling the remaining stock."[28] Later, Melba J. Boyd could only lament that Randall

> Never paid himself, but he always paid his poets, even if it was only $10 a poem. He felt it was important people got paid for their work, even though, too many times, it came out of his own pocket.[29]

An epithet for this period lives in Randall's observation that: "poetry's not a commercial item, and I'm not a good businessman."[30]

Yet, Randall was not completely forgotten by literary circles and the public during the late seventies. He remained a member of such organizations as the Arts Extended Gallery for the Advancement of Culture and Education, the Committee on Small Magazine Editors and Publishers, Kappa Alpha Psi Fraternity, and the Michigan Council for the Arts Advisory Panel on Literature.[31] During this period, Dudley continued to receive recognition and honors for his achievements. In 1976, the Department of English at Wayne State University presented him with the English Alumni Award, and in 1977 came three more awards. Randall was one of five distinguished Michigan artists to receive the first Michigan Arts Awards, with a cash value of $2,500 presented by Governor William G. Milliken in April at the Detroit Institute of Arts; and he also received awards from the International Black Writer's Conference, Chicago, Illinois, and the Institute of Afro-American Studies, Howard University, Washington, D.C.[32] In 1978, he received the honorary Doctor of Literature degree from the University of Detroit.[33] Such tributes continued to reflect the significant contributions which Randall had made to the Black Arts Movement.

Even Broadside Press was not forgotten. In 1976 the last major volume of poetry published by the company during the Black Arts Movement era appeared — Sterling D. Plumpp's *Clinton*, a twenty-six page book, priced at $2.00.[34] This long narrative poem captures the poet's early life experiences in Clinton, Mississippi, a small town in Hinds County, near Jackson, and relates them to his later development in Chicago, Illinois, during the decade of the sixties.[35] Plumpp is recognized nationally as one of the most important black writers based in Chicago from the Black Arts Movement to the present.

Critic Chester J. Fontenot found *Clinton* to be "a remarkable effort to work out the problem created by collapsing the distinction between myth and history, among the past, present, and future. The poem itself becomes a way of rendering — through creative expression — a personal experience in the universal mode."[36] Poet and critic Jerry W. Ward, Jr., views *Clinton* as a "serious" volume of poetry, which "is a strong, autobiographical poem about going from one C into others, up and out of Clinton, Mississippi, into the circle of Chicago and change."[37] In essence, Plumpp explores black history from his own personal field of vision, to assess the meaning of modern life in America from the rural to the urban experience. His work completes the journey first begun by Randall and Margaret Danner in *Poem Counterpoem* (1966), which explored the black memory from its African lineage to its American formation.

Another Broadside publication which also appeared in 1976 was *The Black Position*, an annual, edited and financially supported by Gwendolyn Brooks in Chicago. Although published under the Broadside label, Brooks' Chicago address at 7428 S. Evans Avenue appeared as the publication's official address.[38] This forty page organ, priced at $2.50, contained three articles in 1976: Nora Blakely's (Brooks' daughter) "Take the Load Off, Baby (Psychocultural Pressures of the Black School Child)," Marvin Florence's "Underlife," and George Kent's "The Newark Black Power Conference as Journey of the Self."[39]

Twice during 1976, *The Black Scholar* carried notices of Broadside's books. In the spring of 1976, four books were noted under the journal's "Black Books Round-up" for 1975, including Leaonead Park Bailey, ed., *Broadside Authors and Artists* (1974), Sterling A. Brown, *The Last Ride of Wild Bill and Eleven Narrative Poems* (1975), Nicholas Guillen, *Tengo* (translated by Richard J. Carr, 1974), and Lance Jeffers, *When I Know the Power of My Black Hand* (1974). In the fall of 1976, ten Broadside books were listed, such as Gwendolyn Brooks, *Beckonings* (1975); Linda Bragg, *A Love Song to Black Men* (1975); Sterling Brown, *The Last Ride of Wild Bill*; Chauncey E. Spencer, *Who Is Chauncey Spencer?* (1975); and Henry Blakely, *Windy Place* (1975).[40] Yet, as early as January 1976, Randall was forced to decline any new books for Broadside Press from such writers as Herbert W. Martin, to whom he wrote "'History' is a

Lance Jeffers (November 28, 1919–July 19, 1985) was born in Fremont, Nebraska, but lived in many parts of the United States including San Francisco, New York, Georgia, Alabama, Washington, D.C., and North Carolina during his long career as a significant writer and teacher of African-American literature. He is especially remembered for his great poem "My Blackness Is the Beauty of This Land," and for a body of work which, as Owen Dodson noted in the *CLA Journal* (1978), "pierces hypocrisy, prejudice, black and white, clichés, concessions to the tepid reader, establishments of any kind. Lance Jeffers is spiritually, physically involved in his subject matter, but the effect is wholly universal" (ca. 1970 photo courtesy Broadside Press).

powerful poem, but I'm taking on no additional books for a while."[41] Such words describe the closing of an era. But, a year later, poet Quincy Troupe could write:

> Today there is a host of excellent young (and by young I mean under 45 years of age) African-American poets who are writing better than they have ever written in their lives. Among the outstanding poets composing today are Jayne Cortez, Primus St. John, Lammont Phillips, Judy Simmons, K. Curtis Lyle, Etheridge Knight, Lucille Clifton, Michael A. Harper, June Jordan, Ishmael Reed, Calvin C. Hernton, Amiri Baraka, Haki R. Madhubuti, Carolyn M. Rodgers, Eugene Redmond, Audre Lorde, Al Young, Joyce Carol Thomas, Gerald W. Barrax, Sonia Sanchez, Bob Kaufman, Yvonne, Sam Cornish, Ntozake Shange, Norman Jordan, George Barlow, Carole Gregory Clemmons, Stanley Crough, Alvin Aubert, Nikki Giovanni, Charles Lynch, Ron Welburn, Horace Coleman, Tom Weatherly, Joe Johnson, Conyus, Doughtry Long, Amus Mor, David

Henderson, Elouise Loftin, Sterling Plumpp, and the legendary Watts poet, Ojenke (Alvin Saxon). The poets mentioned above are writing some of the most vigorous, imaginative, and powerful poetry anywhere in the world today.[42]

Dudley Randall, through his work with Broadside Press, had helped bring many of these voices before the public, such as Simmons, Knight, Reed, Madhubuti, Lorde, Sanchez, Barlow, Aubert, Giovanni, Long, Plumpp, and others. His work and insights had helped to shape an entire generation of black poets. But now his own voice was silenced by the pain of debt, of being overworked, and of physical and mental burnout. Nevertheless, new works by Randall were published between 1976 and 1979, including nineteen poems in four anthologies, two magazines and two critical studies, one interview with editor and poet Charles A. Rowell in *Obsidian,* and an introduction to Melba Joyce Boyd's collection of poetry, *Cat Eyes and Dead Wood* (1978).[43] Although this was a period of silence for him, Randall's work was still very much alive, and he would rise again to lift his voice high in the annuals of African-American literature.

Meanwhile, at home in Detroit, Randall and other citizens could observe at close hand a city in crisis. By 1978, journalist Alex Poinsett reported in *Ebony* that:

> the serious problems still plaguing Detroit include a continuing population decline, housing deterioration in some sections, unemployment and the mediocre quality of public school education. [But, in spite of such factors] ... the annual income of a Detroit factory worker is $16,310, compared with the national average of $10,818.[44]

Yet, such figures did not reveal the entire economic situation for black Detroiters. For example, the 1979 median incomes for whites stood at $20,568, contrasted with only $13,695 for blacks in the metropolitan Detroit area.[45] On the other hand, 21.9 percent of the citizens of Detroit had incomes in 1979 which placed them below the poverty level in the city. One study of the period noted that unemployment in Detroit by the mid-seventies "reached the Great Depression level of 23.8 percent."[46] But the greatest volume of unemployment was among the black youth of the city. A 1976 survey of the problem revealed that:

> Unemployment among Detroit's black youth over age 16 is extremely high, variously estimated at from 50 to 75 percent. Precise figures are unknown because officials simply have lost track of thousands of these youngsters.[47]

Such conditions were counterbalanced by the fact that an African-American, Coleman Young, served as Detroit's mayor of the city during the last six years of the seventies. This achievement reflected the political strength of blacks in Detroit. One of the mayor's major policy decisions involved the Detroit Police Department. A study of the period notes that:

> By the end of 1976 Detroit boasted its first black police chief and a top command structure that was half white. One hundred black officers had been hired since Young's election, increasing black representation from 17 percent to 22 percent.[48]

Black Detroiters also operated two economic institutions in the city: the First Independence National Bank of Detroit, established in 1970, and the eighth largest black-owned bank in the United States, with assets in 1978 of $35,378,000, and loans made of

$14,658,000, and the Home Federal Savings and Loan Association, established in 1947, and the ninth largest black-owned savings and loans association in the United States, with assets in 1978 of $21,663,000, and loans made of $18,699,000.[49] Blacks in Detroit also held the honor of owning the first black-owned television station in the continental United States — WGPR-TV, Channel 62. WGPR-TV was established in 1975 by William V. Banks, and reached 880,000 viewers in the Detroit area.[50] Such painstaking gains increased black solidarity and lifted the mood of some black Detroiters during this grim period. But the reality of the situation was that many blacks lived an existence on the margins of society, where a fragile economic and social system did not effectively address their life concerns.

As Broadside Press experienced a period of paralysis in the late seventies, so did a number of other black publishers of books, newspapers, and magazines. Harsh economic times, a decrease in the intensity of the Civil Rights, Black Power, and Black Arts movements of the period 1960–75, and deepening conservatism among whites, all combined to create a new dilemma for much of the nation's black media. On the one hand the gains achieved by blacks, as a result of the Civil Rights Movement, opened up previously closed positions for some of them in such companies as daily newspapers, television, and publishing organizations. Conversely, as some elements among the black middle class grew in numbers and migrated to the suburbs, this created a declining interest in such black media forms as the weekly newspaper, since many blacks preferred to purchase daily, up-to-the-minute news.[51] One study of the period notes that "only about 100 black newspapers were in existence in 1975 and only some 35 of these had a [weekly] circulation exceeding 20,000 per issue."[52] However, journalism scholar Henry G. LaBrie III found in 1979 that "there were 165 black newspapers publishing in 34 states and the District of Columbia. Of this number, 151 reported their circulations which totaled to 2,901,162 weekly." Yet, a 1974 survey by the author observed that blacks owned "213 black newspapers with a total weekly circulation of 4,369,858 (205 papers reporting). The current survey [1979] reflects a 33.6 percent decrease in circulation and a 22.5 percent loss in membership papers."[53] This was the same fate for many black magazines, especially for the radical black journals of the Black Arts Movement. Scholars Abby Arthur Johnson and Ronald Maberry Johnson observe that in the seventies: "they either expired or entered a phase of irregular appearance by commenting on the decade passed and the promises not met."[54] The key problem for all of them lay in the economics of publishing in the United States.

Black publishers were especially hard hit because of their weak economic positions in general, and by a severe distribution system, which prevented them from effectively selling their books to the public. This became even more troublesome for them during this period because of the closure of many black bookstores, and the continued refusal of many white booksellers to carry their products.[55] In the final analysis, black publishers were confronted with an economic system which stigmatized their operations as small, unprofitable, and too large a risk for capital investments or loans. Yet, black publishers, like all other businesses, needed capital. Al Prettyman, an African-American publisher of New York's Emerson Hall, estimated in the late seventies:

> that over a three-year span a small publisher ideally needs $250 thousand to remain in operation just to cover expenses. And $250 thousand he says, is considered "lean."[56]

However, as late as 1966, the average black business in Detroit had starting investments of less than $5,000 (55 percent), and only 7 percent began with over $5,000. (cont. on page 148)

Table 4.2

Black American Publishing Companies, 1970–1979

(alphabetically arranged primarily by state, secondarily by city)

Name	Location	Years in Operation	Publisher/ Editor	Major Focus	Range of Titles	Miscellaneous
Reed, Cannon & Johnson	Berkeley, CA	1974–	Ishmael Reed	Literary, novel, poetry, anthologies	2 in 1974–75	Created by three novelists "to publish authors who otherwise wouldn't be published"
Yardbird Publishing Co.	Berkeley, CA	1971–	Ishmael Reed & Al Young	Anthologies; *Yardbird Reader*, fiction, poetry	5 Yardbird Readers were produced between 1972–76; with at least 5 other books to 1979	Placed a focus on multi-cultural authors and artists
Black Liberation Publishers	East Palo Alto, CA	1971		Literary, poetry, political		Emphasized works with the theme of freedom for black people
Circle Press	Los Angeles, CA	1971	Robert Bowen	Cultural, literary, poetry		Placed a focus on poetry
Kawaida Publications (NIA Cultural Organization)	San Diego, CA	1978		Cultural		Focus on California writers
Journal of Black Poetry Press	San Francisco, CA	1971–78	Joe Goncalves	Cultural, poetry	Titles in black poetry	Emphasized black poetry and political works
Julian Richardson Assoc.	San Francisco, CA	1978	Julian Richardson	Cultural		Placed a major focus on black writers in California
Shabazz Publishing Co.	San Francisco, CA	1971		Cultural, poetry		A major focus on poetry
Associated Publishers	Washington, DC	1921–	Carter G. Woodson, 1921–50; Charles H. Wesley, 1971	Scholarly books	At least 20 titles to the 1970s	Publishing arm of the ASALH, established in 1915

Name	Location	Years in Operation	Publisher/Editor	Major Focus	Range of Titles	Miscellaneous
Drum and Spear Press	Washington, DC	1969–71	Carolyn Carter, director; Judy Richardson, executive director	Educational, historical, political	4 titles between 1969–70	Also based in East Africa, (Dar es Salaam, Tanzania)
Howard University Press	Washington, DC	1972– (actually created by the Howard Univ. Board of Trustees in 1919 but effective only as a univ. press after 1972)	Charles F. Harris, executive director, 1971–; Renee M. Mayfield, managing editor, early 1990s	Scholarly and literary works	Over 37 titles in print to 1978	Published the *Journal of Negro Education* and the *Journal of Religious Thought*
Institute of the Black World	Atlanta, GA	1970s–	Vincent Harding	Political, social, cultural affairs	Books, newsletters, reports	Emphasized black history, economic, social and political works
Afro-Am Publishing Co.	Chicago, IL	1963–1975	David P. Ross; Eugene Winslow	Educational, literary, biography, autobiography	16 titles to 1975	Established "for the purpose of creating and producing materials for African and Afro-American Studies"
DuSable Museum of African-American History Press	Chicago, IL	1961–	Margaret G. Burroughs	Cultural materials, educational, poetry	Books, calendars, art works	Places a major focus on works which contribute to black history, life and culture
Free Black Press	Chicago, IL	1975–78		Cultural		Placed a focus on Chicago area writers
Johnson Publishing Co.	Chicago, IL	1961–	John H. Johnson	Black historical, cultural, social political affairs, biography, reference works	48 books were produced to 1975	Developed to meet the demand for materials on black history

Black American Publishing Companies, 1970–1979 (continued)

Name	Location	Years in Operation	Publisher/ Editor	Major Focus	Titles	Range of Miscellaneous
Nation of Islam Press	Chicago, IL	1956–78		Islamic	Key works by Elijah Muhammad	Temple No. 2 placed a special focus on the black condition in America
Third World Press	Chicago, IL	1967–	Haki R. Madhubuti	Social-historical, cultural, educational	75 titles to 1975	Established "to provide quality Black materials"
Black River Writers	East St. Louis, IL	1978	Eugene Redmond	Poetry, literary	At least 5 titles during the 1970s	Places on emphasis on poetry
Natural Resources Unlimited	Markham, IL	1972–	Joe Mitchell	Poetry	10 titles to 1975	To publish poetry
Black Arts South	New Orleans, LA	1971	Tom Dent	Literary, poetry	At least 4 titles in the 1970s	To publish poetry
Free Southern Theatre	New Orleans, LA	1967–70s	John O'Neal, Jr.	Literary, plays, poetry	Plays and other art works	Promotes the development of black theatre
Tarharka Publishing Co.	Annapolis, MD	1971–	Phaon Sundiata (Goldman)	Scholarly works on Africans worldwide	At least 1 title in the 1970s	Places on focus on Africa
Black Orpheus Press	Rockville, MD	1971–		Scholarly works on Africa	5 or more titles in the 1970s	"Books about Africa that are relevant to the American scene
EuTu Publishing Co.	Amherst, MA	1972–		Cultural, literary, & educational		Materials on subjects which are overlooked
Agascha Productions	Detroit, MI	1970–80	Agadem L. Diara & Schavi Diara	Cultural, political, & social works	6 titles in 1970s	Pan-African Ideology
Balamp Publishing Co.	Detroit, MI	1970–76	James M. Jay	Biography, academic	5 titles were released in the 1970s	Placed a focus on biography & ed.
Black Arts Publications	Detroit, MI	1969–71	Ahmed A. Alhamisi	Poetry & literary books	5 titles in the 1970s	Black Nationalist perspective
Black Star Publishers	Detroit, MI	1970–74		Literary & political	1 or more titles	Published *Inner City*
Broadside Press	Detroit, MI	1965–	Dudley Randall; Gloria House (1977–79)	Poetry; literary	Over 60 books were published between 1965–79	The most important publisher of black poetry in 1965–1975

Name	Location	Years in Operation	Publisher/Editor	Major Focus	Range of Titles	Miscellaneous
Lotus Press	Detroit, MI	1972–	Naomi Long Madgett	Poetry, literary	20 volumes of poetry produced in the 1970s	2nd major publisher of black poetry in the 1970s
Radical Education Program	Detroit, MI	1970		Black affairs	Over a dozen works in the 1970s	"An alternate for young writers"
Jihad Productions (Vita Ya Watu) (People's War) Publishers	Newark, NJ	1967–	Amiri Baraka	Poetry, drama, history, cultural, political works		
Black Academy Press	Buffalo, NY & Bloomfield, NJ (1973–75)	1970–75	S. Okechukwu Mezu	Scholarly books on Africana peoples	30 titles were produced in 1970–75	Published *The Black Academy Review* (1970)
African World Distributors	New York City, NY	1978		Black affairs		
Africana Publishing Co.	New York City, NY	1978		Black affairs		
Afro-Arts, Inc.	New York City, NY	1971	Don Holder	Arts & culture		
Black Dialogue Press	New York City, NY	1970–	Ed Spriggs & Nikki Giovanni	Literary, poetry		Published *Black Dialogue* magazine (1965–1970)
Blyden Press	New York City, NY	1969–75		Children's books, black affairs, educational	3–5 titles in 1970s	
Buckingham Learning Corp.	New York City, NY	1971–73	Oswald White	Educational		
The East	New York City, NY	1965–75		Educational	20 booklets on African affairs to 1975	Youth needs
Emerson Hall Publishers	New York City, NY	1969–75	Alfred E. Prettyman	Social & behavioral sciences, literary	24 books to 1978	Devoted to promoting black authors

Black American Publishing Companies, 1970–1979 (continued)

Name	Location	Years in Operation	Publisher/Editor	Major Focus	Range of Titles	Miscellaneous
Fiction Collective (Brooklyn Col.)	New York City, NY	1978		Literature		
New Dimensions Publishing Co.	New York City, NY	1973–78		Black affairs		
Nok Publishers, Ltd.	New York City, NY	1973–75	Chivuzuz Ude (Nigerian)	African affairs	15 titles to 1975	promotes work on Africa
Oamuru Press	New York City, NY	1978		Black affairs		
Shamal Books	New York City, NY	1978		Black affairs		
Third Press	New York City, NY	1970–86	Joseph Okpaku (Nigerian)	Scholarly, literary, current affairs	93 books to 1975	"Mass-oriented" company
Ashley Books	Port Washington, NY	1978		Black affairs		
More Publishing Co.	Durham, NC	1968–75		Creative writing and nonfiction	69 titles to 1975	
Pan African Center for education materials	Durham, NC	1973		Educational		
Free Lance Press	Cleveland, OH	1952–86	Casper Jordan & Russell Atkins	Literary, poetry	Over 10 books during its publishing history	Produced the organ *Free Lance* (1950–1980)
Vibration Press	Cleveland, OH	1971–78	Norman Jordan	Cultural, poetry		
Commonsense Books	Toledo, OH	1955–75		Protest and self-improvement books		A division of the Black Hope Foundation

Name	Location	Years in Operation	Publisher/Editor	Major Focus	Range of Titles	Miscellaneous
New Pyramid Productions	Chester, PA	1975		Black affairs		
EKO Publications	Philadelphia, PA	1969–75		Literary, educational, fiction		Black materials for black people
Oduduwa Productions	Pittsburgh, PA	1971–78		Cultural, poetry		Produced by the Black Studies Dept., Univ. of Pittsburgh
Winston-Derek Publishers	Nashville, TN	1976–	James Peoples	General, black interest	140 titles to 1989	Themes on American minorities
Energy, Earth Communications	Houston, TX	1970s	Ahmos ZuBolton	Literature, poetry, anthologies	5 titles by 1975	Produced the *Doo* Series magazine

Forty-three percent of these same business operations had incomes under $4,000 and $8,000 yearly.[57] Only a handful of black publishers had operating capital of $250,000 a year, and even fewer could boast of a profit of even $25,000 a year, after expenses were met.[58]

The Broadside Press story illustrates the harshness of the economic environment in America. In spite of its success, the company went under. In fact, in 1973 William Whitsitt, the company's office manager, related to Frenchy Hodges that Broadside was "worth about $250,000 in book stock at list price and about another $250,000 to $500,000 in over-all worth value."[59] In reality, though, the company never had enough capital to meet its obligation and to expand its operations.[60] In a complex economic situation, Randall and Broadside Press could not seek effective help (i.e., loans) from other black businesses in Detroit, which in 1975 were the fifth largest among black-owned business in the ten largest American cities. During this period, there were 4,984 black firms in Detroit, with yearly receipts of $268,395,000.[61] However, the communications networks just did not exist for the mutual aid needed to save Broadside Press.

Nevertheless, although the seventies were a watershed period among black book publishers in America, many prevailed and survived the decade of hardships. Table 4.2 lists the range of active black American publishers between 1970 and 1979.[62] The Big Ten among American black publishers, in terms of either sales or status and influence were located in six cities: Yardbird Publishing Company, Berkeley; Johnson Publishing Company, Chicago; Broadside Press and Lotus Press, Detroit; Howard University Press and the Associated Publishers, Washington, D.C.; Jihad Productions, Vita YaWatu (People's War) Publishers, Newark; and Emerson Hall Publishers and Third Press, New York City. (See Table 4.3.) All of the above cities were major centers of activity during the Black Arts Movement. The publishers and editors of the Big Ten black publishing companies were influential personalities, and major shapers of the intellectual and cultural environment of the sixties and seventies. During the seventies Chicago's Johnson Publishing Company was the largest black publisher in the United States.[63] But the profits at Johnson came not from the book division, but rather from the magazine sales and advertisements in *Ebony* and *Jet*, and from other branches of the company. For in reality, only five books were published by Johnson in 1972.[64] In essence, as noted by a journalist of the period, "most small publishers attempt to publish anywhere from two to seven titles per year."[65] Thus, during any given year of the seventies, the black community was faced with a situation where there were only seventeen to twenty-five active black publishers in this country to promote the black perspective in book publishing.[66] On the other hand, whites controlled at least 2,325 publishing companies in 1972, and 3,397 in 1977.[67] Such statistics reveal the foremost significance of the work of a few black book publishers and their staffs, in attempting to produce and distribute to black people, a variety of world views based on the black experience.[68]

During the Black Arts Movement, Dudley Randall and Broadside Press enjoyed a remarkable degree of cooperation and mutual assistance with Third World Press, Chicago, and Lotus Press, Detroit. The three companies were in fact, the dominant publishers of black poetry in America during the seventies. Randall developed a very close working relationship with Don L. Lee (Haki R. Madhubuti), publisher at Third World Press and the leader among Broadside authors with the most books sold.[69] Likewise, Dudley and Naomi Long Madgett, the publisher of Lotus Press, were close associates, and among the best known black poets who lived and worked in Detroit.[70]

Third World Press was created as an independent black publishing house on August 2, 1967, by Chicago poets Jewel C. Latimore (later known as Johari Amini, Johari M. Kunjufu), Carolyn Rodgers and Don L. Lee.[71] As an alternative to the white mainstream publishers, "Third World Press came into being to provide in-depth reflections of ourselves by ourselves."[72] A 1972 study described the press as "reflecting its community commitment, Third World has established an Institute for Positive Education, which provides lectures, a library, movies and a bookstore, and has also developed a school for neighborhood children and parents."[73]

The company was managed, with few operating funds, out of the writers' apartments and storefronts from 1967 to 1974, and moved during the latter year to new offices on Cottage Grove Avenue.[74] In Chicago, editors at Third World were able to secure the support and encouragement of what critic Houston A. Baker, Jr., calls the "three seminal figures of an established generation — George Kent, Gwendolyn Brooks, and Hoyt W. Fuller... [who] stepped forward and allied themselves with the black arts."[75] Like Broadside, Third World Press' early publishing years were devoted to promoting the publication of black poetry in this country. (See Table 4.4.) Its list of writers included some of the best known black authors in modern America, such as Gwendolyn Brooks, Amiri Baraka, St. Clair Drake, Mari Evans, Hoyt W. Fuller, Sam Greenlee, Angela Jackson, George Kent, Keorapetse Kgositsile, Don L. Lee, Useni Eugene Perkins, Sterling D. Plumpp, Carolyn Rodgers, Askia Muhammad Toure, Margaret Walker, and Chancellor Williams. Although a large number of them were born in the South, during the seventies at least nineteen of the poets lived and worked in Chicago. This pattern demonstrates the importance of Chicago during the Black Arts Movement. Most of the authors were teachers, in addition to being professional writers. Their educational backgrounds also reflected this fact. In the mid-seventies, the company shifted its focus to also include non-fiction and children's books in addition to works of poetry. During its first twelve years in operation the company produced over sixty books and broadsides.[76]

Third World Press made its greatest contribution to the Black Arts Movement by focusing its publishing activities on the works of Chicago's black writers, such as Carolyn Rodgers, Johari Amini, Sterling D. Plumpp, Ebon, Keorapetse Kgositsile, Sam Greenlee, Philip Royster, Angela Jackson, Fred Hord, and Olumo (Jim Cunningham), among others. Many of these poets were also members of the Chicago based Organization of Black American Culture writer's workshop; which included such figures as: Zack Gilbert (an original member); Ebon (1967–69), Olumo (1967–69), Don L. Lee (1967–74), Angela Jackson (1970–present), Sterling D. Plumpp (1968–74), Carolyn Rodgers (1967–71), Philip Royster (1970–73), Johari M. Amini (1967–76), Hoyt W. Fuller (1967–76), and Sam Greenlee (1968–71), among others. George E. Kent also served as OBAC's advisor during the period 1978–80.[77] Although the firm also produced books by authors who lived in other cities, especially New York, Newark, and Detroit, its range of published poets were never as great as that of Broadside Press, which had a much wider geographical diversity of published poetic talent. The vast majority of Third World's books reflected the new black poetry, yet works were also produced by older writers, such as Dudley Randall and Gwendolyn Brooks, although these were in the minority in terms of the books published by Third World Press.

In addition to publishing each other's books, Dudley Randall and Don L. Lee also extended aid to each other in the areas of book distribution, program development,

Table 4.3

Leaders at Big Ten U.S. Black Publishers, 1970–1979

Name	Birth Place	Birth Date	Education	Work Experience	Publishing Experience	Publications
Amiri Baraka	Newark, NJ	Oct. 7, 1934–	Howard Univ., B.A.; Rutgers & Columbia Univ.	Writer, lecturer, teacher, editor, publisher	Major editor, publisher, Jihad Press, Newark, NJ	Over 25 books & plays published to 1979
Charles F. Harris	Portsmouth, VA	January 3, 1934–	Va. State Col., B.A.; New York Univ.	Doubleday, John Wiley & Sons, Random House, Howard Univ. Press	Major publisher, editor, NYC, and Washington, DC	Editor and essayist
John H. Johnson	Arkansas City, AR	January 19, 1918–	Univ. of Chicago, Northwestern Univ.	Businessperson, publisher, editor	Founder Johnson Publishing Co., 1942–, largest & wealthiest U.S. black publisher	Autobiography, key editor and essayist
Naomi Long Madgett	Norfolk, VA	July 5, 1923–	Va. State Univ., B.A.; Wayne St. Univ., M.Ed.; further study, Wayne State, Univ. of Detroit, Ph.D.	Educator, editor, publisher, lecturer	Major publisher of poetry, Lotus Press, Detroit	5 books published to 1979
Haki R. Madhubuti	Little Rock, AR	February 23, 1942–	Chicago City Col., A.A., Wilson Branch; Roosevelt Univ., M.F.A., Univ. of Iowa	Writer, lecturer, educator, editor, and publisher	Major editor & publisher, Third World Press	11 books to 1979, major poets and essayist
Joseph Okpaku	Lokoja, Nigeria	March 24, 1943–	Northwestern Univ., B.A.; M.S., Stanford Univ.; Ph.D., Stanford	Editor, publisher	Major publisher, Third Press, educator	10 books to 1974
Alfred E. Prettyman		1935–		Harper & Row, Emerson Hall, Publishers	Co-founder with Bill Mayot and William Peters of Emerson Hall, Publishers, in 1969	Editor and essayist

Name	Birth Place	Birth Date	Education	Work Experience	Publishing Experience	Publications
Dudley Randall	Washington, DC	January 14, 1914–	Wayne State Univ., A.B.; M.A.L.S., Univ. of Michigan	Librarian, major writer, publisher, editor	Founder of Broadside Press, 1965–	6 books to 1973
Ishmael Reed	Chattanooga, TN	February 22, 1938	Univ. of Buffalo, NY	Writer, lecturer, educator, editor, publisher	Major writer, editor, and publisher, Yardbird Publishing Co., Berkeley, CA	16 books to 1979
Charles H. Wesley	Louisville, KY	Dec. 2, 1891–August 16, 1987	Fisk Univ., B.A.; Yale Univ., M.A.; Howard Univ. Law School; Harvard Univ., Ph.D.	Major historian, major educator (president of Central State Univ., Ohio), lecturer, editor, publisher, clergyman	Publisher of the Associated Publishers, Washington, DC	14 books to 1979

appearances on the literary lecture circuit, news promotion, and book reviews in key black arts journals of the period, such as Third World Press' house organ, *Black Books Bulletin*. Thirteen Broadside Press poets also had books or broadsides published by Third World Press between 1967 and 1979. The poets in this group include Johari Amini, Amiri Baraka, Gwendolyn Brooks, Ebon, Mari Evans, Zack Gilbert, Keorapetse Kgositsile, Don L. Lee, Olumo, Sterling D. Plumpp, Dudley Randall, Carolyn Rodgers, and Margaret Walker.[78] Thus, the two companies were effective in promoting and distributing the work of a significant group of modern black poets in America, while each company sought to grow and develop with the common support of each other. Together, Third World Press and Broadside Press nourished the careers of at least a dozen major African-American poets during the Black Arts Movement, and were very influential in helping dozens of new authors to advance their careers with the publication, in many cases, of their first books.

Dudley Randall has also had a long literary relationship with Naomi Long Madgett. Born in 1923 in Norfolk, Virginia, she was educated at Virginia State University (B.A., 1945), Wayne State University (M.Ed., 1955), and the International Institute for Advanced Studies (Ph.D., 1980). Madgett migrated to Detroit in 1946, and taught English in the city's public schools from 1955 to 1965. She also served as a research associate at Oakland University in Rochester, Michigan, from 1965 to 1966, and as professor of English at Eastern Michigan University, Ypsilanti, 1968–84.[79] By the time Madgett arrived in Detroit, she had already published her first volume of verse, *A Phantom Nightingale* (1941). This was followed with *One and the Many* (1956), and *Star by Star* (1965). Randall and Madgett were among the dozen or so most active black poets in Detroit during the period between the late forties and early sixties. They were also members of Margaret Danner's writer's workshop at Boone House.[80] In 1967, Randall published Madgett's poem "Sunny," as Broadside number 11.[81]

In 1972, Madgett and a group of local Detroit supporters established Lotus Press, as a firm devoted to black poetry. Her fourth book, *Pink Ladies in the Afternoon: New Poems, 1965–1971*, served as the first offering from the new company.[82] Since the early seventies the company's major objectives have been

> to keep the best of black poetry alive by making inexpensive, attractive paperbound volumes available to the bookstores and libraries of the world. To provide a worldwide audience to black poets of excellence, regardless of their ideology, subject matter, or style. Our goal is literary excellence. We are not interested in work that is political without being technically sound; nor are we interested in beginners who have not studied the fundamentals of their craft.[83]

In 1974, Madgett assumed full responsibility for the company. Her economic burdens were similar to conditions at Broadside Press and Third World Press during this period. However, "She knew poetry would never be a profitable pursuit. 'I had to do it. It was an emotional release. Most poets find it therapeutic.'"[84]

Nevertheless, between 1972 and 1979, Lotus Press published eighteen books. (See Table 4.5.[85]) The best known writers on Lotus' list from this period were Naomi Long Madgett, May Miller, Herbert Woodward Martin, Lance Jeffers, James A. Emanuel, and Houston A. Baker, Jr. All of the above poets, except for May Miller, also had books or broadsides of poetry published by Broadside Press. However, unlike Broadside and Third World Press, Lotus Press did not emphasize the new black poetry, but did promote the work of new poets,

Table 4.4

Selected Titles Published by Third World Press, 1967–1979

Author	Title	Year	Form of Publication	Price	Pages
		1960s			
Norman Jordan	*Destination: Ashes*	1967	poetry	$1.50	72
Jewel C. Latimore (Johari Amini)	*Images in Black*	1967	poetry	$0.75	20
Johari Amini	*Black Essence*	1968	poetry	$1.00	17
Ebon	*Revolution*	1968	poetry	$1.00	31
Don L. Lee (Haki R. Madhubuti)	"For Black People and Negroes"	1968	poetry	$0.30	2
Carolyn M. Rodgers	*Paper Souls*	1968	poetry	$1.25	20
Johari Amini	*Spirit Songs* "Folk Fable"	1969	poetry poetry	$1.00 $0.50	20 5
Amiri Baraka	*It's Nation Time*	1969	poetry	$1.00	24
Sterling Plumpp	*Portable Soul*	1969	poetry	$1.00	21
Carolyn Rodgers	*Songs of a Black Bird* "2 Love Raps"	1969	poetry poetry	$1.00 $0.25	39 2
		1970s			
Johari Amini	*Let's Go Somewhere*	1970	poetry	$1.00	33
Amiri Baraka	*J-E-L-L-O*	1970	play	$1.00	38
St. Clair Drake	*The Redemption of Africa and Religion*	1970	history & philosophy	$1.50 (later $1.95) (cloth, $6.95)	82
Keorapetse W. Kgositsile	*For Melba*	1970	poetry	$1.00	25
Luevester Lewis & Cheryl Jolly	*Jacki*	1970	children's book	$1.00 (later $1.50)	20
Sterling Plumpp	*Half Black/Half Blacker*	1970	poetry	$1.00	34
Askia Muhammad Toure	*Ju Ju: Magic Songs for the Black Nation*	1970	poetry	$1.00	20
Charlie Cobb	*Everywhere Is Yours*	1971	poetry	$1.00	18
Hoyt W. Fuller	*Journey to Africa*	1971	prose travel/ history	$1.95 (cloth, $4.95)	95
Zack Gilbert	*My Own Hallelujahs*	1971	poetry	$1.25	42

Author	Title	Year	Form of Publication	Price	Pages
Sam Greenlee	*Blues for an African Princess*	1971	poetry	$1.25	38
Shawna Maglangbayan	*Garvey, Lumumba, Malcolm: Black Nationalist-Separatists*	1971	history/ politics	$1.95 (later $2.50) (cloth $4.95)	118
Ifeanyi Menkiti	*Affirmations*	1971	poetry	$1.00	15
Dudley Randall	*More to Remember*	1971	poetry	$1.95 (cloth $5.00)	80
Philip Royster	*The Back Door*	1971	poetry	$1.00	29
LeRoi Jones (Amiri Baraka)	*Kawaida Studies*	1972	cultural studies	$1.00	20
George Kent	*Blackness and the Adventure of Western Culture*	1972	culture/ literary history	$3.95 (cloth $5.95)	210
Don L. Lee	*Europe and Africa: A Poet's View–Part I*	1972	history	$1.00	20
Sterling D. Plumpp	*Black Rituals*	1972	psychology	$1.95 (cloth $4.95)	110
Margaret Walker	*How I Wrote Jubilee*	1972	literary history	$1.00	38
Lerone Bennett, Jr.	*IBW and Education for Liberation*	1973	history/ politics	$1.00	12
Chike Onwuachi	*Black Ideology in the African Diaspora*	1973	African religion	$4.95	190
Dudley Randall	*After the Killing*	1973	poetry	$1.25	18
Robert F. Williams	*Negroes with Guns*	1973	history/ biography	$1.95 (cloth $4.95)	128
Gwendolyn Brooks	*The Tiger Wore White Gloves or What You Are You Are*	1974	children's book	$3.00	32
Mari Evans	*I Look at Me*	1974	children's book	$2.50 (cloth $4.95)	30
Chester Fuller	*Spend Sad Sundays Singing Songs to Sassy Sisters*	1974	poetry	$1.00	20
Angela Jackson	*Voo Doo/Love Magic*	1974	poetry	$1.50	25
Keorapetse Kgositsile	*The Present Is a Dangerous Place to Live*	1974	poetry	$1.95	35

Author	Title	Year	Form of Publication	Price	Pages
Olumo (Jim Cunningham)	*The Blue Narrator*	1974	poetry	$1.50	28
Sterling Plumpp	*Steps to Break the Circle*	1974	poetry	$1.95 (cloth, $10.00)	30
Chancellor Williams	*The Destruction of Black Civilization: Great Issues of a Race from 4500 B.C. to 2000 A.D.*	1974	history	$5.95 (cloth, $10.00)	385
Useni Eugene Perkins	*Home Is a Dirty Street*	1975	psychology/ sociology	$9.95	200
Mignon Holland Anderson	*Mostly Womenfolk and a Man or Two: A Collection*	1976	short stories	$2.95	128
John Henrik Clarke	*Black-White Alliances: A Historical Perspective*	1976	history	$0.50	23

most notably Toi Derricotte, Paulette C. White, Pamela Cobb (Baraka Sele), Kiarri T-H. Cheatwood, David I. Rice (W. Mondo Eyen we Langa), Willie J. Williams, and the Nigerian poet Kamaldeen Ibraheem. The most distinctive feature of the Lotus Press poets was the traditional focus or nature of much of their work, as it relates to the more conservative to moderate body of black poetry produced in the past.

During the seventies Lotus Press published twenty broadsides of poetry, eleven by men and nine by women. (See Table 4.6.) This list includes work by major poets such as Michael S. Harper, Robert Hayden, June Jordan, Bob Kaufman, Etheridge Knight, Pinkie Gordon Lane, Audre Lorde, Naomi Long Madgett, Gloria C. Oden, Dudley Randall, and Margaret Walker, among others. Thirteen of the twenty poets, or 65 percent of the total, were also published by Broadside Press. Thus, the two companies were very effective in promoting a cross-fertilization of the poetic talents of the era. The Lotus Press broadside authors were geographically distributed by place of birth from the South (six poets, or 30 percent), the East (six) and the Midwest (seven), with the birth sites of two poets, or 10 percent of the total, being unknown. Two American cities dominate the list — Detroit with five poets, and New York City, with four poets. Lotus Press broadside authors averaged 46 years of age, considerably older than Broadside poets. The broadside authors at Lotus Press were a highly educated group (85 percent held college degrees, 60 percent held master's degrees, three held a Ph.D. and one the J.D.), and 80 percent of them made their livings as teachers. Two worked as librarians, one as a social worker, and one each as a merchant marine sailor, an arts administrator, a sculptor, and a dancer.[86]

Between 1972 and 1979, Lotus Press also published fifteen volumes of poetry by individual authors; eight by men, and seven by women. The major poets on the company's list included Houston A. Baker, Jr., Kiarri T-H. Cheatwood, Toi Derricotte, James A. Emanuel, Lance Jeffers, Louie Crew, Naomi Long Madgett, Herbert Woodward Martin, and May Miller, plus six younger authors. Only three of Lotus Press' writers of broadsides — Pamela Cobb, Naomi Long Madgett and Paulette Childress White — also had published volumes

Table 4.5

Lotus Press Publications, 1972–1979

Author	Title	Year	Form of Publication	Pages	Price
Naomi Long Madgett	*Pink Ladies in the Afternoon: New Poems, 1965–71*	1972	poetry	63	$4.00
Naomi Long Madgett, ed.	*Deep River a Portfolio: 20 Contemporary Black American Poets*	1974	broadsides of poetry, with study guide	32	$7.00
Pamela Cobb (Baraka Sele)	*Inside the Devil's Mouth; First Poems*	1975	poetry	42	$3.00
May Miller	*Dust of Uncertain Journey*	1975	poetry	67	$5.00
Paulette C. White	*Love Poem to a Black Junkie*	1975	poetry	37	$4.00
Louie Crew	*Sunspots*	1976	poetry	64	$3.50
Herbert Woodward Martin	*The Persistence of the Flesh*	1976	poetry	68	$3.50
Willie J. Williams	*A Flower Blooming in Concrete*	1976	poetry	35	$3.00
Toi Derricotte	*The Empress of the Death House*	1977	poetry	51	$3.50
Kamaldeen Ibraheem	*Roots, Flowers and Fruits*	1977	poetry	44	$2.00
Lance Jeffers	*O Africa Where I Baked My Bread*	1977	poetry	77	$3.50
Isetta Crawford Rawls	*Flashbacks*	1977	poetry	32	$2.00
James A. Emanuel	*Black Man Abroad: The Toulouse Poems*	1978	poetry	76	$3.50
Naomi Long Madgett	*Exits and Entrances*	1978	poetry	69	$5.00
David I. Rice (W. Mondo Eyen we Langa)	*Lock This Man Up*	1978	poetry	67	$3.50
Houston A. Baker, Jr.	*No Matter Where You Travel, You Still Be Black*	1979	poetry	58	$3.00
Kiarri T-H. Cheatwood	*Valley of the Anointers*	1979	poetry	73	$4.00
Lance Jeffers	*Grandsire*	1979	poetry	55	$3.00

Table 4.6

Broadsides Published by Lotus Press, 1974

Author	Title
Gerald W. Barrax	"(Untitled)"
Jill Witherspoon Boyer	"When Brothers Forget"
Pamela Cobb (Baraka Sele)	"The Aliens"
Michael S. Harper	"Blues Alabama"
Robert Hayden	"The Whipping"
June Jordan	"I Celebrate the Sons of Malcolm"
Bob Kaufman	"Perhaps"
Etheridge Knight	"Crazy Pigeon"
Oliver LaGrone	"Cocoon of Images (Filmland Fantasy)"
Pinkie Gordon Lane	"After the Quarrel"
Audre Lorde	"As I Grow Up Again"
Naomi Long Madgett	"Album: Photo 2"
Glorida C. Oden	"The Carousel"
Raymond R. Patterson	"Black All Day"
Dudley Randall	"Primitives"
Eugene B. Redmond	"Definition of Nature"
William Shelley	"Portrait #5"
James W. Thompson	"Thursday's Collection"
Margaret Walker	"Lineage"
Paulette Childress White	"Big Maybelle"

of poetry selected by the press during this period. Three Broadside Press authors, Houston A. Baker, Jr., James A. Emanuel and Lance Jeffers, were also the authors of Lotus Press books during the seventies. Table 4.7 denotes that a majority of Lotus Press authors were born in either the Midwest or the South, a pattern that also holds true for most of the writers published by both Third World Press and Broadside Press during the Black Arts Movement. While the ages of six of the fifteen published authors at the company are unknown, the sources on the remaining nine members of this group suggest that their average age in 1974 was forty-nine years; which indicates that Lotus Press fostered the development of a much more mature group of writers than perhaps any other major black publisher of poetry during this period. The maturity of this group of writers is also reflected in their advanced educational levels. At least eleven members of this group attended college (ten hold undergraduate degrees, nine received master's degrees, and five hold doctorates). As has been demonstrated at Broadside Press, most Lotus Press authors made their living as writers and teachers.[87]

During a long decade of struggle and work, Naomi Long Madgett made a total commitment to advance Lotus Press, much as Dudley Randall had supported the development of Broadside Press between 1965 and 1975. Madgett later wrote of these years:

> Sensing the need for a showcase for the work of serious black poets, and wishing to insure their integrity and independence regardless of style and subject matter, she became more and more involved, selecting manuscripts of high literary quality and printing and distributing them at her own expense. Never under the illusion that well-crafted poetry would produce financial profit, she took on the commitment of the press as a labor of love. She was aware that, although poetry relates significantly to the experience of every

Table 4.7

Major Lotus Press Authors, 1972–1979

Name	Birth Place	Date	Education	Occupation	Resident in 1970s
Houston A. Baker, Jr.	Louisville, KY	March 22, 1943–	Howard Univ., B.A., Univ. of Calif., M.A., & Ph.D.	Writer, teacher, editor	Charlottesville, VA, & Philadelphia, PA
Kiarri T.-H. Cheatwood	Southeastern U.S.	1940s–	Elmhurst Col., B.A.; Univ. of Mich., Ph.D. studies	Writer, teacher	Chicago, IL in 1974
Pamela Cobb (Baraka Sele)	Detroit, MI		Eastern Mich. Univ., B.A., M.A.	Writer, teacher, arts administrator	Detroit, MI
Louie Crew			Univ. of Ill., Ph.D.	Writer, teacher	Fort Valley, GA
Toi Derricore	Detroit, MI	1941–	Wayne State, B.A.; New York Univ., M.A.	Writer, teacher	Detroit, MI
James A. Emanuel	Alliance, NE	June 15, 1921–	Howard Univ., B.A.; Northwestern Univ., M.A.; Columbia Univ., Ph.D.	Writer, editor, teacher	New York City, NY; France; Poland
Kamaldeen Ibraheem	Nigeria			Writer	Nigeria
Lance Jeffers	Fremont, NE	Nov. 28, 1919–85	Columbia, Univ., B.S.; Univ. of Toronto, M.A.	Writer, teacher	Long Beach, CA
Naomi Long Madgett	Norfolk, VA	July 5, 1923–	Va. State Col., B.A.; Wayne State Univ., M.Ed.; Ph.D.	Writer, teacher, editor,	Detroit, MI
Herbert Woodward Martin	Birmingham, AL	Oct. 4, 1933–	Univ. of Toledo, B.A.; SUNY-Buffalo, M.A., Middlesbury Col., M.A., Lit.; Carnegie-Mellon Univ., D.A.	Writer, teacher	Dayton, OH
May Miller	Washington, DC	1902–	Howard Univ., American Univ., Columbia Univ.	Writer, teacher	Washington, DC
Isetta Crawford Rawls	N/A	1941–	N/A	Writer	N/A
David I. Rice (W. Mondo Eyen we Langa)	Omaha, NE	May 21, 1947–	Creighton Univ., A.A.; Southeast Community College	Writer, activist	Lincoln, NE
Paulette C. White	Detroit, MI	1948–	Wayne State Univ., B.A., Ph.D.	Writer, artist, teacher	Detroit, MI
William J. Williams	N/A	N/A	N/A	Writer	Detroit, MI

culture in the world, it does not enjoy a popular audience in this country. As a result, the major publishers bring out few books of poetry, subsidizing the cost with bestselling novels that are often without permanent value. Knowing the difficulty of getting published by a reputable house — without any requirement that they contribute to the cost — poets were willing to accept copies and discounts in lieu of royalties. Outstanding artists, too, frequently contributed their work for book covers or as occasional illustrations in return for contributors' copies.[88]

Thus, the economics of publishing were a major stumbling block to the rapid growth of the company during the seventies. Yet, Lotus Press did develop a more realistic price list than did either Broadside Press or Third World Press during its early years of evolution. The average volume of poetry at Broadside Press was priced between $1 and $2 in the seventies; however, the average cost at Lotus Press was $4.[89] Nevertheless, the distribution of Lotus books remained a problem, and the company had only eighteen books and twenty broadsides to sell during this period. Such a small mass of products was not very effective in creating a strong financial situation for Lotus Press.[90] But, under Madgett's guidance the company did survive the decade of the seventies.

By the late seventies, Broadside Press had helped to advance the careers of seven major older poets; three black women, Gwendolyn Brooks (1917–), Margaret Danner (1910–82), and Margaret Walker (1915–); plus four black men, Sterling A. Brown (1901–89), James Emanuel (1921–), Lance Jeffers (1919–1985), and Dudley Randall (1914–). Collectively, they represented a generation of poetic giants who were born in the era of World War I and came of age after the Harlem Renaissance of the twenties, during the Great Depression of the thirties. As a group, they had first hand experiences of hardships, sacrifice, and of the deep commitment and dedication required for them to develop into some of the finest poets to emerge in the United States during the twentieth century. A highly educated group, two of them earned the Ph.D. degree, five were awarded the master's degree, and all attended college. (See Table 4.7.) The group also holds more than twenty-five honorary doctorates from some of the leading colleges and universities in this country. The list of other awards which they have received is legend in African-American literature.[91]

The poets were born in two main geographical regions of the country: the South and the Midwest. From the South came Danner from Kentucky, Brown and Randall from Washington, D.C., and Walker from Alabama; while from the Midwest came Brooks from Kansas and Emanuel and Jeffers from Nebraska. Five of the poets have had work experiences at historically black colleges: Brown, Danner, Jeffers, Randall and Walker. All were teachers and literary editors at some stage of their careers.[92]

During the Black Arts Movement, the seven older-generation Broadside poets were recognized by literary critics for their unique contributions to American letters. Table 4.8 describes the opinions of ten critics of the period.[93] Several key themes emerge from these poets' literary works, and from their lives as human beings. First, as a group they expounded a tremendous sense of and dedication to equality and justice in human relations for all people. Secondly, their longevity as practicing poets magnified the range and influence of their artistic creations across three generations of twentieth century readers. Thirdly, their interpretations of African-American and Third World life in general have radiated and promoted a growing awareness and extension of black consciousness both at home and abroad. Such work has offered resistance to racism, colonialism, poverty, and discrimination in modern society.   *(cont. on page 163)*

Table 4.8

Literary Critics on the Work of Seven Major Older Broadside Press Poets

Broadside Press Author	Comments	Year	Critic
Gwendolyn Brooks	"Gwendolyn Brooks started out to write poetry of the ordinary young girl, wife, and mother, to whom her race was only incidental, sometimes annoying, sometimes the occasion for pride. As time has gone on and the conflict in America has deepened and become irreconcilable and the program of pacifist resistance and integration has failed, her poetry has become far more militant and sometimes freer in form. With her own race she is certainly the most popular poet writing today, and so has replaced Langston Hughes, as she has replaced Carl Sandburg as the Poet Laureate of the state of Illinois."	1973	Kenneth Rexroth
Gwendolyn Brooks	A major editor and critic observes of Beckonings that: "The aching loveliness of these poems is sometimes close to unbearable. Through the magic of Gwendolyn Brooks' words, we hold in our souls' eye a vivid image of our beauty, we glimpse what we might yet be. An incredible woman, this poet: she would urge us into our ultimate, our transcendent humanity, with her love."	1975	Hoyt W. Fuller
Sterling A. Brown	A major African-American critic notes that Sterling A. Brown created "a prolific output in a life that spans the era of Booker T. Washington and the era of Black Power [which] makes him not only the bridge between 19th– and 20th– century black literature, but also the last of the great 'race men,' the Afro-American men of letters, a tradition best epitomized by W. E. B. DuBois.... A self-styled 'Old Negro.' Sterling Brown is not only the Afro-American Poet Laureate, he is a great poet."	1992	Henry Louis Gates
Sterling A. Brown	A major historian suggests that Brown incorporates "in his poetry ... the most vital elements of the Afro-American experience and demonstrates how they functioned in history.	1976	Sterling Stuckey
Margaret Danner	"As a group, the African poems are superior to Danner's other poems, and they will undoubtedly form the basis for her future reputation.... As a contributor to Afro-American literature and especially to the Black Arts Movement, and as a poet who clearly understood the ties of African heritage, Danner will be remembered not only as a writer but as a guardian of culture."	1985	June M. Aldridge
Margaret Danner	One critic notes that Danner's poetry raises a central question for African Americans: "'How far is it from Beale Street to Benin City?' or to put it another way, 'what is the cultural distance between the black hands that molded a Senufo Firespitter mask and the black hands that painted the Jeff Donaldson Wall in Chicago?' So Margaret Danner's poetry is concerned with the artistic implications of the African continuum...."	1992	Richard K. Barksdale

Broadside Press Author	Comments	Year	Critic
James A. Emanuel	"For Emanuel thus far, there must an affirmation. A man must be and stand for what he is and has made of himself; he must define himself in terms of human sympathies, people, and affections; he must assert his belief in the solidarity of all men. He will ultimately want to give his own gift back to other individuals.… James Emanuel is a poet of people, as one says of others that they are 'poets of ideas.' … As the champion of a cause, he occupies an important position among the poets of the sixties and seventies. Emanuel is at the forefront among those who have brought about what Stephen Henderson calls/ the awareness that black sensibility itself may be a powerful political catalyst."	1979	Marvin Holdt
James A. Emanuel	"Emanuel has a light, sure touch that can evoke a wide range of responses, from the humorous to the macabre. He is especially attractive in his rapport and empathy with the young."	1969	From the back cover of Emanuel's *The Treehouse and Other Poems* (1968)
Lance Jeffers	An important younger poet of the Black Arts Movement notes that Jeffers "is a very important 'bridge' figure to many young poets who saw in his work a likeness to their own. Jeffers, in both his older and recent work, anticipated and conveyed more clearly than anyone else of his generation the raw river rage that was to flow like a lava river of fire from the great apocalyptic flowering of poetry burst upon the literary scene during the 1960s."	1977	Quincy Troupe
Lance Jeffers	"Anyone who has seen and heard him reading his poems knows that Lance Jeffers is not simply reading — Jeffers is living his poems, such is the intensity of feeling that he communicates.… Jeffers has a sense of continuity, of roots, of heritage.… Lance Jeffers makes his reader see and hear and smell and taste and feel. In other words, Jeffers forces his reader to experience the poem, not just read it. So, much of the magic of this poetry occurs because poet, poem, and reader become one."	1974	Theodore R. Hudson
Lance Jeffers	"His … volume *When I Know the Power of My Black Hand* … gives us the wide range of his concerns and further identifies his special marks as a poet. His central mark is the sheer passion of his lines and their commitment to a great variety of human issues, with the full pressure of historical black experience registered almost pervasively.… Jeffers has the passion and insight of a major poet.…"	1975	George Kent
Dudley Randall	Randall is given major credit as a "pioneer" by one critic, because of his work as the United States distributor for Paul Breman's Heritage Series (London): "to whom contemporary poetry owes a very deep debt."	1971–72	George Kent
Dudley Randall	One author describes that Randall's role during the Black Arts Movement as a publisher and editor of "many outstanding poets, among them … the venerable veterans Margaret Walker and Gwendolyn Brooks."	1977	Quincy Troupe

Literary Critics on the Work of Seven Major Older Broadside Press Poets (continued)

Broadside Press Author	Comments	Year	Critic
Margaret Walker	"She is a walking library of Harlem Renaissance and Post Renaissance knowledge. She has sponsored conferences of great magnitude and power, the Phyllis Wheatley Conference [1973] which was probably the greatest assemblage ever of Black female writers, the Conference on Afrika and Afrikan Affairs, the Plight of the Cities, and other conferences that has placed Jackson State University in the eye of academicians across the country and world."	1978	Ralph "Cheo" Thurman
Margaret Walker	Walker's poem "Harriet Tubman" is given special attention and "praise" by one critic "because she dramatizes for us the creative possibilities of a woman of slavery whose spirit was saturated with the ideal of freedom and who committed herself to that ideal, willingly suffering the consequences."	1975	James D. Tyms

The extent of Broadside's impact on their publishing careers is revealed in Table 4.9. In an era when most black authors could not expect to see their poetry books published widely among historically white American publishers, Broadside took on the challenge, and was very effective in keeping the public's awareness of the seven poets under discussion here.[94]

Their works highlighted a significant portion of the older generation's output during the Black Arts Movement. Furthermore, Broadside's promotion of the seven authors enhanced their careers by helping to generate a greater distribution of their poetic works, especially among black readers in the sixties and seventies; by heightening the critical recognition of their poetic voices (through book reviews and literary studies); and by aiding their financial situations, with the modest royalties which they received from Broadside. Yet, with a large range of new Broadside publications, the authors could also increase the roster of other possible money-making outlets available to them, such as public lectures and poetry readings throughout the United States. Thus, Broadside aided this older generation of writers by serving as a publishing outlet for their newer work, and by helping to keep their names and artistic contributions alive for the educational, psychological, and entertainment needs for the young and old during a period of rapid social change.

Dudley Randall and Broadside Press were key shapers in the careers of four leading, younger poets of the Black Arts Movement: Don L. Lee (Haki R. Madhubuti), Nikki Giovanni, Etheridge Knight, and Sonia Sanchez. Critic Gloria Wade-Gayles refers to the group as the "Broadside Quartet."[95] They were so named because this group best represented the ferment and provocative new voices in black poetry. Randall noted their importance, along with that of Lance Jeffers, in a 1973 article in which he stated that Broadside's earliest and greatest publishing success was achieved with the five poets listed above.[96] Randall took a special interest in promoting the four poets; they also received special assistance from Gwendolyn Brooks, Hoyt W. Fuller, George Kent, John Oliver Killens, Margaret Danner, Joe Goncalves, and Margaret Walker.[97]

The social backgrounds of the younger "Big Four" Broadside poets are listed in Table 3.3 (page 100). One factor immediately stands out: all four of the poets were born in the Deep South. At the height of the Black Arts Movement in 1970, their ages respectively were 27, 28, 39, and 36. Although their roots were in the South, like most other black writers, the Big Four were migrants to other states, where they were able to develop more fully as creative writers.[98] Giovanni (and her sister Gary) spent her childhood in Cincinnati, Ohio (from August 1943 to 1957), but Nikki completed her high school studies (1957–60), in Knoxville Tennessee, where she lived with her maternal grandparents.[99] Don L. Lee was raised during the fifties with his sister on the Lower East side of Detroit, Michigan. After the death of his mother from alcoholism, he went to live with an aunt, and completed his education at the Dunbar Vocational High School, in Chicago, Illinois.[100] Etheridge Knight grew up with four sisters and two brothers in Corinth, Mississippi, and Paducah, Kentucky, and by the late forties, in Indianapolis, Indiana. Knight only attended school through the eighth grade (to age fourteen), and often ran away from home, due to the physical abuse which he suffered from his father.[101] Sonia Sanchez's mother died when she was age one. She grew up with an older sister, Patricia, and a brother, Wilson, in Birmingham, Alabama, with her grandparents. In 1943, Sonia moved with her father, Wilson L. Driver and the rest of the family to Harlem, New York, where she attended George Washington High School.[102]

Table 4.9

Publications by Seven Major Older Poets at Broadside Press, 1965–1979

Author	Books	Tapes of Poetry	Broadsides	Poems in Anthologies
Gwendolyn Brooks	10	2	4	11
Sterling A. Brown	1	0	0	0
Margaret Danner	2	1	1	6
James A. Emanuel	2	3	1	7
Lance Jeffers	2	1	0	2
Dudley Randall	4	3	7	12
Margaret Walker	2	2	1	5

Knight and Lee both served in the U.S. Army. Knight, a medical technician, saw duty during the Korean War, with stops in Guam and Hawaii, and served from 1947 until his discharge in 1957. Lee saw active military duty between 1960 and 1963. Knight developed a serious drug abuse problem during his military tour.[103] In 1960, he committed a robbery in Indianapolis to support his drug habit, and was given an indeterminate sentence of ten to twenty-five years at Indiana State Prison.[104]

During the early to mid-sixties the "Big Four" began their development as serious poets. Nikki Giovanni worked with John Oliver Killens at his Fisk University writer's workshop, which he conducted at the institution from February 1965 to June 1968.[105] Don L. Lee worked as an apprentice curator with Margaret Burroughs, director of the DuSable Museum of African American History, in Chicago, from 1963 to 1967. Lee was also a founding member of Chicago's Organization of Black American Culture writers' workshop in 1967, where he also received the encouragement of Hoyt W. Fuller, the group's first advisor, and George Kent, its second advisor. He was also a member of Gwendolyn Brooks' writers' workshop in Chicago.[106] Etheridge Knight's poetic talents began during his eight years in prison. He wrote to Leaonead Pack Bailey that "I died in Korea from a shrapnel wound and narcotics resurrected me. I died in 1960 from a prison sentence and poetry brought me back to life."[107] While in prison, several national black poets took an interest in Knight's work, and corresponded with him, including Gwendolyn Brooks, Dudley Randall and Sonia Sanchez. Dudley Randall worked closely with Knight, and visited him at Indiana State Prison. According to writer Suzanne Dolezal, Randall met with Knight:

> In a small room reserved for consultations with death row inmates, with iron doors slamming and prisoners shouting in the background, Randall convinced a hesitant Knight of his talent.[108]

Knight's harsh background led Randall to believe that, "He may be a deeper poet than many of the others because he has felt more anguish."[109] Sonia Sanchez married Knight in 1969, after his parole from prison in 1968; however, the marriage was dissolved after one year.[110] Sanchez's early poetic training was received at Hunter College and at New York University in 1956, where she attended Louise Bogan's poetry workshop.

Table 4.10

Publications by Four Major Younger Poets at Broadside Press, 1965–1979

Author	Books	Tapes of Poetry	Broadsides	Poems in Anthologies
Nikki Giovanni	3	1	1	24
Etheridge Knight	2	1	3	15
Don L. Lee (Haki R. Madhubuti)	9	4	3	38
Sonia Sanchez	4	3	2	14

Encouraged by this experience, she organized a writers' workshop that met every Wednesday night in the village; there she met Amiri Baraka (LeRoi Jones) and Larry Neal, poets and critics who became architects of the Black Arts movement and began to read with them in jazz night spots. She also joined the New York CORE and the Reform Democrats Club. At this time she was married to Albert Sanchez, a first generation Puerto-Rican American. He did not understand her intense commitment to causes or her need to write. After four years of marriage and the birth of her first child, Sanchez found herself moving away from the narrowly defined bounds of that relationship.[111]

During the early sixties Sanchez was associated with a number of black writers in New York City.

The "Big Four" poets were extremely important to the operations of Broadside Press. Randall displayed a genius for recognizing this factor early in the company's history. He was also impressed with their unusual poetic talents. The fact that the "Broadside Quartet" were also among the best-selling authors of black poetry in the late sixties and early seventies was another high mark in their primary importance to Broadside. Randall had greatly aided all of their careers by serving either as the publisher of their first books of poetry (Knight and Sanchez), or as the national distributor for their first volumes (Lee and Giovanni). Broadside also published a large body of the group's work in other categories, such as tapes of poetry, broadsides, and poems in anthologies, and the company also published other books by the authors.

Table 4.10[112] indicates the total range of publications by the "Big Four" authors at Broadside for the period 1965–1979.[113] Don L. Lee was the number one best-selling author at Broadside Press. By the early seventies his Broadside books had sold over 100,000 copies in the United States.[114] Broadside's royalty payments at 10 percent of sales did not make any of the writers rich; however, the company could be depended upon to send out financial statements and checks on a regular basis to its authors.[115] Thus, with Randall's and Broadside's support, the "Big Four" authors were able to rapidly expand their writing careers — and their incomes from other sources — during the Black Arts Movement.

The national influence of the "Big Four" poets between the late sixties and 1979 is revealed in Table 4.11, which shows the range and work of the authors as publishers, editors and contributors to journals and magazines.[116] Their collective influence as writers is

Table 4.11

The "Big Four" Poets at Broadside Press as Publishers, Editors, and Magazine/Journal Contributors, 1965–1979

Poet	As Publisher	As Editor of Books	As Editor of Journals	As Contributor of Journals
Nikki Giovanni	Nik-Tom, Ltd. (1970)	*Night Comes Softly* (poetry anthology) (1970)	Managing editor, *Conversation* (1967); Editorial consultant, *Encore* (1972–1979); Editorial board of *Black Dialogue* (1969–1970),	*Encore* (1972–1979); Syndicated columnist for Anderson-Moberg Syndicates, Inc., New York ("One Woman's Voice")
Etheridge Knight	none	*Black Voices from Prison* (1970)	Co-editor, *Black Box*, Washington, DC (1971–1972); Poetry editor, *Motive*, Nashville, TN (1970–1971)	*Negro Digest/Black World*; *Journal of Black Poetry*, *First World*; Contributing editor *New Letters*, University of Mo., Kansas City (1974–1976)
Don L. Lee	Third World Press (1967–)	Black Pages Series	*Black Books Bulletin* (1972–)	*WATU: Journal of Black Art*, Cornell University (1968); *Negro Digest/Black World*; *Black Scholar*; *Color Lines*; *Griot*; *The Zora Neale Hurston Forum*; *Journal of Black Poetry*; *Black Collegian* (1983)
Sonia Sanchez	5X Publishing Co. (1971)	*Three Hundred and Sixty Degrees of Blackness Comin' at You* (1972)	Editorial advisor, *Drum: 1st New England Regional Black Poetry & Photography Anthology* (1975); Editor, *Bildian News* (1975–1977)	*Negro Digest/Black World*; *The Black Scholar*; *Journal of Black Poetry*; *Muhammad Speaks*; *Liberator*; *Black Dialogue*; *Journal of African Studies*; *Soulbook*

also reflected in the range of their poetic works which appeared in some of the major anthologies of the period. A random sample of twenty African-American anthologies published between 1968 and 1979 reveals the high regard which many editors and critics held for their poetry.[117] A total of 161 poems by the four poets appeared in the twenty anthologies, with forty-two by Giovanni, thirty-one by Knight, and forty-four each by Lee and Sanchez. The signature poems of the poets appeared five times each in the twenty anthologies. Giovanni's most anthologized poems for this period were "Nikki-Rosa" and "Knoxville, Tennessee." Knight's included "He Sees Through Stone" and "The Idea of Ancestry." Lee's was "But He Was Cool," and Sanchez's was "right on white america."[118]

Nikki Giovanni, Don L. Lee, Etheridge Knight, and Sonia Sanchez were also among the most famous lecturers and oral interpreters (readers) of their own poetry during the Black Arts Movement. Collectively, they spoke at hundreds of schools, churches, colleges and universities, community centers, conferences, and other events in the late sixties and the seventies. Such public appearances increased their fame and influence, and the demand for their books, tapes, and broadsides of poetry from Broadside Press.[119]

The "Broadside Quartet" were also well-known during the Black Arts Movement years as teachers in American colleges and universities, and in many community-based programs. Table 4.12 lists the major academic appointments which the four poets held during the sixties and seventies.[120] All four were able to survive financially because of the teaching opportunities which opened up to them, due to their fame as poets and creative artists, and because of the pressure generated by the Civil Rights Movement to force American institutions to open their doors more widely to African-American teachers. They were generally offered positions as poets-in-residence for one or two semesters at historically white or black colleges. Of the four poets, Sonia Sanchez and Don L. Lee developed consistent patterns of college and university teaching throughout the late sixties and the seventies. Nikki Giovanni and Etheridge Knight contributed between five and six years each, in the period 1968–73, to teaching at the college level. Giovanni, and Knight to a lesser extent, devoted more energies to public speaking during this period, including the college lecture circuit, than to teaching. Yet, all four poets were supporters of the efforts of students, some black intellectuals and the black community, and helped to foster the development of Black Studies programs and departments during the Black Arts Movement.[121] In fact, according to critic D.H. Melhem, Sonia Sanchez was a major force in 1967–69, while a teacher at San Francisco State University, in helping "to introduce the first Black studies program in the United States; it was chaired by Nathan Hare."[122] Sanchez also worked at the Department of Black Studies at the University of Pittsburgh; chaired the Black Studies Department at Amherst College, in Amherst, Massachusetts; and since 1977 has been affiliated with the Department of Afro-American Studies at Temple University, Philadelphia, Pennsylvania.[123] The "Big Four," like many poets elsewhere, were successful in turning to teaching as a major means of making their livelihoods during difficult economic days — and to use this base as a mechanism from which to continue their writing careers; while at the same time aiding the creation of new student literary talents, and in promoting a love for literature among people. Sonia Sanchez tells of the great rewards which teaching has brought her:

> I get a lot of joy out of teaching. I think it is important for those who have vision to be around students and make them see what this country is about and have them see their

Table 4.12

Teaching Posts of Broadside Press' "Big Four" Authors, 1965–1979

Name	Institution(s)	Location	Dates
Nikki Giovanni	Queens College (CUNY) (Asst. Prof. of Black Studies) Rutgers University	New York City, NY	1968–69
	Livingstone College Campus (Assoc. Prof. of English) *Note:* Giovanni lectured widely in schools and colleges during the seventies (one critic says, "in some years, as many as 200" times)	New Brunswick, NJ	1968–72
Etheridge Knight	Univ. of Pittsburgh (Poet-in-Residence)	Pittsburgh, PA	1968
	Univ. of Hartford (Poet-in-Residence)	West Hartford, CT	1970–71
	Lincoln University (Poet-in-Residence) *Note:* Knight was famous for conducting a series of the Free People's Poetry Workshop, in Memphis, TN; Indianapolis, IN; Minneapolis, MN; and Worcester, MA	Jefferson City, MO	1972–73
Don L. Lee (Haki R. Madhubuti)	Columbia College	Chicago, IL	1968
	Cornell University (Writer-in-Residence)	Ithaca, NY	1968–69
	Northeastern Illinois State College (Poet-in-Residence)	Chicago, IL	1969–70
	University of Illinois (Lecturer)	Chicago, IL	1969–71
	Howard University (Writer-in-Residence)	Washington, DC	1970–75
	Morgan State Univ. (Writer-in-Residence) *Note:* Lee lectured widely in many universities, colleges, community centers, and other forums in the U.S. and abroad during the decades of the sixties and seventies	Baltimore, MD	1972–73
Sonia Sanchez	San Francisco State College (Instructor of Black Studies)	San Francisco, CA	1966–68
	Univ. of Pittsburgh (Instructor of Black Studies)	Pittsburgh, PA	1968–69
	Rutgers University (Asst. Professor)	New Brunswick, NJ	1969–70
	Manhattan Community College	New York City, NY	1971–73
	City College of CUNY (Creative Writing)	New York City, NY	1972
	Amherst College (Assoc. Prof. & Head of Black Studies Dept.)	Amherst, MA	1973–75
	University of Pennsylvania	Philadelphia, PA	1976–77
	Temple University (Prof. of English/Women's Studies; holds the Laura Cornell Chair in English) *Note:* Sanchez is one of the most widely traveled black poets in America	Philadelphia, PA	1977 to present

relationship to their parents.... A teacher can give them a sense of reality, a sense of the future, of what can be, what they can be. It makes them take chances, bring new ideas and new possibilities into the curriculum.[124]

On the other hand, the four poets have also been effective outside of academic classrooms in speaking and teaching in programs at many different kinds of community-based organizations in the United States. Nikki Giovanni was a key member of the SNCC chapter at Fisk University in 1965–67; in 1967, she organized the Cincinnati, Ohio Black Arts Festival; in 1967–68, she worked at the People's Settlement House, Wilmington, Delaware; and between 1972 and 1978, she was a strong financial supporter for *Encore* magazine. Don L. Lee helped to established the Institute of Positive Education at Chicago in 1967, and has served as director of the group since that year. The Institute established an independent elementary school in 1972, called the New Concept Development Center. During the Black Arts Movement, Etheridge Knight hosted a series of the Free People's Poetry workshops in Memphis, Indianapolis, Minneapolis, and Worchester. Sonia Sanchez was supporter of the CORE chapter in New York City; she devoted three years of service to conducting a poetry workshop at the Countee Cullen Library in Harlem, New York, and another three years for a workshop at the Afro-American Historical and Cultural Museum in Philadelphia.[125] Thus, the four Broadside poets were major symbols and messengers of the Black Arts Movement and its program to raise the consciousness of black Americans, in the streets, on the playground, in the schools, and at home.

The critical response by professional literary critics, creative writers, and the general public on the poetry produced by Broadside's "Big Four" authors, for the period between 1967 and 1979, has been "liberal" in its praise and distractions. Few people are neutral (or can be found caught in the middle) on the poetic record of the four poets. The central theme which emerges or dominates a discussion of their work and influence is that collectively they were among the most brilliant and controversial black poets of their generation. A sample of twelve literary opinions written on the four poets was compiled for Table 4.13.[126] Two younger Broadside poets, Nikki Giovanni and Don L. Lee were dominant personalities of the era. In fact, Nikki Giovanni's influence was so great that she became widely known as "the princess of black poetry," a label first given her by Ida Lewis, the editor of *Encore*.[127] Certainly, if Giovanni deserved an honorary title as "the princess of black poetry," then Don L. Lee was the "prince of black poetry":

> Among all new poets, Madhubuti (Don L. Lee) is second only to Nikki Giovanni in the number of accolades and commercial attention he and his poetry have received. A sampling of critics, poets, and scholars who feel he is one of the greatest of the new poets would have to include Stephen Henderson, [Hoyt W.] Fuller, Gwendolyn Brooks, Margaret Walker, Paula Giddings, [Amiri] Baraka, Mari Evans, [Dudley] Randall, and [Addison] Gayle. Gwendolyn Brooks has said he physically resembles Jesus Christ, and her "Introduction" to *Jump Bad* hails him as "the most significant, inventive, and influential black poet in the country." Overlooking, for the moment, the prerequisite of reading "all" the poetry in the "country" before making such a statement, is paradoxical in view of the "collective" policy — and the anti-individualist positions — that allegedly form the cornerstone of the Chicago poetry scene.[128]

Lee's first biographer, Marlene Mosher, reveals in her study that

> by 1971 Lee had sold more books of poetry (some 250,000 copies) than probably all of the black poets who came before him combined.[129]

Such factors help to explain his wide public following during the Black Arts Movement. In essence, the work of Lee and Giovanni describes the human landscape of the sixties and seventies. Giovanni's body of work from the period best represents the black woman's

Table 4.13

Literary Critics on the "Big Four" at Broadside Press

Name of Poet	Comments	Year	Critic
Don L. Lee (Haki R. Madhubuti)	A major black critic observes that Lee is "more widely imitated than any other Black poet with the exception of Imamu Baraka (LeRoi Jones). His unique delivery has given him a popular appeal which is tantamount to stardom. His influence is enormous and is still growing."	Early 1970s	Stephen Henderson
	"I've not seen poetry in Don L. Lee. Anger, bombast, raw hatred, strident, aggrieved, perhaps charismatically crude religious and political canting, propaganda and racist nonsense, yes; and utterly unoriginal in form and style; humorless; cruel laughter bordering on the insane."	1973	Jascha Kessler
	In commenting on Lee's "We Walk the Way of the New World" (1970), a black woman critic writes that his poems focus on "Black men/warriors.../and/draw not only from our unique amerikkkan horror but also from the lush beauty of Mother Africa for inspiration. The Black men/warrior poems are generally sad in tone and seem to wonder if the list of martyrs will ever end.... Don's poems tend to be ... hard-hitting ... [and the] lines rumble like a street gang on the page.... The faults that I find with /his/work are few, but mainly this — I was looking for a level of development in Brother Don's book that I don't seem to see. His third book, Don't Cry, Scream!, was a big jump over Black Pride, his second book, whereas the fourth book's improvement wasn't that great. 'On Seeing Diana (Ross) Go Maddddd,' for example, would've been hip in one of his previous books, but doesn't fit in his latest one now that we've gotten away from the 'dozens' in print."	1971	Liz Gant
Nikki Giovanni	Randall could be critical of some of his major poets; for example, on Nikki Giovanni: "Nikki writes rapidly, and sometimes carelessly. If you point out bad spelling and grammar to her, she'll say defensively, 'Let it stay.' Once she wrote a poem titled 'To Dudley Randle,' and I didn't let that stay. On the other hand, she can write with originality and freshness. She wrote a poem about her first visit to Africa where she looked down from the plane and saw her grandmother sitting in a rocking chair with a lion cub by her side. What other poet would have written of her return to the Motherland like that?"	1975	Dudley Randall
	"The most famous woman poet is Nikki Giovanni, a profound thinker and provocative speaker, whose skills and insights do not always extend into her poetry.... Denounced as an 'individualist' by Madhubuti (Lee) and praised by Margaret Walker and Addison Gayle, Nikki Giovanni has rejected the label 'revolutionary.' ...Much of what Nikki Giovanni was saying in the sixties moved black youth — it was not always safe or chic to disagree even if you wanted to — and some of it was admirable. But these things do not make her work defensible as poetry.... Her poetry lacks lyricism and imagery, and her forced themes show her as a vicarious revolutionary. 'Nikki-Rosa,' her most often quoted poem from the early period, is an exception to the rule. It has a believable, conversation-like language (characteristic of her poetry), and its details honestly tap the inner reaches of the collective black experience, as she unfolds the story of family fun and misfortune.... Nikki Giovanni's importance ... [is] in her personal influence ... which has inspired many young black women to write about themselves and their world."	1976	Eugene Redmond

Name of Poet	Comments	Year	Critic
Nikki Giovanni	The critic deeply dislikes Giovanni's third book, *Re: Creation*, and raises the question: what had happened to the poet? What process had taken place, she wonders (since her first two books), which had led Giovanni to "be transformed (re: created) into an almost declawed, tamed panther with bad teeth"?	1971	Ruth Rambo McClain
Etheridge Knight	Gwendolyn Brooks wrote the Preface to Knight's first poetry collection, *Poems from Prison* (1968): "Vital. Vital. This poetry is a major announcement. It is certainly male — with formidable austerities, dry grins, and a dignity that is scrupulous even when lenient. But there are centers of controlled softness too. The warmth of this poet is abruptly robust. The music that seems effortless is exquisitely carved. Since Etheridge Knight is not your stifled artiste, there is an air in these poems. And there is a blackness, inclusive, possessed and given; freed and terrible and beautiful."	1968	Gwendolyn Brooks
	A Major European editor of Afro-American literature wrote: "Without a doubt the strongest of the new black poets who published "under Dudley Randall's Broadside imprint" was Etheridge Knight. This poet produced "an astonishing first book in which another silent minority suddenly found its voice."	1973	Paul Breman
	Another critic wrote that Knight's first book, *Poems from Prison*, "was a sensitive, anguished, imprisoned poet who could enlarge the range of black poetry."	1975	Jerry W. Ward, Jr.
Sonia Sanchez	Sonia Sanchez's "life-style is perpetually proposed as a link to the ideals and realisation of blackness which so profoundly pervades her work. She has said: 'I think the prime thing with art, of being a writer, be it playwright, a poet, or even a musician, etc., is to really show people what is happening in this country. And then show them they can change it ….' Her work, to a large extent, is centered on five principal levels of concern: (a) the white-woman–black man relationship; (b) Black man–woman relationship; (c) dope, as a reflection of one level of death; (d) politics and (e) loneliness and suicide, the introspection of self, the flight inwards, away from a world that is ever-meanacing and cruel."	1971	Sebastian Clarke
	"Sanchez is one of the few creative artists who have significantly influenced the course of black American literature and culture."	1985	Kalamu ya Salaam
	The writer views Sanchez as a serious artist, among "those who are revolutionaries, [who] want to make this a better world…. This tiny woman with the infant's face attacks the demons of this world with the fury of a sparrow defending his fledglings in the nest … Sanchez is black, and it's a blackness that can't be bought."	1970	Dudley Randall

commitment to black people, and is expressed in the poet's ability to effectively "deal with the South," as she has noted, "because I love it."[130] Yet at the same time, she captures the northern or urban perspective from a black feminist viewpoint. Conversely, Don L. Lee best denotes the black male's commitment to his people from this period. However, Lee's song has at its central core an explicitly urban, northern experience. This is most profoundly expressed in Lee's conclusion to his "Introduction" in *Think Black*:

> America calling,
> negroes.
> can you dance?
> play foot/baseball?
> nanny?
> cook?
> needed now. negroes
> who can entertain
> ONLY.
> others not
> wanted.
> (& are considered extremely dangerous.)[131]

The last two poets in the "Broadside Quartet," Etheridge Knight and Sonia Sanchez are also forerunners of the Black Arts Movement. Perhaps no poet of the period best captures the prison experience for black people as does Etheridge Knight. Poet and critic Eugene Redmond observes:

> Knight roams the deep crevices of the black spiritual and psychic worlds as he combines the language of the prison subculture with the rhythms of black American street speech. He bounces or drives hard — a poetry of "hard bop" — looking at prison life, love and ancestry.[132]

Few poets of the period can equal Sonia Sanchez's poetic achievements in penetrating the unjust nature of American society, and in fostering a political message of black consciousness.

Some of the best known poems by Giovanni, Lee, Knight, and Sanchez from this period follow. Read collectively, they express the anger, frustrations, memories, search for identity, liberation, self-examination, and future hopes of the African-American peoples during the years of the Black Arts Movement.[133] (For Nikki Giovanni's "Nikki-Rosa," and Don L. Lee's "But He Was Cool," see Chapter 2.)

KNOXVILLE, TENNESSEE

> I always like summer
> best
> you can eat fresh corn
> from daddy's garden
> and okra
> and greens
> and cabbage
> and lots of
> barbecue
> and buttermilk

and homemade ice-cream
at the church picnic
and listen to
gospel music
outside
at the church
homecoming
and go to the mountains with
your grandmother
and go barefooted
and be warm
all the time
not only when you go to bed
and sleep
— Nikki Giovanni

THE FUNERAL OF MARTIN LUTHER KING, JR.

His headstone said
FREE AT LAST, FREE AT LAST
But death is a slave's freedom
We seek the freedom of free men
And the construction of a world
Where Martin Luther King could have lived
and preached non-violence
— Nikki Giovanni

RE-ACT FOR ACTION
(for brother H. Rap Brown)

re-act to animals:
                cage them in zoos.
re-act to inhumanism:
                make them human.
re-act to nigger toms:
                with spiritual acts of love &
                forgiveness or with real acts of
                force
re-act to yr/self:
                or are u too busy tryen to be cool
                like tony curtis & twiggy?
re-act to whi-te actors:
                understand their actions;
                faggot actions & actions against
                yr/dreams
re-act to yr/brothers & sisters:
                love.
re-act to whi-te actions:
                with real acts of blk/action.
                BAM BAM BAM
re-act to act against actors
who act out pig-actions against
your acts & actions that keep
you re-acting against their act & actions
stop.

act in a way that will cause them
to act the way you want them to act
in accordance with yr/acts & actions:
                              human acts for human beings

re-act
NOW niggers
& you won't have to
act
false-actions
at
your/children's graves.

                              — Don L. Lee (Haki R. Madhubuti)

THE IDEA OF ANCESTRY

Taped to the wall of my cell are 47 pictures: 47 black
faces: my father, mother, grandmothers (1 dead), grandfathers (both dead), brothers, sisters, uncles, aunts,
cousins (1st & 2nd), nieces, and nephews. They stare
across the space at me sprawling on my bunk. I know
their dark eyes, they know mine. I know their style,
they know mine. I am all of them, they are all of me;
they are farmers, I am a thief, I am me, they are thee.

I have at one time or another been in love with my mother,
1 grandmother, 2 sisters, 2 aunts (1 went to the asylum),
and 5 cousins. I am now in love with a 7 yr old niece
(she sends me letters written in large block print, and
her picture is the only one that smiles at me).

I have the same mane as 1 grandfather, 3 cousins, 3 nephews,
and 1 uncle. The uncle disappeared when he was 15, just took
off and caught a freight (they say). He's discussed each year
when the family has a reunion, he causes uneasiness in
the clan, he is an empty space. My father's mother, who is 93
and who keeps the Family Bible with everybody's birth dates
(and death dates) in it, always mentions him. There is no
place in her Bible for "whereabouts unknown."

Each fall the graves of my grandfathers call me, the brown
hills and red gullies of mississippi send out their electric
messages, galvanizing my genes. Last yr / like salmon quitting
the cold ocean-leaping and bucking up his birthstream / I
hitchhiked my way from L.A. with 16 caps in my pocket and a
monkey on my back. And I almost kicked it with the kinfolks.
I walked barefooted in my grandmother's backyard / I smelled the
    old
land and the woods / I sipped cornwhiskey from fruit jars with the
    men/
I flirted with the women / I had a ball till the caps ran out
and my habit came down. That night I looked at my grandmother
and split / my guts were screaming for junk / but I was almost
contented / I had almost caught up with me.
(The next day in Memphis I cracked a croaker's crib for a fix).

This yr there is a gray stone wall damming my stream, and when
the falling leaves stir my genes, I pace my cell or flop on my bunk

and stare at 47 black faces across the space. I am all of them,
they are all of me, I am me, they are thee, and I have no children
to float in the space between.

— Etheridge Knight

FOR BLACK POETS
WHO THINK OF SUICIDE

Black Poets should live — not leap
From steel bridges (like the white boys do).
Black Poets should live — not lay
Their necks on railroad tracks (like the white boys do).
Black Poets should seek — but not search too much
In sweet dark caves, nor hunt for snipe
Down psychic trails (like the white boys do).

For Black Poets belong to Black People. Are
The Flutes of Black Lovers. Are
The Organs of Black Sorrows. Are
The Trumpets of Black Warriors.
Let All Black Poets die as Trumpets,
And be buried in the dust of marching feet.

-Etheridge Knight

RIGHT ON: WITE AMERICA

1.
it is quite
evident by now
that kennedys
are kill
                able
easily
assasinated
cuz after all
the money and
polish is washed
away in blood
what u got
left cept
poor dirty /
            irish /
                        american
(and we know what that
            means in wite america)
    right on: wite america
2.
white america is saying
stand up & be counted
as a conservative
                or die wite/
liberal if u think u
can be our great/
                wite / president.

and chickens do
come home to roost
cuz
          a / mer / ica /
is now killing her own
after all the
          terrible / blk / deaths
of our
          terrible / blk / yrs.
right on: wite america
          3.
this country might have
been a pio
          neer land
once.
          but.   there ain't
no mo
          indians   blowing
custer's mind
          with a different
image of america.
                    this country
might have
          needed shoot /
outs / daily /
          once.
                    but there ain't
no mo real / wite / all american
                    bad/guys.
just.
     u & me.
                    blk/and un/armed.
this country might have
been a pion
          eer land.   once.
          and it still is.
check out
     the falling
gun shells   on our
          blk/tomorrows.
right on: wite america
          4.
(for: gun/collection/wk/decreed
          by Mayor Alioto
HEAR YE!   HEAR YE!
starting july 4th is
bring in yr/guns/down/to/
yr/nearest/po/lice/station
no questions/asked
                    wk.
and yr/po/lice/dept/
will welcome
all yr/
illegal/guns.   (and they
     won't say a thing)
          cept maybe

                    at the next re/bel/lion
                    maybe just
                              the small sound
                    of murder:
                              yr/own...
                              — Sonia Sanchez

Broadside Press helped to bring these poetic voices before the bar of public opinion to expand the markets for their broadsides, tapes, and books of poetry and to advance their general careers as writers with advice and encouragement from Dudley Randall, Melba Boyd, and other staff members. The case of Broadside's support of Etheridge Knight offers a special insight into the influence and impact of Randall and the company's cultural work during the Black Arts Movement. After his release from Indiana State Prison in 1968, Broadside was instrumental (along with Gwendolyn Brooks) in helping Knight to advance his career as a professional writer. Dudley Randall had been a major influence on the poet during his last years in prison, and of course, Broadside published Knight's first collection of verse, *Poems from Prison*, which became one of the most famous poetry volumes of the Black Arts Movement. In 1967, Randall had written to Knight that "Your book is great! I'll have to beg, borrow, or steal the money to publish it!"[134] Broadside was also effective in its public relations program to bring more attention to Knight's work. This included increasing the sales of *Poems from Prison*, bringing Knight's work to the attention of important critics, writers and editors, and helping to secure speaking engagements for the poet at cultural events, and in schools, colleges, and universities.[135] However, Broadside also made a major financial investment in Knight by advancing him a large number of cash credits, and copies of his Broadside books, against his future royalty credits with the company.

Randall's initial business dealings with Knight were modest. While negotiating a book deal with Knight for *Poems from Prison*, Randall wrote to him in 1967:

> First let's talk terms. I'm not a big publisher. I started by publishing broadsides. Even now I can't publish full-size books. What I planned was 16-page paper-back pamphlets, but found poets keep on sending me good poems.
> [Randall then suggested a first edition to Knight of "500" copies], and see how it goes. [The publisher then went on to say]: If it sells out, we can reprint it. It should be priced so the brothers can afford it — $1.00. You'll get royalties of 10% of the list price; I'm afraid you won't get rich. Copyright will be in your name. All reprint rights will be yours. Will you give me permission to send some of these poems to magazines, to make your name better known and to publicize the forthcoming book?
> [Randall next offered a title for the book]: *Poems from Prison*. [He closed the letter with this line]: There are some changes in grammar and spelling I'd like you to consider. Will write you later.[136]

In his January 1968 contract with Knight, Randall increased the first printing of *Poems from Prison* to 1,000 copies. Knight's royalties from the publisher still stood at 10 percent of the list price of all books sold; and he was also guaranteed 50 percent from all fees received by Broadside for reprint rights, given ten free copies of the book, and allowed to purchase *Poems from Prison* at a special author's discount rate of 40 percent.[137]

Yet, as critic Myles Raymond Hurd points out, "Dudley Randall and other critics and friends [were] quite willing to give" Etheridge Knight "their imprimaturs and monetary blessings."[138] For the poet faced a difficult financial struggle throughout the late sixties and the seventies. Behind Knight's problems lay his prison record, and the fact that he remained addicted to such drugs as heroin.[139] These facts, notwithstanding, Randall remained by his side as a friend and publisher throughout the late sixties and the seventies. He had extended small sums of cash to aid Knight while he was in prison. For example, Randall sent Knight $10 for spending money at Christmastime in December 1967.[140] Beginning in 1968 and continuing to 1976, Randall extended a considerable amount of credit (cash loans) to Knight.

Between 1968 and 1976, Broadside had total sales of $4,766 (at $1 a copy) for *Poems from Prison*.[141] Knight's royalties at 10 percent of total sales came to $476.60 for this period.[142] Knight also made a tape cassette of *Poems from Prison*, which sold for $5.00 a copy. Over eight years, Broadside sold 60 copies of the tape, and Knight also received $30.00 in royalties from these sales. Thus, his total royalties received from Broadside for *Poems from Prison* came to $506.60.

Five years after the publication of *Poems from Prison*, Randall published Knight's book, *Belly Song and Other Poems*, in 1973. He wrote to Knight that: "I've invested a lot in your book, which I consider a fine one: 5,000 copies, including 500 simultaneous hard covers...."[143] *Belly Song* sold very well, and between 1973 and 1976, Broadside had total paperback sales of 2,173, priced at $1.75 each; and 368 cloth volumes at $4.95 each. Knight's royalties for *Belly Song* on a total sale of 2,541 copies was $552.41—$370.26 for the paperback edition and $182.15 for the cloth volume.[144] His total income from book royalties on *Poems from Prison* and *Belly Song* to 1976 was $1,059.01.

But across the years Randall had been very indulgent with Knight's inability to repay Broadside for cash advances given to him against his future royalties, or in his failure to promptly pay the company within thirty days after he had received a shipment of his books to sell to the public during his poetry readings. An examination of Knight's financial statements with Broadside, between March 1970 and May 1974, reveals that on at least ten occasions, he received cash advances, or copies of his books against his future royalties from Broadside, totaling $1,051.54. After a reduction of his royalties during this period, he still owed Broadside $636.14 on May 14, 1974.[145] This was a considerable sum for a struggling black publishing company in America. Finally in July 1974, Randall wrote to Knight:

> I'm sorry that this one time I can't send you a hundred dollars. Our last year's income tax was audited and we owe $4,000 + on it. Besides that, royalties are due. We need every cent we can get and did appreciate your paying on your debt to me. I know you can't pay it all at once, but since you have a steady income you could pay it in small sums—$100 or even $50 at a time. You'd be surprised how fast steady payments will reduce your debt.[146]

Nevertheless the matter did not end there. By October 1974, Knight was deeper in debt to Broadside. Randall informed Knight at this date that:

> You owe us $860.65 and I don't think that I'd help you by letting you get deeper into debt. Sometimes one actually hurts a person by sinking him deeper into debt. I wish my printer had told me long ago, "Randall, no more books till you pay what I owe you." Then I would have limited my publishing and economized, and been in better financial shape. It doesn't help either you or me if you give away the books. I'm not paid for them, yet I have to pay royalties on them, and because they are gone, I have to order more printed and get into debt for the replacements. Pay a substantial sum on the $860, or buy a few for cash. That'll be better for both of us.[147]

Yet, the poet continued to depend on the benevolence of Broadside, even after Randall had sold the company to Broadside/Crummell Press. Aneb Kgositsile (Gloria House), who served as the new editor at Broadside/Crummell, wrote to Knight in 1978 that she was:

> enclosing a check for $100—[an] advance, as you requested. The royalties period we will be starting from is July–Dec. 1977, the time from which Crummell Center has been doing the work.[148]

Meanwhile, from his retirement base at 12651 Old Mill Place in Detroit, Randall, in spite of his own personal setbacks, continued his good efforts to aid Knight. He wrote to the poet in March 1978:

> Dear Etheridge,
>
> Could you call me collect about reading in my place in Minneapolis March 19, or April 19? It'll be reading one night, having an open discussion next morning, and a writers' workshop. Pay is $500 plus expenses.
> I don't think I can do it. I don't think my poems are good enough to read, and I don't know how to run a workshop, & I have nothing to discuss.
> I received the letter from your workshop. Give them all my deepest thanks.
>
> Dudley Randall
>
> P.S. Answer pronto, so I can arrange for you to replace me.[149]

Although this was not a cheerful period for Dudley Randall, he continued to have faith in the work and career of Etheridge Knight. Indeed, throughout the late sixties and the seventies, Randall had stood by Knight through thick and thin. The measurement of his support stands as one of the principal reasons why Etheridge Knight was able to emerge as a significant American poet during the Black Arts Movement.[150]

By 1979, Dudley Randall could look back on an eventful decade of work and struggle in the endeavor to build Broadside Press. The success of his efforts were demonstrated when *Black Enterprise* magazine in 1978 called him "The father of the black poetry movement."[151] Randall was present at the start of "a major age of Black creative writing," and he had been the single most important publisher of black poetry during the sixties and the seventies.[152] As Hoyt W. Fuller observed in *Black World* at the beginning of the seventies, Randall was a key visionary of the era:

> The new Black Literary Movement was sparked by writers who realized that they had nothing to gain by kowtowing to the White Literary Establishment, that, in fact, they risked loss of integrity by submitting to the strictures and the judgment of white critics and editors.... Broadside Press had become one of the most important publishing ventures in the history of Black Literature, and Dudley Randall did it all out of the basement of his home in Detroit.... The whole Movement grew out of the soil of the Black Community, and it is to the Black Community alone that the artists owe their allegiance.[153]

Thus, Randall had effectively served his own community (and the nation), as a publisher, teacher, and poet. He was also among the group of professional librarians during the Black Arts Movement who had labored "as perpetrators of [social] change" to broaden the roles and diversity of American libraries in this country. Indeed, Randall was a spearhead among black intellectuals for the "effort to present the real history of Black America," through the arts, social sciences, and the sciences.[154] Through Randall's influence many African-American women writers were published and promoted, including Gwendolyn Brooks, Margaret Walker, Alice Walker, Audre Lorde, and Sonia Sanchez, among others.[155]

In essence, Randall promoted a large range of older and newer black men and women poets during the Black Arts Movement. Such an approach helped to deepen the published works available on the diversity of the black experience in America, as lived and interpreted by both black men and women poets. As two critics of the period wrote in *Afro-American Writing: An Anthology*, this was especially needed, as the published books by black women writers helps to add "a more complete image of the black woman in literature and a view of the world through her perceptions."[156] At the decade's end, Broadside Press could proudly count among its publications major books written by Sonia Sanchez, Dudley Randall, Lance Jeffers, Gwendolyn Brooks, and Clarence Major, among many others, who offered a black perspective on the human condition to the world.[157] This was the greatest accomplishment of Dudley Randall and Broadside Press between the decades of the sixties and the seventies.

Chapter 5
Revival and Rebirth, 1980–1995

Dudley Randall's long period of depression and "silence" between the years of 1975 and 1980 came to a conclusion when he wrote his first new poem in five years, "The Mini Skirt," on April 4, 1980. A second poem soon followed, entitled "To an Old Man."[1] Returning to poetry helped Randall revive his entire literary life; Alvin Aubert, editor of Detroit's *Obsidian: Black Literature in Review*, which published two new poems by Dudley, observed in mid–1980 that the poet wanted "the world to know that he is out of retirement, teaching, writing and reading his poetry as vigorously as ever."[2] Indeed, the end of the seventies had been a difficult period for Randall, but now, in 1980, he could look forward to another productive period in his long literary career.

Randall and his wife Vivian, continued to make their home at 12651 Old Mill Place, Detroit. Dudley's daughter from his first marriage, Phyllis Ada (Mrs. William Sherron, III), a nurse, also continued to reside in Detroit with her family, which included Dudley's two grandchildren, Venita and William Sherron.[3] During this period Randall's political interests were expressed as an independent, and his religious affiliation was with the Congregational Church.[4]

The eighties were a busy decade for Randall. A major portion of his time was devoted to organizing and promoting the Broadside Poets Theater, which was created by the poet in August 1980. This group served as an outlet in Detroit for monthly poetry readings by old and new local, regional, and national black poets. Like Broadside Press, it was located at the Alexander Crummell Memorial Center, a church in Highland Park, Michigan.

Randall wrote to Etheridge Knight in the summer of 1980:

> Broadside Press is trying to make a comeback. Our Poets Theater is exciting. My rationale is that if a supreme poet like Shakespeare could use theatrical hoopla to make his poems more exciting, like gorgeous costumes, songs, music, dancing, masques, and stage props, we lesser poets could also use the same devices to make our poems exciting. I was thrilled to hear my poems sung. The music expanded and intensified the emotion.[5]

Poet and critic D. H. Melhem notes that during this period, Randall was successful in "drawing black poets from across the country" and this new venture became "his chief commitment to the arts." In fact, poets such as Nikki Giovanni, Gwendolyn Brooks, Etheridge Knight, Audre Lorde, and local writers were active participants in the Broadside Poets Series.[6] In 1984, Leonard Kniffel, a librarian at the Detroit Public Library, described Randall's busy schedule, which included:

The Broadside Press publishing program, coaching young writers at Broadside Poets Theater; coordinating a major reading series, where Broadside poets like [Gwendolyn] Brooks
and [Nikki] Giovanni still perform; attending programs at the Poetry Resource Center,
where he serves on the board; and conducting the annual Poet Laureate Youth Awards
at the Michigan Poetry Festival.... And then there are the countless literary panels and
the University of Detroit's annual poetry awards. The man they are named after does
the judging.[7]

Randall also worked as a U.S. government census worker in 1980.[8]

Randall continued to make literary contributions during the eighties with public readings of his work. His agent for bookings in the early eighties was the Contemporary Forum
of Chicago, Illinois — a company which also handled engagements for such Windy City
poets as Gwendolyn Brooks and Carolyn Rodgers.[9] In fact, Randall's travels as a reading
poet extended from the sixties to the eighties. Among the major highlights of his public
readings over this thirty-year period were visits to the U.S. Library of Congress, Art Camp
(near Moscow, Russia), and many universities and colleges, libraries, and high schools.[10]
Such contributions allowed Randall to take his creative works to the public, and to be a
role model and sage to younger people. The poet noted in 1986 that

> every generation has to learn. It's an inspiration to see what's been done by black peo-
> ple; young people will be able to feel they're able to do the same or bigger, better, greater
> things.[11]

Randall's own life and work served as an example of black creativity to his community.

Recognition for his literary contributions continued to come to Dudley Randall during the eighties. He received three major writing fellowships during the decade, including
a creative artist award in literature from the Michigan Council for the Arts in 1981, a
National Endowment for the Arts fellowship, also in 1981, and a senior fellowship, in 1986.[12]
Such funds helped Randall supplement his retirement income and work and devote part
of his time to future writing projects. One of Randall's greatest honors was awarded on
November 5, 1981, when Mayor Coleman A. Young appointed him as the first Poet Laureate of Detroit. Randall told Howard Blum of the *New York Times* that this recognition
was the capstone of his long career and represented his "real life's work."[13]

Randall was honored along with Sterling A. Brown, at a dinner in the McGregor Memorial Center of Wayne State University, hosted by Mayor Young, and four Wayne State University cooperating sponsors: the Phylon Society, *Obsidian: Black Literature in Review* (Alvin
Aubert, editor), the Institute for the Study of Leisure in the Future, and the Division of Community Relations.[14] Randall also received a check for $500 from the City of Detroit and an
admonition from Mayor Young that Randall's official duties were "to keep on doing what
you're doing."[15] Randall informed journalist Howard Blum that his duties as poet laureate
required him "to go around the city and write about what I think or feel. Part of a poet's
work," he said, "is to look at people. And it's the people in this town that make it such a
poetic place, more than New York, London, even Paris."[16] Randall also felt a special responsibility to nurture younger poetic talents. Dudley recommended that younger writers

> read a lot more. Learn about the old writers as well as the new ones. Keep your mouth
> shut and your eyes and ears open. The best writing is done by people who can put them-
> selves in the other person's place.[17]

In recognition of his continuing services to the city, the Detroit City Council on January 18, 1984, presented a testimonial resolution in Randall's honor. The *Detroit News* noted that "Council President Erma Henderson, who made the presentation ... hailed Randall for his many literary contributions to the city."[18] The city of Detroit claimed in the early eighties that it held the honor of being the only major city in the United States which had an official poet laureate.[19] This gave Dudley Randall a singular honor.

The eighties were a very productive period in the publication of works by Dudley Randall. No doubt, the poet was aided by the fact that at age 66 in 1980, he was now a national treasure among living black poets in the United States. As Herbert Scott, a white poet and professor at Western Michigan University, noted during this period, "In Detroit lives the man who must be considered the dean of Michigan poets: Dudley Randall — a great man, a beautiful poet, a pioneer editor and publisher, the founder of Broadside Press."[20]

Randall's prominent position in American letters is again illustrated by the total range of his publications produced during this decade. He was the author of a new collection of poetry, *A Litany of Friends: New and Selected Poems* in 1981. His 1973 collection of poems, *After the Killing*, went into a first edition, second printing in 1983. Randall was also the editor of two important books during the eighties: *Homage to Hoyt Fuller* in 1984, and *Golden Song: The Fiftieth Anniversary Anthology of the Poetry Society of Michigan, 1935–1985*, with Louis J. Cantoni in 1985. During the eighties, Randall's poems appeared at least forty-one times in seven anthologies, ten journals, programs, newspapers, and broadsides, and were quoted in six scholarly works. His essays, short stories, and interviews were also familiar to American readers during the decade.[21]

When Randall's new book *A Litany of Friends: New and Selected Poems* was published by Lotus Press on November 21, 1981, the public reception was "generally complimentary."[22] Poet Frank Marshall Davis declared that the book's high mark "demonstrate[d] Randall's technical skill."[23] According to critic D. M. Melhem, two major categories emerge in Randall's work of the eighties, "humanist concerns (in sections titled 'Friends,' 'War,' 'Afraica,' and 'Me') and love poetry (in 'Eros,' which, followed in number by 'Friends,' contains the bulk of the new poetry."[24] Indeed, even the front cover of the new book said it all. Drawings by illustrator Scott Holingue captured Randall at his typewriter and the faces of six major Broadside Press poets: Haki R. Madhubuti, Gwendolyn Brooks, Etheridge Knight, Sonia Sanchez, Sterling A. Brown, and Margaret Walker. These were among Randall's closest "litany of friends" who had helped to shape Broadside Press and modern black literature, and encourage the poet during one of the major crisis periods of his life in the late seventies. Randall ended *A Litany of Friends* with "A Poet Is Not a Jukebox":

> A poet is not a jukebox.
> A poet is not a jukebox.
> I repeat, a poet is not a
> > jukebox for someone to shove a quarter in
> > his ear and get the tune they want to hear,
> > or to pat on the head and call "a good little Revolutionary,"
> or to give a Kuumba Liberation Award.
> A poet is not a jukebox.
> A poet is not a jukebox.
> A poet is not a jukebox.
>
> So don't tell me what to write.[25]

This poem is symbolic of Randall's mood after his years of struggle to emerge as a poet, and as he sought to regain his health after the economic crisis of the previous decade. The poem also denotes Randall's commitment not only to his community, but to the individual worth and humanity in the post-industrial urbanized world of the late twentieth century.

In essence, Dudley Randall now viewed his own efforts as a creative artist to be one who "Writes poetry of the Negro. Formal, reflective, with occasional humor."[26] The poet's new mood was also effectively consummated in his poem "The Rite."

> "Now you must die," the young one said,
> "and all your art be overthrown."
> The old one only bowed his head
> as if those words had been his own.
> And with no pity in his eyes
> The young man acted out his part
> and put him to the sacrifice
> and drank his blood and ate his heart.[27]

Randall appeared to be antagonistic toward the new conservative era in which he lived, but hopeful about the future at the same time.

Nonetheless, the eighties were also a stressful and trying period for Dudley Randall as a number of his colleagues, close friends, and major Broadside Press poets died. This list included Robert Hayden (1913–80), Hoyt W. Fuller (1928–81), Owen Dodson (1914–83), George Kent (1920–82), Lance Jeffers (1919–85), James Baldwin (1924–87), Margaret Danner (1915–88), Sterling A. Brown (1901–89), and Nicholas Guillen (1902–89).[28] To honor the memory, contributions, and work of Hoyt W. Fuller, Randall organized the effort to collect and publish some of the best work printed in *Negro Digest* and *Black World* under Fuller's editorship in the sixties and seventies. The book was entitled *Homage to Hoyt Fuller*, and was edited by Randall and published by Broadside Press in 1984. Thirty-one men and sixteen women writers are represented in this important anthology.[29] Twenty-two (or 46 percent) of the forty-seven writers in the anthology were affiliated with Broadside Press (that is, had been previously published by the company). The fourteen black male Broadside writers in *Homage to Hoyt Fuller* were Alvin Aubert, Amiri Baraka, Arna Bontemps, Sterling A. Brown, James Cunningham, Addison Gayle, Jr., Robert Hayden, Lance Jeffers, Etheridge Knight, Haki R. Madhubuti, Sterling D. Plumpp, Dudley Randall, Charles H. Rowell, and Marvin X. The eight black women Broadside authors were Johari Amini, Gwendolyn Brooks, Gloria Davis, Nikki Giovanni, Naomi Long Madgett, Carolyn Rogers, Margaret Walker, and Margaret Burroughs. Although containing the work of numerous brilliant poets, the book's chief significance lay in the early genius of Hoyt W. Fuller in being able to secure the work of a wide range of African-American writers for *Negro Digest* and *Black World* during the years of the Civil Rights Movement in America. Besides the many talented Broadside Press authors, Fuller was able to gain contributions for *Negro Digest* and *Black World* from such figures as Toni Morrison, Mari Evans, Carolyn F. Gerald, Paula Giddings, Robert L. Harris, Jr., Stephen E. Henderson, Langston Hughes, Ishmael Reed, George E. Kent, Woodie King, Jr., Julian Mayfield, Sun Ra, Dawvin T. Turner, Mary Helen Washington, and John A. Williams. Beaufort Cranford, a reporter for the *Detroit News*, described *Homage to Hoyt Fuller* in 1984 as follows:

not just any old collection, this one gathers Randall's selection of the best writing from the pages of now defunct *Black World* magazine into its 354 pages....

Black World magazine, born as *Negro Digest*, ceased publication in 1976. For the past 15 years, Hoyt Fuller was editor, and under him the periodical developed from a reprint magazine into one of the most influential sources of black literature and opinion in the United States.

Fuller, raised in Detroit, was a classmate of Dudley Randall's at Wayne State. In 1955 Fuller left Motown for Chicago to work for *Ebony* magazine, but in two years he quit America altogether for Europe, despairing of this country's future in the face of racial oppression. He returned in 1960, after spending time in emerging Africa, full of new hope that he could help black Americans discover a sense of purpose. In that mind, in 1961 he became editor of *Negro Digest*, renamed *Black World* in 1970.

"I often asked Hoyt to consider publishing a collection," Randall says, "but he was always too busy." So when Fuller died in 1981, Randall dug through his 15 years of personal copies to do the anthologizing himself. "Those years were a period of intense activity in black literature," he says, "and I wanted to see that they were preserved."[30]

Thus, such books as *Homage to Hoyt Fuller* and *A Litany of Friends*, and poems in anthologies and journals, helped to keep Dudley Randall's name and work before the reading public in the United States.[31] His creative activities in the eighties also continued to increase his status as a major living American writer.

At home, in Randall's beloved Detroit, however, conditions became more worrisome in the eighties for the average citizen of the city. For one thing, the city's population continued to decline precariously during this time period. In 1980, Detroit had a black population of 758,939 (63.1 percent) in a total population base of 1,203,339, of which 402,000 were whites. Yet, another 200,000 whites left Detroit in the eighties.[32] Many whites migrated to surrounding suburbs, and were viewed by many blacks as "hostile" toward Detroit's black majority population.[33] Meanwhile, Detroit had the third largest black population among U.S. cities; only New York City and Chicago had more black residents. In Michigan, blacks numbered 1,199,023 (12.9 percent of the state's total population) in 1980, making it the ninth largest black population among American states.[34] Yet, in Detroit the loss of such a large percentage of its population base was a major liability in the city's efforts to secure its tax base, and to promote a better life for the citizens of Detroit:

> The City of Detroit lost nearly 33 percent of its population between 1960 and 1984 ... the highest rate of loss among the ten largest cities in the United States ... During the 1960s the population of the City of Detroit declined by less than 1 percent per year; since 1970 it has declined by nearly 2 percent per year.[35]

Juxtaposed against such alarming population statistics were the economic consequences of decline. A recent study found that between the sixties and the eighties Detroit lost "nearly 70% of its jobs in manufacturing. In 1981, OVER 400,000 Detroiters — one in every three — receives some form of public assistance."[36] Rep. George W. Crockett, Jr., (D) of Michigan, wrote in 1981 that President Ronald Reagan's economic revolution spelled disaster for urban centers in this country. "For Detroit, such a policy means drastic cutbacks in services, from child nutrition to education, from unemployment to urban development."[37] Indeed, the economic crisis of the period is clearly visible in scholar B. J. Widick's statement that "in 1985 blacks in metropolitan Detroit had the highest jobless rate — 28.9 percent — among those living in the nation's 30 largest metropolitan areas."[38] One of the most revealing of the economic indicators of the period is the fact that by 1984, 43 percent of the residents of Detroit lived below the poverty line.[39] Such economic variables were striking examples of the harsh realities of American life for most Detroiters.

Nowhere was the gap between black and white daily lives so evident as in the major social indicators of the eighties.[40] Although Detroit has an excellent housing base from its halcyon days of the past, many dwellings have been destroyed in recent years due to fires, neglect by owners, abandonment, and "urban renewal." In fact, one authority noted that "during 1987 only two single family homes were built" in Detroit. According to the U.S. Census of 1980, Detroit suffered a "net loss of 58,696 homes! This was the largest loss of housing for any city in the United States."[41] Thousands of Detroiters were also homeless during the decade. The black majority population in Detroit suffered from "residential segregation," while most whites had an option to rent or purchase a variety of housing stock in the suburbs.[42]

The *Detroit News* reported in 1987 that:

> Detroit is a city plagued by reality, and myth. The reality is harsh: Highest homicide rate in the United States. Highest teenage murder rate in the country — twice that of any other city. Forty percent of the population living below the poverty line. The myth is that we cannot change it.[43]

Everyday life in the eighties meant dealing with "What's happening in 'Murder City,'" a media description for Detroit.[44] Even children were not safe, and unfortunately were often the perpetuators of violence against other young people. The *Washington Post* reported in 1986 that:

> three hundred sixty-five children, 17 or under, were hit by gunfire in Detroit. Forty-three died ... Roughly one shooting a day, roughly one murder a week, and historically, summer is the deadliest season.[45]

Detroiters also had to contend with a drug crisis in the city, where crack cocaine was cheap, but so costly in terms of human lives.[46] Even the celebration of Halloween each year became a time of dread for Detroit: "'Devil's Night' first began in Detroit in 1983, with a series of fires across the city, on the night before Halloween. It continued to occur throughout the late 1980's."[47]

Many blacks in Detroit also continued to be concerned about the criminal justice system in the city; the issue of police abuse and brutality, especially of younger black men; and of activities associated with the Ku Klux Klan and Nazis in Michigan.[48]

Finally, when citizens of Detroit surveyed their public educational institutions, they found that black students were by and large educated in a segregated system, where in 1980 the percentage of whites in a school of a typical black student was only 9.2 percent.[49] Worse still, according to B. J. Widick, was that the Detroit student

> retention rate dropped from a "high" of 50 percent in 1965–66 to 34.6 percent in 1980. While the rich suburbs spent over $4,000 per pupil, the city schools, with the greatest need in staff, teachers, and training programs, only had $2,670 per pupil.... Perhaps the saddest commentary on the state of education in Detroit was the report that one out of every four high school graduates from the class of 1985 did not pass a proficiency exam which tested minimum reading, writing and math skills.[50]

Collectively then, Detroiters were faced with a strained social system, which almost reached the breaking point during the eighties. But, the city avoided a complete paralysis, perhaps due to the vision and work of its very strong mayor, Coleman Young.

Mayor Young remained Detroit's chief executive official for the eighties. As has been demonstrated, his leadership of the city was challenged by a continuing series of economic crises and social problems during the decade. "In the course of his tenure as mayor of Detroit ... Young and the city of Detroit endured the oil crisis and major layoffs in an auto-base economy."[51]

Journalist Tim Jones of the *Chicago Tribune* points out Young's major achievements in office.

> Despite the heavy odds Young faced, his string of accomplishments is impressive: among them, integrating the Detroit police department, improving minority hiring and helping to win the construction of two new auto assembly plants. Indeed, Young exhibited an uncanny ability to work with corporate leaders especially during the first half of his tenure.[52]

Major Young was most effective in promoting

> pride in the black people of Detroit ... [and in being] a major force in the establishment of black political power in the city. Nor can it be denied that his presence and position have been decisive factors in keeping social peace — avoiding riots on at least two occasions — during his tenure.[53]

In general, political activity is high among black Detroiters; in recent years, fourteen black state representatives and three state senators have been sent to Lansing. Also, two black U.S. representatives have been sent to Congress, and thirty black judges have served in the city's judicial system.[54] The greatest difficulty for blacks has been in turning their political strength into economic power.

In spite of its myriad range of problems, Detroit was able to maintain a rich base of black cultural and social activity during the eighties, with strong currents of African-American music, religion, fine arts, journalism, publishing and writing at work in the city. However, most of Detroit's black artistic groups and individuals had to work overtime just to survive the hard-hitting economic hardships of the period.

This was the general situation which surrounded Dudley Randall as he began to regain his footing in the early eighties. He had maintained an interest in the operations of Broadside/Crummell Press in the late seventies and early eighties by serving as a consultant to the Alexander Crummell Memorial Center, at 74 Glendale Avenue, Highland Park, Michigan.[55] However, no new books, or other materials were published between 1977 and 1981 under the management of the Crummell Center. The focus of the company was now on selling the stock of books and other materials on hand and paying off the debts of Broadside. However, Randall's foresight paid off in the end because "There was a clause in the contract that after five years the press would come back to [him] unless the Crummell Center wanted to retain it. They were changing ministers, and there was no active interest in the press on the part of the parishioners; so they offered it back to me."[56] This was in 1982, and Randall now made Broadside a nonprofit organization.

Yet the eighties were a dangerous period for black publishing and writers in America. Generally, in the contemporary world of American culture during this period, black writers had fallen on "hard times."[57] Black poets, as well as black writers in fiction and nonfiction, found themselves isolated in the publishing business of this nation. "Hard times" for black writers in the eighties and nineties has meant that:

1. Few black books are being published in the United States
2. "...there has been a drop in the number of small black publications that provide both a spring board and an outlet for aspiring writers"
3. There is a loss of publishing opportunities for writers who emerged in the sixties and seventies and also of older established black writers from the twenties to the present
4. The economic problems of publishing are greater today than at any previous period in modern American history
5. Black writers face pressure from the historical burdens of racism — and the decision making policies of American publishers
6. Many white publishers question the commercial viability of black books
7. A change has taken place in the political climate of the country, which affects black publishing opportunities
8. A "blockade" of black writers occurs in bookstores.[58]

Thus, Dudley Randall faced many perplexing hurdles as he resumed the editorship of Broadside Press in 1982. For starters, he had to contend with the fact that the Black Arts Movement was over. Perhaps poet Amiri Baraka [LeRoi Jones] best captured the bitterness of the era when he wrote:

> More and more books by Black writers are simply out of print, and it is more and more difficult for young Black writers to get published. As in the thirties, the fad of publishing Black writers is over. In literature, and in the media generally, the same disgusting evidence of such a rightward motion is obvious. Publishers make certain Negroes famous for putting down the Black Liberation Movement and the sixties, and one well-known backward colored writer came out putting down Malcolm X in his most recent book of essays. In films, once militant-spouting actors play homosexual pimps and normal sick policemen by the dozens. TV gives us Huggie Bear and Rooster, pimps and sidekicks, and more cops. Tarzan is coming back, with Bo Derek as Jane. An entire anti-struggle literature is being mashed on us as real art (remember the late forties and fifties?).[59]

The national mood among black writers of the period was bleak. Article after article told the reading public that "black Writers [are] Pessimistic on Their Publishing Future."[60] And at the end of the eighties, black authors were still faced with a situation where even "school reading lists shunned women and black authors" in this country. The *New York Times* reported in 1989 that:

> required reading lists in the nation's high schools continue to emphasize the works of Shakespeare but largely ignore the literary contributions of women and members of minorities, a new survey says.
> In a sampling of reading lists at nearly 500 public, Roman Catholic and nonsectarian private schools, a federally financed study conducted by the State University of New York at Albany showed only one of the 10 most frequently assigned books was by a woman, and only two minority authors were in the top 53 of the 100 titles listed [Lorraine Hansberry's "Raisin in the Sun" (1959) and Richard Wright's "Black Boy" (1945)]. The only literary work by a woman that was among the 10 most frequently assigned works was Harper Lee's 1961 novel, "To Kill a Mockingbird."[61]

Such hallowing limitations on black writers indicated that there was indeed a continuing need for small black publishers such as Randall's Broadside Press. But how to survive economically and emotionally remained as ever a great burden for Randall and other small black publishers in America. This was apparent to observers of black publishing in the United States because between 1982 and 1984, Randall was only able to publish one broadside and five new books. Table 5.1 indicates the state of publishing at Broadside for the early eighties.[62] The first new Broadside publication since 1976 was Dudley Randall's poem, "For Vivian," which was published in 1982 as Broadside #93. A Broadside flyer announced in 1982:

> The new Broadside is beautifully hand lettered on fine vellum paper by calligrapher Oral Carter, is illustrated in red and gold, and bound in a plain white folder of the same stock, encased in a transparent slip. This new poem, unpublished elsewhere, is printed in a limited edition of 100 copies, signed by the poet and calligrapher. The price is $10.00.[63]

This new poem was written by Randall for his wife. Purchase orders for the Broadside #93 and other materials were once again available from Randall's home at 12651 Old Mill Place, Detroit.[64]

In addition to editing *Homage to Hoyt Fuller*, Randall selected four other manuscripts for publication in the early eighties. Three of the authors, Melba Boyd, Michele S. Gibbs and Aneb Kgositsile were closely identified with Detroit, and the fourth, Sonia Sanchez, was a major Broadside author from the sixties and seventies; all were females. Table 5.2 notes the range of their social backgrounds.[65] Collectively, they represented the generation which came of age during the fifties, and were tremendously impacted by the Civil Rights Movement. A highly educated group, all four writers developed dual careers as educators at the college and university levels, while also making noteworthy contributions as lecturers and editors. Michele S. Gibbs is also known for her artistic work as a muralist.

Melba Joyce Boyd became a very well-known cultural activist in Detroit during the seventies. Besides teaching stints at Cass Tech High School, Eastside Street Academies, Wayne Community College, Shaw College, and Wayne State University — all in Detroit — she was also known for her work as an assistant editor at Broadside Press between 1972 and 1976. By 1982, she was a nationally recognized poet and critic. On her West Coast visit in that same year to participate in the San Francisco African American Historical and Cultural Society's Second Friday Poetry Series, the *Black Scholar* observed:

> Melba Joyce Boyd arrived in San Francisco from Detroit with all that explosive spirit for which folks who get things done are famous. She read from her first collection of verse *Cat Eyes* and *Dead Wood* (Fallen Angel Press, Detroit, 1978); those who had not previously heard her read or read her work before, probably rushed out to find her poetry or reexamined poems once read that her sharp and deep delivery excited greater thought on.[66]

Like Melba Joyce Boyd, Michele S. Gibbs was also active in Detroit's educational life and black cultural scene of the seventies. She was associate director of the Detroit Industrial Mission in 1971–73, and a teacher in Black Studies at the University of Detroit and Wayne State University between 1971 and 1973, and coordinator for Worker's Education at Wayne County Community College, in 1975–76. In the late seventies and early eighties she was a freelance writer, lecturer, educational consultant, and spent 1980 to November 1983 as an artist, writer, and teacher in Grenada, West Indies. Dudley Randall informed the friends of Broadside Press in December 1983 that:

Table 5.1
Broadside Press Books, 1980–1989

Author(s)	Publication	Genre	Price of Book	Pages	Gender of Author
1982					
Melba Boyd (Co-published with Detroit River Press)	Song for Maya	Poetry	$ 5.00	70	F
Dudley Randall	"For Vivian"	Broadside	$10.00	1	M
1983					
Michele S. Gibbs	Sketches from Home	Poetry	$ 5.00	64	F
Aneb Kgositsile	Blood River	Poetry	$ 5.00	38	F
Sonia Sanchez	It's a New Day: Poems for Young Brothas and Sistuhs	Poetry	$ 5.00	32	F
1984					
Dudley Randall, ed.	Homage to Hoyt Fuller	Anthology	$15.00	362	M
1987					
Leslie Reese	Upside Down Tapestry Mosaic History	Poetry	$ 5.00	52	F
1988					
Rayfield Waller	Abstract Blues	Poetry	$ 5.00	62	M
1989					
Michele S. Gibbs	Island Images	Coloring book	$ 5.00	30	F
Aneb Kgositsile	Rainrituals	Poetry	$ 7.00	62	F
Albert Michael Ward	Patches on Mainstreet	Poetry	$ 7.00	58	M

Table 5.2

Social Backgrounds of Broadside Press Authors, 1982–1984

Name	Place of Birth	Date of Birth	Education	Occupation	Resident in 1980
Melba Boyd	Detroit, MI	1950–	Western Mich. Univ. B.A., M.A.; Univ. of Mich., Ph.D.	Educator, writer, editor	Detroit, MI
Michele S. Gibbs	Chicago, IL	April 4, 1946–	Univ. of S. Calif, A.B.; Brown Univ., Ph.D.	Educator, writer, artist	Grenada, WI; Detroit, MI
Aneb Kgositsile	Tampa, FL	Feb. 14, 1941–	Univ. of Calif., B.A., M.A.; Berkeley; Univ. of Mich., Ph.D.	Educator, writer, editor	Detroit, MI
Sonia Sanchez	Birmingham, AL	Sept. 9, 1934–	Hunter Col., B.A.; New York Univ., hon. doct.; Wilberforce Univ.	Educator. writer, editor	Phila., PA

Broadside poet Michele Gibbs, author of *Sketches from Home*, poems from Grenada, returned to Grenada and was arrested and then sent back to the U.S. Every writer dreams of being in the right place at the right time.[67]

This event occurred during a period of political unrest on the island nation of Grenada. One hundred people, including Prime Minister Maurice Bishop (a leftist) were killed in 1983, when Bernard Coard and Hudson Austin led a movement to replace Bishop's government. The United States military and soldiers from other Caribbean islands invaded Grenada on October 25, 1983, to "restore peace" and "to protect the lives of Americans" (including 600 medical students at St. George's University School of Medicine) in Grenada; the foreign forces did not leave the island until 1985.[68]

Aneb Kgositsile (Gloria Larry House) is also a familiar name in Detroit's educational and artistic circles. Besides her work as a professor of the humanities at Wayne State University, she has served as a member of the board of directors of both the Detroit Council of the Arts, and the Poetry Resource Center. Her early service to the Civil Rights Movement included two and one-half years with the Student Non-Violent Coordinating Committee in Alabama, where she wrote the group's famous Vietnam protest statement.[69]

Sonia Sanchez was one of the most active black poets of the seventies and eighties. Since 1977, she has taught African-American literature at Temple University, Philadelphia, Pennsylvania. In 1987, the *Black Scholar* wrote that Sanchez "has lectured at over 500 universities and colleges in the U.S. and has traveled extensively abroad reading her poetry."[70] Poet Kalamu ya Salaam believes that "Sanchez is one of the few creative artists who have significantly influenced the course of black American literature and culture."[71] Not a small achievement for a poet who was born in Birmingham, Alabama.

Meanwhile, Dudley Randall had the problem of selling his new books and continuing to move his older stock of publications, still housed in the Crummell Center. Randall listed ten best-selling Broadside books for November 1983, in his Broadside newsletter of December 1983. The order was as follows:

1. Bill Odarty, *A Safari of African Cooking* (1972), $3.95
2. Dudley Randall, *After the Killing* (1973) $3
3. Dudley Randall, *A Litany of Friends* (1981) $6
4. Sonia Sanchez, *Homecoming* (1969), $3
5. Celes Tisdale, ed., *Betcha Ain't: Poems from Attica* (1974), $3
6. Michele S. Gibbs, *Sketches from Home (Poems from Grenada)* (1983), $5
7. Gwendolyn Brooks, ed., *Jump Bad* (1971), $4
8. Chauncey Spencer, *Who Is Chauncey Spencer?* (1975), $7.95
9. Dudley Randall and Margaret Burroughs, eds., *For Malcolm X* (1967), $4
10. Don L. Lee (Haki R. Madhubuti), *Think Black* (1969), $3[72]

Most of these works had sold well at Broadside for some time, especially Odarty's *A Safari of African Cooking*, Sanchez's *Homecoming*, Tisdale's *Betcha Ain't*, Brooks' *Jump Bad*, Randall and Burrough's *For Malcolm X*, and Lee's *Think Black*. That a new book of Broadside poems by Michele S. Gibbs could also find a strong market was another indication of Randall's abiding faith in the poetic works of younger writers. Broadside became more flexible on its price list during the eighties. By 1983, there was an increase in price from $1 to $3 for *After the Killing*, *Homecoming*, and *Think Black*. *Betcha Ain't* was also increased in price from $2.50 for a paperback edition to $3; and *For Malcolm X* (a strong seller at Broadside for over twenty years) rose from $2.95 to $4 per copy. All the other books on the best ten selling list sold for their original price.[73]

Broadside's 1980 list of available back titles for the early eighties is described in Table 5.3.[74] Most of the items were priced higher than their original prices from the seventies. For example, the average price of a single collection of poetry now sold for $2 to $2.50, versus an original price of only $1 in many cases. Such a low price range, however, was still a golden bargain for poetry lovers, book collectors, and educational institutions. The major works of black men dominate the list across the categories (not counting the Broadside Series, because only a portion of these were still available for purchase by the public). A total of sixty Broadside works appear on the list; 70 percent are by black men and 30 percent are by black women. The works of three writers dominate the list: Gwendolyn Brooks, with seven titles, Don L. Lee (Haki R. Madhubuti) with six, and Dudley Randall with four. These writers were among the best-sellers of Broadside books in the history of the company. However, the available data suggest that Broadside had only modest book, broadside, poster, tape, and record sales during the late seventies and early eighties. In 1981, Randall told scholar Donald Franklin Joyce: "Times are worse than ever, economically."[75]

Randall, like black writers and publishers throughout the United States, lived in a world of few easy answers. It was the world of the eighties where the marketplace for black writing, and especially black poetry, was often disappointing. Critic and poet Jerry W. Ward, Jr., reminded his contemporaries in 1983 that blacks "need[ed] a sociology of African-American literature to account for changes in mode of production (writing and publishing) and in reading patterns (who do black readers read what they read when they read?)"[76] The above problems are complex, given the economic, political and social history of the African-American people from World War II to the present; yet, they have confronted each generation of black poets and publishers, and their audiences in the United States since the nineteenth century.[77] Certainly, Randall was faced with the task of producing black

Table 5.3

Broadside/Crummell Press Publication List, 1979–1980

Author	Title (Broadside Poets)	Edition	Price
Alhamisi	*Holy Ghosts* (1972)	paper	$2.50
Aubert	*Against the Blues* (1972)	paper	$2.00
Barlow	*Gabriel* (1974)	paper	$2.50
Blakely	*Windy Place* (1974)	paper	$2.00
Boyer	*Dream Farmer* (1975)	paper	$2.00
Brooks	*Riot* (1970)	paper	$2.00
Brown	*The Last Ride of Wild Bill* (1975)	paper	$3.00
Danner	*Impressions of African Art Forms* (1960)	paper	$2.00
Giovanni	*Re: Creation* (1970)	paper	$3.00
Guillen	*Tengo* (1975)	paper	$4.25
Hodges	*Black Wisdom* (1971)	paper	$2.00
Jeffers	*When I Know the Power of My Black Hand* (1974)	paper	$2.50
Knight	*Poems from Prison* (1968)	paper	$2.00
Lee	*Don't Cry, Scream!* (1970)	paper	$2.50
Lee	*Think Black* (1967)	paper	$2.00
Lee	*We Walk the Way of the New World* (1970)	paper	$2.50
Madhubuti	*Book of Life* (1973)	paper	$2.50
Plumpp	*Clinton* (1976)	paper	$2.00
Pfister	*Beer Cans Bullets Things and Pieces* (1972)	paper	$2.00
Randall, D.	*Cities Burning* (1966)	paper	$2.00
Randall, J.	*Cities and Other Disasters* (1973)	paper	$2.00
Randall, J.C.	*Indigoes* (1975)	paper	$2.00
Raven	*Blues from Momma and Other Low Down Stuff* (1971)	paper	$0.50
Sanchez	*Home Coming* (1969)	paper	$2.00

Editor	Title (Anthologies)	Edition	Price
Boyer	*The Broadside Annual* (1973)	paper	$2.00
Brooks	*Jump Bad: A New Chicago Anthology* (1971)	paper	$4.00
Randall	*For Malcolm* (1969)	paper	$3.50
Tisdale	*Betcha Ain't: Poems from Attica* (1974)	paper	$2.50

Author	Title (Prose)	Edition	Price
Bailey	*Broadside Authors and Artists* (1974)	cloth	$9.95
Brooks	*A Capsule Course in Black Poetry Writing* (1975)	paper	$3.00
Brooks	*Report from Part One* (1972)	cloth	$5.95
Brooks, ed.	*The Black Position–Number Two* (1972)	paper	$2.00
Brooks, ed.	*The Black Position–Number Three* (1973)	paper	$3.00
Brooks, ed.	*The Black Position–Number Four* (1976)	paper	$2.50
Odarty	*A Safari of African Cooking* (1971)	paper	$3.95
O'Neal	*And Then the Harvest: Three Television Plays* (1974)	paper	$6.00
Randall	*Broadside Memories: Poets I Have Known* (1975)	paper	$5.00
Spencer	*Who Is Chauncey Spencer?* (1974)	cloth	$5.00

Broadside Critics Series

Baker	*A Many-Colored Coat of Dreams: Countee Cullen* (1974)	paper	$2.75
Bell	*The Folks Roots of Contemporary Afro-Amer. Ptry.* (1974)	paper	$2.75
Gayle	*Claude McKay: The Black Poet at War* (1972)	paper	$2.50

Heritage Series – Paul Breman, Ltd., London, England		paper	$2.50
Allen	*Paul Vesey's Ledger* (1975)		
Atkins	*Heretofore* (1968)		

Author	Title (Prose)	Edition	Price
Heritage Series - Paul Breman, Ltd., London, England (cont.)		paper	$2.50
Bontemps	*Personals* (1973)		
Clarke	*Sun Song* (1973)		
Cuney	*Storefront Church* (1973)		
Dodson	*The Confession Stone* (1971)		
Durem	*Take No Prisoners* (1971)		
Esoghene	*The Conflicting Eye* (1973)		
Fair	*Excerpts* (1975)		
John	*Light a Fire* (1973)		
Kendrick	*Through the Ceiling* (1975)		
Rivers	*The Wright Poems* (1972)		
Southerland	*The Magic Sun Spins* (1975)		
Thompson	*First Fire: Poems (1957–60)* (1970)		
Broadside Posters ($2.00) and Voices ($6.00)			
Knight	*For Black Poets Who Think of Suicide*		
Lee	*Rappin' & Readin'* (LP)		
Long	*Angela*		
Major	*The Cotton Club* (cassette)		
Whitsitt	*Black Silhouette*		

publications and developing an audience to buy and read (or listen to) the literature which he published. But he was not alone. Toni Morrison, who was a senior editor at Random House in 1980, noted that she had "never been able to count on 10,000 black buyers to buy anything published by the company I worked for."[78] This made her work all the more difficult in selling new black manuscripts for publication at Random House.

Yet, behind the complexity of the problem lay the issue of illiteracy; the intensity of the media age (especially radio, video, film, and television); the conglomeration of the nation's press, publishing, and cultural outlets in recent decades into the hands of fewer owners; and the economic stagnation of large sectors of the African-American population. These issues have profoundly impacted the growth and development of black culture in America. Authorities as diverse as Jonathan Kozol, Ishmael Reed, and Faith Berry agreed that something was wrong in America during the eighties and the problems included American illiteracy and the obstacles to overcome this burden among the citizenry. The number of Americans who could not read or write stood between 20 and 70 million in the eighties. During this same period the United States ranked twenty-fourth among nations in the number of books purchased. Newspapers experienced a painful decline in this country during the eighties. Kozol observes that a "loss of readership means a loss of competition. The number of cities with competing dailies had declined from 181 to 30 since 1947. Fifty-four daily papers have gone to their death since 1979."[79]

In black America, dozens of magazines, newsletters, and newspapers folded in the eighties and many major black organs suffered a tremendous decline in circulation and income.[80] Such a situation fed into the general state of affairs where "readers competent to understand the written press and find enjoyment in simple verse are an endangered species."[81] For the production of new black poetry books, the outlook was bleaker. Dudley Randall told D. H. Melhem during this period, "I think about an audience for poetry, but I'm afraid the audience for poetry is other poets."[82] Yet, a study by Nicholas Zill and Marianne Wing Lee on *Who Reads Literature?: The Future of the United States as a Nation of Readers*, indicated that in 1985, among U.S. adults aged eighteen and over, many were readers during the previous twelve months. Among blacks, the proportion of the population who read literature stood at 43 percent; those who read poetry, 14 percent; those who did creative writing, 5 percent; and those who read books and magazines, 66 percent.[83] This survey indicates that as in the past, there is a market among blacks for all types of reading materials. Broadside, like most small black publishers had problems with distributing its publications to this market, and for securing economic capital to develop the company. There is hope for the future, if these problems can be surmounted.[84]

However, securing needed capital, especially from white financial institutions, was still a difficult task for small- to middle-size black businesses. As in the past, Broadside also could not successfully tap into the capital produced by larger African-American business operations in Detroit and the state of Michigan. In 1989, *Black Enterprise* listed twenty black-owned firms in Michigan on its list of the top 100 black businesses in the United States. New York state also had twenty, but California led the list with twenty-two.[85] In 1989 and 1990, Michigan contained three of the ten largest U.S. black business operations. In 1990, at number six was Barden Communications, Inc., a Detroit firm which specializes in communications and real estate. This company was established in 1981, had a staff of 308, headed by chief executive officer Don H. Barden, with total 1990 sales of $86 million. Trans Jones Inc./Jones Transfer Company of Monroe, Michigan, held the number seven position on *Black Enterprise*'s list. This transportation services company was created in 1986, had a staff of 1,189, under the guidance of Gary L. White, and total sales in 1990 of $75 million. At number ten stood the Bing Group of Detroit, headed by Dave Bing. This steel processing and metal-stamping operations company was established in 1980. In 1990, the Bing Group employed 173 individuals and had total sales of $61 million. So there was money in the hands of black people in Detroit. In fact, black Americans operated the First Independence National Bank of Detroit, which in 1990 was the fifteenth largest black-owned bank in the United States. First Independence was established in 1970, and by 1990 had a staff of seventy-five, led by Lawrence S. Jones, with assets of $84,971,000, deposits of $81,974,000, and outstanding loans of $29,333,000.[86] But, in a capitalist society, profits, not service, are the norm. Thus, small black publishers in Detroit generally had to survive on their wits, the volunteer services of their families, friends and supporters, and whatever other aid they could secure through public gifts and grants from private and governmental agencies. Yet, regardless of this situation, one journalist argued in 1990 that the overall black economic position in Detroit was a "disappointment." For this writer the central problems were evident in the fact that "only 14 black-owned companies in Detroit earned more than $10 million in 1987, and 6 of them were auto dealerships. Even more revealing, of the 25 largest black-owned companies, just 2 were building firms; their combined income was only $6.6 million."[87]

Nonetheless, for Dudley Randall and other publishers, artists, and community cultural workers in Detroit, even these millions of dollars would never reach their humble but crucial institutions, needed by all in the human struggle to uplift black people at home and abroad, and to promote the common humanity of people everywhere.

At the age of seventy-one in 1985, on the twentieth anniversary of the founding of Broadside Press, Dudley Randall for a second time reluctantly gave up the reins of leadership of Broadside, due to "economic reverses" and a desire on his part to retire from active work. Randall sold the company to Hilda and Donald Vest of Detroit, an active couple on the educational and cultural scene in Detroit.[88] They operate the company from their home

Donald and Hilda Vest, present owners of Broadside Press. Their interests in the arts and black literature encouraged them in 1985 to assume the mantle of leadership of Broadside Press from Dudley Randall.

in northwest Detroit. One of the first tasks which they faced in the mid-eighties was to make an inventory of the 35,000 Broadside books stores at the Crummell Center in Highland Park, Michigan.[89]

Hilda Vest (June 5, 1933–), a poet and former Detroit Public School System elementary teacher (1959–88), is president of Broadside. Hilda's family origins were in Georgia, where her father, Pharr Cyral Freeman (1887–1971) was an M.D. (Meharry Medical School, 1920); and her mother, Blanche Heard Freeman (1901–84), attended Talladega College (Alabama), and was a homemaker. Hilda's education was completed at Wayne State University (B.S. degree in Education, 1958). Donald Vest (1930–) had a long career (1962–87) at Ford Motor Company as a recruiter; he handles the business affairs of the company. Donald's family origins are in Indiana and Michigan. He was born in Ypsilanti, Michigan, and received a B.S. degree from Michigan State University in 1952, and attended

Wayne State University for graduate studies. Don's stepfather, Eugene L. Vest (born in Connersville, Indiana, 1900–67), was self-employed and a laborer; and his mother, Vida C. Vest, was born in Cherry Hill, Michigan (1909–), and worked as a public school teacher in Michigan.[90]

Between 1985 and 1989, according to publisher Hilda Vest, Broadside reprinted works by eight poets that were originally published under Dudley Randall. This list includes Gwendolyn Brooks, Margaret Walker, Sonia Sanchez, Etheridge Knight, Nikki Giovanni, Dudley Randall, Haki R. Madhubuti and Audre Lorde. Table 5.4 shows the major writers and books published by Broadside Press from 1980 through 1995.[91]

Broadside's ten books for the period 1980–89 include one anthology, one coloring book and eight collections of poetry. Seven of these (or 70 percent) have been by women authors: Melba Boyd, Michele S. Gibbs (two books), Aneb Kgositsile (two books), Sonia Sanchez, and Leslie Reese; while three (or 30 percent) have been by men: Dudley Randall, Rayfield Waller, and Albert M. Ward. The average price of a Broadside book is now between $5 and $7, and the average page length of a volume runs to sixty pages, a much larger number than in the early history of Broadside. There are currently thirty-six Broadside titles still in print. The Broadside Classics list includes work in its current catalogue by the following writers: Gwendolyn Brooks, Sterling A. Brown, Nicholas Guillen, Nikki Giovanni, Etheridge Knight, Don L. Lee (Haki P. Madhubuti), Audre Lorde, Dudley Randall, Sonia Sanchez, Margaret Walker, Leaonead Biley, Houston Baker, Jr., Addison Gayle, Jr., Bill Odarty, and Chauncey Spencer. Also in print is *A Capsule Course in Black Poetry Writing*, a co-authored book by Gwendolyn Brooks, Dudley Randall, Haki R. Madhubuti and Keorapetse Kgositsile. Donald Franklin Joyce's study of this period found that:

> Between 1985 and 1989, the best-selling backlist titles of Broadside Press have been *Capsule Course in Black Poetry Writing* by Gwendolyn Brooks, Dudley Randall, Haki Madhubuti [and Keorapetse Kgositsile] (1975) (2,500 copies); *Beckonings* by Gwendolyn Brooks (1975) (3,000 copies); *Book of Life* by Haki Madhubuti (1973) (3,000 copies); and *Last Ride of Wild Bill* by Sterling Brown (1975) (1,000 copies).[92]

In the nineties, the company plans to devote more of its attention to the publication of "new poets." Yet, the company still faces a hard economic future; and in 1990, it was reported that Broadside Press had annual sales of $10,000.[93]

> Broadside markets its books through direct-mail advertising to bookstores, libraries, and educational institutions. The firm distributes its books through national book distribution jobbers and sells direct to bookstores and individuals. It also sends out a newsletter describing recent publications.[94]

Today, a staff of five operates the company: Hilda Vest, publisher; Donald Vest, business manager; Gloria House [Aneb Kgositsile], editor; Willie D. Williams (1951–), photographer and office manager, and one staff assistant. Dudley Randall is a consultant to the new owners, as are Ronald Snelling, a black economist in Detroit, and Ernest Tanks, Jr., a board member of Broadside who works closely with the Vests in the continued development of the company. The current Broadside Board of Directors includes seven individuals. They are Hilda F. Vest, president and secretary; Donald S. Vest, vice president and treasurer; and five members, Earnest Tanks, Jr., Gloria House, Willie Williams, James Emanuel, and Bernice Greene, all of Detroit.[95]   *(cont. on page 202)*

Table 5.4

Nine Major Broadside Press Poets, 1980–1995

Name	Primary residency during this period	Published books	Awards and honors
Gwendolyn Brooks (1917–)	Chicago, IL	*Primer for Blacks* (Chicago: Black Position Press, 1980) *To Disembark* (Chicago: Third World Press, 1981) *Young Poets' Primer* (Chicago: Brooks Press, 1981) *Mayor Harold Washington and Chicago, The I Will Cry* (Chicago: Brooks Press, 1983) *Very Young Poets* (Chicago: Brooks Press, 1983) *The Near Johannesburg Boy and Other Poems* (Chicago: The David Company, 1986) *Blacks* (Chicago: The David Company, 1987) *Gottschalk and the Grande Tavantelle* (Chicago: The David Company, 1988) *Winnie* (Chicago: The David Company, 1988) *Children Coming Home* (Chicago: The David Company, 1991)	Over fifty honorary doctorates. Consultant in Poetry, Library of Congress, 1985–86. Essence Award, 1988. Inducted into the National Women's Hall of Fame, 1988. Frost Medal, Poetry Society of America, 1989. Recipient Lifetime Achievement Award, National Endowment for the Arts, 1989 ($48,000). Gwendolyn Brooks Chair in Black Literature and Creative Writing established in her honor, Chicago State University, 1990. Selected as the 1994 Jefferson Lecturer by the National Endowment for the Humanities (the federal government's highest honor for achievement in the humanities); received a $10,000 honorarium and lectured in Washington, DC, on May 4, and in Chicago on May 11, 1994.
Sterling A. Brown (1901–1989)	Washington, DC	*The Collected Poems of Sterling A. Brown*, ed. by Michael S. Harper (New York: Harper Colophon Books, 1980)	Awarded the Lenore Marshall Poetry Price for his *Collected Poems* (1980). Named poet laureate of Washington, DC, on May 11, 1984, by Mayor Marion Barry.
James A. Emanuel (1923–)	Paris, France	*Snowflakes and Steel: My Life as a Poet, 1971–80* (Durham, NC; Jay B. Hubbell Center, Duke University, 1981) *A Poet's Mind* (New York: Regents, 1983) *The Broken Bowl* (Detroit: Lotus Press, 1983) *Deadly James and Other Poems* (Detroit: Lotus Press, 1987) *The Quagmire Effect* (Detroit: Lotus Press, 1989) *Whole Grain: Collected Poems, 1958–89* (Detroit: Lotus Press, 1991)	Associate Professorship, French National Contingency, University of Toulouse, France, 1979–80.

Name	Primary residency during this period	Published books	Awards and honors
Nikki Giovanni (1943–)	New York City, NY; Cincinnati, OH, and Blacksburg, VA	*Vacation Time: Poems for Children* (New York: William Morrow, 1980) *Those Who Ride the Night Winds* (New York: William Morrow, 1988) *Sacred Crows ... and Other Edibles* (New York: William Morrow, 1988) Edited with Jessie Carney Smith, *Images of Blacks in American Culture: A Reference Guide to Information Sources* (Westport, Conn.: Greenwood Press, 1988) Edited with Cathee Dennison, *Appalachian Elders: A Warm Hearth Sampler* (Pocahontas Press, 1991) *Conversations with Nikki Giovanni*, Edited by Virginia C. Fowler (Jackson: University Press of Mississippi, 1992) *Knoxville, Tennesee* Editor, *Grand/Mothers* *Racism 101* (New York: William Morrow, 1994)	Doctorate of Literate (hon.), College of Mount St. Joseph on Ohio, 1983. Woman of the Year citation, Cincinnati chapter of YWCA, 1983. Elected to the Ohio Women's Hall of Fame, 1985. "Outstanding Woman of Tennessee" citation, 1985. Distinguished Recognition Award, Detroit City Council, 1986. Ohioana Book Award, 1988, for *Sacred Crows ... and Other Edibles*. "Woman of the Year" citation, Lynchburg, Virginia, chapter of NAACP, 1989.
Lance Jeffers (1919–85)	Durham, NC	*Witherspoon* (a noval) (Atlanta, GA: The George A. Flippin Press, 1983)	MacArthur Scholar-at-Large, at Talladega College (Alabama), 1982–83; selected by the United Negro College Fund.
Etheridge Knight (1931–91)	Memphis, TN, and Indianapolis, IN	*Born of a Woman: New and Selected Poems* (Boston: Houghton Mifflin, 1980) *The Essential Etheridge Knight* (Pittsburgh, PA: University of Pittsburgh Press, 1986)	National Endowment for the Arts Fellowship, 1980 ($12,500). Received the Shelley Memorial Award by the Poetry Society of America, 1985. *The Essential Etheridge Knight* (1986), named the winner of the American Book Award, 1987.
Haki R. Madhubuti (1942–)	Chicago, IL	*Earthquakes and Sunrise Mission: Poetry and Essays of Black Renewal, 1973–1983* (Chicago: Third World Press, 1984) *Killing Memory, Seeking Ancestors* (Detroit: Lotus Press, 1987)	Illinois Art Council grant, 1981. National Endowment for the Arts grant, 1982. U.S. African American Cultural Center's Alain Locke Award for Literature, 1985. President of the African American Book Centers, Chicago, Illinois. Author of the year for Illinois by the Illinois Association of

Nine Major Broadside Press Poets, 1980–1995 (continued)

Name	Primary residency during this period	Published books	Awards and honors
Haki R. Madhubuti (cont.)		Editor, *Say That the River Turns: The Impact of Gwendolyn Brooks* (Chicago: Third World Press, 1987)	Teachers of English, 1991. American Book Award, 1991.
		Black Men: Obsolete, Single, Dangerous?: The Afrikan American Family in Transition, Essays in Discovery, Solution, and Hope (Chicago: Third World Press, 1990)	
		Confusion by Any Other Name: Essays Exploring the Negative Impact of the Blackman's Guide to Understanding the Blackwoman (Chicago: Third World Press, 1990)	
		Editor, *Why L.A. Happened: Implications of the '92 Los Angeles Rebellion* (Chicago: Third World Press, 1993)	
		Claiming Earth, Race, Rage, Rape, Redemption: Blacks Seeking a Culture of Enlightened Empowerment (Chicago: Third World Press, 1994)	
Sonia Sanchez (1934–)	Philadelphia, PA	*A Sound Investment* (Chicago: Third World Press, 1980)	Honorary Citizen of Atlanta, GA, 1982. Tribute to Black Women Award, Black Students of Smith College 1982. Lucretia Mott Award of the Academy of Arts and Letters, 1984. American Book Award, Before Columbus Foundation, 1985, for *Homegirls and Handgrenades.* Pennsylvania Governor's Award in the humanities, 1989, for bringing great distinction to herself and her discipline through remarkable accomplishment. The Peace and Freedom Award from the Women International League for Peace and Freedom, 1988.
		I've Been a Woman: New and Selected Poems (Oakland, CA: Black Scholar Press, 1981)	
		Crisis in Culture: Two Speechs by Sonia Sanchez (Black Literation Press, 1983)	
		Homegirls and Handgrenades (New York: Thunder's Mouth Press, 1984)	
		I'm Black When I'm Singing, I'm Blue When I Can't (1982)	
		Under a Soprano Sky (Trenton, NJ: Africa World Press, 1987)	
		Shake Down Memory (Trenton, NJ: Africa World Press, 1991)	

Name	Primary residency during this period	Published books	Awards and honors
Sonia Sanchez (cont.)		*Autumn Blues* (Trenton, NJ): Africa World Press, 1992)	
Margaret Walker (1915–)	Jackson, MS	*Richard Wright, Daemonic Genius: A Portrait of the Man, a Critical Look at His Work* (New York: Warner Books, 1987) *This Is My Century: New and Collected Poems* (Athens: University of Georgia Press, 1989) *How I Wrote Jubilee and Other Essays on Life and Literature*, ed. by Maryemma Graham (New York: The Feminist Press, 1990)	W. E. B. DuBois Award from the Association of Social and Behavioral Scientists, Inc., 1982. The Smithsonian Institution's Black Women: Achievement Against the Odds Award, 1984–86. A Distinguished Alumna Award from the University of Iowa, 1988. A Women of Courage citation, 1988. A Distinguished Professorship in Humanities, established in her honor at Jackson State University, 1988. A Candace Award of Letters, 1989. A Lynhurst Foundation Award, 1989. A Mississippi Library Association Award for Best Book by a Mississippian, 1990. *Jackson Advocate* (Miss.) Special Section, "A 50 Year Salute to Margaret Walker Alexander," October 15, 1992.

Broadside Press celebrated its twenty-fifth anniversary during the month of October 1990, with a series of events held in Detroit, including poetry readings by Etheridge Knight, Leslie Reese and Albert Ward at the Detroit Museum of African-American History. Haki R. Madhubuti was among the out-of-town guests who attended the celebrations in honor of Dudley Randall and Broadside Press.[96] Perhaps the *Detroit Free Press* best summed up the situation with its editorial, which informed Greater Detroit that Broadside Press "has enriched us with African-American poetry."

> If it weren't for Broadside Press, many of us might not know the voice of Nikki Giovanni, who has called Broadside the midwife of the black literary movement of the 1960s and 1970s. Or Etheridge Knight. Or Sonia Sanchez. Or Haki Madhubuti. Or Audre Lord. Or Dudley Randall. Or a host of others.
>
> Mr. Randall, Detroit's poet laureate, founded Broadside Press on a shoestring 25 years ago. Since then, it "has grown by hunches, intuitions, trial and error," Mr. Randall has written. Today, the Detroit-based publishing house — run by Hilda and Don Vest — is an internationally known outlet for the work of African-American poets who are still vastly underrepresented on the lists of the larger publishers.
>
> The 25th anniversary of Broadside is being marked by events around the city — celebrating not only the past but the future of African-American poetry. Some are free and open to the public. They include a poetry reading by Mr. Knight, Leslie Reese and Albert Ward at 1 P.M. today at the Detroit Institute of Arts and the introduction of the HIP (Horizons in Poetry) anthology, at 7 P.M. this evening at the Museum of African-American History.
>
> Were it not for Broadside, many of the works of poets who seek to document the black experience might never have found an audience. Broadside — and its founder — deserve our gratitude.[97]

During the early nineties Broadside published five new books: Ron Allen and Stella Crews, editors, *HIPology* (1990, a poetry anthology of 158 pages priced at $15; Murray Jackson, *Watermelon Rinds and Cherry Pits* (1991), poetry, 98 pages at $7; Sharon Smith-Knight, *Wine Sip and Other Delicious Poems*, 79 pages at $7; Irene Rosemond, compiler, *Reflections: An Oral History of Detroit*, a historical and family/oral history book, 106 pages at $10; and Hilda Vest, *Sorrow's End*, poetry, 72 pages at $8. In 1994, the company published two new books, Monica Morgan's *Freedom's Road: A Photo Journal of South Africa's First All-Race Election*; and a children's book on *Kwanzaa* by playwright Ron Milner. In 1995, Broadside planned to issue new printings of Leslie Reese's *Upside Down Tapestry Mosaic History* and Rayfield Waller's *Abstract Blues*.[98]

The social backgrounds of Broadside's authors and editors of books for the period 1990–95 are described, where the data are known, in Table 5.5. The list contains four men and six women. All have spent part or most of their careers in Detroit. A highly educated group, a majority of them attended Wayne State University and hold an undergraduate degree from that institution. All have had varied professional careers, but the common denominators among them are the field of teaching and their work as poets and editors of African-American literature and culture.[99]

Critics have been kind to the poets and their new books of poetry produced at Broadside under the Vests since 1987. Leslie A. Reese's *Upside Down Tapestry Mosaic History* (1987) was the first volume to appear under the new publishers. It contained a supportive foreword by Detroit's noted poet, Alvin Aubert. Critic Terri L. Jewell wrote in the *Black Scholar*:

Upside Down Tapestry Mosaic History is a strongly crafted first volume for Leslie Reese. If this work is any indication of what she is going into, we are witnessing the arrival of a contemporary poet of note.[100]

Scholar Donald Franklin Joyce was also favorable toward Reese's book. He described the book as:

a remarkable first collection and bodes well for Leslie Reese's future as a poet. Likewise, it bespeaks a celebratory new lease on life for Broadside Press as the first book issued under the new ownership and management of Donald and Hilda Vest.[101]

Broadside's second new publication of poetry was Rayfield Waller's *Abstract Blues: Poems, 1980–87*, issued by the company in 1988. Editor and poet Gloria House (Aneb Kgositsile) wrote:

Leslie Reese was born in 1961 in Detroit, Michigan (ca. 1987 photo courtesy Broadside Press).

Nowhere in modern literature will the reader find more arresting pictures of contemporary social reality, more insightful naming of the deathly hoaxes or subtleties of "progress" and "science." Waller's excellent control of the language pulls us right into the poetic terrain with him, and we nod as he points to "green computer screens glowing lewdly on row after row of coffee colored faces" we hear "a thousand rolex watches chime the catechism of the lunch hour," and we agree with him and Achebe, things are falling apart.[102]

Two more poetry collections were published in 1989 by Broadside, Aneb Kgositsile's (Gloria House) *Rainrituals*, and Albert Michael Ward's *Patches on Mainstreet*. Both poets have had extensive work and service backgrounds in Detroit. These experiences are reflected in their poetry. Critics noted this impact on their creations. Arts correspondent Carolyn Warfied wrote in 1990 that Aneb Kgositsile

has a keen aesthetic sensitivity coupled with a spiritual compassion for the anguish and pressure brought upon society. "To be human is to protect and nurture all, for the death of one is the diminishing of all," she said.

Rainrituals is a captivating reference when the heart seeks the love only solitude can nourish; the place where commitment abides. *Rainrituals* is a rally "to life, which we are determined not to relinquish!"[103]

The social consciousness of poet Albert M. Ward is reflective of the new mood among many black poets in the eighties. This is evident in his signature poem "Patches on Mainstreet."

Table 5.5

Social Backgrounds of Broadside Press Authors, 1985–1995

Name	Place of Birth	Date of Birth	Education	Occupation	Residence in 1989–90
Ron Allen	N/A	N/A	N/A	Writer, editor	Detroit, MI
Stella Crews	Port Huron, MI	Feb. 21, 1950–	Mary Grace Col., 1968–71; Wayne St. 1971–72	Hospital worker, editor, writer, performer	Detroit, MI
Murray Jackson	Philadelphia, PA	Dec. 21, 1926–	Wayne State, B.A., M.A.	Educator, administrator consultant	Detroit, MI
Aneb Kgositsile (Gloria House)	Tampa, FL	February 14, 1941–	Univ. of Calif., Berkeley, A.B., Univ. of Mich., Ph.D.	Educator, writer, editor	Detroit, MI
Leslie Reese	Detroit, MI	Oct. 23, 1961–	Wayne State; Spelman Col.	Writer, media performer	Huntsville, AL, and Detroit, MI
Irene Rosemond	Albany, NY	August 29, 1920–	N/A	Writer	Detroit, MI
Sharon Smith-Knight	Detroit, MI	June 6, 1943–	Univ. of Mich., B.Ed., 1978	Educator, writer	Detroit, MI
Hilda Vest	Griffin, GA	June 5, 1933–	Wayne State, B.S.	Educator, writer, editor, publisher	Detroit, MI
Rayfield Waller	Detroit, MI	March 19, 1960–	Wayne State, B.A.; Cornell Univ., Ph.D. studies	Educator, editor, writer	Ithaca, NY
Albert M. Ward	Detroit, MI	Oct. 16, 1950–	N/A	Business, writer, songwriter, govt. service	Detroit, MI

PATCHES ON MAINSTREET

Not so old
but worn like his coat
he hangs to the side of life
made of brown patches,
pieces of string

Up/Down Woodward
arms hung low,
Patches leans
when he walks past
the downtown windows.

Street folk trust Patches.
He never turns away
when they ask… "Patches,
you got any quarters?"

"God don't like ugly," Patches'd say.
"Seen the best and worst
of all life's offerings,
I'll give you a hard time
If I think yr hustling."

At Grand Circus Park,
the Pigeon lady
feeds her friends
…bits of corn,
her hands like white porcelain,
feet bound
in old newspaper.

Her dolls head silent,
cotton hair tangled with feathers,
a red scarf around her neck,
Patches would say to anyone watching,
"She is innocent, Jesus loves her."

In Kennedy Square,
the cowboy dances.
Rights, lefts, jabs and crosses,
hooks, straights…He practices,
prances, shadow boxes.

Passerbys shake their heads.
Some point, laugh, make comment,
"Look at this fool in cowboy boots
acting like he's a champion."

"I used to do this," Patches hears
between the cowboy's punches
"I used to do this."
The cowboy's words crack/stumble.

Patches wears an old brown hat
where he keeps hope and conversation.
Patches wears two shirts
and sometimes a sweater beneath
his grey tweed jacket.

Patches
not so old
but worn like his coat
hangs to the side of life
in his search for truth
with a shoestring tied
around his soul.[104]

Carolyn Warfield writes that "Albert M. Ward's commitment to humanitarianism spans many years." His poetry also captures this concern and is

reminiscent of growing to manhood in Detroit, [and] security the old Black neighborhoods had. Ward interprets city streets "growing older and not so healthy or as rich as before." Nevertheless, he's convinced "Detroit is holding on because of its Wonderful Roots."[105]

In 1990, critics were especially impressed with Broadside's new anthology of Detroit poets, *HIPology: Horizons in Poetry*, edited by Ron Allen and Stella Crews. Critic Pat Fry's review of the book observed that *HIPology*

is named after a poetry reading series that began in 1982 called "Horizons in Poetry." The monthly series continues every second Tuesday, 8 P.M., at Alexander's, a Detroit restaurant. A featured reader is followed by an open mike performance.

Sixty-five of the 75 poets featured at the poetry readings during the last eight years are published in the anthology.... The HIP poets are representative of the rich ethnic diversity of Detroit's population — African American, Mexican-American, European-American and Asian-American. Appropriately, this latest anthology is dedicated to Dudley Randall.[106]

Surprisingly this anthology reveals just how much the passage of time can make on the poetic talent in a community. Only four poets from the Dudley Randall era (1965–85) at Broadside Press appear in *HIPology*: Alvin Aubert, Naomi Long Madgett, Melba Boyd, and Stella Crews.

Broadside Press published Murray Jackson's *Watermelon Rinds and Cherry Pits* and Sharon Smith-Knight's *Wine Sip and Other Delicious Poems* in 1991. Jackson's poetry, like many of his contemporaries at Broadside, captures the essence of the black historical past in the many moods and phases of the black community in Michigan.

Though this is the poet's first published collection, there are no "beginner's" issues here. Rather this poetry reflects several decades of a full, multifaceted life as husband, father, teacher, pensive observer of community life, lover. These are the notations of an urban villager who knows first hand the nooks and crannies of his people's life, and helps us to recall what has been forgotten, or imagine what we have never known. Here are remembered pool rooms and rent parties, con men and nuns in brown habits, strange in contrast with their ghetto surroundings. Here also are the poet's fine paintings of his beloved cityscapes. All of these images retrieve what has been lost in a eulogy almost palpable.[107]

Sharon Smith-Knight's collection pulls more closely from the tradition of black humor in her quest to capture the black experience in verse. A Michigan critic writes that Sharon Smith-Knight is

Albert Michael Ward was born in 1950 in Detroit, Michigan. Besides his writing interest, he has been very active with urban affairs issues in the Greater Detroit area for over twenty years (photo by Victoria A. Roberts; courtesy Broadside Press).

a poet who is known for her ability to capture even the
most reluctant audiences with her sultry renditions.
In the title poem, she coos:

If you were a vintage bottle of wine
and I could fill my cup
I'd savor your essence for a time
The slowly I'd drink you up.

In "Onions," she affirms:

Memories stored in dark, dry places
are like onions hung in cellars.

Onions peeled, expose layers of feelings
to taste on hungry nights.

Your memory lingers
like the odor of onions
pungent, hard to wash away.
Remembering seasons my soul
and often makes me cry.[108]

In 1992, Broadside published *Reflections: An Oral History of Detroit*, compiled by Irene Rosemond. This book documents the historical experiences of twenty Detroiters through their accounts of the city's past and its influences on the present and the future of its inhabitants: "Reflections" features narratives of individuals who lived in Detroit during the 1920s, 1930s and 1940s and the presentation offer[s] a look at how life was for blacks in Detroit during those years."[109] This book reflects Broadside's efforts to add another dimension to its publication record, by focusing some of the company interests into the social sciences. *Reflections* represents a successful effort by Broadside to tap into the black family/oral history movement, while adding to the life and culture of the modern world.

A new collection of poetry by Hilda Vest, *Sorrow's End*, was published by Broadside in 1993. Critic J. Carl called it "by far her best work to date," saying the Broadside publisher "has a way of painting an expressive picture of the everyday emotions of pain, agony, love and joy while maintaining a strong sense of survival. As the title of the book would suggest: the end of sorrow is the beginning of hope. An outstanding collection."[110]

Collectively, the ten volumes of poetry and one oral history book produced by Broadside Press from 1987 to 1994 radiate five significant themes on the human condition of the African-American people during modern times. These themes are: (1) how does the "past" look to the "present"; (2) disbelief at what has happened to black people, psychologically and socially, since the death of Malcolm X (in 1965) and Martin Luther King, Jr. (in 1968); (3) the phenomenon of the Age of Media and its negative consequences and challenges for African peoples; (4) the vulnerability of blacks; and (5) tasks ahead in the "future world" for human beings.

Between 1985 and 1995, the Vests have continued to operate Broadside Press against the odds of economic hard times, conservative politics, and a social environment where the reading of black books, and especially poetry, is valued much less than during the Black Arts Movement of the sixties and seventies. Writer Junette A. Pinckney observed in 1989 that:

> The Vests had made the decision to join the ranks of independent black publishers based on Hilda's relationship with Randall, who had nurtured her as a poet and invited her to participate in Broadside readings beginning in 1980. "I feel a certain responsibility to carry on the work of someone who was very important, namely, Dudley Randall," Hilda responds when asked why she took on such a formidable task. "Broadside Press is too precious to let it go, and he had too much work in to let it go."[111]

Nonetheless, like their former predecessors at Broadside, the Vests'

> biggest problem is that it [Broadside Press] is under capitalized. The company is developing how-to books that it hopes will become the money-maker to subsidize the poetry volumes that are Broadside's first love. Donald Vest also is submitting proposals to foundations and arts councils as well as looking for partial corporate funding to help with daily costs. "If we could maintain two years of operational funding where we could just hire a secretary and have a copy machine on the premises — we call the copy center down the street our 'satellite office' — we could be self-sustaining by the third year." For the time being, Broadside is funded by book sales and the Vest's personal savings but they are optimistic about the future of the legendary press. "We certainly have bitten off quite a mouthful," says business manager Donald Vest, who used to think he could spend his retirement years doing volunteer work. "But it's an interesting challenge, something we can love doing."[112]

The Vests have tackled the ageless problem of audience development by focusing a part of their energies on increasing book sales to schools and colleges. Donald Vest told the *Detroit News* in 1991, "I hope the recent push for Afrocentric curriculums will inspire schools to use more books by black authors."[113] If this happens, and Broadside sells more books, then the company can also publish more black writers in the future, while at the same time helping to improve the literacy rate among blacks. Hilda Vest is a strong supporter of such efforts and believes that Detroit is a good regional market for literature because "It is a robust city which encompasses many facets of life. This leads to poetry. Unfortunately, poetry is viewed as being elitist."[114]

Nationally, black writers continue to believe in Broadside Press. In the early nineties, according to Donald Vest, the company "received an average 25 manuscripts per month, mostly poetry." But many black writers are so desperate that they even submit unsolicited original manuscripts to Broadside without return postage. The company cannot assume the financial costs of such services, so these manuscripts "are just collecting dust. She [Hilda] is hesitant to throw them away. She recognizes that some represent years of work." The central goal of Broadside today "is to publish quality work. 'That is the salvation of the small press. People look to them for that high quality,' notes Hilda Vest during this period."[115] In Detroit,

> local small presses issue almost exclusively poetry books. Publication averages under five volumes a year per press, with single print runs well under 1,000 copies. Distribution is limited. Many nonprofit publishers operate with art grants and government funds. Others are financed solely by book sales and donations. Most agree that no matter how income is derived, it's never enough. They often put in their own dollars to publish a work. Authors and illustrators are usually paid with copies of their books.
>
> It's especially because of this low scale, say small publishers, that they can provide alternatives for the literary community.[116]

Indeed, this assessment explains many of the reasons for the success of Broadside Press for over twenty-five years. Yet, the total commitment of its editors to Broadside is another irrefutable reason for its long existence in this country.

Meanwhile, during the 1990s Dudley Randall has continued his retirement in Detroit. He grew somewhat less active in this period than he had been in the eighties, but has kept up a public schedule of readings and gives support as a consultant to the Vests' efforts at Broadside Press.[117] Randall's poems were published in the early nineties in such organs as the *Poetry Resource Center of Michigan Newsletter*, and in *The New Cavalcade: African American Writing from 1760 to the Present* (1991), Arthur P. Davis, J. Saunders Redding and Joyce Ann Joyce, editors. Editors are still attracted to his major poems, such as "The Profile on the Pillow."[118] The poet's special place in American letters at this stage of his life (he reached 84 years of age in 1998) is reflected in the fact that eight of his books were still in print or distribution during 1994–95. Broadside Press carried six of his titles in 1990–95, including *For Malcolm X: Poems on the Life and Death of Malcolm X* (1967), co-edited with Margaret Burroughs; *Cities Burning* (1968); *Love You* (1970); *After the Killing* (1973); and *A Capsule Course in Black Poetry Writing* (1975), co-written with Gwendolyn Brooks, Keorapetse Kgositsile, and Haki R. Madhubuti.[119] Bantam Books has reprinted Randall's edited anthology, *The Black Poets: A New Anthology* (1971), several times.[120] Lotus Press continues to distribute Randall's *A Litany of Friends: New and Selected Poems* (1983). Randall thus continues to enjoy a very high status among living black American poets.

Several major Broadside authors died in the early nineties. First came the death at age 59 of critic Addison Gayle, Jr., due to complications from pneumonia, in 1991; followed in 1992 with that of the 58-year-old poet Audre Lorde, due to liver cancer. Both were major American writers and leading voices of black literature and culture during the Black Arts Movement.[121] Each was the author of a major Broadside book; Gayle contributed *Claude McKay: The Black Poet at War* (1972), and Lorde wrote *From a Land Where Other People Live* (1973) and *Cables to Rage* (1973), distributed by Broadside for Paul Breman's Heritage Series of London, England.[122]

Such losses created a void in segments of the black American artistic community. At the same time the general psychological, social, and economic status of African-Americans became increasingly depressing for many in the central cities. Dudley Randall and his family still lived in such an outpost, known nationally by many as "Murder City," and by others as "Motown." Detroit suffered greatly from the sixties to the nineties, and on a personal level, so has Dudley Randall. Writer Ze'ev Chafets captures this sadness in his 1990 best-selling book, *Devil's Night*. Among the many Michigan citizens whom Chafets interviewed for the book was Dudley Randall. Chafet's account of his encounter with Randall illustrates the poet's depressed mood about the human condition during this period, and the state of both black and white race relations in Greater Detroit:

> There is a lovely park across the street from Dudley Randall's house, on the west side of Detroit, but at three in the afternoon it was deserted. At the curb, almost directly opposite the house, two very tough-looking young men sat in a late-model Pontiac. They passed a bottle between them and gazed out the windows, as if they were waiting for someone.
>
> I rang the bell and Dudley Randall had to open several locks to let me in. At seventy-four he was a stooped, tired-looking man with bifocals, dressed in a flannel shirt and Khaki trousers. His living room was lined with books, the walls were covered with African art and there were *National Geographic* magazines and anthologies of poetry stacked on the coffee table. Above the bookcase I saw a plaque, signed by the mayor, proclaiming Randall the Poet Laureate of Detroit.
>
> Randall looked out his front window and gestured at the car in front. "I moved across from the park because I thought it would be nice," he said. "But those two sit there every day and drink whiskey. And then they urinate in the bushes." He made a sad face, offered me a set and took one himself.
>
> Randall has lived his life with books. For years he was a librarian and poet-in-residence at Wayne State University. During that time he founded the Broadside Press, a forum for black poets. But now, retired, he doesn't write anymore, nor does he bother much with literature. "I no longer find truth in the great poets or the great books," he said. There was a pause. "I still read Tolstoy," he added, and fell silent again.
>
> "What's it like being the Poet Laureate of Detroit?" I asked. Randall considered for a moment. "Poetry isn't such a big thing in Detroit," he said finally, in a flat tone.
>
> "What do you think of the city?" I asked, trying hard to make conversation. Friends had told me that Dudley Randall was one of the smartest, most perceptive people in Detroit, but he seemed too discouraged to talk. He looked out the window at the car. "I want to move away," he said. "I'd like to go someplace where it's warm."
>
> A few weeks earlier, on a visit to the mayor's office, I had noticed a poem of Randall's entitled "Detroit Renaissance," which is dedicated to Coleman Young, hanging on a wall in the reception room. Now I asked Randall about it, and he rose slowly, returning with a slim volume of his work, which includes the poem. He sat in silence as I read it to myself.

Cities have died, have burned,
Yet phoenix-like returned
To soar up livelier, lovelier than before.
Detroit has felt the fire
Yet each time left the pyre
As if the flames had power to restore.

First, burn away the myths
Of what it was, and is —
A lovely, tree-laned town of peace and trade.
Hatred has festered here,
And bigotry and fear
Filled streets with strife and raised the barricade.

Wealth of a city lies,
Not in its factories,
Its marts and towers crowding to the sky,
But in its people who
Possess grace to imbue
Their lives with beauty, wisdom, charity.

You have those too long hid,
Who built the pyramids,
Who searched the skies and mapped the planets' range,
Who sang the songs of grief
That made the whole world weak,
Whose Douglass, Malcolm, Martin rung in change.

The Indian, with his soul
Attuned to nature's role;
The sons and daughters of Cervantes' smile;
Pan Tadeysz's children too
Entrust their fate to you;
Souls forged by Homer's, Dante's
Shakespeare's, Goethe's, Yeats' style.

Together we will build
A city that will yield
To all their hopes and dreams so long deferred.
New faces will appear
Too long neglected here;
New minds, new means will build a brave new world.

"Do you still believe it?" I asked. "Will you ever be able to rebuild this city together?"

Randall looked at me and shrugged, a slow movement of tired shoulders. "I guess not," said the Poet Laureate of Detroit. "All the white people have moved away."

And that is the simple truth. The week I met with Randall, the Detroit papers published a University of Chicago study that found, to no one's surprise, that the suburbs of the Motor City are the most segregated in the United States.

Many blacks look beyond the Eight Mile Road border and see America — an undifferentiated, uncaring world of suburban affluence where they are neither liked nor wanted. Actually, the almost four million people of the Metropolitan Detroit area — Wayne, Oakland and Macomb counties — are subdivided by ethnicity. Macomb, to the northeast, is blue-collar territory; a large percentage of its people are second and third generation Polish and Italian refugees from Detroit. Oakland, to the northwest, is the second wealthiest American county among those with a population of over one million, and it is dominated by WASPs and, to a lesser extent, Jews. Detroit itself is located in Wayne County, whose population, outside the city, includes a good number of working-class southern whites, Hispanics, Arabs and ethnics.

In most ways the towns of the tri-county area have little in common; what they share is an estrangement from Detroit. Unlike the suburbs of other major cities, they are not bedroom communities. The average suburbanite almost never visits the city for any reason. As Arthur Johnson, head of the local NAACP, observed, Detroiters know they aren't loved by their neighbors. During the early years of the great white exodus this antipathy was impersonal. It got a face in 1973, with the election of Mayor Coleman Young.

The problem started with Young's inaugural address, in which he warned hoodlums ("whether they're wearing blue uniforms or Superfly suits") to "hit Eight Mile and keep on going." The idea of Detroit policemen crossing the boundary didn't seem to bother suburbanites, but they were mightily exercised by the prospect of a legion of Superfly badasses invading their turf.

A more politic mayor would have tried to mend fences, but Young is not a fence-mender. He dubbed his neighbors "the hostile suburbs" and mounted a campaign of verbal and political harassment that still goes on today. They responded with a hatred usually reserved for enemy heads of state—which, in a way, he is. The mention of the mayor's name is enough to set off tirades from the ritzy salons of Grosse Pointe to the redneck suburbs—places such as Melvindale, "The Little Town with the Big Heart."[123]

But, by 1994 Mayor Young (age seventy-six) was no longer in office, and a new mayor, Dennis Archer (age fifty-three), a lawyer, now sits in City Hall.[124] Many Detroiters are encouraged that he may be able to turn the city around economically, yet this remains to be seen.[125] In essence, blacks in Detroit, as elsewhere in America, live in a country where "more than 36 million Americans live in poverty—and 42% of them are in the cities," according to *Business Week*. Yet, the black community is under tremendous stress since "more than 60% of poor blacks now live in center cities...[where] a stunning 62% [of them reside] in female-headed households, compared with 28% of poor whites."[126]

Such local, state and national conditions did not create a good environment for black writers or publishers. However, many literary figures and institutions continued to press forward in the black community during the early nineties, in spite of economic, political, and social setbacks. As Table 5.4 notes, ten major best-selling Broadside Press poets from the sixties and seventies remained very active in the new period.[127] Five poets in this group represent the older generation of Broadside poets, and include Gwendolyn Brooks, Sterling A. Brown, James A. Emanuel, Lance Jeffers, Margaret Walker, and Margaret Danner who was also a key member of this group; however, she died in 1982.[128]

The remaining four poets on the list, Nikki Giovanni, Etheridge Knight, Haki R. Madhubuti, and Sonia Sanchez, were among the most popular of the younger generation of Broadside poets in the sixties and seventies.[129]

What is most striking about the nine major Broadside poets in Table 5.4 is that after the seventies, most had to turn to white publishers in order to see their manuscripts turned into books. Dudley Randall was happy with this development. In 1982, he told journalist Suzanne Dolezal that he was "gratified that many Broadside poets have gone on to the big publishing houses (Etheridge Knight is with Houghton-Mifflin, poet Audre Lorde is with W. W. Norton, Nikki Giovanni is at William Morrow), but he worries about the new poets."[130]

Only two of the nine poets, Brooks and Madhubuti, did not publish new books in the eighties and nineties with white publishers. In 1981, Brooks published her poetry collection, *To Disembark,* with black-owned Third World Press, under Madhubuti's leadership. However, all of her other books during this era were published by her own company. Five of Madhubuti's books were published by Third World Press in the eighties and early nineties, and his sixth volume, a collection of poetry, was printed by Lotus Press, another black-owned company at the time. On the other hand, James A. Emanuel turned to two white publishers for publication of *Snowflakes and Steel: My Life as a Poet* (Durham, N.C.: Jay B. Hubbell Center, Duke University, 1981) and *A Poet's Mind* (New York: Regents, 1983). His other four books were published by Lotus Press. Sonia Sanchez produced nine books between 1980 and 1994; all but one, *Homegirls and Handgrenades* (Thunder's Mouth Press, 1984), were published by black publishers. New books by Brown, Jeffers, Knight, and Walker were published exclusively by white publishers during the eighties and early nineties.[131] Thus, in spite of the high state of black consciousness which was produced by the Black Arts Movement, many black poets later had to publish with white companies, because the economics of publishing forced the closure of many small black publishing companies, or limited the number of books which many of them could produce from year to year.

Geographically during the eighties and early nineties, the nine poets were concentrated in the Midwest and the South, but only one author, James A. Emanuel, lived abroad in France. Unless they were retired from active work, such as Sterling A. Brown and Margaret Walker, all of the remaining poets held teaching positions at some point during this period. The income produced from teaching aided the economic survival of poets, such as Etheridge Knight. Two of the nine poets died during this period, Sterling A. Brown on January 13, 1989, at age eighty-seven, from leukemia and Etheridge Knight on March 10, 1991, at age fifty-nine, from lung cancer.[132] Both poets were considered giants among American writers of the twentieth century.[133] The collectively high status and national recognition of the nine poets (see Table 5.6) is indicated by the large number of awards and honors which they received between 1980 and 1995. Gwendolyn Brooks stands out as one of the most decorated poets of her generation, followed on this list by Margaret Walker, Nikki Giovanni, Sonia Sanchez, and Haki R. Madhubuti.[134] Thus, long after Broadside Press had stopped producing new books for these poets, they were still mutually beneficial to each other. Broadside continued to distribute their books from the sixties and seventies and to help keep their names and work before the public. Consequently, the income produced by the books of the nine authors aided the economic survival of Broadside during the difficult days of this period.

Broadside's main African-American competition in the publishing of black poetry continued to be Lotus Press in Detroit and Third World Press in Chicago. Both companies produced a significant range of poetic works in the eighties and nineties. Naomi Long Madgett oversaw the operations of Lotus Press during this period, and between 1980 and 1995, she published fifty-seven single-authored books and three anthologies. Table 5.6 lists the books produced by the company.[135] The focus of Lotus continued to be on "literary excellence." Madgett told critic Donald Franklin Joyce in 1986 that at Lotus Press:

> We do not believe there is a white standard and a black standard. Good literature transcends such artificial divisions. But we do not dictate to the author; we are not looking for anything in particular except in terms of excellence. The poet may be as angry, as revolutionary as he/she is conditioned to be — or as ostensibly nonracial in subject matter (and I say "ostensibly" because I do not believe any black poet's work is non-racial, regardless of appearances and superficial observances) — the ultimate questions concerning good and enduring values in art must be answered positively.[136] *(cont. on page 216)*

Table 5.6

Lotus Press Publications, 1980–1995

Author	Title of Book	Year of Publication	Pages	Price
Abba Elethea (James W. Thompson)	*The Antioch Suite-Jazz*	1980	36	$ 3.00
James E. Emanuel	*A Chisel in the Dark: Poems Selected and New*	1980	73	$ 4.00
Ronald Fair	*Rufus*	1980	58	$ 4.00
Naomi Long Madgett	*A Student's Guide to Creative Writing*	1980	134	$11.00
Herbert W. Martin	*The Forms of Silence*	1980	61	$ 4.00
Helen Earle Simcox, ed.	*Dear Dark Faces: Portraits of a People*	1980	104	$ 6.00
Eugene Haun	*Cardinal Paints and Other Poems*	1981	85	$ 5.00
Gayl Jones	*Song for Anninho*	1981	89	$ 4.50
Naomi Long Madgett	*Phantom Nightingale*	1981	60	$ 4.50
Dudley Randall	*A Litany of Friends: New and Selected Poems*	1981	101	$10.00
David L. Rice	*Lock This Man Up*	1981	67	$ 3.50
Philip Royster	*Songs and Dances: Selected Poems*	1981	62	$ 3.50
Ron Welburn	*Heartland: Selected Poems*	1981	67	$ 4.00
Gilbert Allen	*In Everything*	1982	75	$ 4.50
Houston A. Baker, Jr.	*Spirit Run*	1982	38	$ 3.00
Beth Brown	*Light Years: Poems 1973–1976*	1982	76	$ 4.50
Tom Dent	*Blue Lights and River Songs*	1982	75	$ 4.50
Ray Fleming	*Diplomatic Relations*	1982	59	$ 4.00
James C. Kilgore	*African Violet: Poem for a Black Woman*	1982	76	$ 5.00
E. Ethelbert Miller	*Season of Hunger, Cry of Rain, Poems, 1975–80*	1982	68	$ 4.50
Kiarri T-H. Cheatwood	*Psalms of Redemption*	1983	50	$ 4.00
James A. Emanuel	*The Broken Bowl* (New and Uncollected Poems)	1983	85	$ 4.50

Author	Title of Book	Year of Publication	Pages	Price
Naomi F. Faust	All Beautiful Things	1983	105	$ 5.00
Gayl Jones	The Hermit-Woman	1983	77	$ 4.00
May Miller	The Ransomed Wait	1983	77	$ 4.50
Sarah Carolyn Reese	Songs of Freedom	1983	63	$ 5.00
Satiafa (Vivian V. Gordon)	For Dark Women and Others	1983	63	$ 5.00
Jill Witherspoon Boyer	Breaking Camp	1984	61	$ 6.00
Kiarri T-H. Cheatwood	Elegies for Patrice: A Lyrical Historical Remembrance	1984	37	$ 3.00
Sybil Kein	Delta Dancer	1984	89	$ 9.00
Delores Kendrick	Now Is the Things to Praise	1984	117	$ 7.00
Mwatabu Okantah	Collage	1984	68	$ 5.00
Gary Smith	Songs for My Father	1984	78	$ 5.00
Paulette Childress White	The Watermelon Dress	1984	61	$ 6.00
Houston A. Baker, Jr.	Blues Journeys Home	1985	59	$ 5.00
Pinkie G. Lane	I Never Scream: New and Selected Poems	1985	104	$ 7.50
Gunilla Norris	Learning from the Angel	1985	62	$ 5.00
Kiarri T-H. Cheatwood	Bloodstorm: Five Books of Poems and Docu Poems Toward Liberation	1986	160	$ 8.50
Samuel Allen (Paul Vesey)	Every Round and Other Poems	1987	158	$ 9.00
James A. Emanuel	Deadly James and Other Poems	1987	82	$ 9.00
Agnes Nasmith Johnston	Beyond the Moongate	1987	102	$ 7.00
Haki R. Madhubuti	Killing Memory, Seeking Ancestors	1987	58	$ 8.00
Tanure Ojaide	The Eagle's Vision	1987	104	$ 8.00
Nubia Kai	Solos	1988	121	$ 8.50
Naomi Long Madgett, ed.	A Milestone Sampler: 15th Anniversary Anthology	1988	130	$ 9.00
	Octavia and Other Poems (Third World Press)	1988	118	$ 8.00

Author	Title of Book	Year of Publication	Pages	Price
Irma McClaurin	*Pearl's Song*	1988	91	$ 7.00
May Miller	*Halfway to the Sun*	1988	52	$ 5.00
Beth Brown	*Satin Tunnels*	1989	127	$ 8.50
Oliver LaGrone	*Dawnfire and Other Poems*	1989	133	$ 9.00
May Miller	*Collected Poems*	1989	235	$18.00
Atungaye Monifa	*Provisions*	1989	60	$ 5.00
Selene DeMedeiros	*This Is How I Love You*	1990	67	$ 6.00
Naomi F. Faust	*And I Travel by Rhythms and Words*	1990	318	$18.00
Toi Derricotte	*The Empress of the Death House*	1991	51	$ 3.50
James A. Emanuel	*Whole Grain: Collected Poems, 1958–89*	1991	396	$25.00
Naomi Long Madgett, ed.	*Women in Praise of Black Men (An Anthology)*	1992	235	$15.00
Robert Chrisman	*Minor Casualties: New and Selected Poems*	1993	60	$10.00
Naomi Long Madgett, ed.	*Remembrances of Spring:* Collected Poems (in conjunction with Michigan State Univ. Press)	1993	170	$24.95
Adam David Miller	*Forever Afternoon* (in conjunction with Mich. State Univ. Press)	1994	80	$10.00

Madgett's list of forty-four authors and editors of poetic collections is strikingly strong in terms of its range and diversity of literary talent. Several different generations of black poets were published by Lotus in the eighties and nineties. The older generation is represented by such powerful poetic voices as Samuel Allen (Paul Vesey), James A. Emanuel, Oliver LaGrone, Pinkie Gordon Lane, Naomi Long Madgett, May Miller, and Dudley Randall. Talent from the Black Arts Movement era on the list includes Houston A. Baker, Jr., Jill Witherspoon Boyer, Robert Chrisman, Tom Dent, James W. Thompson (Abba Elethea), Dolores Kendrick, Haki R. Madhubuti, Ronald Fair, Gayl Jones, Herbert Woodward Martin, E. Ethelbert Miller, Adam David Miller, Philip Royster, and Ron Welburn. Yet, what is most refreshing about Lotus' publication list is the fact that a majority of its authors were new poetic voices of the late seventies through the eighties and nineties. Madgett's editorial policy from the beginning of Lotus Press in the early seventies had been to support new talent: "I am particularly interested in the black poet who may be well known or who may be just beginning, but whose work I feel is of sound literary merit.... Our idea is that the only criterion is a sound literary standard regardless of subject matter."[137]

Thus, of the forty-four poets on the list during this period, twenty-six, or 59 percent, represent new poetic talent. Poets within this third group include Kiarri T-H. Cheatwood, Toi Derricotte, Naomi F. Faust, Nubia Kai, David L. Rice (W. Mondo Eyen we Langa), and Gary Smith.

Eight Lotus Press poets produced two or more books for the company during the eighties and nineties. Madgett heads the list with six books; followed by James A. Emanuel with four; Kiarri T-H. Cheatwood and May Miller, with three each; and Gayl Jones, Houston A. Baker, Jr., Beth Brown, and Naomi F. Faust with two each. In essence, the company has highlighted the work of the above poets. Madgett is especially appreciative of the poetic contributions made by two of the deans among African-American poets on her list, James A. Emanuel and May Miller. She published the collected works of both poets.[138]

As a small press, Lotus maintained a good gender balance during this period. Out of forty-four authors published by the company, twenty-five, or 57 percent, were men, and nineteen, or 43 percent, were women. However, more women than men were published in Lotus anthologies in the eighties and nineties. In the three anthologies published, *Dear Dark Faces: Portraits of a People* (1980), (Helen Earle Simcox, editor) and *A Milestone Sampler: 15th Anniversary Anthology* (1988) and *Adam of Ife: Black Women in Praise of Black Men* (1992) (both edited by Naomi Long Madgett), there were eighty-one women and thirty-one men represented.[139]

During the period 1980–95, Lotus Press published on the average between four and five new books a year. However, this range of publications decreased greatly to one or two books by 1990–95. Lotus, like Broadside and Third World Press, attempted to keep the costs of its books as low as possible for the buying public. An average Lotus Press book sold for $3 and $6 during this fifteen-year period — (thirty-six books out of sixty produced). Yet, fifteen books were priced between $7 and $9 a copy, three at $10, and six between $11 and $25. Such a wide price range in books was meant to help increase book sales, while also bringing in an increase in cash flow. The average size of a Lotus book was between forty and ninety pages. A large size book increased the range of a poet's work which was available to the public, and allowed the publisher to charge a fair price for the book, and hopefully make a profit too.

While the vast majority of Lotus writers were African-Americans, the company did expand its book list to include authors from other ethnic and cultural groups. By 1992, Lotus had published seven such writers. The list includes four European Americans: Gilbert Allen, Augene Haun, Gunilla Norris, and Ages Nasmith Johnston; two Nigerians: Ojaide Tanure and Kamaldeen Ibraheem; and one Brazilian: Selene DeMedeiros.[140]

During the eighties and nineties Lotus Press replaced Broadside Press as the leading small black publisher of new books of poetry in the United States. Its output of titles was prolific, when compared to that of other companies. Yet, Madgett was disturbed and very "critical of the major white reviewing media's neglect of titles published by black book publishers, but also extends her criticism to the small press reviewers."[141] The problem was of major significance to Lotus, Broadside, and Third World Press, because often their books went unreviewed, and thus unappreciated, with the added burden of small book sales.

Table 5.6, which lists the forty-four authors published by Lotus Press between 1980 and 1994, denotes the significance of this group to American poetry.[142] First, their general social backgrounds are similar to earlier groups of black poets, who were published by Broadside Press, Third World Press, and other contemporary black publishers in America.

The vast majority of the poets are urban dwellers, reflect a range of several generations of poets, are a very highly educated group, and make their living largely by teaching and other service occupations.[143] Many of the Lotus Press poets are closely identified with ten American cities, including New York, Chicago, Detroit, Washington, D.C., New Orleans, Louisiana, Los Angeles, Boston, and San Francisco/Oakland, California; where many of them have lived and worked since the sixties.[144]

On June 25–26, 1987, Lotus Press celebrated its fifteenth anniversary, with a series of programs at Wayne State University, sponsored by Lotus and the Center for Black Studies. Twenty poets and artists associated with Lotus were in attendance during the three days of poetic celebrations in Detroit. Among the poets who read at various programs were Samuel Allen, Jill Witherspoon Boyer, Kiarri T-H. Cheatwood, Ray Fleming, Agnes Nasmith Johnston, Sybil Kein, Dolores Kendrick, Pinkie Gordon Lane, Naomi Long Madgett, Haki R. Madhubuti, Herbert Woodward Martin, May Miller, Philip M. Royster, Satiafa (Vivian V. Gordon), and Paulette Childress White, among others.[145]

Naomi Long Madgett continues to fight for the recognition she believes African-American poets and poetry deserves. She also believes that small publishers should become more efficient in their operations. For that reason, she has fully computerized her operations; this has greatly aided the work of Lotus Press in terms of the production of new books, financial concerns, sales, and bookkeeping.[146] In fact, Madgett is Lotus Press. Nevertheless, she has attracted some volunteer help during the twenty-two years she has operated the press, generally in the form of financial contributions from published poets she has assisted. One of her published poets contributed funds for the company's first computer equipment. Later, Naomi Madgett gave this computer to Broadside Press. Madgett says as late as the mid-eighties Broadside was "doing everything by hand," even under the guidance of then new publishers Hilda and Donald Vest. Madgett has also assisted the Vests with suggestions on book design and other publishing concepts.[147]

The variety of the over sixty-five books produced by Lotus Press since 1972 is impressive. They are handsomely bound, printed and designed. African-American artists — as in the early days of Broadside Press — have been helpful to Lotus by allowing the publisher to use their artistic works, usually without fee, since Lotus doesn't have the budget for such payments. Space is not a problem for Lotus Press, as the company is located at Madgett's former residence which she purchased over three decades ago. She currently lives in another home she and her husband bought on the outer edges of the city.[148]

Madgett identifies the economics of publishing as a major obstacle for small black publishers. The last fifteen years have been especially cruel for such companies, and Madgett had to run Lotus largely unassisted:

> In 1984, Dr. Madgett felt it necessary to retire from teaching in order to comply with the ever increasing demands of the press. While there is some volunteer help, Lotus Press, Inc., remains much more of a one-person commitment than it should be, simply because there are insufficient funds for hiring dependable help. Naomi has never received a salary and still bears many expenses herself, including the donation of office space. Writing grant proposals requires more time than she can afford to spend, and so the critical need for a staff person who could free her for more creative contributions to the community goes unfulfilled.
> In spite of its ongoing struggle, Lotus Press, Inc., through the first quarter of 1991, has published seventy-four titles, sixty-eight of which are still in print. These books have small but worldwide distribution, and some are being used as required reading in

high schools and colleges. Many have received excellent reviews in prestigious journals. Some of the authors' careers have flourished as a result of their having been published by Lotus, a name which commands respect from those who are familiar with the quality of its offerings.[149]

But, back in 1985, Madgett told the *Detroit News*: "In January and February of this year, we came out with four (poetry) books, and I had to use $3,000 of my own money to get them out."[150] Indeed, the struggle to survive economically has been a long and hard one for black publishers. Identifying and reaching a market for black books remains an extraordinarily difficult task for small black publishers. Thus, publishing is a labor of love for Madgett, not one of profit. And, she notes for the record that "Without blacks, black writers would not get published."[151]

The economics of publishing forced Madgett, after the 1992 publication of *Adam of Ife: Black Women in Praise of Black Men*, to bring to an end the "publication of new book titles."[152] However, in 1993, she was able to negotiate a partnership with Michigan State University Press, East Lansing, Michigan, which assumed the publishing costs of producing at least two new Lotus Press books a year, and the distribution of the existing backlist of Lotus publications from 1972 to the present. Madgett announced that the new business arrangement now meant:

> We are no longer publishing books of poetry under the Lotus Press imprint. However, we have not gone out of business. We retain the same name and identity but have shifted our emphasis, now functioning as consultants in poetry and small press publishing.
>
> Naomi Long Madgett, formerly publisher and editor of Lotus Press and continuing as its director, is now Senior Editor of the newly established Michigan State University Press Lotus Poetry Series. Her work can now continue under less stressful conditions. Poets seeking a publisher may still submit their work to her in care of Lotus Press with the understanding that the two manuscripts accepted per year will be published by Michigan State University Press.
>
> Lotus Press books are now being distributed by Michigan State University Press. These volumes are now receiving greater exposure than in the past.[153]

In addition to this fortuitous turn of events, Madgett received several special honors in 1993. First, the Hilton-Long Poetry Foundation of Detroit, announced the creation of the "Naomi Long Madgett Poetry Award," in celebration of the seventieth birthday of the poet. Adam David Miller was selected as the first winner of this award (1993), which included a cash prize of $500 and publication of his collection of poems, *Forever Afternoon*, in 1994, by Michigan State University Press.[154] Second, the Before Columbus Foundation presented Madgett with an American Book Award in 1993, for her work as an American small publisher and poet.[155] Thirdly, during the summer of 1993, Madgett was awarded the Michigan Artist Award, "the top honor given by the Concerned Citizens for the Arts in Michigan."[156] The award was formerly presented to Madgett on October 28, 1993. On receiving the award, Madgett told the *Detroit Free Press*:

> I'm happy that poetry is being recognized as an art form because it is so often neglected, yet it appeals to something basic in all of us. Poetry is something people turn to in times of stress and I'm proud to be among the people they chose to recognize.[157]

Like Dudley Randall, Naomi Long Madgett has been a "long distanced runner" in the struggle to promote the creation, distribution, and preservation of African-American poetry. Like Dudley, she has performed this task as a teacher, editor, publisher, and poet. She reminds readers that when they come to poetry:

> Don't expect to read a poem through once and understand it like prose. It's as if a poet is holding out a hint of an idea. Now you have to reach out and bring your experience to it. A poet doesn't tell it all. A poet uses hints to imply things.[158]

As a black editor and publisher, "She knew poetry would never be a profitable pursuit. 'I had to do it. It was an emotional release. Most poets find it therapeutic.'"[159]

Her legacy to American letters is a rich one.

The third major black-owned publisher of poetry during this period was Third World Press of Chicago. Haki R. Madhubuti, who cofounded the company in 1967 with poets Johari Kunjufu (Johari Amini), and Carolyn Rodgers, has served for twenty-eight years as publisher and chief editor.[160] Writer Paula Giddings noted in 1989 that Third World Press was "the oldest of the Black-owned full-range publishers" active in the United States.[161] By 1990, Third World Press had published over 160 titles by more than 100 black writers.[162] During the course of its history, Third World Press' greatest star has been its publisher, Madhubuti. However, the company has also secured book deals with some of the most important contemporary black writers in the United States, including Gwendolyn Brooks, Gil Scott-Heron, Chancellor Williams, Sonia Sanchez, Useni Eugene Perkins, Frances Cress-Welsing, Joyce Ann Joyce, Nubia Kai, Alphonso Pinkney, and Amiri Baraka, among many others. Thus, Third World Press has emerged in the nineties as one of the strongest black publishers in this country.[163]

Madhubuti and Third World Press have historically had a close working relationship with Broadside Press and Lotus Press. As publishers, Dudley Randall, Naomi Long Madgett, and Haki R. Madhubuti have each published books by the other authors, distributed selected titles of each company's publications, and generally been supportive of the publishing goals of the three independent companies. Such cooperation has aided the development of black literature in America since World War II, and has helped to advance the careers of the three poets. At the same time, however, Madhubuti, Randall, and Madgett have done more to advance the publication of black American poetry than any other three figures in modern history. Their combined efforts have helped to bring attention and acknowledgment to the work of hundreds of black writers.[164]

During the years 1980–95, Third World Press produced sixty-three books, five tapes, one poster, and one journal. A list of the authors and titles for this period appears in Table 5.7. The company's publication list can be divided into seven major genres, or areas of focus: poetry; social sciences and essays (Black Studies, sociology, Women's Studies, psychology, political science, and Urban Studies); literary criticism, drama, and fiction; history and biography; children's literature; a literary journal; and audio/video tapes.[165] Clearly books of poetry dominate Third World Press' list of publications for this period. Yet, the company had in fact been established in the sixties by poets to serve just this purpose. At least it lived up to its creators' original motives for the company. The twenty-two poetry volumes represented 34 percent of all Third World Press books produced during 1980-95. This was no small achievement, given the difficulties of selling poetry in the eighties and nineties.

Third World Press was fortunate in having two of the best-selling black poets in America on its book list: Haki R. Madhubuti, who produced four books and two tapes for the company during this period, and Gwendolyn Brooks, who had four books and one poster distributed by Third World Press.[166] The company also published new books, or new editions of older collections of poetry by six significant black poets, including work by Naomi Long Madgett, Ruby Dee, Gil Scott-Heron, Keorapetse Kgositsile, Kalamu ya Salaam, and Amiri Baraka. Third World Press also published eight books by newer writers and continued to carry thirteen titles "from the revolutionary poets of the sixties to those of the latter seventies."[167] The list of the latter poets includes books by Zack Gilbert, Angela Jackson, Norman Jordan, Johari M. Knujufu, Olumu (Jim Cunningham), Dudley Randall, Carolyn Rodgers, and Phillip Royster, among others. These were among the best-known black creators of poetry in the United States and undoubtedly helped to sell books published by Third World Press.[168]

Equally important to Third World Press during the eighties and nineties has been the publication of new books in the social sciences, humanities, and children's literature. The company has made a major breakthrough by publishing nineteen books in the social sciences. Three of the titles have been best-sellers. Its greatest success has come with historian Chancellor Williams' *The Destruction of Black Civilization*, which has had sixteen printings since 1975, and currently there are over 1 million copies in circulation.[169] This book examines "the rise and fall of Black civilization from early Egypt and Sudan to the present. Williams determines exactly how the highly advanced Black civilization of antiquity was devastated. Williams also examines the crucial issues involved in the exclusion of Black history from Western history books. In addition to providing a framework for study, Williams calls for a new approach in the research, teaching and study of African history."[170] Journalist Calvin Reid writes:

> Among books Madhubuti is particularly proud of is the current top title in several African American bookstores around the country, *The Isis Papers: The Keys to the Colors* by Frances Cress-Welsing, a collection of essays exploring the impact of white supremacy on African Americans. A third-generation physician practicing in Washington, D.C., the author has been on the faculty at Howard University, but she's never thought of writing a book. "I had to nurture her to agree to do the book; she didn't even know the process," Madhubuti says.[171]

Madhubuti's own best-seller, *Black Men: Obsolete, Single, Dangerous? Afrikan-American Families in Transition* (1991), was purchased by 70,000 readers during its first year and a half on the market.[172]

> Madhubuti uses a variety of approaches — poetic verses along with essays, interviews and biographical sketches — to paint a startling portrait of black manhood, black family and black male-female relationships. His interview with a black Chicago police officer about his encounters with his own community — and the overall attitude of young black males on the streets of that city — offer insights into the desperate plight of young black Americans. In the tradition of Martin Luther King, Jr., and Malcolm X, Madhubuti proposes solutions to the ills that plague black Americans through the restoration of the family unit and the development of an autonomous economic community.[173]

Third World Press has also had success in promoting the sale of new books in the humanities and children's literature. Major writers who have published in both areas for the company include Gwendolyn Brooks, Sonia Sanchez, Useni Eugene Perkins, and Mari Evans, whose book *How They Made Biriyani* (1981) is "a family-centered story illustrating (cont. on page 225)

Table 5.7

Publications by Third World Press, 1980–1995

Author	Title	Year of Publication	Pages	Price
Gwendolyn Brooks	*Premier for Blacks* (essays)	1980	16	$ 4.00
	To Disembark (poetry)	1980	70	$ 6.95
Cheikh Anta Diop	*Cultural Unity of Black Africa* (history) (1990, new edition)	1980	236	$14.95
Haki R. Madhubuti	*Enemies: The Clash of Races* (essays)	1980 (new edition)	272	$12.95
Dexter and Patricia Oliver	*I Want to Be* (alphabet)	1980	N/A	$ 5.95
Mari Evans	*How They Made Biriyani* (children's book)	1981	N/A	$ 5.95
Gwendolyn Brooks	*Very Young Poets* (essay)	1983	32	$4.00
Haki R. Madhubuti	*Rise Vision Coming* (poetry) (cassette)	1984		$ 7.00
	Earthquakes and Sunrise Missions: Poetry and Essays of Black Renewal, 1973–83 (essays and poetry)	1984	200	$ 8.95
Bobby Wright	*The Psychopathic Racial Personality and Other Essays* (psychology)	1984	52	$ 5.95
Gregory Millard	*Geechies* (poetry) (distributed by TWP)	1985	70	$ 5.95
Useni Eugene Perkins	*Harvesting New Generations: The Positive Development of Black Youth* (Black Studies)	1985	240	$12.95
Sonia Sanchez	*A Sound Investment* (children's book)	1985 (new edition, 1993)	32	$ 2.95
Gwendolyn Brooks	*The Near Johannesburg Boy* (poetry)	1986	32	$ 4.00
Ruby Dee	*My One Good Nerve*	1986	N/A	$ 8.95
Gwendolyn Brooks	*Blacks* (poetry/fiction)	1987 (dist. by TWP)	512	$36.95 (cloth) $19.55 (paper)
Ruth Garnett	*A Move Further South* (poetry)	1987	64	$ 7.95
Vivian V. Gordon	*Black Women, Feminism, and Black Liberation: Which Way* (Black Women's Studies)	1987	60	$ 5.95
Haki R. Madhubuti	*Say That the River Turns: The Impact of Gwendolyn Brooks* (poetry anthology)	1987	90	$ 8.95

Author	Title	Year of Publication	Pages	Price
Useni Eugene Perkins	*Explosive of Chicago Black Street Gangs* (sociology/Urban Studies)	1987	80	$ 6.95
Gwendolyn Brooks	*Winnie* (poetry)	1988	24	$ 4.00
Naomi Long Madgett	*Octavia and Other Poems* (poetry)	1988	121	$ 8.00
Nora Brooks Blakely	*Shani on the Hill* (fiction)	1989		$ 3.95
Safisha Madhubuti	*The Story of Kwanzaa* (Black Studies)	1989	32	$ 5.95
Jabari Mahiri	*The Day They Stole the Letter J* (children's books)	1989	30	$ 3.95
Useni Eugene Perkins	*The Afrocentric Self-Inventory and Discovery Workbook for African American Youth* (Black Studies)	1989	46	$ 5.95
Kalamu ya Salaam	*What Is Life* (essays)	1989		$ 8.00
Dorothy Palmer Smith	*A Lonely Place Against the Sky* (Biography)	1989		$ 7.95
Alfred Woods	*Manish* (poetry)	1989	54	$ 8.00
Gil Scott-Heron	*So Far, So Good* (poetry)	1990	84	$ 8.00
Darryl Holmes	*Wings Will Not Be Broken* (poetry)	1990	50	$ 8.00
Haki R. Madhubuti	*Black Man, Obsolete, Single, Dangerous?* (essays)	1990	300	$14.95
	Black Men: Obsolete, Single, Dangerous? (lecture) (90 min. video cassette) (90 min. audio cassette)	1990		$29.95
	Confusion: By Any Other Name: Essays Exploring the Negative Impact of the Blackman's Guide to Understanding the Black Woman (Black Studies)	1990	28	$ 3.95
Estella Conwill Alexander	*Jiva Telling Rites: An Initiation* (poetry)	1991	76	$ 8.00
Delores Aldridge	*Focusing: Black Male/Female Relationships* (Black Studies)	1991	79	$ 7.95
Pearl Cleage	*The Brass Bed and Other Stories* (fiction)	1991	74	$ 8.00
Frances Cress Welsing	*The Isis Papers: The Keys to the Colors* (Black Studies/psychology)	1991	236	$14.95

Author	Title	Year of Publication	Pages	Price
Vivian Verdell Gordon	*Kemet and Other Ancient African Civilizations* (history/bibliography)	1991	30	$ 3.95
Nathan Hare	*The Black Anglo-Saxons* (sociology)	1991 (new edition)	144	$12.95
Fred Hord	*Reconstructing Memory: Black Literary Criticism* (literary criticism)	1991	210	$12.95
Ralph Cheo Thurman	*The Future and Other Stories* (short stories)	1991	132	$ 8.00
Haki R. Madhubuti	*Don't Cry, Scream!* (poetry)	1992 (new edition)	66	$ 8.00
	From Plan to Planet: Life Studies: The Need for Afrikan Minds and Institutions	1992 (new edition)	160	$ 7.95
Michael Bradley	*Chosen People from the Caucasus: Jewish Origins, Delusions, Deceptions and Historic Role in the Slave Trade, Genocide and Cultural Colonization* (Jewish Studies/history/anthropology)	1993	288	$23.95
Gwendolyn Brooks	*Maud Martha* (fiction)	1993 (new edition)	192	$ 9.95
Kahil El'Zabar	*MisTaken Brillance* (poetry)	1993	80	$ 8.00
Brian Gilmore	*Elvis Presley Is Alive and Well and Living in Harlem* (poetry)	1993	88	$ 7.95
Joyce A. Joyce	*Warriors, Conjurers and Priests: Defining African-Centered Literary Criticism* (literary criticism)	1993	320	$16.95
Keorapetse Kgositsile	*The Present Is a Dangerous Place to Live*	1993 (new edition)	46	$ 8.00
Acklyn Lynch	*Nightmare Overhanging Darkly* (essays)	1993	276	$14.95
Haki R. Madhubuti	*Why L.A. Happened: Implications of the '92 Los Angeles Rebellion* (Black Studies/Urban Studies)	1993	290	$14.95
"Uncle" Mondo	*Morning of the Bright Bird: Short Stories for African Children*	1993	48	$ 8.95
Mzee Lasana Okpara (formerly Fred Lee Hord)	*Life Sentences: Freeing Black Relationships* (poetry)	1993	85	$ 8.00

Author	Title	Year of Publication	Pages	Price
Useni Eugene Perkins	*Black Fairy and Other Plays* (theater/folktales/drama)	1993	200	$13.95
Alphonso Pinkney	*Lest We Forget: Howard Beach and Other Racial Atrocities* (Urban Studies)	1993	300	$16.95
Sterling D. Plumpp	*Ballad of Harriet Tubman* (poetry)	1993	24	$18.95
Patti Renee Rose	*In Search of Serenity: A Black Family's Struggle with the Threat of Aids* (sociology)	1993	134	$10.95
Byron Sculfield	*Hello! My Name Is Mr. I'm Gonchop* (children's book)	1993	24	$ 5.95
Linda M. Thurston, ed.	*A Call to Action: An Analysis and Overview of the United States Criminal Justice System with Recommendations* (criminal justice/sociology)	1993	112	$ 8.00
Chancellor Williams	*The Rebirth of African Civilization* (history/African Studies)	1993	342	$16.95
Amiri Baraka	*Jesse Jackson and Black People* (essays)	1994	150	$19.95
	Why's Wise, Y's: The Griot's Tale (poetry)	1994	86	$14.95
Frances Cress-Welsing	*Isis Papers: The Keys to the Colors* (lecture) (90 min. VHS videocassette)			$29.95
The Drum and Spear Collective	*Children of Africa: A Coloring Book* (children's fiction)	1994	24	$5.95
Haki R. Madhubuti	*Claiming Earth: Race, Rape, Ritual Richness in America and the Search for Enlightened Empowerment* (essays)	1994	175	$19.95 (cloth)
	Medasi (poetry) (90-min. audiocassette)	N/A		$ 7.00
Kalamu ya Salaam	*Nation of Poets* (poetry voice anthology) (90 min. audiocassette) (90 min. CD)	1990		$ 7.00 $12.00

the values of a family working together,"[174] according to writer Donald Franklin Joyce. Such books are of prime interest to Third World Press, because they emphasize black pride, literacy, and knowledge for black people.[175] The company also distributes five audio and videotapes with lectures and readings by Third World Press writers — Madhubuti, Frances Cress-Welsing, Kalamu ya Salaam, Amiri Baraka, Pearl Cleage, Wanda Coleman, Mari Evans, Askia Muhammad and Sonia Sanchez — from their books, or published poetry with the company.[176] In 1991, Third World Press reactivated *Black Books Bulletin*, its house literary organ, which was active between 1971 and 1981. The new organ was renamed *Black Books*

Bulletin: Words Work, and there were hopes that it would appear bi-monthly. Editor Madhubuti set a goal to

> publish good writing from young, middle-young and established [writers], whose minds have not been frozen or destroyed. We will always champion children because they are our tomorrows, and they need an advocate. We will be a voice for the poor, homeless, the voiceless ignorant, among us, and a sounding panther for the few who are so far ahead of the rest of us that they have been dismissed as intellectually unsound. These utterances will come as editorials, essays, poetry, fiction, visual art and graphics. If you function in any of the genres, please consider our journal.[177]

A number of inferences can also be made from Table 5.10 on the general operations of Third World Press between 1980 and 1995. The company published and distributed works by twenty-five men and twenty women authors during this period; a good gender balance was therefore maintained by the firm. On average, Third World Press produced between one and five books yearly in the eighties, but this range increased to an average of eight to fifteen titles yearly in the late eighties and early nineties. A standard size Third World book contained between thirty and one hundred pages[178] and was priced between $5 and $10 in paperback or between $18.95 and $29.95 in cloth during these years.[179] "Press runs of titles published by Third World Press vary. Initial printings of volumes of poetry are between 2,000 and 3,000 copies. First press runs of prose titles are 4,000 copies with second printings of 5,000 copies."[180] Thus, Third World Press is one of the major black publishers in the United States, because of its commitment to quality and its ability to get work distributed in this country.

Nevertheless, the eighties and early nineties were also difficult years economically for Third World Press. Cunette A. Pinkney notes that the company "lost money for more than 15 years before 'breaking even in 1984 and beginning to make a little,' according to Madhubuti."[181] By 1989, the company's books showed "a series profit."[182] But for years Madhubuti, like Dudley Randall at Broadside Press and Naomi Long Madgett at Lotus Press, "didn't take any salary or expenses. Now, he says dryly, he takes expenses."[183]

In a national effort to aid black publishers and nine bookstore owners, Madhubuti led a movement in 1988 to organize the African-American Publishers and Booksellers Association.[184] This group seeks to promote the financial solvency of black interests in publishing, and promote the distribution of literature (through the African-American Distributors Association) by and on African-Americans at home and abroad. Journalist Joseph Barbato observes that:

> Madhubuti believes his efforts at institution-building offer a "serious model" for black self-reliance. "We're really in the idea business — in terms of the bookstore, the publishing company, and the school." He hopes that the new organization of black presses and booksellers will help build some strength and independence among black publishers in the industry. "Let's say one of our publishers brings out a very important book. As a trade group, it will be our responsibility, for instance, to help that press get proper publicity for the author and the book. We'll not only be a bridge between publishers, we'll be a sounding board, a place where technical advice will be available, especially for new companies. And we include the bookstores because they have similar business concerns."
>
> His plans for the new distribution company are no less ambitious. "One market we have not tapped at the level we can is Africa, especially English-speaking Africa," he

says. "In Nigeria, for instance, English is the official language. We've got to get our books into that market and others, just like the major publishers do."[185]

The efforts of contemporary black publishers such as Broadside press, Lotus Press, and Third World Press have been especially influential in recent years in continuing the pacesetting traditions of excellence in black publishing first promoted by such key figures as Dudley Randall during the Black Arts Movement. The Vests at Broadside, Madgett at Lotus, and Madhubuti at Third World have demonstrated an unusual ability to beat the odds of economic hardships in black publishing, and to forge ahead to continue the ageless dream for black literacy and freedom in America. They stand with Dudley Randall as remarkable individuals who have left an impressive historical and literacy record behind for future generations to duplicate.

Chapter 6

The Achievement of Broadside Press, 1965–1995

B roadside Press stands out as one of the major black American institutions created during the Black Arts Movement of the sixties and seventies, which has survived for thirty years against the odds of economic reversals, changing literary tastes, and political upheaval. The force and vision behind Broadside Press was Dudley Randall; a man who "published Black artists when they couldn't be published anywhere else. Detroit is a unique place because of people like Dudley Randall according to former Detroit Mayor Coleman Young."[1] How did he do it? With guts, total commitment, determination, and the aid of a few friends. Randall also truly believed in the power of black struggle (as witnessed in the examples of Martin Luther King, Jr., Rosa Parks, Ella Baker, and Malcolm X) and the black historical record. He also loved literature, and especially the power, hope, and vision which literary creations offered to human beings in their beauty, grace, and uplift. Indeed, "Dudley Randall's anthologies and his Broadside Press were the keystones of the new Black poetry of the Sixties and Seventies."[2] Randall was also in the right place at the right time. Detroit was a major center of activity in the freedom struggles of the African-American people between the fifties and the seventies. This was especially the case in terms of radical black thought in the United States. Sociologist Alphonso Pinkney writes from the vantage point of 1976:

> It is the present period, however, in which the ideology of black nationalism has had its greatest impact on black artists. Younger black creative writers today, unlike many of their predecessors, are writing specifically for the black community. And if the opening of black bookstores and the sale of books directed toward the black community are indications of success, black people are reading the works of black authors to a greater extent than ever before. For example, three volumes of poetry by Don Lee, *Black Pride, Think Black!* and *Don't Cry, Scream!*, had sold more than 80,000 copies early in 1970. Most of the major black communities now contain at least one bookstore specializing in books by and about blacks, and in the last few years at least 15 new black publishing houses have been established to meet the growing needs of black writers and readers. Black studies programs in colleges and universities no doubt account for much of the success of books by young black writers, but increasingly these books are read by rank-and-file members of the black community.[3]

Dudley Randall was able to seize the opportunity to promote black poetry as a significant contribution to the liberation struggles of black people, while connecting the

228

publishing activities of Broadside to the historical and literary traditions of black America, and to help in fostering a documented record (through poetry) of the period for future generations. The Poetry Resource Center of Michigan noted in 1990:

> Broadside Press is a private non-profit publishing company founded in 1965, but it has long since transcended those boundaries and is now a national treasure. The Press is one of the oldest Black owned publishers in existence and its permanence is consummation of the vision of Dudley Randall. While originally conceived as a vehicle through which poets and writers whose work were not being published by traditional houses could find an outlet for their work, Broadside Press rather quickly achieved national recognition. Through its high ideals and publishing efforts, the creative work of many Black poets and writers became known and several attained national prominence. Others, such as Gwendolyn Brooks, elected to move from large publishing houses to Broadside as an expression of support and ethnic unity.[4]

Yet, Dudley Randall and Broadside Press had always worked under the stresses and strains of existing in a society where fair mindedness could never be taken for granted. Poet and critic D. H. Melhem wrote in 1993:

> Years ago I noted that some of the best writers I knew, were largely either unappreciated or misunderstood by the dominant culture. This realization helped me to focus my critical energies (and some of my poetry, too). An only child reared in a large, multicultural family, I had learned early that a literature of beauty and nobility could be depreciated because it differed from prevailing norms. I saw that in the United States differences were often translated into deficiencies. It was a privilege to study the work of Gwendolyn Brooks, Dudley Randall, Sonia Sanchez, Haki R. Madhubuti, Jayne Cortez, and Amiri Baraka, a privilege to interview them and know them and to interpret the heroic qualities of their lives and works. When no one welcomed my studies, each rejection became a challenge. This family would not be disregarded.[5]

The "heroic" nature of the work of Dudley Randall and Broadside Press extends from the past to the present. He did not allow the possibility of failure to stand in his way, nor the fact that most black writers and publishers were outside of the mainstream circles of American poetry and publishing. This makes his contribution and that of Broadside all the more significant, for as one contemporary newspaper notes: "Detroit's Broadside Press in the sixties and seventies was the publishing equivalent of what Motown was to the nation's recording industry."[6]

Dudley Randall's legacy to Americans extends through four major areas: (1) his work as a professionally trained librarian; (2) his creative efforts as a writer, especially his contributions as a poet, editor, essayist, and critic; (3) his activities as the dominant personality and publisher in the production of books, broadsides, and anthologies of black poetry during the Black Arts Movement; and (4) his literary and historical hallmarks as the leader of the black poetry movement in modern America.

Randall devoted over twenty-five years of his professional life (from the fifties through the mid-seventies) to working in American libraries at the college and community levels. His services as a librarian increased his interest in promoting black literacy; aiding the success rates of students at historically black colleges; increasing the range of young writers produced at American institutions; expanding more positive conditions for the production and distribution of black literature (books, tapes, and other materials), which would aid

the development of libraries, while increasing the data base and range of the works written by black writers; encouraging for students and the general public to read more, especially of black literature; and a life-long concern about censorship in the marketplace of
ideas, and the impact of bookbanning on American libraries and education.[7] A highly educated man, Randall understood throughout his career the impact and meaning of Nicholas
Zill's and Marianne Wing Lee's findings in *Who Reads Literature?: The Future of the United
States as a Nation of Readers*: "The proportion of Americans who read serious literature is
between 10 and 25 percent; contemporary fiction, poetry, and drama attracts at best between
7 and 12 percent of adults."[8] Randall spent a life-time confronting such issues and helping
to make a difference by making available to Americans the works of African-American
poets. Indeed, Randall wanted Americans to travel a much different road from the path
offered by such books as E. D. Hirsch, Jr.'s *Cultural Literacy: What Every American Needs
to Know* (1987). In the same book's appendix, entitled "What Literate Americans Know,"
Hirsch and two of his colleagues, Joseph Kett and James Trefil show only seven black literary figures and themes: Richard Wright's *Black Boy* and *Native Son*; W. E. B. Du Bois;
Martin Luther King, Jr.'s "Letter from a Birmingham Jail"; Malcolm X; Paul Robeson; and
Booker T. Washington.[9] Randall's work aided the struggle to "overcome" such limitations
on the creative spirits of all Americans. Readers will note that no African-American women
appear on the above list.

As a professional librarian, Randall leaves a rich legacy behind to his profession. He
served as a librarian at two of the historically black colleges and universities in the United
States—first at Lincoln University, Jefferson City, Missouri, during 1952 to 1954; and at
Morgan State College [now University], Baltimore, Maryland from 1954 to 1956. His service record also includes extensive community library service for the Wayne County Federated Library System, Wayne, Michigan, 1956–69 and additional higher educational library
service at the University of Detroit, between 1969 and 1976. Randall was one of only several thousand black librarians working in the United States during the period of the fifties
through the seventies. He helped to increase the influence of blacks in a profession where
black people were underrepresented in general, and black men in particular. His colleagues
are highly appreciative of his contributions to the profession across the years.[10]

The work of Dudley Randall as a writer also holds a special place in the literary life
and cultural experiences of African-Americans in modern America. Randall has been composing poetry for over sixty years. He has also been very active as an essayist, critic, and
editor. His productivity is reflected in the thirteen books which he has written as author,
co-author, or editor of since 1966.[11] Yet, it is as a poet that Randall is best known to the
reading public in this country and abroad. In 1974, Donald Barlow Stauffer ranked Randall as "among the best" of contemporary black poets writing in the United States, on a list
that included Don L. Lee, Conrad Kent Rivers, Raymond Patterson, James Emanuel, Sonia
Sanchez, Nikki Giovanni, and Keorapetse Kgositsile.[12] All eight of the poets were associated with Broadside Press—another testimony to Randall's symbolic position of importance in African-American letters. Critic Arnold Rampersad reminds his contemporaries
that the poets of an earlier period, the Harlem Renaissance,

> had played a major role — perhaps the central role — in defining the spirit of the age. In
> literature, as in music (that of Duke Ellington and Louis Armstrong, for example) and
> art (Aaron Douglas and Augusta Savage), the movement laid the foundations for the
> creative representation of African American social and cultural reality in the modern

world. All subsequent African American creativity in these fields has built upon that solid foundation, laid mainly by young men and women of lengthening vision who responded affirmatively to the challenge and the opportunity best symbolized within black America in the decade of the 1920's by Harlem.[13]

Dudley Randall was a "major role" figure for the second Renaissance, the Black Arts Movement of the sixties and seventies as both a writer and publisher. Likewise, Randall was also among "the poets who were the strongest advocates of the Black Aesthetic."[14] He was a promoter of what Kalamu ya Salaam defines as a necessary requirement for black advancement: "a struggle to identify and institutionalize ourselves as a people."[15] Poet and critic Jerry W. Ward, Jr., described an additional vision of Randall as poet and sage at the 1974 Melvin A. Butler Third Annual Memorial Poetry Festival, at Southern University, Baton Rouge, Louisiana:

> Dudley Randall, whose contributions as poet, publisher, prophet are invaluable, set the tenor of the Festival in his brief lecture on the present state of Black poetry. He delineated changes in poetic intent and technique since "Renaissance I" and made these projections: 1) Black poetry will embrace Pan-Africanism; 2) the interchange of ideas among poets of Africa and the Americas will be increasingly fruitful; 3) Black poetry will move from the subdeclamatory to the subjective mode. The audience was stirred by Randall's reading of 24 poems, especially by those from his *After the Killing* and by his student Eileen Tann's "Counter-Poem for Dudley Randall from a Very Green Apple."[16]

Randall's work and life serves as an example of human possibility for his contemporaries, young and old alike. His poetry is also an inspiration to contemporary readers. Certainly, he remains one of the most anthologized poets of his generation; and from the sixties to the present poetry lovers everywhere have found joy and serious reflection upon reading or listening to his masterpieces, including such poems as "Ballad of Birmingham," "The Profile on the Pillow," "Memorial Wreath," "Black Poet, White Critic," "The Southern Road," and "Booker T. and W. E. B.," among many others.[17] Randall's poetry explores the galaxy of the black experience during the twentieth century. It is a body of work in the traditions of black literature — historic, yet individual — which should speak profoundly to future generations on the genius of the man and of his world view on the human condition.

Contemporary issues in the present, such as the various states of consciousness among younger writers, the impact of television on literature and literary activities, gender considerations, and violence in everyday life, especially in American urban centers, offer another element in the assessment of Dudley Randall as a writer and sage during the highlight years of his writing career. Since the sixties Randall has worked with hundreds of younger poets, a humbling experience for many sages. Perhaps Naomi Long Madgett best captures the tasks required of the older generation in working with younger poets. In 1993, she told Mack Puls of the *Detroit News*:

> There are more people writing poetry than reading poetry. Many amateur poets don't have a single book of poetry in their house. You have to study other poets. If you had never taken a piano lesson, would you agree to perform a concert? Of course not. But many people consider themselves poets without studying and understanding poetry.[18]

Like Naomi Long Madgett, Randall has spent a lifetime learning about how to write poetry, and serving as a teacher and guide to younger people on the same subject. Such writers have worked hard to be an elevating impulse, especially, one could argue, for the 476,000 black males and 747,000 black women students in American colleges and universities in 1990.[19] It is a task, however, which must move forward from one generation to the next.

Randall's work as a poet should also remind people of today how a senior poet attempts to deal with such issues as violence on the streets and violence on the minds of the people, as reflected too often in the latter case by American television and media. Randall's lifestyle and poetic creations seek to fulfill what Stephen E. Henderson describes: "one of the chief lessons of the life of Soul … is for black people … to realize the revolutionary potential in their way of life, for Soul means wholeness and energy and healing."[20] And so does the poetry of such artists as Dudley Randall. His verse helps human beings to deal with "grief: expressions in the aftermath of violence"; which can be experienced individually, or collectively in the lives of people, on a daily basis or over an extended time period (i.e., slavery, and later the age of Jim Crow/segregation, down to today's "conservative era").[21]

Still, the plight of black men and women reflects over historical time as an ageless issue of concern to the common community of both. In earlier periods of black literature, black men were the dominant shapers and molders of verse; today, it's the black women's turn. Writer Michael Eric Dyson notes the paradox:

> The identification and development of the womanist tradition in African-American culture has permitted the articulation of powerful visions of black female identity and liberation. Michele Wallace, Bell Hooks, Alice Walker, Audre Lorde, and Toni Morrison have written in empowering ways about the disabling forms of racism and patriarchy that persist in white and black communities. They have expressed the rich resources for identity that come from maintaining allegiances to multiple kinship groups defined by race, gender, and sexual orientation, while also addressing the challenges that arise in such membership.[22]

It is refreshing to reflect on how sincere Dudley Randall was in meeting the gender challenge. The simple truth is that he was fair to black women poets — perhaps the fairest black American editor to black women in history. This legacy, too, remains a central star in Randall's place in black literary history, for he displayed a special strength and ability in being able to recognize and appreciate the contributions of black women writers to black literature — and best of all — to publish and promote a great number of them, such as Nikki Giovanni, Gwendolyn Brooks, Margaret Walker, Sonia Sanchez, and so many others.

A reminiscence on Randall's work as a senior poet and his place in contemporary history, reminds modern readers that the struggle to create a wider circle for the inclusion into the canon of American authors of differing ethnic backgrounds still continues. As recently as 1972, Jay B. Hubbell's *Who Are the Major American Writers* notes only two black American novelists, Ralph Ellison (for *Invisible Man*, 1952) and Richard Wright (for *Native Son*, 1940), among the best writers of fiction during the twentieth century, although James Baldwin's name is mentioned too.[23] No black poet was selected for any of the "lists" reviewed by Hubbell.[24]

But, surprisingly, twenty-one years later, a noted younger black American author could not list a living black poet either, who measured up to his standards of greatness. In 1993, Ralph Wiley wrote in *What Black People Should Do Now: Dispatches from Near the Vanguard*:

> The best writers I know of are dead; which may prove it pays not to become too good at this most peculiar art.... For me the best writers are, in no particular order, DuBois, Dickens, Twain, Wright, Dumas, Baldwin in essay form, Fanon in polemic, and Hurston when she was feeling good about herself.[25]

But on the next page Wiley does manage to find something to say about the living, and lists twenty-five writers that he likes, including Ishmael Reed, Jamaica Kincaid, Wole Soyinka, Charles Johnson, John Wideman, Albert Murray, Samuel Delaney, and Bell Hooks, among others. Such statements suggest the continued invisibility of too many black poets in America. Certainly among the twelve major black American poets since 1960 are Langston Hughes, Gwendolyn Brooks, Margaret Walker, Haki R. Madhubuti, Amiri Baraka, Mari Evans, Nikki Giovanni, Alice Walker, Sonia Sanchez, Etheridge Knight, Dudley Randall, and Robert Hayden. Any list of inclusion must include members of this distinguished group.

As a publisher, Dudley Randall holds a preeminent position among his colleagues during the sixties through the eighties. The keys to understanding Randall's success as a publisher include: (1) his ability to adopt and use the "broadside" and pamphlet formats as an inexpensive way to bring black poetry to the masses; (2) the poet's long-term vision and faith in poetry as an art form which could speak to the human condition of blacks, the very poor, the working class, and the small black middle class in this country; (3) an abiding faith in the Civil Rights Movement and the just cause of blacks; (4) a unique capacity for understanding the cultural scene in the United States during the Black Arts Movement, and a special skill in recognizing promising poets, and as Hilda Vest notes, a vigor "at cultivating new talent"; and (5) a hard-working and creative Broadside Press staff.[26] Randall was also able to tap what sculptor Elizabeth Cattlett refers to as "Responding to Cultural Hunger" among black people. Although Cattlet's special reference was to the fine arts, her reflections are representative of the cultural problems facing black people in the literary world too:

> I realized how often our people are denied art and began to think about the many different ways that this denial is effected; about why it is that Black people, in general, don't visit art museums and symphony halls even when they are permitted entry. It seems to me that the main method of denial was the [during the forties] and continues to be the fostering of an elitist art which further widens class distinctions. The whole system of museums, galleries, critics, the media, even art schools, is all directed towards middle class and wealthy white people. The majority of us are not even considered. Money is very important and plays a basic role in buying, promoting, and selling not only art but artists. To appreciate contemporary visual arts, for example, one must have had certain experiences prior to viewing or participating in it. To visit museums presupposes an interest in their exhibitions. If there is nothing in them relating to us, why spend our little leisure time visiting? These thoughts made me question what kind of art I could offer to young Black people (who would later be professionals) and others who live and worked in the ghettos, if I ever exhibited.[27]

Therefore, Randall was also successful because he was able to break the chains of the past, which largely viewed much of black poetry as a middle and upper class phenomenon. Instead of an elitist formation of black poets and publications, Randall and Broadside Press stressed an egalitarian basis for promoting the work of black poets. According to critic R. Baxter Miller, Randall and Broadside were able to advance their goals because of a policy which emphasized a "tolerance in what he publishes."[28] This flexibility has resulted in over 400 African-American poets being published by Broadside Press over the last three decades. Furthermore, between 1965 and 1995, Broadside has published 101 books, 94 broadsides, 5 posters, and 27 tapes and albums of poetry.[29] Since the sixties this work has reached a largely black audience, basically through black bookstores, direct mail orders from Broadside, purchases of black art, educational and community programs, and by American libraries.[30]

A random sample of four American libraries by the author in 1993 revealed that Broadside's publications are widely distributed and available to the public, and especially to students in such widely distinct regions as Mississippi and Ohio (and of course, throughout the state of Michigan). At the Natchez (Mississippi) Public Library, books by the following Broadside authors were located: Nikki Giovanni, Sonia Sanchez, Dudley Randall, Margaret Walker (all of her books), Clarence Major, and William H. Robinson. Jackson State University Library and Tougaloo College Library, both also in Mississippi, hold extensive collections of Broadside Press publications. For example, Tougaloo's Coleman Library contains all of the books written by Gwendolyn Brooks, and most of the works by such writers as Dudley Randall, Haki R. Madhubuti, Sonia Sanchez, Margaret Danner, Audre Lorde, Sterling A. Brown, Nikki Giovanni, Sterling D. Plumpp, Clarence Major, James Randall, and Etheridge Knight, among many others. This same pattern holds for Sampson Library at Jackson State University. A large range of Broadside Press books are also held by the Cleveland (Ohio) State University Library. The following Broadside authors are represented in this collection: Dudley Randall, Gwendolyn Brooks, Haki R. Madhubuti, James Emanuel, Margaret Danner, Nikki Giovanni, Alvin Aubert, Audre Lorde, Sonia Sanchez, Margaret Walker, James Randall, Sterling A. Brown, Judy D. Simmons, Addison Gayle, Jr., Sterling D. Plumpp, and Lance Jeffers, among others.[31] Indeed, the author has found a very wide distribution of Broadside Press publications throughout the United States during his travels in many states. Broadside Press has been very successful in selling its books to American libraries. Today this high legacy stands as another touchstone for the work of Dudley Randall.[32]

Historian Tony Martin's observations on the impact of the "Black Books Revolution," suggests the scope of Dudley Randall's contribution as a publisher, in light of the political, social, and economic consequences of contemporary history:

> Consciousness has been facilitated by the Black Books Revolution, now about a decade old. For the first time in our history, Black folk now have the capacity to write, publish, distribute and sell their books without total reliance on white or Jewish establishments at any point along the way. The African American public is reading as never before and they are reading their own authors, writing from their own perspective, as never before. Not too long ago many a Black bookstore, on close examination, would be found to be stocking books on Black subjects overwhelmingly written by non Africans and more often than not, by Jews.... The Black Books Revolution is perhaps unique in the avid interest it has stimulated in the non-academic African American community. If anything, the lay population may be reading more of their own material than many of the academics, who have more layers of miseducation to work through before they can emerge into the clear light of self-knowledge.[33]

In summary then, Randall's role as a publisher was to make a way out of nothing for the advancement of black poetry, but he had to achieve this goal without sufficient funding, staff, or other resources, while working at a critical junction in the black freedom struggle in America. Many have been called to the task of black publishing, but few have left the record made by Dudley Randall and Broadside Press.

Dudley Randall's place in literary history is based on his work as a poet, editor, librarian, and publisher from the forties to the present. It is a period in which the poet's career has been especially rich and rewarding, due to the very nature of its longevity, and the many talents which he has expanded upon across the years, to bring joy and happiness to so many people throughout the world, as they read or listen to black literature. Randall was among "the forerunners" of modern black poets, who came of age during the Great Depression and World War II years.[34] But, he was not content to sit idly by and only write poetry. He took effective action to be a part of the campaign to promote black literature and the arts as a component of the freedom struggles of African-Americans in the sixties and seventies by establishing Broadside Press — and by helping to promote literacy, uplift, and black consciousness among his people.[35] In the process, he was able to attract an astonishing number of major and minor poets during the Black Arts Movement to Broadside Press, including Amiri Baraka, Gwendolyn Brooks, Haki R. Madhubuti, Nikki Giovanni, Etheridge Knight, Sonia Sanchez, Lance Jeffers, Margaret Walker, James Emanuel, Margaret Danner, Marvin X, Carolyn M. Rodgers, Doughtry Long, Stephany Fuller, and Keorapetse Kgositsile, among so many others.[36] Only Lotus Press and Third World Press can match Randall's record in publishing so many outstanding black poets during the last quarter of this century in American history. Randall's place as a major publisher in black history is secure on his general publication record alone, but he must also be recognized again for his vision in specifically promoting the writings of black women authors.[37]

Randall also promoted a Pan-African perspective at Broadside Press, in both words and deeds. In 1969, he published Keorapetse Kgositsile's poetry collection, *Spirits Unchained*, and later brought out a tape of the poet reading from this book. Kgositsile remains a highly rated South African poet, editor, and activist among literary circles in the United States, Africa, the Caribbean and Europe.[38] In 1971, Randall brought out a new creative work for Broadside (a cookbook), by Bill Odarty (Bli Odaatey), *A Safari of African Cooking*. A native of Ghana, in West Africa, Odarty's book has been a favorite best-seller at Broadside for almost a quarter of a century. In fact, the book reached a milestone in 1992, with its third edition and fifth printing.[39] Dudley Randall was thus a part of the international efforts of what scholar Phanuel Akubueze Egejuru calls a movement "towards African Literary Independence."[40] This is evident in Randall's efforts to reach out to publish black writers from Africa, such as Kgositsile and Odarty, and by his use of African symbols and images in his own poetry. According to scholar Marion Berghahn:

> Almost naturally Africa became the decisive point of reference in the search for a new and positive image of the individual Afro-American and the group as a whole, as expressed by Dudley Randall and many other black poets: "The age/requires this task;/create/a different image;/Replace/the leer/of the minstrel's burnt-cork face/with a proud, serene/ and classic bronze of Bennin."[41]

A spirit of cooperation was also extended to Caribbean poets by Randall's promotion and distribution of two books of poetry published in 1973 by Paul Breman of London; Eseoghene's (C. Lindsay Barrett) *The Conflicting Eye*, and Frank John's *Light a Fire*. Eseoghene hails from Jamaica, and Frank John was born on Trinidad.

Table 6.1

Dedications of Poems and Books to Dudley Randall, 1967–1994

Author	Title of Dedication	Year
Poems		
Gwendolyn Brooks	"Malcolm X," ("For Dudley Randall")	1967
	"Five Men Agains the Theme 'My Name Is Red Hot, Yo Name Ain Doodley Squat'" ("To: Hoyt and Lerone, Dudley and Haki and Lu")	1975
	"For Dudley Randall on the Tenth Anniversary of Broadside Press"	1976
James A. Emanuel	"For 'Mr. Dudley,' a Black Spy"	1970
Nikki Giovanni	"Poems (For Dudley Randall)"	1969
	"To Dudley Randall"	1975
Murray Jackson	"Dudley Randall"	1991
Alicia L. Johnson	"Our Days Are Numbered"	1969
Sterling D. Plumpp	"(for Dudley Randall)"	1976
James Randall	"Street Games"	1973
	"Letters Home"	1973
Sharon Smith-Knight	"Of Men and Women" ("for Dudley")	1991
Eileen Tann	"A Counterpoem for Dudley Randall"	1974
Preston M. Yancy	"Du Bois and Washington Revered" ("This poem is dedicated to Dudley Randall who served as my model, to Booker T. Washington and W. E. B. DuBois, and to the concept of Black unity.")	1974
Books		
Ron Allen and Stella Crews, eds.	*HIPology: Horizons in Poetry* ("For Dudley Randall")	1990
Gwendolyn Brooks	*Riot* ("For Dudley Randall")	1969
	Report from Part One ("For Clarifiers: Dudley Randall, Don Lee, Walter Bradford, George Kent, Alden Bland, Francis and Val Ward")	1972
	To Disembark ("To Dudley Randall with affection and respect")	1981
Michael Delp, Conrad Hilberry, and Herbert Scott, eds.	*Contemporary Michigan Poetry: Poems from the Third Coast* ("To Dudley Randall")	1988

Poet	Title of Dedication	Year
The Detroit Black Writer's Guild, ed.	*Inner, Inner Visions: A Poetry Anthology* ("This book is dedicated to Dudley Randall, founder of Broadside Press, one of America's oldest black book publishers, for his wide vision and dedication to the arts.")	1994
Don L. Lee (Haki R. Madhubuti)	*Don't Cry, Scream!* (includes a dedication to Dudley Randall and 66 other people)	1969
	Killing Memory, Seeking Ancestors (Dedication to Margaret Burroughs, Margaret Walker, Sterling A. Brown, Dudley Randall: "Giants and memory makers all")	1987
D. H. Melhem	*Heroism in the New Black Poetry* ("To Gwendolyn Brooks, Dudley Randall, Sonia Sanchez, Haki R. Madhubuti, Jayne Cortez, and Amiri Baraka, To all the Black poets mentioned in this study")	1990

In 1974, Randall published a translation by Richard J. Carr of Nicolas Guillen's poetry collection, *Tengo*. First published in Cuba in 1964, this work hails the Cuban Revolution of 1959. Nicolas Guillen (1902–89), was one of the most important New World poets of the twentieth century, and was generally referred to as the national poet of Cuba.[42] Collectively, such efforts as these have promoted a Pan-African state of consciousness at Broadside, which was one of the hallmarks of the Black Aesthetic Movement.[43]

The high esteem in which modern black writers hold Dudley Randall can be ascertained by merely counting the number and variety of times in which his fellow poets have dedicated poems and books in his honor. Table 6.1 offers such a survey review.[44] Between 1967 and 1991, fourteen poems by such poets as Gwendolyn Brooks, James A. Emanuel, Nikki Giovanni, Murray Jackson, Alicia L. Johnson, Sharon Smith-Knight, Sterling D. Plumpp, James Randall, Eileen Tann, and Preston M. Yancy, have been dedicated to Dudley Randall. In addition, since 1969 and 1990, eight books have been dedicated to Randall, by such authors as Ron Allen and Stella Crews, editors of *HIPology: Horizons in Poetry* (1990); Gwendolyn Brooks, author of *Riot* (1969), *Report from Part One* (an autobiography) (1972), and *To Disembark* (1981); Michael Delp, Conrad Hilberry, and Herbert Scott, editors, *Contemporary Michigan Poetry: Poems from the Third Coast* (1988); Don L. Lee (Haki R. Madhubuti), author of *Don't Cry, Scream!* (1969), and *Killing Memory, Seeking Ancestors* (1987); and D.H. Melhem, author of *Heroism in the New Black Poetry* (1990). Such an impressive list of dedications speaks volumes about the reception and goodwill held by American writers for the life and work of Dudley Randall.

Two short paragraphs by Dudley Randall in *A Capsule Course in Black Poetry Writing* (1975), seems to sum up the poet's perspective on the tasks and future challenges facing any writer.

PROLOGUE

What is a poet?
A poet is one who writes poetry.
Why do you want to be a poet? To become famous and appear on TV?

Then rob a bank. You'll be on the six o'clock news.
To make money?
Go into business. It's a surer way.
To effect social change?
Become a politician.
    Poets write because they must. Because they have an inner drive. Whether or not any
one hears of them, whether or not they make a cent, whether or not they affect a
single person, poets write and will continue to write. Poets' medium is language. Do
you love words? The sound of them, the rhythm of them, their differences and
similarities, the way they paint pictures, stir emotions? If you were a prisoner and
wrote a letter, would you say, "I'm incarcerated," or would you say, "I'm in jail"? If
you would say, "I'm in jail," then you are sensitive to words, and may be a poet. Read
on.[45]

In reality, Randall has lived his life as a poet by placing special attention and "sensitivity
to words." The poet speaks as a single individual, or voice, yet interprets the broad scope
of the human experience. Perhaps Margaret Walker (a poet of Randall's generation) — offers
an explanation for the question: "What do you see as being the task of Black writers today?"
Responding to *The Black Nation* magazine in 1982, Walker answers:

    Well, I think the task has always been, the Black writer is supposed to be avant-garde.
    He's like the philosopher or the social scientist, he implements the new concepts of the
    universe. He seeks to inform the mass audience of his people for whom he writes of
    their human and spiritual destiny. He seeks to prepare them for the days ahead in which
    they may truly see a world of common humanity.[46]

    Yet, like many writers everywhere, Randall and Walker have lived through an age where
they both had to challenge the status quo as writers, in order to develop and grow as poets,
teachers, literary artists, and members of the black community. Across the decades
each writer has had to face the challenge of such issues as: "Can Poetry Matter?"; "Who
Reads Literature?"; and if "44 percent of American adults do not read even one book
in the course of a year," how can black writers in the nineties and beyond influence
the over 10,000,000 "underclass" among black people in the United States to do so, let
alone a majority of the 20,000,000 working and middle class black elements too?[47] This is
the great paradox which has faced black writers in America for generations. Yet, historically, many black writers have remained hopeful about the future, although many of them
have been, or are often impoverished by a brutal economic system which loves the arts, but
only so long as they remain behind closed doors.[48] Truly, Dudley Randall's work at Broadside Press indicates the limitations and the challenges which lie ahead for black people in
America as writers, editors, and publishers.[49] It is a challenge which each generation must
painstakingly advance by securing black publishing and media interests wherever black people live.
    Dudley Randall's role in the advancement of the black community during the twen-
tieth century invokes the historic memories of the contributions of black abolitionists of
the nineteenth century, in the ongoing struggle to overthrow slavery and secure equal rights
for all Americans. Men and women such as Frederick Douglass (1817–95), Harriet Tub-
man (1820–1913), David Walker (1785–1830), and Sojourner Truth (1797–1883), among
so many other thousands from an earlier era, helped to galvanize a nation toward social
reform.[50] Randall's work in the twentieth century helped to continue this great tradition

by aiding the black community's use of the written word to assist in the struggle to over-come oppression in his own times and to promote the transformation of the people's world view, identity, and sense of consciousness. Like the abolitionists, Dudley Randall worked for decades to foster creative change and human awareness and understanding.[51] This is the rich legacy which he achieved through Broadside Press, his own personal writing, and the life giving literature which he gave to the people.

Appendix A: Chronology
of Broadside Press

1965

Dudley Randall (born on January 14, 1914, in Washington, D.C.) establishes Broadside Press from his home at 12651 Old Mill Place in Detroit, Michigan, with $12 of his personal funds. During the Civil Rights Movement, Broadside Press comes to be described as "the most important black press in America." During the period 1963–1969, Randall works as head of the reference-interloan department of the Wayne County, Michigan, Federated Library System. From the 1960s to the present he holds memberships in such organizations as the American Library Association, the Detroit Society for the Advancement of Culture and Education, the International Afro-American Museum, the Michigan Library Association, the Michigan Poetry Society, and the National Association for the Advancement of Colored People.

Randall publishes the first "broadsides" (single poems printed on one sheet of paper). The first broadsides are Randall's own "The Ballad of Birmingham" and "Dressed All in Pink," published in September 1965.

1966

Randall attends the First Black Writer's Conference during the month of May at Fisk University, Nashville, Tennessee.

Randall travels to Paris, France; Prague, Czechoslovakia; and the Soviet Union.

Randall receives the Tompkins Award for poetry and fiction from Wayne State University, Detroit, Michigan.

Randall (with Margaret Danner) publishes *Poem Counterpoem*, the first book of poetry published by Broadside Press. The first press run is 500 copies.

1967

Randall and Margaret Burroughs serve as the editors of *For Malcolm: Poems on the Life and Death of Malcolm X*, the second book produced by Broadside Press.

1968

Margaret Danner's *Impressions of African Art Forms* (originally printed in 1960) is reprinted by Broadside Press.

James Emanuel's first book of poetry, *The Treehouse and Other Poems,* appears under the Broadside seal.

Broadside Press becomes the distributor for Nikki Giovanni's second book, *Black Judgement.*

Sonia Sanchez's *Homecoming* is published.

Etheridge Knight's *Poems from Prison* is published; by 1975 it will be in its third printing.

Don L. Lee's (Haki R. Madhubuti's) second book, *Black Pride*, is published. This work is the third book produced by Broadside. It becomes an early best-seller for the company. Lee's first book, *Think Black!*, privately printed in 1967, is reprinted in a new edition by Broadside in 1968.

Dudley Randall publishes *Cities Burning.*

Broadside Press becomes the United States distributor for Paul Breman's Heritage Series of London, England, which is devoted to black poetry collections by such writers as Conrad Kent Rivers, Russell Atkin, Arna Bontemps, Owen Dodson, Ray Durem, Robert Hayden, Audre Lorde, Clarence Major, Dudley Randall and Ishmael Reed, among others.

1969

Gwendolyn Brooks selects Broadside Press as the publisher for her poetry collection entitled *Riot.*

Don L. Lee's *Don't Cry, Scream!* is published. This is the first Broadside book to appear as both a cloth and a paperback.

Randall is editor of *Black Poetry: A Supplement to Anthologies Which Exclude Black Poets.* According to D. H. Melhem in *Heroism in the New Black Poetry* (Lexington: The University Press of Kentucky, 1990), this work "was the first such anthology to appear under the imprint of a Black publisher." By 1973, there will be 25,000 copies of this volume in print.

Broadside Press publishes collections of poetry by Nancy Arnex and Beatrice Murphy, Jon Eckels, Keorapetse Kgositsile, Sonia Sanchez, Stephany Fuller, and Marvin X.

During the period 1969–1975 the office staff at Broadside Press includes: Dudley Randall, publisher and editor; Ruth Elois Whitsitt Fondren (1931–1972), office manager; Melba J. Boyd, assistant editor; and Bill Whitsitt, office manager.

Randall teaches in the English Department of the University of Michigan at Ann Arbor.

The second edition of *For Malcolm* becomes the second Broadside book published in both a paperback and a cloth edition.

Broadside Press becomes the distributor for Ahmed Alhamisi and Harun Kofi Wangara, editors, *Black Arts: An Anthology of Black Creations* (Detroit: Black Arts Publications, 1969).

1970

During the period 1970–1975, Randall serves as a reference librarian and poet-in-residence at the University of Detroit; he also teaches at the University of Michigan, Ann Arbor.

Between 1970 and 1976 Randall serves as a member of the Michigan Council for the Arts and on its advisory panel on literature; he also serves as a member of New Detroit, Inc.

Randall travels to Ghana, Togo, and Dahomey, and is a student of African arts at the University of Ghana.

Don L. Lee's *Don't Cry, Scream!* appears in a third edition, with 5,000 copies. Lee's *We Walk the Way of the New World* is published. *Time* magazine noted on April 6, 1970, that Don L. Lee's first three books of poetry, *Think Black!, Black Pride,* and *Don't Cry, Scream!* have "sold some 80,000 copies" by 1970.

Broadside Press produces "Broadside on Broadway: Seven Poets Read," in its Broadside Voices series, including the following poets: Dudley Randall, Jerry Whittington, Frenchy Hodges, Sonia Sanchez, Gwendolyn Brooks, Don L. Lee, and Margaret Walker.

Randall publishes *Love You* with Paul Breman (London, England: Breman).

Broadside receives a grant from the Coordinating Council of Literary Magazines.

James Emanuel's *Panther Man* is published.

Nikki Giovanni's *Re: Creation* is published.

Lance Jeffers' *My Blackness Is the Beauty of This Land* is printed.

Sonia Sanchez's *We a BaddDDD People* is printed.

Margaret Walker's *Prophets for a New Day* is published.

By the end of this year Broadside Press has produced sixteen books and thirty-two broadsides of poetry.

1971

Gwendolyn Brooks is the author of *Family Pictures* and serves as the editor of the anthologies *A Broadside Treasury* and *Jump Bad, a New Chicago Anthology.*

Don L. Lee's *Directionscore: Selected and New Poems* appears. Lee is also the author of *Dynamite Voices: Black Poets of the 1960s.* This book becomes the first volume of criticism published by Broadside Press.

Bill Odarty's *A Safari of African Cooking,* "the only book of African cookery in the American book trade compiled by a black African," is published.

Randall's *More to Remember: Poems of Four Decades* published by Third World Press.

Randall serves as editor of *The Black Poets* (New York: Bantam Books, Inc.).

1972

Ahmed Alhamisi's *Holy Ghosts* is published.

Alvin Aubert's *Against the Blues* is published.

Jill Witherspoon Boyer serves as the editor of *The Broadside Annual,* a yearly anthology of poetry published from 1972 through 1974.

Gwendolyn Brooks' autobiography, *Report from Part One,* is published by Broadside Press. By 1973, there will be more than 10,000 copies of this book in print. Melba J. Boyd, assistant editor at Broadside, will note in 1975 that this book is the company's "most significant publication."

Addison Gayle's *Claude McKay: The Black Poet at War* is published as the second volume in the Broadside Critical Series.

Pearl Lomax's *We Don't Need No Music* appears.

Randall reads at a poetry festival entitled "The Forerunners" at Howard University, Washington, D.C. During the year he receives a citation from the Metropolitan Detroit English Club.

James Randall is the author of *Cities and Other Disasters.*

1973

Etheridge Knight's *Belly Song and Other Poems* is published.

Don L. Lee's *From Plan to Planet-Life Studies: The Need for Afrikan Minds and Institutions* appears. *Think Black!* reaches a third edition, 16th printing, in June 1973.

Audre Lorde's third book, *From a Land Where Other People Live* is published and is nominated for a National Book Award.

Randall's *After the Killing* is published by Third World Press.

Randall receives the Kuumba Liberation Award and participates in a seminar for socio-literature in the East West Culture Learning Institute at the University of Hawaii.

Margaret Walker's *October Journey* is printed.

1974

Leaonead Bailey is the compiler of *Broadside Authors and Artists.* Melba J. Boyd credits this work as another "most significant" book in the history of Broadside Press.

Houston A. Baker is the author of *A Many Colored Coat: Countee Cullen,* another work in the Broadside Critics series.

George Barlow's *Gabriel* is published.

Bernard Bell's *Folk Roots of Afro-American Poetry,* a work in the Broadside Critics series, is published.

Sterling Brown's *The Last Ride of Wild Bill* is published.

Cuba's Nicholas Guillen is the author of *Tengo* (translated by Richard Carr). This work becomes Broadside's first publication of a poetry work in translation.

Lance Jeffers' *When I Know the Power of My Black Hand* is published.

Haki R. Madhubuti's *Book of Life* is published.

Sonia Sanchez's *A Blues Book for Black Magical Women* is published.

Celes Tisdale serves as the editor of *Betcha Ain't: Poems from Attica.*

1975

The offices of Broadside Press move to 12652 Livernois, Detroit.

Randall receives an Arts Award in Literature from the Michigan Foundation for the Arts. He serves on the Detroit Council of the Arts and is selected for the Distinguished Alumnus Award of the University of Michigan's School of Library Science.

By this year there are over 95,000 copies of Don L. Lee's (Haki R. Madhubuti's) books in print. The author's *Think Black!* appears in a new printing by Broadside, with over 25,000 copies in print.

A Capsule Course in Black Writing appears, written by Dudley Randall, Gwendolyn Brooks, Haki R. Madhubuti, and Keorapetse Kgositsile.

Randall publishes *Broadside Memories: Poets I Have Known.*

Under the Broadside Voices series, the company has produced by this date ten tapes of poets reading their own books, including works by James Emanuel, Dudley Randall, Etheridge Knight, Sonia Sanchez, Jon Eckels, Beatrice and Nancy Arnez, Marvin X, Keorapetse Kgositsile, Don L. Lee (Haki R. Madhubuti), and Stephany Fuller.

The Broadside Press Tenth Anniversary Dinner is held on September 27, 1975, in the Riverview Room at Cobo Hall, Detroit.

According to Melba J. Boyd, four of the most successful Broadside authors who have aided "the growth of Broadside" in its first ten years of history are Haki R. Madhubuti (Don L. Lee), Etheridge Knight, Sonia Sanchez, and Audre Lorde.

By the end of this year Broadside Press has published eighty-nine Broadsides, eight anthologies, and over sixty collections of poetry and criticism.

1976

Between 1976 and 1977 Broadside Press suffers a series of financial problems, due to increasing debt and the literary commitments made by Dudley Randall to authors.

Writer D. H. Melhem in *Heroism in the New Black Poetry* refers to this period as the "silence" era (quoting Randall) in the life and work of Dudley Randall. Financial and health problems force Randall to curtail his daily activities in running Broadside Press. This period of silence lasts from 1976 to 1980. Randall will only begin to write poetry again on April 4, 1980.

1977

The Alexander Crummell Memorial Church (Episcopal) in Highland Park, Michigan, purchases Broadside Press from Randall, who assumes a post as consultant to the new owners.

Randall is active in the Arts Extended Gallery for the Advancement of Culture and Education, the Committee on Small Magazine Editors and Publishers, and Kappa Alpha Psi fraternity.

Randall receives an award from the International Black Writer's Conference, Chicago, Illinois. He also receives an award from the Institute of Afro-American Studies, Howard University, Washington, D.C.

Late 1970s

A period of "silence" for Dudley Randall (1976–1980). He begins to write poetry again on April 4, 1980, and around the same time becomes active again in literary affairs.

1980

Randall serves as a United States government census worker.

1981

Randall is awarded a Creative Artist Award in Literature from the Michigan Council for the Arts. He also receives a fellowship from the National Endowment for the Arts. Naomi Long Madgett, publisher of Lotus Press, Detroit, publishes Randall's *A Litany of Friends: New and Selected Poems.* (His last book to appear in print was published in 1973.) On November 9, 1981, a special ceremony honoring Dudley Randall on his appointment by Mayor Coleman A. Young as the city of Detroit's first Poet Laureate, is held at Wayne State University in Detroit.

1982

Randall resumes ownership of Broadside Press.

1984

Randall serves as the editor of Broadside's *Homage to Hoyt Fuller,* an anthology.

1985

Randall retires at the age of 71. Hilda and Donald Vest of Detroit, Michigan, purchase Broadside Press from Randall.

1985–1989

The company concentrates on reprinting eight poets published under the Randall-led Broadside Press: Gwendolyn Brooks, Margaret Walker, Sonia Sanchez, Etheridge Knight, Nikki Giovanni, Dudley Randall, Haki R. Madhubuti, and Audre Lorde.

1990–1995

The twenty-fifth anniversary of Broadside Press is celebrated in Detroit, Michigan. It is reported that Broadside Press has annual sales of $10,000, and there are thirty-six Broadside titles still in print. Ten new books are published. Broadside Press celebrates its thirtieth anniversary in the fall of 1995.

Appendix B:
Broadside Press Authors
and Artists, 1965–1995

Name	*Place of Birth*
A	
Lloyd Addison (1931–)	Boston, Massachusetts
Allen Adkins	
Rico Africa	
Kwadwo Akpan	
Nanina Alba (1917–68)	Montgomery, Alabama
Paula Denise Alexander (1951–)	Las Vegas, Nevada
Ahmed Alhamisi (1940–)	Savannah, Georgia
Ron Allen	
Samuel Allen [Paul Vesey] (1917–)	Columbus, Ohio
Richard Alonso	
James Amaker	
Johari M. Amini [Kunjufu] (1935–)	Philadelphia, Pennsylvania
Kuweka Amiri [Mwandishe] [Sterling X] (1953–)	Chester, Pennsylvania
Sonebeyatta Amungo [Robert Hagan] (1956–)	Detroit, Michigan
JoAnn Anderson (1953–)	Detroit, Michigan
T. W. Anderson	
Nancy L. Arnex (1928–)	Baltimore, Maryland
Russell Atkins (1927–)	Cleveland, Ohio
Alvin Aubert (1930–)	Luchter, Louisiana
B	
Leaonead Pack Bailey (1906–)	Hinton, West Virginia
Houston A. Baker, Jr. (1943–)	Louisville, Kentucky
Dirk Bakker	
Toni Cade Bambara (1939–96)	New York City, New York
Amiri Baraka (1934–)	Newark, New Jersey
Irv Barat	
George Barlow (1948–)	Berkeley, California
Leonard Baskin	
Romare Bearden (1912–98)	Charlotte, North Carolina
Bernard, Bell (1936–)	Washington, D.C.
Lerone Bennett, Jr. (1928–)	Clarksdale, Mississippi
Kenneth Benson	
Chantal Sandre Berry (1948–)	Newark, New Jersey

Name	Place of Birth
Faruq Z. Bey	
Sadiq Bey	
McLane Birch, III (1942–)	Little Rock, Arkansas
Henry Blakely (1916–97)	Chicago, Illinois
Arna Bontemps (1902–73)	Alexandria, Louisiana
Melba Joyce Boyd (1950–)	Detroit, Michigan
Edward Boyer	
Hersey Boyer	
Jill Witherspoon Boyer (1947–)	Detroit, Michigan
Arthur Phillip Boze (1945–)	Washington, D.C.
Walter Louis Bradford (1937–)	Chicago, Illinios
Linda Bragg (1939–)	Akron, Ohio
Paul Breman (1931–)	Bussum, Holland
Gwendolyn Brooks (1917–)	Topeka, Kansas
Lewis Alexander Brooks	
Daniel Brown	
Joseph Clifton Brown (1908–)	Jackson, Mississippi
Robert T. Brown (1936–)	New Haven, Connecticut
Sterling A. Brown (1901–89)	Washington, D.C.
Dennis Brutus (1924–)	Harare, Zimbabwe
George Edward Buggs (1947–)	Brooklyn, New York
Carolyn Burke	
Paula Denise Alexander Burnett (1951–)	Las Vegas, Nevada
Yusuf Burni [Joseph Pannell]	Washington, D.C.
Margaret Burroughs (1917–)	St. Rose, Louisiana

C

Marcella Caine (1915–)	Stanford, Montana
Mary Ann Cameron	
Charles E. Cannon (1946–)	Durham, North Carolina
Richard Carr	
Harold Carrington (1938–)	Atlantic City, New Jersey
Karl W. Carter	
Hernan Catellano-Giron	
Chico	
Chinosole	
Carl Clark (1932–)	Brinkley, Arkansas
Sebastian Clark (1948–)	Trinidad
Evelyn Clarke (1935–)	Tarboro, North Carolina
Carol Gregory Clemmons (1945–)	Youngstown, Ohio
Lucille Clifton (1936–)	Depew, New York
Eugenia Collier (1928–)	Baltimore, Maryland
Mike Cook (1939–)	Chicago, Illinois
Susan Cox [Sandara Kamusikiri] (1949–)	Greenville, South Carolina
Walter Cox	
Stella Crews (1950–)	Port Huron, Michigan
Countee Cullen (1903–46)	Baltimore, Maryland
William Waring Cuney (1906–)	Washington, D.C.

D

Bill Dabney	
Margaret Danner (1915–82)	Pryorsburg, Kentucky
Larry Darby	
Gloria Davis	
Ossie Davis (1917–)	Cogsdell, Georgia
Rhonda M. Davis (1941–)	Chicago, Illinois
Bill Day	

Name	Place of Birth
Betty DeRamus	
Melvin Dixon (1950–92)	Stamford, Connecticut
Owen Dodson (1914–83)	Brooklyn, New York
Jeff Donaldson (1932–)	Pine Bluff, Arkansas
Saundra Douglas	
C. Gene Drafts (1946–)	Boston, Massachusetts
Ray Durem (1915–)	Seattle, Washington
Leisia Duskin	
Ebon [Ebon Dooley] (1942–)	Milan, Tennessee

E

Jon Eckels (1940s–)	Indianapolis, Indiana
Pearl Eckles	
George Robert Elie [Brother Amar; Amar Sekau Mshaka]	
Curtis Ellis	
James A. Emanuel (1921–)	Alliance, Nebraska
Ronald L. Emmons (1948–)	Chicago, Illinois
Emory	
Eseoghene [C. Lindsay Barrett]	Lucea, Jamaica
Mari Evans (1923–)	Toledo, Ohio

F

Sarah W. Fabio (1928–79)	Nashville, Tennessee
Ronald Fair (1937–)	Chicago, Illinois
Eugene Feldman	
B. Felton [Elmer Buford] (1934–)	Cleveland, Ohio
Sweiji Fiddo	
Julia Fields (1938–)	Uniontown, Alabama
Jose-Angel Figuerosa (1946–)	Mayaguez, Puerto Rico
Ray Fleming (1945–)	Cleveland, Ohio
Dennis Wilson Folly (1954–)	Hanover County, Virginia
Kent Foreman	Chicago, Illinois
LeRoy Foster (1948–74)	Detroit, Michigan
Bill Frederick (1943–)	Philadelphia, Pennsylvania
Jerry Frosh (1949–)	Canton, Georgia
Hoyt W. Fuller (1927–81)	Atlanta, Georgia
Stephany Fuller (1947–)	Chicago, Illinois

G

Larry Gabriel	
Jose L. Garza	
Addison Gayle, Jr. (1932–91)	Newport News, Virginia
Bruce C. Geary [K. Sayif M. Shabazz] (1942–)	Worcester, Massachusetts
Carolyn F. Gerald [Carolyn Flower] (1930s–)	Louisiana
Charles Gervin	
Michele S. Gibbs (1946–)	Chicago, Illinois
Paula Giddings (1947–)	Yonkers, New York
El Gilbert	
Zack Gilbert (1928–97)	McMullen, Missouri
Nikki Giovanni (1943–)	Knoxville, Tennessee
David M. Glicker	
Joe Goncalves (1937–)	Boston, Massachusetts
Carmin Auld Goulbourne [Carmen Auld Blanchette] (1912–)	El Cristo, Cuba

Name	Place of Birth
Glenda Gracia (1948–)	Philadelphia, Pennsylvania
Le Graham [Ahmed Alhamisi] (1940–)	Savannah, Georgia
Carl H. Green (1945–)	Philadelphia, Pennsylvania
Nicholas Guillen (1902–89)	Camaguey, Cuba

H

Bob Hamilton (1928–)	Cleveland, Ohio
Micheal S. Harper (1938–)	Brooklyn, New York
Doug Harris	
Robert L. Harris, Jr. (1938–)	Detroit, Michigan
Kaleema Hasen	
Darnell Felix Hawkins (1946–)	Sherrill, Arkansas
Isaiah Hawkins	
Robert Hayden (1913–80)	Detroit, Michigan
Bruce Heath	
David Henderson (1942–)	Harlem, New York
Errol A. Henderson	
Stephen E. Henderson (1925–)	Key West, Florida
Lolita Hernandez	
Chester Higgins, Jr. (1946–)	Lexington, Kentucky
Everett Hoagland, III (1942–)	Philadelphia, Pennsylvania
Frenchy Jolene Hodges (1940–)	Dublin, Georgia
Frank Horne (1899–1973)	New York City, New York
Theodore R. Horne (1937–)	Washington, D.C.
Langston Hughes (1902–67)	Joplin, Missouri
Mildred Hunt	
Kim Hunter	

I

Femi Funmi Ifetayo [Regina Micou] (1954–)	Detroit, Michigan

J

Mae Jackson (1946–)	Earl, Arkansas
Murray Jackson (1926–)	Philadelphia, Pennsylvania
Geoffrey Jacques	
Jamail [Robert Sims]	
Jamal [Joseph Kitt]	
Lance Jeffers (1919–85)	Fremont, Nebraska
Ted Joans (1928–)	Cairo, Illinois
Frank John (1941–)	Trinidad
Alicia L. Johnson (1944–)	
Charles Johnson	
Christine C. Johnson (1911–)	Versailles, Kentucky
Alice H. Jones	
June Jordan (1936–)	New York City, New York

K

Nubia Kai	Detroit, Michigan
Angeline Kaimala	
Sybil Kean (1942–)	New Orleans, Louisiana
Dolores Kendrick (1927–)	Washington, D.C.
Peggy Kenner (1937–)	Chicago, Illinois
George Kent (1920–82)	Columbus, Georgia
Robert Kesby	

Name	Place of Birth
Aneb Kgositsile [Gloria House] (1941–)	Tampa, Florida
Keorapetse Kgositsile (1938–)	Johannesburg, South Africa
Mabarut Khalimalik	
Carl Killibrew	
Hodari Kinamo (1940–)	Jonesville, Louisiana
Henri Umbaji King	
Woodie King, Jr. (1937–)	Alabama
Alvin Kingcade (1950–)	Philadelphia, Pennsylvania
Porter Kirkwood	
Etheridge Knight (1931–91)	Corinth, Mississippi

L

Oliver LaGrone (1906–)	McAlester, Oklahoma
Omar Lama	
Clear Land	
Pinkie Gordon Lane (1923–)	Philadelphia, Pennsylvania
Dave Lee	
George V. Lee	
Lyn A. Levy [Lyn Knight] (1943–)	Boston, Massachusetts
Arine Lewis	
Jacelyn Andrette Lewis (1950–)	
Roy Lewis (1940–)	Natchez, Mississippi
Paul Lichter	
M.L. Liebler	
Linyatta [Doris Turner]	
David Edward Llorens (1939–73)	Chicago, Illinois
Elouise Loftin (1950–)	Brooklyn, New York
Pearl M. Lomas [Pearl Cleage] (1948–)	Springfield, Massachusetts
Doughtry Long (1942–)	Atlanta, Georgia
Talita Long (1948–)	Brooklyn, New York
Lori Lunford	
James Rowser Lucas (1931–)	Falmouth, Virginia

M

Theodore McCain, Jr.	
Charles McClary	
Art McFallan	
Patricia McIlnay (1934–)	Battle Creek, Michigan
Claude McKay (1890–1948)	Jamaica
Rick McKenzie	
Jahra Michele McKinney	
Ray McKinney	
Dee Dee McNeil	
Marvin McQueen	
Naomi Long Madgett (1923–)	Norfolk, Virginia
Haki R. Madhubuti [Don L. Lee] (1942–)	Little Rock, Arkansas
Barbara Mahone [Barbara Diane Mahone McBain] (1944–)	Chicago, Illinois
Clarence Major (1936–)	Atlanta, Georgia
Mabarut Khalil Malik	
Harvey A. Marcelin	
Herbert Woodward Martin (1933–)	Birmingham, Alabama
John Mason	
Julian Mayfield (1928–84)	Greer, South Carolina
Mbenbe [Milton Smith] (1946–)	Kansas City, Missouri
Rhonda Mills	

Name	Place of Birth
Ron Milner (1938–)	Detroit, Michigan
Joe Mitchell	
Monica Morgan	
Wardell Montgomery, Jr.	
Toni Morrison (1931–)	Lorain, Ohio
Donald Mosley	
Mshaka [Willie Monroe]	
Beatrice M. Murphy (1908–)	Monessen, Pennsylvania
Mukhtarr Mustapha (1943–)	Freetown, Sierra Leone

N

Michael Nance	
Schaarazetta Natalege	
Kofi Natambu	
Lawrence P. Neal (1937–81)	Atlanta, Georgia
Betty H. Neals	
A.X. Nicholas (1930s–)	
Marion Nicholes [Marion Elizabeth Alexander Nicholes] (1944–)	New York City, New York
Bahala T. Nkrumah	
Kim Nolte-Avalon	
George E. Norman (1923–)	
John Lee Norris	

O

Bill Odarty (1938–)	Ghana, West Africa
Ademola Olugbefola (1941–)	St. Thomas, Virgin Islands
Olumo [Jim Cunningham] (1936–)	Webster Grove, Missouri
Regina O'Neal [Regina Louise Solomon O'Neal]	Detroit, Michigan
Ray B. Orford (1935–)	Chicago, Illinois

P

Harold E. Packwood	
James Patterson (1933–)	
Raymond Patterson (1929–)	New York City, New York
Reginald Payne	
Julianne D. Perry (1952–)	Durham, North Carolina
Arthur Pfister (1949–)	New Orleans, Louisiana
Clarence Phillips	
Frank Lamont Phillips (1950s–)	Memphis, Tennessee
Lawrence Pike	
Ibn Pori Pitts	
Sterling D. Plumpp (1940–)	Clinton, Mississippi
John Porter	
Helen Pulliam (1945–)	Buena Vista, Mississippi

Q

Helen G. Quigless (1944–)	Washington, D.C.

R

Sun Ra [Herman Blount] (1914–)	Birmingham, Alabama
Dudley Randall (1914–)	Washington, D.C.
James Andrew Randall, Jr. (1938–)	Detroit, Michigan
James Randall (1943–)	Bolton, North Carolina
Jon Randall (1942–)	Detroit, Michigan
John Raven (1936–)	Washington, D.C.
Ishmael Reed (1938–)	Chattanooga, Tennessee

Name	Place of Birth
Leslie Reese (1961–)	Detroit, Michigan
Sarah Carolyn Reese	Logansport, Indiana
Rod Reinhart	
Edward Richer (1930–)	Mason City, Iowa
Lawrence C. Riley (1947–)	Detroit, Michigan
Conrad Kent Rivers (1933–68)	Atlantic City, New Jersey
Victor A. Roberts	
Robert L. Robinson (1946–)	Detroit, Michigan
William H. Robinson (1922–)	Newport, Rhode Island
Carolyn Rodgers (1945–)	Chicago, Illinois
Rod Rodgers	
Benjamin Howard Rogers (1949–)	Sioux City, Iowa
Irene Rosemond (1920–)	Albany, New York
Cyprian Rowe	
Charles H. Rowell (1930s–)	Near Auburn, Alabama
Philip Royster (1943–)	Chicago, Illinois
Sandra Royster (1942–)	Chicago, Illinois
Rod Rudnick	
Tony Rutherford [Umar Abdul-Rahim Hassan] (1945–)	Detroit, Michigan
Wilbert E. Rutledge, Jr. (1940–)	Kansas City, Missouri

S

Sonia Sanchez (1934–)	Birmingham, Alabama
Trinidad Sanchez	
Steven Schreiner	
Sharon Scott (1951–)	Chicago, Illinois
Tom Sellers [Thomas Peyton Sellers] (1949–)	Summit, New Jersey
Ali Shabaz (1929–)	Memphis, Tennessee
Hill Shabaz (1912–)	Detroit, Michigan
Chaka Shango [Horance Coleman] (1943–)	Dayton, Ohio
Ed Sherman	
Gerald Simmons, Jr. [Ulozi]	
Judy Dothard Simmons (1944–)	Westerly, Rhode Island
Edward Simpkins	
John Sinclair (1941–)	Flint, Michigan
Joseph T. Sketter, Jr.	
Sharyn Jeanne Sketter (1945–)	New York City, New York
Jeanne Newkirk Smith (1936–)	New York City, New York
Johnny Smith	
Sharon Smith-Knight (1943–)	Detroit, Michigan
Chauncey E. Spencer	Lynchburg, Virginia
John Spencer	
Edward S. Spriggs (1934–)	Cleveland, Ohio
Shirley Stark (1927–)	New York, New York
Ruth Steed (1947–)	Marianna, Florida
Marie Stephens	
Frederick Gerald Stepp	
Keith Sterling	
Christopher Sutherland	
Ellease Sutherland (1943–)	

T

Teresa M. Tan	
Eileen Tann	
Omari Kenyatta Tarajia [Richard C. James, III]	
Eleanora E. Tate (1948–)	Canton, Missouri
Cledie Collins Taylor (1926–)	Bolivor, Arkansas

Name	Place of Birth
Prentiss Taylor (1951–)	Chicago, Illinois
Rockie D. Taylor [Tejumola Ologboni] (1945–)	Salina, Kansas
Dennis Teichman	
Mozehin Tejani	
William Anthony Thigpen (1948–71)	Detroit, Michigan
Beverly Thomas (1948–)	St. Louis, Missouri
Carolyn Thomas (1944–)	Detroit, Michigan
Richard Thomas (1939–)	Detroit, Michigan
James W. Thompson (1935–)	Detroit, Michigan
Celes "Les" Tisdale (1941–)	Salters, South Carolina
LaDonna Jean Tolbert (1956–)	Detroit, Michigan
Melvin B. Tolson (1898–1966)	Moberly, Missouri
Jean Toomer (1894–1967)	Washington, D.C.
Askia Muhammad Toure [Roland Snellings] (1938–)	Raleigh, North Carolina
Saundra Towns	
Darwin T. Turner (1931–91)	Cincinnati, Ohio
Chris Tysh	

V

Hilda Vest (1933–)	Griffin, Georgia
Mick Vranich	

W

Alice Walker (1944–)	Eatonton, Georgia
Evan K. Walker	
Margaret Walker (1915–)	Birmingham, Alabama
Rayfield, Waler (1960–)	Detroit, Michigan
Kofi Wangara [Harold G. Lawrence] (1928–)	Detroit, Michigan
Malaika Ayo Wangara [Joyce E. Whitsitt Lawrence] (1938–)	Mt. Clemens, Michigan
Albert M. Ward (1950–)	Detroit, Michigan
Frances Ward (1935–)	Atlanta, Georgia
Val Gray Ward (1933–)	Mt. Bayou, Mississippi
Roberto Warren	
Mary Helen Washington (1941–)	Cleveland, Ohio
Sam Washington	
Thomas Washington, Jr.	
Raymond X. Webster	
Albert Wendt	
Patricia Whitsitt	
John A. Williams (1925–)	Jackson, Mississippi
Tyrone Williams	
Willie Williams	
James D. Wilson	
Reginald Wilson	
Sigmonde Wimberli [Kharlos Tucker] (1938–)	
Habte Wolde [Alozo Jennings] (1945–)	Patterson, New Jersey
Ruby Woods	
Shirley Woodson (1936–)	Pulaski, Tennessee
James Ralph Worley (1921–)	Welch, West Virginia
Deonne B. Wright	
Jay Wright (1935–)	Albuquerque, New Mexico

X

Hurley X [Hurley Smith]	
Marvin X [Fitnah Nazzam al of Nazzam A Sudan] (1944–)	Fowler, California
Sanford X	
Sterling X [Kuweka Amiri Mwandishi] (1953–)	Chester, Pennsylvania

Notes

Chapter 1

1. Dudley Randall, interview with the author, Detroit, Mich., April 9, 1992; Frenchy Jolene Hodges, "Dudley Randall and the Broadside Press" (M.A. thesis, Atlanta University, 1974), 8.
2. Randall, interview with the author, April 9, 1992.
3. E. Franklin Frazier, *Negro Youth at the Crossways: Their Personality Development in the Middle States* (New York: Schocken Books, 1940, 1967), 7–8, 33–36.
4. Gwendolyn Fowlkes, "An Interview with Dudley Randall," *The Black Scholar* 6, no. 9 (June 1975): 87; D.H. Melhem, *Heroism in the New Black Poetry: Introductions and Interviews,* see Chapter 2, "Dudley Randall: The Poet as Humanist" (Lexington: University Press of Kentucky, 1990), 42.
5. Fowlkes, "An Interview with Dudley Randall," 87.
6. Hodges, "Dudley Randall and the Broadside Press," 8.
7. Carole Marks, *Farewell — We're Good and Gone: The Great Black Migration* (Bloomington: Indiana University Press, 1989), 1.
8. Ibid., 3. On the early history of blacks in Detroit see David M. Katzman, *Before the Ghetto: Black Detroit in the Nineteenth Century* (Urbana: University of Illinois Press, 1973).
9. Florette Henri, *Black Migration: Movement North 1900–1920. The Road from Myth to Man* (Garden City, N.Y.: Anchor Press/Doubleday, 1976), 265–67; Elliott M. Rudwick, *Race Riot at East St. Louis, July 2, 1917* (Carbondale: Southern Illinois University Press, 1964).
10. Hodges, "Dudley Randall and the Broadside Press," 8.
11. Ibid.; Charles H. Wesley, *Negro Labor in the United States, 1850–1925* (New York: Russell and Russell, 1927), 293, 298; Melvin G. Holli, ed., *Detroit* (New York: New Viewpoints, 1976), 147; Allen H. Spear, "East St. Louis Race Riot (1917)" in *Encyclopedia of African American Civil Rights: From Emancipation to the Present,* ed. Charles D. Lowery and John F. Marszalek (Westport, Conn.: Greenwood, 1992), 163.
12. DeWitt S. Dykles, Jr., "The Search for Community: Michigan Society and Education, 1945–1980," in *Michigan, Visions of Our Past,* ed. Richard J. Hathaway (East Lansing: Michigan State University Press, 1989), 298.
13. Donald R. Deskine, Jr., *Residential Mobility of Negroes in Detroit, 1837–1965* (Ann Arbor: University of Michigan Press, 1972), 265; Darlene Clark Hine, "Black Migration to the Urban Midwest: The Gender Dimension, 1915–1945," in *The Great Migration in Historical Perspective: New Dimensions of Race, Class and Gender,* ed. Joe William Trotter, Jr. (Bloomington: Indiana University Press, 1991), 128.
14. Randall, interview with the author, April 9, 1992.
15. David Gordon Nielson, *Black Ethos, Northern Urban Negro Life and Thought, 1890–1930* (Westport, Conn.: Greenwood, 1977), 74.
16. A.X. Nicholas, "A Conversation with Dudley Randall," *Black World* 21, no. 2 (December 1971): 27; R. Baxter Miller, "Dudley Randall," in *Dictionary of Literary Biography,* vol. 41, *Afro American Poets Since 1955,* ed. Trudier Harris and Thadious M. Davis (Detroit: Gale Research Co., 1985), 266.
17. Melhem, *Heroism in the New Black Poetry,* 42.

18. Charles H. Rowell "In Conservation with Dudley Randall," *Obsidian* 2 (Spring 1976): 33; "Black Books Bulletin Interviews Dudley Randall," (Winter 1972): 24. On the Harlem Renaissance era see David Levering Lewis, *When Harlem Was in Vogue* (New York: Alfred A. Knopf, 1981); Cary D. Wintz, *Black Culture and the Harlem Renaissance* (Houston, Tex.: Rice University Press, 1988); Gerald Early, ed., *My Soul's High Song: The Collected Writings of Countee Cullen, Voice of the Harlem Renaissance* (New York: Anchor Books, 1991); Cynthia Earl Kerman and Richard Eldridge, *The Lives of Jean Toomer: A Hunger for Wholeness* (Baton Rouge: Louisiana State University Press, 1987).

19. R. Baxter Miller, "Endowing the World and Time: The Life and Work of Dudley Randall," in *Black American Poets Between Worlds 1940–1960*, ed. R. Baxter Miller (Knoxville: University of Tennessee Press, 1986), 77; Melham, *Heroism in the New Black Poetry*, 42.

20. "Black Books Bulletin Interviews Dudley Randall," 23. On Garveyism in Detroit see David Allen Levine, *Internal Combustion: The Races in Detroit, 1915–1926* (Westport, Conn.: Greenwood, 1976), 100–3.

21. Rowell, "In Conversation with Dudley Randall," 32. In another interview Randall relates that his "father also managed the campaigns or was active in the campaigns of black office-seekers. None of them were elected, and people said he was hitting his head against a stone wall. It wasn't until after his death that Detroit elected its first black official." See "Black Books Bulletin Interviews Dudley Randall."

22. "Black Books Bulletin Interviews Dudley Randall," 23.

23. Randall, interview with the author, April 9, 1992.

24. Hodges, "Dudley Randall and the Broadside Press," 9–10.

25. Richard W. Thomas, *Life for Us Is What We Make It: Building Black Community in Detroit, 1915–1945* (Bloomington: Indiana University Press, 1992), 137–40; Scott Nearing, *Black American* (New York: Schocken Books, 1929), 111.

26. Forrester Washington, "Police Brutality" in *Detroit Perspectives: Crossroads and Turning Points,* ed. Wilma Wood Henrickson (Detroit: Wayne State University Press, 1991), 338.

27. The next four states with the largest estimated Ku Klux Klan membership lists were: New Jersey with 720,220; Texas, 450,000; Kentucky, 441,560; and Ohio, 400,000. See Lenwood G. Davis and Janet L. Sims-Wood, *The Ku Klux Klan: A Bibliography* (Westport, Conn.: Greenwood, 1984), 622–23.

28. Michael and Judy Ann Newton, *The Ku Klux Klan: An Encyclopedia* (New York: Garland Publishing, Inc., 1991), 388; Kenneth T. Jackson, "The Ku Klux Klan in Michigan," in *A Michigan Reader,* ed. Robert M. Warner and C. Warren Vander Hill (Grand Rapids, Mich.: William B. Eerdmans Publishing Co., 1974), 169–82; Nora Faires, "Transition and Turmoil: Social and Political Development in Michigan, 1917–1945," in *Michigan: Visions of Our Past,* 205; Raymond R. Fragnoli, *The Transformation of Reform: Progressivism in Detroit — and After, 1912–1933* (New York: Garland Publishing, Inc., 1982), 309.

29. Edward Byron Reuter, *The American Race Problem* (New York: Thomas Y. Crowell Co., 1970), 346; Nearing, *Black America,* 269.

30. Thomas, *Life for Us Is What We Make It,* 179; C. Eric Lincoln and Lawrence H. Mamiya, *The Black Church in the African American Experience* (Durham, N.C.: Duke University Press, 1990), 119–20.

31. Thomas, *Life for Us Is What We Make It,* 187.

32. *Detroit Contender,* November 13, 1920, May 7, 1921; *Detroit Independent,* June 10, September 16, 1927; *The Detroit Blue Book, a National Weekly Newspaper: A Complete Survey of Negro Life and Activities in Greater Detroit for 1929* (Detroit: Detroit Independent Publishing Co., 1929), 22; *Classified Detroit Negro Business Directory 1927* (Detroit: Detroit Negro Business League, 1927), 20; John D. Stevens, "The Black Press Looks at 1920s Journalism," *Journalism History* 7, no. 3–4 (Autumn/Winter 1980): 109. See also Frank Angelo, *On Guard: A History of the Detroit Free Press* (Detroit: Detroit Free Press, 1981).

33. Thomas, *Life for Us Is What We Make It,* 53, 194–201, 229–30; Jesse Thomas Moore, Jr., *A Search for Equality: The National Urban League 1910–1961* (University Press: Pennsylvania State University Press, 1981), 73; Levine, *Internal Combustion: The Race in Detroit, 1915–1926,* 100–1; Nancy J. Weiss, *The National Urban League, 1910–1940* (New York: Oxford University Press, 1974), 143.

34. Harvey C. Jackson, Jr., "Summary History of the ASNLH," *Negro History Bulletin* 26, no. 1

(October 1962): 1; Alfred Young, "The Historical Origin and Significance of National Afro-American (Black) History Month Observance," *Negro History Bulletin* 43, no. 1 (January/February/March 1980): 6–8.

35. "Dudley Randall," (Detroit: Detroit Public Library, Biography and Criticism Department, VF, n.d.); Hodges, "Dudley Randall and the Broadside Press," 9; Dudley Randall, interview with the author, Detroit, Mich., October 14, 1995.

36. Hodges, "Dudley Randall and the Broadside Press," 9.

37. Reuter, *The American Race Problem,* 45.

38. B.J. Widick, *Detroit: City of Race and Class Violence* (Chicago: Quadrangle Books, 1972), 43–44.

39. Broadus Mitchell, *Depression Decade: From New Era Through New Deal 1929–1941,* vol. IX, *The Economic History of the United States* (New York: Holt, Rinehart and Winston, 1947), 103–4.

40. Raymond Wolters, *Negroes and the Great Depression: The Problem of Economic Recovery* (Westport, Conn.: Greenwood, 1970), 115–16

41. Joyce Shaw Peterson, "Black Automobile Workers in Detroit, 1910–1930," *The Journal of Negro History* 64, no. 3 (Summer 1979): 177.

42. Ibid., 179.

43. Kuniko Pupa, *Black Worker's Struggles in Detroit's Auto Industry, 1935–1975* (Detroit: Century Twenty-One Publishing, 1980), 10.

44. Ibid., 13.

45. Joyce Shaw Peterson, "Autoworkers Confront the Depression, 1929–1933," *Detroit in Perspective,* 6, no. 2 (Fall 1982): 48.

46. *All About Michigan Almanac* (Hartland, Mich.: H/S/O Publications, 1989), 39.

47. Iris Cloyd, ed., *Who's Who Among Black Americans* (Detroit: Gale Research Co., 1990), 1045; Melhem, *Heroism in the New Black Poetry,* 43; Dudley Randall, interview with the author, Detroit, Mich., October 14, 1995.

48. Hodges, "Dudley Randall and the Broadside Press," 9.

49. Ibid., 11. Postal service jobs were viewed as an important area for black employment during the Age of Segregation in the United States. One study notes that "The entire postal service employed 25,390 Negroes in 1928, about 9 percent of the total force. In Detroit Negroes constitute about 16.4 percent of the postal staff. In Chicago they constitute 31 percent; in New York 16 percent. They are thus unmistakably a factor to be reckoned with." See Sterling D. Spero and Abram L. Harris, *The Black Worker: Negro and the Labor Movement* (New York: Columbia University Press, 1931, 1959; reprint, New York: Atheneum, 1969), 122.

50. "The Negro in Detroit, 1926," 147.

51. Jane H. Bayes, *Minority Policies and Idealogies in the United States* (Novato, Calif.: Chandler and Sharp Publishers, 1982), 31; Henry J. Young, *Major Black Religious Leaders Since 1940* (Nashville, Tenn.: Abingdon, 1979), 66–68.

52. Young, *Major Black Religious Leaders Since 1940,* 32; C. Eric Lincoln, *The Black Muslims in America* (Boston: Beacon Press, 1961), 16–17; Wardell J. Payne, ed., *Directory of African American Religious Bodies: A Compendium by the Howard University School of Divinity* (Washington, D.C.: Howard University Press, 1991), 139–40, 142–43.

53. Hathaway, *Michigan: Visions of Our Past,* 210; A.O. Edmonds, *Joe Lewis* (Grand Rapids, Mich.: William B. Eerdmans Publishing Co., 1973).

54. On this period see Danny Duncan Collum, ed., *African Americans in the Spanish Civil War: This Ain't Ethiopia But It'll Do* (New York: G.K. Hall & Co., 1992); William R. Scott, *The Sons of Sheba's Race: African-Americans and the Italo-Ethiopian War, 1935–1941* (Bloomington: Indiana University Press, 1992); John Hope Franklin and Alfred A. Moss, Jr., *From Slavery to Freedom: A History of Negro Americans* (New York: McGraw-Hill, 1988), 385, 406.

55. "Black Books Bulletin Interviews Dudley Randall," 24.

56. Rowell, "In Conversation with Dudley Randall," 34. During the 1930s Robert Hayden worked as a journalist at the *Michigan Chronicle,* established in 1936, and operated by the *Chicago Defender*'s Robert S. Abbott Publishing Company. Over the next ten years, the *Michigan Chronicle* became one of the most important black weekly newspapers in the state. See *Blacks in Detroit* (Detroit: Detroit Free Press, 1983), 64.

57. Dudley Randall, interview with the author, Detroit, Mich., October 14, 1995.

58. Melhem, *Heroism in the New Black Poetry*, 45. Rowell, "In Conversation with Dudley Randall," 34. The black press in Michigan served as one possible outlet for the work of struggling writers in the state. During the 1930s there were twenty active black press organs in Michigan, with sixteen of these in Detroit. During this period Robert Hayden was recognized as the music and drama critic for the *Michigan Chronicle* under the editorship of Louis E. Martin. Earlier, in 1936, Hayden secured a position as director of the Federal Writers' Project investigation into local black Detroit history and folklore. Dudley Randall is noticeable for his absence from such activities during the 1930s. On the black press in Michigan for the 1930s see George James Fleming, "A Survey of Negro Newspapers in the United States" (B.A. thesis, University of Wisconsin, 1931), 88, 97; Ulysses W. Boykin, *A Handbook on the Detroit Negro* (Detroit: The Minority Study Associates, 1943), 112–13; *Michigan Chronicle*, April 14, 1956; *Negro Newspapers and Periodicals in the United States* (Washington, D.C.: Department of Commerce, 1939), 7; Roland E. Wolseley, *The Black Press, U.S.A.* (Ames: Iowa State University Press, 1990), 85. On Robert Hayden for this period see Sterling A. Brown, Arthur P. Davis, and Ulysses Lee, eds., *The Negro Caravan* (New York: Dryden Press, 1941; reprint, New York: Arno Press and the New York Times, 1970), 404; James O. Young, *Black Writers of the Thirties* (Baton Rouge: Louisiana State University Press, 1973), 193.

59. Randall, interview with the author, Detroit, Mich., October 14, 1995; Cloyd, *Who's Who Among Black Americans 1990*, 1045; Randall, interview with the author, April 9, 1992.

60. Boykin, *A Handbook on the Detroit Negro*, 111; Lawrence M. Sommers, *Michigan: A Geography* (Boulder, Col.: Westview Press, 1984), 179.

61. Boykin, *A Handbook on the Detroit Negro,* 111.

62. Hodges, "Dudley Randall and the Broadside Press," 11; Melhem, *Heroism in the New Black Poetry,* 43, 66.

63. Paul T. Murray, "Blacks and the Draft: A History of Institutional Racism," *Journal of Black Studies* 2, no. 1 (September 1971): 64; Otto Lindenmeyer, *Black and Brave: The Black Soldier in America* (New York: McGraw-Hill, 1970), 88; Franklin and Moss, *From Slavery to Freedom,* 391.

64. See Richard O. Hope, *Racial Strife in the United States Military: Toward the Elimination of Discrimination* (New York: Praeger, 1979); Mary Penick Motley, ed., *The Invisible Soldier: The Experience of the Black Soldier, World War II* (Detroit: Wayne State University Press, 1987); Wilbur C. Rich, *Coleman Young and Detroit Politics: From Social Activist to Power Broker* (Detroit: Wayne State University Press, 1989), 53; Franklin and Moss, *From Slavery to Freedom,* 396–406; Neil A. Wynn, *The Afro-American and the Second World War* (New York: Holmes and Meier Publishers, 1976).

65. Patrick S. Washburn, "J. Edgar Hoover and the Black Press in World War II," *Journalism History* 13, no. 1 (Spring 1986): 26–33; Lee Finkle, *Forum for Protest: The Black Press During World War II* (Cranbury, N.J.: Fairleigh Dickinson University Press, 1975); John D. Stevens, "World War II and the Black Press," in *Perspectives of the Black Press: 1974*, ed. Henry LaBrie, III (Kennebunkport, Maine: Mercer House Press, 1974), 27–37; Patrick S. Washburn, *A Question of Sedition: The Federal Government's Investigation of the Black Press During World War II* (New York: Oxford University Press, 1986), 263.

66. Walton Bean, *California: An Interpretive History* (New York: McGraw-Hill, 1986), 430–31; Michi Weglyn, *Years of Infamy: The Untold Story of America's Concentration Camps* (New York: Morrow Quill Paperbacks, 1976), 4–5; John Tateishi, *And Justice for All: An Oral History of the Japanese Americans Detention Camps* (New York: Random House, 1984), vii; Roger Daniel, *Concentration Camps USA: Japanese Americans and World War II* (New York: Holt, Rinehart and Winston, 1972), 70–71, 157.

67. Thomas, *Life for Us Is What We Make It,* 143–48; John G. Van Deusen, *The Black Man in White American* (Washington, D.C.: Associated Publishers, 1944), 55; Dominic J. Capeci, Jr., *Race Relations in Wartime Detroit: The Sojourner Truth Housing Controversy of 1942* (Detroit: Wayne State University Press, 1984).

68. Ray Marshall, *The Negro and Organized Labor* (New York: John Wiley and Sons, 1965), 52;

69. Rayford W. Logan, ed., *What the Negro Wants* (Chapel Hill: University of North Carolina Press, 1944), 14.

70. Homer Hawkins and Richard Thomas, "White Policing of Black Populations: A History

of Race and Social Control in America," in *Out of Order?: Policing Black People,* ed. Ellis Cashmore and Eugene McLaughlin (New York: Routledge, 1991), 81.

71. Thomas, *Life for Us Is What We Make It,* 172. Riots also occurred in 1943 in Los Angeles, California; Beaumont, Texas, and Mobile, Alabama. See Harvard Sitkoff, "The Detroit Race Riot of 1943," in *Blacks in White American Since 1865: Issues and Interpretations,* ed. R.C. Twombly (New York: David McKay Co., 1971), 315–32; and Harvard Sitkoff, "Racial Militancy and Interracial Violence in the Second World War," *Journal of American History* 58 (1971): 671.

72. Widick, *Detroit: City of Race and Class Violence,* 111. See also Dominic J. Capeci, Jr. and Martha Wilkerson, *Layered Violence: The Detroit Riot of 1943* (Jackson, Miss.: University Press of Mississippi, 1991), 20–21, 27, 30–31, 146–49, 193; Thurgood Marshall, "The Gestapo in Detroit," *Crisis* 50 (August 1943): 232–33.

73. Melhem, *Heroism in the New Black Poetry,* 44; Hodges, "Dudley Randall and the Broadside Press," 12.

74. Hodges, "Dudley Randall and the Broadside Press," 12. See also Eric F. Goldman, *The Crucial Decade and After: America 1945–1960* (New York: Vintage Books, 1960), 13, 49–50.

75. J. Irving E. Scott, *Negro Studies and Their Colleges* (Boston: Meador Publishing Co., 1949), 174. In 1947, there were only 2 black students out of 650 at Alma College, 70 out of 2,206 at Michigan State College (now University), and 85 out of 7,500 at the University of Detroit. *Afro-American Encyclopedia* (North Miami, Fla.: Educational Book Publishers, 1974), 1846. By 1974, over 27,000 men had been initiated into the Kappa Alpha Psi Fraternity, Inc. See also *Jet Magazine.* May 3, 1982, 21, December 6, 1982, 18; Ann Allen Shockley and Sue P. Chandler, *Living Black American Authors: A Biographical Directory* (New York: R.R. Bowker Co., 1973), 131; William L. Crump, *The Story of Kappa Alpha Psi: A History of the Beginning and Development of a College Greek Letter Organization, 1911–1991* (Philadelphia, Pa.: Kappa Alpha Psi Fraternity, 1991).

76. Randall, interview with the author, April 9, 1992; Henrietta Epstein, "Randall's Broadside Press," *South End* (Detroit, Mich.), February 2, 1972.

77. Miller, "Endowing the World and Time," 78.

78. Randall, interview with the author, April 9, 1992.

79. Rowell, "In Conversation with Dudley Randall," 40; Fowlkes, "An Interview with Dudley Randall," 88; Dudley Randall, *Cities Burning* (Detroit: Broadside Press, 1968), 3.

80. Miller, "Endowing the World and Time," 82; Melhem, *Heroism in the New Black Poetry,* 48–49.

81. Melhem, *Heroism in the New Black Poetry,* 47–49. See also James A. Emanuel and Theodore L. Gross, eds., *Dark Symphony: Negro Literature in America* (New York: Free Press, 1968), 489; Margaret Danner and Dudley Randall, *Poem Counterpoem* (Detroit: Broadside Press, 1966), 13.

82. Rowell, "In Conversation with Dudley Randall," 34; Emanuel and Gross, *Dark Symphony,* 482.

83. Rowell, "In Conversation with Dudley Randall," 34. On this period see Arthur P. Davis, *From the Dark Tower: Afro-American Writers, 1900–1960* (Washington, D.C.: Howard University Press, 1981), 120–25, 147–53, 180–93.

84. "Black Books Bulletin Interviews Dudley Randall," 24; Wolseley, *The Black Press, U.S.A.,* 64. In 1943, African-Americans spent $133,770,000 on reading material in the United States. Yet, buying black poetry was not a major area of purchase by them, or most other Americans. See Charlotte Perry, compiler, *Official Business and Professional Guide of Detroit 1946* (Detroit: Charlotte Perry, Publisher, 1946), 37.

85. *A Profile of the Detroit Negro,* 21; *U.S. New and World Report* (May 7, 1962), 53; Edward G. Carmines and James A. Stimson, *Issue Evolution: Race and the Transformation of American Politics* (Princeton: Princeton University Press, 1989), 33. In 1950, there were 442,296 blacks in population of 6,371,766 people in Michigan. See Hathaway, *Michigan: Visions of Our Past,* 298.

86. Jacqueline Jones, *The Disposed: America's Underclasses from the Civil War to the Present* (New York: Basic Books, 1992), 209.

87. See Charles Wartman, "The Fifties: The Look of Togetherness," in *Detroit Perspectives, Crossroads and Turning Points,* ed. Wilma Wood Henrickson (Detroit: Wayne State University Press, 1991), 451–56.

88. H.V. Savitch, "The Politics of Deprivation and Response," in *Racism and Inequality: The Policy Alternatives,* ed. Harrell R. Rodgers, Jr. (San Francisco: W.H. Freeman and Co., 1975), 18; Jack Greenburg, *Race Relations and American Law* (New York: Columbia University Press, 1959), 293, 305.

89. Sab A. Lecitan, William B. Johnson, and Robert Taggard, *Still a Dream: The Changing Status of Blacks Since 1960* (Cambridge, Mass.: Harvard University Press, 1975), 15.

90. Stanley Lecitan, *A Piece of the Pie: Black and White Immigrants Since 1880* (Berkeley: University of California Press, 1980), 64. For a recent assessment of the black experience in Detroit see Elaine Latzman Moon, *Untold Tales, Unsung Heroes: An Oral History of Detroit's African American Community, 1928–1967* (Detroit: Wayne State University Press, 1994), 23–36.

91. Hodges, "Dudley Randall and the Broadside Press," 12.

92. Jonathan Marwil, *A History of Ann Arbor* (Ann Arbor: University of Michigan Press, 1990), 150. The small number of black students at the University of Michigan is evident by the number of them in the Class of 1962: only 11 of 2,105 were black.

93. Ibid., 144.

94. Ibid., 142.

95. Christine Nasso, ed., *Contemporary Authors: A Bio-Bibliographical Guide to Current Authors and Their Work*, vols. 25–28 (Detroit: Gale Research Co., 1977), 578.

96. Hodges, "Dudley Randall and the Broadside Press," 12; Shockley and Chandler, *Living Black American Authors,* 131; E.J. Josey and Ann Allen Schockley, eds., *Handbook of Black Librarianship* (Littleton, Col.: Libraries Unlimited, Inc., 1977), 162. In 1950, there were only 1,465 professionally trained black librarians in the United States. More were needed. See Jesse E. Gloster, *Economics of Minority Groups* (Houston, Texas: Premier Printing Co., 1973), 55.

97. *Barron's Profiles of American Colleges* (Hauppauge, N.Y.: Barron's Educational Series, Inc., 1992), 863.

98. J. Irving E. Scott, *Negro Students and Their Colleges* (Boston: Meador Publishing Co., 1949), 73–74. See also W. Sherman Savage, *The History of Lincoln University* (Jefferson City, Mo.: Lincoln University, 1939): Lorenzo J. Greene, Gary R. Kremer, and Anthony F. Holland, *Missouri's Black Heritage* (Saint Louis: Forum Press, 1980; reprint, Columbia: University of Missouri Press, 1993).

99. Hodges, "Dudley Randall and the Broadside Press," 9.

100. Josey and Shockley, *Handbook of Black Librarianship,* 162.

101. Scott, *Negro Students and Their Colleges,* 69.

102. August Meier, *A White Scholar and the Black Community, 1945–1965: Essays and Reflections* (Amherst: University of Massachusetts Press, 1992), 18.

103. Ibid., 117.

104. Hodges, "Dudley Randall and the Broadside Press," 12; Leaonead Pack Bailey, ed., *Broadside Authors and Artists: An Illustrated Biographical Directory* (Detroit: Broadside Press, 1974), 97.

105. Bailey, *Broadside Authors and Artists,* 97.

106. Hodges, "Dudley Randall and the Broadside Press," 12; Fowlkes, "An Interview with Dudley Randall," 88.

107. Bailey, *Broadside Authors and Artists,* 97. Randall, interview with the author, April 9, 1992.

108. On the role of librarians in American society, and especially of issues revolving around the perceptions and stereotyping of librarians see Pauline Wilson, *Stereotype and Status: Librarians in the United States* (Westport, Conn.: Greenwood, 1982), 6–9, 188–21; David Shavit, *The Politics of Public Librarianship* (Westport, Conn.: Greenwood, 1986), xii; Frances M. Jones, *Defusing Censorship: The Librarian's Guide to Handling Censorship Conflicts* (Phoenix, Ariz.: Oryx Press, 1983), 77–87.

109. Rowell, "In Conversation with Dudley Randall," 40. See also Martin Luther King, Jr., *Stride Toward Freedom: The Montgomery Story* (New York: Harper and Row, 1958); Richard Kluger, *Simple Justice for Equality* (New York: Vintage Books, 1977).

110. Dave Ferguson, "Dudley Randall ... Poet in Residence," *The Varsity News* (University of Detroit), September 16, 1969, 3.

111. Davis, *From the Dark Tower: Afro-American Writers, 1900–1960,* 203–26; Woodie King, Jr., "Lorraine Hansberry's Children: By Black Artists and a Raisin in the Sun," *Freedomways* 19, no. 4 (First Quarter, 1979): 219–21.

112. Randall, "Bio-Bibliographical Sketch," 1.

113. Noel Heermance, "Midwest Journal," in *Black Journals of the United States: Historical Guides to the World's Periodicals and Newspapers,* ed. Walter C. Daniel (Westport, Conn.: Greenwood, 1982), 246–47.

114. Dudley Randall, "Booker T. and W.E.B.," *Midwest Journal* 5 (Winter 1952-53).

115. Miller, "Endowing the World and Time," 79. See also Melhem, *Heroism in the New Black Poetry,* 50–51; Emanuel and Gross, *Dark Symphony,* 489.

116. Randall, "Bio-Bibliographical Sketch," 1. During the fifties the *Michigan Chronicle* continued to serve as an outlet for black writers in Detroit. In 1955, the paper had a circulation of 35,000. Randall contributed work to the *Chronicle.* See Trammer, "Identity Crisis in the Black Press," 64; Bailey, *Broadside Authors and Artists,* 97.

117. *Black Enterprise Magazine,* May 1978.

Chapter 2

1. Letter from Douglas A. Whitaker, County Librarian, Wayne County Public Library Wayne, Michigan, June 1, 1993, to the author. Randall worked in a position where professionally trained blacks with advanced degrees were still rare. In 1960, there were only 3,144 professionally trained black librarians working in this country. See Jesse E. Gloster, *Economics of Minority Groups* (Houston, Tex.: Premier Printing Co., 1973), 55.

2. Frenchy Jolen Hodges, "Dudley Randall and the Broadside Press," (M.A. thesis, Atlanta University, 1974), 12–13.

3. Whitaker to the author, June 1, 1993.

4. Ann Allen Shockley and Sue P. Chandler, *Living Black American Authors, a Biographical Directory* (New York: R.R. Bowker Co., 1973), 131; William Joseph Reeves, *Librarians as Professionals* (Lexington, Mass.: Lexington Books/D.C. Heath and Co., 1980), 3, 20; Jeffrey L. Salter and Charles A. Salter, *Literacy and the Library* (Englewood, Col.: Libraries Unlimited, Inc., 1991).

5. Nationally, many librarians were concerned during the 1960s with the small number of black professionally trained librarians in the United States. One study notes that between 1962 to 1966, only 372 blacks (4 percent) received master of arts in library science degrees (out of 9,204 graduates) of 25 accredited library schools; and of this number, one institution, historically black Atlanta University (now Clark-Atlanta University), graduated 202 students. Many black library school students and graduates complained that racism in library school programs was a major challenge for them to overcome in reaching their goals of becoming professional librarians. Another revealing statistic is evident in the fact that by 1960, 85 percent of all workers in librarianship were women. In too many cases they were underpaid and overworked. See Helen E. Williams, "Experiences of Blacks in Predominantly White Library Schools, 1962–1974: An Era of Transition," in *Activism in American Librarianship,* ed. Mary Lee Bundy and Frederick J. Stielow (Westport, Conn.: Greenwood, 1987), 154–55; Lois W. Banner, *Women in Modern America: A Brief History* (New York: Harcourt Brace Jovanovich, 1974), 257. For this period see also E.J. Josey, ed., *The Black Librarian in America* (Metuchen, N.J.: Scarecrow Press, 1970), ix, 40, 113; Annie L. McPheeters, *Library Service in Black and White: Some Personal Recollections, 1921–1980* (Metuchen, N.J.: Scarecrow Press, 1988).

6. D.H. Melhem, *Heroism in the New Black Poetry: Introductions and Interviews* (Lexington: University Press of Kentucky, 1990), 43. By the mid–1960s Wayne State University had 2,500 black students enrolled at the institution. One study notes that this total was "more than in the Big Ten and the Ivy League combined." See B.J. Widick, "Mayor Cavanagh and the Limits of Reform," in *Detroit Perspectives: Crossroads and Turning Points,* ed. Wilma Wood Henrickson (Detroit: Wayne State University Press, 1991), 489.

7. Widick, "Mayor Cavanagh and the Limits of Reform," 489.

8. Christine Nasso, ed., *Contemporary Authors: A Bio-Bibliographical Guide to Current Authors and Their Works,* vols. 25–28, First Revision (Detroit: Gale Research Co., 1977), 578.

9. Ibid.; Shockley and Chandler, *Living Black American Authors,* 131.

10. Wilbur C. Rich, *Coleman Young and Detroit Politics: From Social Activist to Power Broker* (Detroit: Wayne State University Press, 1989), 25; Donald R. Deskins, Jr., *Residential Mobility of Negroes in Detroit, 1837–1965* (Ann Arbor: University of Michigan Press, 1972), 392.

11. Deskins, *Residential Mobility of Negroes in Detroit, 1837–1965,* 392; DeWitt S. Dykes, Jr., "The Search for Community: Michigan Society and Education, 1945–1980s," in *Michigan: Visions of Our Past,* ed. Richard J. Hathaway (East Lansing: Michigan State University Press, 1989), 298.

12. Joe T. Darden, Richard C. Hill, June Thomas, and Richard Thomas, *Detroit: Race and Uneven Development* (Philadelphia, Pa.: Temple University Press, 1976), 203.

13. Denise J. Lewis, "Victory and Defeat for Black Candidates," *The Black Politician: A Quarterly Journal of Current Political Thought* 2, no. 4 (April 1971): 35.

14. See Tim Kiska, *Detroit Powers and Personalities* (Rochester Hills, Mich.: Momentum Books, 1989), 44–45; Rich, *Coleman Young*, 85; Bruce A. Ragsdale and Joel B. Treese, *Black Americans in Congress, 1870–1989* (Washington, D.C.: Office of the Historian, U.S. House of Representatives, Raymond W. Smock, Historian and Director, U.S. Government Printing Office, 1990) 25–26, 39–40; Mark Kram, "Rosa Parks," in *Contemporary Black Biography*, ed. Michael L. LaBlanc (Detroit: Gale Research Co., 1992), 189–92.

15. Roberta H. Brisbane, *Black Activism: Racial Revolution in the United States, 1954–1970* (Valley Forge, Pa.: Judson Press, 1974), 165. See also Clint C. Wilson, II, *Black Journalists in Paradox: Historical Perspectives and Current Dilemmas* (Westport, Conn.: Greenwood, 1991), 21.

16. Sab A. Levitan, William B. Johnson, and Robert Taggart, *Still a Dream: The Changing Status of Blacks Since 1960* (Cambridge, Mass.: Harvard University Press, 1975), 15.

17. Stephanie Coontz, *The Way We Never Were: American Families and the Nostalgia Trap* (New York: Basic Books/HarperCollins, 1992), 233.

18. Reynolds Farley and Walter R. Allen, *The Color Line and the Quality of Life in America* (New York: National Committee for Research on the 1980 Census and the Russell Sage Foundation, 1987), 141, 154. See also Kalt E. Taeuber and Alma F. Taeuber, "Negroes in Cities: Residential Segregation and Neighborhood Change," in *Studies in American Urban Society,* ed. Frank L. Sweetser (New York: Thomas Y. Crowell Co., 1970), 104–9; Albert J. Mayer and Thomas F. Holt, "Race and Residence in Detroit," in *A City in Racial Crisis: The Case of Detroit Pre and Post the 1967 Riot,* ed. Leonard Gordon (New York: Wm. C. Brown Co. Publishers, 1971), 3–9; On black social conditions in Detroit during the 1960s see also Elaine Latzman Moon, *Untold Tales Unsung Heroes: An Oral History of Detroit's African American Community 1918–1967* (Detroit: Wayne State University Press, 1994), 368–403. "The Urban Housing Dilemma of Blacks in Michigan: 1960–1970," in *Blacks and Chicanos in Urban Michigan,* ed. Homer C. Hawkins and Richard W. Thomas (East Lansing: Michigan History Division, Michigan Department of State, 1979), 7–11.

19. Mark E. Neithercat, *Detroit Twenty Years After: A Statistical Profile of the Detroit Area Since 1967,* (Detroit: Center for Urban Studies Wayne State University, 1987), 27, 33. In 1960, the median years of school completed by Detroit Whites was 10.2, and 9.9 for nonwhites. See Joeal D. Aberback and Jack L. Walker, *Race in the City: Political Trust and Public Policy in the New Urban System* (Boston: Little, Brown and Co. 1973), 31.

20. *Crisis,* (February 1961): 114, 116.

21. Richard W. Thomas, "The Black Urban Experience in Detroit: 1916–1967," in *Blacks and Chicanos,* ed. Hawkins and Thomas, 65; Harry Cook and Joyce Walker-Tyson, "Politics and the Pulpit: A Tradition" in *Blacks in Detroit,* 56–59; "The Black Christian Nationalist Church," *Black World* 23, no. 3 (January 1974): 88–89.

22. *The Negro Handbook* (Chicago: Johnson Publishing Co., 1966), 385; Frank B. Sawyer, ed., *U.S. Negro World 1967* (New York: U.S. Negro World, 1967), 33; *Michigan Chronicle,* January 16, 1960; *Detroit Tribune,* March 10, 1962; *The Illustrated News* 1 (October 23, 1961): 1–4; *The Illustrated News* 2 (February 19, 1962): 1–4; *The Illustrated News* 4 (November 2, 1964): 1; *B.T. Washington Association Guide to Better Service* (Detroit: B.T. Washington Association, 1968), 34; Irving J. Sloan, *The American Negro: A Chronology and Fact Book* (Dobbs Ferry, N.Y.: Oceana Publications, 1965), 80; *Newspaper Resources of Metropolitan Detroit Libraries: A Union List* (Detroit: Wayne State University Library, 1965); *The Ghetto Speaks* 2 (December 1, 1968): 1–8; *Negro Newspapers in the United States 1966* (Jefferson City, Mo.: Lincoln University, 1966), 6; *Second Baptist Advocate* (January 1963); *Detroit Free Press,* June 26, 1966.

23. Trammer, "Identity Crisis in the Stack Press," 64.

24. *Michigan Chronicle,* January 7, 1961, December 28, 1963, January 8, June 25, 1966; Detroit Board of Education, *Black Personalities of Detroit* (Detroit: Detroit Public Schools, 1975), 31.

25. Kenneth L. Kusmer, "The Black Urban Experience in American History," in *The State of Afro-American History,* ed. Darlene Clark Hine (Baton Rouge: Louisiana State University Press, 1986), 116.

26. See Robert Conot, *American Odyssey: A History of a Great City* (Detroit: Wayne State

University Press, 1986), 528–31; *Detroit: Race and Uneven Development*, 204–5; Ida Lewis, "Conversation: The Reverend Albert B. Cleage, Jr.," *Essence* 1, no. 8 (December 1970): 22–27; Rich, *Coleman Young*, 82; "The Fight Against Discrimination in Detroit: A Look at the NAACP," *Negro History Bulletin* 26 (October 1962): 19, 29. The membership figures of several major African-American organizations in Detroit during the 1960s are revealing. For example, in 1963, the Detroit branch of the NAACP had 29,402 members; only the Chicago branch had a greater number with 33,708. ORE's Detroit branch on the other hand, had only 30 to 40 members in 1961, 72 in October 1964, and 100 in late 1965. The *Detroit Free Press* estimated in 1962 that Temple no. 1 of the Nation of Islam (Black Muslims) in Detroit had 375 members, with 102 children in the Muslim school. See NAACP, in *Freedom's Vanguard: Report for 1963* (New York: NAACP, July 1964), 25; August Meier and Elliott Rudwick, *CORE: A Study in the Civil Rights Movement, 1942–1968* (New York: Oxford University Press, 1973), 151, 227, 359; *Detroit Free Press*, June 26, 1966.

27. Rhoda Lois Blumberg, *Civil Rights: The 1960s Freedom Struggle* (Boston: Twayne Publishers, 1984, 1991), 4. The major civil rights movement event in Detroit during the early 1960s was the Detroit March led by Martin Luther King, Jr., on July 23, 1963, in which from 150,000 to 200,000 Detroiters took part, 95 percent of whom were African-Americans. See *Detroit: Race and Uneven Development*, 134.

28. "Bio-Bibliographical Sketch of Dudley Randall," 2; Rosey E. Pool, ed., *Beyond the Blues: New Poems by American Negroes* (Lympne, Kent, England: The Hand and Flower Press, 1962), 165–67; Arna Bontemps, ed., *American Negro Poetry* (New York: Hill and Wang, 1963), 121–22; Langston Hughes, ed., *New Negro Poets: USA* (Bloomington: University Press, 1964), 41, 43, 59; Preston M. Yancy, compiler, *The Afro-American Short Story: A Comprehensive, Annotated Index with Selected Commentaries* (Westport, Conn.: Greenwood, 1986), 135–36.

29. See Parm Mayer, "The Stars Are Out," *Phylon* 23, no. 4 (Winter 1962): 412–13; Nick Aaron Fords "The Fire Next Time? A Critical Survey of Belles Lettres By and About Negroes Published in 1963," *Phylon* 25, no. 2 (Summer 1964): 131; Miles M. Jackson, "Significant Belles Lettres By and About Negroes Published in 1964," *Phylon* 26, no. 3 (September 1965): 223–24.

30. Donald Franklin Joyce, "Magazines of Afro-Americans," *American Libraries* 7, no. 11, December 1976): 681–82; *Washington Post*, May 14, 1981, C6; Eugene Redmond, "Stridency and the Sword: Literary and Cultural Emphasis in Afro-American Magazines," in *The Little Magazine in America: A Modern Documentary History*, ed. Elliott Anderson and Mary Kinzie (Yonkers, N.Y.: Pushcart Press 1978), 548, 550–51; Roland E. Wolseley, *The Black Press, U.S.A.* (Ames: Iowa State University Press, 1990), 146.

31. *Negro Digest* 19, no. 1 (November 1969): 78.

32. Wolseley, *The Black Press, U.S.A.*, 178; John Hope Franklin and Alfred A. Moss, Jr., *From Slavery to Freedom: A History of African Americans* (New York: McGraw-Hill, 1994), 414.

33. These 8 poems have remained very popular with editors throughout Randall's career.

34. Melhem, *Heroism in the New Black Poetry*, 42–43.

35. James A. Emanuel and Theodore L. Gross, eds., *Dark Symphony: Negro Literature in America* (New York: Free Press, 1968), 489.

36. Larry Neal, ed. by Michael Schwartz, *Visions of a Liberated Future: Black Arts Movement Writings* (New York: Thunder's Mouth Press, 1989), 222.

37. Redmond, "Stridency and the Sword: Literary and Cultural Emphasis in Afro-American Magazines," 564; Addison Gayle, Jr., ed., *The Black Aesthetic* (Garden City, N.Y.: Doubleday & Co., 1972).

38. Elaine Showalter, "A Criticism of Our Own: Autonomy and Assimilation in Afro-American and Feminist Literary Theory," 172, quoting Houston A. Poker, Jr., "Generational Shifts and the Recent Criticism of Afro-American Literature," *Black American Literature Forum* 15 (Spring 1981): 6.

39. E.A. Boateng, *A Political Geography of Africa* (New York: Cambridge University Press, 1978), 162, 193, 262–63; Larry Neal, "The Social Background of the Black Arts Movements," *The Black Scholar* 18 (January/February 1987): 16. See also Frantz Fanon, *The Wretched of the Earth* (New York: Grove Press, 1966), *Black Skins, White Masks* (New York: Grove Press, 1967), *A Dying Colonialism* (New York: Grove Press, 1968), *Towards the African Revolution* (New York: Grove Press, 1969); M. Frank Wright, "Frantz Fanon: His Work in Historical Perspective," *The Black Scholar* 6, no. 10 (July/August 1975): 19–29.

40. R. Baxter Miller, "Endowing the World and Time: The Life and Work of Dudley Randall," in *Black American Poets Between Worlds, 1940–1960,* ed. R. Baxter Miller (Knoxville: University of Tennessee Press, 1986), 78–81.

41. Amiri Baraka, "Black Literature and the African-American Nation: The Urban Voice," in *Literature and the Urban Experience,* ed. A.C. Watts and Michael C. Jaye (New Brunswick, N.J.: Rutgers University Press, 1981), 155; Melba Boyd, "The Detroit Writer: A Report," *Black Creation* 6 (1974–75): 76–77; LeRoi Jones (Amiri Baraka), *Black Music* (New York: William Morrow, 1968), 133; Jeanne E. Saddter, "Ron Milner: The People's Playwright," *Essence* 5, no. 7 (November 1974): 20; Diane Haithman, "Stage Was Set for Stardom," in *Blacks in Detroit,* 96–97.

42. Melhem, *Heroism in the New Black Poetry,* 44.

43. A.X. Nicholas, "A Conversation with Dudley Randall," *Black World* 21, no. 2 (December 1971): 28.

44. Miller, "Endowing the World and Time: The Life and Work of Dudley Randall," 34; Charles Rowell, "In Conversation with Dudley Randall," *Obsidian* 2 (Spring 1976): 34; Miller, Miller, "Dudley Randall," 966–67; Abraham Chapman, ed., *Black Voices: An Anthology of Afro-American Literature* (New York: New American Library, 1968), 468.

45. Rowell, "In Conversation with Dudley Randall," 34. See *Negro History Bulletin* 24, no. 1 (October 1962). This special issue was highlighted at the Detroit convention of the ASNLH in 1962. The Detroit branch of the Association was established in 1924. In 1964, the *Negro History Bulletin* published a second special Detroit edition and the group also met in Detroit during that same year. See *Negro History Bulletin* 27, no. 5 (February 1964); *Negro History Bulletin* 28, no. 2 (November 1964): 27–28.

46. Pool, *Beyond the Blues* 86–87, 111–14, 138–139, 142–43, 147–149, 165–67, 174.

47. Dudley Randall, ed., *The Black Poets: A New Anthology* (New York: Bantam Books, 1971), xxiii. See Langston Hughes and Arna Bontemps, eds., *The Poetry of the Negro, 1746–1949* (Garden City, N.Y.: Doubleday & Co., 1949, 1970), 305–6, 620.

48. Angela Y. Davis, "Remembering Carole, Cynthia, Addie Mae & Denise," *Essence* 24, no. 5 (September 1993): 92, 122–123, 126; Frank Sikora, *Until Justice Rolls Down: The Birmingham Church Bombing Case* (Tuscaloosa, Ala.: University of Alabama Press, 1991), 3–19; Peter M. Bergman and Mort N. Bergman, *The Chronological History of the Negro in America* (New York: New American Library, 1969), 579; Adam Fair Clough, *To Redeem the Soul of America, the Southern Christian Leadership Conference and Martin Luther King, Jr.* (Athens: University of Georgia Press, 1987), 483.

49. "Ballad of Birmingham," in Margaret Danner and Dudley Randall, *Poem Counterpoem* (Detroit: Broadside Press, 1969), 4.

50. "Dressed All in Pink," in Dudley Randall, *Cities Burning* (Detroit: Broadside Press, 1968), 10. See also Melhem, *Heroism in the New Black Poetry,* 44.

51. Melhem, *Heroism in the New Black Poetry,* 44.

52. A.X. Nicholes, "A Conversation with Dudley Randall" *Black World* 21, no. 2 December 1971): 27–28. D.H. Melhem also notes that Randall was encouraged to think of becoming a new publisher after a "meeting with Margaret Danner at a party for ... Hoyt Fuller editor of the journal Black World." See Melhem, *Heroism in the New Black Poetry,* 44. On the largest civil rights march of the period, see Thomas Gentile, *March on Washington: August 28, 1963* (Washington D.C.: New Day Publications, 1983).

53. Dudley Randall, interview with the author, October 11, 1991; Bradford Chambers, "Why Minority Publishing?" *Publishers Weekly* 199, no. 11 (March 15, 1992): 44; Kiffel, "Poet in Motion," 160.

54. Melba Joyce Boyd, "Out of the Poetry Ghetto: The Life/Art Struggle of Small Black Publishing Houses," *The Black Scholar* (July/August 1985): 13–14; Dudley Randall, *Broadside Memories: Poets I Have Known* (Detroit: Broadside Press, 1975), 23. Parts of this work were published by Randall earlier in "Broadside Press: A Personal Chronicle," *Black Academy Review* 1, no. 1 (1970); and reprinted in *The Black Seventies,* ed. Floyd B. Barbour (Boston: Porter Sargent Publishers, 1970), 138–148.

Frenchy Hodges notes that in 1965, Randall was interested in publishing his work so that he could better protect it through the copyright laws of the United States. See Hodges, "Dudley Randall and the Broadside Press," 13.

Readers should also be aware that between 1960 and 1964 black Detroit did not have a major literary magazine, nor a significant publishing company, other than the *Michigan Chronicle,* which was a weekly newspaper.

The printer for Broadside publications was the Harlo Printing Company, at 16721 Hamilton, Detroit, Michigan. See James A. Emanuel, *The Treehouse and Other Poems* (Detroit: Broadside Press, 1968), 4.

55. Nick Aaron Ford, ed., *Black Insights, Significant Literature by Black Americans, 1760 to the Present* (Wolthan, Mass.: Ginn and Co., 1971), 317; Nicholas, "A Conversation with Dudley Randall," 31; James Sullivan, "Real Cool Pages: The Broadside Press Broadside Series," *Contemporary Literature* 32, no. 4 (Winter 1991): 552–72. Joe C. Brown's broadside, "Ghetto Manchild," published in 1966, was not given a number in the Broadside Series, and is generally referred to as a special broadside by the company. See Leaonead Pack Bailey, ed., *Broadside Authors and Artists: An Illustrated Biographical Directory* (Detroit: Broadside Press, 1974), 32. On the importance of broadsides in the nation's history and the special collections held by a leading society, see "broadsides," *Massachusetts Historical Society Miscellany,* 54 (Winter 1993): 5–6.

56. Randall, *Broadside Memories,* 23.

57. Eugene B. Redmond, *Drumvoices, the Mission of Afro-American Poetry: A Critical History* (Garden City, N.Y.: Anchor Press/Doubleday, 1976), 330.

58. *Detroit News,* July 7, 1983, F4.

59. "Black Books Bulletin Interviews Dudley Randall," *Black Books Bulletin* (Winter 1972): 24; *Detroit Free Press,* April 11, 1982, 11.

60. Nelson George, *Where Did Our Love Go?: The Rise and Fall of the Motown Sound* (New York: St. Martin's Press, 1985), ix–x; *All About Michigan Almanac* (Hartland, Mich.: H/S/O Publications, 1989), 32; Alan Wells, "Black Artists in American Popular Music 1955–1985" *Phylon* 48, no. 4 (Winter 1987): 309–12; Gerald Early, "One Nation Under a Groove," *The New Republic,* Issues 3,991 and 3,992 (July 15 & 22, 1991): 30–41; Jerry Wexler and David Ritz, *Rhythm and the Blues: A Life in American Music* (New York: Alfred A. Knopf, 1993), 206–15; Herschel Johnson "Motown: The Sound of Success," *Black Enterprise* 4, no. 11 (June 1974): 71–74, 77, 79–80.

61. On black organizations in Detroit see Labomyr R. Wynar, *Encyclopedia Directory of Ethnic Organizations in the United States* (Littletown, Col.: Libraries Unlimited, 1975), 44–52; *Detroit Free Press,* June 26, 1966 and April 3, 1973.

62. *Journal of Black Poetry* 1, no. 12 (Summer/Fall 1969): 80; *Black World* (March 1975): 76–79; Shockley and Chandler, *Living Black American Authors,* 179–80; Henry Alsup, Jr., *Cold Heart Sweet* (Detroit: Ink & Soul, 1976), ii; Randall, *The Black Poets,* 335–37, 339; W. Lawrence Hogue, *Discourse and the Other: The Production of the Afro-American Text* (Durham, N.C.: Duke University Press, 1986), 55. Two of the most famous black writer's workshops during the 1960s and 1970s were located in New York City and Chicago. In the former, the Umbra Workshop influenced a number of East Coast writers. While in the latter, black writers organized the Orgnization of Black American Culture in 1967. See Lorenzo Thomas, "The Shadow World: New York's Umbra Workshop and Origins of the Black Arts Movement," *Callaloo* 1, no. 4 (October 1978): 53–72; David Henderson, ed., *Umbra Anthology 1967–1968* (New York: Umbra Workshop, 1967); Carole A. Parks, ed., *Nommo: A Literary Legacy of Black Chicago (1967–1987)* (Chicago: The Organization of Black American Culture Writer's Workshop, 1987). See also LeRoi Jones and Larry Neal, eds., *Black Fire: An Anthology of Afro-American Writing* (New York: William Morrow & Co., 1968); Gerald A. McWorter, *Guide to Scholarly Journals in Black Studies* (Chicago: Peoples College Press, 1981); Carolyn Fowler, *Black Arts and Black Aesthetics, Bibliography* (Atlanta, Ga.: Carolyn Foster, 1976); Wolseley, *The Black Press, U.S.A.,* 87–89, 142, 146.

63. Manning Marable, *Race, Reform and Rebellion: The Second Reconstruction in Black America, 1945–1982* (Jackson: University Press of Mississippi, 1984), 66–127; Steven F. Lawson, *Running for Freedom: Civil Rights and Black Politics in America Since 1941* (New York: McGraw-Hill, 1991), 66–145; James C. Harvey, *Black Civil Rights During the Johnson Administration* (Jackson: University and College Press of Mississippi, 1973); Robert F. Williams, *Negroes with Guns* (Chicago: Third World Press, 1973).

64. Dudley Randall, interview with author, Detroit, Mich., October 11, 1991.

65. Although Gwendolyn Brooks began to publish with Broadside Press in 1969, her last contract with Harper & Row, resulted in the publication of *The World of Gwendolyn Brooks* in 1971.

See Harry B. Shaw, Gwendolyn Brooks (Boston: Twayne Publishers, 1980), 36; George E. Kent, *A Life of Gwendolyn Brooks* (Lexington: University Press of Kentucky, 1990), 192–224. D.H. Melhem, *Gwendolyn Brooks: Poetry of the Heroic Voice* (Lexington: University Press of Kentucky, 1987), 155; *Detroit News*, October 10, 1984, D2; *New York Times,* May 13, 1981, 19. To this list one might also add two other Detroiters, the poet Robert Hayden (1913–1980), who taught at Fisk University, Nashville, Tennessee, and later at the University of Michigan, Ann Arbors, and who strongly supported Randall as a writer and publisher; and the Rev. Albert Cleage, Jr., the minister of Detroit's Shrine of the Black Madonna, who also supported black literacy and educational needs in Detroit by establishing a bookstore on the site of the church at 13535 Livernois. See Shockley and Chandler, *Living Black American Authors,* 29–30; Aprele A.M. Elliott, "A Dramatic Analysis of Rev. Albert Cleage's Role in the Black Protest Movement from 1960 to 1969" (Ph.D. thesis, Wayne State University, 1984). On correspondence between Randall and Fuller in the 1960s and early 1970s see Hoyt W. Fuller papers, Clark-Atlanta University Library, Atlanta, Georgia.

66. *South End Press* (Detroit: Wayne State University), February 2, 1972.

67. Randall, *Broadside Memories,* 28; Randall, interview with author, October 11, 1991.

68. Randall, *Broadside Memories,* 58; Dudley Randall, interview with author, Detroit, Mich., June 27, 1994.

69. Carolyn Fowler notes the importance of the pamphlet format in black publishing during the Black Arts Movement. See Carolyn Fowler, "A Contemporary American Genre: Pamphlet/Manifesto Poetry," *Black World* 23, no. 8 (June 1974): 4–19.

70. A one-year subscription for the Broadside Series cost $6.00 in 1969. See *Catalogues of Broadside Press* (Detroit: Broadside, October 1969), 3; Bailey, *Broadside Authors and Artists*: *Negro Digest* (April 1968): 82; Miller, "Dudley Randall," 267; Randall, *Broadside Memories,* 23; Carrington Bowner, "An Interview with Nikki Giovanni," *Black American Literature Forum* 18, no. 1 (September 1984): 30. Broadside Press also produced a smaller set of "Broadside Posters," during this period, which were "Large, illustrated posters by outstanding artists, featuring poems by Sonia Sanchez, Etheridge Knight ('For Black Poets Who Think of Suicide'), and other poets." These were generally priced between $1.00 and $1.50 to $2.00 See *Catalogues of Broadside Press,* 1969, 3; *Catalogues of Broadside Press,* 1975, 5.

71. Melhem, *Heroism in the New Black Poetry,* 45; Randall, *Broadside Memories,* 23; Woodie King, Jr., ed., *The Forerunners, Black Poets in America* (Washington, D.C.: Howard University Press, 1975), xi–xxix. Addition to Chapter 2, Note 71, p. 188. Three of the major black poets of the twentieth century died in the mid–1960s. Randall noted the passing of M.B. Tolson on August 23, 1966, Jean Toomer in April 1967, and Langston Hughes in May 1967, and their significance to black literature, in a *Negro Digest* article. See Dudley Randall, "Three Giants Bone," *Negro Digest,* (November 1967): 87.

72. Bailey, *Broadside Authors and Artists,* 18, 24–25, 30–31, 41–42, 47–48, 50–51, 58–60, 63–64, 47–68, 70, 72, 75–76, 79, 83–84, 89, 93–94, 97–98, 101, 116–118, 120; Shockley and Chandler, *Living Black American Writers,* 88, 118. Among key historically black colleges and universities which the Broadside Series poets attended were Howard University, with two poets, LeRoi Jones and James A. Emanuel, and Lincoln University (Pa.), with Langston Hughes and Raymond Patterson. Other poets attended such Nashville, Tennessee, institutions as Fisk University (Sarah E. Webster Fabio), and Tennessee A. & I. State University (Ahmed Alhamisi). The key historically white colleges and universities which many of the poets attended were Columbia University: LeRoi Jones, James A. Emanuel, Langston Hughes, Doughtry Long and Melvin B. Tolson; Northwestern University: Margaret Walker; Roosevelt University, with Margaret Danner and Don L. Lee; Wayne State University: Robert E. Hayden, Harold Lawrence (Harun Kofi Wangara), Naomi Long Madgett, Dudley Randall, Carolyn Reese, and Tony Rutherford; and the University of Michigan, Ann Arbor: Alhamisi Hayden, Randall, and Rutherford. Since historically white southern schools were closed to blacks prior to the civil rights movement of the sixties, many blacks were forced to attend northern schools, especially for advanced degrees and professional studies in many fields. See Mary Berry and John Blassingame, *Long Memory: The Black Experience in America* (New York: Oxford University Press, 1982), 279–281.

73. *Catalogues of Broadside Press,* 1969, 1–4; 1975, 1–5.

74. Randall, *Broadside Memories,* 23; Marilyn K. Basel, "Dudley (Felker) Randall," in *Con-

temporary Authors, New Revision Series, V, ed. Deborah A. Straub (Detroit: Gale Research Co., 1988), 469. See also Hoyt W. Fuller, "Cultural Notes, Reverberations from a Writer's Conference," *African Forum* 1, no. 2 (Fall 1965): 78–84.

75. Miller, "Dudley Randall," 267. The first edition of *Poem Counterpoem* contained five hundred copies, signed by the authors. See Randall, *Broadside Memories,* 24.

76. Dudley Randall and Margaret G. Burroughs, eds., *For Malcolm X: Poems on the Life and the Death of Malcolm X* (Detroit: Broadside Press, 1966); Randall, *Broadside Memories,* 24.

77. Randall and Burroughs, *For Malcolm X,* 130.

78. *Detroit Free Press,* April 11, 1982, 11. In 1984, Lenwood G. Davis and Marsha L. Moore noted the importance of *For Malcolm X,* when they included an appendix section on "Poetry Inspired by Malcolm X," in a new work devoted to the black leader. See Lerwood G. Davis and Marsha L. Moore, compilers, *Malcolm X: A Selected Bibliography* (Westport, Conn.: Greenwood, 1984), 115–23.

79. Several white American poets appeared in *For Malcolm X,* including Marcella Caine, Bill Frederick, and Edward Richer. See Randall and Burroughs, *For Malcolm X,* 8, 24, 37, 83, 85, 93, 96, 98, 109; Bailey, *Broadside Authors and Artists,* 37, 54, 101.

80. The earliest Broadside tapes of poetry were recorded by James A. Emanuel, reading his collection of poems in *The Treehouse and Other Poems*; Etheridge Knight interpreting his work in *Poems from Prison*; and Dudley Randall reading from his book, *Cities Burning.* In 1969, 50 copies of each volume were produced, autographed and numbered, and priced at $5 each. See "New Broadside Venture," *Negro Digest* 18, no. 5 (March 1969): 86.

81. See Armistead Scott Pride, "The Names of Negro Newspapers," *American Speech* 29, no. 2 (May 1954): 114–18; Julius E. Thompson, *The Black Press in Mississippi 1865–1985: A Directory* (West Cornwall, Conn.: Locust Hill Press, 1988); Bailey, *Broadside Authors and Artists.*

82. On the historical importance of "names" to the African-American community see Richard Poe, "Negro: By Definition," *Negro History Bulletin* 40, no. 1 (January/February 1977): 668–70; Michael C. Beaubien, "The Capitalization of 'Black'"; *The Black Observer* (Carbondale: Southern Illinois University), (April 1985): 10; Berry and Blassingame, *Long Memory,* 110, 391–93; Nathan Hare, "Rebels Without a Name," *Phylon,* 23, no. 3 (Fall 1962): 271–77; Scott Cummings and Robert Carrere, "Black Culture, Negroes, and Colored People: Racial Image and Self-esteem Among Black Adolescents," *Phylon* 36, no. 3 (September 1975): 238–48; F. James Davis, *Who Is Black?: One Nation's Definition* (University Park, Pa.: Pennsylvania State University Press, 1991), 5, 30; Pride, "The Names of Negro Newspapers," 114–18.

83. Rich, *Coleman Young and Detroit Politics,* 19; Widick, *Detroit: City of Race and Class Violence,* 195.

84. R.J. Johnson, *The American Urban System: A Geographical Perspective* (New York: St. Martin's Press, 1982), 238.

85. See Stokely Carmichael and Charles V. Hamilton, *Black Power: The Politics of Liberation in America* (New York: Vintage Books, 1967). Carmichael defined Black Power as "…a call for black people to begin to define their own goals, to lead their own organizations and to support those organizations. It is a call to reject the racist institutions and values of this society." See also Marable, *Race, Reform and Rebellion,* 95–127.

86. Robert H. Brisbane, *Black Activism: Racial Revolution in the United States, 1954–1970* (Valley Forge, Pa.: Judson Press, 1974), 139–49, 161, 162, 169, 179.

87. See especially Frances Fox Piven and Richard A. Cloward, *Poor People's Movements, Why They Succeed, How They Fail* (New York: Vintage Books, 1979), 295, 299; Jones A. Geschwender, *Class, Race, and Worker Insurgency: The League of Revolutionary Black Workers* (New York: Cambridge University Press, 1977), xi–xii, 16–84, 87–102, 162–187, 190–205; Chokwe Lumumba, "Short History of the U.S. War on the R.N.A.," *The Black Scholar* 12 (January/February 1981): 72–81; Robert L. Norfolk, Jr., "The Black Studies Revolt and Radical Black Student Unions 1967–72," (Detroit: Pan-African Research & Documentation Project, Discussion Paper 2, May 1992); Darden, Hill, J. Thomas, and R. Thomas, Detroit: *Race and Uneven Development,* 207.

88. Herbert H. Haines, *Black Radicals and the Civil Rights Mainstream, 1954–1970* (Knoxville: University of Tennessee Press, 1988), 67; Bruce A. Rubenstein and Lawrence E. Ziewacz, *Michigan: A History of the Great Lakes State,* 253; Alphonso Pinkney, *Black Americans* (Englewood Cliffs, N.J.: Prentice Hall, 1969), 206. Georgakos and Surkin, *Detroit: I Do Mind Dying: A Study in Urban Revolution*; John Hensey, The *Algiers Motel Incident* (New York: Bantam Books, 1968). A recent study also notes that during the rebellion "well over

1,000 buildings had been burned to the ground and 2,700 businesses ransacked." See Darden, Hill, J. Thomas, and R. Thomas, *Detroit: Race and Uneven Development*, 72. Two interesting additional insights into the 1967 Detroit rebellion are offered in studies by Rhoda Lois Blumber and Peter H. Rossi. Rossi notes that the Detriot revolt had a tremendous impact on blacks in other cities in Michigan, because it "was followed by similar outbreaks in half a doze Michigan cities." While Blumberg states that "participants in the ... Detriot ... riot had a higher level of education than comparable others." Perhaps some individuals in the latter case were interested in reading — and thus may have been among those blacks in Detroit who supported black publishers, such as Broadside Press, and read black newspapers, such as the *Michigan Chronicle*. See Peter H. Rossi, ed., "Introduction," *Ghetto Revolts* (New Brunswick, N.J.: Transaction Books, 1973), 5; Blumberg, *Civil Rights: The 1960s Freedom Struggle*, 164.

89. *Michigan Chronicle*, March 1968; Wilson, *Black Journalists in Paradox*, 20–21; Darden, Hill, J. Thomas and R. Thomas, *Detroit: Race and Uneven Development*, 224–25; Homer Hawkins and Richard Thomas, "White Policing of Black Populations: A History of Race and Social Control in America," in *Out of Order: Policing Black People*, ed. Ellis Cashmore and Eugene McLaughlin (New York: Routledge, 1991), 66, 79–80, 83–84; Sidney Fine, *Violence in Model City: The Cavanagh Administration, Race Relations, and the Detriot Riot of 1967* (Ann Arbor: University of Michigan Press, 1989), 27–31, 372–73, 380–81; William Turner, *Power on the Right* (Berkeley, Calif.: Ramparts Press, 1971), 231–34; George Napper, *Blacker Than Thou: The Struggle for Campus Unity* (Grand Rapids, Mich.: William. B. Eerdmans Publishing Co., 1973), 35. Although the University of Michigan (Randall's old graduate school) was but 24 miles from Detroit, in Ann Arbor, the institution was not receptive to African-Americans during the 1960s. In fact, by 1967, Michigan had 34,000 students, but only 450 were black, and there were only 25 black professors among a total faculty of 2,500. See "Michigan," *Negro History Bulletin* 30, no. 5 (May 1967): 20.

90. Darden, Hill, J. Thomas and R. Thomas, *Detriot: Race and Uneven Development*, 202–7; Lewis, "Victory and Defeat for Black Candidates," 34–36, 66–73.

91. Although Detroit blacks were not successful during the decade in electing a black as a mayor of Detroit, blacks in Michigan by 1966 had more black state legislators than any other state. Georgia was second. See Victor H. Bernstein, "Why Negroes Are Still Angry," in *Black History: A Reappraisal*, ed. Melvin Drimmer (Garden City, N.Y.: Anchor Books/Doubleday, 1969), 515.

92. "Dudley Randall," (Detroit: Detroit Public Library), *Biography and Criticism* VF, n.d., 1.

93. Ibid.; Hodges, "Dudley Randall and the Broadside Press," 13.

94. Nicholas, "A Conversation with Dudley Randall," 28–29.

95. Whitaker to the author, June 1, 1993; Hodges, "Dudley Randall and the Broadside Press, 14. The tour group consisted of Margaret and Charles Burroughs, their son, Paul; Sylvester Britton, a graphic artist of Chicago; Wesley South, a Chicago broadcaster and staff member of the *Chicago Defender*; Geraldine McCullogh, a sculptor of Maywood, Illinois; Ruth Woddy, a Los Angeles, California artist; Gary A. Rickson, a Boston, Massachusetts, artist; and Dudley Randall. See Hodges, "Dudley Randall and the Broadside Press," 14.

During the Russian tour Dudley had an opportunity "in Moscow ADS read his own translations of Russian poems into English." See Abraham Chapman, ed. *Black Voices: An Anthology of Afro-American Literature* (New York: New American Library, 1968), 468.

96. Hodges, "Dudley Randall and the Broadside Press," 15.

97. Ibid., 14; Randall, "Bio-Bibliographical Sketch," 1; Theresa Gunnels Rush, Carol Fairbanks Myers and Esther Spring Arota, *Black American Writers Past and Present: A Bibliographical and Bibliographical Dictionary*, vol. II: J–Z (Metuchen, N.J.: Scarecrow Press, 1975), 607; Whitaker to the author, June 1, 1993.

98. *Ten: An Anthology of Detroit Poets*, 17; Randall, interview with the author, April 9, 1992.

99. Basel, "Dudley (Felker) Randall," 329; Josey and Shockley, *Handbook of Black Librarianship*, 163; Shockley and Chandler, *Living Black American Authors*, 131; Coleman Young and Lonnie Wheelers, *Hard Stuff: The Autobiography of Coleman Young* (New York: Viking, 1994), 1980.

100. On Malcolm X see Oba T'Shaka, *The Political Legacy of Malcolm X* (Chicago: Third World Press, 1983); Eugene Victor Wolfenstein, *The Victims of Democracy: Malcolm X and the Black Revolution* (Berkeley: University of California Press, 1981); Bruce Perry, *Malcolm: The Life of a Man Who*

Changed Black America (Barrytown, N.Y.: Station Hill Press, 1991); C. Eric Lincoln, *The Black Muslims in America* (Grand Rapids, Mich.: William B. Eerdmans Publishing Co., 1994). On Langston Hughes see especially Arnold Rampersad, *The Life of Langston Hughes*, vol. II, *I Dream a World, 1947–1967* (New York: Oxford University Press, 1988); James A. Emanuel, *Langston Hughes* (Boston: Twayne Publishers, 1967). On Martin Luther King, Jr. see especially James H. Cone, *Martin and Malcolm and America: A Dream or a Nightmare* (Maryknoll, N.Y.: Orbis Books, 1991); David J. Garrow, *Bearing the Cross: Martin Luther King, Jr. and the Southern Christian Leadership Conference* (New York: William Morrow and Co., 1986). On Robert Kennedy see Edwin O. Gauthman and Jeffrey Shulman, eds., *Robert Kennedy in His Own Words* (New York: Bantam Books, 1988).

101. Miller, "Dudley Randall," 269; *Detroit Free Press*, April 11, 1981, 11.

102. Hodges, "Dudley Randall and the Broadside Press," 16–17.

103. Ibid. [from an interview with Dudley Randall on July 1, 1973], 17.

104. Dave Ferguson, "Dudley Randall ... Poet in Residence," *The Varsity News* (University of Detroit), (September 16, 1969): 3.

105. *Black World* 19, no. 5 (December 1969): 33.

106. Randall, *Broadside Memories*, 27; *Catalogue of the Heritage Series* (London, England: Paul Breman Limited, 1974), 1–4; *Catalogues of Broadside Press*, 1969, 4; *Catalogues of Broadside Press*, 1975, 1–5; Sonia Sanchez, ed., *Three Hundred and Sixty Degrees of Blackness Coming at You: An Anthology of the Sonia Sanchez Writers Workshop at Countee Cullen Library in Harlem* (New York: 5X Publishing Co., 1971); Ahmed Alhamisi and Kofi Wangara, eds., *Black Arts: An Anthology of Black Creations* (Detroit: Black Arts Publications, 1969); Virginia C. Fowler, *Nikki Giovanni* (New York: Twayne Publishers, 1992), 26.

107. Bailey, *Broadside Authors and Artists*, 30–31; Paul Breman, ed., *You Better Believe It: Black Verse in English from Africa, the West Indies and the United States* (Baltimore, Md.: Penguin Books, 1973), 525–26; *Contemporary Authors* (Detroit: Gale Research Co., 1992), 114.

108. Breman, *You Better Believe It*, 525.

109. Ibid., 122; Dudley Randall, review of *You Better Believe It* in *Okike: An African Journal of New Writing* 1, no. 5 (June 1974): 71.

110. Robert Hayden, ed., *Kaleidoscope: Poems by American Negro Poets* (New York: Harcourt, Brace and World, 1967), ix.

111. *Negro Digest* was the single most important journal for the publication of Dudley Randall's work between 1965 and 1969. See the following issues: 1965: February, April, May, June, August, and September; 1966: January, March, April, May, August, September, and November; 1967: March and November; 1968: January, April, and September; and 1969: February and September. See also Randall, "Bio-Bibliographical Sketch," 22–23.

112. See Rosey E. Pool, ed., *Ik Ben de Nieuwe Neger* (The Hague: Bert, Bakker, 1965), 159, 183; Langston Hughes, ed., *Negro American Poetry* (Paris, France: Editions Seghers, 1966), 166–67; Hayden, *Kaleidoscope*, 131–35; Arnold Adolf, ed., *I Am the Darker Brother: An Anthology of Modern Poems* (New York: Macmillan, 1968), 50; Chapman, *Black Voices*, 468, 471; Emanuel and Gross, *Dark Symphony*, 490–92; *Ten: An Anthology of Detroit Poets*, 17–22; Ahmed Alhamisi and Kofi Wangara, eds., *Black Arts: An Anthology of Black Creations* (Detroit: Black Arts Publications, 1969), 111–12; Lillian Faderman and Barbara Bradshaw, eds., *American Ethnic Writing: Speaking for Ourselves* (Glenview, Ill.: Scott, Foresman and Co. 1969), 62–63; Clarence Mayor, ed., *The New Black Poetry* (New York: International Publishers, 1969), 103–4; Dudley Randall, ed., *Black Poetry* (Detroit: Broadside Press, 1969), 16–18; Darwin T. Turner, ed., *Black American Literature: Poetry* (Columbus, Ohio: Charles E. Merrill, 1969), 107–8.

113. Randall, *Broadside Memories*, 24, 26.

114. Ibid., 26.

115. "Black Books Bulletin Interviews Dudley Randall," 25.

116. See also Redmond, "Stridency and the Sword," 544, 568; King, *Forerunners: Black Poets in America*, 15–16, 21–22, 99–100, 105–6; Kirkland C. Jones, *Renaissance Man from Louisiana: A Biography of Arna Wendell Bontemps* (Westport, Conn.: Greenwood, 1992), 156–61; Kent, *A Life of Gwendolyn Brooks*, 192–224; Rampersad, *The Life of Langston Hughes*; Ford, *Black Insights*, 317; Boyd, "The Detroit Writer: A Report," 76–77; Mayor, *The New Black Poetry*, 103, 153. *Black Books Bulletin* notes that Randall's "Black Poetry was the first anthology of black poetry to be published by a black publishing company." See "Black Books Bulletin Interviews Dudley Randall," 23. See also Randall, *Broadside Memories*, 28, 32.

117. Gayle, *The Black Aesthetic*, xxii–xxiii. Not all black contemporaries of the Black Arts Movement agreed with its ideology. Bayard Rustin took exception to some of its conclusion. Speaking before the students at Clark College, Atlanta, Georgia, in a convocation address on March 5, 1968, Rusin stated that: "Young Negroes are now so frustrated that they are substituting sloganism for analysis. They are examining their navels when they should be examining economic and social programs." Did young blacks and their most radical leaders really understand America? To Rustin the answer seemed to be no. "If I refuse to use the word 'honky,' if I refuse to insult white people, and if I refuse to call them dirty names, it is not because I do not understand them. On the contrary, it is because I understand them infinitely better than Malcolm X or Stokely Carmichael ever have. If Stokely and Malcolm really understood white America, they would know that the society is so intensely brutal, that its only response to anti-white abuse and anti-white stoganism is to throw blacks in jail, deprive them of Civil liberties, drive them into exile or shoot them. So it is because I know how brutal this society can be, that I will not take the chance of urging Negroes to expose themselves uselessly to such brutality." See Bayard Rustin, "Convocation Address," in *On Being Black, Writings by Afro-Americans from Frederick Douglass to the Present*, ed. Charles T. Davis and Daniel Warden (Greenwich, Conn.: Fawcett Publications, 1970), 319–20. See also Bayard Rustin, *Down the Line: The Collected Writings of Bayard Rustin* (Chicago: Quadrangle Books, 1971).

118. *Contemporary Authors*, 1977, 578.

119. Redmond, *Drumvoices*, 330; Donald Franklin Joyce, *Black Book Publishers in the United States: A Historical Dictionary of the Presses, 1817–1990* (Westport, Conn.: Greenwood, 1991), 63–64; Emanuel and Gross, *Dark Symphony* 488; Adolf, *The Poetry of Black America*, 533; Josey and Shockley, *Handbook of Black Librarianship*, 163; "Black Books Bulletin Interviews Dudley Randall," 23; George Thomas Kurian, *The Directory of American Book Publishing: From Founding Fathers to Today's Conglomerates* (New York: Simon and Schuster, 1975), 83, 234; Thomas, "The Shadow World," 53–73; Redmond, "Stridency and the Sword," 543–44, 553–54, 556, 558–59, 566.

120. Owachekwa Jemie, *Langston Hughes: An Introduction to the Poetry* (New York: Columbia University Press, 1976), 185–86.

121. *Negro Digest* 17, nos. 11–12 (September/October 1968): 53.

122. "Dudley Randall: Detroit Public Library, Biography and Criticism VNF Collection," article by Tom Pawlick (*Detroit News*, or *Detroit Free Press*, no date), 3–4. See also Barrington Bonner, "An Interview with Nikki Giovanni," *Black American Literature Forum* 18, no. 1 (Spring 1984) 30.

123. *The CLA Journal* and the *Negro History Bulletin* did not review a single book by Broadside Press during the years 1965–1969. Perhaps the editors of both organs considered the books of Broadside Press to be too radical for a review of them to appear in their publications.

124. Randall, *Broadside Memories*, 25.

125. "Dudley Randall," Biography and Criticism VF Collections 3; Randall, *Broadside Memories* 24–26; *Detroit Fress Press*, April 11, 1982, 11. Randall could not break down the white barriers of majority population owned stores even in Detroit. Only one Detroit bookstore a black one, Vaughn's, carried all of Broadside's titles. White bookstores were generally negative toward black books produced by allegedly "radical" black publishers. See Randall, *Broadside Memories*, 31.

126. Redmond, "Stridency and the Sword," 559. See also Abby Arthur Johnson and Ronald Maberry Johnson, *Propaganda and Aesthetics: The Literary Politics of Afro-American Magazines in the Twentieth Century* (Amherst: University of Massachusetts Press, 1979), 161–93; Wolseley, *The Black Press U.S.A.*, 173–74.

127. Redmond, "Stridency and the Sword," 556.

128. Ibid., 550, 564; *Negro Digest* 19, no. 1 (November 1969): 78.

129. Redmond, *Drumvoices*, 329.

130. Bailey, *Broadside Authors and Artists*, 19, 55, 78, 91, 105–6; Orde Coombs, ed., *We Speak as Liberators: Young Black Poets* (New York: Dodd, Mead and Co., 1970), 242, 244; Breman, *You Better Believe It*, 493; Gwendolyn Brooks, ed., *Jump Bad: A New Chicago Anthology* (Detroit: Broadside Press, 1971), 183–84; *Negro Digest* 19, no. 1 (November 1969): 98.

131. May, Strauls, and Trosky, *Black Writers*, 340, 503, 586; Page, *Selected Black American*

Authors: An Illustrated Bio-Bibliography, 3–4, 8–9, 99; Jerry W. Ward, Jr., interview with the author (telephone), Tougaloo College, Tougaloo, Mississippi, July 9, 1993; Carolyn Fowler, *A Knot in the Thread: The Life and Work of Jacques Roumain* 4 (Washington, D.C.: Howard University Press, 1980); Brooks, *Jump Bad*, 183–84.

132. May, Strauls, and Trosky, *Black Writers*, 340, 503, 586; Page, *Selected Black American Authors: An Illustrated Bio-Bibliography* 3–4, 8–9, 99.

133. See Houston A. Baker, Jr., *A Many Colored Coat of Dreams: The Poetry of Countee Cullen* (Detroit: Broadside Press, 1974); Brooks, *Jump Bad*, 128–197; Nikki Giovanni, *Black Feeling, Black Talk* (1968) *Black Judgement* (1968), were both distributed by Broadside Press; "Nikki-Rosa" in Randall, *Black Poetry*, 48; Randall and Burroughs, *For Malcolm X*, 19; Sonia Sanchez, *Home Coming* (Detroit: Broadside Press, 1968).

134. Gustan Berle, *The Small Business Information Handbook* (New York: John Wiley and Sons, 1990), 18–21; Steven Solomon, *Small Business USA: The Role Small Companies Play in Sparking America's Economic Transformation* (New York: Crown Publishers, 1986), 22–25, 232–47.

135. Berle, *The Small Business Information Handbook*, 18–21; Solomon, *Small Business USA*, 22–25, 232–47; *Book, Promotion, Sales and Distribution: A Management Training Course* (London and Paris: Book House Training Centre and UNESCO, 1991), 6–7, 16–23, 74–75, 132–33; "Accounting for Small Business: *Black Enterprise* 23, no. 4 (November 1992): 37, 40; J. William Snorgrass, "Freedom of the Press and Black Publications," *Western Journal of Black Studies* 4, no. 3 (Fall 1980): 172–78; Kenneth O'Reilly, *"Racial Matters": The FBI's Secret File on Black America, 1960–1972* (New York: Free Press/Macmillan, 1989), 261–92, 325–29.

136. John P. Dessauer, "The U.S. Book Industry Today," in *American Books Abroad: Toward a National Policy*, ed. William M. Child and Donald E. McNeil (Washington, D.C.: Helen Dwight Reid Educational Foundation, 1986), 6.

137. Dudley Randall, "Black Emotion and Experience: The Literature for Understanding," *American Libraries* 4, no. 2 (February 1973): 87–88.

138. Wolseley, *The Black Press, U.S.A.*, 169. See also Jennifer Jordan, "Cultural Nationalism in the 1960s: Politics and Poetry," in *Race Politics, and Culture: Critical Essays on the Radicalism of the 1960s*, ed. Adolph Reed, Jr. (Westport, Conn.: Greenwood, 1986), 39.

139. Leonard Kniffel, "Poet in Motion," *Monthly Detroit* 7, no. 6 (June 1984): 160.

140. Randall, *Broadside Memories*, 28.

141. Benjamin Quarles, "Black History Unbound," in *Black Mosaic: Essays in Afro-American History and Historiography* (Amherst: University of Massachusetts Press, 1988), 196.

142. Randall, *Broadside Memories*, 39; Bailey, *Broadside Authors and Artists*, 53, 108, 110–11, 113, 123; Melhem, *Heroism in the New Black Poetry*, 82; Dennis Thompson, *The Black Artist in America: An Index to Reproductions* (Metuchen, N.J.: Scarecrow Press, 1991), 85, 104, 168, 268, 315.

143. Randall, *Broadside Memories*, 38.

144. See Carol Polsyrove, "Making Books: In the Publishing Business, Small Can Be Beautiful," *The Progressive* 45, no. 9 (September 1981): 47–49.

145. Michael Loudon, "Dudley Randall," in *Critical Survey of Poetry: English Language Series*, vol. 6, ed. Frank N. Magill (Englewood Cliffs, N.J.: Salem Press, 1982), 2312.

146. Redmond, "Stridency and the Sword," 544.

147. Margaret Danner, "This Is an African Worm," in Margaret Danner and Dudley Randall, *Poem Counterpoem*, 11.

148. Emanuel, "The Negro," in *The Tree House and Other Poems*, 12.

149. Don L. Lee's *Think Black* was originally published privately in Chicago by the author, and reprinted by Broadside Press in 1968.

150. Trudier Harris, "African-American Literature: A Survey," in *Africana Studies: A Survey of Africa and the African Diaspora*, ed. Mario Azevedo (Durham, N.C.: Carolina Academic Press, 1993), 336.

151. See Lindsay Patterson, ed., *An Introduction to Black Literature in America: From 1746 to the Present* (New York: Associated Publishers and the Association for the Study of Negro Life and History 1969), 223.

152. Redmond, *Drumvoices*, 349.

153. Don L. Lee, "But He Was Cool or: He Even Stopped for Green Lights," in *Don't Cry, Scream!* (Detroit: Broadside Press, 1969), 24–25. See also Randall, *Black Poetry*, 41–42.

154. Giovanni, "Nikka-Rosa," in *Black Judgement*, 10. See also Randall, *Black Poetry*, 48.

155. Mercer Cook and Stephen E. Henderson, *The Militant Black Writer in Africa and the United States* (Madison: University of Wisconsin Press, 1969), 65.

156. See Vincent Harding, *Beyond Chaos: Black History and the Search for the New Land* (Atlanta, Ga.: Institute of the Black World, Black Paper No. 2, 1970), 1–31.

157. Jon Eckels, "White Collar Job," in *Home Is Where the Soul Is* (Detroit: Broadside Press, 1969), 14.

158. Etheridge Knight, *Poems from Prison* (Detroit: Broadside Press, 1968), 18.

159. Marvin X. *Black Man Listen* (Detroit: Broadside Press, 1969), 24.

160. Keorapetse Kgositsile, *Spirits Unchained* (Detroit: Broadside Press, 1969), 8. See also Emmanuel Sinelson, "Black America and the Black South African Literary Consciousness," in *Perspectives of Black Popular Culture*, ed. Harry B. Shaw (Bowling Green, Ohio: Bowling Green State University Popular Press, 1990), 162–64.

161. Richard K. Barksdale, "Urban Crisis and the Black Poetic Avant-Garde," in *Praise Song of Survival* (Urbana, Ill.: University of Illinois Press, 1992), 65–67. See also Keorapetse Kgositsile, "Paths to the Future," *Negro Digest* 17, nos. 11–12 (September/October 1968): 38–48, Leila Azzam and Aisha Governeur, *The Life of the Prophet Muhammad* (London: Islamic Texts Society, 1985); C. Eric Lincoln, *The Black Muslims of America* (Grand Rapids, Mich.: William B. Eerdmans Publishing Co. and Trenton, N.J.: Africa World Press, 1994), 16–17, 107, 273–76.

162. Redmond, *Drumvoices*, 244.

163. Richard Barksdale and Kenenth Kinnamons eds., *Black Writers of America* (New York: Macmillan, 1972), 809.

164. Ibid. Critics Richard A. Long and Eugenia W. Collier lists the following major Broadside authors in their chronology of the most significant books published by African-American writers during the 1960s: James A. Emanuel, *The Treehouse and Other Poems* (1968); Nikki Giovanni, *Black Feeling, Black Talk* (1968); Etheridge Knight, *Poems from Prison* (1968); Don L. Lee *Black Pride* (1968), *Think Black* (1968); Dudley Randall, *Cities Burning* (1968); Dudley Randall and Margaret Danner, *Poem Counterpoem* (1968); Gwendolyn Brooks, *Riot* (1969); Nikki Giovanni, *Black Judgment* (1969); Don L. Lee, *Don't Cry, Scream!* (1969); and Sonia Sanchez, *Home Coming* (1969). See Richard A. Long and Eugenia W. Collier eds., *Afro-American Writing: An Anthology of Prose and Poetry*, vol. 1 (New York: New York University Press, 1972), iii.

165. Ralph Cohen, ed., *New Directions in Literary History* (Baltimore: Johns Hopkins University Press, 1974), 1–3. See also Manfred Veumann, [translated by Peter Heath], "Literary Production and Reception" *New Literary History* 8, no. 1 (Autumn 1976): 107–26.

166. Randall, *Broadside Memories*, 28. Authors also received 2–5 free copies of their publications from Broadside. See Broadside Press letter to Etheridge Knight, June 10, 1966, Knight Papers, University of Toledo, Ohio.

167. On the national situation for American poets see Mary Biggs, *A Gift That Cannot Be Refused: The Writing and Publishing of Contemporary American Poetry* (Westport, Conn.: Greenwood, 1990).

168. *On Broadside News* see *Negro Digest* 19, no. 2 (December 1969): 33.

169. Josey and Shockley *Handbook of Black Librarianship*, 163, quoting *Black Books Bulletin* (Winter 1972).

170. *Contemporary Authors*, New Revision Series (Detroit: Gale Research Co., vol. 23, 1988), 225. Randall's aid to other poets included writing introductions to their books. See Lee, *Black Pride* (1968), 7–8; and Stephany Fuller, *Moving Deep* (1969), 7–9. He also aided the advancement of other poets through his services as guest editor of such magazines as the *Journal of Black Poetry*, and other publications. See Johnson and Johnsons *Propaganda and Aesthetics*, 184.

171. See James P. Draper, ed., *Black Literary Criticism*, vol. 2 (Detroit: Gale Research Co., 1992), 1307.

172. See "Perspectives," *Negro Digest* 18, no. 7 (May 1969): 49.

173. Gwendolyn Brooks, "Malcolm X," in Randall and Burroughs, *For Malcolm X*, 3. See also Gwendolyn Brooks, *In the Mecca* (New York: Harper and Row, 1968), 39.

174. Lee, *Don't Cry, Scream!*, 5.

175. Nikki Giovanni, in *Negro Digest* 18, no. 11 (September 1969): 96.

Chapter 3

1. R. Baxter Miller, "Dudley Randall," in *Dictionary of Literary Biography*, vol. 41, *Afro-American Poets Since 1955*, ed. Trudier Harris and Thadious M. Davis (Detroit: Gale Research Co., 1985), 269; *Who's Who Among Black Americans 1977–78* (Northbrook, Ill.: Who's Who Among Black Americans, 1977), 738.

2. Frenchy Jolen Hodges, "Dudley Randall and the Broadside Press," (M.A. thesis, Atlanta University, 1974), 16–17. During this period Randall remained active in the professional librarian organizations, including the American Library Association and the Michigan Library Association. See Ann Allen Shockley and Sue P. Chandler, *Living Stack American Authors: A Biographical Directory* (New York: R.R. Bowker Co., 1973), 131. For this period see also E.J. Josey, "The Civil Rights Movement and American Librarianship: The Opening Road," in *Activism in American Librarianship, 1962–1973*, ed. J. Stielow (Westport, Conn.: Greenwood, 1987), 13–20.

3. *Who's Who Among Black Americans, 1980–81*, 657; Miller, "Dudley Randall," 269.

4. Letter from Vivian Barnett Spencer-Randall, Detroit, Mich., May 17, 1992, to the author; Dudley Randall, interview with author, Detroit, Mich., April 9, 1992; Hodges, "Dudley Randall and the Broadside Press," 21.

5. Randall, interview with author, April 9, 1992.

6. Hodges, "Dudley Randall and the Broadside Press," 19; James A. Page, compiler, *Selected Black American Authors: An Illustrated Bio-Bibliography* (Boston: G.K. Hall & Co., 1977), 225.

7. Hodges, "Dudley Randall and the Broadside Press," quoting from her interview with Dudley Randall on July 1, 1973.

8. Miller, "Dudley Randall," 269; Martha Brown and Sue Shott, "Interview with Dudley Randall," *The Speak Easy Culture* 3 (May 1973): 27; D.H. Melhem, *Heroism in the New Black Poetry* (Lexington: University Press of Kentucky, 1990), 51.

9. *Directory of Active Michigan Poets* (Detroit: Poetry Society of Michigan, 1982), 40; Melhem, *Heroism in the New Black Poetry*, 45; Miller, "Dudley Randall," 268–69.

10. R. Baxter Miller, "Endowing the World and Time: The Life and Work of Dudley Randall," in *Black American Poets Between Worlds, 1940–1960*, ed. R. Baxter Miller (Knoxville: University of Tennessee Press, 1986), 86–87; *Black World* 21, no. 11 (September 1972): 50; *Black World* 23, no. 11 (September 1974): 80–81; *Broadside News*, no. 22 (April 1973): 1; no. 29 (October 1974): 1; *Broadside News*, no. 30 (December 1974): 1; Dudley Randall, letter to Virginia Brocks-Shedd, Detroit, Mich., November 12, 1973 (Tougaloo, Miss.: Tougaloo College Library VF).

11. Melba Joyce Boyd, "Out of the Poetry Ghetto: The Life/Art Struggle of Small Black Publishing Houses," *The Black Scholar* 16, no. 4 (July/August 1985): 14.

12. Hodges, "Dudley Randall the Broadside Press," 21.

13. Boyd, "Out of the Poetry Ghetto: The Life/Art Struggle of Small Black Publishing Houses," 14.

14. Donald B. Gibson, ed., *Modern Black Poets: A Collection of Critical Essays* (Englewood Cliffs, N.J.: Prentice-Hall, Inc., 1973), 166.

15. Stephen Henderson, *Understanding the New Black Poetry* (New York: William Morrow, 1973), 391–92.

16. Dudley Randall, *I Love You* (London: Paul Breman, 1970); Dudley Randall, *More to Remember* (Chicago: Third World Press, 1971); Dudley Randall, ed., *The Black Poets* (New York: Bantam Books, 1971); Dudley Randall, *After the Killing* (Chicago: Third World Press, 1973); Dudley Randall, *Broadside Memories: Poets I Have Known* (Detroit: Broadside Press, 1975); Dudley Randall, with Gwendolyn Brooks, Keorapetse Kgositsile, and Haki R. Madhubuti, *A Capsule Course in Black Poetry Writing* (Detroit: Broadside Press, 1975).

17. Jim Walker, Review of *The Black Poets*, in *Black Creation* 3, no. 3 (Spring 1972): 55.

18. Frank Marshall Davis, Review of *After the Killing*, in *Black World* 23, no. 11 (September 1974): 85.

19. See William Adams, Peter Conn and Barry Slepian, eds., *Afro-American Literature: Poetry* (Boston: Houghton Mifflin Co., 1970), 27–28; Arnold Adoff, ed., *Black Out Loud: An Anthology of Modern Poems by Black Americans* (New York: Macmillan, 1970), 5; Sue Abbott Boyd, ed., *Poems by Blacks*

(Fort Smith, Ark.: South and West, Inc., 1970), 61–62; Bradford Chambers and Rebecca Moon, eds., *Right On: An Anthology of Black Literature* (New York: New American Library, 1970), 252; Francis S. Freeman, ed., *The Black American Experience: A New Anthology of Black Literature* (New York: Bantam Books, 1970), 95–96; Langston Hughes and Arna Bontemps, eds., *The Poetry of the Negro, 1746–1970* (Garden City, N.Y.: Doubleday & Co., 1970), 305–6; Francis E. Kearns, ed., *Black Identity: A Thematic Reader* (New York: Holt, Rinehart, & Winston, 1970) 295–96; Darwin T. Turner, ed. *Black American Literature. Essays Poetry Fiction, Drama* (Columbus, Ohio: Charles E. Merrill Publishing Co., 1970), 263–64; Houston A. Baker, Jr., ed., *Black Literature in America* (New York: McGraw-Hill, 1971), 337–38; Gwendolyn Brooks, ed., *A Broadside Treasury* (Detroit: Broadside Press, 1971), 121–28; Patricia L. Brown, Don L. Lee and Francis Ward, eds., *To Gwen with Love: An Anthology Dedicated to Gwendolyn Brooks* (Chicago: Johnson Publishing Co., 1971), 82; Arthur P. Davis and Saunders Redding, eds., *Cavalcade: Negro American Writing from 1960 to the Present* (Boston: Houghton Mifflin Co., 1971), 774–75; Nick Aaron Ford, ed., *Black Insights: Significant Literature by Black Americans: 1760 to the Present* (Waltham, Mass.: Ginn and Co., 1971), 318; Robert Hoyden, David J. Burrows, and Frederick R. Lapides, eds., *Afro-American Literature: An Introduction* (New York: Harcourt Brace Jovanovich, 1971), 137; Alma Murray and Robert Thomas, eds., *The Science* (New York: Scholastic Book Services, 1971), 90–91, 187; Randall, *The Black Poets,* 139–48; Barbara Dodds Stanford, ed., *I Too Sing America: Black Voices in American Literature* (New York: Hoyden Book Co., 1971), 76–77; Leonard Weisman and Elfreda S. Wright, eds., *Black Poetry for All Americans* (New York: Globes, 1971), 17; Raoul Abdul, ed., *Magic of Black Poetry* (New York: Dodd, Mead & Co., 1972), 84–85; Richard Barksdale and K. Kinnamon, eds., Black Writers of *America: A Comprehensive Anthology* (New York: Macmillan, 1972), 813–14; Bernard W. Bell, ed., *Modern and Contemporary Afro-American Poetry* (Boston: Allyn and Bacon, 1972), 69–71; Abraham Chapman, ed., *New Black Voices* (New York: Mentors, 1972), 322–25; Gloria M. Simmons, Helene D. Hutchinson, and Henry E. Simmons, eds., *Black Culture: Reading and Writing Black* (New York: Holt, Rinehart and Winston, 1972), 239; Arnold Adoff, ed., *The Poetry of Black Americans: Anthology of the 20th Century* (New York: Harper & Row Publishers, 1973), 138–42; Paul Breman, ed., *You Better Believe It: Black Verse in English* (Baltimore, Md.: Penguin Books, 1973), 143–44; Hugh Fox, ed., *The Living Underground: An Anthology of Contemporary American Poetry* (Troy, N.Y.: Whitston Publishing Co., 1973), 329–31; Henderson, *Understanding the New Black Poetry,* 233–34; Ronnie M. Lane, ed., *Face the Whirlwind* (Grand Rapids, Mich.: Pilot Press Books, 1973), 43–48; Lindsay Patterson, ed., *A Rock Against the Wind: Black Love Poems: An Anthology* (New York: Dodd, Mead & Co., 1973), 49, 107, 128–29, 139; Clyde Taylor, ed., *Vietnam and Black America: An Anthology of Protest and Resistance* (Garden City, N.Y.: Anchor Press/Doubleday, 1973), 138; Arna Bontemps, ed., *American Negro Poetry* (New York: Hill and Wang, 1974), 121–22; John Ciardi and Miller Williams, eds., *How Does a Poem Mean* (Boston: Houghton Mifflin Co., 1975), 94; Woodie King, Jr., ed. *The Forerunners: Black Poets in America* (Washington, D.C.: Howard University Press, 1975), 101–3; Quincy Troupe and Rainer Schulte, eds., *Giant Talk: An Anthology of Third World Writings* (New York: Vintage Books, 1975), 67.

20. Melhem, *Heroism in the New Black Poetry,* 51.

21. Randall, "The Profile on the Pillow," in *Love You,* 3.

22. Randall, *More to Remember,* 67–69.

23. *Black World* 19, no. 11 (September 1970): 59–60; *Black World* 21, no. 11 (September 1972): 64; *Black World* 22, no. 4 (February 1973): 53; *Black World* 22, no. 11 (September 1973): 72–73; *Black World* 23, no. 1 (September 1974): 70; *Michigan in Books* 11, no. 3 (Winter 1970-71): 2; *Essence* 1, no. 10 (February 1971): 46; *Essence* (April 1971): 25; *Essence* 4, no. 1 (May 1973): 96; *Journal of Black Poetry* (Fall/Winter 1971): 1; *Hoo Doo* 1, no. 1 (1972): 30; *Okike: An African Journal of New Writing,* no. 5 (June 1974): 45–49.

24. See Floyd B. Barbour, ed., *The Black Seventies* (Boston: Porter Sargent, 1970), 139–48; Addison Gayle, Jr., ed., *The Black Aesthetic* (Garden City, N.Y.: Doubleday, 1972), 2; Gibson, *Modern Black Poets,* 84–92; *Black World,* 1970–1975; Sonia Sanchez, ed., *We Be Word Sorcerers: 25 Stories by Black Americans* (New York: Bantam Books, 1972), 189–90; *Broadside on Broadway: Seven Poets Read* (Detroit: Broadside Press, 1970).

25. Lawrence M. Sommers, *Michigan: A Geography* (Boulder, Col.: Westview Press, 1984), 21; *The Official Associated Press Almanac, 1973* (New York: Almanac Publishing Co., 1973), 142, 144.

26. *Black Enterprise* 2, no. 20 (March 1972): 80, 82.

27. Wilbur C. Rich, *Coleman Young and Detroit Politics: From Social Activist to Power Broker* (Detroit: Wayne State University Press, 1989), 91–108; Ronald Stephens, "A Review Essay, Coleman Young: The Man and His Times," *The Black Scholar* 21, no. 3 (Summer 1990/Summer 1991): 41.

28. "Victory in Detroit," *Freedomways* 13, no. 4 (Fourth Quarter 1973): 280.

29. Rich, *Coleman Young and Detroit Politics*, 208–9; "Tough for the New Mayor" *The Economist* 251, no. 6820 (May 11, 1974): 54.

30. Remer Tyson, "Detroit Hangs in There: Mayor Young a Year Later," *The Nation* 220, no. 8 (March 1, 1975): 237.

31. Sanjukta Banjeri, *Deferred Hopes: Blacks in Contemporary America* (New York: Advent Books, Inc., 1987), 188.

32. Michael A. Jenkins and John W. Shepherd,"Decentralizing High School Administration in Detroit: An Evaluation of Alternative Strategies of Political Control," in *Black America, Geographic Perspectives*, ed. Robert T. Ernst and Lawrence Huggs (Garden City, N.Y.: Anchor Books/Doubleday, 1976), 771; Mark E. Neithercat, *Detroit Twenty Years After: A Statistical Profile of the Detroit Area Since 1967* (Detroit: Center for Urban Studies, Wayne State University, 1987), 29.

33. "Detroit: Motor City Becomes Murder City Amid a Flurry of Homicides," *Black Enterprise* 3, no. 9 (April 1973): 19; "Detroit's Heroin Subculture," *Newsweek* (February 28, 1972): 18–19. See also Lawrence E. Gary and Lee P. Brown, eds., *Crime and Its Impact on the Black Community* (Washington, D.C.: Institute for Urban Affairs and Research, Howard University, 1975).

34. "Detroit: Some Post-Riot Progress, But Tension Continues," *Black Enterprise* 2, no. 20 (March 1972): 78.

35. Neithercat, *Detroit Twenty Years After*, 8.

36. Ibid., 22; Donald C. Bacon, "A Bitter New Generation of Jobless Young Blacks,"*U.S. News and World Report*, 71, no. 13 (September 27, 1976): 64.

37. "The State of the Race," *Black Enterprise* 21, no. 1 (August 1990): 60.

38. *Black Enterprise* 2, no. 20 (March 1972): 83.

39. *Black Enterprise* 8, no. 21 (June 1978): 125.

40. Ernest Holsendolph, "The Black Enterprise 100 Story: Strong Growth in a Tough Year" *Black Enterprise* 4, no. 11 (June 1974): 37, 39.

41. Carlton B. Goodlett, "Mass Communication, U.S.A.: Its Feet of Clay," *The Black Scholar* 6, no. 3 (November 1974): 3.

42. See Joe T. Darden, Richard Child Hill, June Thomas, and Richard Thomas, *Detroit: Race and Uneven Development* (Philadelphia, Pa.: Temple University Press, 1987), 11–65; Robert Hargreaves, *Superpower: A Portrait of America in the 1970's* (New York: St. Martin's Press, 1973), 13, 15, 544; Ze'ev Chafeti, *Devil's Night: And Other Tales of Detroit* (New York: Random House, 1990) 23–25; Joeal D. Aberback and Jack L. Walker, *Race in the City: Political Trust and Public Policy the New Urban System* (Boston: Little, Brown and Co., 1973), 10.

43. Randall, *Broadside Memories,* 28.

44. Barksdale and Kinnamon, *Black Writers of America*, 808.

45. Ibid. *Broadside News* noted in 1970 that "Operations have moved from a room in the publisher's home to a boarded-up storefront with more space and part-time help for faster, more efficient service. Gwendolyn Brooks has donated a mimeograph machine to Broadside, and Nikki Giovanni is making a collage out of Broadside ads and brochures." See *Broadside News*, no. 5 (June 1970): 1.

46. Gayle, *The Black Aesthetic*, xxii.

47. "Black Books Bulletin Interview Dudley Randall,"*Black Books Bulletin* (Winter 1972): 24; James Sullivan "Real Cool Pages: The Broadside Press Broadside Series," *Contemporary Literature* 32, no. 4 (Winter 1991): 552–572.

48. *Catalogues of Broadside Press* (Detroit: Broadside Press, 1975); Len Fulton, ed., *Directory of Little Magazines, Small Presses, Underground Newspapers, 1970* (Paradise, Calif.: Dustbooks, 1970), 10; Len Fulton and James Boyer May, eds., *Directory of Little Magazines Small Presses, and Underground Newspapers, 1971–72* (Paradise, Calif.: Dustbooks, 1971), 22; Fulton and May, *International Directory of Little Magazines and Small Presses, 1973–74*, 17; Etheridge Knight Collection, Toledo, Ohio: The Ward M. Canady Center, University of Toledo.

49. Bailey, *Broadside Authors and Artists*, 19–20, 28–29, 31–35, 38–39, 43–44, 51–53, 55–58, 70–72, 76, 89–9 94–99, 102–9, 111, 116, 119; Michael Harper, *Debridement* (Garden City, N.Y.:

Doubleday & Co., 1973), 113; Ted Wilentz and Tom Weatherly, eds., *Natural Process: An Anthology of New Black Poetry* (New York: Hill and Wang, 1970), 42; Linda Metzger, Deborah A. Straub, Hal May, and Susan M. Trosky, eds., *Black Writers: A Selection of Sketches from Contemporary Authors* (Detroit: Gale Research Co., 1989), 111–12, 340, 345–46, 491; "Broadsides 34–92," E. Knight Collection, The Ward M. Canady Center; James A. Page and Joe Minroh, *Selected Black American, African, and Caribbean Authors: A Bio-Bibliography* (Littleton, Col.: Libraries Unlimited, 1985), 57; Susan M. Trosky, ed., *Contemporary Authors*, vol. 132 (Detroit: Gale Research Co., 1991), 98; "Melvin Dixon, 42, Professor and Author," *New York Times*, October 29, 1992.

50. *Catalogues of Broadside Press,* 1975; Hodges, "Dudley Randall and the Broadside Press," 49, 69.

51. Keorapetse W. Kgositsile, "Paths to the Future," *Negro Digest* 17, nos. 11–12 (September/October 1968): 40.

52. Gwendolyn Brooks, *A Broadside Treasury* (Detroit: Broadside Press, 1971), 13–188.

53. Gwendolyn Brooks, ed., *Jump Bad: A New Chicago Anthology* (Detroit: Broadside Press, 1971), 7–188.

54. Jill Witherspoon Boyer, ed., *The Broadside Annual* (Detroit: Broadside Press, 1972), 722.

55. Boyer, ed., *The Broadside Annual, 1973*, 9–22. Boyer edited a third "The Broadside Annual, 1974" however, this publication was never published. The *Broadside News* informed readers in 1974 that: "Poets selected are Arthenia Bates, Melba Boyd, Leroy Calliste, Janice Cobb, Charles Cording, Eugenia Collier, Jacqueline Harris, Charlene Pinkney, Elizabeth Swados, Ted Thomas, Rudy Wallace, Jerry Ward, Jr., and Paulette White. We are awaiting the return of full information requested from the poets before sending the book to the printer." See *Broadside News*, no. 28 (August 1974): 1.

56. Scott Christinson, "Our Black Prisons," in *The Criminal Justice System and Blacks,* ed. Daniel Georges-Abeyie (New York: Clark Boardman Co., 1984), 270.

57. Boi D. Townsey, "The Incarceration of Black Men," in *Black Men*, ed. Lawrence Gary (Beverly Hills, Calif.: Sage Publishers, 1981), 231.

58. Other prison poets who published with Broadside Press include Etheridge Knight from Indiana State Prison, Michigan City, Indiana; Bruce C. Geary (Sayif Shabazz), from Walpole State Prison and Norfolk State Prison, Virginia; and Ronald Emmons, from a prison in Istanbul, Turkey. See Etheridge Knight, *Belly Song and Other Poems* (Detroit: Broadside Press, 1973), 66; Boyer, *The Broadside Annual, 1972*, 21.

59. *Catalogues of Broadside Press,* 1970–1975.

60. Chauncey E. Spencer, *Who Is Chauncey E. Spencer?* (Detroit: Broadside Press, 1975); *Catalogues of Broadside Press,* 1974–1975, 1–6. See also Charles E. Francis, *The Tuskegee Airmen: The Men Who Changed a Nation* (Boston: Branden Publishing Co., 1993); Joanne V. Gabbin, *Sterling A. Brown: Building the Black Aesthetic Tradition* (Charlottesville: University Press of Virginia, 1985), 57.

61. Hodges, "Dudley Randall and the Broadside Press," quoting from her interview with Dudley Randall of July 15, 1973, 48. See also *Catalogues of Broadside Press,* 1968–1975.

62. Hodges, "Dudley Randall and the Broadside Press," 48.

63. Randall, *Broadside Memories*, 26; Marlene Mosher, *New Directions from Don L. Lee* (Hicksville, N.Y.: Exposition Press, 1975), 128. See also Don L. Lee "Reads *Don't Cry, Scream!*" (Detroit: Broadside Press Voices, 1969), and "Reads *We Walk the Way of the New World*" (Detroit: Broadside Press Voices, 1970).

64. Hodges, "Dudley Randall and the Broadside Press," 48.

65. *Catalogues of Broadside Press,* 1974–75; Randall, *Black Poets*, 347; *Broadside News*, no. 6 (August 1970): 1.

66. Broadside's poets also made key recordings of their poetry outside of the company. See *Poet's Audio Center Catalogue* (Washington, D.C.: Poet's Audio Center, 1992), 1–3, 5; "Robert Hayden, Naomi Long Madgett and Dudley Randall Read the Six Poems They Want to Be Remembered By" (Orchard Lake, Mich.: Oakland Community College, 50 minutes, 8 mm, B/W).

67. Randall, *Broadside Memories*, 26; Broadside, *Broadside Authors and Artists*, 17–18, 20, 22, 26–27, 30, 49, 59, 65, 80–81, 85, 87, 97, 101, 102, 116; Broadside, *You Better Believe It*, 85, 132, 143, 145, 151, 161, 181, 208, 268, 312, 370, 401, 425, 443, 478; *Catalogues of the Heritage Series* (London,

England: Paul Breman, Limited, 1974); *Catalogues of Broadside Press*, 1972–1975; *Journal of Black Poetry* 1, no. 15 (Fall/Winter 1971): 108; *Journal of Black Poetry* 1, no. 16 (Summer 1972): 16; *Broadside News*, no. 4 (March 1970): 1; *Broadside News*, no. 20 (November 1972): 1. *Broadside News* informed the public in 1972 that "Mae Jackson's CAN I POET WITH YOU, formerly published by Black Dialogue Press and distributed by Broadside Press, is now a Broadside publication. CAN I POET WITH YOU was out of print for a while but is now available for only $1.00." See *Broadside News*, no. 20 (November 1972): 1.

68. Bailey, *Broadside Authors and Artists*; Breman, *You Better Believe It*.

69. Dudley Randall, "Black Publisher, Black Writer: An Answer," *Black World* 26, no. 5 (March 1975): 35.

70. Charles H. Rowell, "In Conversation with Dudley Randall," *Obsidian* 2 (Spring 1976): 36.

71. Randall, "Black Publishing Black Writer: An Answer," 34.

72. Melhem, *Heroism in the New Black Poetry*, 47.

73. "Black Books Bulletin Interviews Dudley Randall," 26.

74. See Anthony O. Putman, *Marketing Your Services: A Step-by-Step Guide for Small Businesses and Professionals* (New York: John Wiley & Sons, 1990), 87.

75. Aurelia Toyer Miller, Review of "D. Parke Gibson, $70 Billion in the Black: American's Black Consumers," *The Review of Black Political Economy* 10, no. 1 (Fall 1979): 116–17.

76. Ibid., 115.

77. Hodges, "Dudley Randall and the Broadside Press," 28.

78. Randall, *Broadside Memories*, 41; Hodges, "Dudley Randall and the Broadside Press," 28–29.

79. Hodges, "Dudley Randall and the Broadside Press," 28.

80. Ibid.

81. Randall, *Broadside Memories*, 45.

82. Hodges, "Dudley Randall and the Broadside Press," 29; Dudley Randall, interview with the author, Detroit, Mich., June 27, 1994.

83. Hodges, "Dudley Randall and the Broadside Press," from her interview with Dudley Randall on July 15, 1973, page 30.

84. Ibid., 34; Randall, *Broadside Memories*, 8, 11, 13, 15–16, 18, 21, 26–28, 38–39, 52.

85. Hodges, "Dudley Randall and the Broadside Press," 31.

86. Ibid., 36.

87. Ibid., 34.

88. Ibid., 37–38.

89. Ibid., 39.

90. Linda S. Habbard, ed., *Publishers Directory 1992* (Detroit: Gale Research Co., 1992), 571.

91. Hodges, "Dudley Randall and the Broadside Press," 41.

92. Ibid., 41.

93. Ibid.

94. Ibid., 42.

95. *Catalogues of Broadside Press*, 1967–1975.

96. Hodges, "Dudley Randall and the Broadside Press," 43.

97. Randall, *Broadside Memories*, 25, 31.

98. Marcus D. Pohlmann, *Black Politics in Conservative America* (New York: Longman, 1990), 199.

99. Randall, *Broadside Memories*, 28, 31, 52; Hodges, "Dudley Randall and the Broadside Press," 43; David Armstrong, *Alternative Media in America* (Los Angeles: J.P. Tarcher, 1981), 50–51, 172–73, 214, 218, 374–75; Roland E. Wolseley, *The Black Press, U.S.A.* (Ames: Iowa State University Press, 1990), 214. In 1972, *Broadside News* announced to its readers that "Reviews of many Broadside books and broadsides and of Heritage books are to be found in the current Free Lance magazines, ($2.00, 6005 Grand Avenue, Cleveland, Ohio)." See *Broadside News*, no. 18 (August 1972): 1.

100. Hodges, "Dudley Randall and the Broadside Press," 43–45.

101. *Black Academy Review* 1, no. 1 (Spring 1970): 39; *Black Academy Review* 1, no. 3 (Fall 1970): 63; *CLA Journal* 14, no. 3 (March 1971): 362; *Black Theatre*, #5 (1971): 54; *The Black Scholar* 3, no. 4 (1973): 41; *Black Creation* 6 (1974–75): 97.

102. See Julius E. Thompson, *The Black Press in Mississippi, 1865–1985* (Gainesville, Fla.: University Press of Florida, 1993), 1, 11 60, 79–80.

103. "Profile of Black Businessmen in Detroit in 1966," (Detroit: Detroit Public Library Vertical Files, Business and Finance Division, dated July 21, 1976), one page.

104. Ibid.

105. Hodges, "Hodges Randall and the Broadside Press," 50; "Black Books Bulletin Interviews Dudley Randall," 25.

106. "Black Books Bulletin Interviews Dudley Randall," 25; *International Directory of Little Magazines and Small Presses, 1973–74,* 17. On the tasks of the marketing manager, see Merlin Stone, *Marketing and Economics* (London: Macmillan, 1980), 1–6.

107. Hodges, "Dudley Randall and the Broadside Press," 50–51.

108. Ibid., 52; *Catalogues of Broadside Press,* 1972.

109. The author has taken the liberty of rounding-off Dudley Randall's *Black Poetry*, priced at $0.95 per copy, to $1.00 each for this grand total sum of $38,311.00. In some cases, these figures do not reflect all of each author's total number of active books carried on Broadside's list, but only their top or lowest selling volumes for 1972 only. Using the paperback rates only, the following figures summarize the total number of books sold in 1972, by the top and bottom selling authors at Broadside Press:

Nikki Giovanni, 8,960 sales	=	$13,440.00
Don L. Lee, 6,688 sales	=	10,032.00
Gwendolyn Brooks, 3,598 sales	=	9,370.00
Dudley Randall, 2,553 sales	=	2,553.00
Sonia Sanchez, 1,944 sales	=	2,916.00
James A. Emmanuel, 338 sales	=	338.00
Doughtry Long, 173 sales	=	259.50
Beatrice M. Murphy and		
Nancy L. Arnex, 189 sales	=	189.00
James Randall, Jr., 190 sales	=	190.00
Everett Hoagland, 191 sales	=	191.00
Dudley Randall, 207 sales	=	207.00
John Raven, 210 sales	=	105.00
Margaret Danner, 230 sales	=	230.00
Keorapetse Kgositsile, 243 sales	=	243.00

110. Readers may wish to note that Randall did not include a new edition, or even list 7 of the lowest selling Broadside books of 1972, in his 1974–75 catalogue, only 3 of the lowest sellers on the 1974–75 list; including, Danner's *Impression of African Art Forms,* Emanuel's *Panther Man,* and Randall's *Cities Burning.* See *Catalogues of Broadside Press, 1974–1975,* 1–2.

111. On the importance of the Black Studies Movement for this period see: Floyd W. Hayes, III, "Preface to the Student," "Preface to the Instructor," and "African American Studies: Trends, Developments and Future Challenges," in *A Turbulent Voyage: Readings in African American Studies,* ed. Hayes (San Diego, Calif.: Collegiate Press, 1992), xi–xlvii, 1–23; Talmadge Anderson, *Introduction to African American Studies: Cultural Concepts and Theory* (Dubuque, Iowa: Kendall/Hunt Publishing Co., 1993), 31, 49; James L. Conyers, Jr. "A Descriptive and Evaluate Analysis of Selected African American Studies Departments and Programs (Ph.D. thesis, Temple University, 1992).

112. Imani L.B. Fryar, "The Black Woman Writer," *Journal of Black Studies* 20, no. 4 (June 1990): 461; James C. Anyike, *African American Holidays: A Historical Research and Resource Guide to Cultural Celebrations* (Chicago: Popular Truth, 1991).

113. See Robert H. Brisbane, *Black Activism: Racial Resolution in the United States, 1954–1970* (Valley Forge, Pa.: Judson Press, 1974), 109–24, 134–47, 162–63, 193–221, 236; Manning Marable, *Race, Reform, and Rebellion: The Second Reconstruction in Black America, 1945–1982* (Jackson: University Press of Mississippi, 1984), 96–102, 104–7, 118–19, 121–26; Oba T'Shaka, *The Political Legacy of Malcolm X* (Chicago: Third World Press, 1983), 24–37; Victor Wolfenstein, *The Victims of Democracy: Malcolm X and the Black Revolution* (Berkeley: University of California Press, 1981), 4–11, 22–23.

114. Brisbane, *Black Activism*, 236.

115. Eugene B. Redmond, *Drumvoices: The Mission of Afro-American Poetry, A Critical History* (Garden City, N.Y.: Anchor Books, 1976), 396, 406, 415–17; "Clarence Major Issues" *African American Interview* 20, no. I (Spring 1994): 5–140; Fowler, *Nikki Giovanni*, xiii–xv; Demetrice A. Worley and Jesse Perry, Jr., eds., *African American Literature: An Anthology of Nonfiction, Fiction, Poetry and Drama* (Lincolnwood, Ill.: National Textbook Co., 1993), 197, 237, 249, 259, 289, 295, 305, 309; Elaine Maria Upton, "Audre Lorde 1934–1992," in *Contemporary Lesbian Writers of the United States: A Bio-Bibliographical Critical Sourcebook,* Sandra Pollack and Denise T. Knight, eds. (Westport, Conn.: Greenwood, 1993), 316–24. Readers may wish to note that this volume was dedicated to Audre Lord; "Mari Evans," "Audre Lord," "Sonia Sanchez," "Margaret Walker," in *The Feminist Companion to Literature in English: Women Writers from the Middle Ages to the Present*, ed. Virginia Blain, Patricia Clements and Isobel Grunoy (New Haven, Conn.: Yale University Press, 1990), 347–48, 670, 943, 1124–25.

116. Mosher, *New Directions from Don L. Lee,* 137–41; Gloria T. Hull, Patricia Bell Scott, and Barbara Smith, eds., *All the Women Are White, All the Blacks Are Men, But Some of Us Are Brave: Black Women's Studies* (New York: The Feminist Press, 1982), 337–78; Brooks, Kgositsile, Madhubuti, and Randall, *A Capsule Course in Black Poetry Writing*; Mari Evans, *I Am a Black Woman: Poems by Mari Evans* (New York: William Morrow & Co., 1970).

117. Vincent Harding, *Beyond Chaos: Black History and the Search for the New Land* (Atlanta: Institute of the Black World, 1970).

118. See Harding, *Beyond Chaos: Black History and the Search for the New Land,* 2, 30–31; Nikki Giovanni and Margaret Walker, *A Poetic Equation: Conversations Between Nikki Giovanni and Margaret Walker* (Washington D.C.: Howard University Press, 1971), xi–xiv, 48–49; Mosher, *New Directions from Don L. Lee,* 40, 72–72, 95; Doris L. Laryea, "A Black Poet's Vision: An Interview with Lance Jeffers," *CLA Journal* 26 (June 1983): 422–33; D.H. Melhem, "Sonia Sanchez: Will and Spirit" *Melus* 12, no. 3 (Fall 1985): 94; James A. Emanuel, "Black Man Abroad," *Black American Literature Forum* 13, no. 3 (Fall 1979): 79–85. As early as 1967, some black writers were impressed with Harold Cruse's *The Crisis of the Negro Intellectual: From Its Origin to the Present* (New York: William Morrow, 1967), and the author's argument about the need for a national black struggle in the United States to promote cultural nationalism. See also Harold Cruse, *Rebellion or Revolution?* (New York: William Morrow, 1968); Redmond, "Stridency and the Sword," 562; Joe Goncalves, "Book Review," *Journal of Black Poetry* 1, no. 11 (Spring 1969): 63–64; Ernest Kaiser, "Recent Books," *Freedomways* 7, no. 4 (Fall 1967): 378–79.

119. On the new black history see especially works by the following authors: Vincent Harding, *There Is a River: The Black Struggle for Freedom in America* (New York: Harcourt Brace Jovanovich, 1981); John W. Blassingame, *The Slave Community: Plantation Life in the Antebellum South* (New York: Oxford University Press, 1972, 1979); Lerone Bennett, Jr., *The Challenge of Blackness* (Chicago: Johnson Publishing Co., 1972); Mary F. Berry and John W. Blassingame, *Long Memory: The Black Experience in America* (New York: Oxford University Press, 1982); Abdul Alkalimat and Associates, *Introduction to Afro-American Studies: A Peoples College Primer* (Chicago: Twenty-First Century Books and Publications, 1973, 1986).

120. Gwendolyn Brooks, ed., *The Black Position: An Annual*, Numbers 1–4 (Detroit: Broadside Press, 1971, 1972, 1973, 1976).

121. Ibid., no. 2 (1972): 1; Fulton and Ferber, *International Directory of Little Magazines and Small Presses*, 40; *Black World* 21, no. 2 (December 1971): 77; *Black World* 22, no. 12 (October 1973): 87.

122. Brooks, *The Black Position*, no. 2 (1972): 3.

123. Ibid., 1971, 1972, 1973.

124. Ibid.; *Black World* 23, no. 6 (April 1974): 93.

125. Charles H. Wesley, *The Quest for Equality: From Civil War to Civil Rights* (Washington, D.C.: Association for the Study of Negro Life and History, 1968), 200–1; Franklin and Moss, *From Slavery to Freedom*, 476–79; Brisbane, *Black Activism*, 276–83; Shockley and Chandler, *Living Black American Authors*, 12–13, 21, 88, 94–95, 117.

126. Don L. Lee, *From Plan to Planet: Life Studies, The Need for Afrikan Minds and Institutions* (Detroit: Broadside Press and Institute of Positive Education, 1973), 21–24, 137–42; William Worthy, "The American Negro Is Dead" *Esquire* 68, no. 5 (November 1967): 126, 167–68; "The Negro in Viet Nam" Special Issue, *Time*, May 26, 1967; Gerald Gill, "From Maternal Pacifism

to Revolutionary Solidarity: African-American Women's Opposition to the Vietnam War," in *Sights on the Sixties*, ed. Barbara L. Tischler (New Brunswick, N.J.: Rutgers University Press, 1992), 177–80.

127. Bailey, *Broadside Authors and Artists*, 18, 28, 37, 45, 72, 74, 89, 97–99; *New York Times*, October 5, 1991, 28; Shockley and Chandler, *Living Black American Authors*, 47, 92; Jon C. Randall, *Indigoes* (Detroit: Broadside Press, 1975), 18; Charles E. Cannon, *Saint Nigger* (Detroit: Broadside Press, 1972), 26; Chester M. Hedgepeth, Jr., *Twentieth Century African-American Writers and Artists* (Chicago: American Library Association, 1991), 151–52. Charles E. Cannon was among the younger Broadside Press poets (U.S. Marine Corps, 1966–68), who served in Vietnam. See Bailey, *Broadside Authors and Artists*, 37.

128. Bontemps, *Personals*, 35; Cannon, *Saint Nigger*, 16; Cuney, *Storefront Church*, 20; Eckels, *Home Is Where the Soul Is*, 24–25; Emanuel, *The Treehouse and Other Poems*, 24; Giovanni, *Black Judgement*, 11–13; Jeffers, *When I Know the Power of My Black Hand*, 13; Knight, *Belly Song and Other Poems*, 26; Lee, *Black Pride*, 27; Audre Lorde, "Viet Nam Addenda," in *The New York Head Shop and Museum* (Detroit: Broadside Press, 1974), 46; Randall, *After the Killing*, 9; Wolde, *Enough to Die For*, 34; Marvin X, *Black Man Listen*, 24.

129. Lorde, *The New York Head Shop and Museum*, 46.

130. William Waring Cuney, "Say Amen," in *Storefront Church* (London: Paul Breman Ltd., 1973), 20.

131. Don L. Lee, "Message to a Black Soldier," in *Black Pride* (Detroit: Broadside Press, 1968), 27.

132. Lorenzo Thomas, "Marvin X (Marvin E. Jackmon, Nazzam Al Fitnah Muhajir, El Muhajir)," in *Afro-American Writers After 1955: Dramatists and Prose Writers*, ed. T. M. Davis and T. Harris (Detroit: Gale Research Co., 1985), 179.

133. Ibid. See also "Marvin X, Attack Justice Must Be Done," in *Vietnam and Black American: An Anthology of Protest and Resistance*, ed. Clyde Taylor (Garden City, N.Y.: Anchor Press/Doubleday, 1973), 280–84, 321.

134. Sharon Harley, Stephen Middleton, and Charlotte Stokes, *The African-American Experience: A History* (Englewood Cliffs, N.J.: Glove Book Co., 1992), 353; Felix (Pete) Peterson, "Vietnam Battle Deaths: Is There a Race or Class Issue?" *Focus* 15, no. 7 (July 1987): 3–4.

135. Hodges, "Dudley Randall and the Broadside Press," 30.

136. Ibid.

137. Audre Lorde, questionnaire to the author, St. Croix, Virgin Islands, August 12, 1991; Ntozake Shange, questionnaire to the author, Philadelphia, Pa., October 10, 1991; Sharyn J. Skeeter, "Black Women Writers: Levels of Identity," *Essence* 4, no. 1 (May 1971): 58–59, 76, 89; Jacqueline Jones Royster, "Perspectives on the Intellectual Tradition of Black Women Writers," in *The Right to Literacy*, ed. Andrea A. Lunsford, Helene Moglen and J. Slevin (New York: Modern Language Association of America, 1990), 103–12.

138. Patricia Hill Collins, *Black Feminist Thought: Knowledge, Consciousness, and the Politics of Empowerment* (New York: Routledge, 1991), 65. See also Jeffrey M. Elliot, ed., *Conversations with Maya Angelou* (Jackson: University Press of Mississippi, 1989), 198–99; Cheryl A. Wall, ed., *Changing Our Own Words: Essays on Criticism, Theory, and Writing by Black Women* (New Brunswick, N.J.: Rutgers University Press, 1989); Joyce A. Joyce, "Black Woman Scholar, Critic, and Teacher: The Inextricable Relationship Between Race, Sex, and Class," *New Literary History* 22, no. 3 (Summer 1991): 543–65.

139. Collins, *Black Feminist Thought*, 147–51, 230. Seven Broadside authors are quoted extensively in Collins' book: Gwendolyn Brooks, 14, 80, 82, 111, 137; Nikki Giovanni, 89, 104, 110, 157, 233; June Jordan, 39, 108, 115, 129, 136, 195, 197, 210, 213, 232–33; Audre Lorde 26, 71, 91, 93–94, 98, 110, 164–65, 184, 188, 193–94, 196, 229–30; Sonia Sonchez, 35, 81, 105; Alice Walker, 5, 9, 12–13, 17, 31, 36–37, 39, 68, 85, 87, 89, 97–98, 107, 112, 117, 127, 130, 134, 136–37, 151, 163–64, 167–68, 170, 173–74, 176, 186–88, 193, 214–15, 231, 236; and Margaret Walker, 40, 85. On Black Women and the Women's Movement see Deborah King, "Black Women and Feminism," in *Women's Studies Encyclopedia, I: Views from the Sciences*, ed. Helen Tierney (Westport, Conn.: Greenwood, 1989), 42–44; and "Womanism," "Womanish." Ibid., 389–90.

140. Annette Gilliam, "Essence Women: Barbara Sizemore," *Essence* 5, no. 11 (March 1975): 21. On the worldwide phenomenon of severe economic conditions for black women, see "Statistics on

African Women," *Africa Report* 26, no. 2 (March/April 1981): 65–66; "The Rich — and Not So Rich — Nations of the Third World," *U.S. News and World Report* (March 14, 1983): 52.

141. Alex M. Herman, "A Statistical Portrait of the Black Woman Worker," *The Black Collegian* 8, no. 5 (May/June 1978): 30.

142. Bell Hooks, *Talking Back: Thinking Feminist, Thinking Black* (Boston: South End Press, 1989), 143.

143. Ibid., 143–44.

144. Collins, *Black Feminist Thought*, 98. See also Bell Hooks, *Yearning: Race, Gender and Cultural Politics* (Boston: South End Press, 1990), 11.

145. Calvin C. Hernton, *The Sexual-Mountain and Black Women Writers: Adventures in Sex, Literature, and Real Life* (New York: Anchor Press, 1987), 40–41.

146. "An Emerge Interview: A Race Man and a Scholar" *Emerge* 1, no. 4 (February 1990): 60.

147. Erlene Stetson, "Black Women In and Out of Print," in *Women in Print, I: Opportunities for Women's Studies Research in Language and Literature*, ed. Joan E. Hartman and Ellen Messer-Davidow (New York: Modern Language Association, 1982), 87–88.

148. Manning Marable, *Black American Politics: From the Washington Marches to Jesse Jackson* (London: Verso, 1985), 48–49. For a contemporary perspective on the issue of homophobia among some black Americans see Phillip Brian Harper, "Eloquence and Epitaph: Black Nationalism and the Homophobic Impulse in Responses to the Death of Max Robinson," in *Writing Aids: Gay Literature, Language, and Analysis,* ed. Timothy F. Murphy and Suzanne Poirier (New York: Columbia University Press, 1993), 117–39.

149. Collins, *Black Feminist Thought*, 192–93, 196.

150. Ann Allen Shockley, "The Black Lesbian in American Literature: An Overview," in *Homegirls: A Black Feminist Anthology,* ed. Barbara Smith (New York: Kitchen Table, Women of Color Press, 1983), 90.

151. Lorde, questionnaire to the author, August 12, 1991.

152. Ibid.

153. Audre Lorde letter to the author St. Croix, Virgin Island, August 12, 1991. See also Lorde's autobiography: Audre Lorde, *Zami: A New Spelling of My Name* (Trumansburg, N.Y.: Crossing Press, 1982).

154. Dudley Randall's FBI file was not available for this study. However, under the Freedom of Information Act a request was made by the author for the file of Broadside Press. The FBI responded that: "A search of the central records system at FBI headquarters revealed that Broadside Press was not the subject of a main finite investigation. This organization however appears in four cross references. A cross-reference is defined as a mention of a particular topic, or individual in a file on another individual, organization, event, activity or the like." For Broadside, such "cross-references" included mentions of *The Black Scholar* and *The Militant.* See U.S. Department of Justice, FBI, Washington, D.C., letter to the author, June 15, 1993; Freedom of Information Act no. 349,923, Confidential Memorandum, Domestic Intelligence Divisions no. 100-0-43835 67D, July 26, 1972. See also Ward Churchill and Jim Vander Wall, *The Cointelpro Papers: Documents from the FBI's Secret Wars Against Domestic Dissent* (Boston: South End Press, 1990), 10–92, 108–9, 117–223, 355; Natalie Robins, *Alien Ink: The FBI's War on Freedom of Expression* (New York: William Morrow & Co., 1992), 319–22, 365, 408–48.

155. Kenneth O'Reilly, *Racial Matters: The FBI's Secret File on Black America 1960–1972* (New York: Free Press, 1989), 248, 270, 336.

156. Manning Marable, *Race, Reform and Rebellion: The Second Reconstruction in Black America*, 142–43, 148; Steven F. Lawson, *Running for Freedom Civil Rights and Black Politics in America Since 1941* (New York: McGraw-Hill, 1991), 128, 130, 135; Herb Boyd "Blacks and the Police State: A Case Study of Detroit," *Black Scholar* 12 (January/February 1981): 58–61; Baxter Smith "Somebody's Watching You," *The Black Collegian* 6, no. 5 (May/June 1976): 62–63; The *Interreligious Foundation for Community Organization News* (Winter 1979); Nelson Blackstock, *Cointelpro: The FBI's Secret War on Political Freedom* (New York: A Pathfinder Book, 1975); Doug McAdam, *Political Process and the Development of Black Unsurgency, 1930–1970* (Chicago: University of Chicago Press, 1982), 218–20.

157. *Black World* 24, no. 9 (July 1976) 49; Carole Parks "10th Anniversary Celebration in Detroit: The Broadside Story" *Black World* 25, no. 3 (January 1976): 84–90.

158. Parks, "10th Anniversary Celebration in Detroit," 84–90; Dudley Randall letter to Herbert W. Martin, Detroit, Mich., January 6, 1976, in Martin Papers, Box 3, Folder 29, The Ward M. Canady Center, University of Toledo; *Broadside News*, no. 31 (May 1975): 1; *Broadside News*, no. 32 (August 1975): 1; Broadside Press open letter to all authors, June 30, 1975. Dudley Randall selected 16 poems by 5 men and 8 women poets for his *Broadside Memories: Poets I Have Known* (1975), which was produced to honor the work of Broadside Press on its tenth anniversary. The poets represented in the book were Gwendolyn Brooks, "A Black Wedding Song" and "Friend"; Nikki Giovanni, "Nikki-Rosa"; Etheridge Knight, "The Idea of Ancestry" and "For Black Poets Who Think of Suicide"; Audre Lorde, "For Each of You"; Haki R. Madhubuti, "Blackwoman"; Sonia Sonchez, "Black Magic"; Dudley Randall, "Detroit Renaissance" and "The Profile on the Pillow"; Carolyn M. Rodgers, "For H. W. Fuller"; Jill Witherspoon Boyer, "For Mama"; Jon C. Randall, "Because Is Why"; Linda Brown Bragg, "Going to Africa"; Harold G. Lawrence, "Black Madonna"; and Lucille Clifton, "All of Us Are All of Us." See Randall, *Broadside Memories*, 8, 10, 12, 14, 16, 18 20–21, 23, 54–57, 61.

159. Parks, "10th Anniversary Celebration in Detroit," 84–90; *Michigan Chronicle*, September 20, 1975, C4, September 27, 1975, B8, October 11, 1975, A2, December 6, 1975, A1; *Detroit Free Press,* September 27, 1975, A3–4; *Detroit News*, April 12, 1977, 6–8.

160. Parks, "10th Anniversary Celebration in Detroit," 84–85.

161. Randall, *Broadside Memories*, 25, 33; Dudley Randall, "New Books for Black Readers,"*Publishers Weekly* 204, no. 117 (October 22, 1973): 51.

162. Randall, *Broadside Memories*, 25.

163. Millers, "Endowing the World and Time," 82.

Chapter 4

1. Melba Joyce Boyd, "Out of the Poetry Ghetto: The Life/Art Struggle of Small Black Publishing Houses," *The Black Scholar* 16, no. 4 (July/August 1985): 15.

2. Dudley Randall, *Broadside Memories: Poets I Have Known* (Detroit: Broadside Press, 1975), 28.

3. Ibid., 31.

4. *Black World* magazine was discontinued in April 1976, because it was not a financial success; according to John H. Johnson, he was forced to cease publishing the organ when its circulation "dropped from 100,000 to 15,000." *Black World* was succeeded by *First World*, which Hoyt W. Fuller established at Atlanta, Georgia, in 1979. See *Black World* 25, no. 6 (April 1976); *First World* 2, no. 4 (1980): 42; D.H. Melhem, *Heroism in the New Black Poetry* (Lexington: University Press of Kentucky, 1990), 78; Abby Arthur Johnson and Ronald Maberry Johnson, *Propaganda & Aesthetics: The Literary Politics of Afro-American Magazines in the Twentieth Century* (Amherst: University of Massachusetts Press, 1979), 196–97; John H. Johnson with Lerone Bennett, Jr., *Succeeding Against the Odds: The Autobiography of a Great American Businessman* (New York: Amistad Press, 1989), 289.

5. *Detroit Free Press,* April 11, 1982, 11.

6. *Catalogues of Broadside Press* (Detroit: Broadside Press, 1966–1976). Readers should also be aware that Broadside Press produced twenty-one tape recordings of poetry between 1967–1976; each was priced at $5.00.

7. Dudley Randall interview with author, Detroit, Mich., April 9, 1992.

8. Ahmed A.A. Alhamisi, "On Spiritualism and the Revolutionary Spirit," in *Black Art, Black Culture*, ed. Joe Goncalves (San Francisco, Calif.: Journal of Black Poetry Press, 1972), 25–26.

9. Dempsey J. Travis, "Black Business: Obstacles to Their Success," *The Black Scholar* 4, no. 4 (January 1973): 19.

10. "Black Books Bulletin Interviews Dudley Randall," *Black Books Bulletin* 1 (Winter 1972): 25.

11. Sheila Smith-Hobson, "Black Book Publishing: Protest, Pride and Little Profit," *Black Enterprise* 8, no. 10 (May 1978): 39. Ms. Hobson points out the tragic fact that during the seventies

on the average: "Costs to publish one title are estimated at $8,000; 1,000 books are usually printed of one title." But few black publishers could cover such costs. Naomi Long Madgett, publisher of Lotus Press, notes the predominant situation for black publishers of poetry: "If a book of poems sells 800 copies that is considered good." See *Detroit News,* January 2, 1985, 12-A. On the historical problems of black publishers see Donald Joyce, *Gatekeepers of Black Culture: Black-Owned Book Publishing in the United States, 1817–1981* (Westport, Conn.: Greenwood, 1983).

12. Dudley Randall, "Black Publisher, Black Writer: An Answer," *Black World* 26, no. 5 (March 1975): 33–34.

13. Bradford Chambers, "Why Minority Publishing?" *Publishers Weekly* 199, no. 11 (March 15, 1971): 54.

14. Leonard Kniffel, "Poet in Action," *Monthly Detroit* 7, no. 6 (June 1984): 161. Even on the issue of contracts many black publishers could only plan to offer effective documents sometime in the future of their operations. Randall offered this reflection on the issue: "Because of a lack of funds, they [black publishers] can't afford to pay advances. In my own contracts, there is no mention of advances." In fact, Randall's contracts with one of his major writers, Haki R. Madhubuti, were an oral agreement between the two writers that Broadside Press would reprint his *Think Black!* and publish his second book, *Black Pride*; for the latter of which Randall wrote an "Introduction." See R. Baxter Miller, "Endowing the World and Time: The Life and Work of Dudley Randall," in *Black American Poets Between Worlds, 1940–1960,* ed. R. Baxter Miller (Knoxville: University of Tennessee Press, 1986), 81–82; Randall, "Black Publisher, Black Writer: An Answer," 34. See also the *Detroit Free Press,* September 27, 1975, A4.

15. *Newsweek* 81, no. I (January 1973): 20–21, 88 (October 11, 1976): 37–38.

16. Lloyd Hogan, *Principles of Black Political Economy* (Boston: Routledge & Kegan Paul, 1984), 157.

17. Alphonso Pinkney, *The Myth of Black Progress* (New York: Cambridge University Press, 1984), 102. The crisis in income distribution was especially extreme for black female-headed households during this period. In 1976, the median income of such families was estimated at $5,069. However, the Bureau of Labor Statistics recommended a minimum budget of at least $9,838 as a "low standard of living budget for a family of four." See Alex M. Herman, "A Statistical Portrait of the Black Woman Worker," *The Black Collegian* 8, no. 5 (May/June 1978): 30.

18. Hogan, *Principles of Black Political Economy,* 158. A 1964 study indicated that black families in the United States spent 11 percent less on reading materials and 50 percent less on education than whites, in terms of the allocation of disposable income among urban families. But in order to "cope" with the extra stressful conditions of living in America, black families in 1964 spent 29.4 percent more on tobacco, 25 percent more on alcoholic beverages, 22.5 percent more on clothing, and 36 percent more on personal care, than did white families. Yet, the data suggest that they also spent 28.4 percent less than whites on medical care. (Perhaps many blacks of the period were fearful about the quality and or expense of such care — unless they were very ill to begin with!) See Frank G. Davis, *The Economics of Black Community Development* (Chicago: Markham Publishing Co., 1972), 187.

19. "The State of Black America 1977," *The Black Scholar* 9, no. 1 (September 1977): 3, 28. Some readers may find it shocking, but the United States also contained 17,770,000 whites in 1975, who also existed "below the official poverty level" in this country.

20. George E. Kent, *A Life of Gwendolyn Brooks* (Lexington: University Press of Kentucky, 1990), 192.

21. Ibid., 225.

22. Randall, *Broadside Memories,* 16. See also Miller's "Endowing the Word of Time," 82.

23. Randall, *Broadside Memories,* 28.

24. Kniffel, "Poet in Motion," 160.

25. "Black Books Bulletin Interviews Dudley Randall," 26.

26. Chambers, "Why Minority Publishing?" 45.

27. *Detroit Free Press,* September 27, 1975, A4.

28. Kniffel, "Poet in Motion," 161.

29. *Detroit Free Press,* April 11, 1982, 11.

30. Ibid.; Melhem, *Heroism in the New Black Poetry,* 41.

31. E.J. Josey and Ann Allen Shockley, eds., *Handbook of Black Librarianship* (Littleton, Col.:

Libraries Unlimited, 1977), 163; *Who's Who Among Black Americans,* 1977–1978 (Northbrook, Ill.: Who's Who Among Black Americans, 1977), 738.

32. *Directory of Active Michigan Poets* (Detroit: The Poetry Society of Michigan, 1982), 40; *Detroit News,* April 12, 1977, B6.

33. Chester M. Hedgepath, Jr., *Twentieth Century African-American Writers and Artists* (Chicago: American Library Association, 1991), 250; *Who's Who Among Black Americans,* 1985, 693.

34. Sterling D. Plumpp, *Clinton* (Detroit: Broadside Press, 1976).

35. Jerry W. Ward, Jr., "Sterling D. Plumpp: A Son of the Blues," *The Southern Quarterly: A Journal of the Arts in the South* 29, no. 3 (Spring 1991), 30–31.

36. Chester J. Fontenat, Review of *Clinton, Black American Literature Forum* 11, no. 3 (Fall 1977): 119.

37. Jerry W. Ward, Jr., Review of *Clinton, Obsidian* 5, nos. 1 & 2 (Spring/Summer 1979): 134.

38. *The Black Position,* no. 4 (1976): 1–2; Len Fulton, ed., *Directory of Little Magazines and Small Presses, 1977* (Paradise, Calif.: Dustbook, 1977), 40.

39. Ibid., 1–36.

40. *The Black Scholar* 7, no. 7 (April 1976): 5–6; *The Black Scholar* 8, no. 2 (October 1976): 32. A general survey of the *Black Scholar* for the period 1972–1976, reveals that Broadside Press could not afford to invest advertisement funds in the journal on a monthly, or even quarterly basis.

41. Dudley Randall to Herbert W. Martin, January 6, 1976, Detroit, Mich. See H.W. Martin Papers, Box 3, Folder no. 29, 1972–83, University of Toledo.

42. Quincy Troupe, "Introduction," in *Celebrations: A New Anthology of Black American Poetry,* ed. Arnold Adoff (Chicago: Follett Publishing Co., 1977), xv.

43. See *Ebony* 32 (August 1977): 30; James D. Tyms, *Spiritual (Religious) Values in the Black Poet* (Washington, D.C.: University Press of America, 1977), 107; Phyllis R. Klotman, *Another Man Gone: The Black Runner in Contemporary Afro-American Literature* (Port Washington, N.Y.: Kennikat Press, 1977), 6; Adoff, *Celebrations: A New Anthology of Black American Poetry,* 8–10, 60–61, 109, 150, 200, 221–23; Joan Cannady, ed., *Black Images in American Literature* (Rochelle Park, N.J.: Hayden Book Co., 1977), 134; Conrad Hilberry, Herbert Scott and James Tipton, eds., *The Third Coast: Contemporary Michigan Poetry* (Detroit: Wayne State University Press, 1976), 191–97; X.J. Kennedy, ed., *An Introduction to Poetry* (Boston: Little, Brown and Co., 1978), 382–83; Charles H. Rowell, "In Conversation with Dudley Randall," *Obsidian* 2 (Spring 1976): 32–44; Melba Joyce Boyd, *Cat Eyes and Dead Wood* (Highland Park, Mich.: Fallen Angel Press, 1978), 4–5. Randall's published poems during this period included a wide-range of his earlier work, such as "Ballad of Birmingham," "Black Magic," "Black Berry Sweet," "Booker T. and W.E.B.," "After the Killing," "Frederick Douglass and the Slave Breaker," "The Idiot," "George," "Informer," "Green Apples," "Memorial Wreath," "Roses and Revolution," and "The Southern Road," among others.

44. Alex Poinsett, "Motor City Makes a Comeback," *Ebony* 33, no. 6, (April 1978): 36.

45. Joe T. Darden, Richard C. Hill, June Thomas, and Richard Thomas, *Detroit: Race and Uneven Development* (Philadelphia, Pa.: Temple University Press, 1987), 76.

46. Mark E. Neithercut, *Detroit Twenty Years After: A Statistical Profile of the Detroit Area Since 1967* (Detroit: Center for Urban Studies, Wayne State University, 1987), 8; Melvin G. Holli, "Detroit Today: Locked Into the Past," *The Midwest Quarterly* 19 (Spring 1978): 251.

47. Donald C. Bacon, "A Bitter New Generation of Jobless Young Blacks," *U.S. News and World Report,*" 71, no. 13 (September 27, 1976): 64.

48. Darden, Hill, J. Thomas, and R. Thomas, *Detroit: Race and Uneven Development,* 216. On Coleman Young's reelection in 1977 as mayor of Detroit, see Rich, *Coleman Young and Detroit Politics,* 106–12.

49. *Black Enterprise* 8, no. 11 (June 1978): 125, 129.

50. Claude L. Matthews, "Detroit's WGPR: Struggling Start for Black TV," *Black Enterprise* 7, no. 4 (November 1976): 63–65. In 1978, Greater Detroit was served by 10 television stations, which reached an audience of 848,300 television households (99 percent) in southeastern Michigan. See *Information Please Almanac: Atlas and Yearbook 1979* (New York: Information Please Publishing, 1978), 706.

51. Wolseley, *The Black Press, U.S.A.,* 20–23, 398–400; Jannette L. Dates, "Print News," in *Split Image: African Americans in the Mass Media,* ed. Jannette L. Dates and William Barlow (Washington, D.C.: Howard University Press, 1990), 358–60, 366–67, 377–85.

52. Harry A. Ploski and James Williams, eds., *Reference Library of Black America*, V (New York: Afro-American Press, 1990), 1256.

53. Henry G. LaBrie, III, *A Survey of Black Newspapers in America* (Kennebunkport, Maine: Merser House Press, 1979), 13. But of the over 4 million circulation figures for the early 1970s, LaBrie argues that "only 517,000 is confirmed to be audited! Thus, the black press is largely a 'free' newspaper which is home-delivered or available in supermarkets and drug stores. It relies more than ever on advertising but continues to highlight news which the larger establishment dailies ignore." In 1973, 2,500 people were employed by black newspapers, including 250 whites. See Henry G. LaBrie, III, "The Future of the Black Press: A Silent Crusade," *Negro History Bulletin* 36, no. 8 (December 1973): 166, 169. See also Clint C. Wilson II, *Black Journalists in Paradox: Historical Perspectives and Current Dilemmas* (Westport, Conn.: Greenwood, 1991), 85–89. While the black newspaper fought to survive in the 1970s, African-Americans were also interested in increasing their numbers at historically white-owned newspapers and other media outlets in the United States. However, several studies of the period found a high level of stubborn resistance to black integration of the white press. A 1974 report by the American Society of Newspaper Editors noted that blacks held only 1 percent of the professional newsroom positions in this country. By 1978, this figure had increased to 4 percent; however, there were still "no minority employees at two-thirds" of U.S. newspapers; and only about 850 black journalists worked on daily papers. As late as 1979, the *Detroit Free Press* employed 155 journalists, but only 10 (6.4 percent) of this total were minorities. See Ernest C. Hynds, *American Newspapers in the 1970s* (New York: Hastings House Publishers, 1975), 151; *New York Times*, April 12, 1978, 42; Gerald R. Gill, *Meanness Mania: The Changed Mood* (Washington, D.C.: Howard University Press, 1980), 33.

54. Johnson and Johnson, *Propaganda and Aesthetics: The Literary Politics of Afro-American Magazines in the Twentieth Century*, 196. See also Roland E. Wolseley, *The Black Press, U. S. A.* (Ames: Iowa State University Press, 1990), 170.

55. Sheila Smith-Hobson, "Black Book Publishing: Protest, Pride and Little Profit," *Black Enterprise* 8, no. 10 (May 1978): 39, 47.

56. Ibid., 39.

57. "Profile of Black Businessmen in Detroit in 1966," 1.

58. On this period see also Berkeley G. Burrell, "Black Business and the Crime of Uneconomic Communities," in *Crime and Its Impact on the Black Community*, ed. Lawrence E. Gary and Lee P. Brown (Washington, D.C.: Institute for Urban Affairs Howard University 1975), 31–37; Richard Simmons, Jr., "The Black Business Community: Survival or Failure," *Journal of Afro-American Issues* 3, nos. 3 & 4 (Summer/Fall 1975): 442–53.

59. Frenchy Jolen Hodges, "Dudley Randall and the Broadside Press," (M.A. thesis, Atlanta University, 1974), 51.

60. Randall, "Black Publisher, Black Writer: An Answer," 33–34.

61. Burrell, "Black Business and the Crime of Uneconomic Communities," 38.

62. Donald Franklin Joyce, *Gatekeepers of Black Culture: Black-Owned Book Publishing in the United States, 1817–1981* (Westport; Conn.: Greenwood, 1983), 76, 84–85, 87, 89, 94–95, 107, 131–34, 176–77, 181–82, 189, 195–97, 208; Donald Franklin Joyce, *Black Book Publishers in the United States: A Historical Dictionary of the Presses, 1817–1990* (Westport, Conn.: Greenwood, 1991), 32–36, 51–55, 89–92, 112–16, 218–22; Task Force on Alternatives in Print, *Alternatives in Print, 1973–74: The Annual Catalog of Social Change Publications* (San Francisco, Calif.: Glide Publications, 1973), 43, 46, 82–83, 90–91, 159, 175, 186–87, 305–6; Dudley Randall, ed., *The Black Poet: A New Anthology* (New York: Bantam Books, 1971), 335–37; Ann Allen Shockley and Sue P. Chandler, *Living Black American Authors: A Biographical Directory* (New York: R.R. Bowker Co., 1973), 179–80; "Black and White Book Publishing," *Negro History Bulletin* 34, no. 8 (December 1971): 172–73; *Black Academy Review* 2, no. 3 (Fall 1971): 68–72; *Black World* 19, no. 8 (June 1970): 50; *The Black Scholar* 6, no. 7 (April 1975): 42; *The Black Scholar* 7, no. 7 (April 1976): 8, 16, 47; *The Black Scholar* 8, no. 3 (December 1976): 65; *The Black Scholar* 8, no. 5 (March 1977):53; *The Black Scholar* 10, no. 2 (October 1978): 39, 45; *The Black Scholar* II, no. 1 (September/October 1979): 54, 62; "Black Book Publishers," *Black Enterprise* 3, no. 2 (September 1972): 39–42.

63. According to John H. Johnson, the chief executive officer of Johnson Publishing Company, by 1985: "The company grossed $154,860,000 ... and was no. 1 for the second straight year on the

Black Enterprise list of the top one hundred Black businesses." See John H. Johnson, with Lerone Bennett, Jr., *Succeeding Against the Odds: The Autobiography of a Great American Businessman* (New York: Amistad Press 1989) 353; Wolseley, *The Black Press, U.S.A.*, 88; Joyce, *Black Book Publishers in the United States*, 138.

64. Bigsby, *The Second Black Renaissance: Essays in Black Literature*, 50.

65. Smith-Hobson, "Black Book Publishing: Protest, Pride and Little Profit," 39.

66. Shockley and Chandler, *Living Black American Authors*, 179–80, list 17 active black publishers for 1973 while Carole Parks, *Black World* 24, no. 7, (March 1975): 72–79 lists 21 publishers for that year.

67. Benjamin M. Compaine, Christopher H. Sterling, Thomas Guback and J. Kendrick Noble, Jr., *Who Owns the Media?: Concentration of Ownership in the Mass Communication Industry* (White Plains, N.Y.: Knowledge Industry Publications, 1982), 105.

68. Boyd, "Out of the Poetry Ghetto: The Life/Art Struggle of Small Black Publishing Houses," 12–24; Smith-Hobsons "Black Book Publishing: Protests Pride and Little Profit," 39–40, 42, 44, 47; Wilson, *Black Journalists in Paradox,* 63.

In spite of the hardships at home in Detroit, Dudley Randall and Broadside sponsored the "Broadside Press Annual Poetry Awards" for 1975–76, with a yearly prize of $100.00 "to a poet who was published for the first time in *Black World* and to a poet who previously had published in the magazine." See *Black World* 25, no. 3, (January 1976): 50. Of course, by April 1976, *Black World* was no longer published by Johnson Publishing Company. See Robert L. Harris, Jr., national committee of concern over the demise of *Black World*, "Black World Magazine Discontinued," *The Black Scholar* 7, no. 7 (April 1976): 30.

69. Randall, *Broadside Memories*, 16; Dudley Randall, "New Books for Black Readers," *Publishers Weekly* 204, no. 17 (October 22, 1973): 51.

70. Miller, "'Endowing the World and Time': The Life and Work of Dudley Randall."

71. *Catalogues of Third World Press* (Chicago, Ill.: Third World Press, 1989), 1.

72. *Catalogues of Third World Press* (Chicago, Ill.: Third World Press, 1975), 16. See also Joyce, *Gatekeepers of Black Culture: Black-Owned Book Publishing in the United States*, 88.

73. Smith-Hobson, "Black Book Publishing," 40. See also Marlene Mosher, *New Directions from Don L. Lee* (Hicksville, N.Y.: Exposition Press, 1975), 106.

74. Smith-Hobson, "Black Book Publishing: Protest, Pride and Little Profit," 40.

75. Houston A. Baker, Jr., *Afro-American Poetics: Revisions of Harlem and the Black Aesthetic* (Madison: University of Wisconsin Press, 1988), 161.

76. Joyce, *Black Book Publishers in the United States: A Historical Dictionary of the Presses, 1817–1990*, 208; *Catalogues of Third World Press*, 1968–1979.

77. Carole A. Parks, ed., *Nommo: A Literary Legacy of Black Chicago (1967–1987)* (Chicago, Ill.: The Organization of Black American Culture Writers' Workshop, 1987), 337–42.

78. See *Black Books Bulletin* 1, no. 1 (Fall 1971): 33, 56. The Broadside Press authors who published two or more publications with Third World Press during the 1960s and 1970s were Johari Amini, 5; Amiri Baraka, 3; Keorapetse Kgositsile, 2; Don L. Lee, 2; Sterling D. Plumpp, 4; Dudley Randall, 2; and Carolyn Rodgers, 3. See *Catalogues of Broadside Press, 1968–1975*; *Catalogues of Third World Press, 1968–1979*.

79. Michigan Association for Media in Education, *Michigan Authors* (Ann Arbor: Michigan Association for Media in Education, 1980), 217; *Who's Who Among Black Americans,* 1988.

80. Randall, *Broadside Memories*, 36.

81. Naomi Long Madgett, "Sunny," (Detroit: Broadside Press, 1967). As an active critic during the Black Arts Movement, Dudley Randall also reviewed books written by Naomi Long Madgett. See his critique of *Pink Ladies in the Afternoon* in *Black World* 23, no. 11 (September 1974): 52, 84–85.

82. Joyce, *Black Book Publishers in the United States,* 141; Mark Puls, "For the Patient Reader, Detroit Poet's Imagination, Sensitivity Stir the Soul," *Detroit News,* September 30, 1993.

83. Donald Franklin Joyce, "Reflecting on the Changing Publishing Objectives of Secular Black Book Publishers, 1900–1986," in *Reading in America: Literature and Social History*, ed. Cathy N. Davidson (Baltimore: Johns Hopkins University Press, 1989), 234–35.

84. Puls, "For the Patient Reader."

85. *Catalogues of Lotus Press,* 1988, 1990.

86. Shockley and Chandler, *Living Black American Writers*, 10, 68, 70, 84, 86, 92, 94, 100, 157; James A. Page, compiler, *Selected Black American Authors: An Illustrated Bio-Bibliography* (Boston: G.K. Hall & Co., 1977), 13, 150, 158, 161, 182–83, 210, 213–14, 228–29, 262; Pamela Cobb (Baraka Sele), letter to the author, December 6, 1993, San Francisco, Calif.; James Vinson and D.L. Kirkpatrick, eds., *Contemporary Poets* (New York: St. Martin's Press, 1985), 439; *Who's Who Among Black Americans*, 1988, 412; Leaonead Pack Bailey, *Broadside Authors and Artists: An Illustrated Biographical Directory* (Detroit: Broadside Press, 1974), 29.

87. James Vinson, ed., *Contemporary Poets* (London: Macmillan, 1980), 435–37; *Catalogues of Lotus Press*, 1975, 1979; Toi Derricotte, *The Empress of the Death House* (Detroit: Lotus Press, 1978), 53; Toi Derricotte, letter to the author, December 7, 1993, Potomac, Maryland; Pamela Cobb (Baraka Sele), telephone interview with the author, December 21, 1993, San Francisco, Calif.; Louie Crew, ed., *The Gay Academia*, (Palm Springs, Calif.: ETC Publications, 1978, viii–ix; Pamela Cobb (Baraka Sele), letter to the author; Kiarri T-H. Cheatwood, letter to the author, December 8, 1993, Richmond, Virginia, *Valley of the Anointers* (Detroit: Lotus Press, 1979), 75; *Catalogues of Lotus Press*, 1988, 1990, 1991; Shockley and Chandler, *Living Black American Authors*, 8, 79, 104, 106; Page, *Selected Black American Authors*, 182–83, 187–88, 195–96; Paulette Childress White, *The Watermelon Dress* (Detroit: Lotus Press, 1984), 63; Naomi Long Madgett, ed., *Adam of Ife: Black Women in Praise of Black Men* (Detroit: Lotus Press, 1992), 224, 230; David L. Rice, letter to the author, December 3, 1993, Lincoln, Neb.; *Omaha (Neb.) World Herald*, March 23, 1993, 1, 5.

88. Naomi Long Madgett, "A Short History of Lotus Press, 1972–1992," in *Lotus Press Newsletter* (Detroit: Lotus Press, 1992), 2.

89. *Catalogues of Lotus Press*, 1972–1979.

90. See Julius E. Thompson, "An Afternoon with Naomi Long Madgett," *Jackson (Miss.) Advocate*, November 14, 1991, 148.

91. Bailey, *Broadside Authors and Artists*, 31–33, 41–42, 47–48, 66, 97–98, 120.

92. Ibid.

93. Quincy Troupe, "Introduction," in *A New Anthology of Black American Poetry*, ed. Arnold Adoff (Chicago, Ill.: Follett Publishing Co., 1977), xi, xiv; Ralph "Cheo" Thurman, "A Chat with Dr. Margaret Walker Alexander," *Jackson Advocate*, August 31, 1978, 8; George E. Kent, "Notes on the 1974 Black Literary Scene," *Phylon* 36, no. 2 (June 1975): 195; James D. Tyms, "The Black Poet and a Sense of Self—The Praise of Famous Men," *The Journal of Religious Thought* 32, no. I (Spring/Summer 1975): 30–31; Marvin Holdt "James A. Emanuel: Black Man Abroad," *Black American Literature Forum* 13, no. 3 (Fall 1979): 85; Sterling Stuckey, quoted in Stephen E. Henderson, "Sterling A. Brown: Poet, & Scholar Is Honored as Great American Original," *Ebony* 31, no. 12 (October 1976): 134; Henry Louis Gates, quoted in "Sterling Brown, 1901–1989," in *Black Literary Criticism*, ed. James P. Draper (Detroit: Gale Research Co., 1922), 282; Kenneth Rexroth, *American Poetry in the Twentieth Century* (New York: Seabury Press, 1973), 155–56; Hoyt W. Fuller, "Comment," noted in Beth Brown, Review of Beckonings, *The Black Scholar* 15, no. 6 (November/December 1984): 63; George E. Kent, "Struggle for the Image: Selected Books by or About Blacks During 1971," *Phylon* 33, no. 4 (Winter 1972): 316; Theodore R. Hudson, Review "When I Knew the Power of My Black Hand" by Lance Jeffers, *CLA Journal* 18, no. 1 (September 1974): 133, 135; Richard K. Barksdale, "Margaret Danner and the African Connection," in *Praise Song of Survival: Lectures and Essays, 1957–89* (Urbana: University of Illinois Press, 1992) 128–29; Helen Houston, "Margaret Danner," quoting June M. Aldridge from a *Dictionary of Literary Biography*, vol. 42, 1985, in *Notable Black American Women* ed. Jessie Carney Smith (Detroit: Gale Research Co., 1922), 249–50.

94. Bailey, *Broadside Authors and Artists*, 31–33, 41, 42, 47–48, 66, 97–98; Dudley Randall and Margaret Burroughs, eds., *For Malcolm X* (Detroit: Broadside Press, 1967), 3, 6–7, 32–33; Dudley Randall, ed., *Black Poetry* (Detroit: Broadside Press, 1969), 16–18, 20–26, 28; Gwendolyn Brooks, ed., *A Broadside Treasury* (Detroit: Broadside Press, 1971), 33–38, 39–42, 44–47, 72, 121–28, 150–54, 167.

95. Gloria Wade-Gayles, "Sonia Sanchez," in *Notable Black American Women*, ed. Jessie Carney Smith (Detroit: Gale Research Co., 1922) 976.

96. Randall, "New Books for Black Readers," 51. Four other younger Broadside poets were also major voices of the Black Arts Movement. They were Clarence Major, Audre Lorde, Keorapetse Kgositsile and Marvin X. All four poets published a significant collection of poetry with Broadside during this era. In addition, Major was one of the most productive writers, and edited a highly regarded anthology, *The New Black Poetry* (1969). Lorde was perhaps the most noted gay writer among

black women poets of the period. Kgositsile was without doubt the most famous younger African writer in exile, who lived in the United States during the 1960s and 1970s. Finally, Marvin X emerged during this period as a leading proponent of a pro–Muslim (Nation of Islam) philosophy and way of life among black poets. See Clarence Major, *The Cotton Club: New Poems* (Detroit: Broadside Press, 1972); "Clarence Major," in Draper, *Black Literary Criticism*, II, 1323–39; Audre Lorde, *From a Land Where Other People Live* (Detroit: Broadside Press, 1973); Anna Wilson, "Audre Lorde and the African Tradition: When the Family Is Not Enough," in *New Lesbian Criticism: Literary and Cultural Readings*, ed. Sally Munt (New York: Columbia University Press, 1922), 75–93; Joan Martin, "The Unicorn Is Black: Audre Lorde in Retrospect," in *Black Women Writers (1950–1980): A Critical Evaluation*, ed. Mari Evans (New York: Anchor Press/Doubleday, 1984), 277–91; Keorapetse Kgositsile, *Spirits Unchained* (Detroit: Broadside Press, 1969); O.R. Dathorne, *The Black Mind: A History of African Literature* (Minneapolis: University of Minneapolis Press, 1974) 304–5; Marvin X, *Black Man Listen: Poems and Proverbs* (Detroit: Broadside Press, 1969); Lorenzo Thomas, "Marvin X (Marvin E. Jackmon, Nazzam Al Fitnah Muhajir El Muhajir)," in *Afro-American Writers After 1955: Dramatists and Prose Writers*, ed. T.M. Davis and T. Harris (Detroit: Gale Research Co., 1985), 177–84.

97. Zala Chandler, "Voices Beyond the Veil: An Interview of Toni Cade Bambara and Sonia Sanchez, in *Wild Women in the Whirlwind: Afro-American Culture and the Contemporary Literary Renaissance*, ed. Joanne M. Braxton and Andree Nicola McLaughlin (New Brunswick, N.J.: Rutgers University Press, 1990), 357.

98. Eight other major Broadside authors were also born in one of the former eleven states of the Confederacy: Addison Gayle, Jr. (Newport News, Va., on June 2, 1932); Naomi Long Madgett (Norfolk, Va., on July 5, 1923); Clarence Major (Atlanta, Ga., on December 31, 1936); Arthur Pfister (New Orleans, La., on September 20, 1949); Ishmael Reed (Chattanooga, Tenn., on February 22, 1938); Askia Muhammad Toure (Raleigh, N.C., on October 13, 1938; Alice Walker (Eaton, Ga., on February 9, 1944); and Margaret Walker (Birmingham, Ala., on July 7, 1915). See Bailey *Broadside Authors and Artists*, 54, 83, 85, 94, 100, 118–20; M. Thomas Inge, "Contemporary Southern Black Writers: A Checklist," *Mississippi Quarterly: The Journal of Southern Culture* 31, no. 2 (Spring 1978): 188–90; Julian Mason, "Black Writers of the South," *Mississippi Quarterly: The Journal of Southern Culture* 31, no. 2 (Spring 1978): 169–83.

99. Virginia C. Fowler, *Nikki Giovanni* (New York: Twayne Publishers, 1922), xiii, 2.

100. "Haki R. Madhubuti," in *Black Literary Criticism*, II, 1306.

101. "Etheridge Knight," in *Black Literary Criticism*, II, 1210.

102. Melhem, "Sonia Sanchez: The Will and the Spirit," in *Heroism in the New Black Poetry*, 133.

103. Bailey, *Broadside Authors and Artists*, 55, 72, 75, 105; George Barlow, "Etheridge Knight," in *The Before Columbus Foundation Poetry Anthology: Selections from the American Book Awards, 1980–1990*, ed. J.J. Phillips, I. Reed, G. Strods and S. Wang, (New York: W.W. Norton & Co., 1992), 171.

104. "Etheridge Knight," in *The New Cavalcade: African American Writing from 1760 to the Present* (Washington, D.C.: Howard University Press, 1991), II: 384; Bailey, *Broadside Authors and Artists*, 72, 74.

105. Barlow, "Etheridge Knight," 171; "Etheridge Knight," in *The New Cavalcade* II, 384.

106. Carolyn Mitchell, "Nikki Giovanni," in *Black Women in America: An Historical Encyclopedia*, ed. Darlene Clark Hine, Elsa Barkley Brown, and Rosalyn Terborg-Penn (Brooklyn, N.Y.: Carlson Publishers, 1993), I: A–L, 488; John Oliver Killens, "The Half Ain't Never Been Told," in *Contemporary Authors: Autobiography Series*, II, ed. Adele Sarkissian (Detroit: Gale Research Co., 1985), 296.

107. Theodore R. Hudson, "Don Luther Lee in *Contemporary Poets*, Vinson and Kirkpatrick, 484; Parks, *Nommo: A Literary Legacy of Black Chicago*, 340; Randall, *Broadside Memories*, 16; Melhem, "Haki R. Madhubti/Don L. Lee: Prescriptive Revolution," in *Heroism in the New Black Poetry*, 86, 120.

108. Bailey, *Broadside Authors and Artists*, 72.

109. "Etheridge Knight," in *Black Literary Criticism*, II: 1210; "Etheridge Knight," in *Contemporary Authors*, vol. 23 (1988): 225.

110. "Etheridge Knight," in *The New Cavalcade*, II: 384.

111. Melhem, "Sonia Sanchez: The Will and the Spirit," 88, 133; Joanne V. Gabbin, "Sonia Sanchez: A Soft Reflection of Strength," *The Zora Neale Hurston Forum* 1, no. 2 (Spring 1987): 54.

While living in Chicago in 1975–77, Sanchez, along with Haki R. Madhubuti, "established a weekly writers' group that gave public readings." Gabbin, "Sonia Sanchez," 55. "Sonia Sanchez," in *Black Literary Criticism*, 1647.

112. Brooks, *A Broadside Treasury*, 25, 27, 48–69, 73–120, 136–46, 155; Randall and Burroughs, *For Malcolm X*, 21, 38–39, 43, 55, 64, 73–74; Brooks, *Jump Bad*, 30–46; Randall, *Black Poetry*, 29–32, 37–38, 41–45, 48.

113. Hodges, "Dudley Randall and the Broadside Press," 95–98; *Catalogues of Broadside Press, 1967–1979*. Critic Deborah A. Stanley observes that: "In a *Mademoiselle* article, Sheila Weller noted that Black Judgement sold six thousand copies in three months, making that volume five to six times more sellable than the average." See Deborah A. Stanley, "Nikki Giovanni," in *Contemporary Authors: A Bio-Bibliographical Guide to Current Writers in Fiction, General Non-Fiction, Poetry, Journalism, Drama, Motion Pictures, Television, and Other Fields*, ed. Susan M. Trosky, New Revision Series, vol. 41 (Detroit: Gale Research Co., 1994), 180. She also quotes Mozella G. Mitchell from her article on Giovanni in *Dictionary of Literary Biography*, "that Giovanni's poems of that period brought her prominence as one of the three leading figures of the new black poetry between 1986 and 1971."

114. *Catalogues of Broadside Press, 1967–1979*.

115. Hodges, "Dudley Randall and the Broadside Press," 51; Randall, *Broadside Memories*, 27–28, 31; Boyd, "Out of the Poverty Ghetto: The Life/Art Struggle of Small Black Publishing Houses," 13–14. Nikki Giovanni was the most success Broadside author on the college lecture tour circuit during the Black Arts Movement. Journalist M. Cordell Thompson noted in 1972 that: "Nikki says she does not feel embarrassed about the $1000 to $1500 she negotiates for a college lecture. She also offers no apologies for the fact that she has a business manager and press agent to help handle the money side of her creative life. 'I can't do it so I leave it to people who have the skills to do it, and I respect that,' she says. 'I want to be reasonably comfortable and I do it by making the lectures. I am a poet, so I write poetry, I read poetry. I only make about 12 cents from every book of mine sold.'" See M. Cordell Thompson, "Nikki Giovanni: Black Rebel with Power in Poetry," *Jet* 42, no. 9 (May 25, 1972): 22.

116. Johnson and Johnson, *Propaganda and Aesthetics*, 183–4; Nikki Giovanni, ed. *Night Comes Softly* (New York: Niktom Ltd., 1970), 88; Frederick D. Murphy, "Nikki," *Encore American & Worldwide News* 4, no. 9 (May 5, 1975): 34; *Black Books Bulletin* 2, nos. 3–4 (Winter 1974): 2; *The Black Scholar* 10, nos. 6–7 (March/April 1979): 1; *Black Collegian* 13, no. 4, (February/March 1983): 126, 128; Mosher, *New Directions from Don L. Lee*, (Hicksville, N.Y.: Exposition Press, 1975), 42, 46, 64–92, 106.

117. LeRoi Jones and Larry Neal, eds., *Black Fire: An Anthology of Afro-American Writing* (New York: William Morrow & Co., 1968), 250–55; Ahmed Alhamisi and Kofi Wangara, eds., *Black Arts: An Anthology of Black Creations* (Detroit: Black Arts Publications, 1969) 15–16, 95–98, 117–18, 131–33; Ted Wilentz and Tom Weatherly, eds., *Natural Process: An Anthology of New Black Poetry* (New York: Hill and Wang, 1970), 21–31, 124–33; Arnold Adoff, ed., *Black Out Loud: An Anthology of Modern Poems by Black Americans* (New York: Macmillan, 1970), 2, 9, 22, 29, 30, 32, 42, 56, 58; Adam David Miller, ed., *Dices or Black Bones: Black Voices of the Seventies* (Boston: Houghton Mifflin Co., 1970), 70–79; Darwin T. Turner, ed., *Black American Literature: Essays, Poetry, Fiction, Drama* (New York: Charles E. Merrill, 1970), 279–82; June Jordan, ed., *Soulscript: Afro-American Poetry* (Garden City, N.Y.: Zenith Books/Doubleday, 1970), 22, 92–94, 104; Clarence Major, ed., *The New Black Poetry* (New York: International Publishers, 1970), 53–54, 80–83, 114; Orde Coombs, ed., *We Speak as Liberators: Young Black Poets* (New York: Dodd, Mead & Co., 1970), 51–55, 96–98, 158–59; Frances S. Freedman, ed., *The Black American Experience: A New Anthology of Black Literature* (New York: Bantam, 1970), 230–31; Alan Lomax and Raoul Abdul, eds., *3000 Years of Black Poetry: An Anthology* (New York: Dodd Mead & Co., 1970), 256–57; Nick Aaron Ford, ed., *Black Insights: Significant Literature by Black Americans, 1760 to the Present* (Waltham, Mass.: Ginn and Co., 1971), 358–60; Alma Murray and Robert Thomas, eds., *Major Black Writers* (New York: Scholastic Book Services, 1971), 189, 198–99, 203; Randall, *The Black Poets*, 203–10, 231–42, 195–309, 318–29; Arthur P. Davis and Saunders Redding, eds., *Cavalcade: Negro American Writing from 1760 to the Present* (Boston: Houghton Mifflin Co., 1971), 777–78, 811–19; Gloria M. Simmons, Helene D. Hutchinson, and Henry E. Simmons, eds., *Black Culture: Reading and Writing Black* (New York: Holt, Rinehart and Winston, 1972), 34–35, 174, 195, 199, 260; Woodie King, ed., *Black Spirits: A Festival of New Black Poets in America* (New York: Vintage Books/Random House, 1972) 74–80, 114–19, 186–92; Paul Breman, ed., *You Better Believe It: Black Verse in English* (Baltimore, Md.: Penguin Books, 1973), 305–9,

364–68, 449–59, 474–79; Quincy Troupe and Rainer Schulte, eds., *Giant Talk: An Anthology of Third World Writings* (New York: Vintage Books/Random House, 1975), 206, 286–87, 206–8, 427–28, 439–40; Arnold Adoff, ed., *Celebrations: A New Anthology of Black American Poetry* (Chicago: Follet Publishing Co., 1997), 2, 22–23, 26–27, 32–35, 50, 77–78, 98–99, 119–20, 126–28, 132, 146, 148–49, 180, 223–24, 244.

118. Giovanni's "My Poem," appeared in four anthologies of this sample; followed by three times for "For Saundra," two times each for "The Time Import of Present Dialogue: Black vs. Negro," and "Poem (No Name no. 2)," and 19 single poems were also published. Etheridge Knight's poems, "It Was a Funky Deal" and "For Black Poets Who Think of Suicide," were published three times, followed by two times for "The Violent Space;" 13 single poems in the anthologies. Don L. Lee's poem "Back Again, Home," "A Poem Looking for a Reader," "Re-Act for Action," "The Self-Hatred of Don L. Lee," and "Big Momma" were selected three times each for the sample anthologies; and 22 single poems also appeared once in the sample. Sonia Sanchez's "Poem at Thirty," appeared in three anthologies, and "Summary," "To All Sisters." "Indianapolis/Summer 1969/Poem," "don't wanna be," and "Present," were selected by two editors each; 26 single poems were also published.

119. Mitchell, "Nikki Giovanni," 487; Brown-Guillory, "Sonia Sanchez," 1003; Miller, "Dudley Randall," 268; Hudson, "Don Luther Lee," 485; James, "Etheridge Knight," 549; Hudson, "Sonya Sanchez," 737–38; Fred Lee Hord, "Two Black Poets and Responsible Power; The Power of Truth," in *Reconstructing Memory: Black Literary Criticism* (Chicago: Third World Press, 1991), 103–24, 188–94; Regina B. Jennings, "The Blue/Black Poetics of Sonia Sanchez," in *Language and Literature in the African American Imagination*, ed. Carol Aisha Blackshire-Belay (Westport, Conn.: Greenwood, 1992), 125; Randall, *Broadside Memories*, 16; Murphy, "Nikki," 30; Hodges, "Dudley Randall and the Broadside Press."

120. Fowler, Nikki Giovanni, xiii–xv; Bailey, *Broadside Authors and Artists*, 74–75; Jerry B. McAninch, "Haki R. Madhubuti," in *American Poets Since World War II: Part 2: L–Z*, ed. Donald J. Greiver (Detroit: Gale Research Co., 1980), 34; Charles L. James, "Etheridge Knight," in *Contemporary Poets* (New York: St. Martin's Press, 1985), 459; *New York Times*, March 14, 1991; Wade-Gayles, "Sonia Sanchez," 976; H.M. Zell, C. Bundy, V. Coulan, eds., *A New Reader's Guide to African Literature* (New York: Africana Publishing Co./Holmes and Meier Publishers, 1983), 398.

121. Melhem, "Sonia Sanchez: The Will and the Spirit," 133–34; Mosher, *New Directions from Don L. Lee*, 4, 5, 9, 93–120; Fowler, *Nikki Giovanni*, 11, 13; Etheridge Knight, *Born of a Woman: New and Selected Poems* (Boston: Houghton Mifflin Co., 1980), 1212. The influence of the black studies movement is also revealed in the intense interest of the four poets on Africa. All reflected on the African background in their poetry, and all traveled to Africa during the Black Arts Movement era. Haki R. Madhubuti's African travel included trips in 1969, when he made his first visit to the continent to attend the First Pan-African Festival, in Algiers, Algeria; in 1974, to attend the Sixth Pan-African Congress in Dar-es Salaam, Tanzania; and in 1976, at the invitation of the Senegalese government, when he was a delegate at the meeting of Encounter: African World Alternatives. In 1973, Nikki Giovanni toured 9 African countries on a goodwill trip sponsored by the Department of State, which took her to Ghana, Lesotho, Swaziland, Botswana, South Africa, Zambia, and Tanzania. Etheridge Knight received a travel grant to Africa in 1973. Sonia Sanchez has made several trips to Africa. See Melhem, *Heroism in the New Black Poetry*, 87, 446–47; Fowler, *Nikki Giovanni*, 57, 69–71, 83; Bailey, *Broadside Authors and Artists*, 72; Nikki Giovanni, "The Whole Point Is to Share," *International Educational and Cultural Exchange* 10, no. 1, (Summer 1974): 20–22.

122. Melhem, "Sonia Sanchez: The Will and the Spirit," 133–34.

123. Wade-Gayles, "Sonia Sanchez," 976. Sonia Sanchez notes that during the Black Arts Movement she had to move from job to job, due to government surveillance and being "white-balled" by university administrators; because she "was too political" and a writer. At one point in the early 1970s she could not secure a job in New York State, and was forced to accept a teaching post at Amherst College, Amherst, Massachusetts. "That's what they do to you. If they can't control what you write, they make alternatives for you and send you to places where you have no constituency." See Claudia Tate, ed., "Sonia Sanchez," in *Black Women Writers at Work* (Harpenden, Herts, England: Old Castle Books, 1983), 136. See also Kenneth O'Reilly, *"Racial Matters": The FBI's Secret File on Black America, 1960–1972* (New York: Macmillan, 1991), 271–76, 334–35.

124. Melhem, "Sonia Sanchez: The Will and Spirit," 73.

125. Fowler, *Nikki Giovanni*, 12, 17; Mitchell, "Nikki Giovanni," 483; McAninch, "Haki R. Madhubuti," 34; Hudson, "Don Luther Lee," 484; Melhem, "Haki R. Madhubuti," 87; Barlow, "Etheridge Knight," 172; Melhem, "Sonia Sanchez," 134. The "Big Four," poets were also helpful to other authors by writing prefaces and introductions to their books. For example Nikki Giovanni wrote an "Introduction" for Mae Jackson's *Can I Poet with You* (1969), and in 1972 she wrote a "Foreword" to Woodie King's anthology, *Black Spirits*. Don L. Lee wrote an "Introduction" for the same book. See Mae Jackson, *Can I Poet with You* (New York: Black Dialogue Publishers, 1969); Eugene B. Redmond, *Drumvoices: The Mission of Afro-American Poetry, A Critical History* (Garden City, N.Y.: Anchor Books, 1976), 364; King, *Black Spirits*, xi–x, xvii–xxvii.

126. *The Black Scholar* (June 1975): 90; Redmond, *Drumvoices,* 361–64; Ruth Rambo McClain, review of *Re: Creation, Black World* 20, no. 4 (February 1971): 62–64; Gwendolyn Brooks, "Preface," in Etheridge Knight, *Poems from Prison* (Detroit: Broadside Press, 1968), 9; Breman, *You Better Believe It*, 305; Jerry W. Ward, Jr. Review of *Poems from Prison, Obsidian: Black Literature in Review* 1, no. 1 (Spring 1975): 88–90; "Haki R. Madhubuti," in *Black Literary Criticism*, 1307; Jascha Kessler, quoted from *Poetry* (February 1973), by McAninch, in Greiner, ed., *American Poets Since World War II, Part 2: L–Z*, 34; Liz Gant, review of *We Walk the Way of the New World, Black World* 20, no. 6 (April 1971): 84–87; Sebastian Clarke, review of *Homecoming* and *We a BaddDDD People*, in *Black Literary Criticism*, 1649; Kalamu ya Salaam, "Sonya Sanchez," in *Dictionary of Literary Biography*, vol. 41, *Afro-American Poets Since 1955*, 295–306; Dudley Randall, "Introduction," in Sanchez, *We a BaddDDD People* (Detroit: Broadside Press, 1968), 9–10.

127. Redmond, *Drumvoices*, 361. See also Murphy, "Nikki," 2.

128. Redmond, *Drumvoices*, 389.

129. Mosher, *New Directions from Don L. Lee*, 5. Lee was the first Broadside author to receive a book devoted to his life and work as a creative artist.

130. David R. Goldfield, *Black, White, and Southern: Race Relations and Southern Culture 1940 to the Present* (Baton Rouge: Louisiana State University Press, 1990), 22.

131. Lee, *Think Black!*, 6.

132. Redmond, *Drumvoices*, 385–86.

133. "Nikki-Rosa," "Knoxville, Tennessee," "My Poem," and "The Funeral of Martin Luther King, Jr.," in Nikki Giovanni, *Black Judgement* (Detroit: Broadside Press, 1968), 8, 10, 15, 35; "Back Again Home," and "React for Action," in Don L. Lee (Haki R. Madhubuti), *Think Black!*, (Detroit: Broadside Press, 1969), 7, 16, "But He Was Cool," and "A Poem Looking for a Reader," in *Don't Cry, Scream!* (Detroit: Broadside Press, 1969), 24–25, 61–62; "It Was a Funky Deal," "The Idea of Ancestry," "He Sees Through Stone," in Etheridge Knight, *Poems from Prison* (Detroit: Broadside Press, 1968), 13, 16–17, 27, and "For Black Poets Who Think of Suicide," in Etheridge Knight, *Belly Song and Other Poems* (Detroit; Broadside Press, 1973), 45; "right on: wite America," in Sonia Sanchez, *We a BaddDDD People* (Detroit: Broadside Press, 1970), 25–28; "Summary," and "to all sisters," in Sonia Sanchez, *Home Coming* (Detroit: Broadside Press, 1969), 14, 22.

134. Dudley Randall, letter to Etheridge Knight, October 21, 1967; Etheridge Knight Papers, University of Toledo, Ohio Library; all major correspondence which follows is from this collection.

135. Dudley Randall, letters to Etheridge Knight, Detroit, Mich., August 19, 1967, May 30, 1968, August 26, 1968, October 3, 1968, April 26, 1970, and June 20, 1973.

136. Dudley Randall, letter to Etheridge Knight, October 31, 1967.

137. Publisher's contract between Broadside Press and Etheridge Knight, January 2, 1968.

138. Myles Raymond Hurd, "The Corinth Connection in Etheridge Knight's 'The Ideal of Ancestry,'" *Notes on Mississippi Writers*, 25, no. 1 (January 1993): 7. Knight also received support for book sales from other black poets. For example, Randall informed Knight in 1968 that the following sales of *Poems from Prison* had been made: (1) Don L. Lee sold 25 copies during a tour of California; (2) Gwendolyn Brooks purchased 25 copies; (3) "Mari Evans called from Indianapolis and said your book was so great she wanted to push all other books under the counter, including her own forthcoming book. She ordered 12, to give to influential people"; (4) "San Francisco State College ordered 60 of your book for classes, then 30, the 25 more"; (5) Cornell [University] ordered 100 of them; through Don [L. Lee] of course." Dudley Randall, letter to Etheridge Knight, May 30, October 3, 1968. See also Melba J. Boyd, letter to Etheridge Knight, August 27, 1973.

139. On Knight's arrest and charge with the possession of heroin while he taught at the University of Hartford (Conn.) in 1971 see *The Hartford Courant*, March 14, 1971, 3. At his hearing, the

paper noted that Knight was "placed on probation after the executive director of the state commission on the arts [Anthony S. Keller] asked for leniency in his case."

140. Dudley Randall, letter to Etheridge Knight, December 6, 1967.

141. See Broadside Press Royalty Statements on *Poems from Prison*: Dudley Randall to Etheridge Knight, letter, July 4, 1968, Detroit, Mich.; Broadside Press Royalty Report to Etheridge Knight, February 21, 1972, June 20, 1973, October 1, 1973, June 27, 1974, November 24, 1974, July 9, 1975, December 31, 1975, and May 10, 1976. See Broadside Press Royalty Statements on *Belly Song and Other Poems*: June 26, 1974, November 24, 1974, July 9, 1975, December 31, 1975, and May 10, 1976.

142. This figure does not include the ten free copies which were given to Knight, the five free copies that went to the illustrator of *Poems from Prison*, Frederick Goldstepp, nor the 22 review copies mailed to the editors of such periodicals as *Negro Digest*, *Ebony*, *Time*, *Free Lance*, *Poetry*, Negro Bibliography Service, and individual critics such as John H. Clarke, Clarence Major, William Healey, and D. Georgakas, among others. See Dudley Randall, letter to Etheridge Knight, July 4, 1968; Knight, *Poems from Prison*, 6.

143. Dudley Randell, letter to Etheridge Knight, November 30, 1973. Randall's 1973 contract with Knight actually called for a first printing of "1,000 minimum copies." A second contract for the book in 1974 also contained this number. However, the publisher increased the percentage of royalties available to the author. The contract read as follows: "Royalties after 10,000 copies of the book have been sold shall be 12½ percent. Royalties after 15,000 copies have been sold will be 15 percent." Contract between Broadside Press and Etheridge Knight, January 3, 1973, July 12, 1974.

144. Broadside Press Royalty Reports to Etheridge Knight, June 26, November 24, 1974; July 9, December 31, 1975, and May 10, 1976. The total book value of Broadside's sales of *Belly Song* was $3,702.75 for paperback sales, and $1,821.60 for cloth condition sales, giving a total of $5,424.35, to 1976 for the company. Knight also received small sums from Broadside for the fees received by the company from reprints of Knight's work by others. For example, in 1972, he received a check for $20.00 for the use of his poem "Shine" in Randall's anthology *Black Poet*; $65 in 1973, for his poems to appear in Henderson anthology, *Understanding the New Black Poetry*; and $25 in 1974, for the Australian Broadcasting Commission to use his poem, "He Sees Through Stone," in a broadcast entitled "Contemporary American Poets." Dudley Randall, letter to Etheridge Knight, January 17, 1972, June 12, 1973, and July 26, 1974.

145. The following sums were advanced to Knight by Broadside Press during the period 1970–1974: March 30, 1970: $108; May 13, 1970: $50; December 7, 1972: $217.20; December 31, 1972: $210.10; February 23, 1973: $50; September 24, 1973: $100; November 2, 1973: $25; December 10, 1973: $141.24; April 11, 1974: $50; May 14, 1974: $100. Totals: $1,051.54. See Broadside Press financial statement to Etheridge Knight, May 14, 1974. Knight often wrote to Randall for copies of his Broadside books. For example, in 1971, he wrote to the publisher: "Send me a box of *Poems from Prison*. I got a couple of readings coming up in January and I want to have some books on hand to sell. Charge it to my already overburdened bill." Etheridge Knight, letter to Dudley Randall, December 13, 1971, Nashville, Tennessee. (Randall's note on this letter requested the staff to send Knight 100 copies of his book.) Ibid. See also Etheridge Knight, letter to Dudley Randall, December 15, 1973.

146. Dudley Randall, letter to Etheridge Knight, July 12, 1974.

147. Dudley Randall, letter to Etheridge Knight, October 27, 1974. Knight reduced his debt to Broadside to $549.03 by November 24, 1975, and to $402.88, by July 9, 1975, and still further to $281.03 by December 31, 1975. However, by May 10, 1976, he again owed the company $561.34. See Broadside Royalty Reports to Etheridge Knight for the above dates.

148. Aneb Kgositsile, letter to Etheridge Knight, March 5, 1978, Highland Park, Mich. Broadside/Crummel Press also sent Knight 50 copies each of *Belly Song* and *Poems from Prison* in March 1978, at a 40 percent author's discount rate, and billed him for $85.29. See Invoice no. 10250, Broadside/Crummel Press, March 6, 1978. Three years earlier, in 1975, Knight requested Randall's advice and aid on an offer from the University of Toledo Library (the Ward M. Canady Center), which wished to purchase and house his literary papers. Randall responded positive, and the papers were processed in 1987. See Noel Stock, letter to Etheridge Knight, October 2, 1975, Toledo, Ohio; Etheridge Knight, letter to Noel Stock, October 6, 1975, Indianapolis, Indiana; Etheridge Knight, letter to Dudley Randall, October 6, 1975, Indianapolis, Indiana; "Biographical Sketch on Etheridge Knight," Ward M. Canady Center, University of Toledo Library, Collection no. 016 (1991), 1–3.

149. Dudley Randall, letter to Etheridge Knight, March 6, 1978, Detroit, Mich.

150. Ironically, Broadside/Crummel Press was not in a financial position in 1979 to publish Knight's fourth book, *Born of a Woman: New and Selected Poems.* The poet had to turn to a major white publisher, Houghton Mifflin Company, for support. His contract with Houghton Mifflin gave him an advance of $1,000—("against all monies earned under the terms of this agreement"), with a royalty base of 10 percent on all copies sold, and a first printing, softcover, trade edition of 25,000 copies. See Jonathan Galassi to Etheridge Knight, October 17, 1979, New York City, N.Y. Knight's new book was priced at $5.95 a copy, and this had a possible market value of $148,750, with Knight's share at 10 percent of this sum coming to $14,875. See Etheridge Knight, *Born of a Woman: New and Selected Poems* (Boston: Houghton Mifflin Co., 1980). Knight's earlier books had been of moderate size. *Poems from Prison* contained 28 poems, in a volume of 30 pages; *Belly Songs*, 41 poems and 62 pages; however, *Born of a Woman* consisted of 87 poems, in a book of 138 pages.

151. Smith-Hobson, "Black Book Publishing: Protest, Pride and Little Profit," 44.

152. *Harvard Journal of Afro-American Affairs* 2, no. 2 (1971): 116.

153. Hoyt W. Fuller, "A Warning to Black Poets," *Black World* 19, no. 11 (September 1970): 50.

154. Bessie R. Grayson, "A Black Librarian's Challenge to the Publishing World," in *What Black Librarians Are Sayings*, ed. E.J. Josey (Metuchen, N.J.: Scarecrow Press, 1972), 279.

155. *Catalogues of Broadside Press,* 1967–1979; Winifred D. Wandersee, *On the Move: American Women in the 1970s* (Boston: Twayne Publishers/G.K. Hall & Co., 1988), 72–74.

156. Richard A. Long and Eugenia W. Collier, eds., *Afro-American Writing: An Anthology of Prose and Poetry* (University Park, Pa.: Pennsylvania State University Press, 1985), 628.

157. Ibid., 629.

Chapter 5

1. D.H. Melhem, *Heroism in the New Black Poetry: Introductions and Interviews* (Lexington: University Press of Kentucky, 1990), 41, 69; D.H. Melhem, "Dudley Randall: A Humanist's View," *Black American Literature Forum* 17, no. 4 (Winter 1983): 157.

2. *Obsidian: Black Literature in Review* 6, nos. 1 and 2 (Spring/Summer 1980): 6, 179–81.

3. Dudley Randall, interview with author, Detroit, Mich., April 9, 1992.

4. Deborah A. Straub, ed., *Contemporary Authors,* New Revision Series, vol. 23 (Detroit: Gale Research Co., 1988), 329.

5. Melhem, *Heroism in the New Black Poetry,* 41; Melhem, "Dudley Randall: A Humanist's View" 157; Marilyn K. Basel "Dudley (Felker) Randall, 1914–," in *Black Writers: A Selection of Sketches from Contemporary Authors,* ed. Hal May, Deborah A. Straub, and Susan M. Trosky (Detroit: Gale Research Co., 1988), 470. *The Black Scholar* informed its readers in 1980 that Dudley Randall and Melba Joyce Boyd viewed this new effort as an attempt "to present poetry in a more attractive form as entertainment that promotes culture and a better understanding of poetry." See *The Black Scholar* 11, no. 7 (September/October 1980): 90. Donald Franklin Joyce also notes that Randall began the Broadside Theater: "to revive community interest in the press and to raise funds for reprintings and new publications." See Donald Franklin Joyce, *Black Book Publishers in the United States: A Historical Dictionary of the Presses 1817–1990* (Westport, Conn.: Greenwood, 1991), 66. Dudley Randall offered Etheridge Knight $100, plus transportation in 1980 to appear on a future Broadside Poets Theater Program. See Dudley Randall, letter to Etheridge Knight, August 21, 1980, Detroit, Mich.

6. Melhem, *Heroism in the New Black Poetry* 41; *Detroit News,* July 24, 1980; "Giovanni, Brooks, Knight, Lorde at Broadside Press Poets Theater," *Poetry Resource Center Newsletter and Calendar* (August 1980): 1; *Michigan Chronicle,* August 14, 1982, p. C6; Third Anniversary of the Broadside Poets Theater, Program, August 7, 1983 (Highland Park, Mich.: Alexander Crummell Memorial Center, 1983), 1–4. The Broadside Poets Theater Committee consisted of six individuals: Willie Williams, Hilda Vest, Harry Rux, Dudley Randall, Margaret Montgomery, and Aneb Kgositsile. At the August 7, 1983, program three poets read from their works: Etheridge Knight, Melba Joyce Boyd, and Dudley Randall.

7. Leonard Kniffel, "Poet in Motion," *Monthly Detroit* 7, no. 6 (June 1984): 163.

8. Melhem, *Heroism in the New Black Poetry,* 82.

9. The Contemporary Forum, "A Selective Guide: Multi-Cultural Programs for the 90's, Speakers — Performers," (Chicago: The Contemporary Forum, 1990), 3–4. Beryl Zitch served as the artists' representative for the Contemporary Forum. In addition to Gwendolyn Brooks and Carolyn Rodgers, her list of clients in 1990 included: Sam Greenlee, Dorothy Spruill Redford, Ivan Van Sertima, Claude Brown, Nora Blakely, Clarence Page, Haki Madhubuti, Joy Harjo, Merri Dee, Angela Jackson, Manuel Galvan, Alice Childress, Camille Yarbrough, Ralph Ellison, Chuck Stone, Margaret Burroughs, Etheridge Knight, Lerone Bennett, Jr., and James Comer, among active writers; and performers, such as: Ossie Davis and Ruby Dee, L.D. Frazier, Sybil Kein, the Chocolate Chips, Linda Humes, William Marshall, Coleman and Stuart, and Hannah Jon Taylor.

10. Dudley Randall, Public Statement to the director of Cultural Programs, 24 October 1980; a copy is held in the VF of the Language and Literature Division, Detroit Public Library. Randall often appeared in public schools to promote the study of literature and writing of poetry. On his April 26–27, 1983, creative writer-in-school residence at Cass Technical High School, a leading educational institution in Detroit, see the *Michigan Chronicle*, April 23, May 7, 1983. On his 1986 reading at the Library of Congress, Washington, D.C., see *Michigan Chronicle,* March 22, 1986, A1.

11. Dudley Randall in a quote in the *Detroit Free Press*, February 2, 1986.

12. Basel, "Dudley (Felker) Randall," 329; Iris Cloyd, ed., *Who's Who Among Black Americans* (Detroit: Gale Research Co., 1990), 1045.

13. Howard Blum, "In Detroit, Poet Laureate's Work Is Never Done," *New York Times*, January 30, 1984, A8.

14. *Detroit News*: November 6, 1981; *Obsidian: Black Literature in Review* 6, no. 3 (Winter 1980): 1.

15. *New York Times,* January 30, 1984.

16. Ibid.

17. Michael A. Tucker, "Detroit Poet Laureate," *Detroit News*, November 6, 1981, A1.

18. *Detroit News*, January 19, 1984, F2.

19. *New York Times*, January 30, 1984, A8.

20. Herbert Scott, "Contemporary Poetry in Michigan," in Michigan Council for the Humanities, *Literary Michigan: A Sense of Place, a Sense of Time* (Lansing, Mich.: Michigan Council for the Humanities, 1988), 22.

21. On Randall's book production during the 1980s see: Dudley Randall, *A Litany of Friends: New and Selected Poems* (Detroit: Lotus Press, 1981); Dudley Randall, *After the Killing* (Chicago: Third World Press, 1973), First Edition, Second Printing, 1983; Dudley Randall, ed., *Homage to Hoyt Fuller* (Detroit: Broadside Press, 1984); Dudley Randall and Louis J. Cantoni, eds., *Golden Song: The Fiftieth Anniversary Anthology of the Poetry Society of Michigan, 1935–1985* (Detroit: Harlo, 1985). On Randall's work in anthologies see: "The Rite" and "Blackberry Sweet," in *Dear Dark Faces: Portraits of a People*, ed. Helen Earle Simcox (Detroit: Lotus Press, 1980), 50, 69; "Slave Names," "Be Kind to Me," "My Muse," and "The Future Looms," in *The Otherwise Room: A Poetry Anthology*, ed. Joyce Jones, Mary McTaggart and Maria Mootry (Carbondale, Ill.: The Poetry Factory, 1981), 71, 130, 184, 187–88; S.J. Kennedy and D. Kennedy, eds., *Knock at a Star* (Boston: Little, Brown, 1982); "The Profile on the Pillow," "Incident," Randall, ed., in *Homage to Hoyt Fuller,* 123–24; "For Kim Weston," Randall and Cantoni, eds. in *Golden Song,* 92; "'The Ballad of Birmingham," Edgar V. Roberts and Henry E. Jacobs, eds., in *Literature: An Introduction to Read and Writing* (Englewood Cliffs, N.J.: Prentice-Hall, 1986), 767–68; "Ballad of Birmingham," "Booker T. and W.E.B.," and "A Poet Is Not a Jukebox," Richard Ellmann and Robert O'Clair, eds., in *Modern Poems: A Norton Introduction* (New York: W.W. Norton and Co., 1989), 490–94. On Randall's poetry in journals, programs, newspapers and broadsides see: "In Africa," and "A Poet Is Not a Jukebox," in *Obsidian* 6, nos. 1 and 2 (Spring/Summer 1980): 179–81; "A Leader of the People," *The Black Scholar* 11, no. 7 (September/October 1980): 91; "The Mini Skirt," *First World* 2, no. 4 (1980): 10; "To an Old Man," *Obsidian* 7, no. 1 (Spring 1981): 38; "Profile on the Pillow," *Ebony* 36 (August 1981): 56; "Wooing a Woman: Probing the Circle," *The Black Scholar* 12, no. 5 (September/October 1981): 20–21; "The Profile on the Pillow," *Detroit Free Press,* February 24, 1983; "For Vivian," *Broadside #93* (Detroit: Broadside Press, 1982); "Motown Polka," "Be Kind to Me," "Old Detroit (For Sister Barbara Johns)," "Silly Jim (After Mother Goose)," "For Kim," "To Poets Who Preach in Prose," "Women of Ghana," "For Vivian," and "The Girls in Booths," in *Black American Literature Forum* 17, no. 4 (Winter 1983): 168–70; "The Profile on the Pillow," *Essence* 15 (August 1984): 132; "Love Song of a

Hippo," *Open Places*, no. 34 (Spring 1957): 184; "The Profile on the Pillow," *Phase Two* (n.d.). On the use of Randall's work in scholarly studies see: "Booker T. and W.E.B.," quoted in Joyce Pettis, "The Black Poet as Historian," *Umoja* 4, no. 1 (Spring 1980): 50; "The Melting Pot," quoted in Anne Wortham, *The Other Side of Racism: A Philosophical Study of Black Race Consciousness* (Columbus: Ohio State University Press, 1981), 204–5; "Women," in Jacquelyn Hillsman, *The Experimental Movement: The World of Dudley Randall, Poet Laureate of Detroit* (Detroit: The Experimental Movement, 1984), 6; "Black Poet, White Critic," quoted in William J. Harris, *The Jazz Aesthetic* (Columbia: University of Missouri Press, 1985), 88; "Booker T. and W.E.B.," quoted in Abdul Alkalimat and Associates, *Introduction to Afro-American Studies: A Peoples College Primer* (Chicago: Twenty-First Century Books and Publications, 1986), 227; "Booker T. and W.E.B" quoted in Ceola Ross Baber, "The Artistry and Artifice of Black Communication," in Geneva Gay and Willie L. Baber, eds., *Expressively Black Ethnic Identity* (New York: Praeger Publishers, 1987), 98. On Randall's essay production during the 1980s see: "Robert Hayden," James Vinson, ed., in *Contemporary Poets* (New York: St. Martin's Press, 1980), 664–66; "The Most Important Books of the 1970s," in *The Black Scholar* 12, no. 2 (March/April 1981): 86–87; "Sterling Brown as Seen by a Publisher," in *Sterling A. Brown: A Umum Tribute*, ed. Black History Museum Committee (Philadelphia, Pa.: Black History Museum Umum Publishers, 1982), 45–46; "Report on the Black Arts Convention," in *Homage to Hoyt Fuller*, 20–24; "Introduction," in Aneb Kgositsile [Gloria House], *Blood River (Poems), 1964–1983* (Detroit: Broadside Press, 1983). On Randall's short stories, see "Incident on a Bus" in *Homage to Hoyt Fuller*, 64–65. On an important interview with Randall, see A.X. Nicholas, "A Conversation with Dudley Randall," in *Homage to Hoyt Fuller*, 266–74.

22. *Detroit News*, November 6, 1981; Basel, "Dudley (Felker) Randall," 469.

23. Basel, "Dudley (Felker) Randall," 469. Critic R. Baxter Miller also speaks favorably of this work. In 1985, he wrote: "Randall's book *A Litany of Friends* (1981) contains twenty-four reprints and forty-eight new poems. Six appeared first in *Poem, Counterpoem* (1966), four in *Cities Burning* (1968), and one in *Love You* (1970). Fourteen others appeared first in *More to Remember* (1971), and nine came out in *After the Killing* (1973). Grouped by topics such as friends, eros, war, Africa, and self, the verses demonstrate Randall's technical skill." See R. Baxter Miller, "Dudley Randall," *Dictionary of Literary Biography*, vol. 41, *Afro-American Poets Since 1955* (Detroit: Gale Research Co., 1985), 41. Editors and critics during the 1980s continued to be attracted to Dudley Randall's older poetic works. His work was selected on 14 occasions to appear in anthologies during the 1980s, and the most frequent poem selected was his masterpiece, "Ballad of Birmingham," in two anthologies. Yet, the most frequent older poem selected by editors of journals were his poems "The Profile on the Pillow" (3 times), and "For Vivian" (2 times). However, scholars were still very impressed with another of his early masterpieces, the historical poem "Booker T. and W.E.B." (which was quoted 3 times in six scholarly works written during this period).

24. Melhem, *Heroism in the New Black Poetry*, 57.

25. Randall, *A Litany of Friends*, 101.

26. John M. Reilly, "Dudley (Felker) Randall," in *Contemporary Poets*, 691.

27. Dudley Randall, "The Rite," in Simcox, *Dear Dark Faces: Portraits of a People*, 50.

28. On Robert Hayden see Vilma Ruskin Potter, "Reconsiderations and Reviews: A Remembrance for Robert Hayden: 1913–1980," *Melus* 8, no. 1 (Spring 1981): 51–55; *New York Times*, February 27, 1980, B5; and in "A Robert Hayden Special Issue," *Obsidian: Black Literature in Review* 8, no. 1 (Spring 1981): 6–211. On Hoyt W. Fuller see: C. Gerald Fraser, "Hoyt W. Fuller: A Literary Critic and Editor of Black Publications," *New York Times*, May 13, 1981, 19; *The Washington Post*, May 14, 1981, C6; *Chicago Tribune*, May 14, 1981, C20; Africana Studies and Research Center, Cornell University, "Commemorative Colloquium in Honor of Hoyt W. Fuller, Writer, Editor, Literary Critic: Conference Theme, The Role of the Black Writer in the American Social Fabric: Confronting Issues of Philosophic and Theoretical (literary) Criticism," October 5–6, 1984, Ithaca, New York. Dudley Randall spoke at this conference on October 5, 1984, with a presentation entitled, "Black World and the Writer," 4. On Margaret Danner see Hedgepeth, *Twentieth Century African-American Writers and Artists* (1991), 68; Helen Houston, "Margaret Danner," in *Notable Black American Women*, ed. Jessie Carney Smith (Detroit: Gale Research Co., 1992), 249–50. On Lance Jeffers see Hedgepeth, *Twentieth Century African-American Writers and Artists*, 151–52; Doris L. Laryea, "A Black Poet's Vision: An Interview with Lance Jeffers," *CLA Journal* 26, no. 4 (June 1983): 422–33; "In Memoriam: Lance Jeffers, November 28, 1919–July 19, 1985," *The Black Scholar* 16, no. 4

(July/August 1985): 73. On Sterling A. Brown see James P. Draper, ed., *Black Literary Criticism*, vol. 1 (Detroit: Gale Research Co., 1992), 281–82; Ntongela Masilela, "Sterling A. Brown: The Last of the Harlem Renaissance Greats," *Presence Africaine: Cultural Review of the Negro World*, no. 148 (Fourth Quarter 1988): 170–75; *New York Times*, January 7, 1989, B11. On George Kent see James A. Page and Joe Min Roh, *Selected Black American, African and Caribbean Authors: A Bio-Bibliography* (Littleton Col.: Libraries Unlimited, 1985), 159–60.

29. Randall, *Homage to Hoyt Fuller*, 11–354.

30. Beaufort Cranford, "Anthology Honors the Best Writing," *Detroit News*, October 10, 1984, D2.

31. R. Baxter Miller, "Dudley Randall," in *Dictionary of Literary Biography*, vol. 4, *Afro-American Poets Since 1955: Dramatists and Prose Writers*, ed. T.M. Davis and T. Harris (Detroit: Gale Research Co., 1985), 272–73.

32. D.L. Johnson, *We, the Black Americans* (Washington, D.C.: U.S. Government Printing Office, 1986), 5; John D. Kasarda, "Urban Change and Minority Opportunities," in *The New Urban Reality*, ed. Paul E. Peterson (Washington, D.C.: The Brookings Institution, 1985), 52; *USA Today*, February 28, 1991, A9.

33. *Detroit Free Press*, October 30, 1990, 7-A. See also Joe T. Darden, Richard Child Hill, June Thomas, and Richard Thomas, *Detroit: Race and Uneven Development* (Philadelphia, Pa.: Temple University Press, 1987), 11–65.

34. Johnson, *We, the Black Americans*, 6; *The New Book of American Rankings* (New York: Facts on File Publications, 1984), 46.

35. Mark E. Neithercut, *Detroit Twenty Years After: A Statistical Profile of the Detroit Area Since 1967* (Detroit: Center for Urban Studies, Wayne State University, 1987), 4–5.

36. Dan Luria and Jack Russell, "Rational Reindustrialization," in *Detroit Perspectives, Crossroads and Turning Points*, ed. Wilma Wood Henrickson (Detroit: Wayne State University Press, 1991), 551.

37. George W. Crockett, Jr., "Michigan Blitzed: A Reagan Budget Case Study," *Freedomways* 21, no. 2 (Second Quarter 1981): 88.

38. B.J. Widick, *Detroit: City of Race and Class Violence* (Detroit: Wayne State University Press, 1989), 234.

39. Neithercut, *Detroit Twenty Years After*, 8.

40. See "Gap Widens Between Michigan Blacks, Whites," *Jackson (Miss.) Advocate*, August 10, 1989, A8.

41. "Conscience, and Housing," in Wilma Wood Henrickson, *Detroit Perspectives: Crossroads and Turning Points* (Detroit: Wayne State University Press, 1991), 553–54.

42. John O. Calmore, "To Make Wrong Right: The Necessary and Proper Aspirations of Fair Housing," in *The State of Black America*, ed. Janet Dewart (New York: National Urban League, 1989), 90–92. See also Isabel Wilkerson, "Foie Gras and Vivaldi on Woodward," *New York Times*, October 6, 1987, A16; Tom Hundley, "Detroit Clears Out Its Ruins, but Only Pheasants Are Moving In," *Chicago Tribune*, December 31, 1989, A10.

43. Frank Viviano, "What's Happening in Murder City," *The Progressive* 45, no. 9 (September 1981) 38, 40–42; *Detroit News*, November 15, 1987, A21.

44. Viviano, "What's Happening in Murder City," 40–42.

45. Jim Naughton, "In Murder City, the Mothers' Crusade," *The Washington Post*, June 22, 1987, B1.

46. *Detroit Free Press*, November 15, 1987, J1–6 Isabel Wilkerson, "Detroit Crack Empire Showed All Earmarks of Big Business," *New York Times*, December 18, 1988, A1.

47. Ze'ev Chafets, *Devil's Night: And Other True Tales of Detroit* (New York: Random House, 1990), 3–4. Chafets also observes that "according to the FBI, there were 686 homicides in Detroit in 1987 — almost 63 per 100,000." (Since then, the rate has declined slightly, and Washington, D.C., has become the nation's leader.) See also "City's Bloodiest Summer Weekend — 43 People Are Shot, 12 Killed," *Detroit News*, August 24, 1986, 1, A18–19; "Detroit Efforts Fail to Stern Arson on Eve of Halloween," *New York Times*, November 11, 1986, A14.

48. See Herb Boyd, "Blacks and the Police State: A Case Study of Detroit," *The Black Scholar* 12, no. 1 (January/February 1981): 58–61; James P. Danky and Frank Hennessy, "Radical Right Publishing in America: The Heart of Darkness," *New Pages: News and Reviews of the Progressive Book*

Trade, no. 9 (1985): 5–13; Bill Stanton, *Klanwatch: Bringing the Ku Klux Klan to Justice* (New York: Grove Weidenfeld, 1991), 87; *The Ku Klux Klan: An Encyclopedia* (1991), 162. Race relations with whites in the suburbs remained an issue of contention between Detroit and its neighbors. One author notes that city officials in nearby Dearborn passed a law "barring outsiders from its parks." The act was later disallowed by a Wayne County circuit judge. See Isabel Wilkerson, "Race Raised as Issue in Variety of Disputes at Detroit's Borders," *New York Times,* October 10, 1986, A14.

49. Gary Orfield, "School Desegregation Needed Now: Support for Busing Grows but National Policy Has Been at a Stand-still in the 1980s," *Focus: The Monthly Newsletter of the Joint Center for Political Studies,* 151, no. 7 (July 1987): 7.

50. Widick, *Detroit: City of Race and Class Violence,* 248–49. On the interests of black students to promote the development of a Department of Africana Studies at Wayne State University during this period see Daryl Fears, "Students Say Black Center Gets Low-class Treatment," *Detroit Free Press,* April 14, 1989, A13; Stephen Jones, WSU Protest Comes to End as Students Claim Victory," *Detroit Free Press,* April 24, 1989, 1, A15. For a national view of this period see Luke Tripp, "The Political Views of Black Students During the Reagan Era," *The Black Scholar* 22, no. 3 (Summer 1992): 45–52.

51. Ronald Stephens, "Coleman Young: The Man and His Times," *The Black Scholar* 21, no. 3 (Summer 1991): 41.

52. *Chicago Tribune,* February 20, 1994, Section 14, 10. See also Wilbur C. Rich, *Coleman Young and Detroit Politics: From Social Activist to Power Broker* (Detroit: Wayne State University, 1989), 224–63; Bette Woody, *Managing Crisis Cities: The New Black Leadership and the Politics of Resource Allocation* (Westport, Conn.: Greenwood, 1982), 22–32.

53. Widick, *Detroit: City of Race and Class Violence,* 266. The spirits of the City were also lifted in 1984 when the Detroit Tigers won the World Series. See *Detroit Monthly City Guide* (1991–92), 9.

54. Ernest Dillard, "The Cry of White Racism," in Henrickson, *Detroit Perspectives, Crossroads and Turning Points,* 566.

55. Basel, "Dudley (Felker) Randall," 330; Donald Franklin Joyce, "Reflections on the Changing Publishing Objectives of Secular Black Book Publishers, 1900–1986," in *Reading in America: Literature and Social History,* ed. Cathy N. Davidson (Baltimore, Md.: Johns Hopkins University Press, 1989), 233. Detroit poet and educator Aneb Kgositsile (Gloria House) served as editor of Broadside/Crummell Press in 1977–80. See Joyce, *Black Book Publishers in the United States,* 65.

56. Kniffel, "Poet in Motion," 163.

57. Mel Watkins, "Hard Times for Black Writers," *The New York Review of Books,* February 22, 1981, page 33.

58. Ibid., 26.

59. Amiri Baraka , "Black Literature and the Afro-American Nation: The Urban Voice," in *Literature and the Urban Experience,* ed. Michael C. Jaye and Ann C. Watts (New Brunswick, N.J.: Rutgers University Press, 1981), 157.

60. *New York Times,* November 27, 1980, C19. See also C. Gerald Fraser, "Black Writers Are Wary on Publishing Outlook," November 27, 1980, 15; Dhoruba Moore, "Strategies of Repression Against the Black Movement," *The Black Scholar* 12, no. 3 (May/June 1981) 10-16; Toni Morrison, "This Beleaguered, Guilt-Ridden, Frustrated Species — The Individual Artist," *The Cultural Post* (National Endowment for the Arts) 7, no. 1 (May/June 1981): 24–25; John A. Williams "Quick Hit at Racial Censorship," *American Book Review* 5 (November/December 1982): 7; Paul Desruisseaux, "Minority Writers Find Their Work Treated as a Cultural Curiosity," *The Chronicle of Higher Education* 25, no. 18 (January 12, 1983): 8; Eve Pell, *The Big Chill: How the Reagan Administration, Corporate America, and the Religious Conservatives Are Subverting Free Speech and the Public's Right to Know* (Boston: Beacon Press, 1984); Michael Coffey, "Black Writers Debate 'Being Human in the 20th Century,'" *Publishers Weekly* 235, no. 7 (February 17, 1989) L16–17; Will Nixon, "Better Times for Black Writers?" *Publishers Weekly* 235, no. 7 (February 17, 1989) L16–17, 35–40; Will Nixon, "Black Male Writers: Endangered Species?" *American Visions* 5, no. 1 (February 1990): 24–28.

61. *New York Times,* June 21, 1989, B6.

62. *Catalogues of Broadside Press* (Detroit: Broadside Press, 1983); Melba Boyd, *Song for Maya* (Detroit: Broadside Press and Detroit River Press, 1982); Michele S. Gibbs, *Sketches from*

Home (Detroit: Broadside Press, 1983); Aneb Kgositsile, *Blood River* (Detroit: Broadside Press, 1983); Sonia Sanchez, *It's a New Day: (Poems for Young Brothas and Sistuhs)* (Detroit: Broadside Press, 1983); Dudley Randall, ed., *Homage to Hoyt Fuller* (Detroit: Broadside Press, 1984). In 1983, Randall also reprinted (at $3.00 a copy), a Tenth Anniversary Edition of Gwendolyn Brooks *Beckonings* (Detroit: Broadside Press, 1975). For a review of this work by Beth Brown see *The Black Scholar* 15, no. 6 (November/December 1984): 63–64.

63. "Broadside Press Flyer," (Detroit: Broadside Press, 1982). See "Small/Fine Presses Folder," Ward M. Canady Center Library, University of Toledo, Ohio.

64. "Broadside Press Flyer."

65. On Melba Boyd see Melba Boyd, *Cat Eyes and Deadwood* (Highland, Mich.: Fallen Angel Press, 1978), 52; Roseann P. Bell, Bettye J. Parker, and Beverly Guy-Sheftall, eds., *Sturdy Black Bridges: Visions of Black Women in Literature* (Garden City, N.Y.: Anchor Books/Doubleday, 1979), 418. On Michele S. Gibbs see Gibbs, *Sketches from Home*, 64; Hilda Vest, Publisher/Editor of Broadside Press, letter and vitae on Michele Gibbs, to the author, December 26, 1991, Detroit, Michigan. On Aneb Kgositsile, see Kgositsile, *Blood River*, 8, 42; Hilda Vest, letter and vitae to the author, December 26, 1991. On Sonia Sanchez see Laurie Collier and Joyce Nakamura, eds., *Major Authors and Illustrators for Children and Young Adults* (Detroit: Gale Research Co., 1993), 2014–17; Fred Lee Hord, *Reconstructing Memory: Black Literary Criticism* (Chicago: Third World Press, 1991), 103–24.

66. Dorothy Randall-Tsuruta, quoted in *The Black Scholar* 13, nos. 4 and 5 (Summer 1982): 45.

67. Hilda Vest, letter, and vitae of Michele S. Gibbs, to the author, December 26, 1991; *Broadside Press Newsletter* 36 (December 1983): 1.

68. Joyce Eisenberg, *Places and Peoples of the World: Grenada* (New York: Chelsea House Publishers, 1988) 12–13; Ronald H. Spector, *U.S. Marines in Grenada* (Washington, D.C.: U.S. Government Printing Office, 1987), 1–35; "Grenada," *The World Book Encyclopedia,* vol. 8 (Chicago World Book, Inc., 1993), 389–90.

69. Hilda Vest, letter, and vitae of Aneb Kgositsile, to the author, December 26, 1991; Kgositsile, *Blood River*, 42; Almed Alhamisi and Harun Kofi Wangara, eds., *Black Arts* (Detroit: Black Arts Publications, 1969), 112.

70. *The Black Scholar* 18, no. 1 (January/February 1987): 31.

71. Kalamu ya Salaam, "Sonia Sanchez," in *Dictionary of Literary Biography,* vol. 4, *Afro-American Poets Since 1955* (Detroit: Gale Research Co., 1985), 295–306.

72. *Broadside Press News* 36 (December 1983): 1.

73. Ibid.

74. *Catalogues of Broadside Press* (Detroit: Broadside Press, 1980), 1.

75. Donald Franklin Joyce, *Gatekeepers of Black Culture: Black-Owned Book Publishing in the United States 1817–1981* (Westport, Conn.: Greenwood, 1983), 130. See also Joyce, *Black Book Publishers in the United States,* 65–66, 68.

76. Jerry W. Ward, Jr. "Retreat Into Possibility: A Literary View of the Eighties," (Tougaloo, Miss.: Unpublished Paper, Tougaloo College, February 18, 1983), 3.

77. On the historical nature of black poets and the black press see Blyden, Jackson, *The Waiting Years: Essays on American Negro Literature* (Baton Rouge: Louisiana State University Press, 1976); Eugene B. Redmond, *Drumvoices: The Mission of Afro-American Poetry: A Critical History* (Garden City, N.Y.: Anchor Press/Doubleday, 1976); Wolseley, *The Black Press, U.S.A.*; Henry Lewis Suggs, ed., *The Black Press in the South, 1865–1979* (Westport, Conn.: Greenwood, 1983); Joyce, *Black Book Publishers in the United States.*

78. *New York Times*, November 27, 1980, 15.

79. Jonathan Kozol, "There Is Little to Celebrate," in *Illiteracy in America,* ed. Gary E. McCuen (Hudson, Wis.: Gary E. McCuen Publications, 1988), 17, 19. See also Jonathan Kozol, "Michigan Is a Textbook Example of Inequality," *Detroit News,* October 8, 1991, C1, and Jonathan Kozol, *Savage Inequalities: Children in America's Schools* (New York: Harper Perennial, 1991); Ishmael Reed, *Writin' Is Fightin': Thirty-Seven Years of Boxing on Paper* (New York: Atheneum, 1988), 185–86; Faith Berry, "A Question of Publishers and a Question of Audience," *The Black Scholar* 17, no. 2 (March/April 1986): 41–49. *Black Enterprise* noted in 1989 that: "Of the approximately 1,100 television stations in the United States, only 13 are black-owned and of the 9,000 commercial radio stations across the country, only 170 are owned by blacks. Less than 2% of the broadcast properties in this country are owned and controlled by blacks." See "Broadcast News," *Black Enterprise,* 20, no. 5 (December

1989): 101. On national patterns of media ownership in this country a study published in 1984 notes: "The concentration and centralization of power in the media world is as considerable, in some cases even more so, than in other branches of industry, commerce, and banking. In 1978, 5% of firms producing newspapers accounted for 48% of daily circulation.... Since 1948, less than half of the U.S. population has lived in a city with a daily paper.... In 1978 just 35 cities enjoyed more than one daily paper (2.3% of the total).... In mass market paperbacks, the top eight firms in 1976 accounted for 81% of total sales." See John Downing, *Radical Media: The Political Experience of Alternative Communication* (Boston: South End Press, 1984), 37.

80. Students of the black press in America note that there were at least 350 such organs in the United States during the early 1970s; however, by the early 1990s "over 200 black newspapers ceased publication." A study by Jean Folkerts observes that the audited circulation of six black newspapers showed a tremendous decline in readership during the eighties. Data from this study are highlighted below.

Newspaper (City, year founded)	Audited Circulation 1980	1985	1990
New York Amsterdam News (New York, 1909)	81,200	50,000	31,584
Michigan Chronicle (Detroit, 1936)	41,712	32,000	24,516
L. A. Sentinel (Los Angeles, 1933)	34,100	29,356	23,886
Afro-American (Baltimore, 1892)	26,400	12,500	11,614
Mobile Beacon (Mobile, Ala., 1954)	7,560	4,678	4,672
Louisiana Weekly (New Orleans, 1926)	17,370	9,600	4,651

See John Hope Franklin and Alfred A. Moss, Jr., *From Slavery to Freedom: A History of African Americans* (New York: McGraw-Hill Publishing Co., 1994), 379; Harry A. Ploski and James Williams, eds., *Reference Library of Black America* (Detroit: Gale Research Co., 1990), 1253; Jean Folkerts, "From the Heartland" in *The Future of News*, ed. Philip S. Cook, Douglas Gomery, and Lawrence W. Lichty (Baltimore: Johns Hopkins University Press, 1992), 131. *The Chicago Defender* also experienced a loss of readers, and its circulation of 36,541 in 1967 dropped to 22,611 by 1986. Clint C. Wilson, II, observes that there were approximately 185 active black newspapers in this country in 1989–1990. See Wolseley, *The Black Press, U.S.A.*, 341; Clint C. Wilson, II, *Black Journalists in Paradox: Historical Perspectives and Current Dilemmas* (Westport, Conn.: Greenwood, 1991), 178. See also Julius E. Thompson, *The Black Press in Mississippi, 1865–1985* (Gainesville: University Press of Florida, 1993), 115–16; Jannette L. Dates and William Barlow, eds. *Split Image: African Americans in the Mass Media* (Washington, D.C.: Howard University Press, 1990) 382–85.

81. Kozol, "There Is Little to Celebrate," 19.

82. Melhem, *Heroism,* 61.

83. The percentages among all adults of this survey were 56 percent for those who read literature, 18.6 percent for those who read poetry, 6.2 percent for those who did creative writing, and 85.6 percent for those who read books and magazines. See Nicholas Zill and Marianne Winglee, *Who Reads Literature?: The Future of the United States, as a Nation of Readers* (Cabin John, Md./Washington, D.C.: Seven Locks Press, 1990), 45.

84. Joyce, *Gatekeepers of Black Culture,* 130.

85. *Black Enterprise* 19, no. 1 (June 1989): 196.

86. *Black Enterprise* 21, no. 1 (June 1991): 107, 177. In 1990, the largest black-owned business firm in the United States was TLC Beatrice International Holdings, Inc., of New York City, which was established in 1987 and headed by Reginald Lewis (C.E.), who managed a staff of 5,000. TLC Beatrice International specializes in the distribution of food products. Its 1990 total sales were $1,496,000,000. The second largest U.S. black-owned firm in 1990 was Johnson Publishing

Company (publishing, broadcasting, cosmetics, and hair care products), of Chicago, Illinois, created by John H. Johnson in 1942. In 1990, he managed a staff of 2,382, and had total sales of $252,187,000.

87. Ze'ev Chafets, "The Tragedy of Detroit," *New York Times Magazine*, Section 6, July 29, 1990, page 50. In 1982, according to a survey of minority-owned business enterprises, by the U.S. Department of Commerce, Bureau of the Census, there were 6,798 such firms in Detroit, with receipts of $272,405,000. In Michigan there were 12,270 minority businesses, with total receipts of $470,329,000. *See Facts About Blacks* (Los Angeles, Calif.: Jeffries Associates, Inc., 1986), 19.

88. Joyce, *Black Book Publishers in the United States*, 66. In fact, economic conditions were so bad by the mid–1980s that Randall told the *Detroit News*: "There's no light at the end of the tunnel in this business." The paper noted that "His firm, Broadside Press, is finding it increasingly difficult to pay a mounting pile of bills. The business is so far in the red that he isn't publishing any new titles." For Randall, the issue came down to the fact that "Books about blacks are not selling. People just are not as interested as they once were back in the 1960s. Back then, blacks bought many more books than they are buying now." See *Detroit News*, January 2, 1985, A1, A12.

89. *Catalogues of Broadside Press* (Detroit: Broadside Press, 1990), 2; "Broadside Press," (Detroit: Broadside Press, 1990), 1–4.

90. Joyce, *Black Book Publishers in the United States*, 66; Interview with Hilda Vest by the author, June 15, 1994, Detroit, Mich.; Interview with Donald Vest by the author, June 15, 1994, Detroit, Mich.

91. *Catalogues of Broadside Press,* 1990; *Detroit Free Press*, October 20, 1990; Hilda Vest, letter to the author, December 26, 1991, Detroit, Mich.

92. Joyce, *Black Book Publishers in the United States,* 66.

93. Darren L. Smith, ed., *Black American Information Directory, 1990–1991* (Detroit: Gale Research Co., 1990), 298; *Catalogues of Broadside Press,* 1990, 1991. Although Broadside's books generally were priced between $5.00 to $7.00 after 1985, this was still very much below the average list price for a U.S. produced book in the period 1987–1989. The average list price for a book produced in this country was $32.40 in December 1987, $34.56 in December 1988, and $36.58 in December 1989. It is hardly surprising therefore that Broadside's profits were so low in 1990. The company just did not bring in enough cash for its book products. See Celia Wagner, "Book Pricing Update #2," *Against the Grain* 2, no. 1 (February 1990): 18.

94. Joyce, "Reflections on the Changing Publishing Objectives of Secular Black Book Publishers, 1900–1986," 233.

95. Smith, *Black American Information Directory 1990–1991*, 298; Interview with Ronald Snelling, with the author, October 10, 1993, Detroit, Mich.; Interview with Willie Williams, with the author, July 15, 1994, Detroit, Mich; Broadside Press Board of Directors List, Hilda Vest, to the author, July 20, 1994.

96. Thompson, "Interview with Dudley Randall." The new owners of Broadside observed in 1991 that "A positive, and valuable outgrowth of the 25th anniversary celebration is the establishment of the Friends of Broadside. The Friends is an informal group of concerned individuals who provide financial support for the Press in its ongoing quest for economic self reliance through the community. While the initial contributions were used to defray the expenses for the anniversary, there is, however a continuing need for operating funds. Individuals making contributions of $25.00 or more will be recognized as Friends of Broadside. As such you will receive a periodic newsletter and notification of all events sponsored by Broadside." See *Broadside Press Newsletter* (Detroit: Broadside Press, 1991), 3.

97. *Detroit Free Press*, October 20, 1990.

98. *Catalogues of Broadside Press* (Detroit: Broadside Press, 1994); Hilda Vest, interview with the author, June 15, 1994.

99. Hilda Vest, interview with the author, June 15, 1994; Bailey, *Broadside Authors and Artists*, 40; Aneb Kgositsile, *Blood River* (Detroit: Broadside Press, 1983), 42; Albert M. Ward, *Patches* (Detroit: Broadside Press 1989), 56; Sharon Smith-Knight, *Wine Sip and Other Delicious Poems* (Detroit: Broadside Press, 1991), 79; Murray Jackson, *Watermelon Rinds* (Detroit: Broadside Press, 1991), 89. In 1994, Broadside will publish Monica Morgan, *Freedom's Road: A Photo Journal of South Africa's First All-Race Election*; and Ron Milner's *Kwanzaa*, a children's book. In 1995, the company will print Leslie Reese's *Upside Down Tapestry Mosaic History* and Rayfield Waller's *Abstract Blues*.

100. Terri L. Jewell, review of Leslie A. Reese, *Upside Down Tapestry Mosaic History* in *The Black Scholar* 21, no. 3 (Summer 1990/Summer 1991): 49. See Alvin Aubert, "Foreword," in Leslie A. Reese, *Upside Down Tapestry Mosaic History* (Detroit: Broadside Press, 1987), iii–iv. For other comments on the poet and her collection of poems see also *Detroit Free Press*, March 30, 1988, B3, April 24, 1988, C7; "Review in Brief," *Poetry Resource Center Newsletter* (Detroit, Mich.), November 1988, 2. The Broadside Press Series (single broadsides of poetry) was reactivated in 1989, with the publication of Rayfield Waller's poem, "Upon Hearing of James Baldwin Dead." See Rayfield Waller, "Upon Hearing of James Baldwin Dead" (Detroit: Broadside Press, 1989).

101. Joyce, *Black Book Publishers in the United States*, 69.

102. Gloria House, "Introduction," in Rayfield Waller, *Abstract Blues: Poems, 1980–1987,* vii. In 1989, Broadside also published Michele Gibbs' *Island Images: A Coloring Book for the Young of All Ages.* The focus of the themes in the book are on black life and culture in the Caribbean.

103. Carolyn Warfield, "New Publications from Broadside Press," review of Aneb Kgositsile, *Rainrituals, Michigan Citizen,* October 7, 1990, page 12. See also Bill Harris, *River Mist* (Detroit, Mich.), January 31, 1989; J. Overmyer, *Choice* (July/August 1991): 183.

104. Albert Michael Ward, *Patches on Mainstreet* (Detroit: Broadside Press, 1989), 15–16.

105. Warfield, "New Publications from Broadside Press," review of Albert M. Ward, *Patches on Mainstreet.*

106. Pat Fry, "Poetry: HIPology: Horizons in Poetry; Detroit's Broadside Press Celebrates 25 Years," review of Ron Allen and Stella Crews, eds., *HIPology: Horizons in Poetry* in *People's Weekly World* (Detroit), November 10, 1990, page 18. See also Thom Jurek, "Diversions," review of Ron Allen and Stella Crews, eds., *HIPology: Horizons in Poetry,* in *Metro Arts* (Detroit), (1990); "Readings," *Orbit* (December 1993): 27; *The New England Review of Books* (Leverett, Mass.), July 1992; Neil Ollivierra, "Hot Dates," *Metro Times,* (Detroit), October 17, 1990; Scott Martelle, "Odes to Tough City: Writers Bare Their Anger, Souls in Detroit's Poetic Renaissance," *Detroit News,* October 3, 1988, C1–2; Chris Golembiewski, "Book 'Em: Bookstores Write New Chapter in Service," *Lansing (Mich.) State Journal,* June 6, 1991, C1, C7.

107. Gloria House, "Introduction," in Murray Jackson, *Watermelon Rinds and Cherry Pits* (Detroit: Broadside Press, 1991), x.

108. "Broadside Press Presents Sharon Smith-Knight," *Poetry Resource Center of Michigan Newsletter and Calendar* (November 1991): 1; Sharon Smith-Knight, *Wine Sip and Other Delicious Poems* (Detroit: Broadside Press, 1991), 15–16.

109. *Detroit Free Press,* (n.d., 1990), 15, 18.

110. J. Carl, review of Hilda Vest, *Sorrow's End, National Entertainment Plus Magazine* (March 1994): 10; Hilda Vest, *Sorrow's End* (Detroit: Broadside Press, 1993).

111. Junette A. Pinkney, "Independent Black Publishing," *American Visions* 4, no. 2 (April 1989): 51–52. On the decline of black consciousness and pride, a hallmark of the Black Arts Movement, a key Detroit observer noted in 1985 that: "We don't see expressions of black pride like we had back then [the 1960s], and we have stopped looking for them, says Edward Vaughn, owner of Vaughn's a now seldom-open bookstore. 'Blacks are not reading to such a degree that bookstores are closing in lots of cities, and there's less publishing,' adds Vaughn, a mayoral aid [to Coleman Young] and former state representative." See *Detroit News*, January 1, 1985, A12. The Rev. Albert B. Cleage, Jr., founder and Holy Patriarch of the Shrine of the Black Madonna of the Pan-African Orthodox Christian Church celebrated the 40th anniversary of the group in October 1993.

112. Pinkney, "Independent Black Publishing," 52. The reality of the economic situation facing Broadside is revealed in Donald Vest's 1991 observation that "It costs about $7,000 to get 2,000 copies of a novel ready for a bookstore, and that's a considerable amount for us." See the *Detroit News,* January 31, 1991.

113. See Keith Sterling, "Hilda Vest: The Beacon of Broadside Press," *Michigan Chronicle,* September 16, 1989, A5. But dealing with the public school system and higher educational institutions requires fortitude. Journalist Chauncey Bailey observes that in 1989, when Donald Vest "invited 20 English department heads from Detroit high schools, Highland Park High School and Wayne County Community College to a workshop, 'only three teachers showed up.' 'We wanted to explain how they could incorporate the impact of race and gender in creative writing,' he said." See the *Detroit News,* January 31, 1991.

114. Sterling, "Hilda Vest: The Beacon of Broadside Press." Hilda Vest told the *Michigan*

Chronicle that "The Broadside Press has a goal to publish four titles a year. We are considering expanding our market to novels and short stories, and we would consider other things, such as African cookbooks." To help increase a liberal audience for poetry, the Vests have fostered making Broadside writers "available for poetry readings, instructional seminars and book signing events." The company also provides consultants for "academic instruction and criticism." See *Broadside Press Newsletter* (Detroit: Broadside Press, 1991), 3.

115. *The Michigan Chronicle,* September 16, 1989, A5.

116. See Perri Giovannucci, "Detroit Small Presses," *City Arts* (Detroit, n.d., 1989?), 25.

117. Dudley Randall, interview with the author, October 11, 1991, Detroit, Mich.; Donald Vest, interview with the author, June 15, 1994, Detroit, Mich. On Randall's speaking engagements for this period see Program Conference — "Words in the Mourning Time," a celebration of Robert Hayden's poetry, Department of English, University of Michigan, Ann Arbor, February 22–25, 1990; Program Conference — The First Annual Conference on Black Literature, Creative Writing, Criticism and Publishing, "Black Literature and Knowledge: Developing a Liberating Worldview," Honoring Gwendolyn Brooks, Chicago State University, October 18–19, 1991.

118. Thomas H. Brennan, ed., *Writings on Writing: A Compendium of 1209 Quotations from Authors on Their Craft* (Jefferson, N.C.: McFarland, 1994), 76.

119. *Catalogues of Broadside Press,* 1990–1995.

120. Dudley Randall, ed., *The Black Poets: A New Anthology* (New York: Bantam Books, 1971).

121. On Addison Gayle, Jr., see the *New York Times,* October 5, 1991; on Audre Lorde see the *New York Times,* November 1992. During this period several other major black writers also died, including the critic Darwin Turner, at age 59, in 1991; and Ralph Ellison, the novelist, who wrote *Invisible Man* (1952), and died at age 80, in 1994. On Turner see the *Chicago Tribune,* February 22, 1991, A10; on Ellison see the *New York Times,* April 17, 1994, 38.

122. For a contemporary interpretation on black literature and Gayle and Lorde see Joyce Ann Joyce, *Warriors, Conjurers and Priests: Defining African-Centered Literary Criticism* (Chicago: Third World Press, 1994), 26–27, 29, 111, 252.

123. Chafets, *Devil's Night,* 124–28. On Chafets' background and the mixed reactions to his book see Peter Gavrilovich, "Author of 'Devil's Night' Faces the Heat in Detroit," *Detroit Free Press,* October 30, 1990, A7.

124. Redmond, *Drumvoices,* 306–7, 423; Randall, *Broadside Memories,* 25, 32.

125. Conditions have been harsh in Detroit during the early 1990s. Journalist Thomas J. Bray observes that a mid–1991 analysis of the city's plight by the Citizens Research Council of Michigan, a nonprofit community group, highlights the major challenges facing Detroit in the 1990s, including: "Population declined from a peak of 1.8 million in 1950 to about 1 million in the 1990 census. That's a loss of more than 800,000. Only 10 U.S. cities have a population of more than 800,000. Detroit's population in 1920 was 993,000. Less than half of Detroit's adult population is in the civilian labor force, compared to about 65 percent nationwide. Nearly half are on some form of welfare. The effective buying income of the median household ($19,394) is the lowest of major U.S. cities." And on it goes. See Thomas J. Bray, "Archer: Good Start, Big Problems," *Detroit News,* Fall 1993.

126. Ronald Grover, Gloria Lau, and Jane Birnbaum, "The Economic Crisis of Urban America," *Business Week,* no. 3266 (May 18, 1992): 38, 40. See also *New York Times,* October 7, 1991; *Chicago Tribune,* January 8, 1991, and November 3, 1993.

127. See Laurie Collier and Joyce Nakamura, eds., *Major Authors and Illustrators for Children and Young Adults* (Detroit: Gale Research Co., 1993), 2014–17; George E. Kent, *A Life of Gwendolyn Brooks* (Lexington: University Press of Kentucky, 1990), 273–74; Joanne V. Gabbin, *Sterling A. Brown: Building the Black Aesthetic Tradition* (Westport, Conn.: Greenwood, 1985). John Oliver Killens and Jerry W. Ward, eds., *Black Southern Voices: An Anthology of Fiction, Poetry, Drama, Nonfiction, and Critical Essays* (New York: Meridian Penguin, 1992), 234; Virginia C. Fowler, *Nikki Giovanni* (New York: Twayne Publishers, 1992), 169–70; Helen Houston, "Margaret Danner," in *Notable Black American Women,* ed. Jessie Carney Smith (Detroit: Gale Research Co., 1992), 249–50; Rachel C. Kranz, *The Biographical Dictionary of Black Americans* (New York: Facts on File, 1992), 159; James A. Emanuel, *Whole Grain: Collected Poems, 1958–1989* (Detroit: Lotus Press, 1991); Lance Jeffers, *Witherspoon* (a novel) (Atlanta, Ga.: George A. Flippin Press, 1983); *New York Times,* March 14, 1991; *Indianapolis Recorder,* March 16, 1991; Julius E. Thompson, "The Public Response to Haki R. Madhubuti, 1968–1988," *The Literary Griot: International Journal of Black Expressive Cultural Stud-*

ies 4, nos. 1 and 2 (Spring/Fall 1992): 16–37; "A 50 Year Salute to Margaret Walker Alexander," *Jackson Advocate*, October 15, 1992, B1–12.

128. Arthur P. Davis, Saunders Redding, and Joyce Ann Joyce, eds., *The New Cavalcade* (Washington, D.C.: Howard University Press, 1991), 60.

129. Broadside Press also greatly influenced the careers of poets Aurde Lorde, Keorapetse W. Kgositsile, Clarence Majors, Sterling Plumpp, and Marvin X. Collectively, these writers had a profound impact upon the Black Arts Movement and on the cultural scene of the eighties and nineties.

130. Suzanne Dolezal, "Poet," *Detroit Free Press*, April 11, 1982, page 11. See also Marilyn K. Basel, "Dudley Randall," in *Black Writers: A Selection of Sketches from Contemporary Authors*, 470.

131. *Broadside News* announced in August 1980 that its 10 best-selling books in July 1980 were: (1) Sanchez, *A Blues Book for Blue Black Magical Women*; (2) Brown, *The Last Ride of Wild Bill*; (3) Brooks, *Report from Part One*; (4) Brooks, *Jump Bad*; (5) Lee, *Don't Cry, Scream!*; (6) Jeffers, *When I Know the Power of My Black Hand*; (7) Bailey, *Broadside Authors and Artists*; (8) Walker, *Prophets for a New Day*; (9) Brooks, *Beckonings*; and (10) Gayle, *Clause McKay*. Thus, 8 of the 10 best-selling books during the summer of 1980 were by an author listed on Table 5.6. Gwendolyn Brooks with 3 titles was especially important to book sales at Broadside Press, as was Haki R. Madhubuti. See *Broadside News*, no. 34 (August 1980): 1.

132. *New York Times*, January 17, 1989, B11; *Indianapolis (Ind.) Star*, March 12, 1991.

133. Killens and Ward, *Black Southern Voices*, 234, 246.

134. Gwendolyn Brooks also stands out among Broadside poets because she holds the record for the highest number of publications (17) published by a single Broadside author by the company. See D.H. Melhem, *Gwendolyn Brooks: Poetry and the Heroic Voice* (Lexington: University Press of Kentucky, 1987), 257–58. On the other hand, Haki R. Madhubuti is the holder of the title of best-selling author in the history of Broadside Press. A recent study observes that "By 1991, some seventeen titles and more than three million copies of Madhubuti's books were in print." See Roy Neil Graves, "The Poetry of Haki R. Madhubuti," in *Masterpieces of African American Literature*, ed. Frank N. Magill (New York: HarperCollins, 1992), 431; Marlene Mosher, *New Directions from Don L. Lee* (Hicksville, N.Y.: Exposition Press, 1975), 5. Madhubuti produced 16 publications for Broadside Press (9 books, 3 broadsides, 3 tapes, and 1 album) between 1968 and 1975.

135. *Catalogues of Lotus Press*, 1980–1995; *Michigan State University Press Catalogue*, (East Lansing, Mich.: Fall/Winter 1993), 4–5; (Spring/Summer 1994), 4–5.

136. Joyce, *Black Book Publishers in the United States* (in a quote from a questionnaire by Naomi Long Madgett) to the author, February 6, 1986, page 42.

137. Joyce, *Black Book Publishers in the United States* (in a quote from an interview with Naomi Long Madgett), November 6, 1975, page 141.

138. Naomi Long Madgett, interview with the author, Detroit, Mich., October 18, 1991; Julius E. Thompson, "An Afternoon with Naomi Long Madgett, *Jackson Advocate*, November 14, 1991. See Emanuel, *Whole Grain: Collected Poems*; May Miller, *Collected Poems* (Detroit: Lotus Press, 1989).

139. Thirty-seven Broadside poets were selected for the three anthologies. Seventeen appeared in *Dear Dark Faces*; 9 in *A Milestone Sampler*; and 11 in *Adam of Ife*. See Helen Earle Simcox, ed., *Dear Dark Faces: Portraits of a People* (Detroit: Lotus Press, 1980); Naomi Long Madgett, ed., *A Milestone Sampler: 15 Anniversary Anthology*, (Detroit: Lotus Press, 1988), and Naomi Long Madgett, ed., *Adam of Ife: Black Women in Praise of Black Men* (Detroit: Lotus Press, 1992).

140. *Catalogues of Lotus Press*, 1988, 1992.

141. Joyce, *Gatekeepers of Black Culture*, 132.

142. *Catalogues of Lotus Press*, 1980–1994.

143. Joyce, *Black Book Publishers in the United States*, 141–44.

144. See Sherille Phelps, ed., *Who's Who Among Black Americans, 1994–95* (Detroit: Gale Research Co., 1994), 24, 62, 388, 459, 464, 478, 813, 872, 937, 1026, 1277, 1544; Sascha Feinstein and Yusef Komunyakaa, eds., *The Jazz Poetry Anthology* (Bloomington: Indiana University Press, 1991), 262, 275; James A. Page and Joe Min Roh, *Selected Black American, African, and Caribbean Authors: A Bio-Bibliography* (Littleton, Col.: Libraries Unlimited, 1985), 4, 51, 90, 189.

145. *Fifteenth Anniversary Celebration of Lotus Press, Inc.* (Detroit: Lotus Press, June 25–27, 1987), 1–10. Dudley Randall was not able to attend the celebrations.

146. Naomi Long Madgett, interview with the author, October 18, 1991, Detroit, Mich.

147. Ibid.

148. Thompson, "An Afternoon with Naomi Long Madgett."

149. Naomi Long Madgett, *Lotus Press: The Inside Story*, (Detroit: Lotus Press, 1992), 1–2.

150. Chauncey Bailey, "Struggle to Survive: Black Writers' Publishers See Red Ink," *Detroit News*, January 2, 1985, A1.

151. Ibid., A12.

152. Madgett, *Lotus Press: The Inside Story*, 2.

153. "We've Made Some Changes!" (Detroit: Lotus Press, 1993), 1; American Booksellers Association, *Exhibition Directory and Convention Guide* (Miami, Fla.: American Booksellers Association, May 29–June 1, 1993).

154. Announcement of the Hilton-Long Poetry Foundation, "Naomi Long Madgett Poetry Award," (Detroit: Hilton-Long Poetry Foundation, 1993), 1–2; *Michigan State University Press Catalogue* (Spring/Summer 1994), 4.

155. The Before Columbia Foundation, *American Book Awards, 1993* (Oakland, Calif.: The Before Columbus Foundation, 1993). See also J.J. Phillips, Ishmael Reed, Gundars Strods, and Shawn Wong, eds., *The Before Columbus Foundation Poetry Anthology: Selections from the American Book Awards, 1980–1990* (New York: W.W. Norton and Co., 1992), xv–xvii; *Detroit News and Free Press*, June 6, 1994, J7.

156. The Herald-Palladium (St. Joseph/Benton Harbor, Mich.), August 15, 1993.

157. Carol Teegardin, "Detroit Poet Honored with State Arts Award," *Detroit Free Press*, August 14, 1993, A13.

158. Mark Puls, "For the Patient Reader, Detroit's Poet's Imagination, Sensitivity Stir the Soul," *Detroit News*, September 30, 1993.

159. Ibid.

160. *Catalogues of Third World Press,* (1993–1994) (Chicago: Third World Press, 1993) 1; Joyce, *Black Book Publishers in the United States*, 208.

161. Paula Giddings, "About People: Book Marks," *Essence* 19, no. 11 (March 1989): 26.

162. Will Nixon, "Better Times for Black Writers?" *Publishers Weekly* 235, no. 7 (February 17, 1989): 40.

163. Paula Giddings notes that two other black-owned publishers have made major contributions to black book production in the United States: Kitchen Table, Women of Color Press, Lathan, New York, established in 1981 by Barbara Smith and Audre Lorde; and Africa World Press created in 1979 by Kassahun Checole, a native of Eritrea. See Gidding, "About People: Book Marks," 26.

164. Haki R. Madhubuti's contributions also include service to the New Concept Development Center, a private elementary school (to grade three), and the African-American Book Center, located in Chicago. Along with Third World Press, the above groups are all a part of the Institute of Positive Education. See John Allison, "Knowledge Is Power," *American Bookseller* (February 1990): 168.

165. *Catalogues of Third World Press*, 1980–1995.

166. Ibid.; Joyce, *Black Book Publishers in the United States,* 207–11.

167. *Catalogues of Third World Press*, 1989, 31.

168. Five major Broadside Press poets had works of poetry published or distributed by Third World Press between 1980 and 1995. They were Keorapetse Kgositsile, 1 book; Sonia Sanchez, 1 book; Naomi Long Madgett, 1 book; Haki R. Madhubuti, 4 books; and Gwendolyn Brooks, 4 books.

169. Pinkney, "Independent Book Publishing," 52; Joseph Barbato, "New Alliance Brings Black Publishers, Booksellers Together," *Publishers Weekly* 234, no. 24 (December 9, 1988): 39; Connie Goddard, "Aiming for the Mainstream," *Publishers Weekly* 239, no. 4 (January 20, 1992): 29.

170. *Catalogues of Third World Press*, 1990, 10.

171. Goddard, "Aiming for the Mainstream," 29.

172. Ibid.

173. Bruce Bean, "Book Review," *Los Angeles Times,* n.d., 1990. Paula Giddings notes that "The book's first printing of 7,500 sold out within four weeks. 'There hasn't been such a strong reaction to any of my books since "*Don't Cry, Scream!*" [1969],' Madhubuti says." See Paula Giddings, "Haki Madhubuti: A Guide for Black Men," *Essence* 21, no. 21 (June 1990): 44. Madhubuti also had a best-seller in his collection of essays, *Enemies: The Clash of Races* (1978), which by the end of 1991 had sold over 75,000 copies. See Goodard, "Aiming for the Mainstream," 29.

174. Giddings, "About People: Book Marks," 26; Joyce, *Gatekeepers of Black Culture,* 129. See also Joyce, *Black Book Publishers in the United States,* 208. The social backgrounds of many Third World Press authors for the years 1980–95 reveal that most have had a Chicago connection —(i.e., born in the city, or lived and worked there during some stage of their careers). Like earlier groups of black writers in New York and Detroit, the Chicago writers of the period are a highly educated group. Many have had dual careers as teachers, writers, and editors. See Page, *Selected Black American Authors,* 12, 26–27, 80–81, 114–15, 153, 157, 163–64, 182, 215, 219, 241, 295.

175. Allison, "Knowledge Is Power," 168.

176. *Catalogues of Third World Press,* 1993–1994, 42–43.

177. Haki R. Madhubuti, "From the Editor," *Black Books Bulletin: Words Work* 8 (1991): iii.

178. The exact range of pages for books produced at Third World Press between 1980–1994 follows:

1–50	*51–69*	*70–100*	*101–150*	*151–199*	*200–249*	*250–300*	*Above 300*
19	7	11	6	2	5	6	5

Unknown: 2.

The range of books produced yearly at Third World Press follows:

1980: 4; 1981: 1; 1984: 2; 1985: 3; 1987: 4; 1988: 1; 1989: 5; 1990: 4; 1991: 9; 1992: 8; 1993: 17; 1994: 4. See *Catalogues of Third World Press,* 1980–1994.

179. A survey of the paperback price list for Third World Press during 1980–1994, reveals that 9 books were priced below $5.00; 38 at $5.01 to $9.99; 13 books at $10 to $14.99; 6 at $15 to $19.99 and only 1 book between $20.00 and $29.99. See *Catalogues of Third World Press,* 1980–1994.

180. Joyce, *Black Book Publishers in the United States,* 208.

181. Pinkney, "Independent Black Publishing," 52.

182. Ibid.

183. "A Weathervane for Black Writers," *Los Angeles Times,* November 18, 1988, Part V, 5.

184. In 1988–89, the African-American Publishers and Booksellers Association's members included Broadside Press (Detroit), Black Classic Press (Baltimore), Twelve Gates Publications (Indianapolis), Blackwood Press (Atlanta), Third World Press, Path Press, and Urban Research Press, all of Chicago, and bookstores, such as African-American Literature Service (Columbia, Md.), Akbar's Books (St. Louis) and 21st Century Books (Chicago). See Joseph Barbata, "New Alliance Brings Black Publishers, Booksellers Together," *Publishers Weekly* 234, no. 24 (December 9, 1988): 39.

185. Ibid.

Chapter 6

1. Pat Fry, "Detroit's Broadside Press Celebrates 25 Years" *People's Weekly World* (November 10, 1990): 18.

2. Marilyn Nelson Waniek, review of Dudley Randall's *A Litany of Friends,* in *Callaloo* 6, no. 1 (February 1983): 164.

3. Alphonso Pinkney, *Red, Black, and Green: Black Nationalism in the United States* (Cambridge: Cambridge University Press, 1976), 78.

4. *Poetry Resource Center of Michigan Newsletter and Calendar* (October 1990): 1.

5. D.H. Melhem, "The Writer's Behavior," *Confrontation,* no. 51 (Summer 1993): 31.

6. "Broadside Press and Lotus Press Keep Pumping Them Out," *Michigan Chronicle,* February 12, 1992, page 23.

7. On the complexity of these issues see David Harman, *Illiteracy: A National Dilemma* (New York: Cambridge Book Co., 1989), 4–5; Jonathan Kozol, *Illiterate America* (New York: New American Library, 1985), 4–5, 32–35, 230–33; Katherine H. Adams, *A History of Professional Writing Instruction in American Colleges: Years of Acceptance, Growth, and Doubt* (Dallas, Texas: Southern Methodist University Press, 1993), 14–15, 70–73, 100–1, 152–54; Denise Kimagner, "3-Year Project Seeks to Develop Degree-Level Writing Programs at Historically Black Colleges," the *Chronicle of Higher Education* XL, no. 3 (September 8, 1993): A20; "Report: Students Read Too Little," *Chicago Tribune,* May 29, 1992, A4; William Noble, *Bookbanning in America: Who Bans Books? And*

Why (Middlebury, Vt.: Paul S. Eriksson Publisher, 1990), 203–4; Jane Smiley, "Censorship in a World of Fantasy," *Chicago Tribune*, February 15, 1994, A13.

8. Nicholas Zill and Marianne Winglee, *Who Reads Literature? The Future of the United States as a Nation of Readers* (Washington, D.C.: Seven Locks Press, 1990), from the back cover.

9. See E.D. Hirsch, Jr., *Cultural Literacy: What Every American Needs to Know* (Boston: Houghton Mifflin Co., 1987), 158, 168, 184, 186, 190, 200, 213–14.

10. R. Baxter Miller, "'Endowing the World and Time': The Life and Work of Dudley Randall," in *Black American Poets Between Worlds, 1940–1960*, ed. R. Baxter Miller (Knoxville: University of Tennessee Press, 1986), 78; Ann Allen Shockley, "Librarians, Archivists, and Writers: A Personal Perspective," in *The Black Librarian in America Revisited*, ed. E.J. Josey (Metuchen, N.J.: Scarecrow Press, 1994), 322–23.

11. Hal May, Deborah A. Straub, and Susan M. Trosky, eds., *Black Writers: A Selection of Sketches from Contemporary Authors* (Detroit: Gale Research Co., 1988), 468.

12. Donald Barlow Stauffer, *A Short History of American Poetry* (New York: E.P. Dutton & Co., 1974), 426.

13. Arnold Rampersad, "The Poetry of the Harlem Renaissance," in *The Columbia History of American Poetry*, ed. Jay Parin and Brett C. Miller (New York: Columbia University Press, 1993), 476.

14. Jennifer Jordan, "Cultural Nationalism in the 1960s: Politics and Poetry," in *Race, Politics, and Culture: Critical Essays on the Radicalism of the 1960s*, ed. Adolph Reed, Jr. (Westport, Conn.: Greenwood, 1986), 39.

15. Kalamu ya Salaam, "African American Cultural Empowerment: A Struggle to Identify and Institutionalize Ourselves as a People," in *Voices from the Battlefront: Achieving Cultural Equity*, ed. Marta Moreno Vega and Cheryll Y. Greene (Trenton, N.J.: Africa World Press, 1993), 119.

16. Jerry W. Ward, Jr., "Report on a Poetry Festival: Melvin A. Butler Third Annual Memorial," *Black World* XXIII, no. 11 (September 1974): 80.

17. Rosey E. Pool, ed., *Beyond the Blues: New Poems by American Negroes* (Lympne Kent, England: The Hand and Flower Press, 1962), 165–66; Langston Hughes, ed., *New Negro Poets: USA* (Bloomington: Indiana University Press, 1964), 41, 59; Robert Hayden, ed., *Kaleidoscope: Poems by American Negro Poets* (New York: Harcourt, Brace & World, 1967), 131–32; Dudley Randall, ed. *The Black Poets* (New York: Bantam Books, 1971), 143–44, 147; Stephen Henderson, ed., *Understanding the New Black Poetry: Black Speech and Black Music as Poetic References* (New York: William Morrow & Co., 1973), 233–34; R.S. Gwynn, ed., *Poetry: A HarperCollins Pocket Anthology* (New York: HarperCollins, 1993), 215–16.

18. Mark Puls, "For the Patient Reader, Detroit Poet's Imagination, Sensitivity Stir the Soul," *Detroit News*, September 30, 1993. In 1994, Naomi Long Madgett was awarded an honorary doctorate from Michigan State University, in recognition of her contributions to American literature. Naomi Long Madgett, letter to the author, Detroit, Mich., July 25, 1994. See especially Dudley Randall, Part V, in *A Capsule Course in Black Poetry Writing*, with Gwendolyn Brooks, Keorapetse Kgositsile and Haki R. Madhubuti (Detroit: Broadside Press, 1975), 35–53. Readers can observe the intensity of the current period (1990s), and its impact on younger black poets, by consulting the comments of writer Michael Robinson. Writing in *American Visions*, in 1994, Robinson paints a bleak picture of the contemporary situation for black poets. He notes that "Only a handful [of poets] from the last generation — Amiri Baraka, Nikki Giovanni, Sonia Sanchez, June Jordan and Quincy Troupe — have become well-known and well respected Grafters of words and verse. The poets who have emerged in their wake struggle for recognition. They toil in obscurity, refining their craft at occasional readings in softly lit basement clubs, their compensation often barely sufficient for the late-night cab ride home. Most don't bemoan their lack of organization or the fact that, unlike the Black Arts Movement of a generation ago, they are not connected to a vibrant political current. For many, their predecessors — the village elders of black poetry — are bodies of knowledge who point the way. As Tracie Morris puts it, 'Amiri Baraka, Sonia Sanchez and Nikki Giovanni are still involved and are living institutions — walking, talking, breathing, living institutions.'" See Michael Robinson, "Raves: Poets Come in from the Cold," *American Visions* 9, no. 4 (August/September 1994): 15–16, 18.

19. "Minority Enrollment Figures Set Record Highs," the *National College Newspaper*, 5 (March 1992): 6. On a contemporary study of black life see Clarence Lusane, *African Americans at the*

Crossroads: The Restructuring of Black Leadership and the 1992 Elections (Boston, Mass.: South End Press, 1994).

20. See Stephen E. Henderson, "'Survival Motion': A Study of the Black Writer and the Black Revolution in American," in *The Militant Black Writer in Africa and the United States*, Mercer Cook and Stephen E. Henderson (Madison: University of Wisconsin Press, 1969), 128–29; Dudley Randall, *After the Killing* (Chicago: Third World Press, 1973): Dudley Randall, *Cities Burning* (Detroit: Broadside Press, 1968).

21. In the contemporary world one can certainly note "violence" in the fact that "the Los Angeles School System has 32 psychiatric social workers for 610,000 students." And in foreign lands, "The Khmer Rouge is estimated to have killed 1.5 million people, 80% of them men." Or the over 500,000 plus Tutsis and Hutus killed by Hutu militias in Rwanda in the Spring of 1994. See Margaret DiCanio, *The Encyclopedia of Violence: Origins, Attitudes, Consequences* (New York: Facts on File, 1993), 109–11; *Chicago Tribune*, July 25, 1994, A5. Many contemporary authors have described the mixed impact of American television and media on people. Some believe that the medium has not lived up to its potential. Yet, the fact remains, as Marcus D. Pohlmann notes that "more than 98 percent of all American homes currently have at least one television set, and it is turned on an average 6 to 7 hours each day. (The average 6-year-old has spent more time in front of the television than at school.)" See Marcus D. Pohlmann, *Black Politics in Conservative America* (New York: Longman, 1990), 198. See also Yahya Kamalipour, "The Brain Drain: What Television Is Doing to Us...," *Chicago Tribune*, May 2, 1994, A13.

22. See Michael Eric Dyson, Chapter 13, "The Plight of Black Men," in *Reflecting Black: African-American Cultural Criticism* (Minneapolis: University of Minnesota Press, 1993), 185. On the international dimensions of several of Broadside's most important black women poets, such as Sonia Sanchez and Audre Lorde see especially Chapter 6, "Lust for a Working Tomorrow: U.S. Women's Poetry of Solidarity and Struggle," in *Poetics of Resistance: Women Writing in El Salvador, South Africa and the United States*, Mary K. DeShazer (Ann Arbor: University of Michigan Press, 1994), 241–99.

23. See Jay B. Hubbell, *Who Are the Major American Writers* (Durham, N.C.: Duke University Press, 1972), 228–29, 298. No African-American novelist is mentioned on any "best book" list of the period in this book, not even Toni Morrison who was awarded the Nobel Prize in Literature in 1993. See William Grimes, "Toni Morrison Is '93 Winner of Nobel Prize in Literature," *New York Times*, October 8, 1993, A1, B10.

24. Hubbell, *Who Are the Major American Writers*, 298–99.

25. Ralph Wiley, *What Black People Should Do Now: Dispatches from Near the Vanguard* (New York: Ballantine Books, 1993), 126–27.

26. See James Sullivan, "Real Cool Pages: The Broadside Press Broadside Series," *Contemporary Literature* XXXII, no. 4 (Winter 1991): 552–72; "Poetry from Broadside Press," the *Friends of the Lilly Library Newsletter* [Indiana University], no. 16 (Spring 1991): 5–6; Dudley Randall, *Broadside Memories: Poets I Have Known* (Detroit: Broadside Press, 1975), 23–33; "Broadside Press and Lotus Keep Pumping Them Out," *Michigan Chronicle*, February 12, 1992.

27. Elizabeth Catlett, "Responding to Cultural Hunger," in *Reimaging America: The Arts of Social Change,* ed. Mark O'Brien and Craig Little (Philadelphia, Pa.: New Society Publishers, 1990), 244–45.

28. Miller, "'Endowing the World and Time,'" 77.

29. See Randall, *Broadside Memories*, 33; Junette A. Pinkney, "Independent Black Publishers," *American Visions* (April 1989): 52–53; *Detroit Free Press*, April 11, 1982; *Black World* 24, no.5 (March 1975): 35.

30. Donald Franklin Joyce, *Black Book Publishers in the United States: A Historical Dictionary of the Presses 1817–1990* (Westport, Conn.: Greenwood, 1991), 63–70; *Broadside Memories*, 28. Broadside's continuing influence on black literature in the 1990s was highly expressed at one of the most important African-American literary festivals and conferences in the country since 1970, when 14 Broadside writers appeared at the Furious Flower Conference: A Revolution in African American Poetry, on September 29–October 1, 1994, at James Madison University, Harrisonburg, Virginia. The program organizer, Joanne V. Gobbin, invited 15 Broadside poets to appear on the program, including: Samuel Allen, Alvin Aubert, Amiri Baraka, Gwendolyn Brooks, Eugenia Collier, Mari Evans, Nikki Giovanni, Michael S. Harper, Pinkie Gordon Lane, Naomi Long Madgett, Haki Madhubuti, Sterling Plumpp (did not attend), Raymond Patterson, Sonia Sanchez,

and Askia T. Mohammad. See *Furious Flower Conference: A Revolution in African American Poetry Program* (Harrisonburg, Va.: James Madison University, 1994); B. Denise Hawkins, "A Furious Flowering of Poetry: Conference to Document, Analyze Black Arts Movement of the 60s," *Black Issues in Higher Education* 11, no. 13 (August 25, 1994): 41–42.

31. Cleveland State University Library Catalog, Cleveland, Ohio, reviewed by the author, April 26, 1993; Natchez Public Library Catalog, Natchez, Mississippi, reviewed by the author, August 16, 1993; Tougaloo College Library Catalog, Tougaloo, Mississippi, reviewed by the author, August 16, 1993; Jackson State University Library Catalog, Jackson, Mississippi, reviewed by the author, August 17, 1993. On the special role and contributions of black American libraries see Jessie Carney Smith, "Special Collections of Black Literature in the Traditionally Black College," *College and Research Libraries* 35, no. 5 (September 1974): 322–35; Jessie Carney Smith, *Black Academic Libraries and Research Collections: An Historical Survey* (Westport, Conn.: Greenwood, 1977), 53, 74–81; "First Conference of African American Librarians Convenes in Ohio," *The Black Scholar* 23, no. 1 (Winter/Spring 1993): 33.

32. Randall, *Broadside Memories*, 23–33; Donald Franklin Joyce, *Gatekeepers of Black Culture: Black-Owned Book Publishing in the United States, 1817–1981* (Westport, Conn.: Greenwood, 1983), 183–84; Dudley Randall, interview with the author, October 11, 1991, Detroit, Michigan. Indeed, Randall's success as a publisher is all the more amazing because of the suffocating statistics which he was up against. Two are noted here. Journalist Neal Shine wrote in 1991 that: "One study of adults between the ages of 21 and 25 showed that 80 percent could not read a bus schedule, 73 percent could not understand a newspaper story and 63 percent could not follow written map directions.... There are an estimated 800,000 functionally illiterate adults in Michigan, more than half of them in the Detroit area." See the *Detroit Free Press*, October 6, 1991, G3. Such issues had an impact on Randall's work to foster audience development for Broadside publications. Secondly, Randall worked as a publisher in a society where the economic pie was unequally divided between whites, blacks, and other groups. Economist Don Mark Walder observed in 1981 that: "While Blacks now constitute approximately 11.6% of the U.S. population and receive 7.5% of income, they own only 1% of all income producing wealth. The sales of black firms trail far behind at less than .2% of total business sales. The amount of capital that Blacks can obtain through currently available sources has been investigated by Dorsey and Knight and been found to be woefully inadequate — less than 5% of the amount required to achieve parity over a period of 20 years." See Don Mark Walder, "The Potential for Black Business," *The Review of Black Political Economy* 11, no. 3 (Spring 1981): 310.

33. Tony Martin, *The Jewish Onslaught: Dispatches from the Wellesley Battlefront* (Dover, Mass.: Majority Press, 1993), 42.

34. See Woodie King, Jr., ed., *The Forerunners: Black Poets in America* (Washington, D.C.: Howard University Press, 1975), 99–103.

35. See William W. Cook, "The Black Arts Poets," in *The Columbia History of American Poetry*, ed. Jay Parini and Brett C. Miller (New York: Columbia University Press, 1993), 674–706. Readers can witness Dudley Randall's closeness to many of the Black Arts Movement poets by simply viewing his inscription on a gift copy of his book, *A Litany of Friends*, that the poet autographed for Lance Jeffers. It reads: "For Lance who had faith in me and gave me his royalties and praised me. My thanks, my love, from Dudley 2/10/82." See Lance Jeffers Papers, Tougaloo College Library Archives, Tougaloo, Mississippi. The author is thankful to Dr. Jerry W. Ward, Jr., English Department, Tougaloo College, for bringing this information to his attention. Jerry W. Ward, Jr., letter to the author, Tougaloo, Mississippi, May 29, 1994.

36. Contemporary critics still bemoan the under-representation of black women writers in the canon of African-American literature. However, Dudley Randall must be given credit by all for his significant efforts to help correct this historic problem. See Faith Berry, "A Question of Publisher and a Question of Audience," *The Black Scholar* 17, no. 2 (March/April 1986): 41–49; Acklyn Lynch, "Black Women Writers in the Past Two Decades: Voices Within the Veil," in *Nightmare Overhanging Darkly: Essays on African American Culture and Resistance* (Chicago: Third World Press, 1992), 189–205. Randall even found space at Broadside for white poets, including John Sinclair, head of the White Panther Party, noted by one authority as "a radical white youth group inspired by the Black Panthers." See David Armstrong, *Alternative Media in America* (Los Angeles: J.P. Tarcher, Inc., 1981), 172; Dudley Randall and Margaret Burroughs, eds., *For Malcolm X* (Detroit: Broadside Press, 1967), 58, 94, 110.

37. Randall, *Broadside Memories*, 5, 8–11, 18–19, 33; Bailey, *Broadside Authors and Artists* 17, 19–24, 27–29, 31–32, 34, 36, 38–43, 49–51, 55–57, 62–63, 65, 67–69, 76–78, 80–81, 83, 84, 86–88, 91–92, 96, 101, 103–6, 108–9, 111–13, 115–16, 119–21, 123.

38. See Leaonead Pack Bailey, *Broadside Authors and Artists: An Illustrated Biographical Directory* (Detroit: Broadside Press, 1974), 70; Emmanuel S. Nelson, "Black America and the Black South African Literary Consciousness," in *Perspectives of Black Popular Culture*, ed. Harry B. Shaw (Bowling Green, Ohio: Bowling Green State University Popular Press, 1990), 155–65.

39. Bill Odarty, *A Safari of African Cooking* (Detroit: Broadside Press, 1971, 1992); Bailey, *Broadside Authors and Artists*, 89.

40. See Phanuel Akubueze Egejuru, *Towards African Literary Independence: A Dialogue with Contemporary African Writers* (Westport, Conn.: Greenwood, 1980), 15–31, 55–70. On a related theme see Ngugi wa Thiong'o, *Decolonising the Mind: The Politics of Language in African Literature* (London: James Currey, Ltd., and Nairobi, Kenya: Heinemann Kenya, 1986).

41. Dudley Randall, "A Different Image," in *Black Poets: A New Anthology*, 142, quoted in Marion Berghahn, *Images of Africa in Black American Literature* (London: The Macmillan Press, Ltd., 1977), viii.

42. See Eseoghene, *The Conflicting Eye* (London: Paul Breman, 1973), 26; Frank John, *Light a Fire* (London: Paul Breman, 1973), 22; Paul Breman, ed., *You Better Believe It* (Baltimore, Md.: Penguin Books, 1973), 442, 446; *Catalogues of Broadside Press* (Detroit: Broadside Press, 1974–1975). Nicolas Guillen, *Tengo,* translated by Richard J. Carr (Detroit: Broadside Press, 1974); "Nicolas Guillen," *The Encyclopedia Americana*, International Edition, vol. 13 (Danbury, Conn.: Grolier, Inc., 1994), 580.

43. Addison Gayle, Jr., ed., *The Black Aesthetic* (Garden City, N.Y.: Anchor Books/Doubleday, 1972), xxi.

44. Gwendolyn Brooks, "Malcolm X," in *For Malcolm X*, ed. Randall and Burroughs (1967), 3, and *In the Mecca* (New York: Harper & Row, 1968), 39, "Five Men Against the Theme 'My Name Is Red Hot, Yo Name Ain Doodley Squat,'" in *Beckonings* (Detroit: Broadside Press, 1975), 6, "For Dudley Randall on the Tenth Anniversary of Broadside Press," *Black World* XXV, no. 3, January 1976): 91; James A. Emanuel, "For 'Mr. Dudley,' A Black Spy," in *Panther Man* (Detroit: Broadside Press, 1970), 14–15; Nikki Giovanni, "Poems (For Dudley Randall)," *The Afro-American Woman Magazine* 1 (March/April 1969): 22, also in Nikki Giovanni, *Black Feeling, Black Talk, Black Judgement* (New York: William Morrow & Co., 1970); "To Dudley Randall," noted in *The Black Scholar* 6, no. 9 (June 1975): 90; Murray Jackson, "Dudley Randall," in *Watermelon Rinds and Cherry Pits* (Detroit: Broadside Press, 1991), 25; Alicia L. Johnson, "Our Days Are Numbered," (Detroit: Broadside Press, Broadside No. 30, 1969), and in Gwendolyn Brooks, ed., *A Broadside Treasury* (Detroit: Broadside Press, 1971), 176; Sharon Smith-Knight, "Of Men and Women," for Dudley, in *Wine Sip and Other Delicious Poems* (Detroit: Broadside Press, 1991), James Randall, "Street Games," and "Letters Home," in *Cities and Other Disasters* (Detroit: Broadside Press, 1973), 12–13, 15–20; Sterling D. Plumpp, "(For Dudley Randall)," *Black World* XXV, no. 3 (January 1976): 82–83; Eileen Tann, "A Counterpoem for Dudley Randall," (Detroit: Broadside Press, Broadside No. 83, 1974); Preston M. Yancy "Du Bois and Washington Revered," *Black World* XXIII, no. 4 (February 1974): 84; Ron Allen and Stella Crews, eds., *HIPology: Horizons in Poetry* (Detroit: Broadside Press, 1990); Gwendolyn Brooks, *Riot* (Detroit: Broadside Press, 1969), 5; Gwendolyn Brooks, *Report from Part One* (Detroit: Broadside Press, 1972), 6; Gwendolyn Brooks, *To Disembark* (Chicago: Third World Press, 1981); Michael Delp, Conrad Hilberry, and Herbert Scott, eds., *Contemporary Michigan Poetry, Poems from the Third Coast* (Detroit: Wayne State University Press, 1988), 9; Don L. Lee, *Don't Cry, Scream!* (Detroit: Broadside Press, 1969), 5; Don L. Lee (Haki R. Madhubuti), *Killing Memory, Seeking Ancestors* (Detroit: Lotus Press, 1987), v; Melhem, *Heroism in the New Black Poetry*, vi.

45. Dudley Randall, from Part V in *A Capsule Course in Black Poetry Writing*, with Gwendolyn Brooks, Keorapetse Kgositsile, and Haki R. Madhubuti (Detroit: Broadside Press, 1975), 35. "*Black Nation* Interviews Margaret Walker," *The Black Nation: Journal of Afro-American Thought* 2, no. 1 (Fall/Winter 1982): 14. Walker went on to recommend the following advice to young writers: "The first thing they have to do is think hard about the reality of our lives. The second thing is to read everything that they can find so that they have models on which to base their work, and to develop the craft and to work to develop the art."

46. "*Black Nation* Interviews Margaret Walker," 14.

47. See Clint C. Wilson, II, *Black Journalists in Paradox: Historical Perspectives and Current*

Dilemmas (Westport, Conn.: Greenwood, 1991), 152–53; Dana Gioia, *Can Poetry Matter?: Essays on Poetry and American Culture* (Saint Paul, Minn.: Graywolf Press, 1992), 1–24; Nicholas Zell and Marianne Winglee, *Who Reads Literature?: The Future of the United States as a Nation of Readers* (Washington, D.C.: Seven Locks Press, 1990), 44–75; Michigan Literacy, Inc., "40 Facts About Adult Illiteracy in the United States of America" (Detroit: Detroit Public Library, 1993), 5, quoting a report by the U.S. Department of Education; Billy J. Tidwell, ed., *The State of Black America 1994* (New York: National Urban League, 1994), 14.

48. See Chapter 8, "'Mama How Come Black Men Don't Get to Be Heroes?': Colorizing American Experience," in Laurence Goldstein, *The American Poet at the Movies: A Critical History* (Ann Arbor: University of Michigan Press, 1994), 199–222, 272–74. Works by contemporary black poets in Detroit continue to appear. See Daphne Williams Ntir, ed., *Consonance and Continuity in Poetry: Detroit Black Writers* (Detroit: Bedford Publishers, 1988).

49. An interesting dispute developed in 1975–76, between Dudley Randall, Hoyt W. Fuller, and novelist John A. Williams. In March 1975, editor Fuller published a special issue of *Black World* on a "Survey of Black Publishing." Williams submitted an article on "Black Publisher, Black Writer: An Impasse," in which he challenged black publishers to be fairer with black writers in terms of their contracts, publication schedules, and other concerns of authors. A year later, Williams complained in a new essay, "Sandbagging at *Black World*," in *Yardbird Reader* (1976), that Fuller had allowed Dudley Randall to write a rebuttal article in the same March 1975 issue of *Black World*, "Black Publisher, Black Writer: An Answer," without informing Williams about it. This left a bitter sentiment in Williams' opinion of both Fuller and Randall. See John A. Williams, "Black Publisher, Black Writer: An Impasse," *Black World* XXIIII, no. 5 (March 1975): 28–31; John A. Williams, "Sandbagging at *Black World*," *Yardbird Reader* 5 (Berkeley, Calif.: Yardbird Publishing, Inc., 1976), 11–12; Dudley Randall, "Black Publisher, Black Author: An Answer," *Black World* XXIV, no. 5 (March 1975): 32–37.

50. See Columbus Salley, *The Black 100: A Ranking of the Most Influential African-Americans Past and Present* (New York: Citadel Press/Carol Publishing Co., 1993), 9–14, 37–40, 48–51, 60–61, 174; Benjamin Quarles, *Black Abolitionists* (New York: Oxford University Press, 1969).

51. Shirley J. Yee's study on nineteenth century black women abolitionists makes an observation about them that also applies to black men abolitionists, and to many twentieth century "abolitionists," as well. "Central to the experiences of black female abolitionists were community-building, political organizing, and forging a network of personal and professional friendships with other activists." See Shirley J. Yee, *Black Women Abolitionists: A Study in Activism, 1828–1860* (Knoxville: University of Tennessee Press, 1992), 2. The current managers of Broadside Press, Hilda and Donald Vest, remain hopeful about the future and the black writer. Their current goals suggest that "Future programs will focus on three specific areas: First, publication of new works; Second, reprinting of select volumes; and Third, reactivation of the Broadside Poets Theater. To fund these programs, Broadside Press hopes to generate support from a variety of sources. We would appreciate an opportunity to discuss funding options that may be consistent with your commitment to support cultural and literary endeavors. We hope to keep an historically significant institution alive. Your tax deductible contribution can help make that possible." In 1990, the Society of African-American Poets Association of Detroit, presented Broadside Press with an "Award of Merit," for outstanding achievement in "Poetry Reading, Lecturing, Publishing, and Support." See *Broadside Press Newsletter* (Detroit: Broadside Press, 1994), 1; Hilda Vest, interview with the author, Detroit, Michigan, June 15, 1994; Award of Merit by the Society of African-American Poets Association (Detroit: SOA-PAD, 1990).

Selected Bibliography

The personal papers of Dudley Randall and the office files of Broadside Press (1965–1995) have not yet been deposited in an archival collection. However, a large body of Mr. Randall's correspondence exists in the personal papers of many American literary figures, including Etheridge Knight, Margaret Danner, George Kent, Haki R. Madhubuti, Herbert W. Martin, Margaret Burroughs, Hoyt W. Fuller, Margaret Walker, Gwendolyn Brooks, and others. Currently, the best sources available for use by students and scholars are the Etheridge Knight Papers and the Herbert W. Martin Papers, located at the Ward M. Canady Center, the University of Toledo Library, Toledo, Ohio; and the Hoyt William Fuller Collection, 1940–1981, Woodruff Library, Clark-Atlanta University Library, Atlanta, Georgia. The best single source on documents relating to the early history of Broadside Press is the M.A. thesis, "Dudley Randall and the Broadside Press," written by Frenchy Jolene Hodges in 1974 at Clark-Atlanta University. This study also greatly profited from the rich archival holdings of the Burton Historical Collection of the Detroit Public Library, Detroit, Michigan; and from the excellent African-American literature collections of the latter institution, the Purdy/Kresge Library of Wayne State Unviersity, and the University of Detroit Library.

Manuscript Collections

Amistad Collection, Tulane University, New Orleans, Louisiana
Chicago Historical Society, Chicago, Illinois
Etheridge Knight Collection and Herbert W. Martin Papers
The Hoyt William Fuller Collection, 1940–1981, Woodruff Library, Clark-Atlanta University, Atlanta, Georgia
Library of Congress, Washington, DC
Margaret Walker Collection, Jackson State University Library, Jackson, Mississippi
Moorland-Springarn Research Center, Howard University, Washington, DC
Schomburg Collection of Black History, Literature and Art, New York Public Library, New York City, New York
Tougaloo College Archives, Tougaloo, Mississippi
The Ward M. Canady Center, University of Toledo Library, Toledo, Ohio

Interviews

Melba J. Boyd, June 16, 1994, Detroit, Michigan
Naomi Long Madgett, October 18, 1991, Detroit, Michigan
Dudley F. Randall, October 11, 1991, Detroit, Michigan
_____. April 9, 1992, Detroit, Michigan
_____. June 27, 1994, Detroit, Michigan
_____. October 14, 1995, Detroit, Michigan

Ronald Snelling, October 10, 1993, Detroit, Michigan
Donald Vest, June 15, 1994, Detroit, Michigan
Hilda Vest, June 15, 1994, Detroit, Michigan
Willie Williams, July 15, 1994, Detroit, Michigan

Selected Letters Received

Samuel Allen   Pearl M. Cleage Lomax
Alvin Aubert   Audre Lorde
Melba Boyd   Naomi Long Madgett
Paul Breman   Clarence Major
Gwendolyn Brooks   Herbert Woodward Martin
Margaret G. Burroughs   D. H. Melhem
Kiarri T-H. Cheatwood   Sterling D. Plumpp
Pamela Cobb [Baraka Sele]   Dudley F. Randall
Stalla A. L. Crews   James A. Randall, Jr.
Toi Derricote   Eugene Redmond
James A. Emanuel   Philip Royster
Carolyn Flower   Edward Simpkins
Nikki Giovanni   Vivian Barnett Spencer-Randall
Fred Lee Hord   Donald Vest
Lance F. Jeffers   Hilda Vest
Donald Franklin Joyce   Jerry W. Ward, Jr.
Woodie King, Jr.   Ron Welburn
Pinkie Gordon Lane   Douglass A. Whitaker
W. Mondo Eyen We Langa [David L. Rice]   Willie Williams

Questionnaires Received (Selected Listing)

Samuel Allen, Winthrop, Mass., August 22, 1991; Maya Angelou, Winston-Salem, N.C., August 16, 1991; Molefi Asante, Philadelphia, Pa., July 15, 1991; Alvin Aubert, Detroit, Mich., July 29, 1991; Bernard W. Bell, University Park, Pa., November 13, 1991; David Bradley, Philadelphia, Pa., August 8, 1991; Gwendolyn Brooks, Chicago, Ill., July 20, 1991; Dennis Brutus, Pittsburgh, Pa., September 18, 1991; Margaret T. Burroughs, Chicago, Ill., July 17, 1991; Pearl M. Cleage, Atlanta, Ga., September 23, 1991; Cyrus Colter, Chicago, Ill., September 18, 1991; Melvin Dixon, Washington, D.C., September 18, 1991; Rita Dove, Charlottesville, Va., September 10, 1991; James A. Emanuel, Paris, France, August 26, 1991; Carolyn Fowler, Atlanta, Ga., October 4, 1991; Edmund Barry Gaither, Boston, Mass., August 12, 1991; Henry Louis Gates, Jr., Boston, Mass., August 6, 1991; Nikki Giovanni, Blacksburg, Va., September 15, 1991; Nathan Hare, San Francisco, Calif., August 6, 1991; Robert L. Harris, Jr., Ithaca, N.Y., July 23, 1991; Epsy Y. Hendricks, Lorman, Miss., August 7, 1991; Darlene Clark Hine, E. Lansing, Mich., July 11, 1991; Wendell P. Holbrook, Newark, N.J., September 18, 1991; Fred L. Hord, Galesburg, Ill., August 31, 1991; Kristin Hunter, Philadelphia, Pa., September 4, 1991; Blyden Jackson, Chapel Hill, N.C., August 5, 1991; Murray Jackson, Ann Arbor, Mich., May 6, 1992; Sylvia M. Jacobs, Durham, N.C., August 13, 1991; June Jordan, Berkeley, Calif., September 1, 1991; Woodie King, Jr., New York, N.Y., July 17, 1991; Richard Long, Atlanta, Ga., July 30, 1991; Audre Lorde, St. Croix, V.I., August 12, 1991; Naomi Long Madgett, Detroit, Mich., July 20, September 6, 1991; Clarence Major, Davis, Calif., August 24, 1991; Herbert Woodward Martin, Dayton, Ohio, October 23, 1991; D. H. Melhem, New York, N.Y., August 18, 1991; R. Baxter Miller, Knoxville, Tenn., July 30, 1991; Loften Mitchell, Jamaica, N.Y., December 30, 1991; Raymond R. Patterson, Merrick, N.Y., July 15, 1991; Arnold Rampersad, Princeton, N.J., August 14, 1991; Eugene B. Redmond, East St. Louis, Ill., September 12, 1991; Philip M. Royster, Chicago, Ill., September 16, 1991; Ntozake Shange, Philadelphia, Pa., October 10, 1991; Ann Allen Shockley, Nashville, Tenn., October 31, 1991; Rayfield Allen Waller, Ithaca, N.Y., April 21, 1992; Jerry W. Ward, Jr., Tougaloo,

Miss., July 12, 1991; Mary Helen Washington, Washington, D.C., September 11, 1992; Ron Welburn, Danbury, Conn., August 17, 1991; Richard Wesley, Newark, N.J., October 24, 1991; John Wideman, Amherst, Mass., August 16, 1991

Journals

Africa Report, 1981
African American Review, 1993
Against the Grain, 1990
The American Rag, 1978
American Vision, 1990
Black Academy Review, 1970
Black American Literature Forum, 1984
Black Books Bulletin, 1972–1995
The Black Collegian, 1978
Black Creation, 1972–1975
Black Enterprise, 1972–1995
The Black Nation, 1982
The Black Scholar, 1969–1995
Black Theatre, 1971
Black World, 1970–1972
Broadside News, 1970–1972
Business Week, 1992
Callaloo, 1978
CLA Journal, 1965–1995
Contemporary Literature, 1991
Crisis, 1943, 1961
Ebony, 1965–1980
Emerge, 1990
Encore: American & World Wide News, 1977
Esquire, 1967
Essence, 1971, 1974–1975
Expressive Cultural Studies, 1992
First World, 1979
Focus: The Monthly Newsletter of the Joint Center for Political Studies, 1987
Freedomways, 1973, 1979
Hoo Doo, 1972
Jet, 1972
Journal of Afro-American Issues, 1975

Journal of Black Poetry, 1969–1975
Journal of Black Studies, 1971, 1990
The Journal of Religious Thought, 1975
Journalism History, 1980
The Langston Hughes Review, 1993
The Literary Griot: International Journal of Black Melus, 1985
Midwest Journal, 1952–1953
Mississippi Quarterly: The Journal of Southern Culture, 1978
Monthly Detroit, 1984
The Nation, 1975
Negro Digest, 1965–1969
Negro History Bulletin, 1962, 1964, 1980
New Literary History, 1991
The New Republic, 1991
Newsweek, 1972
Notes on Mississippi Writers, 1993
Obsidian: Black Literature in Review, 1975–1995
Okike: An African Journal of New Writing, 1974
Open Places, 1985
Phylon, 1962–1989
The Progressive, 1981
Publisher's Weekly, 1969–1995
The Southern Quarterly: A Journal of the Arts in the South, 1991
The Speak Easy Culture, 1973
Time, 1967
Umbra, 1967–68
Umoja, 1980
U.S. News and World Report, 1962, 1976, 1983
The Varsity News (University of Detroit), 1969
Yardbird Reader, 1975
Zora Neale Hurston Forum, 1987

Newspapers

Chicago Tribune, 1989–1994
The Detroit Blue Book, A National Weekly Newspaper, 1929
Detroit Contender, 1920–1921
Detroit Free Press, 1960–1995
Detroit Independent, 1927
Detroit News, 1960–1995
Detroit Tribune, 1962
The Hartford (Conn.) Courant, 1971
Jackson Advocate, 1975–1995

Lansing (Mich.) State Journal, 1991
Los Angeles Times, 1990
Michigan Chronicle, 1955–1956, 1960–1995
Michigan Citizen, 1990
New York Times, 1960–1995
River Mist (Detroit), 1989
Washington Post, 1981
World Herald (Lincoln, Neb.), 1993

Secondary Sources

Abdul, Raoul, ed. *Magic of Black Poetry.* New York: Dodd, Mead & Co., 1972.

Aberback, Joeal D. and Jack L. Walker. *Race in the City: Political Trust and Public Policy in the New Urban System.* Boston: Little, Brown and Co., 1973.

"Accounting for Small Business." *Black Enterprise* 23, no. 4 (November 1992): 37, 40.

Adams, Kathrine. *A History of Professional Writing Instruction in American Colleges: Years of Acceptance, Growth, and Doubt.* Dallas, Texas: Southern Methodist University Press, 1993.

Adams, William, Peter Conn and Harry Slepian, eds. *Afro-American Literature: Poetry.* Boston: Houghton Mifflin Co., 1970.

Adoff, Arnold, ed. *I Am the Darker Brother: An Anthology of Modern Poems.* New York: The Macmillan Co., 1968.

_____, ed. *Black Out Loud: An Anthology of Modern Poems by Black Americans.* New York: The Macmillan Co., 1970.

_____, ed. *The Poetry of Black Americans: Anthology of the 20th Century.* New York: Harper & Row, Publishers, 1973.

_____, ed. *Celebrations: A New Anthology of Black Poetry.* Chicago: Follett Publishing Co., 1977.

Afro-American Encyclopedia. North Miami, Fla.: Educational Book Publishers, 1974.

Albert, Judith Clavir and Stewart Edward Albert, eds. *The Sixties Papers: Documents of a Rebellious Decade.* New York: Praeger Publishers, 1984.

Alhamisi, Ahmed. *Holy Ghosts.* Detroit: Broadside Press, 1972.

_____, and Kofi Wangara, eds. *Black Arts: An Anthology of Black Creations.* Detroit: Black Arts Publications, 1969.

Alkalimat, Abdul. *Introduction to African-American Studies: A Peoples College Primer.* Chicago: Twenty-First Century Books and Publications, 1986.

All About Michigan Almanac. Hartland, Mich.: Hisio Publications, 1989.

Allen, Ron and Stella Crews, eds. *HIPology: Horizons in Poetry.* Detroit: Broadside Press, 1990.

Allen, Samuel. *Paul Vesey's Ledger.* London: Paul Breman, 1975.

Allison, John. "Knowledge Is Power." *American Bookseller* (February 1990): 168.

Alsup, Henry, Jr. *Cold Heart Sweet.* Detroit: Ink & Soul, 1976.

Anderson, Elliott and Mary Kinzie, eds. *The Little Magazine in America: A Modern Documentary History.* Yonkers, N.Y.: The Pushcart Press, 1978.

Anyike, James C. *African American Holidays: A Historical Research and Resource Guide to Cultural Celebrations.* Chicago: Popular Truth, 1991.

Armstrong, David. *Alternative Media in America.* Los Angeles: J. P. Trarcher, Inc., 1981.

Aubert, Alvin. *Against the Blues.* Detroit: Broadside Press, 1972.

Azevedo, Mario, ed. *Africana Studies: A Survey of Africa and the African Diaspora.* Durham, N.C.: Carolina Academic Press, 1993.

Bacon, Donald C. "A Bitter New Generation of Jobless Young Blacks." *U.S. News and World Report* 71, no. 13 (September 27, 1976): 61–62, 64, 67.

Bailey, Leaonead Pack, compiler. *Broadside Authors and Artists: An Illustrated Biographical Directory.* Detroit: Broadside Press, 1974.

Baker, Houston, A., Jr., ed. *Black Literature in America.* New York: McGraw-Hill, 1971.

_____, ed. *A Many Colored Coat of Dreams: The Poetry of Countee Cullen.* Detroit: Broadside Press, 1974.

_____, ed. *Afro-American Poetics: Revisions of Harlem and the Black Aesthetic.* Madison: University of Wisconsin Press, 1988.

Baker, Kim and Sunny Baker. *How to Promote, Publicize, and Advertise Your Growing Business: Getting the Word Out Without Spending a Fortune.* New York: John Wiley & Sons, 1992.

Baker, Stephen. *The Advertiser's Manual.* New York: John Wiley & Sons, 1988.

Banerji, Sanjukta. *Deferred Hopes: Blacks in Contemporary America.* New York: Advent Books, 1987.

Banner, Louis W. *Women in Modern America: A Brief History.* New York: Harcourt Brace Jovanovich, 1974.

Barbato, Joseph. "New Alliance Brings Black Publishers, Booksellers Together." *Publishers Weekly* 234, no. 24 (December 9, 1988): 39.

Barbour, Floyd, ed. *The Black Seventies.* Boston: Porter Sargent Publishers, 1970.

Barksdale, Richard K. *Praisesong of Survival: Lectures and Essays, 1957–1989.* Urbana: University of Illinois Press, 1992.

_____, and Kenneth Kinnamon, eds. *Black Writers in America.* New York: The Macmillan Co., 1972.

Barlow, George. *Gabriel.* Detroit: Broadside Press, 1974.

Barron's Profiles of American Colleges. Hauppauge, New York: Barron's Educational Series, 1992.

Bayes, Jane H. *Minority Politics and Ideologies in the United States.* Novato, Calif.: Chandler and Sharp Publishers, 1982.

Bean, Walton. *California: An Interpretive History.* New York: McGraw-Hill, 1968.

Bell, Bernard W., ed. *Modern and Contemporary Afro-American Poetry.* Boston: Allyn and Bacon, 1972.

_____, ed. *The Folk Roots of Contemporary Afro-American Poetry.* Detroit: Broadside Press, 1974.

Bell, Morag. *Contemporary Africa: Development, Culture and the State.* New York: Longman, 1986.

Bell, Roseann, Bettye J. Parker and Beverly Guy-Sheftall, eds. *Sturdy Black Bridges: Visions of Black Women in Literature.* Garden City, N.Y.: Anchor Books/Doubleday, 1979.

Berghahn, Marion. *Images of Africa in Black American Literature.* London: The Macmillan Press, Ltd., 1977.

Bergman, Peter M. and Mort N. Bergman. *The Chronological History of the Negro in America.* New York: New American Library, 1969.

Berle, Guston. *The Small Business Information Handbook.* New York: John Wiley & Sons, 1990.

Bernstein, Irving. *Promises Kept: John F. Kennedy's New Frontier.* New York: Oxford University Press, 1991.

Berry, Faith. "A Question of Publishers and a Question of Audience." *The Black Scholar* 17, no. 2 (March/April 1986): 41–49.

Berry, Mary and John Blassingame. *Long Memory: The Black Experience in America.* New York: Oxford University Press, 1982.

Bigsby, C.W.E. *The Second Black Renaissance: Essays in Black Literature.* Westport, Conn.: Greenwood Press, 1980.

"Black Book Publishers." *Black Enterprise* 3, no. 2 (September 1972): 39–42.

"Black Books Bulletin Interviews Dudley Randall." *Black Books Bulletin* 1, no. 2 (Winter 1972): 22–26.

Black History Museum Committee, ed. *Sterling A. Brown: A Umum Tribute.* Philadelphia, Pa.: Black History Museum Umum Publishers, 1982.

"Black World Magazine Discontinued." *The Black Scholar* 7, no. 7 (April 1976): 38.

"Blacks in Detroit." Detroit: *The Detroit Free Press,* 1983.

Blackshire-Belay, Carol Aisha. *Language and Literature in the African American Imagination.* Westport, Conn.: Greenwood Press, 1992.

Blackwell, James E. *Mainstreaming Outsiders: The Production of Black Professionals.* Dix Hills, N.Y.: General Hall, 1987.

Blain, Virginia, Patricia Clements and Isobel Grundy, eds. *The Feminist Companion to Literature in English: Women Writers from the Middle Ages to the Present.* New Haven, Conn.: Yale University Press, 1990.

Blumberg, Rhoda Lois. *Civil Rights: The 1960s Freedom Struggle.* Boston: Twayne Publishers, 1991.

Boateng, E.A. *A Political Geography of Africa.* New York: Cambridge University Press, 1978.

Boggs, James and Grace Lee Boggs. *Revolution and Evolution in the Twentieth Century.* New York: Monthly Review Press, 1974.

Bok, Marcia. *Civil Rights and the Social Programs of the 1960s: The Social Justice Functions of Social Policy.* Westport, Conn.: Praeger Publishers, 1992.

Bolkosky, Sidney. *Harmony and Dissonance: Voices of Jewish Identity in Detroit, 1914–1967.* Detroit: Wayne State University Press, 1991.

Bontemps, Arna. *Personals.* London: Paul Breman, 1963 ed. *American Negro Poetry.* New York: Hill and Wang, 1963.

Book, Promotion, Sales and Distribution: A Management Training Course. London and Paris: Book House Training Centre and UNESCO, 1991.

Booker T. Washington Guide to Better Service. Detroit: Booker T. Washington Association, 1968.

Boskin, Joseph. *Sambo: The Rise and Demise of an American Jester.* New York: Oxford University Press, 1986.

Bowner, Carrington. "An Interview with Nikki Giovanni." *Black American Literature Forum* 18, no. 1 (September 1984): 29–30.

Boyd, Herb. "Blacks and the Police State: A Case Study of Detroit." *Black Scholar* 12, no. 1 (January/February 1981): 58–61.

Boyd, Melba. "The Detroit Writer: A Report." *Black Creation* 6 (1974-75): 76–77.
_____. *Cat Eyes and Deadwood.* Highland Park, Mich.: Fallen Angel Press, 1978.
_____. *Sons for Maya.* Detroit: Broadside Press and Detroit River Press, 1982.
_____. "Out of the Poetry Ghetto: The Life/Art Struggle of Small Black Publishing Houses." *The Black Scholar* 16, no. 4 (July/August 1985): 12–24.
Boyd, Sue Abbott, ed. *Poems By Blacks.* Fort Smith, Ark.: South and West, Inc., 1970.
Boyer, Jill Witherspoon. *Dream Farmer.* Detroit: Broadside Press, 1975.
_____, ed. *The Broadside Annual.* Detroit: Broadside Press, 1972, 1973.
Boyken, Ulysses W. *A Handbook on the Detroit Negro.* Detroit: The Minority Study Associates, 1943.
Boze, Arthur. *Black Words.* Detroit: Broadside Press, 1972.
Bragg, Linda Brown. *A Love Sons to Black Men.* Detroit: Broadside Press, 1974.
Braxton, Joanne M. and Andree Nicola McLaughlin, eds. *Wild Women in the Whirlwind: Afro-American Culture and the Contemporary Literary Renaissance.* New Brunswick, N.J.: Rutgers University Press, 1990.
Breman, Paul, ed. *You Better Believe It: Black Verse in English from Africa, the West Indies and the United States.* Baltimore, Md.: Penguin Books, 1973.
Brennan, Thomas H., ed. *Writings on Writings: A Compendium of 1209 Quotations from Authors on Their Craft.* Jefferson, N.C.: McFarland, 1994.
Brisbane, Robert H. *Black Activism: Racial Revolution in the United States, 1954–1970.* Valley Forge, Pa.: Judson Press, 1974.
Broadside on Broadway: Seven Poets Read. Detroit: Broadside Press, 1970.
Brooks, Gwendolyn. *Riot.* Detroit: Broadside Press, 1969.
_____. *Family Pictures.* Detroit: Broadside Press, 1970.
_____. *Aloneness.* Detroit: Broadside Press, 1971.
_____. *Report from Part One.* Detroit: Broadside Press, 1972.
_____. *To Disembark.* Chicago: Third World Press, 1981.
_____, ed. *A Broadside Treasury.* Detroit: Broadside Press, 1971.
_____, ed. *Jump Bad: A New Chicago Anthology.* Detroit: Broadside Press, 1971.
_____, ed. *The Black Position: An Annual.* Detroit: Broadside Press, 1971, 1972, 1973, 1976.
Brooks, Thomas R. *Walls Come Tumbling Down: A History of the Civil Rights Movement, 1940–1970.* Englewood Cliffs, N.J.: Prentice-Hall, 1974.
Brown, Lloyd W. *Amiri Baraka.* Boston: Twayne Publishers, 1980.
Brown, Martha and Sue Shott, "Interview with Dudley Randall." *The Speak Easy Culture* 3 (May 1973): 4–5, 27–29, 31.
Brown, Patricia L., Don L. Lee and Frances Ward, eds. *To Gwen with Love: An Anthology Dedicated to Gwendolyn Brooks.* Chicago: Johnson Publishing Co., 1971.
Brown, Sterling A. *The Last Ride of Wild Bill.* Detroit: Broadside Press, 1975.
Brown, Sterling A., Arthur P. Davis and Ulysses Lee, eds. *The Negro Caravan.* New York: The Dryden Press, 1941; reprint ed., New York: Arno Press and the New York Times, 1970.
Brownell, Blaine and David R. Goldfield, eds. *The City in Southern History: The Growth of Urban Civilization in the South.* Port Washington, N.Y.: National University Publications/Kennikat Press, 1977.
Browning, Rufus P., Dale Rogers Marshall and David H. Tabb, eds. *Racial Politics in American Cities.* New York: Longman, 1990.
Bundy, Mary Lee and Frederick J. Stielow, eds. *Activism in American Librarianship.* Westport, Conn.: Greenwood Press, 1987.
Burns, Stewart. *Social Movements of the 1960s: Searching for Democracy.* Boston: Twayne Publishers/G.K. Hall & Co., 1990.
Button, James W. *Black Violence: Political Impact of the 1960s Riots.* Princeton: Princeton University Press, 1978.
Cannady, Joan, ed. *Black Images in American Literature.* Rochelle Park, N.J.: Hayden Book Co., 1977.
Cannon, Charles E. *Saint Nigger.* Detroit: Broadside Press, 1972.
Capeci, Dominic J., Jr. *Race Relations in Wartime Detroit: The Sojourner Truth Housing Controversy of 1942.* Detroit: Wayne State University Press, 1984.

_____, and Martha Wilkerson. *Layered Violence: The Detroit Rioters of 1943.* Jackson: University Press of Mississippi, 1991.

Carmichael, Stokely and Charles V. Hamilton. *Black Power: The Politics of Liberation in America.* New York: Vintage Books, 1967.

Carmines, Edward G. and James A. Stimson. *Issue Evolution: Race and the Transformation of American Politics.* Princeton: Princeton University Press, 1989.

Case, Sue-Ellen. *Feminism and Theatre.* New York: Routledge, 1988.

Cashmore, Ellis and Eugene McLaughlin, eds. *Out of Order?: Policing Black People.* New York: Routledge, 1991.

Catalogues of Broadside Press. Detroit: Broadside Press, 1968–1995.

Catalogues of Lotus Press. Detroit: Lotus Press, 1974–1994.

Catalogues of the Heritage Series. London: Paul Breman, 1970, 1974.

Catalogues of Third World Press. Chicago: Third World Press, 1969–1995.

Chafeti, Ze'ev. *Devil's Night: And Other Tales of Detroit.* New York: Random House, 1990.

Chambers, Bradford. "Why Minority Publishing?" *Publishers' Weekly* 199, no. 11 (March 15, 1971): 35–50.

_____, and Rebecca Moon, eds. *Right On: An Anthology of Black Literature.* New York: New American Library, 1970.

Chapman, Abraham, ed. *Black Voices: An Anthology of Afro-American Literature.* New York: New American Library, 1968.

_____, ed. *New Black Voices.* New York: Mentor, 1972.

Cheatwood, Kiarri T-H. *Valley of the Anointers.* Detroit: Lotus Press, 1979.

Child, William M. and Donald E. McNeil, eds. *American Books Abroad: Toward a National Policy.* Washington, D.C.: The Helen Dwight Reid Educational Foundation, 1986.

Childs, John Brown. *Leadership, Conflict, and Cooperation in Afro-American Social Thought.* Philadelphia, Pa.: Temple University Press, 1989.

Churchill, Ward and Jim Vander Wall. *The CointelPro Papers: Documents from the FBI's Secret War Against Domestic Dissent.* Boston: South End Press, 1990.

Ciardi, John and Miller Williams, eds. *How Does a Poem Mean.* Boston: Houghton Mifflin Co., 1975.

Classified Detroit Negro Business Directory 1927. Detroit: Detroit Negro Business League, 1927.

Cleage, Pearl. *The Brass Bed and Other Stories.* Chicago: Third World Press, 1991.

Clive, Alan. *State of War: Michigan in World War II.* Ann Arbor: University of Michigan Press, 1979.

Clough, Adam Fair. *To Redeem the Soul of America: The Southern Christian Leadership Conference and Martin Luther King, Jr.* Athens: University of Georgia Press, 1987.

Cloyd, Iris, ed. *Who's Who Among Black Americans.* Detroit: Gale Research Co., 1990.

Cohen, Ralph, ed. *New Directions in Literary History.* Baltimore, Md.: Johns Hopkins University Press, 1974.

Coleman, James W. *Blackness and Modernism: The Literary Career of John Edgar Wideman.* Jackson: University Press of Mississippi, 1989.

Collier, Laurie and Joyce Nakamura, eds. *Major Authors and Illustrators for Children and Young Adults.* Detroit: Gale Research Co., 1993.

Collins, Patricia Hill. *Black Feminist Thought: Knowledge, Consciousness, and the Politics of Empowerment.* New York: Routledge, 1991.

Compaine, Benjamin M., Christopher H. Sterling, Thomas Guback, and J. Kendrick Noble, Jr. *Who Owns the Media?: Concentration of Ownership in the Mass Communication Industry.* White Plains, N.Y.: Knowledge Industry Publications, 1982.

Conot, Robert. *American Odyssey: A History of a Great City.* Detroit: Wayne State University Press, 1986.

Contemporary Authors. Detroit: Gale Research Co., 1992.

Cook, Chris and David Killingray. *African Political Facts Since 1945.* New York: Facts on File, 1991.

Cook, Mercer and Stephen E. Henderson. *The Militant Writer in Africa and the United States.* Madison: University of Wisconsin Press, 1969.

Cook, Philip S., Douglas Gomery and Lawrence W. Lichty, eds. *The Future of News: Television — Newspapers — Wire Services News — Magazines.* Washington, D.C.: The Woodrow Wilson Center Press; and Baltimore, Md.: Johns Hopkins University Press, 1992.

Coombs, Orde, ed. *We Speak as Liberators: Young Black Poets*. New York: Dodd, Mead and Co., 1970.

Coontz, Stephanie. *The Way We Never Were: American Families and the Nostalgia Trap*. New York: Basic Books/HarperCollins Publishers, 1992.

Cooper, James R. *Twilight's Last Gleaming: The Price of Happiness in America*. Buffalo, N.Y.: Prometheus Books, 1992.

Crew, Louie, ed. *The Gay Academic*. Palm Springs, Calif.: ETC Publications, 1978.

Crockett, George W., Jr. "Michigan Blitzed: A Reagan Budget Case Study." *Freedomways* 21, no. 2 (Second Quarter 1981): 87–92.

Cronon, Edmund David. *Black Moses: The Story of Marcus Garvey and the Universal Negro Improvement Association*. Madison: University of Wisconsin Press, 1962.

Cuney, William Waring. *Storefront Church*. London: Paul Breman, 1973.

Daniel, Roger. *Concentration Camps USA: Japanese Americans and World War II*. New York: Holt, Rinehart and Winston, 1972.

Daniel, Walter C., ed. *Black Journals of the United States: Historical Guides to the World's Periodicals and Newspapers*. Westport, Conn.: Greenwood Press, 1982.

Danner, Margaret. *Impressions of African Art Forms*. Detroit: Broadside Press, 1968.

_____, and Dudley Randall. *Poem Counterpoem*. Detroit: Broadside Press, 1966.

Darden, Joe T., Richard Child Hill, June Thomas, and Richard Thomas. *Detroit: Race and Uneven Development*. Philadelphia, Pa.: Temple University Press, 1987.

Dates, Jannette L. and William Barlow, eds. *Split Image: African Americans in the Mass Media*. Washington, D.C.: Howard University Press, 1990.

Dathorne, O. R. *The Black Mind: A History of African Literature*. Minneapolis, Minn.: University of Minneapolis Press, 1974.

Davidson, Cathy N., ed. *Reading in America: Literature and Social History*. Baltimore, Md.: Johns Hopkins University Press, 1989.

Davies, Philio John and Fredric A. Waldstein, eds. *Political Issues in America: The 1990s*. New York: Manchester University Press, 1991.

Davis, Angela Y. "Remembering Carole, Cynthia, Addie Mae and Denise." *Essence* 24, no. 5 (September 1993): 92–93, 126.

Davis, Arthur P. "The New Poetry of Black Hate." *CLA Journal* 13, no. 4 (June 1970): 382–91.

_____. *From the Dark Tower: Afro-American Writers, 1900–1960*. Washington, D.C.: Howard University Press, 1981.

_____, with Saunders Redding, and Joyce Ann Joyce, eds. *The New Cavalcade: African American Writing from 1760 to the Present*. 2 vols. Washington, D.C.: Howard University Press, 1991.

Davis, Charles T. and Daniel Walden, eds. *On Being Black: Writings by Afro-Americans from Frederick Douglass to the Present*. Greenwich, Conn.: Fawcett Publications, 1978.

Davis, F. James. *Who Is Black?: One Nation's Definition*. University Park: Pennsylvania State University Press, 1991.

Davis, Frank G. *The Economics of Black Community Development*. Chicago: Markham Publishing Co., 1972.

Davis, King E. "Jobs, Income, Business and Charity in the Black Community." *The Black Scholar* 9, no. 4 (December 1977): 2–11.

Davis, Lenwood G. and Janet L. Sims-Wood. *The Ku Klux Klan: A Bibliography*. Westport, Conn.: Greenwood Press, 1984.

_____, and Marsha L. Moore, compilers. *Malcolm X: A Selected Bibliography*. Westport, Conn.: Greenwood Press, 1984.

Davis, T.M. and T. Harris, eds. *Afro-American Writers After 1955: Dramatists and Prose Writers*. Detroit: Gale Research Co., 1985.

De Jongh, James. *Vicious Modernism: Black Harlem and the Literary Imagination*. New York: Cambridge University Press, 1990.

Derricotte, Toi. *The Empress of the Death House*. Detroit: Lotus Press, 1978.

Deskins, Donald R., Jr. *Residential Mobility of Negroes in Detroit, 1837–1965*. Ann Arbor: University of Michigan Press, 1972.

"Detroit: Motor City Becomes Murder City Amid a Flurry of Homicides." *Black Enterprise* 3, no. 9 (April 1973): 19.

"Detroit: Some Post-Riot Progress, But Tension Continues." *Black Enterprise* 2, no. 20 (March 1972): 75, 77–78, 80, 82–82

The Detroit Black Writer's Guild, ed. *Inner, Inner Visions: A Poetry Anthology.* Detroit: Detroit Black Writer's Guild, Inc., 1994.

The Detroit Blue Book, A National Weekly Newspaper: A *Complete Survey of Negro Life and Activities in Greater Detroit for 1929.* Detroit: Detroit Independent Publishing Co., 1929.

Detroit Board of Education. *Black Personalities of Detroit.* Detroit: Detroit Public Schools, 1975.

Deusen, John G. Van. *The Black Man in White America.* Washington, D.C.: Associated Publishers, 1944.

DiCanio, Margaret. *The Encyclopedia of Violence: Origins, Attitudes, Consequences.* New York: Facts on File, 1993.

Directory of Active Michigan Poets. Detroit: The Poetry Society of Michigan, 1982.

Dodson, Owen. *The Confession Stone: Song Cycles.* London: Paul Breman, 1971.

Downing, John. *Radical Media: The Political Experience of Alternative Communication.* Boston: South End Press, 1984.

Drake, St. Clair. "The Black Experience in Black Historical Perspective," in *Black Experience: Analysis and Synthesis.* San Rafael, Calif.: Leswing Press, (1972), 308–19.

Draper, James P., ed. *Black Literary Criticism* 4 vols. Detroit: Gale Research Co., 1992.

Drimmer, Melvin, ed. *Black History: A Reappraisal.* Garden City, N.Y.: Anchor Books/Doubleday, 1969.

Dykes, Dewitt S., Jr. "The Search for Community: Michigan Society and Education, 1945–1980s," in *Michigan: Visions of Our Past.* Edited by Richard J. Hathaway. East Lansing: Michigan State University Press, 1989.

Dyson, Michael Eric. *Reflecting Back: African-American Cultural Criticism.* Minneapolis: University of Minnesota Press, 1993.

Early, Gerald. *Tuxedo Junction: Essays on American Culture.* New York: The Ecco Press, 1989.

_____. "One Nation Under a Groove." *The New Republic,* Issues 3,991 and 3,992 (July 15 & 22, 1991): 30–41.

_____, ed. *My Soul's High Sons: The Collected Writings of Countee Cullen: Voice of the Harlem Renaissance.* New York: Anchor Books, 1991.

Eckels, John [Askia Akhnaton]. *Home Is Where the Soul Is.* Detroit: Broadside Press, 1969.

_____. *Our Business in the Streets.* Detroit: Broadside Press, 1971.

Egejuru, Phanuel Akubueze. *Towards African Literary Independence: A Dialogue with Contemporary African Writers.* Westport, Conn.: Greenwood Press, 1980.

Eisenberg, Joyce. *Places and Peoples of the World: Grenada.* New York: Chelsea House Publishers, 1988.

Elliot, Jeffrey M., ed. *Conversations with Maya Angelou.* Jackson: University Press of Mississippi, 1989.

Ellmann, Richard and Robert O'Clair, eds. *Modern Poems: A Norton Introduction.* New York: W. W. Norton & Co., 1989.

"An Emerge Interview: A Race Man and a Scholar." *Emerge* 1, no. 4 (February 1990): 60.

Emmanuel, James A. *The Treehouse and Other Poems.* Detroit: Broadside Press, 1968.

_____. *Panther Man.* Detroit: Broadside Press, 1970.

_____. "Black Man Abroad." *Black American Literature Forum* 13, no. 3 (Fall 1979): 79–85.

_____, and Theodore L. Gross, eds. *Dark Symphony: Negro Literature in America.* New York: The Free Press, 1968.

Epstein, Barbara. *Political Protest and Cultural Revolution: Nonviolent Direct Action in the* 1970s *and* 1980s. Berkeley: University of California Press, 1991.

Ernst, Robert T. and Lawrence Huggs, eds. *Geographic Perspectives.* Garden City, N.Y.: Anchor Books/Doubleday, 1976.

Eseoghene [C. Lindsay Barrett]. *The Conflicting Eye.* London: Paul Breman, 1973.

Evans, Mari, ed. *Black Women Writers (1950–1980): A Critical Evaluation.* New York: Anchor Press/Doubleday, 1984.

Fabre, Michel. *From Harlem to Paris: Black American Writers in France, 1840–1980.* Urbana: University of Illinois Press, l991.

Facts About Blacks. Los Angeles, Calif.: Jeffries and Associates, 1986.

Faderman, Lillian and Barbara Bradshaw, eds. *American Ethnic Writing: Speaking for Ourselves*. Glenview, Ill.: Scott, Foresman & Co., 1969.

Farley, Reynolds and Walter R. Allen. *The Color Line and the Quality of Life in America*. New York: National Committee for Research on the 1980 Census and the Russell Sage Foundation, 1987.

Ferguson, Dave. "Dudley Randall ... Poet in Residence." *The Varsity News* [University of Detroit]. (September 16, 1969): 3.

Fetrow, Fred M. *Robert Harden*. Boston: Twayne Publishers, 1984.

Fine, Sidney. *Violence in the Model City: The Cavanagh Administration: Race Relations and the Detroit Riot of 1967*. Ann Arbor: University of Michigan Press, 1989.

Fishburn, Katherine. *Women in Popular Culture: A Reference Guide*. Westport, Conn.: Greenwood Press, 1982.

Fisher, Sethard. *From Martin to Mainstream: The Social Progress of Black Americans*. New York: Praeger Publishers, 1982.

Fleming, James. "A Survey of Negro Newspapers in the United States." B.A. thesis, University of Wisconsin, 1931.

Floyd, Samuel A., Jr., ed. *Black Music in the Harlem Renaissance: A Collection of Essays*. Westport, Conn.: Greenwood Press, 1990.

Foner, Jack D. *Blacks and the Military in American History: A New Perspective*. New York: Praeger Publishers, 1974.

Fontenot, Chester, Jr., ed. *Writing About Black Literature*. Lincoln: The Nebraska Curriculum Development Center, University of Nebraska, 1976.

_____, ed. Review of *Clinton*. *Black American Literature Forum* 11, no. 3 (Fall 1977): 119.

Ford, Nick Aaron. "The Fire Next Time?: A Critical Survey of Belles Lettres By and About Negroes Published in 1963." *Phylon* 25, no. 2 (Summer 1964): 123–34.

_____, ed. *Black Insights: Significant Literature by Black Americans, 1760 to the Present*. Waltham, Mass.: Ginn & Co., 1971.

Forsythe, Dennis, ed. *Black Alienation, Black Rebellion*. Washington, D.C.: College and University Press, 1975.

Fowler, Carolyn. "A Contemporary American Genre: Pamphlet Manifesto Poetry." *Black World* 23, no. 8 (June 1974): 4–19.

_____. *Black Arts and Black Aesthetics: A Bibliography*. Atlanta, Ga.: Privately printed, 1976.

Fowler, Virginia C. *Nikki Giovanni*. Boston: Twayne Publishers, 1992.

Fowlkes, Gwendolyn. "An Interview with Dudley Randall." *The Black Scholar* 6, no. 9 (June 1975): 87–90.

Fox, Fugh, ed. *The Living Underground: An Anthology of Contemporary American Poetry*. Troy, N.Y.: Whiston Publishing Co., 1973.

Fragnoli, Raymond R. *The Transformation of Reform: Progressivism in Detroit—and After, 1912–1933*. New York: Garland Publishing, 1982.

Franklin, John Hope and Alfred A. Moss, Jr. *From Slavery to Freedom: A History of African Americans*. New York: McGraw-Hill, 1994.

Frazier, E. Franklin. *Negro Youth at the Crossways: Their Personality Development in the Middle States*. New York: Schocken Books, 1940, 1967.

Freedman, Frances S., ed. *The Black American Experience: A New Anthology of Black Literature*. New York: Bantam, 1970.

Fryar, Imani L.B. "The Black Woman Writer." *Journal of Black Studies* 20, no. 4 (June 1990): 443–66.

Fujita, Kuniko. *Black Worker's Struggles in Detroit's Auto Industry, 1935–1975*. Detroit: Century Twenty-One Publishing, 1980.

Fuller, Hoyt W. "Cultural Notes: Reverberations from a Writer's Conference." *African Forum* 1, no. 2 (Fall 1965): 78–84

_____. "A Warning to Black Poets." *Black World* 19, no. 11 (September 1970): 50.

Fuller, Stephany. *Moving Deep*. Detroit: Broadside Press, 1969.

Fulton, Len, ed. *Directory of Little Magazines, Small Presses, Underground Newspapers 1970*. Paradise, Calif.: Dustbooks, 1970.

_____, and James Boyer May, eds. *Directory of Little Magazines, Small Presses, and Underground Newspapers, 1971–72*. Paradise, Calif.: Dustbooks, 1971.

Gabbin, Joanne V. *Sterling A. Brown: Building the Black Aesthetic Tradition*. Westport, Conn.: Greenwood Press, 1985.

_____. "Sonia Sanchez: A Soft Reflection of Strength." *The Zora Neale Hurston Forum* 1, no. 2 (Spring 1987): 47–56.

_____, and Lee P. Brown, eds. *Crime and Its Impact on the Black Community.* Washington, D.C.: Institute for Urban Affairs, Howard University, 1975.

Gary, Lawrence E., ed. *Black Men.* Beverly Hills, Calif.: Sage Publishers, 1981.

Gay, Geneva and Willie L. Baber, eds. *Expressively Black: The Cultural Basis of Ethnic Identity.* New York: Praeger Publishers, 1987.

Gayle, Addison, Jr., ed. *The Black Aesthetic.* Garden City, N.Y.: Doubleday & Co., 1972.

_____, ed. *Claude McKay: The Black Poet at War.* Detroit: Broadside Press, 1972.

George, Nelson. *Where Did Our Love Go?: The Rise and Fall of the Motown Sound.* New York: St. Martin's Press, 1985.

Georges-Abeyie, Daniel, ed. *The Criminal Justice System and Blacks.* New York: Clark Boordman Co., 1984.

Geschwender, James A. *Class, Race, and Worker Insurgency: The League of Revolutionary Black Workers.* New York: Cambridge University Press, 1967.

Gibbs, Michele S. *Sketches from Home.* Detroit: Broadside Press, 1983.

Gibson, Donald B. *The Politics of Literary Expression: A Study of Major Black Writers.* Westport, Conn.: Greenwood Press, 1981.

_____, ed. *Modern Black Poets: A Collection of Critical Essays.* Englewood Cliffs, N.J.: Prentice Hall, Inc., 1973.

Giddings, Paula. "About People: Book Marks." *Essence* 19, no. 11 (March 1989): 26.

_____. "Haki Madhubuti: A Guide for Black Men." *Essence* 21, no. 2 (June 1990): 44.

Gill, Gerald R. *Meanness Mania: The Chanced Mood.* Washington, D.C.: Howard University Press, 1980.

Gilliam, Annette. "Essence Women: Barbara Sizemore." *Essence* 5, no. 11 (March 1975): 21.

Gioia, Dana. *Can Poetry Matter?: Essays on Poetry and American Culture.* Saint Paul, Minn.: Graywolf Press, 1992.

Giovanni, Nikki. *Black Feeling, Black Talk.* Detroit: Broadside Press, 1968.

_____. *Black Judgement.* Detroit: Broadside Press, 1968.

_____. *Black Feeling, Black Talk, Black Judgement.* New York: William Morrow & Co., 1970.

_____. *Re: Creation.* Detroit: Broadside Press, 1970.

_____. "The Whole Point Is to Share." *International Educational and Cultural Exchange* 10, no. 1 (Summer 1974): 20–22.

_____, and Margaret Walker. *A Poetic Equation: Conversations Between Nikki Giovanni and Margaret Walker.* Washington, D.C.: Howard University Press, 1974.

Gitlin, Todd. *The Sixties: Years of Hope, Days of Rage.* New York: Bantam Books, 1987.

Glikin, Ronda. *Black American Women in Literature: A Bibliography, 1976 Through 1987.* Jefferson, N.C.: McFarland, 1989.

Gloster, Jesse E. *Economics of Minority Groups.* Houston, Texas: Premier Printing Co., 1973.

Goddard, Connie. "Aiming for the Mainstream." *Publishers Weekly* 239, no. 4 (January 20, 1992): 28–32, 34.

Goldfield, David R. *Black, White, and Southern: Race Relations and Southern Culture, 1940 to the Present.* Baton Rouge: Louisiana State University Press, 1990.

Goldman, Eric F. *The Crucial Decade and After: America, 1945–1960.* New York: Vintage Books, 1960.

_____. *The Tragedy of Lyndon Johnson.* New York: Dell Publishing Co., 1969.

Goldstein, Laurence. *The American Poet at the Movies: A Critical History.* Ann Arbor: The University of Michigan Press, 1994.

Goncalves, Joe, ed. *Black Art, Black Culture.* San Francisco, Calif.: Journal of Black Poetry Press, 1972.

Goodlett, Carolton B. "Mass Communication, U.S.A.: Its Feet of Clay." *The Black Scholar* 6, no. 3 (November 1974): 2–6.

Gordon, Leonard, ed. *A City in Racial Crisis: The Case of Detroit Pre and Post the 1967 Riot.* New York: Wm. C. Brown Co. Publishers, 1971.

Graham, Hugh Davis. *The Civil Rights Era: Origins and Development of National Police, 1960–1972.* New York: Oxford University Press, 1990.

Greenberg, Jack. *Race Relations and American Law.* New York: Columbia University Press, 1959.

Greiver, Donald J., ed. *American Poets Since World War II: Part 2: L–Z.* Detroit: Gale Research Co., 1980.

Grossman, James R. *Land of Hope: Chicano, Black Southerners, and the Great Migration.* Chicago: The University of Chicago Press, 1989.

Grover, Ronald, Gloria Lau, and Jane Birnbaum. "The Economic Crisis of Urban America." *Business Week,* no. 3266 (May 18, 1992): 38–46.

Guillen, Nicolas. *Tengo.* Translated by Richard J. Carr. Detroit: Broadside Press, 1974.

Gutknecht, Douglas B. "The Rise and Fall of the Marcus Garvey Movement, 1916–25: The Uses and Abuses of Cultural-Expressive Dimensions for Social Change" in *Cultural Politics: Radical Movements in Modern History.* Edited by Jerold M. Starr. New York: Praeger, 1985.

Gwynn, R.S., ed. *Poetry: A HarperCollins Pocket Anthology.* New York: HarperCollins College Publishers, 1993.

Habbard, Linda, S., ed. *Publishers Directory 1992.* Detroit: Gale Research Co., 1992.

Haines, Herbert H. *Black Radicals and the Civil Rights Mainstream, 1954–1970.* Knoxville: University of Tennessee Press, 1988.

Harding, Vincent. *Beyond Chaos: Black History and the Search for the New Land.* Atlanta, Ga.: Institute of the Black World, Black Paper No. 2, 1970.

Hargreaves, Robert A. *A Portrait of America in the 1970's.* New York: St. Martin's Press, 1973.

Harley, Sharon, Stephen Middleton, and Charlotte Stokes. *The African-American Experience: A History.* Englewood Cliffs, N.J.: Glove Book Co., 1992.

Harris, Norman. *Connecting Times: The Sixties in Afro-American Fiction.* Jackson: University Press of Mississippi, 1988.

Harris, Trudier. *Exorcising Blackness: Historical and Literary Lynching and Burning Rituals.* Bloomington: Indiana University Press, 1984.

_____, and Thadious M. Davis, eds. *Dictionary of Literary Biography.* Vol. 41. *Afro-American Poets Since 1955.* Detroit: Gale Research Co., 1985.

Harris, William J. *The Jazz Aesthetic.* Columbia: University of Missouri Press, 1985.

Harper, Michael. *Debridement.* Garden City, N.Y.: Doubleday & Co., 1973.

Hartman, Joan E. and Ellen Messer-Davidow, eds. *Women in Print, I: Opportunities for Women's Studies Research in Language and Literature.* New York: Modern Language Association, 1982.

Hatch, James V. *Sorrow Is the Only Faithful One: The Life of Owen Dodson.* Urbana: University of Illinois Press, 1993.

Hathaway, Richard J., ed. *Michigan: Visions of Our Past.* East Lansing: Michigan State University Press, 1989.

Hawk, Beverly G., ed. *Africa's Media Image.* New York: Praeger Publishers, 1992.

Hawkins, Homer C. and Richard W. Thomas, eds. *Blacks and Chicanos in Urban Michigan.* East Lansing: Michigan History Division, Michigan Department of State, 1979.

Hayden, Robert, ed. *Kaleidoscope: Poems by American Negro Poets.* New York: Harcourt, Brace and World, 1967.

_____, and David J. Burrows, and Frederick R. Lapides, eds. *AfroAmerican Literature: An Introduction.* New York: Harcourt Brace Jovanovich, 1971.

Hedgepeth, Chester M., Jr. *Twentieth Century African-American Writers and Artists.* Chicago: American Library Association, 1991.

Henderson, David, ed. *Umbra Anthology, 1967–1968.* New York: Umbra Workshop, 1967.

Henderson, Stephen, ed. *Understanding the New Black Poetry.* New York: William Morrow, 1973.

Henri, Florette. *Black Migration: Movement North, 1900–1920, the Road from Myth to Man.* Garden City, N.Y.: Anchor Press/Doubleday, 1976.

Henrickson, Wilma Wood, ed. *Detroit Perspectives: Crossroads and Turning Points.* Detroit: Wayne State University Press, 1991.

Herman, Alex M. "A Statistical Portrait of the Black Woman Worker." *The Black Collegian* 8, no. 5 (May/June 1978): 30, 32.

Hernton, Calvin C. *The Sexual Mountain and Black Women Writers: Adventures in Sex, Literature, and Real Life.* New York: Anchor Press, 1987.

Herron, Jerry. *Universities and the Myth of Cultural Decline.* Detroit: Wayne State University Press, 1988.

Hine, Darlene Clark. "Black Migration to the Urban Midwest: The Gender Dimension, 1915–1945," in *The Great Migration in Historical Perspective: New Dimensions of Race, Class, and History.* Edited by Joe William Trotter, Jr. Bloomington: Indiana University Press, 1991.

_____, ed. *The State of Afro-American History.* Baton Rouge: Louisiana State University Press, 1986.

_____, Elsa Barkley Brown, and Rosalyn Terborg-Penn, eds. *Black Women in America: An Historical Encyclopedia.* Brooklyn, N.Y.: Carlson Publishers, 1993.

Hirsch, E.D., Jr. *Cultural Literacy: What Every American Needs to Know.* Boston: Houghton Mifflin Co., 1987.

Hoagland, Everett. *Black Velvet.* Detroit: Broadside Press, 1970.

Hodges, Frenchy Jolene. *Black Wisdom.* Detroit: Broadside Press, 1971. "Dudley Randall and the Broadside Press." M.A. thesis, Atlanta University, 1974.

Hogan, Lloyd. *Principals of Black Political Economy.* Boston: Routledge & Kegan Paul, 1984.

Hogue, W. Lawrence. *Discourse and the Other: The Production of the Afro-American Text.* Durham, N.C.: Duke University Press, 1986.

Holdt, Marvin. "James A. Emanuel: Black Man Abroad." *Black American Literature Forum* 13, no. 3 (Fall 1979): 79–85.

Holleb, Doris B. *Colleges and the Urban Poor: The Role of Public Higher Education in Community Service.* Levington, Mass.: Lexington Books, 1972.

Holli, Melvin G. "Detroit Today: Locked Into the Past." *The Midwest Quarterly* 19, no. 3 (Spring 1978): 251–59.

_____, and Peter d'A. Jones, eds. *Biographical Dictionary of American Negroes, 1820–1980.* Westport, Conn.: Greenwood Press, 1981.

Holsendolph, Ernest. "The Black Enterprise 100 Story: Strong Growth in a Tough Year." *Black Enterprise* 4, no. 11 (June 1974): 31–33, 45.

Hooks, Bell. *Talking Back: Thinking Feminist, Thinking Black.* Boston: South End Press, 1989.

_____. *Yearning: Race, Gender, and Cultural Politics.* Boston: South End Press, 1990.

Hoover, Dwight W. *A Teacher's Guide to American Urban History.* Chicago: Quadrangle Books, 1971.

Hord, Fred Lee. *Reconstructing Memory: Black Literary Criticism.* Chicago: Third World Press, 1991.

Hubbell, Jay B. *Who Are the Major American Writers.* Durham, N.C.: Duke University Press, 1972.

Hughes, Langston, ed. *New Negro Poets: USA.* Bloomington: Indiana University Press, 1964.

_____, ed. *Negro American Poetry.* Paris, France: Editions Seghers, 1966.

Hughes, Langston and Arna Bontemps, eds. *The Poetry of the Negro, 1746–1970.* New York: Doubleday & Co., 1949, 1970.

Hull, Gloria T., Patricia Bell Scott, and Barbara Smith, eds. *All the Women Are White, All the Blacks Are Men, But Some of Us Are Brave: Black Women's Studies.* New York: The Feminist Press, 1982.

Hurd, Myles Raymond. "The Corinth Connection in Etheridge Knight's 'The Ideal of Ancestry.'" *Notes on Mississippi Writers* 25, no. 1 (January 1993): 1–9.

Hynds, Ernest C. *American Newspapers in the 1970s.* New York: Hastings House, Publishers, 1975.

"In Memoriam: Lance Jeffers, November 28, 1919–July 19, 1985." *The Black Scholar* 16, no. 4 (July/August 1985): 73.

Inge, M. Thomas. "Contemporary Southern Black Writers: A Checklist." *Mississippi Quarterly: The Journal of Southern Culture* 31, no. 2 (Spring 1978): 188–90.

Issel, William. *Social Change in the United States, 1945–1983.* New York: Schocken Books, 1985.

Jackson, Blyden and Louis D. Rubin, Jr. *Black Poetry in America: Two Essays in Historical Interpretation.* Baton Rouge: Louisiana State University Press, 1974.

Jackson, Harvey C., Jr. "Summary History of the Detroit Branch of the ASNLH." *Negro History Bulletin* 26, no. 1 (October 1962): 84.

Jackson, Irene V., ed. *More Than Dancing: Essays on Afro-American Music and Musicians.* Westport, Conn.: Greenwood Press, 1985.

Jackson, Mae. *Can I Poet with You.* New York: Black Dialogue Publishers, 1969.

Jackson, Miles M. "Significant Belles Lettres By and About Negroes Published in 1964." *Phylon* 26, no. 3 (September 1965): 223–24.

Jackson, Murray. *Watermelon Rinds and Cherry Pits.* Detroit: Broadside Press, 1991.

Janken, Kenneth Robert. *Rayford W. Loran and the Dilemma of the African-American Intellectual.* Amherst: University of Massachusetts Press, 1993.

Jaye, Michael C. and Ann Chalmers Watts, eds. *Literature and the Urban Experience: Essays on the City and Literature*. New Brunswick, N.J.: Rutgers University Press, 1981.

Jeffers, Lance. *My Blackness Is the Beauty of This Land*. Detroit: Broadside Press, 1970.

_____. *When I Know the Power of My Black Hand*. Detroit: Broadside Press, 1974.

Jemie, Onwachekwa. *Langston Hughes: An Introduction to the Poetry*. New York: Columbia University Press, 1976.

Jennings, James. *The Politics of Black Empowerment: The Transformation of Black Activism in Urban America*. Detroit: Wayne State University Press, 1992.

Joe, Tom, and Cheryl Rogers. *By the Few, for the Few: The Reagan Welfare Legacy*. Lexington, Mass.: Lexington Books, 1985.

John, Frank. *Light a Fire*. London: Paul Breman, 1973.

Johnson, Abby Arthur and Ronald Maberry Johnson. *Propaganda and Aesthetics: The Literary Politics of Afro-American Magazines in the Twentieth Century*. Amherst: University of Massachusetts Press, 1979.

Johnson, Dwight L. *We, the Black Americans*. Washington, D.C.: U.S. Department of Commerce, Bureau of the Census, U.S. Government Printing Office, 1986.

Johnson, Herschel. "Motown: The Sound of Success." *Black Enterprise* 4, no. 11 (June 1974): 71–74, 77, 79–80.

Johnson, John H. with Lerone Bennett, Jr. *Succeeding Against the Odds: The Autobiography of a Great American Businessman*. New York: Amistad Press, 1989.

Johnson, R. J. *The American Urban System: A Geographical Perspective*. New York: St. Martin's Press, 1982.

Jones, Frances M. *Defusing Censorship: The Librarian's Guide to Handling Censorship Conflicts*. Phoenix, Ariz.: The Oryx Press, 1983.

Jones, Jacqueline. *The Dispossessed: America's Underclass from the Civil War to the Present*. New York: Basic Books/HarperCollins Publishers, 1992.

Jones, Joyce, Mary McTaggart and Maria Mootry, eds. *The Otherwise Room: A Poetry Anthology*. Carbondale, Ill.: The Poetry Factory, 1981.

Jones, Kirkland C. *Renaissance Man from Louisiana: A Biography of Arna Wendell Bontemps*. Westport, Conn.: Greenwood Press, 1992.

Jones, LeRoi [Amiri Baraka]. *Black Music*. New York: William Morrow & Co., 1968.

_____, and Larry Neal, eds. *Black Fire: An Anthology of Afro-American Writing*. New York: William Morrow & Co., 1968.

Jordan, June, ed. *Soulscript: Afro-American Poetry*. Garden City, N.Y.: Zenith Books/Doubleday, 1970.

_____, ed. *Technical Difficulties: African American Notes on the State of the Union*. New York: Pantheon Books, 1992.

Josey, E.J., ed. *The Black Librarian in America*. Metuchen, N.J.: The Scarecrow Press, 1970, 1994.

_____, ed. *What Black Librarians Are Saving*. Metuchen, N.J.: The Scarecrow Press, 1972.

_____, and Ann Allen Shockley, eds. *Handbook of Black Librarianship*. Littleton, Col.: Libraries Unlimited, 1977.

Joyce, Donald Franklin. "Magazines of Afro-American Thought on the Mass Market: Can They Survive?" *American Libraries* 7, no. 11 (December 1976): 678–83.

_____. *Gatekeepers of Black Culture; Black-Owned Book Publishing in the United States, 1817–1981*. Westport, Conn.: Greenwood Press, 1983.

_____. *Black Book Publishers in the United States: A Historical Directory of the Presses, 1817–1990*. Westport, Conn.: Greenwood Press, 1991.

Joyce, Joyce Ann. "Black Woman Scholar, Critic, and Teacher: The Inextricable Relationship Between Race, Sex, and Class." *New Literary History* 22, no. 3 (Summer 1991): 543–65.

_____. *Warriors, Conjurers and Priests: Defining African Centered Literary Criticism*. Chicago: Third World Press, 1994.

The Kaiser Index to Black Resources 1948–1986, O-S, vol. 4, *T-Z*, vol. 5. Brooklyn, New York: Carlson Publishers, 1992.

Karon, Berthan P. *Black Scars*. New York: Springer Publishing Co., 1975.

Katzman, David M. *Before the Ghetto: Black Detroit in the Nineteenth Century*. Urbana: University of Illinois Press, 1973.

Kay, Ernest, ed. *International Who's Who in Poetry.* Cambridge, England: International Biographical Centre, 1977.

Kearns, Francis E., ed. *Black Identity: A Thematic Reader.* New York: Holt, Rinehart, & Winston, 1970.

Kendrick, Dolores. *Through the Ceiling.* London: Paul Breman, 1975.

Kennedy, S.J. and D. Kennedy, eds. *Knock at a Star.* Boston: Little, Brown, and Co., 1982.

Kennedy, X.J., ed. *An Introduction to Poetry.* Boston: Little, Brown, and Co., 1978.

Kent, George E. "Struggle for the Image: Selected Books By or About Blacks During 1971." *Phylon* 33, no. 4 (Winter 1972): 304–23."

———. "Notes on the 1974 Black Literary Scene." *Phylon* 36, no. 2 (June 1975): 182–203.

———. *A Life of Gwendolyn Brooks.* Lexington: University Press of Kentucky, 1990.

Kgositsile, Aneb [Gloria House]. *Bloodriver (Poems), 1964–1983.* Detroit: Broadside Press, 1983.

———. *Rainrituals.* Detroit: Broadside Press, 1989.

Kgositsile, Keorapetse. "Paths to the Future." *Negro Digest* 17, nos. 11–12 (September/October 1968): 38–48.

———. *Spirits Unchained.* Detroit: Broadside Press, 1969.

Killens, John Oliver and Jerry W. Ward, Jr., eds. *Black Southern Voices: An Anthology of Fiction, Poetry, Drama, Nonfiction, and Critical Essays.* New York: Meridian Penguin, 1992.

King, Woodie, Jr., ed. *Black Spirits: A Festival of New Black Poets in America.* New York: Vintage Books/Random House, 1972.

———. "Lorraine Hansberry's Children: Black Artists and a Raisin in the Sun." *Freedomways* 19, no. 4 (Fourth Quarter 1979): 219–22.

Kisha, Tim. *Detroit Powers and Personalities.* Rochester Hills, Mich.: Momentum Books, 1989.

Klotman, Phyllis R. *Another Man Gone: The Black Runner in Contemporary Afro-American Literature.* Port Washington, N.Y.: Kennikat Press, 1977.

Kniffel, Leonard. "Poet in Motion." *Monthly Detroit* 7, no. 6 (June 1984): 160–63.

Knight, Etheridge. *Poems from Prison.* Detroit: Broadside Press, 1968.

———. *Belly Song and Other Poems.* Detroit: Broadside Press, 1973.

———. *Born of a Woman: New and Selected Poems.* Boston: Houghton Mifflin Co., 1980.

———, ed. *Voices from Prison.* New York: Pathfinder Press, 1970.

Kornweibel, Theodore, Jr. "The Most Dangerous of All Negro Journals: Federal Efforts to Suppress the Chicago Defender During World War I." *American Journalism* 11, no. 2 (Spring 1994): 154–68.

Kozol, Jonathan. *Illiterate America.* New York: New American Library, 1985.

Kramer, Victor A., ed. *The Harlem Renaissance Re-examined.* New York: AMS Press, 1987.

Kranz, Rachel C. *The Biographical Dictionary of Black Americans.* New York: Facts on File, 1992.

Krieglstein, Werner. *The Dice-Playing God: Reflecting on Life in a Post-Modern Age.* New York: University Press of America, 1991.

Kumar, Narendra and S. K. Ghai, eds. *Afro/Asian Publishing: Contemporary Trends.* New Delhi, India: Institute of Book Publishing, 1992.

Kurian, George Thomas. *The Directory of American Book Publishing: From Founding Fathers to Today's Conglomerates.* New York: Simon and Schuster, 1975.

LaBlanc, Michael L., ed. *Contemporary Black Biography: Profiles from the International Black Community.* Vol. 1. Detroit: Gale Research Co., 1992.

LaBrie, Henry G., III, "The Future of the Black Press: A Silent Crusade." *Negro History Bulletin* 36, no. 8 (December 1973): 166–69.

———. *A Survey of Black Newspapers in America.* Kennebunkport, Maine: Mercer House Press, 1979.

Lambert, Wallace E. and Donald M. Taylor. *Coping with Cultural and Racial Diversity in Urban America.* New York: Praeger Publishers, 1990.

Lane, Ronnie M., ed. *Face the Whirlwind.* Grand Rapids, Mich.: Pilot Press Books, 1973.

Langer, Judith A., ed. *Language Literacy and Culture: Issues of Society and Schooling.* Norwood, N.J.: Ablex Publishing Corp., 1987.

Laryea, Doris L. "A Black Poet's Vision: An Interview with Lance Jeffers." *CLA Journal* 26, no. 4 (June 1983): 422–33.

Lawson, Steven F. *Running for Freedom; Civil Rights and Black Politics in America Since 1941.* New York: McGraw-Hill, 1991.

Lee, Don L. [Haki R. Madhubuti]. *Think Black.* Detroit: Broadside Press, 1968.

_____. *Black Pride.* Detroit: Broadside Press, 1968.

_____. *Don't Cry, Scream!.* Detroit: Broadside Press, 1969.

_____. "Reads *Don't Cry, Scream!.*" Detroit: Broadside Press, 1969.

_____. *We Walk the Way of the New World.* Detroit: Broadside Press, 1970.

_____. "Reads *We Walk the Way of the New World.*" Detroit: Broadside Press, 1970.

_____. *Directionscore: Selected and New Poems.* Detroit: Broadside Press, 1971.

_____. *Book of Life.* Detroit: Broadside Press, 1973.

_____. *From Plan to Planet: Life Studies: The Need for Afrikan Minds and Institutions.* Detroit: Broadside Press and Institute of Positive Education, 1973.

Levine, David Allen. *Internal Combustion: The Races in Detroit 1915–1926.* Westport, Conn.: Greenwood Press, 1976.

Levine, George, ed. *Aesthetics and Ideology.* New Brunswick, N.J.: Rutgers University Press, 1994.

Levittan, Sab A., William B. Johnson, and Robert Taggart. *Still a Dream: The Changing Status of Blacks Since 1960.* Cambridge, Mass.: Harvard University Press, 1975.

Levy, Lyn. *Singing Sadness Happy.* Detroit: Broadside Press, 1972.

Lewis, David Levering. *District of Columbia: A Bi-centennial History.* New York: W. W. Norton & Co.; and Nashville: American Association for State and Local History, 1976.

_____. *When Harlem Was in Vogue.* New York: Alfred A. Knopf, 1981.

Lewis, Denise J. "Victory and Defeat for Black Candidates." *The Black Politician: A Quarterly Journal of Current Political Thought* 2, no. 4 (April 1971): 34–36, 66–73.

Lewis, Ida. "Conversation: The Reverend Albert B. Cleage, Jr." *Essence* 1, no. 8 (December 1970): 22–27.

Lieberson, Stanley. *A Piece of the Pie: Black and White Immigrants Since 1880.* Berkeley: University of California Press, 1980.

Lincoln, C. Eric. *The Black Muslims in America.* Boston: Beacon Press, 1961, 1994.

Lindenmeyer, Otto. *Black and Brave: The Black Soldier in America.* New York: McGraw-Hill, 1970.

Locke, Don C. *Increasing Multicultural Understanding: A Comprehensive Model.* Newbury Park, Calif.: Sage Publications, 1992.

Logan, Rayford W., ed. *What the Negro Wants.* Chapel Hill: University of North Carolina Press, 1944.

Lomax, Alan and Raoul Abdul, eds. *3000 Years of Black Poetry: An Anthology.* New York: Dodd, Mead & Co., 1970.

Lomax, Pearl Cleage. *We Don't Need No Music.* Detroit: Broadside Press, 1972.

_____. *Black Love, Black Hope.* Detroit: Broadside Press, 1971.

Long, Doughtry. *Song for Nia.* Detroit: Broadside Press, 1971.

Long, Richard and Eugenia W. Collier, eds. *Afro-American Writing: An Anthology of Prose and Poetry.* 2 vols. New York: New York University Press, 1972.

Lorde, Audre. *Cables to Rage.* London: Paul Breman, 1970.

_____. *From a Land Where Other People Live.* Detroit: Broadside Press, 1973.

_____. *The New York Head Shop and Museum.* Detroit: Broadside Press, 1974.

Lowery, Charles D. and John F. Marszalek, eds. *Encyclopedia of African-American Civil Rights: From Emancipation to the Present.* Westport, Conn.: Greenwood Press, 1992.

Lumumba, Chokwe. "Short History of the U.S. War on the R.N.A." *The Black Scholar* 12, no. 1 (January/February 1981): 72–81.

Lunsford, Andrea A., Helene Mogle and J. Slevin, eds. *The Right to Literacy.* New York: The Modern Language Associaton of America, 1990.

Lynch, Acklyn. *Nightmare Overhanging Darkly: Essays on African American Culture and Resistance.* Chicago: Third World Press, 1992.

Madgett, Naomi Long, ed. *Adam of Ife: Black Women in Praise of Black Men.* Detroit: Lotus Press, 1992.

Magill, Frank N., ed. *Critical Survey of Poetry: English Language Series.* Vol. 6. Englewood Cliffs, N.J.: Salem Press, 1982.

_____, ed. *Masterpieces of African American Literature.* New York: HarperCollins Publishers, 1992.

Magner, Denise. "3-Year Project Seeks to Develop Degree Level Writing Program at Historically Black Colleges." *The Chronicle of Higher Education* XL, no. 3 (September 8, 1993): A20.

Mahone, Barbara. *Sugarfields.* Chicago: By the author, 1970.

Major, Clarence. *The Cotton Club.* Detroit: Broadside Press, 1972.

_____. *The Dark and Feeling: Black American Writers and Their Work.* New York: The Third Press, 1974.

_____, ed. *The New Black Poetry.* New York: International Publishers, 1970.

Majors, Richard and Janet Mancini Billson. *Cool Pose: The Dilemmas of Black Manhood in America.* New York: The MacMillan Co., 1992.

Mamiya, Lawrence H. *The Black Church in the African American Experience.* Durham, N.C.: Duke University Press, 1990.

_____. *Race, Reform and Rebellion: The Second Reconstruction in Black America, 1945–1982.* Jackson: University Press of Mississippi, 1984.

Marable, Manning. *Black American Politics: From the Washington Marches to Jesse Jackson.* London, England: Verso, 1985.

Marks, Carole. *Farewell — We're Good and Gone: The Great Black Migration.* Bloomington: Indiana University Press, 1989.

Markwalder, Don. "The Potential for Black Business." *The Review of Black Political Economy* 11, no. 3 (Spring 1981): 303–12.

Marshall, Roy. *The Negro and Organized Labor.* New York: John Wiley & Sons, 1965.

Marshall, Thurgood. "The Gestapo in Detroit." *Crisis* 50 (August 1943): 232–33.

Martin, Tony. *The Jewish Onslaught: Despatches from the Wellesley Battlefront.* Dover, Mass.: The Majority Press, 1993.

Marvin X. *Black Man Listen.* Detroit: Broadside Press, 1969.

Marwil, Jonathan. *A History of Ann Arbor.* Ann Arbor: University of Michigan Press, 1990.

Mason, Julian. "Black Writers of the South." *Mississippi Quarterly: The Journal of Southern Culture* 31, no. 2 (Spring 1978): 169–83.

Matthews, Claude L. "Detroit's WGPR: Struggling Start for Black TV." *Black Enterprise* 7, no. 4 (November 1976): 63, 65, 73, 76.

Max, D.I. "The End of the Book." *The Atlantic Monthly* 274, no. 3 (September 1994): 62, 64, 67–68, 70–71.

Mayer, Parm. "The Stars Are Out." *Phylon* 23, no. 4 (Winter 1962): 412–13.

McAdam, Doug. *Political Process and the Development of Black Insurgency, 1930–1970.* Chicago: University of Chicago Press, 1982.

McClane, Kenneth A. *Wall: Essays, 1985–1990.* Detroit: Wayne State University Press, 1991.

McCuen, Gary E., ed. *Illiteracy in America.* Hudson, Wis.: Gary E. McCuen Publications, 1988.

McWorter, Gerald A. *Guide to Scholarly Journals in Black History.* Chicago: Peoples College Press, 1981.

Meier, August. *A White Scholar and the Black Community, 1945–1965: Essays and Reflections.* Amherst: University of Massachusetts Press, 1992.

_____, and Elliott Rudwick. *CORE: A Study in the Civil Rights Movement, 1942–1968.* New York: Oxford University Press, 1973.

Melhem, D.H. "Sonia Sanchez: Will and Spirit." *Melus* 12, no. 3 (Fall 1984): 73–98.

_____. *Gwendolyn Brooks: Poetry and the Heroic Voice.* Lexington: University Press of Kentucky, 1987.

_____. *Heroism in the New Black Poetry: Introductions and Interviews.* Lexington: University Press of Kentucky, 1990.

_____. "The Writer's Behavior." *Confrontation,* no. 51 (Summer 1993): 31.

Melton, J. Gordon. *Religious Leaders of America: A Biographical Guide to Founders and Leaders of Religious Bodies, Churches, and Spiritual Groups in North America.* Detroit: Gale Research Co., 1991.

Metzger, Linda, Deborah A. Straub, Hal May, and Susan M. Trosky, eds. *Black Writers: A Selection of Sketches from Contemporary Authors.* Detroit: Gale Research Co., 1989.

"Michigan." *Negro History Bulletin* 30, no. 5 (May 1967): 20.

Michigan Association for Media in Education. *Michigan Authors.* Ann Arbor: Michigan Association 'for Media in Education, 1980.

Michigan Council for the Humanities. *Literary Michigan: a Sense of Place, a Sense of Time*. Lansing: The Michigan Council for the Humanities, 1988.

Miller, Adam David, ed. *Dices or Black Bones: Black Voices of the Seventies*. Boston: Houghton Mifflin Co., 1970.

Miller, Aurelia Toyer. Review of "D. Parke Gibson, $70 Billion in the Black: America's Black Consumers." *The Review of Black Political Economy* 10, no. 1 (Fall 1979): 116–17.

Miller, E. Ethelbert, ed. *In Search of Color Everywhere: A Collection of African American Poetry*. New York: Stewart, Tabori and Chang, 1994.

Miller, R. Baxter, ed. *Black American Poets Between Worlds, 1940–1960*. Knoxville: University of Tennessee Press, 1986.

Mitchell, Broadus. *Depression Decade: From New Era Through New Deal, 1929–1941*. Vol. IX, *The Economic History of the United States*. New York: Holt, Rinehart and Winston, 1947.

Moon, Elaine Latzman. *Untold Tales, Unsung Heroes: An Oral History of Detroit's African American Community, 1918–1967*. Detroit: Wayne State University Press, 1994.

Moore, Jesse Thomas, Jr. *A Search for Equality: The National Urban League, 1910–1961*. University Park: Pennsylvania State University Press, 1981.

Mosher, Marlene. *New Directions from Don L. Lee*. Hicksville, N.Y.: Exposition Press, 1975.

Mueller-Hartmann, Andreas. "Houston A. Baker, Jr., The Development of a Black Literary Critic." *International Journal of Black Oral and Literary Studies* 1, no. 2 (Spring 1989): 100–11.

Munt, Sally, ed. *New Lesbian Criticism: Literary and Cultural Readings*. New York: Columbia University Press, 1992.

Murphy, Beatrice M. and Nancy L. Arnez. *The Rocks Cry Out*. Detroit: Broadside Press, 1969.

Murray, Alma and Robert Thomas, eds. *Major Black Writers*. New York: Scholastic Book Services, 1971.

_____, eds. *The Scene*. New York: Scholastic Book Services, 1971.

Murray, Paul T. "Blacks and the Draft: A History of Institutional Racism." *Journal of Black Studies* 2, no. 1 (September 1971): 57–76.

Murphy, Frederick D. "Nikki." *Encore: American and Worldwide News* 4, no. 9 (May 5, 1975): 30–34.

NAACP. *In Freedom's Vanguard; Report for 1963*. New York: NAACP, July 1964.

Napper, George. *Blacker Than Thou: The Struggle for Campus Unity*. Grand Rapids, Mich.: Wm. B. Eerdmans Publishing Co., 1973.

Nasso, Christine, ed. *Contemporary Authors: A Bio-Bibliographical Guide to Current Authors and Their Works*. Vols. 25–28. Detroit: Gale Research Co., 1977.

NBC News and Rand McNally. *World Atlas & Almanac, 1991*. New York: NBC News and Rand McNally & Co., 1991.

Neal, Larry. Edited by Michael Schwartz. *Visions of A Liberated Future: Black Arts Movement Writings*. New York: Thunder's Mouth Press, 1989.

Neale, Caroline. *Writing Independent History: African Historiographs, 1960–1980*. Westport, Conn.: Greenwood Press, 1985.

Nearing, Scott. *Black America*. New York: Schocken Books, 1929.

The Negro Handbook. Chicago: Johnson Publishing Co., 1966.

Negro Newspapers and Periodicals in the United States, 1938. Washington, D.C.: Department of Commerce, 1939.

Negro Newspapers in the United States, 1966. Jefferson City, Mo.: Lincoln University, 1966.

Neithercat, Mark E. *Detroit Twenty Years After: A Statistical Profile of the Detroit Area Since 1967*. Detroit: Center for Urban Studies, Wayne State University, 1987.

The New Book of American Rankings. New York: Facts on File Publications, 1984.

Newton, Michael and Judy Ann Newton. *The Ku Klux Klan: An Encyclopedia*. New York: Garland Publishing, 1991.

Nicholas, A.X. "A Conversation with Dudley Randall." *Black World* 21, no. 2 (December 1971): 26–34.

Nicholes, Marion. *Lifestyles*. Detroit: Broadside Press, 1971.

Nielsen, Aldon Lynn. *Reading Race: White American Poets and the Racial Discourse in the Twentieth Century*. Athens: University of Georgia Press, 1988.

Nielson, David Gordon. *Black Ethos: Northern Urban Negro Life and Thought, 1890–1930*. Westport, Conn.: Greenwood Press, 1977.

Nixon, Will. "Better Times for Black Writers?" *Publishers Weekly* 235, no. 7 (February 17, 1989): 35–40.

_____. "Black Male Writers: Endangered Species?" *American Visions* 5, no. 1 (February 1990): 24–28.

Noble, William. *Bookbanning in America: Who Bans Books? And Why.* Middlebury, Vt.: Paul S. Eriksson Publisher, 1990.

Ntir, Daphne Williams. *Consonance and Continuity in Poetry: Detroit Black Writers.* Detroit: Bedford Publishers 1988.

O'Brien, Mark and Craig Little, eds. *In Reimaging in America: The Arts of Social Chance.* Philadelphia, Pa.: New Society Publishers, 1990.

The Official Associated Press Almanac, 1973. New York: Almanac Publishing Co., 1973.

Okihiro, Gary Y., ed. *Ethnic Studies: Selected Course Outlines and Reading Lists from American Colleges and Universities.* Vol. 1. New York: Markus Wiener Publishing, 1989.

O'Reilly, Kenneth. *"Racial Matters": The FBI's Secret File on Black America, 1960–1972.* New York: The Free Press/The Macmillan Co., 1989.

Ostendorf, Berndt. *Black Literature in White America.* Totowa, N.J.: Barnes & Noble Books, 1982.

Page, James A., compiler. *Selected Black American Authors: An Illustrated Bio-Bibliography.* Boston: G. K. Hall & Co., 1977.

_____, & Joe Min Roh, compilers. *Selected Black American, African, and Caribbean Authors: A Bio-Bibliography.* Littleton, Col.: Libraries Unlimited, 1985.

Parin, Jay and Brett C. Miller, eds. *The Columbia History of American Poetry.* New York: Columbia University Press, 1993.

Parks, Carole. "10th Anniversary Celebration in Detroit: The Broadside Story." *Black World* 25, no. 3 (January 1976): 84–90.

_____, ed. *Nommo: A Literary Legacy of Black Chicano (1967–1987).* Chicago: The Organization of Black American Culture Writer's Workshop, 1987.

Parrish, Michael. *Anxious Decades: America in Prosperity and Depressions 1920–1941.* New York: W.W. Norton & Co., 1992.

Patterson, Lindsay, ed. *An Introduction to Black Literature in America: From 1746 to the Present.* New York: Associated Publishers and the Association for the Study of Negro Life and History, 1969.

_____, ed. *A Rock Against the Wind: Black Love Poems, an Anthology.* New York: Dodd, Mead, 1973.

Payne, Wardell J., ed. *Directors of African American Religious Bodies: A Compendium by the Howard University School of Divinity.* Washington, D.C.: Howard University Press, 1991.

Perry, Charlotte, compiler. *The Official Business and Professional Guide of Detroit 1946.* Detroit: Charlotte Perry, Publisher, 1946.

Peterson, Felix (Pete). "Vietnam Battle Deaths: Is There a Race or Class Issue?" *Focus* 15, no. 7 (July 1987): 34.

Peterson, Joyce Shaw. "Black Automobile Workers in Detroit, 1910–1930." *The Journal of Negro History* 64, no. 3 (Summer 1979): 177–190.

_____. "Autoworkers Confront the Depression, 1929–1933." *Detroit in Perspective* 6, no. 2 (Fall 1982): 47–71.

Peterson, Paul E., ed. *The New Urban Reality.* Washington, D.C.: The Brookings Institution, 1985.

Pettis, Joyce. "The Black Poet as Historian." *Umoja* 4, no. 1 (Spring 1980): 50.

Pfister, Arthur. *Beer Cans, Bullets, Things & Pieces.* Detroit: Broadside Press, 1972.

Phelps, Sherille, ed. *Who's Who Among Black Americans 1994–95.* Detroit: Gale Research Co., 1994.

Phillips, J.J., I. Reed, G. Strods and S. Wang, eds. *The Before Columbus Foundation Poetry Anthology: Selections from the American Book Awards, 1980–1990.* New York: W.W. Norton & Co., 1992.

Pinckney, Alphonso. *Black Americans.* Englewood Cliffs, N.J.: Prentice Hall, 1969.

_____. *Red, Black, and Green: Black Nationalism in the United States.* Cambridge: Cambridge University Press, 1976.

_____. *The Myth of Black Progress.* New York: Cambridge University Press, 1984.

Pinckney, Darryl. *High Cotton.* New York: Farrar, Straus, Giroux, 1992.

Pinckney, Junette A. "Independent Black Publishing." *American Visions* 4, no. 2 (April 1989): 50–54.

Piven, Frances Fox and Richard A. Cloward. *Poor People's Movements: Why They Succeed, How They Fail.* New York: Vintage Books, 1979.

Ploski, Harry A. and James Williams, eds. *Reference Library of Black America*. New York: Afro-American Press, 1990.

Plumpp, Sterling D. *Clinton*. Detroit: Broadside Press, 1976.

Poet's Audio Center Catalogue. Washington, D.C.: Poet's Audio Center, 1992.

Pohlmann, Marcus D. *Black Politics in Conservative America*. New York: Longman, 1990.

Poinsett, Alex. "Motor City Makes a Comeback." *Ebony* 33, no. 6 (April 1978): 29–32, 34, 36–38, 40.

Pollack, Sandra and Denise D. Knight, eds. *Contemporary Lesbian Writers of the United States: A Bio-Bibliographical Critical Sourcebook*. Westport, Conn.: Greenwood Press, 1993.

Polsgrove, Carol. "Making Books: In the Publishing Business, Small Can Be Beautiful." *The Progressive* 45, no. 9 (September 1981): 47–49.

Pool, Rosey E., ed. *Beyond the Blues: New Poems by American Negroes*. Lympne, Kent, England: The Hand and Flower Press, 1962.

_____, ed. *Ik Ben de Nieuwe Newer*. The Hague, Holland: Bert, Bakker, 1965.

Potter, Vilma Ruskin. "Reconsiderations and Reviews: A Remembrance for Robert Hayden, 1913–1980." *Melus* 8, no. 1 (Spring 1981): 51–55.

Pride, Armistead. "The Names of Negro Newspapers." *American Speech* 29, no. 2 (May 1954): 114–18.

Putman, Anthony O. *Marketing Your Services: A Step-by-Step Guide for Small Businesses and Professionals*. New York: John Wiley & Sons, 1990.

Quarles, Benjamin. *Black Mosaic: Essays in Afro-American History and Historiography*. Amherst: University of Massachusetts Press, 1988.

Ragsdale, Bruce A. and Joel D. Treese, eds. *Black Americans in Congress, 1870–1989*. Washington, D.C.: U.S. Government Printing Office, 1990.

Randall, Dudley and Margaret G. Burroughs, eds. *For Malcolm X: Poems on the Life and Death of Malcolm X*. Detroit: Broadside Press, 1966.

Randall, Dudley. *Cities Burning*. Detroit: Broadside Press, 1968.

_____. "The Creative Arts," in *Black Expression: Essays By and About Black Americans*. Edited by Addison Gayle, Jr. New York: Weybright & Talley, 1969.

_____. "Broadside Press: A Personal Chronicle." *Black Academy Review* 1, no. 1 (1970): 40–47.

_____ *Love You*. London: Paul Breman, 1970.

_____. *More to Remember*. Chicago: Third World Press, 1971.

_____. *After the Killing*. Chicago: Third World Press, 1973.

_____. "Black Emotion and Experience: The Literature for Understanding." *American Libraries* 4, no. 2 (February 1973): 86–90.

_____. "New Books for Black Readers." *Publishers Weekly* 204, no. 17 (October 22, 1973): 48–51.

_____. Review of "You Better Believe It." *Okike: An African Journal of New Writing* 1, no. 5 (June 1974): 71.

_____. "Black Publisher, Black Author: An Answer." *Black World* 24, no. 5 (March 1975): 32–37.

_____. *Broadside Memories: Poets I Have Known*. Detroit: Broadside Press, 1975.

_____, ed. *Black Poetry: A Supplement to Anthologies Which Exclude Black Poets*. Detroit: Broadside Press, 1969.

_____, ed. *The Black Poets: A New Anthology*. New York: Bantam Books, 1971.

_____, ed. *Homage to Hoyt Fuller*. Detroit: Broadside Press, 1984.

_____, with Gwendolyn Brooks, Keorapetse Kgositsile, and Haki R. Madhubuti. *A Capsule Course in Black Poetry Writing*. Detroit: Broadside Press, 1975.

_____, and Louis J. Cantoni, eds. *Golden Song: The Fiftieth Anniversary Anthology of the Poetry Society of Michigan, 1935–1985*. Detroit: Harlo, 1985.

Randall, James, Jr. *Don't Ask Me Who I Am*. Detroit: Broadside Press, 1970.

_____. *Cities and Other Disasters*. Detroit: Broadside Press, 1973.

Randall, Jon C. *Indigoes*. Detroit: Broadside Press, 1975.

Raven, John. *Blues for Momma and Other Low Down Stuff*. Detroit: Broadside Press, 1971.

Reardon, Joan. *Poetry by American Women, 1975–1989: a Bibliography*. Metuchen, N.J.: The Scarecrow Press, 1990.

Redding, J. Saunders. "The Black Arts Movement in Negro Poetry." *The American Scholar* 42, no. 2 (Spring 1973): 330–36.

Redmond, Eugene B. *Drumvoices: The Mission of Afro-American Poetry, A Critical History*. Garden City, N.Y.: Anchor Books, 1976.

Reed, Adolph, Jr., ed. *Race, Politics, and Culture: Critical Essays on the Radicalism of the 1960s.* Westport, Conn.: Greenwood Press, 1986.

Reed, Ishmael. *Writin' Is Fightin': Thirty-Seven Years of Boxing on Paper.* New York: Atheneum, 1988.

Reese, Leslie. *Upside Down Tapestry Mosaic History.* Detroit: Broadside Press, 1987.

Reeves, William Joseph. *Librarians as Professionals.* Lexington, Mass.: Lexington Books; and Washington, D.C.: Heath and Co., 1980.

Reuter, Edward Byran. *The American Race Problem.* New York: Thomas Y. Crowell Co., 1970.

Rexroth, Kenneth. *American Poetry in the Twentieth Century.* New York: The Seabury Press, 1973.

Rich, Wilbur C. *Coleman Young and Detroit Politics: From Social Activist to Power Broker.* Detroit: Wayne State University Press, 1989.

Rieff, David. *Los Angeles: Capital of the Third World.* New York: Simon & Schuster, 1991.

Rivers, Conrad Kent. *The Wright Poems.* London: Paul Breman, 1972.

Roberts, Edgar V. and Henry E. Jacobs, eds. *Literature: An Introduction to Reading and Writing.* Englewood Cliffs, N.J.: Prentice-Hall, 1986.

Robins, Natalie. *Alien Ink: The FBI's War on Freedom of Expression.* New York: William Morrow & Co., 1992.

Robinson, Michael. "Raves: Poets Come in from the Cold." *American Visions* 9, no. 4 (August/September 1994): 14–18.

Rodgers, Harrell R., Jr., ed. *Racism and Inequality: The Policy Alternatives.* San Francisco, Calif.: W.H. Freeman & Co., 1975.

Rollock, Barbara. *Black Authors and Illustrators of Children's Books: A Biographical Dictionary.* New York: Garland Publishing, 1992.

Rose, Peter I. *Mainstream and Margins: Jews, Blacks and Other Americans.* New Brunswick, N.J.: Transaction Books, 1983.

Rosemond, Irene, compiler. *Reflections: An Oral History of Detroit.* Detroit: Broadside Press, 1992.

Rossi, Peter H. *Ghetto Revolts.* New Brunswick, N.J.: Transaction Books, 1975.

Rowell, Charles H. "In Conversation with Dudley Randall." *Obsidian* 2, no. 1 (Spring 1976): 32–44.

Rubin, Louis D., Jr., ed. *The History of Southern Literature.* Baton Rouge: Louisiana State University Press, 1985.

Rudwick, Elliott M. *Race Riot at East St. Louis, July 2, 1917.* Carbondale: Southern Illinois University Press, 1964.

Rush, Theressa Gunners, Carol Fairbanks Myers and Ester Spring Arata. *Black American Writers, Past and Present: A Biographical and Bibliographical Directory.* 2 vols. Metuchen, N.J.: The Scarecrow Press, 1975.

Russell, Anne D. *Blacks in Pontiac.* Pontiac, Mich.: Privately printed, 1977.

Saddler, Jeanne E. "Ron Milner: The People's Playwright." *Essence* 5, no. 7 (November 1974): 20.

Salaam, Kalamuya. "Sonia Sanchez." *Dictionary of Literary Biography,* Vol. 4, *Afro-American Poets Since 1955.* Detroit: Gale Research Co., 1985.

Salley, Columbus. *The Black 100: A Ranking of the Most Influential African-Americans, Past and Present.* New York: Citadel Press/Carol Publishing Co., 1993.

Sanchez, Sonia. *Homecoming.* Detroit: Broadside Press, 1969.

_____. *We a BaddDDD People.* Detroit: Broadside Press, 1970.

_____. *A Blues Book for Blue Black Magical Women.* Detroit: Broadside Press, 1974.

_____. *It's a New Day: (Poems for Brothas and Sistuhs).* Detroit: Broadside Press, 1983.

_____, ed. *Three Hundred and Sixty Degrees of Blackness Coming at You: An Anthology of the Sonia Sanchez Writers Workshop at Countee Cullen Library in Harlem.* New York: 5X Publishing Co., 1971.

_____, ed. *We Be Word Sorcerers: 25 Stories by Black Americans.* New York: Bantam Books, 1972.

Sarkissian, Adele, ed. *Contemporary Authors: Autobiography,* Series II. Detroit: Gale Research Co., 1985.

Sawyer, Frank B., ed. *U.S. Negro World 1967.* New York: U.S. Negro World, 1967.

Schulberg, Budd, ed. *From the Ashes: Voices of Watts.* New York: New American Library, 1967.

Schultz, Bud and Ruth Schultz. *It Did Happen Here: Recollections of Political Repression in America.* Berkeley: University of California Press, 1989.

Scott, J. Irving E. *Negro Students and Their Colleges.* Boston: Meador Publishing Co., 1949.

Segal, Ronald. *The Race War.* London: Jonathan Cape, 1966.

Shavit, David. *The Politics of Public Librarianship.* Westport, Conn.: Greenwood Press, 1986.

Shaw, Harry B. *Gwendolyn Brooks.* Boston: Twayne Publishers, 1980.

_____, ed. *Perspectives of Black Popular Culture*. Bowling Green, Ohio: Bowling Green State University Popular Press, 1990.

Shockley, Ann Allen and Sue P. Chandler. *Living Black American Authors: A Biographical Directory*. New York: R.R. Bowker Co., 1973.

Sikora, Frank. *Until Justice Rolls Down: The Birmingham Church Bombing Case*. Tuscaloosa: University of Alabama Press, 1991.

Silk, Catherine and John Silk. *Racism and Anti-racism in American Popular Culture: Portrayals of African-Americans in Fiction and Film*. Manchester, England: Manchester University Press, 1990.

Simcox, Helen Earle, ed. *Dear Dark Faces: Portraits of a People*. Detroit: Lotus Press, 1980.

Simmons, Gloria M., Helene D. Hutchinson, and Henry E. Simmons, eds. *Black Culture: Reading and Writing Black*. New York: Holt, Rinehart and Winston, 1972.

Simmons, Judy Dothard. *Judith's Blues*. Detroit: Broadside Press, 1973.

Simmons, Richard R. "The Black Business Community: Survival or Failure." *Journal of Afro-American Issues* 3, nos. 3 & 4 (Summer/Fall 1975): 442–53.

Sitkoff, Harvard. "Racial Militancy and Interracial Violence in the Second World War." *Journal of American History* 58, no. 3 (December 1971): 661–81.

Skeeter, Sharyn J. "Black Women Writers: Levels of Identity." *Essence* 4, no. 1 (May 1971): 58–59, 76, 89.

Sloan, Irving J. *The American Negro: A Chronology and Fact Book*. Dobbs Ferry, N.Y.: Oceana Publications, 1965.

Smallwood, Carol, ed. *Michigan Authors*. Hillsdale, Mich.: Hillsdale Educational Publishers, 1993.

Smith, Barbara, ed. *Homegirls: A Black Feminist Anthology*. New York: Kitchen Table, Women of Color Press, 1983.

Smith, Baxter. "Somebody's Watching You." *The Black Collegian* 6, no. 5 (May/June 1976): 62–63.

Smith, Darren L., ed. *Black American Information Directory 1990–1991*. Detroit: Gale Research Co., 1990.

Smith, David Lionel. "The Black Arts Movement and Its Critics." *American Literary History* 3, no. 1 (Spring 1991): 93–110.

Smith, Jessie Carney, ed. *Notable Black American Women*. Detroit: Gale Research Co., 1992.

Smith, Theophus M. *Confusing Culture: Biblical Formations of Black America*. New York: Oxford University Press, 1994.

Smith-Hobson, Sheila. "Black Book Publishing: Protest, Pride and Little Profit." *Black Enterprise* 8, no. 10 (May 1978): 39–40, 42, 44, 47

Smith-Knight, Sharon. *Wine Sip and Other Delicious Poems*. Detroit: Broadside Press, 1991.

Snorgrass, William. "Freedom of the Press and Black Publications." *Western Journal of Black Studies* 4, No. 3 (Fall 1980): 172–78.

Solomon, Steven. *Small Business USA: The Role of Small Companies in Sparking America's Economic Transformation*. New York: Crown Publishers, 1986.

Sommers, Lawrence M. *Michigan; A Geography*. Boulder, Col.: Westview Press, 1984.

Southerland, Ellease. *The Magic Sun Spins*. London: Paul Breman, 1975.

Southern, Eileen, ed. *Readings in Black American Music*. New York: W.W. Norton & Co., 1983.

Spencer, Chauncey E. *Who Is Chauncey E. Spencer?* Detroit: Broadside Press, 1975.

Spero, Sterling and Abram L. Harris. *The Black Worker: The Negro and the Labor Movement*. New York: Columbia University Press, 1931, 1959.

Stanford, Barbara Dodds, ed. *I, Too, Sing America: Black Voices in American Literature*. New York: Hayden Book Co., 1971.

Stanton, Bill. *Bringing the Ku Klux Klan to Justice*. New York: Grove Weidenfeld, 1991.

"The State of Black America 1977." *The Black Scholar* 9, no. 1 (September 1977): 2–8.

The State of Black America, 1992, 1994. New York: The National Urban League, Inc., 1992, 1994.

Stauffer, Donald Barlow. *A Short History of American Poetry*. New York: E. P. Dutton & Co., 1974.

Stephens, Ronald. "Coleman Young: The Man and His Times." *The Black Scholar* 21, no. 3 (Summer 1990–91): 41.

"Sterling A. Brown: Poet, Scholar, Is Honored as Great American Original." *Ebony* 31, no. 12 (October 1976): 128–30, 132, 134, 136.

Stevens, John D. "The Black Press Looks at 1920's Journalism." *Journalism History* 7, nos. 3–4 (Autumn/Winter 1980): 109–13.

Stewart, Jeffrey C., ed. *Race Contacts and Interracial Relations: Lectures on the Theory and Practice of Race by Alain LeRoy Locke.* Washington, D.C.: Howard University Press, 1992.

Stielow, J., ed. *Activism in American Librarianship, 1962–1973.* Westport, Conn.: Greenwood Press, 1987.

Stone, Merlin. *Marketing and Economics.* London: The Macmillan Press Ltd., 1980.

Straub, Deborah A., ed. *Contemporary Authors, New Revision Series.* Vol. V. Detroit: Gale Research Co., 1988.

Sullivan, James. "Real Cool Pages: The Broadside Press Broadside Series." *Contemporary Literature* 32, no. 4 (Winter 1991): 552–72.

Sweetser, Frank L., ed. *Studies in American Urban Society.* New York: Thomas Y. Crowell Co., 1970.

Task Force on Alternatives in Print. *Alternatives in Print, 1973–74: The Annual Catalog of Social Change Publications.* San Francisco, Calif.: Glide Publications, 1973.

Tate, Claudia, ed. *Black Women Writers at Work.* Harpenden, Herts, England: Old Castle Books, 1983.

Tateishi, John. *And Justice for All: An Oral History of the Japanese American Detention Camps.* New York: Random House, 1984.

Taylor, Clyde, ed. *Vietnam and Black America: An Anthology of Protest and Resistance.* Garden City, N.Y.: Anchor Press/Doubleday, 1973.

Thigpen, William, Jr. *Down Nickel Paved Streets.* Detroit: Broadside Press, 1972.

Third World Press Catalogues. Chicago: Third World Press, 1968–1995.

Thomas, Lorenzo. "The Shadow World: New York's Umbra Workshop and Origins of the Black Arts Movement." *Callaloo* 1, no. 4 (October 1978): 53–72.

Thomas, Richard W. *Life for Us Is What We Make It: Building Black Community in Detroit, 1915–1945.* Bloomington: Indiana University Press, 1992.

Thompson, Carolyn. *Frank.* Detroit: Broadside Press, 1970.

Thompson, Dennis. *The Black Artist in America: An Index to Reproductions.* Metuchen, N.J.: The Scarecrow Press, 1991.

Thompson, James W. *First Fire: Poems, 1957–1960.* London: Paul Breman, 1970.

Thompson, Julius E. *The Black Press in Mississippi 1865–1985: A Directory.* West Cornwall, Conn.: Locust Hill Press, 1988.

_____. "The Public Response to Haki R. Madhubuti, 1968–1988." *The Literary Griot: International Journal of Black Expressive Cultural Studies* 4, nos. 1 & 2 (Spring/Fall 1992): 16–37.

_____. *The Black Press in Mississippi 1865–1985.* Gainesville: University Press of Florida, 1993.

Thompson, M. Cordell. "Nikki Giovanni: Black Rebel with Power in Poetry." *Jet* 42, no. 9 (May 25, 1972): 18–24.

Tidwell, Billy J., ed. *The State of Black America 1994.* New York: National Urban League, 1994.

Tierney, Helen, ed. *Women's Studies Encyclopedia.* Vol. 1. *Views from the Sciences.* Westport, Conn.: Greenwood Press, 1989.

Tischler, Barbara L. *Sights on the Sixties.* New Brunswick, N.J.: Rutgers University Press, 1992.

Tisdale, Celes, ed. *Betcha Ain't: Poems from Attica.* Detroit: Broadside Press, 1974.

Travis, Dempsey J. "Black Business: Obstacles to Their Success." *The Black Scholar* 4, no. 4 (January 1973): 19–21.

Trosky, Susan M., ed. *Contemporary Authors: A Bio-Bibliographical Guide to Current Writers in Fiction, General Nonfiction, Poetry Journalism, Drama, Motion Pictures, Television, and Other Fields.* New Revision Series. Vol. 41. Detroit: Gale Research Co., 1994.

Trotter, Joe William, Jr., ed. *The Great Migration in Historical Perspective: New Dimensions of Race, Class, and Gender.* Bloomington: Indiana University Press, 1991.

Troupe, Quincy and Rainer Schulte, eds. *Giant Talk: An Anthology of Third World Writings.* New York: Vintage Books, 1975.

T'Shaka, Oba. *The Political Legacy of Malcolm X.* Chicago: Third World Press, 1983.

Turner, Darwin T., ed. *Black American Literature: Poetry.* Columbus, Ohio: Charles E. Merrill, 1969.

_____, ed. *Black American Literature: Essays, Poetry Fiction, Drama.* Columbus, Ohio: Charles E. Merrill Publishing Co., 1970.

Turner, William. *Power on the Right.* Berkeley, Calif.: Ramparts Press, 1971.

Twombly, R.C., ed. *Blacks in White America Since 1865: Issues and Interpretations.* New York: David McKay Co., 1971.

Tyms, James D. "The Black Poet and a Sense of Self—The Praise of Famous Men." *The Journal of Religious Thought* 32, no. 1 (Spring/Summer 1975): 22–35.

Spiritual (Religious) Values in the Black Poet. Washington, D.C.: University Press of America, 1977.

Tyson, Remer. "Detroit Hangs in There: Mayor Young a Year Later." *The Nation* 220, no. 8 (March 1, 1975): 237–40.

Vega, Marta Moreno and Cheryll Y. Greene, eds. *Voices from the Battlefront: Achieving Cultural Equity.* Trenton, N.J.: Africa World Press, 1993.

Vendler, Helen. "Good Black Poems One by One." *The New York Times Book Review* (September 29, 1974): 3, 11, 14.

Vest, Hilda. *Sorrow's End.* Detroit: Broadside Press, 1993.

Vinson, James and D. L. Kirkpatrick, eds. *Contemporary Poets.* New York: St. Martin's Press, 1985.

Wagner, Celia. "Book Pricing Update #2." *Against the Grain* 2, no. 1 (February 1990): 18.

Waldron, Edward E. *Walter White and the Harlem Renaissance.* Port Washington, New York: National University Publications, Kennikat Press, 1978.

Walker, Margaret. *Prophets for a New Day.* Detroit: Broadside Press, 1970.

_____. *October Journey.* Detroit: Broadside Press, 1973.

Wailer, Rayfield. *Abstract Blues.* Detroit: Broadside Press, 1988.

Wandersee, Winifred. *On the Move: American Women in the 1970s.* Boston: Twayne Publishers/G.K. Hall & Co., 1988.

Ward, Albert Michael. *Patches on Mainstreet.* Detroit: Broadside Press, 1989.

Ward, Jerry W., Jr. "Report on a Poetry Festival: Melvin A. Butler Third Annual Memorial." *Black World* 23, no. 11 (September 1974): 80–83.

_____. Review of *Clinton. Obsidian* 5, nos. 1 & 2 (Spring/Summer 1979): 133–41.

_____. "Sterling D. Plumpp: A Son of the Blues." *The Southern Quarterly: A Journal of the Arts in the South* 29, no. 3 (Spring 1991): 5–36.

Warner, Robert M. and C. Warren V. Hill, eds. *A Michigan Reader.* Grand Rapids, Mich.: William B. Eerdmans Publishing Co., 1974.

Washburn, Patrick S. *A Question of Sedition: The Federal Government's Investigation of the Black Press During World War II.* New York: Oxford University Press, 1986.

_____. "J. Edgar Hoover and the Black Press in World War II." *Journalism History* 13, no. 1 (Spring 1986): 26–33.

Watts, Thomas D. and Roosevelt Wright. *Black Alcohol Abuse and Alcoholism: An Annotated Bibliography.* New York: Praeger Publishers, 1986.

Weglyn, Michi. *Years of Infamy: The Untold Story of America's Concentration Camps.* New York: Morrow Quill Paperbacks, 1976.

Weisman, Leonard & Elfreda S. Wright, eds. *Black Poetry for All Americans.* New York: Globe, 1971.

Weiss, Nancy J. *The National Urban League, 1910–1940.* New York: Oxford University Press, 1974.

Wells, Alan. "Black Artists in American Popular Music, 1955–1985." *Phylon* 48, no. 4 (Winter 1987): 309–12.

Wesley, Charles H. *Negro Labor in the United States, 1850–1925.* New York: Russell & Russell, 1927.

_____. *The Quest for Equality: From Civil War to Civil Rights.* Washington, D.C.: The Association for the Study of Negro Life and History, 1968.

Wexler, Jerry and David Ritz. *Rhythm and the Blues: A Life in American Music.* New York: Alfred A. Knopf, 1993.

White, Paulette Childress. *The Watermelon Dress.* Detroit: Lotus Press, 1984.

Who's Who Among Black Americans 1977–1978. Northbrook, Ill.: Who's Who Among Black Americans, 1977, 1985.

Widick, B. J. *Detroit: City of Race and Class Violence.* Chicago: Quandrangle Books, 1972.

Wilentz, Ted and Tom Weatherly, eds. *Natural Process: An Anthology of New Black Poetry.* New York: Hill and Wang, 1970.

Wiley, Ralph. *What Black People Should Do Now: Dispatches from Near the Vanguard.* New York: One World/Ballantine Books, 1993.

Willhelm, Sidney M. *Black in a White America.* Cambridge, Mass.: Schenkman Publishing Co., 1983.

Williams, John A. "Black Publisher, Black Writer: An Impasse." *Black World* 24, no. 5 (March 1975): 28–31.

_____, and Charles F. Harris, eds. *Amistad* 1. New York: Vintage Books, 1970.

Williams, Pontheolla T. *Robert Harden: A Critical Analysis of His Poetry.* Urbana: University of Illinois Press, 1987.

_____. Wilson, Clint C., II. *Black Journalists in Paradox: Historical Perspectives and Current Dilemmas.* Westport, Conn.: Greenwood Press, 1991.

Wilson, Pauline. *Stereotype and Status: Librarians in the United States.* Westport, Conn.: Greenwood Press, 1982.

Wolde, Habte [Henry Alonzo Jennings]. *Enough to Die For.* Detroit: Broadside Press, 1972.

Wolfenstein, Victor. *The Victims of Democracy: Malcolm X and the Black Revolution.* Berkeley: University of California Press, 1981.

Wolff, Miles. *Lunch at the Five and Ten, the Greensboro Sit-Ins: A Contemporary History.* New York: Stein and Day, Publishers, 1970.

Wolseley, Roland E. *The Black Press, U.S.A.* Ames: Iowa State University Press, 1990.

Wolters, Raymond. *Negroes and the Great Depression: The Problem of Economic Recovery.* Westport, Conn.: Greenwood Publishing Corp., 1970.

Woodward, C. Vann. *Thinking Back: The Perils of Writing History.* Baton Rouge: Louisiana State University Press, 1986.

Worley, Demetrice A. and Jesse Perry, Jr., eds. *African American Literature: An Anthology of Nonfiction, Fiction, Poetry and Drama.* Lincolnwood, Ill.: National Textbook Co., 1993.

Worthy, William. "The American Negro Is Dead." *Esquire* 68, no. 5, (November 1967): 126–29, 167–68.

Wright, M. Frank. "Frantz Fanon: His Work in Historical Perspective." *The Black Scholar* 6, no. 10 (July/August, 1975): 19–29.

Wynar, Labomyr R. *Encyclopedia Directory of Ethnic Organizations in the United States.* Littletown, Col.: Libraries Unlimited, 1975.

Wynn, Neil A. *The Afro-American and the Second World War.* New York: Holmes and Meier Publishers, 1976.

Yancy, Preston M., compiler. *The Afro-American Short Story: A Comprehensive Annotated Index with Selected Commentaries.* Westport, Conn.: Greenwood Press, 1986.

Yee, Shirley J. *Black Women Abolitionists: A Study in Activism, 1828–1860.* Knoxville: University of Tennessee Press, 1992.

Young, Alfred. "The Historical Origin and Significance of National Afro-American (Black) History Month Observance." *Negro History Bulletin* 45, no. 1 (January/February/March 1980): 6–8.

Young, Henry J. *Major Black Religious Leaders Since 1940.* Nashville, Tenn.: Abingdon, 1979.

Young, James O. *Black Writers of the Thirties.* Baton Rouge: Louisiana State University Press, 1973.

Zell, H.M., C. Bundy, and V. Coulan, eds. *A New Reader's Guide to African Literature.* New York: Africana Publishing Co./Holmes and Meier Publishers, 1983.

Zieger, Robert H. *American Workers, American Unions, 1920–1985.* Baltimore, Md.: Johns Hopkins University Press, 1986.

Zill, Nicholas and Marianne Winglee. *Who Reads Literature?: The Future of the United States as a Nation of Readers.* Cabin John, Md./Washington, D.C.: Seven Locks Press, 1990.

Index